Dr. Seuss Goes to War

ALSO BY RICHARD H. MINEAR

Victors' Justice: The Tokyo War Crimes Trial

Hiroshima: Three Witnesses (editor and translator)

Through Japanese Eyes (editor)

Japanese Tradition and Western Law: Emperor, State, and Law in the Thought of Hozumi Yatsuka

Requiem for Battleship Yamato (editor and translator)

Black Eggs: Poems by Kurihara Sadako (editor and translator)

When We Say Hiroshima (editor and translator)

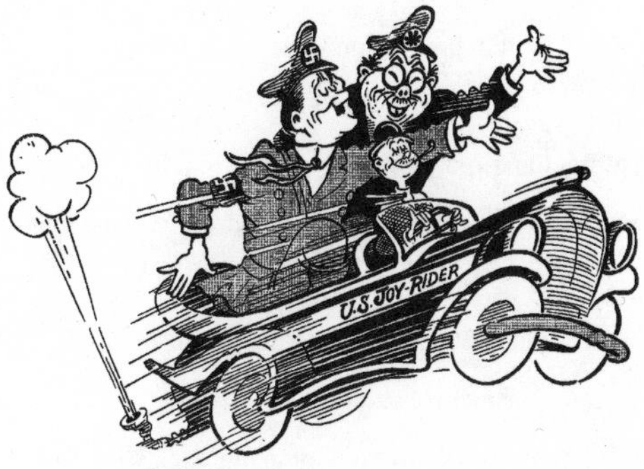
U.S. JOY-RIDER

Dr. Seuss Goes to War

The World War II Editorial Cartoons of Theodor Seuss Geisel

RICHARD H. MINEAR

Published in cooperation with the Dr. Seuss Collection
at the University of California, San Diego

THE NEW PRESS
NEW YORK

For permission to reprint portions of Ralph Ingersoll's papers,

the publisher thanks The Ralph Ingersoll Papers, Special Collections, Boston University.

Published in the United States by The New Press, New York, 1999

Paperback edition, 2001

Distributed by W. W. Norton & Company, Inc., New York

The New Press was established in 1990 as a not-for-profit alternative to the large, commercial publishing houses

currently dominating the book publishing industry. The New Press operates in the public interest

rather than for private gain, and is committed to publishing, in innovative ways,

works of educational, cultural, and community value that are often deemed insufficiently profitable.

The New Press

450 West 41st Street, 6th floor

New York, NY 10036

www.thenewpress.com

Book design by BAD

Printed in the United States of America

2 4 6 8 10 9 7 5 3 1

Contents

Introduction ART SPIEGELMAN

What? Dr. Seuss, beloved purveyor of genial rhyming nonsense for beginning readers, stuff about cats in hats and foxes in socks, started as a feisty political cartoonist who exhorted America to do battle with Hitler? Yeah, right! And Ad Reinhardt–the guy who painted austere black-on-black abstractions–used to draw comic strips explaining modern art to the uninitiated! Both these unlikely phenomena in fact did occur in the pages of what may well have been America's most remarkable daily newspaper, New York's *PM*. This short-lived "popular front" tabloid eschewed all paid advertising, though it did print announcements of department store bargains as news items. (It also first published "Barnaby," a once-revered intellectual comic strip by Crockett Johnson, who later created the Harold and the Purple Crayon kid books.)

In some happier alternate universe, *PM* is still being published daily and Dr. Seuss was awarded a Pulitzer Prize for his anti-Fascist *PM* cartoons of 1941 and 1942. Actually, Dr. Seuss did get a Pulitzer in the universe we inhabit: a special citation in 1984 "for his contribution over nearly half a century to the education and enjoyment of America's children and their parents." Presumably, though, most of that award committee was as unaware of the heretofore "lost" cartoons in this volume as the rest of us. While it's true that most of these cartoons lack the weight and gravitas of the cartoons by Herblock that did

get the Pulitzer in 1942, they are still very impressive evidence of cartooning as an art of persuasion.

These cartoons rail against isolationism, racism, and anti-Semitism with a conviction and fervor lacking in most other American editorial pages of the period. These are virtually the only editorial cartoons outside the communist and black press that decried the military's Jim Crow policies and Charles Lindbergh's anti-Semitism. Dr. Seuss said that he "had no great causes or interest in social issues until Hitler," and explained that "*PM* was against people who pushed other people around. I liked that." More of a humanist than an ideologue — one of those Groucho rather than Karl Marxists — Dr. Seuss made these drawings with the fire of honest indignation and anger that fuels all real political art. If they have a flaw, it's an absolutely endearing one: they're funny.

Many of the editorial cartoonists of the time used grease crayon for their effects, evidence of their roots in the Honoré Daumier tradition. Dr. Seuss's twisted roots, on the other hand, were in the vaudeville tradition of early comic strips and gag cartoons. Theodor Geisel (Dr. Seuss's "real" name) began his career in the late 1920s, doing gag cartoons for the two most important humor magazines of the time, *Judge* and *Life*. He received his first renown for a long-lived series of cartoons advertising a bug spray called *Flit*. (One of the more memorable images reprinted in this volume has Seuss's Uncle Sam eagle about to shoot a Flit spray gun labeled "U.S. Defense Bonds and Stamps" at enormous Adolf, Tojo, and Benito bugs.) In 1935, he briefly turned out a comic strip for King Features called "Hejji." And he produced four well-received children's books before hooking up with *PM*, though his grand-scale success as a children's book artist didn't come until the late 1950s. But the idioms of the picture book, the comics, gag cartoons, and advertising informed his *PM* work. Over the past twenty to thirty years the newspaper editorial cartoon has reduced its ambition, basically becoming a gag cartoon with political subject matter. Dr. Seuss's political cartoons were, perhaps, ahead of their time in seeking to entertain as well as convince. This is by no means to deny Seuss's earnestness, it's just that — much as with Chaplin's *The Great Dictator* — comedy was too frail a weapon to deal mortal blows to Hitler.(On the other hand, it's also true that the far more vitriolic cartoons of George Grosz and John Heartfield were no more adequate to the task.)

One of the great pleasures in this collection of drawings (beyond the not inconsiderable one of getting a painless history lesson on the side) is the affirmation of just how good the good Doctor really was: good at communicating his ideas clearly and just plain old-fashioned good. He called 'em as he saw 'em, and most of the time he was on the side of the angels. The greatest pleasure, though, lies in watching the artist develop his goofily surreal vision while he delivers the ethical goods. The unique galumphing menagerie of Seussian fauna, the screwball humor and themes that later enraptured millions (as well as earning millions of dollars for the artist), come into focus in these early drawings that were done with urgency on very short deadlines.

The *PM* cartoons make us more aware of the political messages often embedded within the sugar pill of Dr. Seuss's signature zaniness. For better or worse, the didactic moralist struggled for supremacy over the iconoclastic jokester in much of his mature — could that be the right adjective? — work. *Yertle the Turtle* (visually prefigured in a stack of turtles forming a victory V in a March 20, 1942, cartoon) is an anti-fascist tract. *The Sneetches* is clearly a plea for racial tolerance (what are those stars on thar bellies, if not Magen Davids?). An environmental message overwhelms any of the nonsense in *The Lorax*, and the polemic for nuclear disarmament in *The Butter Battle Book* created a blizzard of controversy when it first appeared in 1984.

The Cat in the Hat's red-and-white-striped leaning tower of a stove-pipe has become an American icon only slightly less recognizable than the Disney mouse ears. Seeing the slightly battered lid on the Seuss bird that represents the United States in many of the *PM* drawings (presumably it's an eagle, though it looks as much like a Sneetch and suspiciously like the prominently beaked Theodor Geisel himself) is disorienting enough to bring on an epiphany: the prototype for the cat's famous headgear is actually an emblem deployed in countless political cartoons: Uncle Sam's red-and-white-striped top hat! The Cat in the Hat is America!

And now, rescued from the newsprint where they moldered unseen for over half a century, the cartoons let us know what happens when Horton hears a *Heil*.

Some Important Dates

Oct. 3, 1935	Italian invasion of Ethiopia
May 1, 1937	U. S. Neutrality Act
July 7, 1937	Sino-Japanese War
Oct. 1, 1938	German seizure of Sudetenland (Czechoslovakia)
Nov. 9, 1938	*Kristallnacht* pogrom in Germany
Sept. 1, 1939	German invasion of Poland
Sept. 17, 1939	Soviet Union occupation of east Poland
Apr. 9, 1940	German invasion of Norway and occupation of Denmark
May 10, 1940	German invasion of Belgium, the Netherlands, France, and Luxemburg
June 14, 1940	German entry into Paris
July 10, 1940	Battle of Britain (to Spring 1941)
Nov. 5, 1940	Roosevelt victory over Wendell Willkie in Presidential election
June 22, 1941	German invasion of Soviet Union
Aug. 1, 1941	United States ban on gasoline export to Japan
Sept. 15, 1941	German siege of Leningrad (to Jan. 1943)
Sept. 30, 1941	German attack on Moscow (to December 1941)
Dec. 7, 1941	Japanese attack on Pearl Harbor, Wake, Guam, Philippines, British Malaya, Hong Kong, and Thailand
Dec. 8, 1941	United States declaration of war on Japan
Dec. 11, 1941	United States declaration of war on Germany and Italy
Jan. 20, 1942	Nazi decision on "Final Solution" at Wannsee Conference
Feb. 15, 1942	Singapore surrender to Japan
Feb. 19, 1942	U.S. Executive Order 9066, relocating Japanese Americans on the West Coast to internment camps
May 6, 1942	Allied surrender of Corregidor Island (Philippines)
June 3–6, 1942	United States defeat of Japanese at Midway
Sept. 13 1942	Battle of Stalingrad (to February 2, 1943)
———	
May 7, 1945	German unconditional surrender at Reims
Sept. 2, 1945	Japanese surrender aboard USS *Missouri* in Tokyo Bay

Dr. Seuss and *PM*

Theodor Seuss Geisel was born in 1904 in Springfield, Massachusetts.

A prosperous small city on the Connecticut River in western Massachusetts, Springfield boasted a Mulberry Street and Terwilliger and McElligot clans. Today there is a Dr. Seuss Room in the building that houses its New England Historical Society, and there are plans for a larger national memorial. Theodor was third-generation American, the second child and only son of one of the prosperous German-American families in Springfield. An older sister was born in 1902. On both sides of the family, his grandparents had emigrated to the United States from Germany. His father's parents emigrated before 1870 and established a brewery in Springfield: Kalmbach and Geisel. The brewery became known as "Come back and guzzle." The brewery prospered until Prohibition took effect in 1920 and killed it.

German was the language of the Geisel household. The family's religion was Evangelical Lutheran, with services conducted in German. During World War I, Theodor, then a Boy Scout, sold U. S. war bonds. His grandfather, the immigrant Geisel, bought $1,000 worth. Theodor was one of ten Springfield Boy Scouts to win an award for successful sales.

After graduating from the Springfield public schools, Theodor enrolled at Dartmouth College, in the class of 1925. While still in high school, he had drawn cartoons, and at Dartmouth he gravitated to the college humor magazine. A run-in with the college authorities over bootleg liquor forced him to publish his cartoons under an alias, so he chose his middle name, Seuss (the German pronunciation of Seuss rhymes with Royce). The "Dr." part came later. During his senior year, Theodor wrote to his father that he would get a college fellowship for postgraduate study at Oxford. His father boasted of this to the editor of the local paper, who mentioned it in print. The fellowship did not materialize, but, to preserve family pride, the elder Geisel footed the bill for the year at Oxford. That year convinced Theodor that academia was not for him. However, it exposed him to Great Britain, to France, and to Germany. The next year he spent in Paris, with trips to Switzerland, Austria, and Italy. "Dr. Seuss" never did earn a Ph.D., but when he became successful his alma mater conferred on him an honorary doctorate.

From 1927 to 1941 Dr. Seuss lived in New York City. He drew humor cartoons for an obscure humor magazine, *Judge*, which billed itself as "the world's wittiest weekly," and occasionally for more prestigious journals such as the *Saturday Evening Post*. One of his cartoons incorporated the bug-spray Flit, and it caught the eye of the wife of the advertising executive responsible for the account of Standard Oil of New Jersey, which manufactured Flit. For the next seventeen years Dr. Seuss was on the payroll of Esso

(Ess-O, S[tandard] O[il of New Jersey]), earning the then-sizable income of $12,000 per year. So, during the Depression, when many Americans suffered severe financial hardship, Dr. Seuss did not. According to Dr. Seuss, "It wasn't the greatest pay, but it covered my overhead so I could experiment with my drawings." In a major break with his Republican father in 1932 he voted for Franklin Delano Roosevelt. Sometime after, Dr. Seuss moved to a spacious apartment at 1160 Park Avenue with a foyer, a large living room, a dining room, and two bedrooms.

The salary from Esso allowed for travel, both at home and abroad. On board ship returning from one trip to Europe, Dr. Seuss was struck by the rhythm of the ship's engines. After landfall he produced the line, "And to *think* that I *saw* it on *Mulberry Street.*" It became the title of his first book. Twenty-seven publishers rejected the book before a Dartmouth acquaintance at Vanguard Press bumped into Dr. Seuss on a New York sidewalk. Vanguard published the book in 1937. In 1938, Vanguard published Dr. Seuss's *The Five Hundred Hats of Bartholomew Cubbins.* After Vanguard merged with Random House, Random House published *King's Stilts* (1939) and *Horton Hatches the Egg* (1940).

Fame and fortune did not come immediately. In its first six years *Mulberry Street* sold 32,000 copies. *King's Stilts* sold fewer than 5,000 copies in year one and only 400 in year three. *Horton Hatches the Egg* sold 6,000 in year one and 1,600 in year two. The real takeoff in sales came in the years after the war. In 1957, Dr. Seuss published *The Cat in the Hat*, his breakthrough book. One source in 1959 puts Dr. Seuss's cumulative sales at 1,500,000 copies; in 1979, the then-current total was 80,000,000; and today's numbers are higher still. In any case, by 1941 Dr. Seuss had a steady income from Esso and the beginnings of a career as author of unconventional children's books.

But all was not well with the world. In September 1931, Japan seized Manchuria, igniting Asia's fifteen-year war. In September 1939, Germany invaded Poland and plunged Europe into six years of war. Dr. Seuss had strong views. His opposition to Italian fascism led him to set pen to paper for his first editorial cartoon. The cartoon exemplified the sharp wit, the wealth of detail, and many of the stylistic elements that were to characterize Dr. Seuss's work for the next two years. In the cartoon, Virginio Gayda, editor of *Il Giornale d'Italia*, a major publication of the fascist regime, is suspended before a giant typewriter, banging away. He wears the fez that Italy's fascist militia adopted for their uniform. Pieces of the typewriter fly off in several directions, and steam issues improbably from three vents. A *steam* typewriter? Who but Dr. Seuss could have imagined it? The steam does in the observer bird at top right (note the crosses for eyes, a sure sign that the bird is dead). As we shall see, onlooking birds and other creatures play important roles in Dr. Seuss's wartime cartoons. The paper emerging from Gayda's typewriter becomes a banner that extends back over his head, where a winged Mussolini holds up the free end. This is Dr. Seuss's first version of Mussolini, but most of the elements we will see in later cartoons are already in place. The cartoon suggests that poisoned prose comes from this captive press: if Gayda is not captive, why can't he stand on his own two feet?

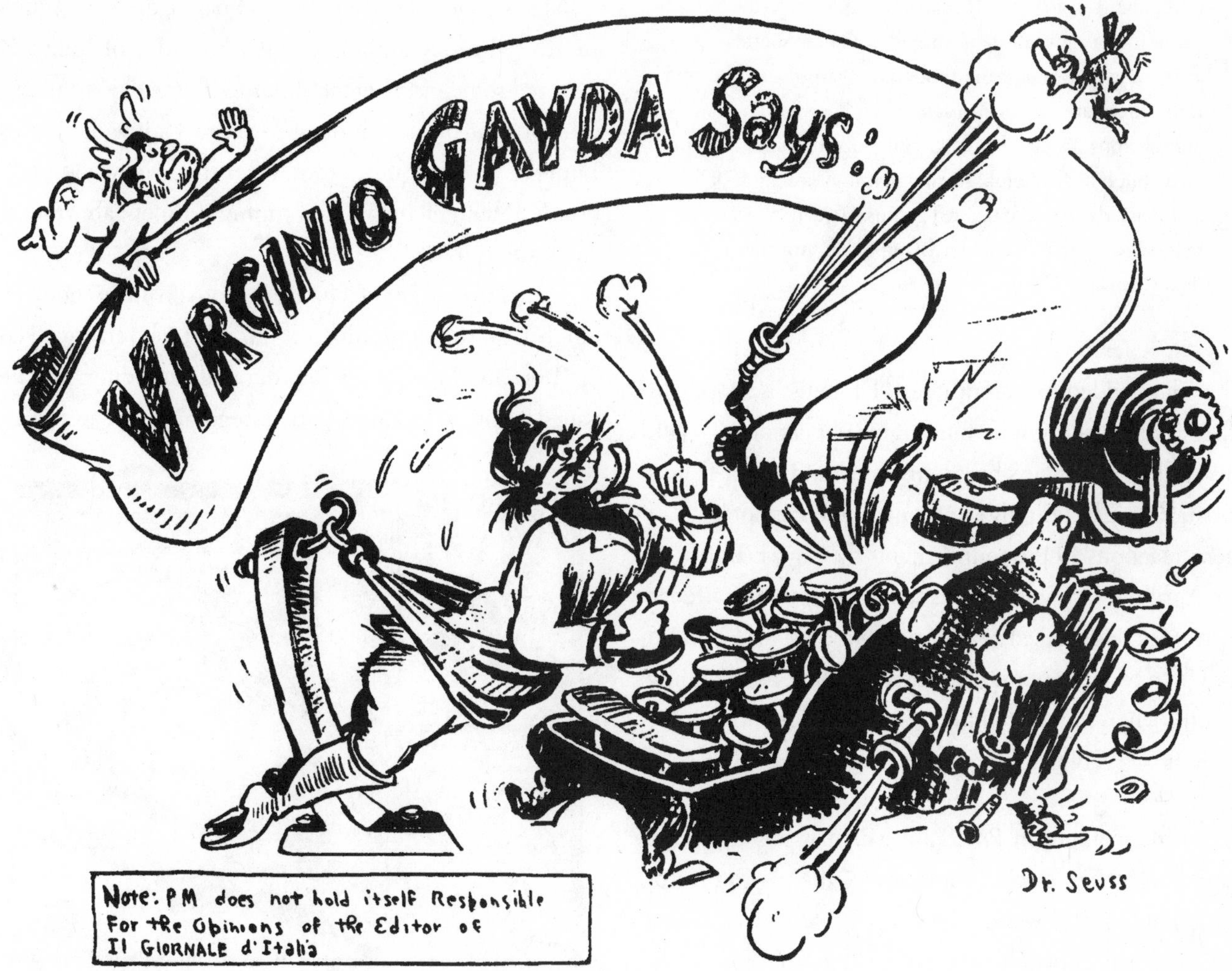
VIRGINIO GAYDA Says:
Note: PM does not hold itself Responsible For the Opinions of the Editor of Il GIORNALE d'Italia
Dr. Seuss

Dr. Seuss showed it to a friend who worked for *PM*, a left-wing daily newspaper published in New York from 1940–1948. The friend passed it on to *PM*'s editor, Ralph Ingersoll, who liked it. The cartoon appeared at the end of January 1941. Below it was this note:

Dear Editor: If you were to ask me, which you haven't, whom I consider the world's most outstanding writer of fantasy, I would, of course, answer: "I am." My second choice, however, is Virginio Gayda. The only difference is that the writings of Mr. Gayda give me a pain in the neck. This morning, the pain became too acute, and I had to do some-

> thing about it. I suddenly realized that Mr. Gayda could be made into a journalistic asset, rather than a liability. Almost every day, in amongst the thousands of words that he spews forth, there are one or two sentences that, in their complete and obvious disregard of fact, epitomize the Fascist point of view. Such as his bombastically deft interpretation of a rout as a masterly stroke of tactical genius. He can crow and crawl better than any other writer living today. Anyhow...I had to do a picture of Gayda.
>
> —Dr. Seuss

The editor added, in parentheses, "Dr. Seuss is a topflight advertising artist, most famous for his Flit cartoons." With this cartoon, Dr. Seuss began his career at *PM*. In February and March, he published only three cartoons, all of them reactions to pronouncements by Gayda. But from late April on, Dr. Seuss published three or more cartoons each week. He worked as editorial cartoonist for *PM* from early 1941 to January 1943, nearly two full years, spanning months when the United States was at peace and months when it was very much at war.

In his monograph on *PM*, Paul Milkman describes the paper as "A New Deal in Journalism;" the play on words is intentional. *PM* was a new deal in many ways. It cost five cents per copy when its competitors sold for two or three cents. It ran no comics (at least at first), crossword puzzles, or stock market reports. It specialized in photographs and other visuals using an improved "hot ink" printing process; the issue of November 26, 1942, for example, carried eight full pages of war maps, most of them full-page spreads and one of them a two-page spread. It accepted no advertising. It continued no stories onto back pages. It pioneered radio pages, the early equivalent of the newspaper television guides of today. It attracted some of the greatest names of the day in American journalism and letters. Erskine Caldwell, James Thurber, I. F. Stone, James Wechsler, Heywood Hale Broun, Lillian Hellman, and Jimmy Cannon: all wrote at one time for *PM*.

Most important, *PM* was outspoken in its politics. Ralph Ingersoll, a prominent journalist who had worked for *Time* and *Life*, was its founder and first editor, and he issued political position papers regularly. For example,

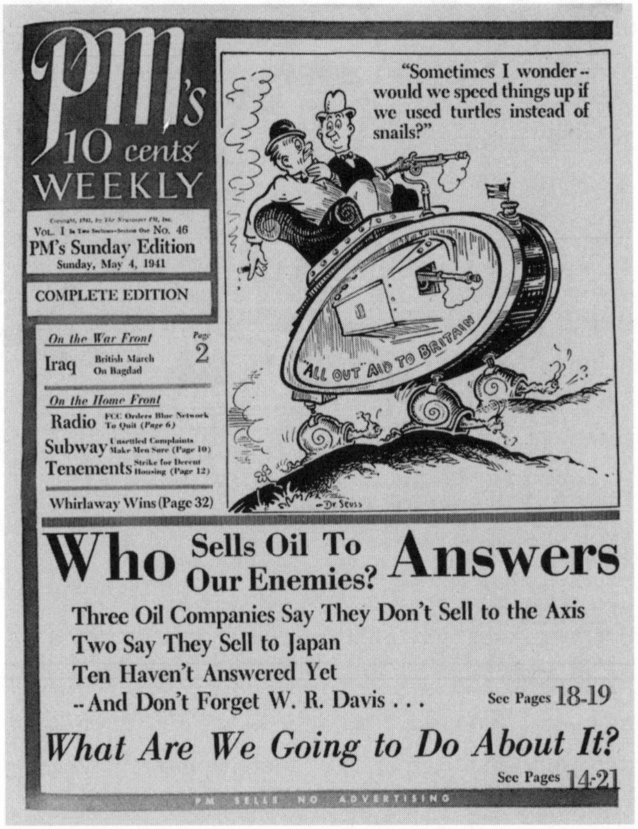

PM's
10 cents
WEEKLY

Vol. I No. 46
PM's Sunday Edition
Sunday, May 4, 1941

COMPLETE EDITION

On the War Front — Page 2
Iraq — British March On Bagdad

On the Home Front
Radio — FCC Orders Blue Network To Quit (*Page 6*)
Subway — Unsettled Complaints Make Men Sore (Page 10)
Tenements — Strike for Decent Housing (Page 12)

Whirlaway Wins (Page 32)

"Sometimes I wonder--would we speed things up if we used turtles instead of snails?"
ALL OUT AID TO BRITAIN
Dr Seuss

Who Sells Oil To Our Enemies? Answers

Three Oil Companies Say They Don't Sell to the Axis
Two Say They Sell to Japan
Ten Haven't Answered Yet
--And Don't Forget W. R. Davis . . . See Pages 18-19

What Are We Going to Do About It? See Pages 14-21

PM SELLS NO ADVERTISING

this is one of his formulations of the *PM* stance: "We are against people who push other people around, just for the fun of pushing, whether they flourish in this country or abroad. We are against fraud and deceit and greed and cruelty and we seek to expose their practitioners. We are for people who are kindly and courageous and honest.... We propose to applaud those who seek constructively to improve the way men live together. We are American and we prefer democracy to any other form of government." Or again: "The Fascist philosophy [represents] a live threat to everything we believe in, beginning with a democratic way of life.... We do not believe either the study of the works of Karl Marx or membership in the Communist Party in America is antisocial."

PM
5 cents
NEW YORK DAILY
Copyright, 1941, by The Newspaper PM, Inc.
Vol. I – No. 23
Thursday, May 8, 1941
Mostly Cloudy and Mild
COMPLETE EDITION
What's Going On in the Mediterranean? Page 12
An Effort to Separate Some Facts From Fiction
British Down 23 Night Raiders Page 2
Defense Industries Queried on Why They Won't Hire Negroes Page 8
Auto Tax Asked To Hit Profits Page 4
Canada Trains 20,000 Fliers a Year for RAF Page 11
U. S. Spreads Net To Trap Aliens Page 4
TALK
TALK
TALK
TALK
TALK
TALK
TALK
Dr. Seuss
WILLKIE: If U. S. Delivers the Goods NOW England Will Win Page 5
KNOX: Don't Let Our Enemies Destroy Britain's Sea Power Page 4
But What Are We Going To DO About It?
PM SELLS NO ADVERTISING

On December 8, 1941, in the immediate aftermath of the Japanese attack on Pearl Harbor, Ingersoll sent a "Memo to the Staff" setting down "what [he] had to say" that day. It includes this section:

> 3. That with the declaration of war, *PM*'s first job was done. The first serious job that *PM* undertook was giving the people of America the facts about the threat of Fascist aggression—at home and abroad. When the Fascists attacked us yesterday, this job was finished. We have nothing more to say about the threat for it has now materialized in the open attack that we have been so long convinced was inevitable.
>
> 4. That this is our satisfaction: that our warnings have contributed to the preparedness of this country....
>
> 5. That today we begin a new task. That this task is WINNING THE WAR.

Ingersoll surely claimed too much for *PM*, both in preparing the United States for war and in winning the war, but such was his ambition and *PM*'s sense of mission. *PM*'s daily circulation was about 150,000. In those days there were seven other mass-circulation dailies in New York City, including the *New York Times* (daily circulation: roughly 500,000) and the *Daily News* (daily circulation: over 2,000,000). As we shall see, the latter paper was the particular target of *PM*'s outrage.

On January 6, 1941, Ingersoll had further thoughts:

> At present our particular interests are:

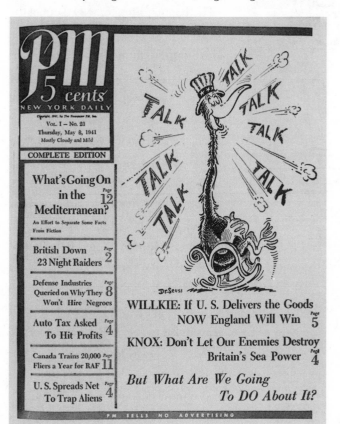

> FOR—ALL OUT PRODUCTION OF WEAPONS...that comes ahead of everything for our stake is human lives. (We always take Victory for granted; we work to speed victory to save lives.)
>
> FOR—INTELLIGENT TRAINING OF OUR ARMED FORCES....
>
> FOR—INTELLIGENT LEADERSHIP....
>
> FOR—DEMOCRACY AT HOME. The war against Fascism continues at home as well as abroad. It is one war, wherever. At home we now wage it in the name of winning the war on the field of battle. The big word MORALE covers it—too much like a tent to suit us.... LABOR'S INTERESTS ARE SYNONYMOUS WITH OURS—AND WITH THE COUNTRY'S....
>
> AGAINST—DEMOCRACY'S RECORDED ENEMIES. By the time the Fascists attacked Pearl Harbor and Hitler and Mussolini declared war on us, the Professional Isolationists had revealed themselves as American Enemies of Democracy.... We experienced hunters of American Enemies of Democracy have a special obligation—and privilege—to expose them. It takes doing. But we'll find ways to do it.

PM signed on to the New Deal of President Roosevelt, but it did so—in the words of historian Paul Milkman—"at precisely the moment when Roosevelt was abandoning New Deal politics to create an interventionist coalition." As the Administration moved toward the right, *PM* endorsed intervention but clung to the Administration's earlier social commitments.

Michael Denning's *The Cultural Front* speaks of the Popular Front of the 1930s and early 1940s, that coming together of industrial unionists, Communists, independent socialists, community activists, and emigré antifascists behind a three-part program: antifascism and anti-imperialist solidarity; social democratic electoral politics; and civil liberties. Writes Denning: "The Popular Front emerged out of the crisis of 1929, and it remained the central popular democratic movement over the following three decades." Among the intellectuals, it brought together older "patrician" modernists such as Malcolm Cowley and Edmund Wilson and younger "plebeian" writers and artists: producer John Houseman, filmmaker Fritz Lang, playwright Bertolt Brecht, writers Ayako Ishigaki and Franz Werfel, composers Kurt Weill and Béla Bartók. Denning labels *PM* "the Popular Front tabloid."

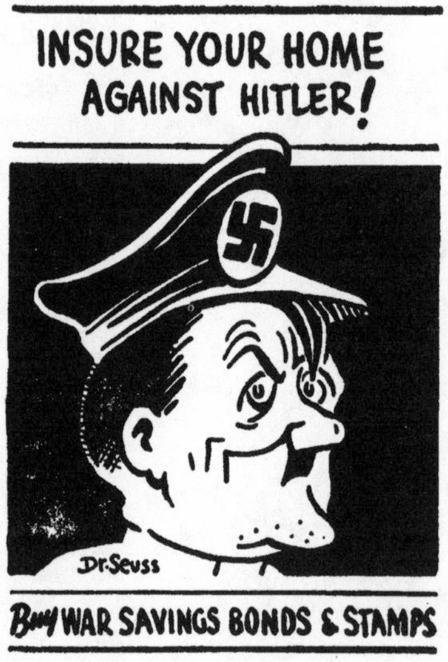
INSURE YOUR HOME
AGAINST HITLER!
Dr. Seuss
Buy WAR SAVINGS BONDS & STAMPS

July 28, 1942

Editor Ingersoll himself later had second and third thoughts about *PM* and its activism. This is clear from accounts of these years in his papers at Boston University. In one outline he wrote: "'A New Kind of Newspaper' was to have been A *Crusade* all right—but a crusade not *for* any political or social reform but simply *against* the stupidity, the dullness, the lack of imagination and ingenuity—and the occasional venality—of the Big Business American Newspapers of the Twentieth Century. If there were any politics in this, they were reactionary rather than radical. They sought to go back to simpler days when the newspaper business was not to sell advertising space but to tell *news*. This was the diametrical opposite of the concept of the propagandist. Yet *PM* had become the propagandist to end all propagandizing (and itself!)." To the last sentence Ingersoll appended in pencil: "*—the warmonger of all times*." The date of this addition is not clear, but the insertion speaks eloquently to Ingersoll's second thoughts.

For the years 1941 and 1942, Dr. Seuss drew editorial cartoons for *PM*. *PM* was on the left in American politics, but what defined the spectrum? What were the issues? Who were the players? Fifty-two percent of those Americans eligible to vote went to the polls in November 1940 to vote in the presidential election pitting President Franklin Delano Roosevelt, a Democrat elected first in 1932 and reelected in 1936, against Wendell Willkie, a Democrat-turned-Republican. The war in Europe and Asia was a major issue. Should the United States oppose the Germans and aid the British? How? To what extent? At what risk? Willkie supported Roosevelt's foreign policy—aid for Britain—but attacked New Deal social programs. The result was Roosevelt's third victory and an unprecedented third term, although Roosevelt's margin of victory was much narrower than in either 1932 or 1936: Willkie won 22,000,000 votes to Roosevelt's 27,000,000 and eighty-two votes in the electoral college (in 1936, the Republican candidate had won eight). What is more, Republicans held on to most of their striking gains of 1938 in the House. Roosevelt won the election in part by promising not to take the United States into the war.

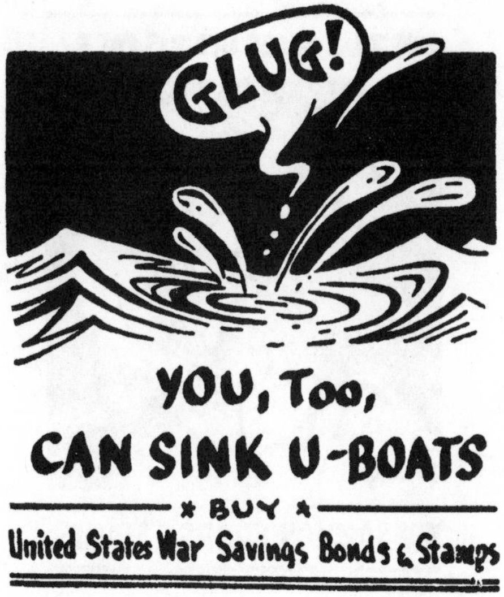
GLUG!
YOU, Too,
CAN SINK U-BOATS
BUY
United States War Savings Bonds & Stamps

May 24, 1942

However, in his State of the Union address (January 6, 1941) President Roosevelt called for "full support of all those resolute peoples everywhere, who are resisting aggression and are thereby keeping war away from our hemisphere," and he spoke disparagingly of the noninterventionists: "We must always be wary of those who with sounding brass and a tinkling cymbal preach the 'ism' of appeasement. We must especially beware of that small group of selfish men who would clip the wings of the American eagle in order to feather their own nests." Four days later he submitted to Congress a bill to allow shipments on credit to Britain and other nations fighting Germany. This was the Lend-Lease Act, which, somewhat amended, passed Congress late in March. The House vote was 260-165, with 135 of 159 Republicans voting no; and the Senate vote was sixty to thirty-one, with seventeen of twenty-seven Republicans voting no.

The rhetoric was heated, in part because this was a significant step away from neutrality, in part because the bill as submitted gave the President great power. Senator Clark of Missouri, a Democrat like the President, stated: "It is simply a bill to authorize the President to declare war...and to establish a totalitarian government." Senator LaFollette of Wisconsin, a Progressive, called the bill "a bill for Congress to abdicate." Socialist leader Norman Thomas derided it as "dictatorship in the name of defending democracy." Roosevelt's long-time antagonist Republican Representative Hamilton Fish of New York said: "It looks as if we are bringing Nazism, fascism, and dictatorship to America and setting up a Führer here." Roosevelt did have the support of Wendell Willkie, who as defeated Presidential nominee could claim to speak for the Republican Party.

WIPE THAT SNEER OFF HIS FACE!
Dr. Seuss
BUY
WAR SAVINGS BONDS & STAMPS

October 13, 1942

Where was the American public on the issue of war and peace? Public opinion polls show that from the start of the fighting in September 1939 the American public preferred a British to a German victory by an overwhelming margin, but by the same overwhelming margin the public opposed American entry into the war. Particularly after the fall of France in June 1940, a majority of the American public was willing to help the British cause by any means short of fighting. Germany's military victories had increased public distaste for Hitler, but the public was not ready yet for war. Still, by 1941, when Dr. Seuss began drawing his editorial cartoons, the "isolationist" coalition had begun to fray badly.

It was into this volatile picture that Dr. Seuss plunged. He joined forces with *PM* to produce the cartoons in this volume. After the initial few months, during which the cartoons appeared anywhere in *PM*'s twenty news pages, they appeared most often on the editorial page, usually as the only illustration on that page. Side by side with the signed editorials, the cartoons enjoyed a prominence of place exceeded only by the cover, and a half dozen *PM* covers themselves carry Dr. Seuss's cartoons. Occasionally there are smaller Dr. Seuss drawings elsewhere, in among the letters to the editor or promoting the sale of war bonds. Two such signed drawings depict Hitler and "Japan." A third, unsigned but clearly from the pen of Dr. Seuss, depicts the aftermath of the sinking of a German submarine.

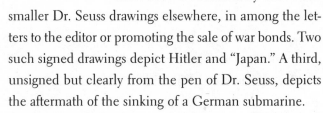

The Home Front

On December 7, 1941, the Japanese attacked Pearl Harbor.

On December 11, Japan's European ally Germany declared war on the United States. The United States was at war, and the war began with a massive military setback. On December 8, Dr. Seuss published his first cartoon reacting to the changed situation. (The number in the margin gives the page on which the cartoon appears.) It did not show Japan or Pearl Harbor. Instead, it showed a bird, "Isolationism," demolished by an explosion, "WAR." For months before December 7 "isolationism" and "isolationists" had been Dr. Seuss's targets. Dr. Seuss (and *PM*) had long wanted the United States to intervene in the European war. Editor Ralph Ingersoll named "Professional Isolationists" as "American Enemies of Democracy" (note the capital letters). Pearl Harbor did not change Dr. Seuss's campaign against these domestic enemies embodied by Charles A. Lindbergh, the America First movement, and Father Charles Coughlin; anti-black racists and anti-Semites; and the opponents of New Deal social programs.

Hitler was the most frequent subject of Dr. Seuss's wartime editorial cartoons, but Charles A. Lindbergh came in second, at least for the year 1941. Lindbergh was the first person to fly solo across the Atlantic, a feat that stunned the world in 1927 and turned him into an authentic international hero. In the 1930s, however, Lindbergh spoke in admiring tones of Hitler's regime, and in early 1941 Lindbergh joined the anti-interventionist organization America First and began speaking out against the interventionist steps of the Roosevelt administration, notably the Lend-Lease Act. On September 11, 1941, in Des Moines, Iowa, Lindbergh made a speech in which he made a distinction between the "Jewish race" and "Americans." That speech included these sentences:

> I am not attacking either the Jewish or the British people. Both races I admire. But I am saying that the leaders of both the British and Jewish races, for reasons which are understandable from their viewpoint as they are inadvisable from ours, for reasons which are not American, wish to involve us in the war. We cannot blame them for looking out for what they believe to be their own interests, but we must look out for ours. We cannot allow the natural passions and prejudices of other peoples to lead our country to destruction.

The charge of anti-Semitism has stuck to Lindbergh's name ever since, and it served to discredit as well the "isolationist" cause to which he had lent his prestige.

I keep "isolationist" in quotation marks because, as in the Ingersoll position paper, it is a rhetorical label that simplifies a highly complex phenomenon. Those opposing

28

American involvement in the war in Europe did so with a variety of motives. Some were pacifists. Others looked back to Versailles and the harsh peace it imposed on Germany; these people saw a part of Hitler's foreign policy as a reaction to Versailles and thus were reluctant to endorse sharp criticism of it. Others distrusted great-power politics of any kind, but particularly support for Britain and the British empire. Others feared the changes war would bring to the United States. Still others distrusted President Roosevelt. The "anti-isolationists" or "interventionists" read the situation differently: that Hitler and Nazi Germany were a threat not simply to Germany's European neighbors but to civilization, that aiding Britain would enable Britain to fight on, that a British collapse would leave the United States alone in a hostile world. However, those advocating this position, as *PM* did, labored under the difficulty that for political reasons the Roosevelt administration had to camouflage its desire to intervene in the war in Europe.

Between "isolationists" and those advocating intervention lay a large divide. In *Second Chance: The Triumph of Internationalism in America During World War II*, a book critical of "isolation," Robert A. Divine suggests that the "internationalists" (proponents since Wilsonian times of an active role for the United States in international affairs) were a relatively homogeneous group. He lists these characteristics:

> Virtually all were old-stock Protestant Americans. Descendants of English and Scottish settlers, they were Anglophiles who believed that the United States had inherited England's role as arbiter of world affairs. As representatives of a social class that had taken on many of the characteristics of a caste, they showed little sympathy for the plight of colonial peoples. The world they wanted to save was limited to Europe and its overseas possessions; they took Latin America for granted and neglected the Orient. Bankers, lawyers, editors, professors, and ministers predominated; there were few salesmen or clerks and no workmen in their ranks. The business community was represented by men who dealt in the world markets.... Small manufacturers, real-estate brokers, and insurance executives were conspicuously absent. Above all, the internationalists lived in the Northeast, with only isolated cells scattered through the provinces in university towns and such cosmopolitan centers as San Francisco and New Orleans.

In more recent times in the United States, the leading "internationalist" organizations—the Foreign Policy Association, the Council on Foreign Relations, and later the Trilateral Commission—have come under attack. The times have changed, but the fault line endures.

Complicating the picture for President Roosevelt was the fact that key parts of his electoral base—Southerners and Irish Americans—were generally against intervention, at least early on. But that was not a concern for *PM* and Dr. Seuss. In their biography of Dr. Seuss, *Dr. Seuss and Mr. Geisel*, Judith and Neil Morgan report that Dr. Seuss had written a bit of doggerel about Lindbergh and hung it on his studio wall. It speaks of Lindbergh's having flown the Atlantic "With fortitude and a ham sandwich" but concluded that Lindbergh "shivered and shook/At the sound of the gruff German landgwich." By the time of Pearl Harbor, Dr. Seuss had depicted Lindbergh in a dozen cartoons. On April 28, 1941, Dr. Seuss drew "The Lindbergh Quarter," which includes the ostrich that becomes Dr. Seuss's representation of "isolationism."

29

This is the bird that the explosion of war blows up into the air on December 8. This was not an innovation. Dr. Seuss had drawn an ostrich with its head in the sand before the war. Then the issue was "Sex, sex, everywhere Sex! Even ostriches hiding their heads have ulterior motives." Nor was the image new in the national debate: in his State of the Union speech of January 3, 1940, President Roosevelt had said, "I hope that we shall have fewer ostriches in our midst. It is not good for the ultimate health of ostriches to bury their heads in the sand." But Dr. Seuss was to put it
30 to good use. On April 29, Dr. Seuss drew smiling simpletons lining up to don "ostrich bonnets" offered by the "Lindy Ostrich Service, Inc."

31 In mid-May 1941, Dr. Seuss depicted Uncle Sam happily in a separate bed from Europe with its contagious diseases: "Stalin-itch, Hitler-itis, Blitz Pox, Nazi Fever, Fascist Fever, Italian Mumps." The latter had killed the cat stretched out beneath the bed labeled "Europe." Later
32 that same month Dr. Seuss depicted Uncle Sam sitting atop a nest in a forest with only one other tree still standing. Trees labeled Poland, France, Holland, Norway, Greece, Jugoslavia, and "etc." have fallen victim to the assault of a woodpecker with the face of Hitler and a ferocious beak. The only other tree left is England, and the woodpecker has already cut its trunk halfway through. Says Uncle Sam, "Ho hum! When he's finished pecking down that last tree he'll quite likely be tired."

A drawing of May 23 urged people to listen to radio coverage of an event at Madison Square Garden featuring Lindbergh ("the Colonel"), the socialist Norman Thomas, and Senator Burton Wheeler. The drawing is Dr. Seuss's, but the note underneath must have come from the editor: "*PM* isn't in the habit of drumming up listeners for appeasement meetings. But sometimes it is worth listening to people just to note what they *don't* say." The questions *PM* wanted the "isolationists" to answer were these: "If Britain is defeated, do you think we will have more democracy, or less, in the U. S. A.? If Britain is defeated, do you think the U. S. A. will be

Yes—By All Means—Listen, and Think!

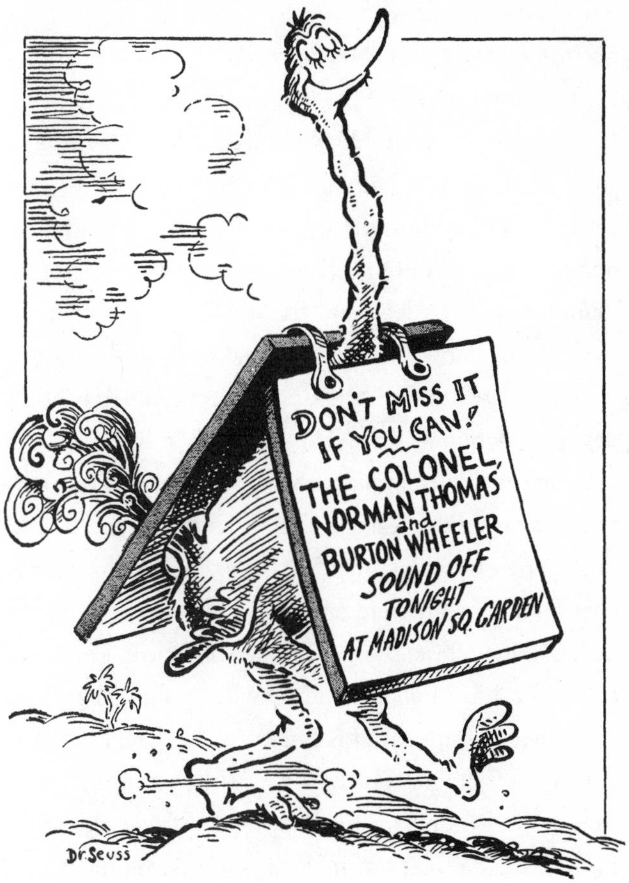
DON'T MISS IT IF YOU CAN!
THE COLONEL, NORMAN THOMAS and BURTON WHEELER SOUND OFF TONIGHT AT MADISON SQ. GARDEN
Dr. Seuss

more secure, or less, from attack by Hitler? Which will bring militarism more quickly to the U. S. A., and make it last longer—a British victory or a Hitler victory?" The notice concluded: "If Lindbergh, Wheeler, and Thomas fail to answer these simple questions, it doesn't matter much what else they may say. Because in the answers to these questions lie the real issues facing America today." This cartoon raises a question I cannot answer: Did Dr. Seuss draw his editorial cartoons to order? Or did he have free rein? This drawing and several others appear to have been specifically commissioned, but often there is no immediate connection between Dr. Seuss's editorial cartoon and the rest of the editorial page.

33 A cartoon in late May showed a blithe "America First" lolling in a bathtub labeled "American hemisphere." With him in the tub are a crocodile, a shark, an octopus, and a lobster, all wearing swastikas. Note the drainpipe with its leak and the right rear leg of the tub (well off the floor). On May 29, Lindbergh made a speech in which he stated: "Mr. Roosevelt claims that Hitler desires to dominate the world. But it is Mr. Roosevelt who advocates world domination when he says it is our business to control the wars of Europe and Asia, and that we in America must dominate islands lying off the African coast." (Lindbergh's reference was to Fernando de Noronha, an island off the coast of Brazil, not Africa). Lindbergh called for "new policies and new leadership." Dr. Seuss

34 responded on June 2: in his cartoon of that date Lindbergh pats a Nazi dragon on the head while warning against Roosevelt. Dr. Seuss further developed these ideas early in July in a cartoon not included in this volume. In the

cartoon a flock of ostriches parades with a sign "Lindbergh for President in 1944!" while an ominous hooded figure ("U. S. fascists") skulks behind, carrying a smaller sign: "Yeah, but why wait till 1944?"

35 On June 9, Dr. Seuss depicted Hitler as an artist. (Of course, Hitler was a failed artist.) He is at work on a portrait of a female "Germania" surrounded by the torch of truth, a dove of peace, and a happy workman; she sits atop a volume labeled "Law," and across her ample bosom is the word "Plenty." Note the two Hitler-faced *putti* with haloes. John Cudahy was a Democrat who had served as ambassador to Belgium (1939–1940). A hardline opponent of the Soviet Union, Cudahy went to Germany and interviewed Hitler; the interview appeared in the *New York Times* in early June 1941. In an editorial *PM* characterized the incident as "boosting Nazi propaganda."

36 Two days later, Dr. Seuss drew "By the Way...Did Anyone Send that Aid to Britain?" Eight old men sit around a table; the calendar on the wall read 1951, ten years in the future. The men have long beards, are festooned with cobwebs, and their beards intertwine. Even the cat has a beard. A skeptic might ask: If the ten years between 1941 and 1951 have not brought Nazi victory, why the worry? But short-term delay, not long-term outcome, is Dr. Seuss's point here. In late June, an unhappy "Amer-
37 ica First" tries to blunt the thorns of a cactus labeled "Stiffening U. S. Foreign Policy." (Count the steps on the impossible stepladder!) In July, Dr. Seuss drew two cartoons under the title, "The Great U. S. Sideshow"; both show freaks of nature. One (July 3, not included in this volume) shows a literally gutless "Appeaser"—there is

nothing at all between his front and back suspenders. In the other (July 8), "America First" and a Nazi are joined at the beard. This was a theme Dr. Seuss and *PM* emphasized: connections between "isolationists" in the United States and the enemies abroad—fascism and Nazism.

On July 16, Dr. Seuss drew a happy whale on a mountain-top chortling: "I'm saving my scalp/Living high on an Alp.../(Dear Lindy! He gave me the notion!)" Particularly in 1941 Dr. Seuss incorporated rhymes and puns into his cartoons. The first of these (not included here) came in June and showed "Uncle Sam" at home ("Home Sweet Home") in his armchair, feet up on a hassock, glass with straw in it on a table by his side, blithely ignoring a "blitz": "Said a bird in the midst of a Blitz,/"Up to now they've scored very few hitz,/So I'll sit on my canny/Old Star Spangled Fanny.../And on it he sitz and he sitz."

There are others. On July 18 (a cartoon not included in this volume), two isolationist clams commented on the dangers of the Atlantic Ocean: "Cried a clam with an agonized shout,/'Don't be so aggressive, you lout!/That's Hitler's Atlantic;/You'll make the man frantic!/Good gracious, don't stick your Neck Out'!" And in August a limerick accompanies a cartoon of Stalin knitting. But that was the last. Perhaps indicating Dr. Seuss's maturation as an editorial cartoonist, he later was to de-emphasize words and focus instead on balancing words and image.

On an August cover, "The Appeaser" (is it Lindbergh?) offers lollipops to Nazi dragons. A September cartoon has Lindbergh attempting to mate the American eagle and a jellyfish. (Note that the jellyfish has eyes—two of them; note also the beards and mustaches of the learned audience.) In September, "America First" assures Uncle Sam, as they stand beside a railroad track, that the Nazi express roaring toward them will turn off onto a very flimsy "Appeasement Junction." Lindbergh made his Des Moines speech, on September 11. One week later, in "Spreading the Lovely Goebbels Stuff," Dr. Seuss draws Lindbergh atop a "Nazi Anti-Semite Stink Wagon." (Paul Joseph Goebbels was Hitler's Minister of Propaganda.) On September 26 Dr. Seuss drew "Appeaser's Mirror," a critique of defeatism: a fun house mirror—"Take one look at yourself and despair!"—gives a healthy Uncle Sam a black eye, a long beard, and a crutch. On October 1, a mother labeled "America First" reads the tale of "Adolf the Wolf" to her frightened children; she reassures them: "...and the wolf chewed up the children and spit out their bones... But those were *Foreign Children* and it really didn't matter."

Four days later—two full months before Pearl Harbor—came the hilarious "I was weak and run-down." Before: "I had circles under my eyes. My tail drooped. I had a foul case of Appeasement... THEN I LEARNED ABOUT 'GUTS' that amazing remedy For all Mankind's Woes." After: "I FEEL STRONG ENOUGH TO PUNCH MISTER HITLER RIGHT IN THE SNOOT!"

Senator Burton Wheeler (D-Montana) was a staunch opponent of intervention. On October 17, he said: "I can't conceive of Japan being crazy enough to want to go to war with us." One month later, he added: "If we go to war with Japan, the only reason will be to help England." On November 7, to pillory Wheeler, Dr. Seuss invoked the story of Admiral George Dewey, the

American hero of the battle of Manila Bay in the Spanish-American War. Dewey was the attacker, and he became famous for saying to the captain of his flagship: "You may fire when you are ready, Gridley." Dr. Seuss's admiral is Wheeler, and he speaks from the bottom of the ocean; a torpedo has blown out the port side of his flagship. The Nazi sub that did the deed lurks not far away as Wheeler fulminates: "You may fire when I am damn good and ready, Gridley." At the end of November—still before Pearl Harbor—Dr. Seuss relegates "Isolationism" to a museum along with a pair of dinosaurs.

In early 1942, *PM* launched a campaign to convince the government to act against the anti-Semitic Roman Catholic priest Charles E. Coughlin. Coughlin had a radio show and published a magazine, *Social Justice*, that *PM* wanted banned from the U. S. mail. On March 30, *PM* printed a ten-page attack on Father Coughlin that included a ballot for readers to sign and mail to the attorney general. In April *Social Justice* was banned from the mail for violating the Espionage Act of 1942. As Paul Milkman comments, "*PM*'s zeal to silence the fascist and pro-fascist mouthpieces shows an alarming absence of concern for civil liberties." Dr. Seuss contributed a number of cartoons to this campaign. On February 9, 1942, he drew "Still Cooking with Goebbels Gas." Earlier he had linked Lindbergh and Goebbels; here it is Coughlin and Goebbels and "The same old Down-with-England-and-Roosevelt Stew." On March 23, "Vater Coughlin" appears as engineer on "The Berlin-Tokyo Rome + Detroit" railroad, pulling freight cars loaded with "Axis propaganda." (Coughlin's home base was just outside Detroit.) Note the swastika on the front of the locomotive and the steam that blasts the unfortunate onlooker in the face. On March 30, he had Hitler himself reading *Social Justice* and phoning Coughlin: "Not bad, Coughlin...but when are you going to start printing it in German?"

Few of Dr. Seuss's editorial cartoons dealt with the postwar world. When his last editorial cartoon appeared in January 1943, the end of the war was still more than two years off. But beginning at the end of August 1942, Dr. Seuss *did* plan the peace or at least restate his opposition to American "isolationism." In August, he ridiculed "The Gopher Hole of Isolation." Then came five cartoons dedicated to this theme in December 1942 (of twenty-one in all) and one in January 1943 (of four). We don't know the date on which Dr. Seuss decided to leave *PM*, but in his last five weeks, the fight against "isolationism" was very much on his mind. On December 14, a giant Uncle Sam was shown watching tiny figures at work on FOUNDATIONS FOR POST-WAR ISOLATIONISM. A huge sign read: "DANGER! SMALL MEN AT WORK!" In a Christmas Day cartoon, a man peeks out from a shelter after the cyclone of war has passed; the title, "With a Whole World to Rebuild..." underlines the pettiness of the shelter-dweller, who thinks only of patching up his fence, labeled "ISOLATION." Finally, on New Year's Day 1942, Dr. Seuss depicted a seedy gentleman labeled "REACTION" offering an "Isolation Lollipop" to Baby 1943. Dr. Seuss may not have drawn the postwar settlement, but he went on record against U. S. "isolationism."

As we have seen, Dr. Seuss portrayed the United States in two ways: as human Uncle Sam and as bird.

Uncle Sam wears a bow tie, cutaway, striped pants, and top hat; unlike Dr. Seuss's other top hats (on the heads of folks he is ridiculing), this hat has stars around the band and vertical stripes. The bird—witness the cartoon show-
41 ing Lindbergh attempting to crossbreed eagle and jellyfish—is an eagle, though bird lovers may be forgiven if they don't recognize it as such. And note that the eagle's wings often end, virtually, in fingers. Dr. Seuss's use of this bird to represent the United States drew a rebuke from one reader, who complained in a letter to the editor (December 18, 1941): "Much as I admire and appreciate the work of Dr. Seuss, I question the fitness of continuing to picture our Uncle Sam as an ostrich. At least he should be transformed into an Eagle." Without correcting the reader's misapprehension, Ralph Ingersoll reprinted one of Dr. Seuss's Uncle Sams and this sentence: "He looks pretty perky to us."

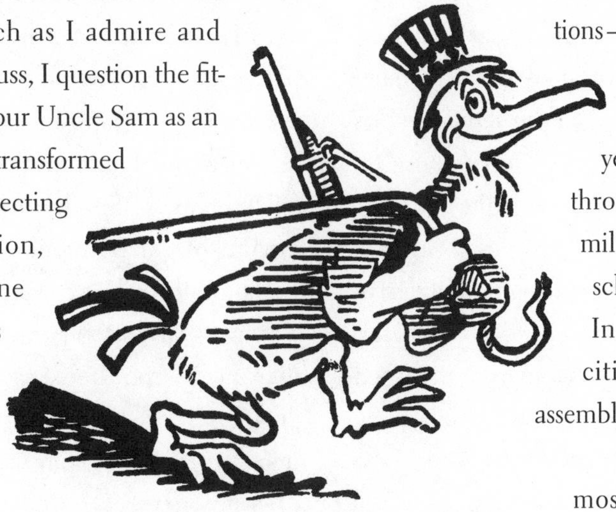

He looks pretty perky to us.—Ed.

December 18, 1941

Dr. Seuss never drew President Franklin Delano Roosevelt. His representations of the United States were Uncle Sam and an eagle, and, sometimes, in a sense "YOU + ME." Dr. Seuss idolized Roosevelt. He quoted Roosevelt and honored him by conferring on him the first membership in his imaginary
188 "Society of Red Tape Cutters," as we will see. But he never *drew* Roosevelt. It is not that Roosevelt was not suitable material for caricature: before and during the war American cartoonists often depicted him, jaunty demeanor, cigarette in holder at a confident angle, and—despite the fact that in real life he was confined to a wheelchair—often standing or striding. But Dr. Seuss's United States is always an idealized figure distinct from its president. In the next chapters we will contrast that treatment with Dr. Seuss's treatment of Germany, Italy, and Japan.

In American society in the early 1940s, relations among the races—primarily, black-white relations—were rocky at best. During the 1930s, there were on average more than ten lynchings per year. Jim Crow laws were in place throughout the country. The U. S. military was still segregated, as were schools and major league baseball. In 1943, riots paralyzed northern cities when black workers joined assembly lines that had been all-white.

Dr. Seuss saved some of his most biting cartoons for issues of anti-black racism and anti-Semitism.
In April 1942, he showed a "Discrim- 56
inating Employer"—castigating "Jewish Labor" and "Negro Labor": "*I'll* run Democracy's War. You stay in your Jim Crow Tanks!" Note the evil expression on the employer's face, and note that Dr. Seuss's "Negro" differs from his "Jew" only in skin tone. On June 11, 1942 Uncle
Sam uses a Flit gun to disinfect American brains. Says 57
John Q. Public as a "racial prejudice bug" blows out of his

Richard H. Minear

ear, "Gracious, was *that* in my head?" As many other Americans await their turn to be spritzed, the cat in the lower right corner smiles approvingly. On June 16, an estimated 18,000 blacks gathered at Madison Square Garden to hear A. Philip Randolph kick off a campaign against discrimination in the military, in war industries, in government agencies, and in labor unions. On June 26, a

58 Seuss cartoon, "The Old Run-Around," shows "Negro Job-Hunters" entering a maze which leads only to dead ends, not to "U. S. War Industries." (How *any* job-hunters were to get to "U. S. War Industries" is a puzzle.)

59 In a cartoon later that month an angry Uncle Sam taps an organist labeled "War Industry" on the shoulder: "Listen, Maestro...if you want to get *real harmony*, use the black keys as well as the white!" Cobwebs on the black keys underline the fact that they haven't been used. In July's

60 "War Work to Be Done," a white employer posts a sign on a woodpile: "No Colored Labor Needed." Two blacks comment: "There seems to be a white man in the woodpile!" (The original expression is "There seems to be a nigger in the woodpile." The term "nigger" was clearly pejorative, but the origins of the expression are obscure; it may have meant simply something unexpected.) In August a

61 black bird of "Race Hatred" perches on the shoulder of segregationist Democratic Governor Eugene Talmadge of Georgia. Note that the bird wears a black hood (why not the white hood of the Ku Klux Klan?) and that Talmadge's whip dwarfs the fenced-in state of Georgia. It is not easy to tell which of the tiny figures are black and which white, but the figures themselves are all similar, as are the houses in front of which they stand.

As we have seen, Dr. Seuss linked racism and anti-Semitism and opposed both. Anti-Semitism was one focus of his assault on Charles Lindbergh. A *PM* cover of September 22, 1941, stated the case in reaction to Lindbergh's speech of September 11 at Des Moines. Dr. Seuss placed 62 a chagrined Uncle Sam in stocks, and a sign hanging from his beak reads, "I am part Jewish." The "sheriffs" who have placed him there are Lindbergh and Senator Gerald P. Nye (D-Wisconsin), one-time New Deal ally of President Roosevelt. A later cartoon involving Nye (April 26, 1942; not included here) depicted him as the hind part of a horse. According to Seuss biographers Judith and Neal Morgan, Ralph Ingersoll feared a lawsuit. But what arrived in the mail from Senator Nye was something else: "[The] issue of Sunday, April 26...carried a cartoon, the original of which I should very much like to possess. May I request its mailing to me?"

In a grim cartoon of July 20, 1942, ten bodies hang by 101 their necks from trees, each one bearing the stark label "Jew"; Hitler stands with Pierre Laval, an additional noose at the ready. On October 21, 1941 (a cartoon not included here), Dr. Seuss drew "Japan" puzzling over *Mein Kampf* and musing, "Now what in blazes am I going to use for Jews?" A photo of Hitler hangs on the wall, signed, "Your Old Pal, Adolf." Shortly before Christmas 1942 Dr. Seuss depicted "Race Hatred" as Adolf 63 Hitler's "annual gift to civilization"; a "U. S. anti-Semite" stands poised to help Hitler wrap the present. A wreath on the wall is filled with swastikas.

December 28, 1942, was the eighty-sixth anniversary of the birth of Woodrow Wilson, the American president who a generation earlier had attempted unsuccessfully to take the United States into the League of Nations that was, in large measure, his creation. Henry A. Wallace, President Roosevelt's vice-president, used the occasion to deliver a speech that focused on postwar issues; the speech was carried on NBC radio. Here is one excerpt: "The United Nations [i. e., the war-time allies, not the postwar organization, which didn't exist yet] must back up military disarmament with psychological disarmament—supervision, or at least inspection, of the school systems of Germany and Japan, to undo so far as possible the diabolical work of Hitler and the Japanese war lords in poisoning the minds of the young." Dr. Seuss weighed in two days later. On December 30, in "'Psychological Disarmament' of Axis Youth," Uncle Sam uses power-driven bellows to blow germs out of the brain of a Nazi boy. Uncle Sam holds a child "Japan" by the scruff of his neck; he's next. This cartoon is a reworking of the cartoon of June 1942 in which it is *American* heads that need to be debugged. *Thinking* on race needed to change, whether here in the United States or in Nazi Germany. Dr. Seuss was not simply echoing the Roosevelt Administration, for he was also echoing his own earlier cartoon; still, the conjunction indicates how closely Dr. Seuss was attuned to the politics of the day. (This is one of the two cartoons included in this collection that do not have Dr. Seuss's signature; the other is the cartoon on p. 217. Many of his cartoons have *both* signature and printed credit.)

Dr. Seuss's campaign for civil rights and against racism and anti-Semitism had one major blind spot: Americans of Japanese descent. At the time of Pearl Harbor, nearly 120,000 Americans of Japanese descent lived on the West Coast. Two-thirds were U. S. citizens by virtue of having been born in the United States. Many of the others were prevented by law from becoming citizens. Soon after Pearl Harbor, the American government ordered the forced relocation and internment of all Americans of Japanese descent living on the West Coast. On February 13, 1942, just days before the Roosevelt administration's decision to incarcerate all Japanese Americans living on the West coast, Dr. Seuss drew "Waiting for the Signal From Home..." It shows the West Coast—Washington, Oregon, and California—and a horde of smiling, bespectacled, virtually identical Asians lining up to pick up blocks of TNT from a warehouse labeled "Honorable 5th Column." A smiling fellow on the roof looks through a telescope out to sea for that "signal from home." It is a scurrilous cartoon. For one thing, no Japanese American on the West Coast was ever convicted of an act of sabotage. General John DeWitt, the individual most responsible for the incarceration, could not have asked for more effective propaganda. To its eternal discredit, *PM* never attacked head-on the incarceration of the Japanese Americans. This cartoon bears a distinct resemblance to the cartoon (December 10, 1941) that shows Japanese as alley cats: the sheer numbers, the sweep of the crowd from right rear to left front, the interchangeable faces.

How could so antiracist and progressive a man as Dr. Seuss and so antiracist and progressive a paper as *PM* indulge in such knee-jerk racism? We see here a blind spot of the wartime New York left. A few people spoke out against America's concentration camps, but only a few; more failed to see a civil rights issue of monumental consequence. No reader of *PM* wrote in to protest this cartoon—at least, no such letter appeared among the letters to the editor. As we have seen, there were letters against Dr. Seuss's eagle. As we shall see, there were letters against his attack on the pacifist preacher John Haynes Holmes and against his slander of dachshunds. But there was no letter against this stark example of mainstream American racism against Asians in America.

In its domestic politics, as we have seen, the newspaper *PM* supported the New Deal vociferously. President Roosevelt moved right, in part because of Republican electoral gains beginning in 1936, but *PM* stayed the course. Even as "Dr. New Deal" became "Dr. Win the War," *PM* committed itself to the New Deal goals that "Dr. Win the War" preferred to downplay. We find these commitments in Dr. Seuss's cartoons, too, albeit in less strident forms. Most of these cartoons appeared in 1942, after the United States joined the war. In one of his political position papers, Ralph Ingersoll had written, "Labor's interests are synonymous with ours—and with the country's." Dr. Seuss, too, concerned himself with labor, but his commitment seemed significantly less strong than *PM*'s. In 66 November 1941, he showed Hitler welcoming news of American labor unrest. The point of the cartoon is in part Hitler's control of information, in part American labor unrest. But the unrest Dr. Seuss has in mind is not primarily between labor and business but *within* labor: between the American Federation of Labor and the upstart Congress of Industrial Organizations, and within the C. I. O. itself. Dr. Seuss's sympathies are not obvious. Was he

merely opposed to labor unrest and for unity and maximum productivity in time of war? A cartoon of March 26, 1942 decries antilabor policies in more unequivocal fash- 67 ion: "Gassing the Troops on Our Own Front Line." But in October (in a cartoon not included here) Dr. Seuss derided John L. Lewis, president of the United Mineworkers and a power in the C. I. O. The cartoon is "The Lord Giveth, and the Lord Taketh Away," and in it Lewis is the lord, and he reaches down out of a cloud with a piece of coal. A strike had brought coal production to a halt, and Dr. Seuss did not approve.

The committed pro-labor cartoons of other cartoonists of this era are strikingly different from Dr. Seuss's cartoons. They feature men in open-throated shirts, sleeves rolled up, in overalls, wearing caps, perhaps, but not hats. Dungarees often sport union badges. Miner's lamps are common, as are lunch pails. So are women, spectacularly so in the cartoons that focus on Rosie the Riveter. These cartoons depict a world quite different from Dr. Seuss's.

On May 18, 1942 Dr. Seuss showed a "Reactionary 68 Wrecking Crew of Congress" advancing with a huge wrecking ball on the "U. S. Social Structure." One bearded fellow, eyes closed, drives the crane; another, eyes open, says: "We're just going to knock out the Unnecessary Floors designed by F. D. R.!" Nine days later, amid much Congressional discussion of taxes, there appears a 69 cartoon lambasting a "tax-exempt securities loop hole for rich." A rich man (top hat, bow tie, spats) climbs up on the rump of a snooty figure labelled "House Ways and Means Committee" to climb through the loophole. The "Committee" points John Q. Citizen—tiny in comparison—to the Income Tax Window: "G'wan, small fry. You pay at the turnstile!" News reports in June showed that New York City had more unemployed people than any other city in the United States. In June, Dr. Seuss pleaded the cause of "400,000 New York unemployed." In October a cartoon attacked the poll tax: "Democracy's Turnstile: Vote Here (If you can afford it)." Here again the crowd is all male and all white. (The poll tax—an annual tax for the right to vote—was an issue with clear racial implications, for it was southern states that had poll taxes.) A later cartoon (November 16, 1942) attacks a prime instrument of conservative opposition to the New Deal, the filibuster. A huge creature, part dog, part dragon, flies through the sky over the Capitol in Washington, D. C. A diminutive Senator Theodore Bilbo (D-,

Mississippi), prominent filibusterer, stands on the back of the beast, using its thirty-foot-long ears as reins. Attached to him is the label "Poll tax bloc." Bilbo's career (and life) ended several years later as Congress investigated the charge that he had intimidated blacks from voting. More than twenty-five years elapsed after the appearance of Dr. Seuss's editorial cartoons before poll taxes were abolished. In 1964, the Twenty-fourth Amendment outlawed poll taxes for primary and general elections for national offices; at that time five states still had poll taxes. Because of a general sense that that constitutional amendment was ineffective, Congress passed the Voting Rights Act of 1965, which authorized a legal test of all poll taxes; two years later, in 1966, the Supreme Court extended the ban to all elections.

He Never Knew What Hit Him

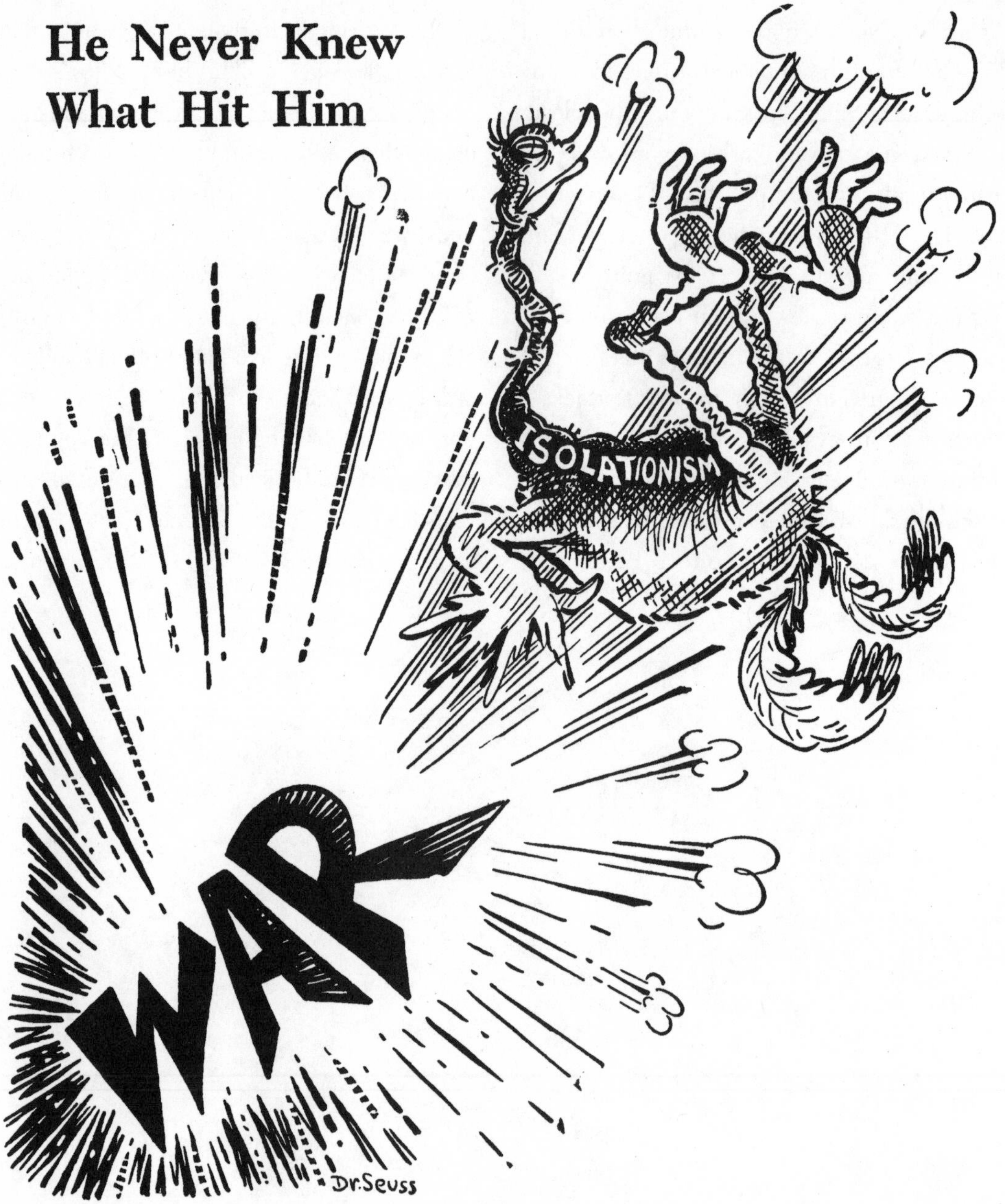
ISOLATIONISM
WAR
Dr. Seuss

28 — December 8, 1941

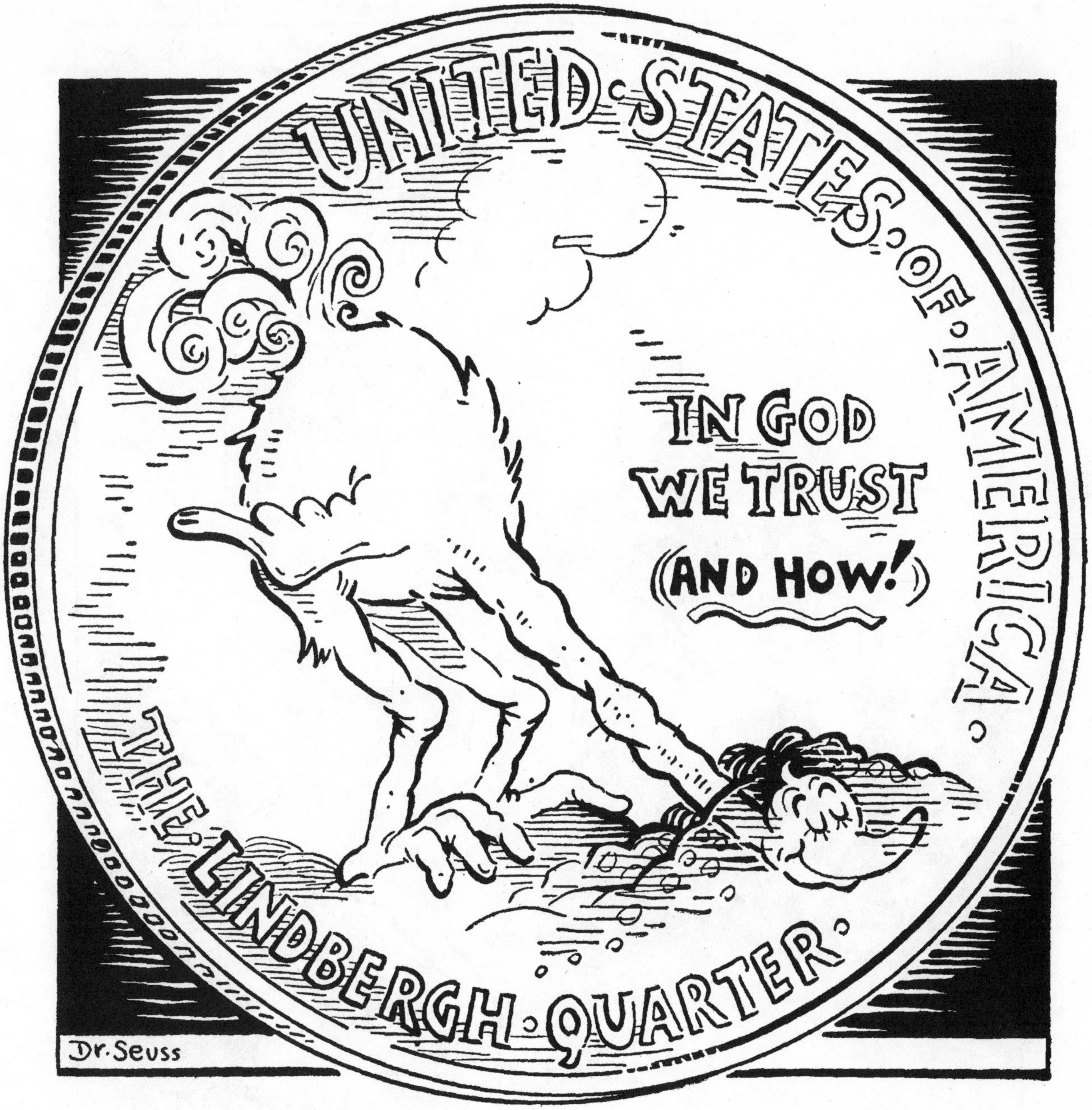
UNITED STATES OF AMERICA
IN GOD
WE TRUST
(AND HOW!)
THE LINDBERGH QUARTER
DR. SEUSS

"Since when did we swap our ego for an ostrich?"

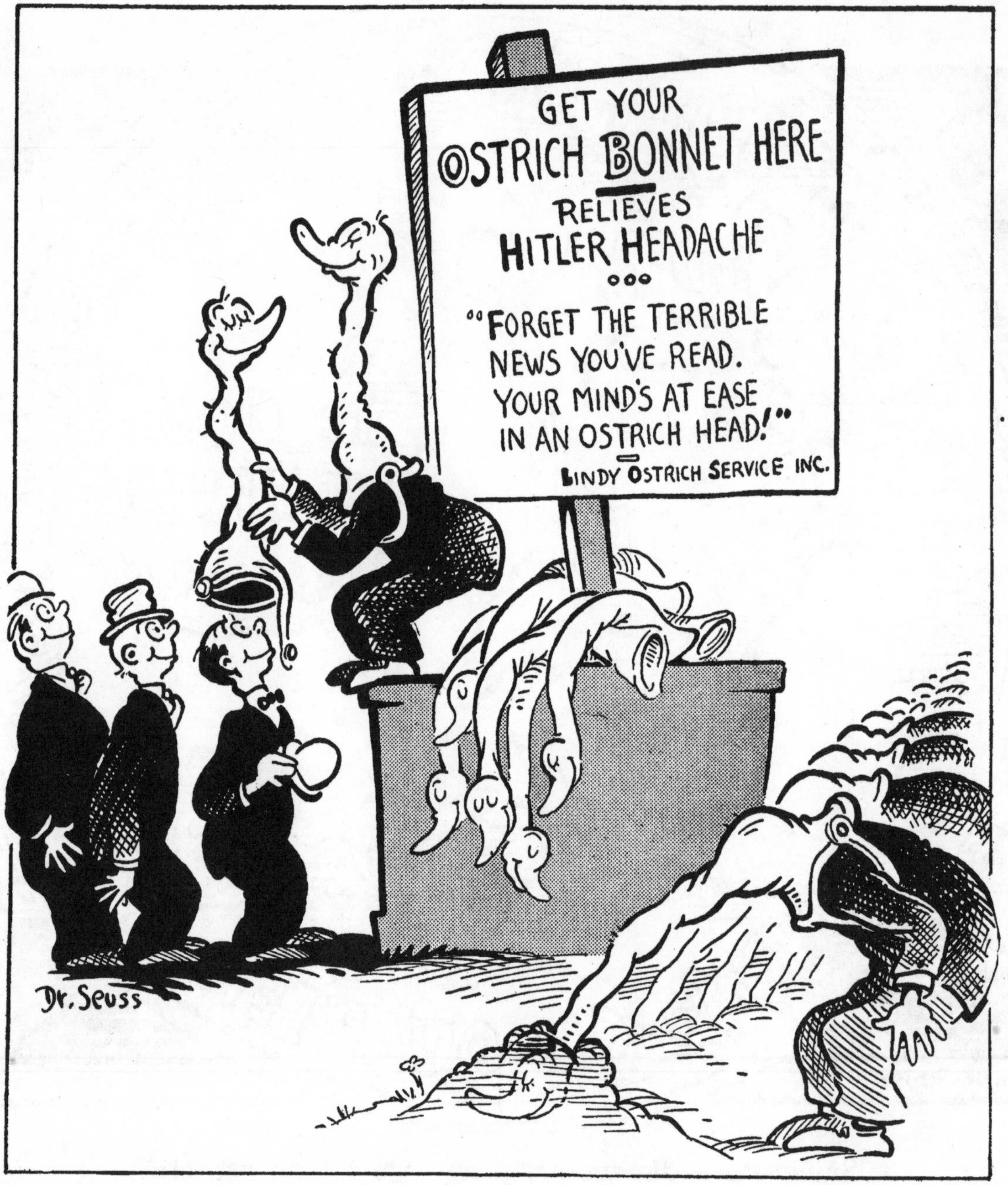
GET YOUR
OSTRICH BONNET HERE
RELIEVES
HITLER HEADACHE
"FORGET THE TERRIBLE
NEWS YOU'VE READ.
YOUR MIND'S AT EASE
IN AN OSTRICH HEAD!"
LINDY OSTRICH SERVICE INC.
Dr. Seuss

We Always Were Suckers for Ridiculous Hats . . .

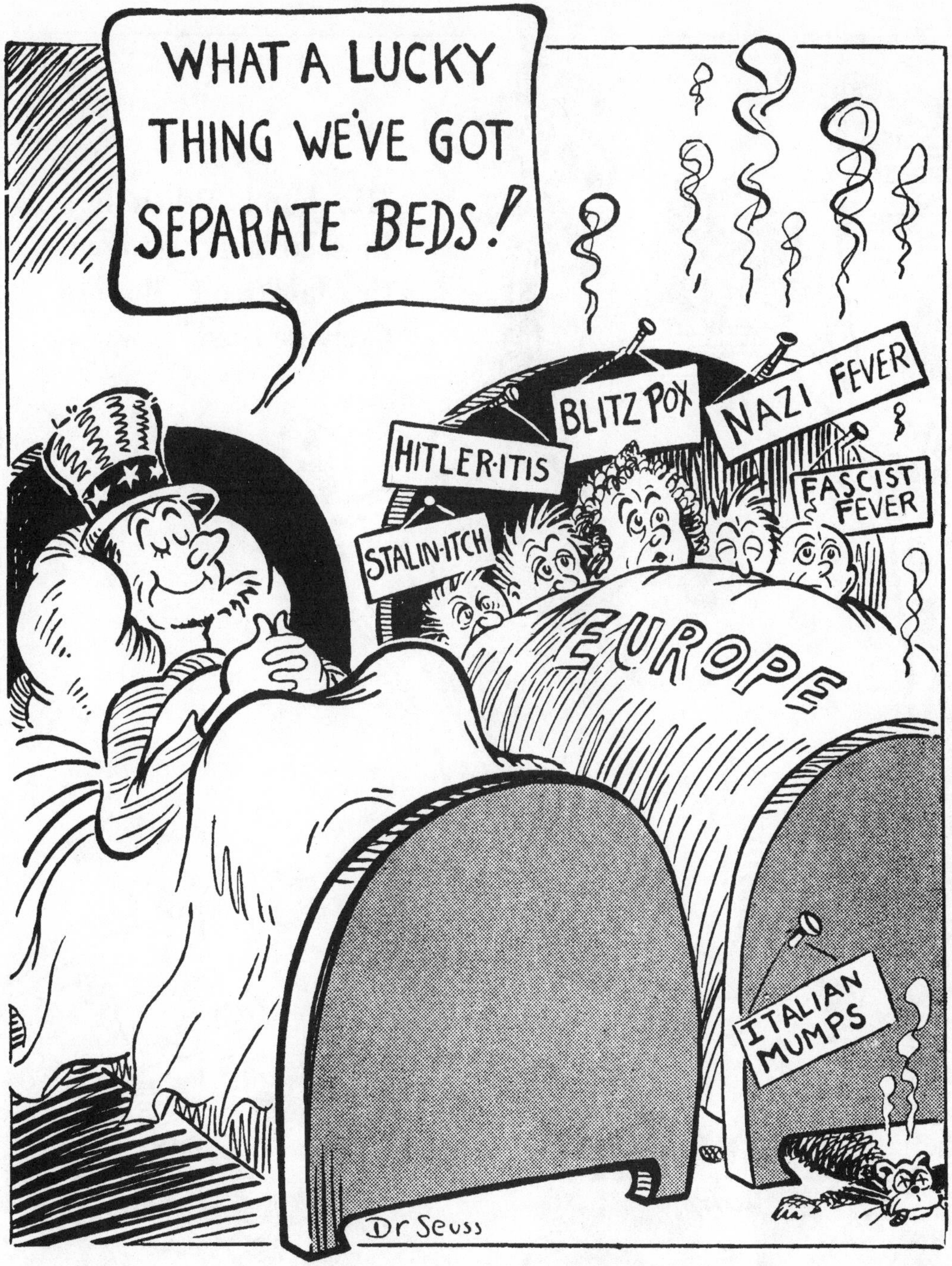
WHAT A LUCKY THING WE'VE GOT SEPARATE BEDS!
HITLER-ITIS
BLITZ POX
NAZI FEVER
STALIN-ITCH
FASCIST FEVER
EUROPE
ITALIAN MUMPS
Dr Seuss

Ho Hum! No chance of contagion.

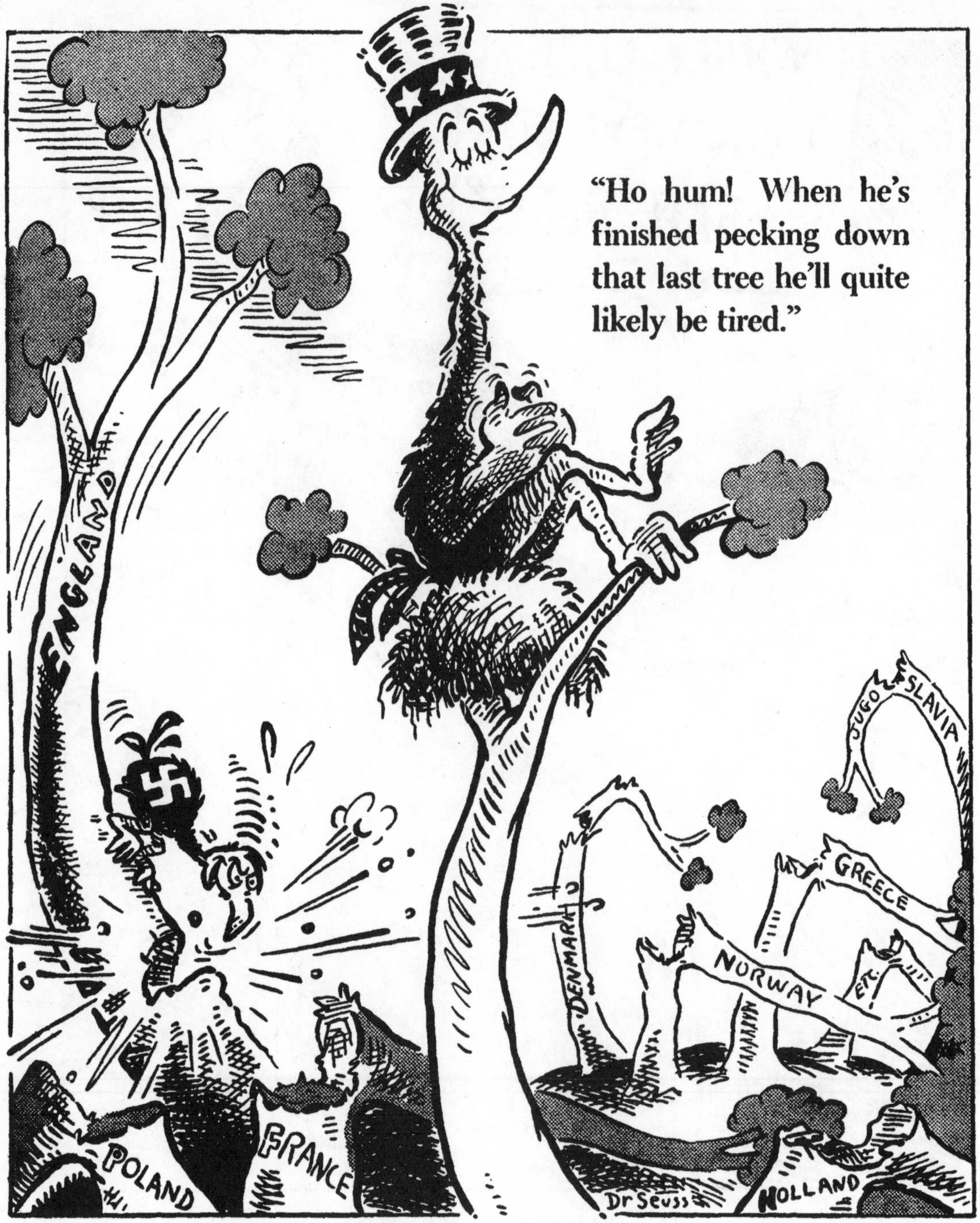
"Ho hum! When he's finished pecking down that last tree he'll quite likely be tired."
ENGLAND
JUGO SLAVIA
GREECE
DENMARK
NORWAY
ETC.
POLAND
FRANCE
HOLLAND
Dr Seuss

32 — May 22, 1941

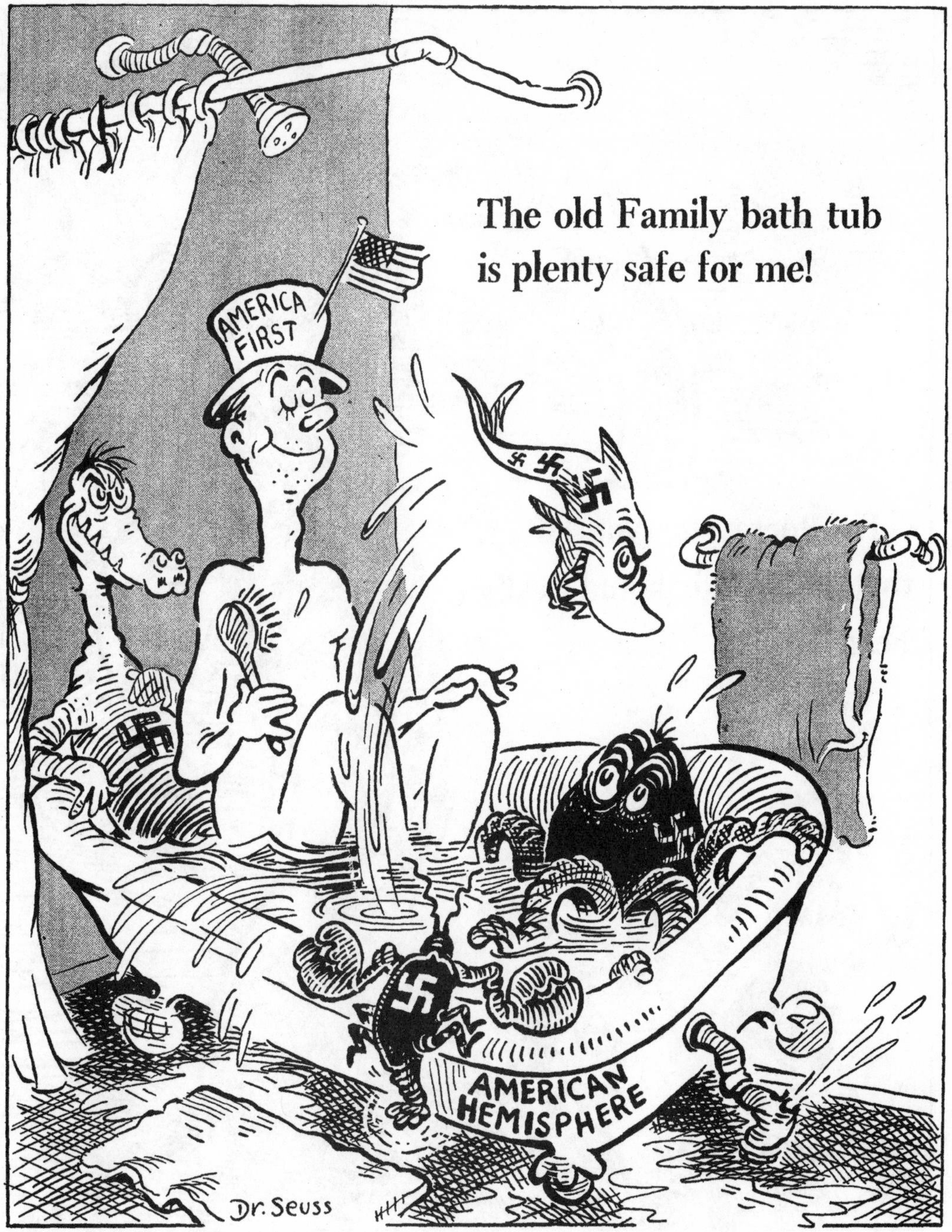
The old Family bath tub
is plenty safe for me!
AMERICA FIRST
AMERICAN HEMISPHERE
Dr. Seuss

33 — May 27, 1941

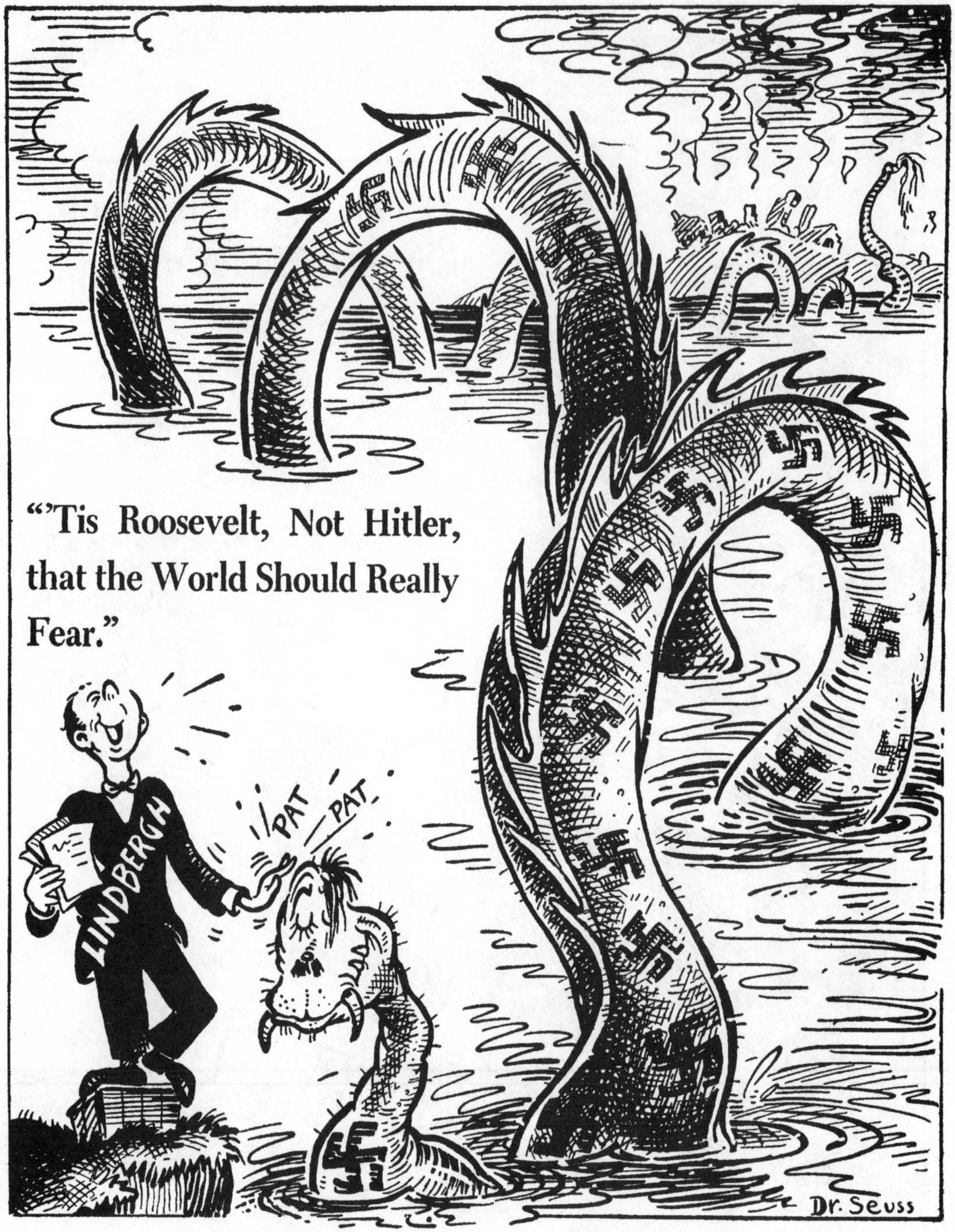
"'Tis Roosevelt, Not Hitler, that the World Should Really Fear."
LINDBERGH
PAT
PAT
Dr. Seuss

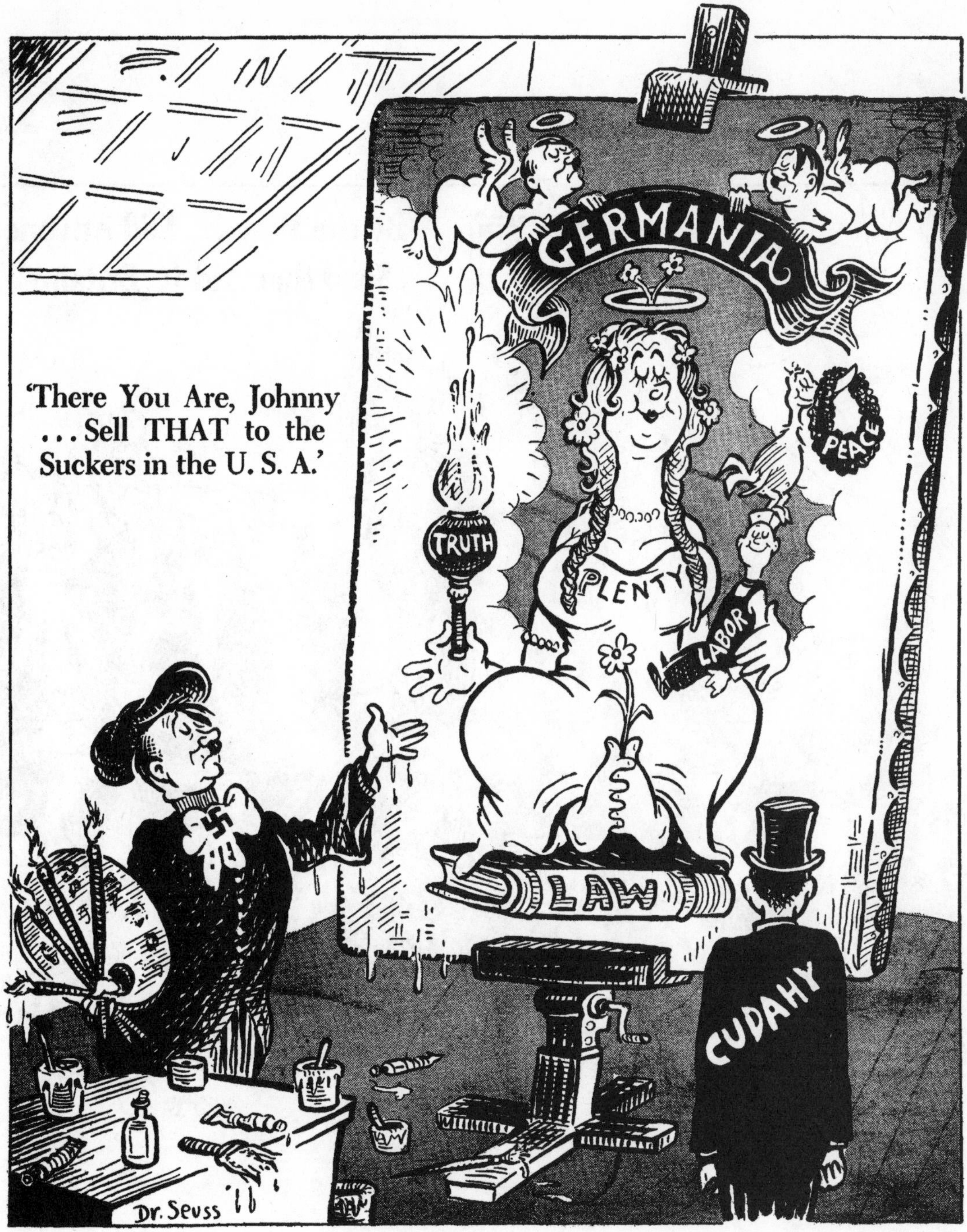
'There You Are, Johnny
. . . Sell THAT to the
Suckers in the U. S. A.'
GERMANIA
TRUTH
PLENTY
LABOR
PEACE
LAW
CUDAHY
Dr. Seuss

35 — June 9, 1941

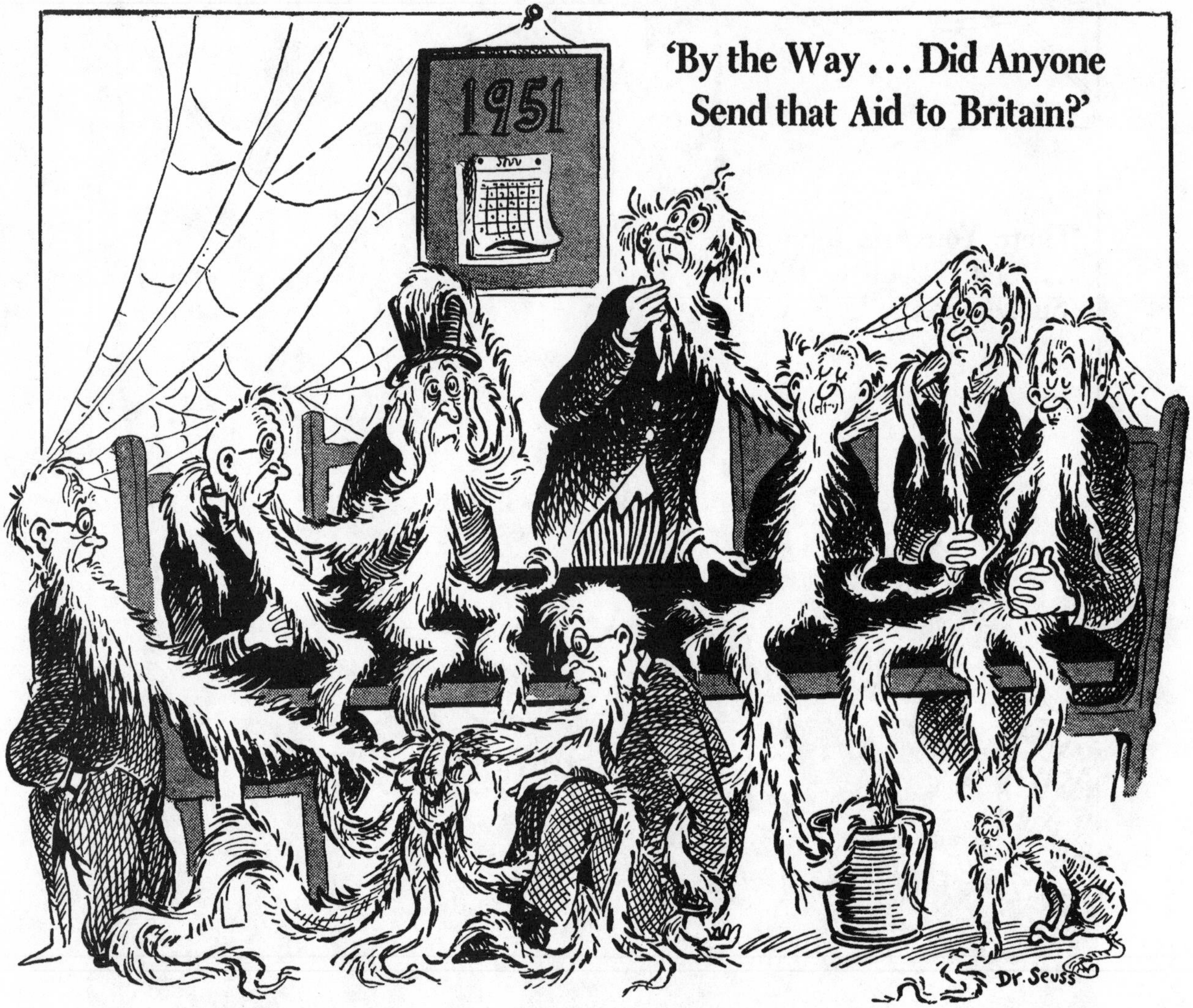
1951
DR. SEUSS
'By the Way . . . Did Anyone Send that Aid to Britain?'

36 — June 10, 1941

"Dear me . . . such spines! Someone's apt to get hurt!

CORKS
AMERICA FIRST
STIFFENING U.S. FOREIGN POLICY
DR SEUSS

37 — June 27, 1941

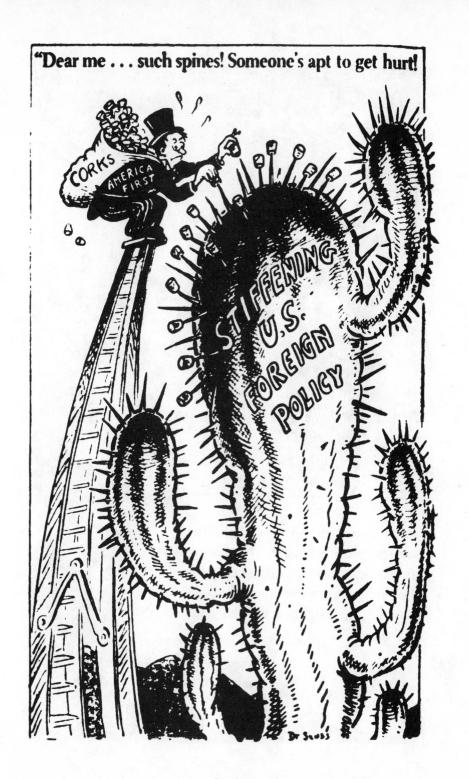

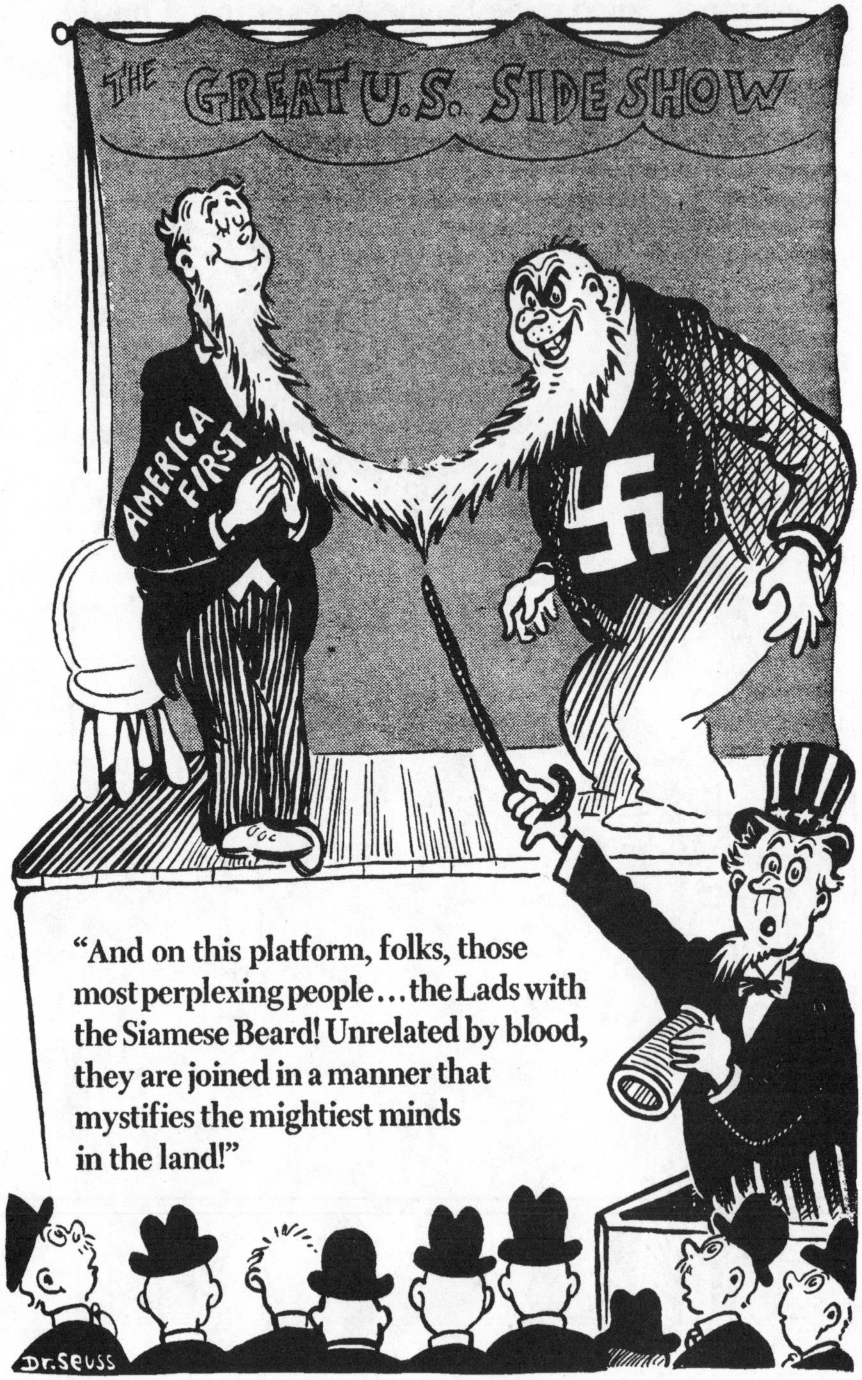
THE GREAT U.S. SIDE SHOW
AMERICA FIRST
"And on this platform, folks, those most perplexing people . . . the Lads with the Siamese Beard! Unrelated by blood, they are joined in a manner that mystifies the mightiest minds in the land!"
DR. SEUSS

38 — July 8, 1941

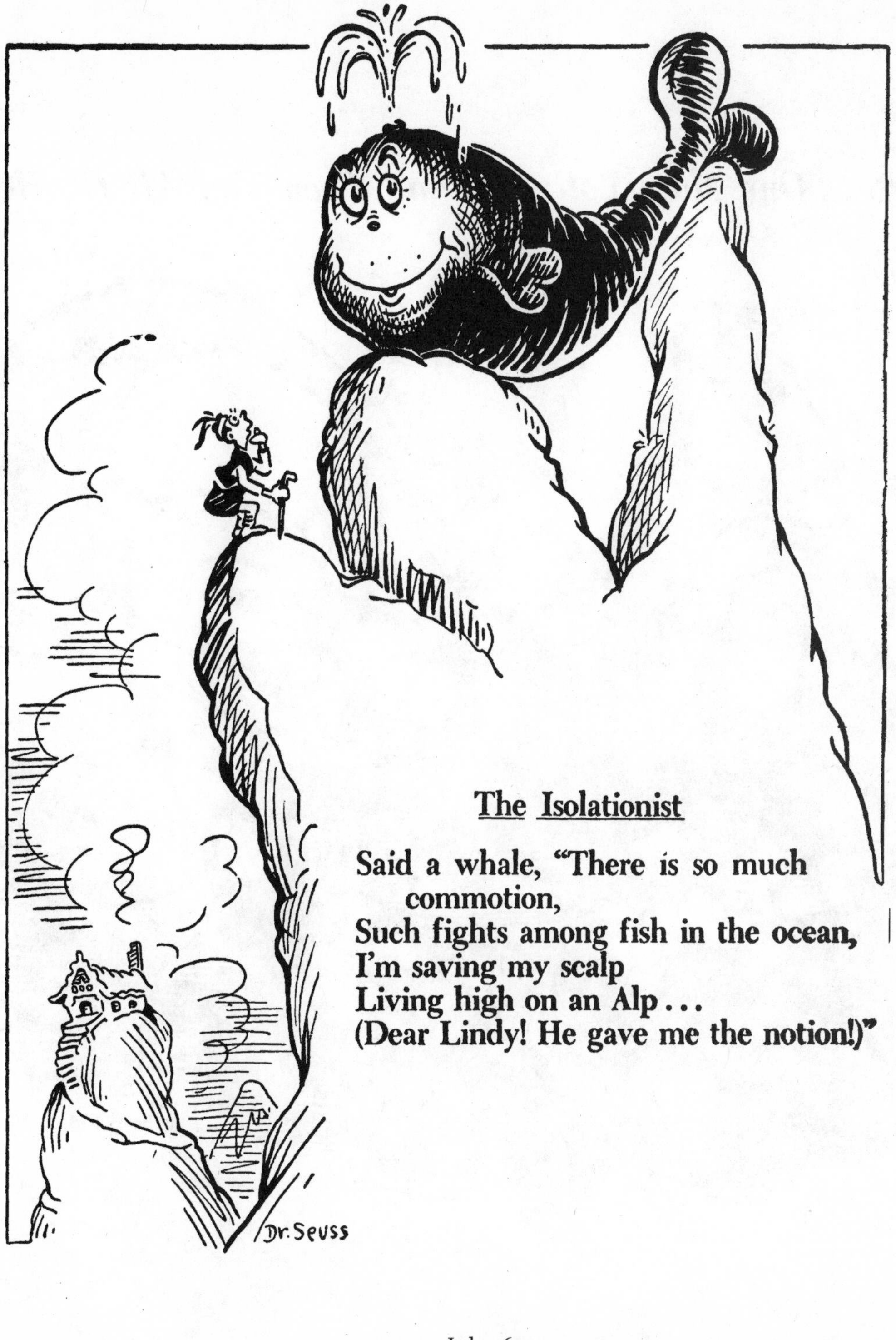
The Isolationist
Said a whale, "There is so much commotion,
Such fights among fish in the ocean,
I'm saving my scalp
Living high on an Alp . . .
(Dear Lindy! He gave me the notion!)"
Dr. Seuss

39 — July 16, 1941

'Remember . . . One More Lollypop, and Then You All Go Home!'

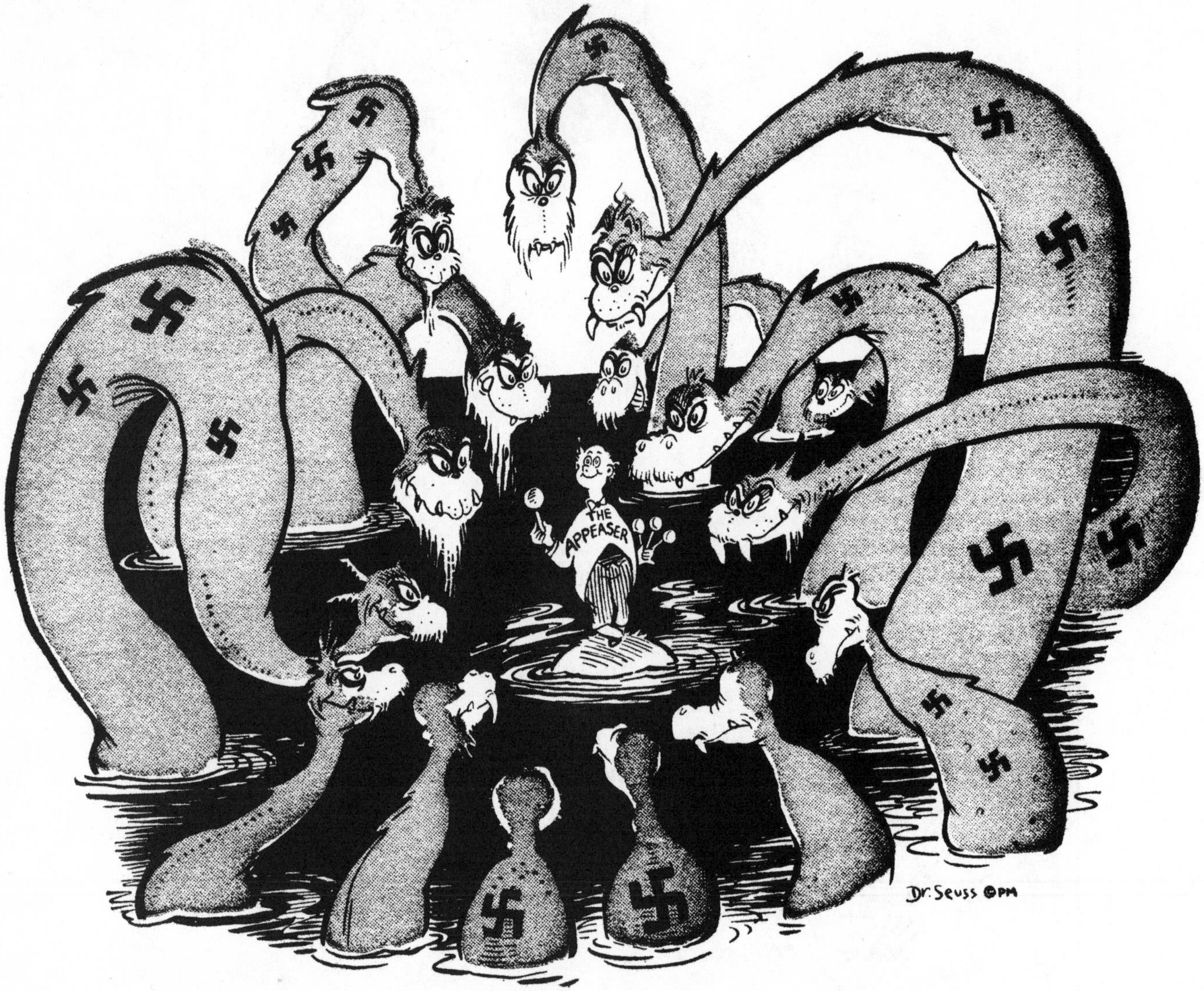
THE APPEASER
Dr. Seuss ©PM

40 — August 13, 1941

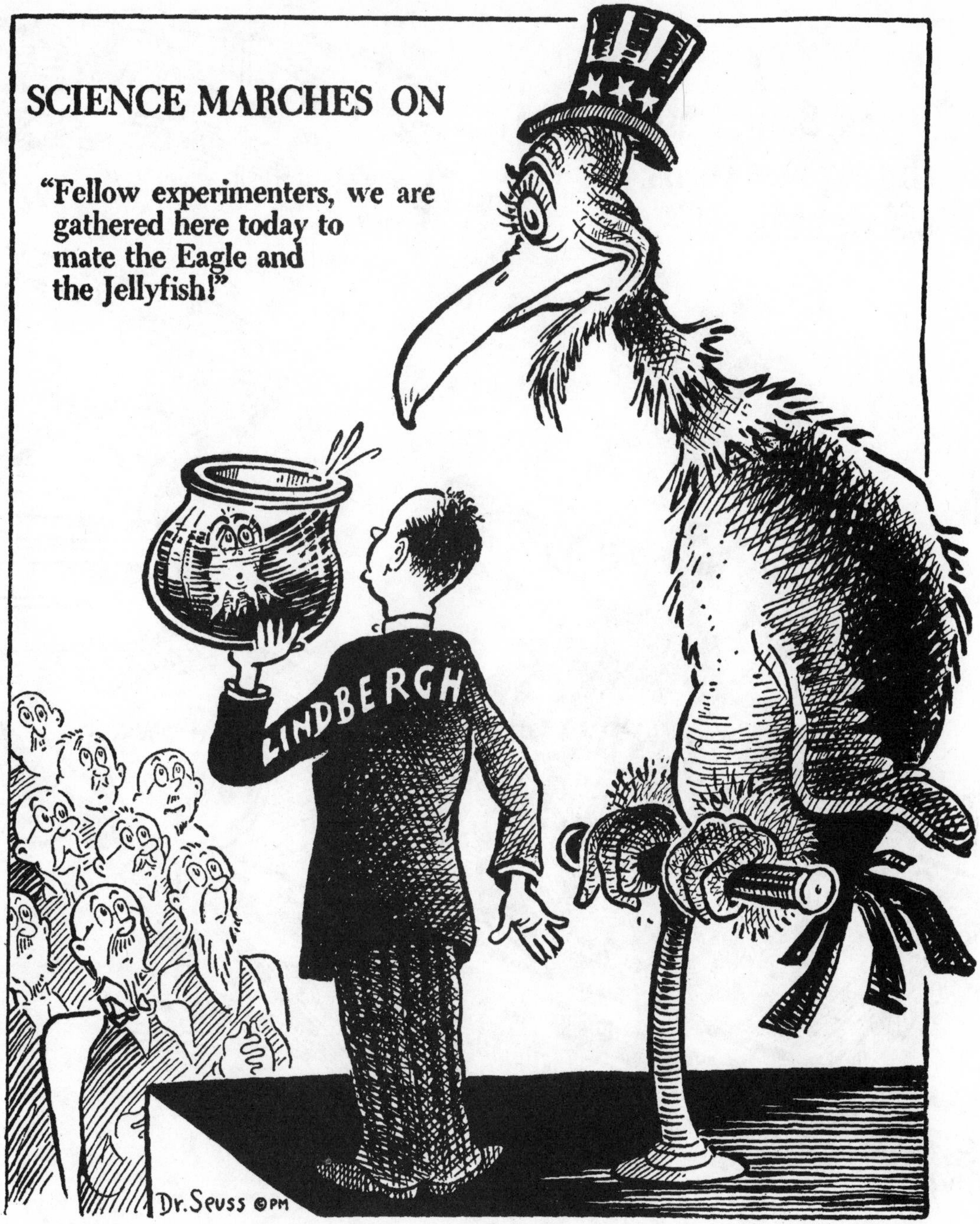
SCIENCE MARCHES ON
"Fellow experimenters, we are gathered here today to mate the Eagle and the Jellyfish!"
LINDBERGH
Dr. Seuss ©PM

41 — September 2, 1941

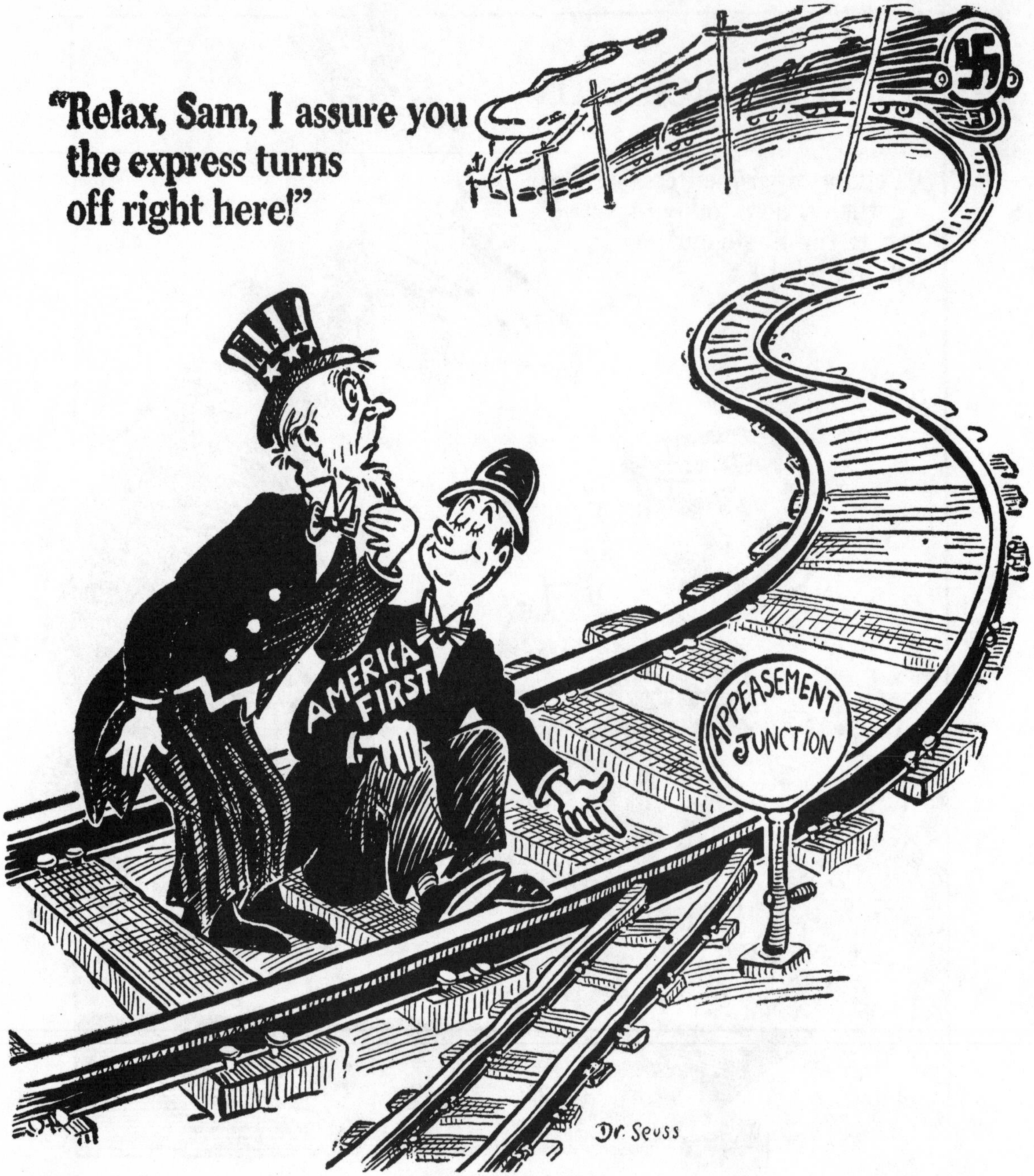
"Relax, Sam, I assure you the express turns off right here!"
AMERICA FIRST
APPEASEMENT JUNCTION
Dr. Seuss

42 — September 9, 1941

Spreading the Lovely Goebbels Stuff

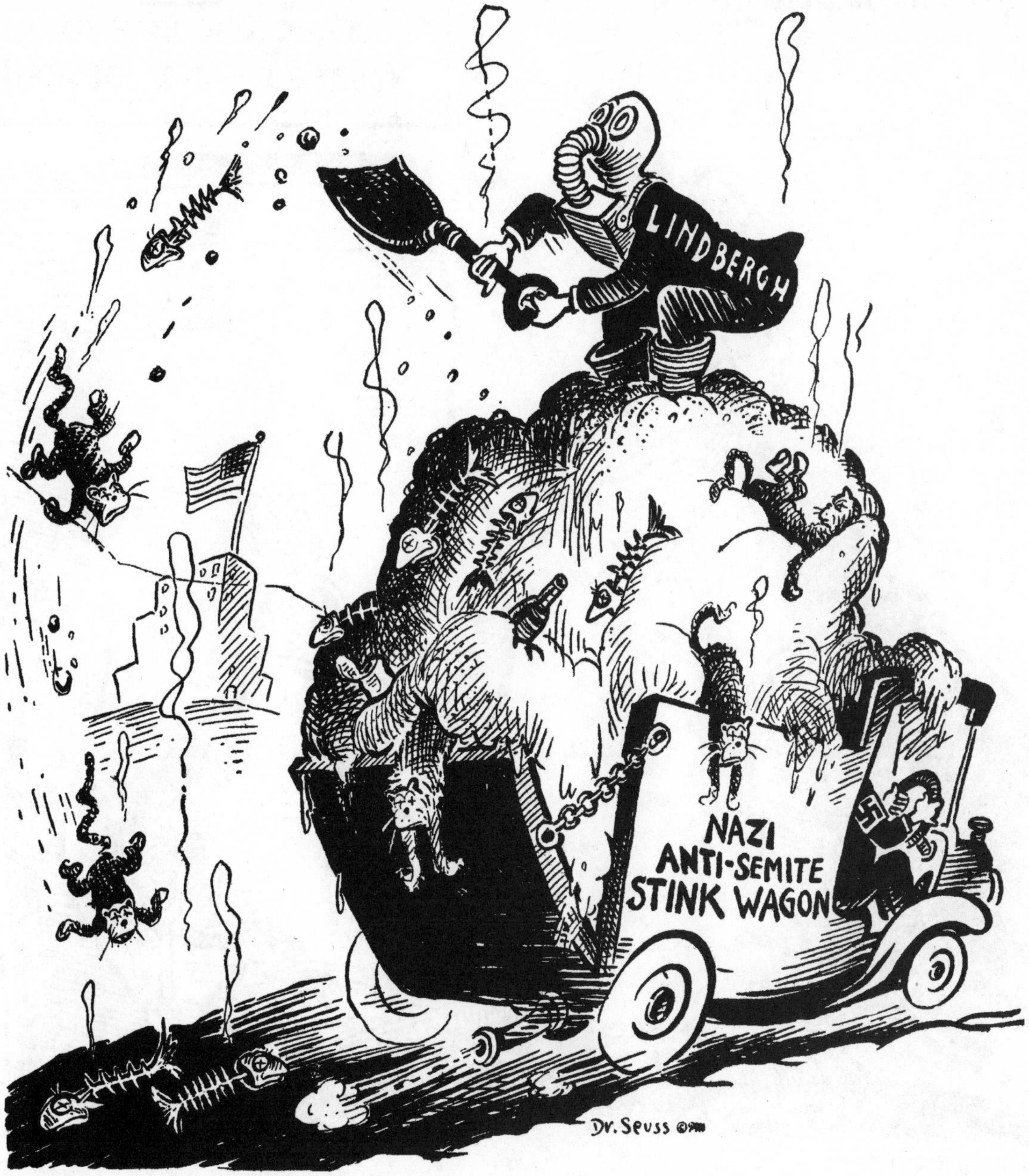
LINDBERGH
NAZI
ANTI-SEMITE
STINK WAGON
DR. SEUSS

43 — September 18, 1941

“Jeepers! Is that Me”

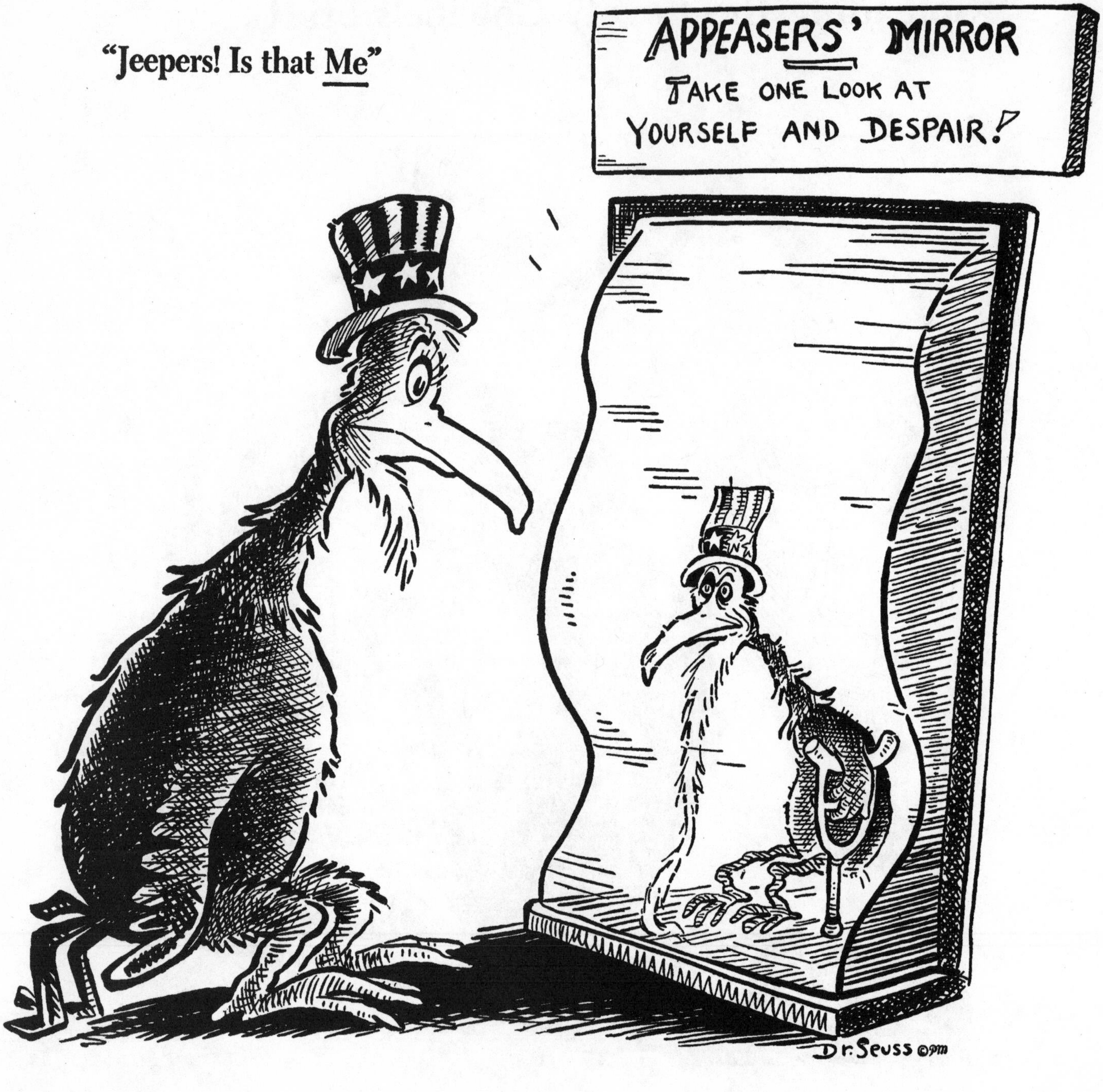
APPEASERS' MIRROR
TAKE ONE LOOK AT YOURSELF AND DESPAIR!
Dr. Seuss ©pm

. . . and the Wolf chewed up the children and spit out their bones . . .
But those were Foreign Children and it really didn't matter."

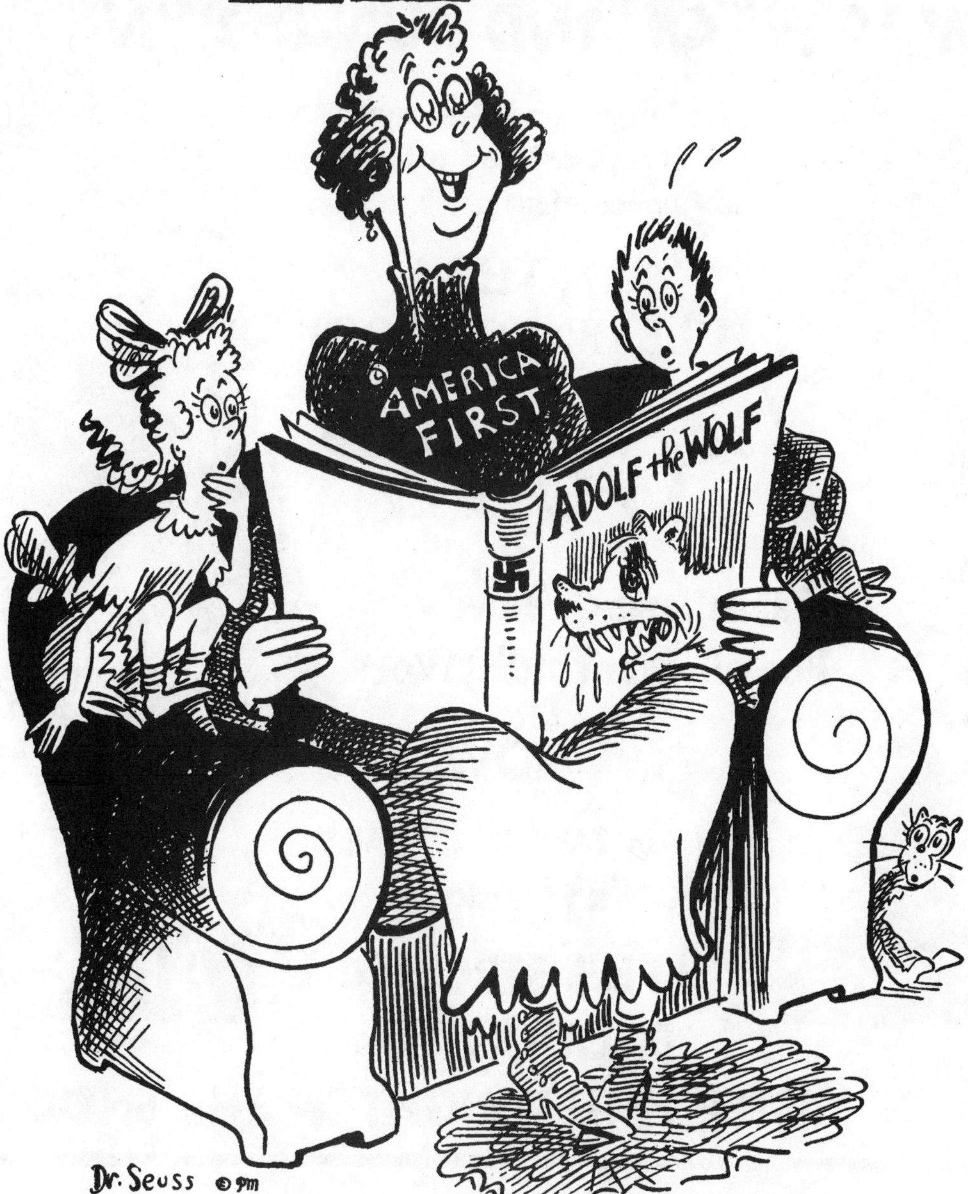
AMERICA FIRST
ADOLF the WOLF
Dr. Seuss

45 — October 1, 1941

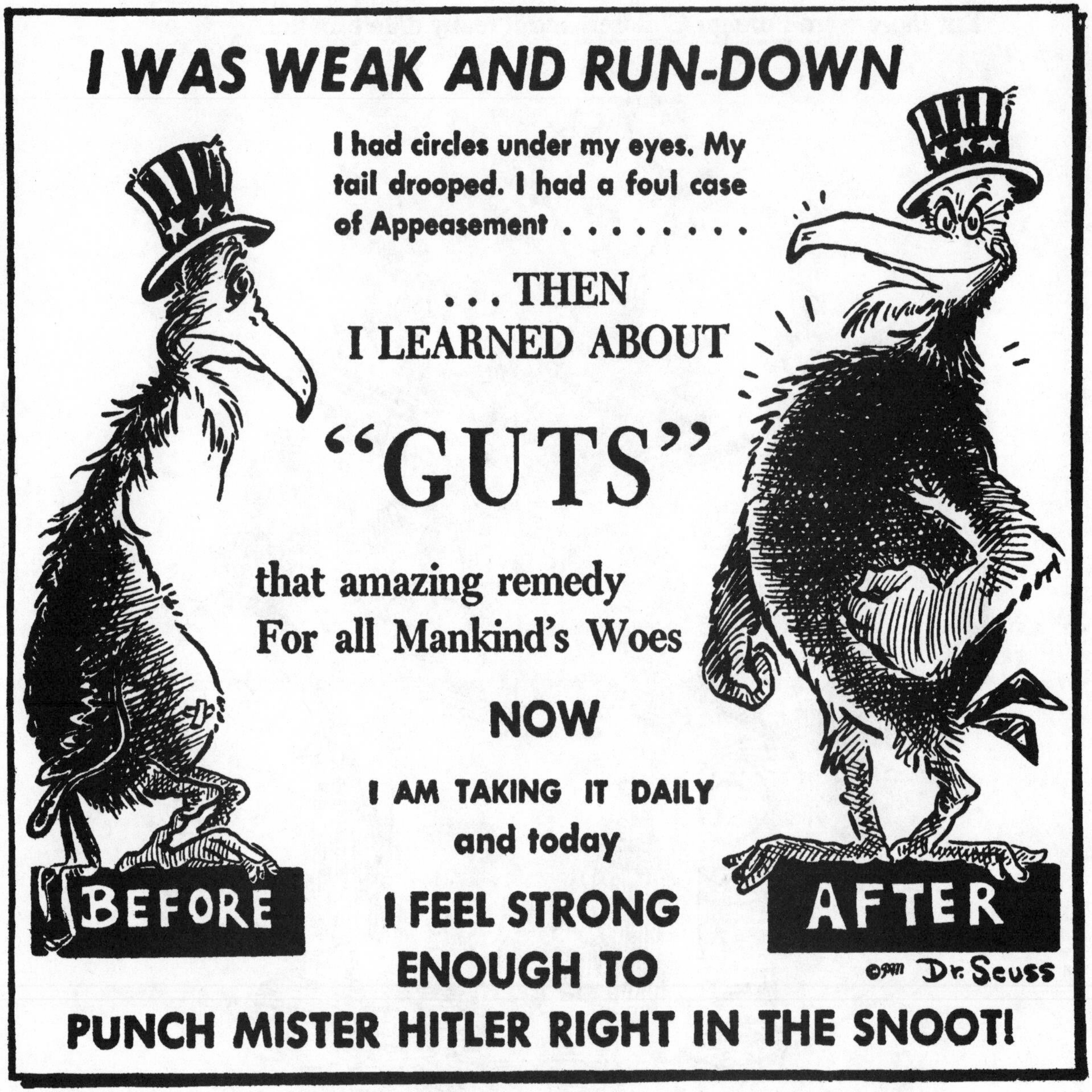
I WAS WEAK AND RUN-DOWN
I had circles under my eyes. My tail drooped. I had a foul case of Appeasement . . . .
. . . THEN
I LEARNED ABOUT
"GUTS"
that amazing remedy
For all Mankind's Woes
NOW
I AM TAKING IT DAILY
and today
I FEEL STRONG
ENOUGH TO
PUNCH MISTER HITLER RIGHT IN THE SNOOT!
BEFORE
AFTER
©1941 Dr. Seuss

46 — October 5, 1941

'You may fire when I am damn good and ready, Gridley!'

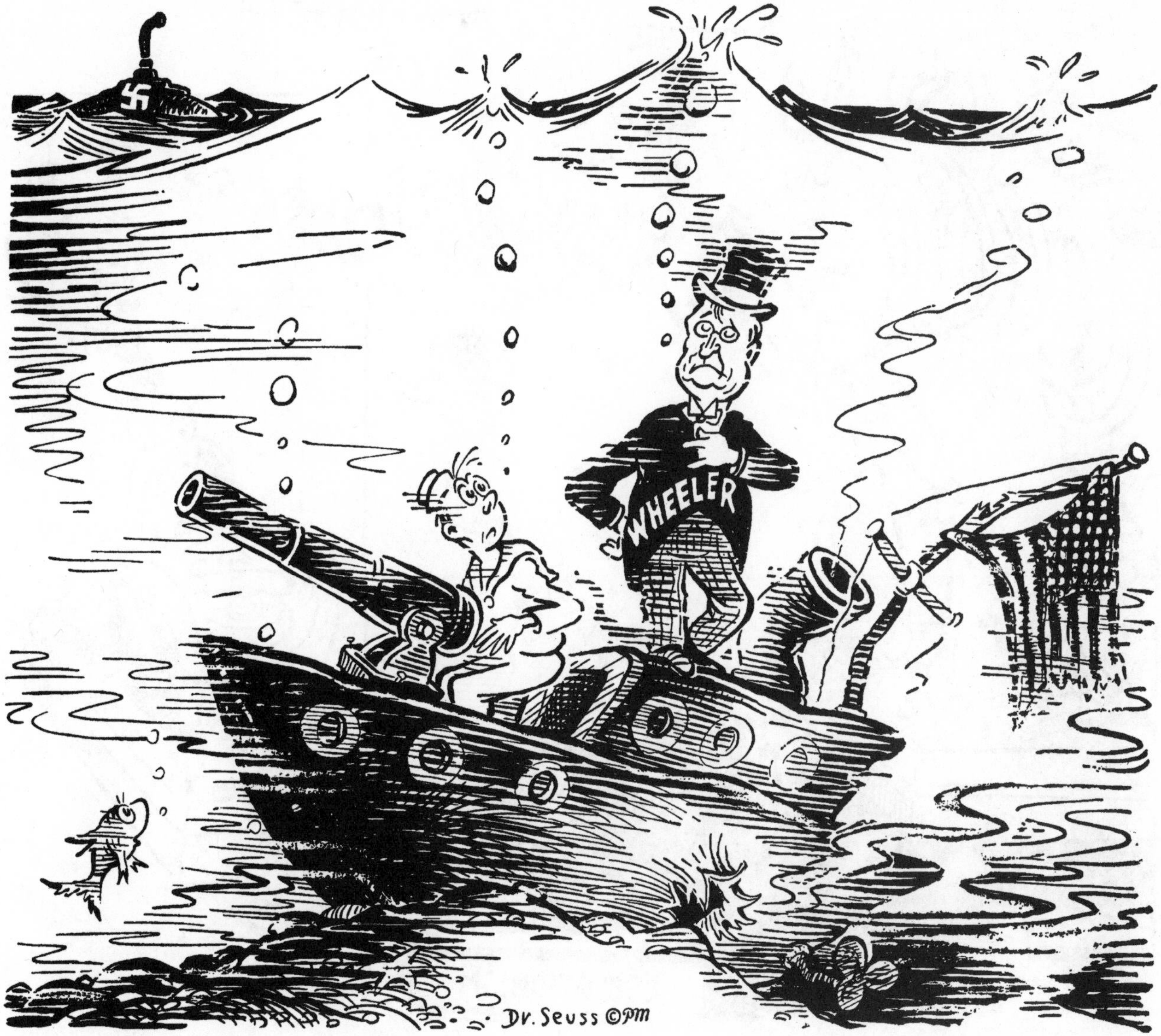
WHEELER
Dr. Seuss ©PM

47 – November 7, 1941

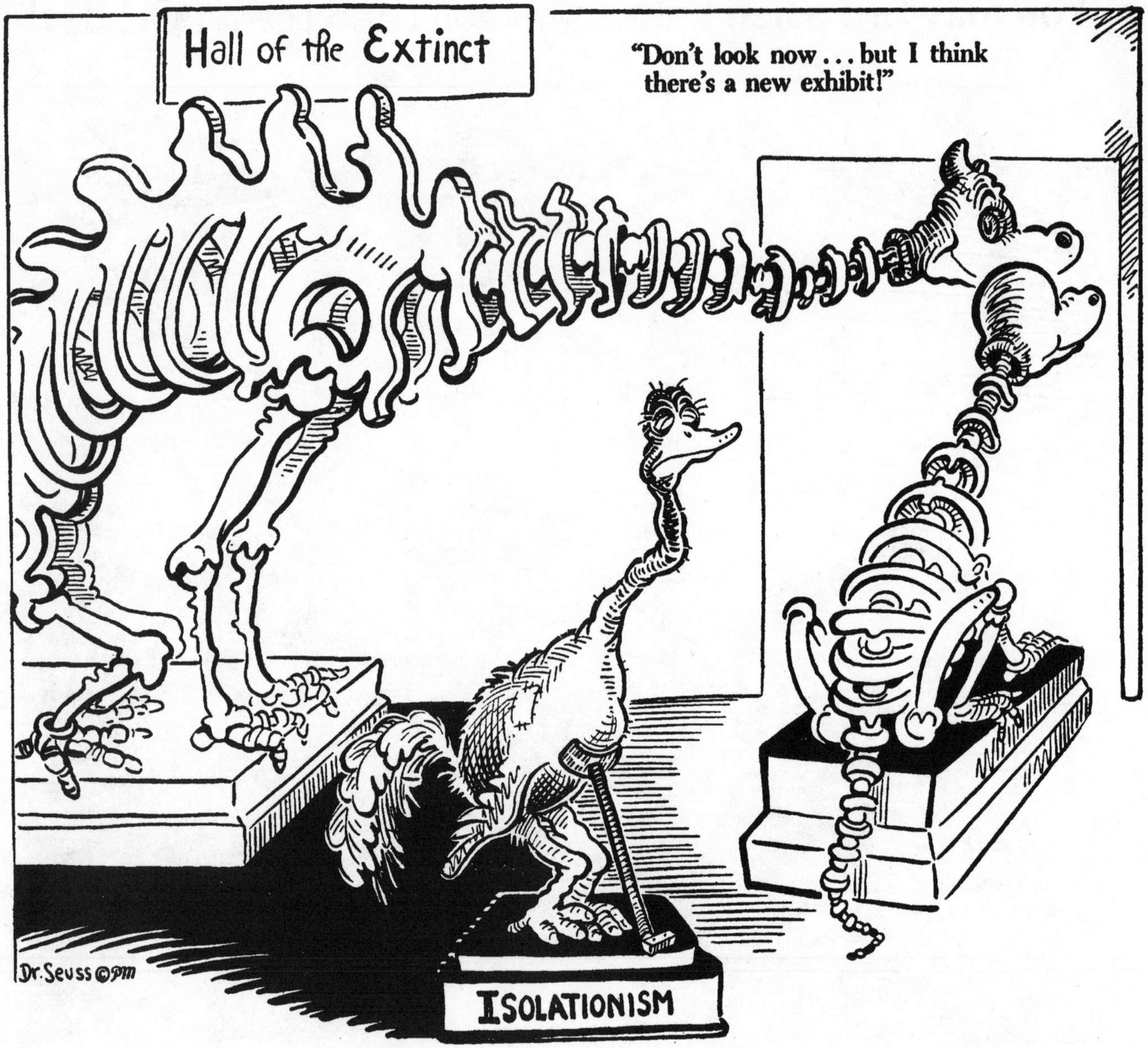
Hall of the Extinct
"Don't look now . . . but I think there's a new exhibit!"
Dr. Seuss
ISOLATIONISM

48 — November 25, 1941

Still Cooking With Goebbels Gas

THE SAME OLD DOWN-WITH-ENGLAND-AND-ROOSEVELT STEW

FR. COUGHLIN

DR. SEUSS

From Father Coughlin's *Social Justice*: "At last the British sun began to set, and upon the land of the exploited yellow man there began to rise the dawn of freedom. Today 300 million Orientals—believe it or not—are beginning to chant Britain's requiem in the words of 'Asia for Asiatics.' . . . The end for England before midsummer is not inconceivable. . . . The Truman report is an adroit attempt to exculpate President Roosevelt's personal muddling in the matter of industrial preparedness."

Speaking of Railroads . . . *Here's* One to Take Over!

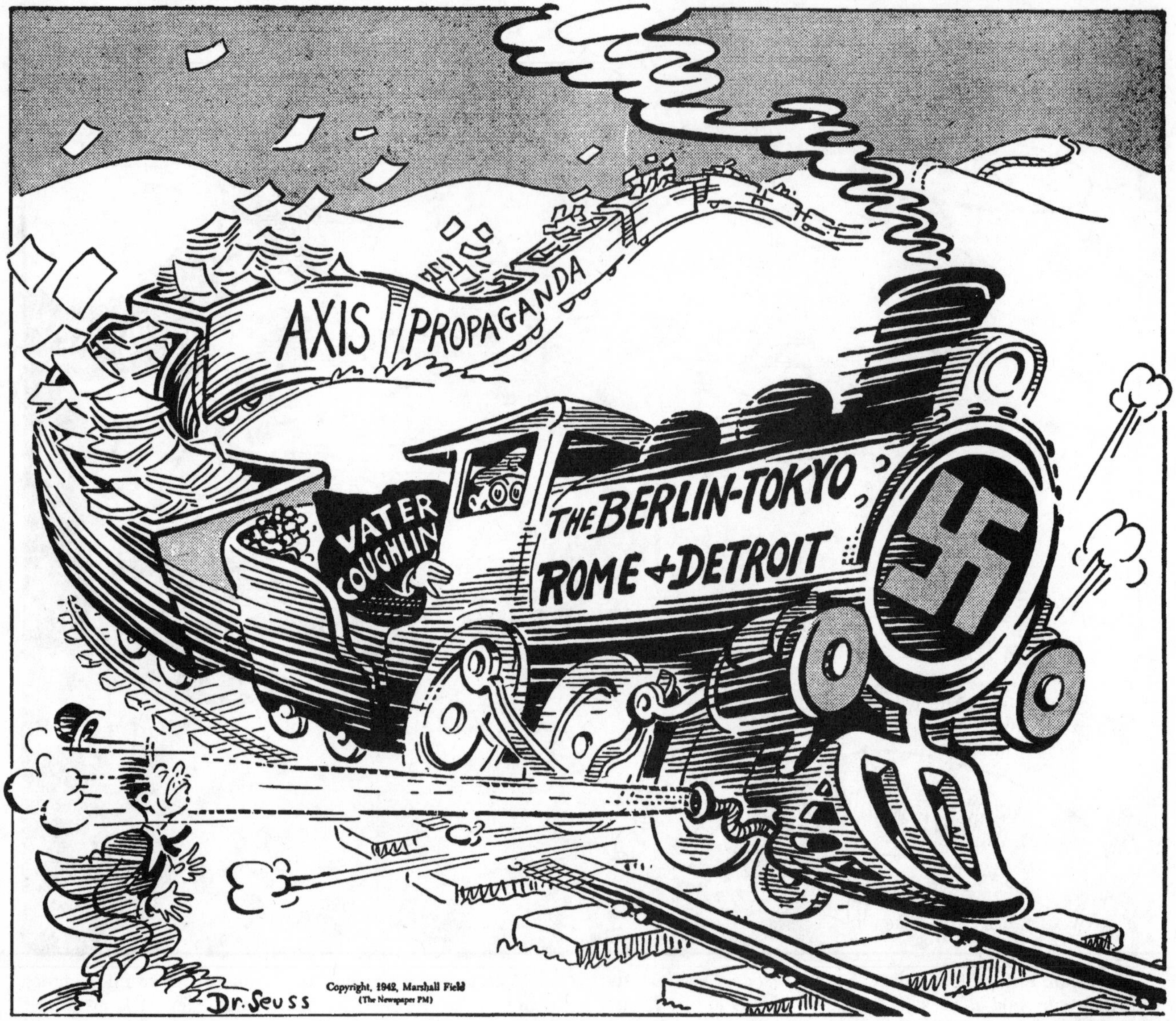
AXIS PROPAGANDA
VATER COUGHLIN
THE BERLIN-TOKYO ROME + DETROIT
DR. SEUSS
Copyright, 1942, Marshall Field
(The Newspaper PM)

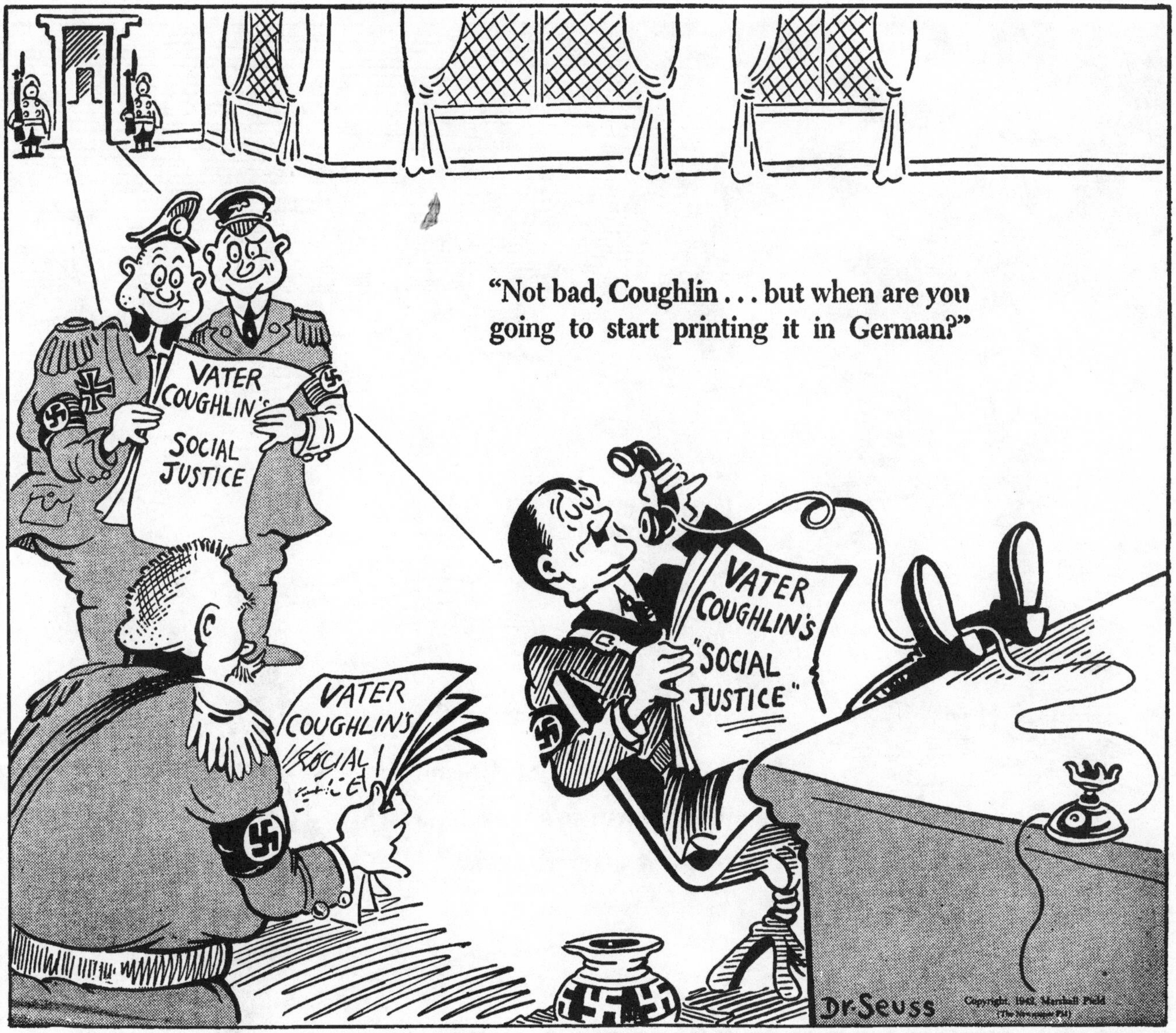
VATER COUGHLIN's SOCIAL JUSTICE
VATER COUGHLIN'S "SOCIAL JUSTICE"
VATER COUGHLIN'S
Dr. Seuss
Copyright, 1942, Marshall Field
"Not bad, Coughlin . . . but when are you going to start printing it in German?"

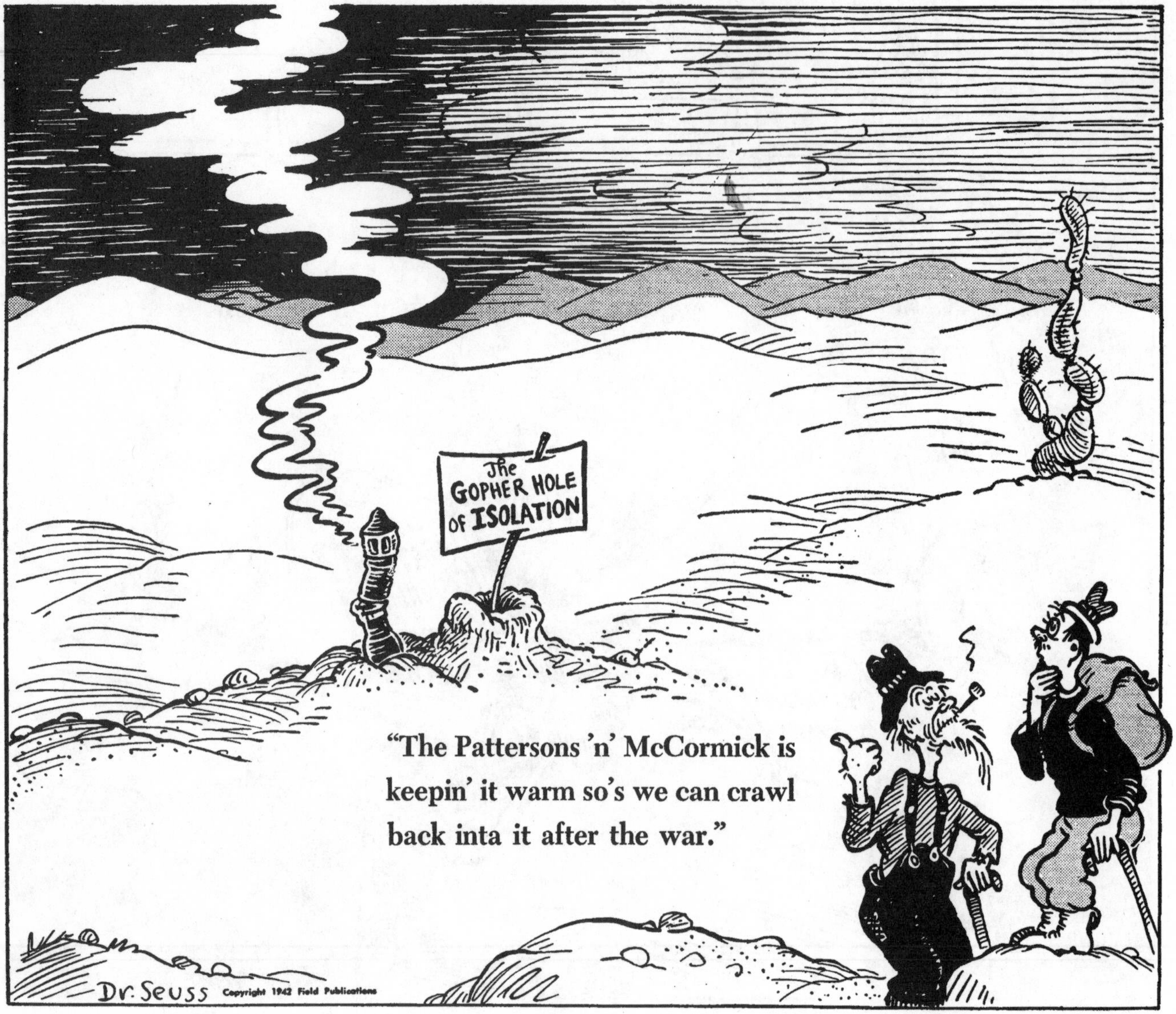
The GOPHER HOLE OF ISOLATION
Dr. Seuss
Copyright 1942 Field Publications

"The Pattersons 'n' McCormick is keepin' it warm so's we can crawl back inta it after the war."

Busy as Beavers

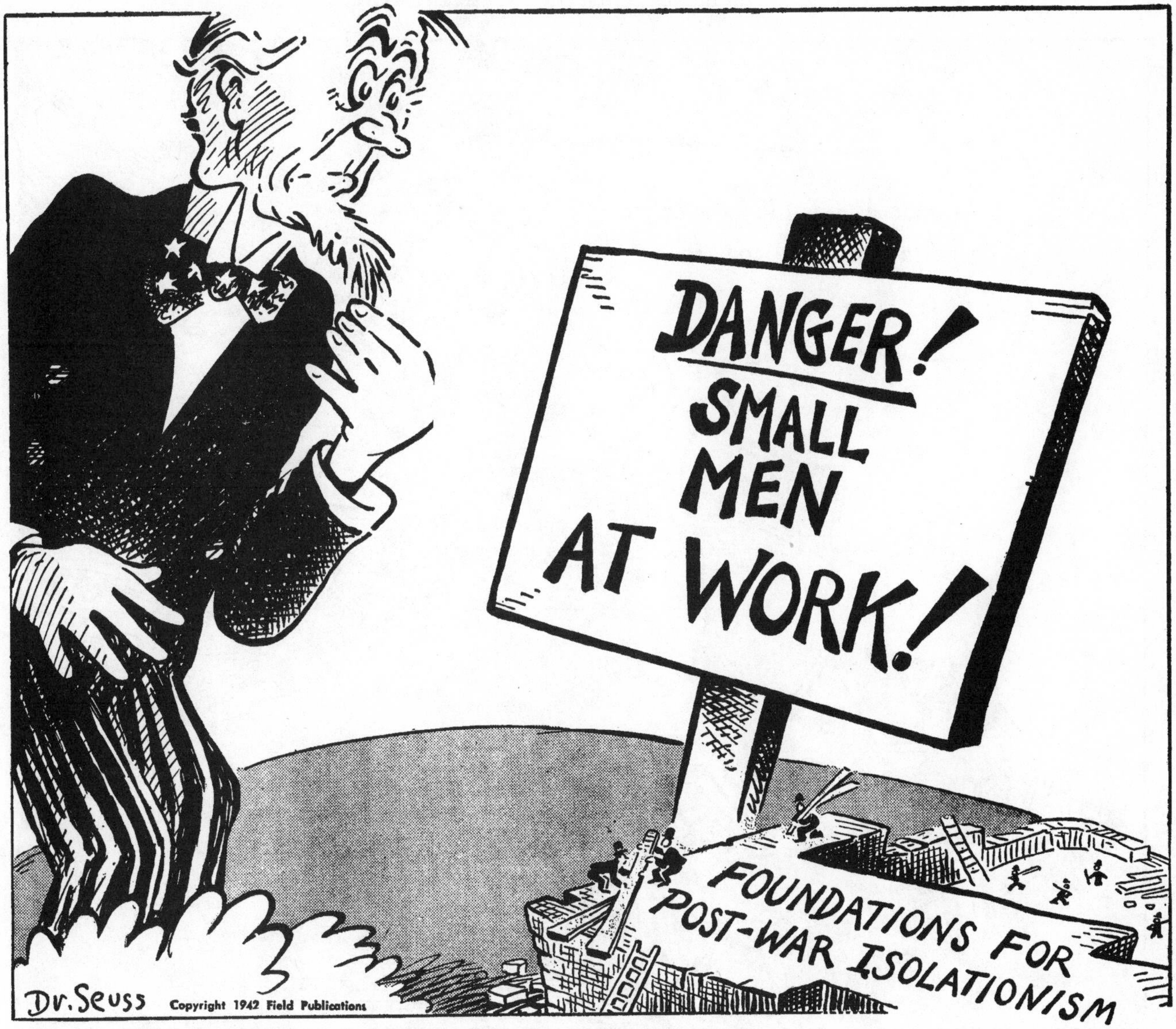
DANGER!
SMALL
MEN
AT WORK!
FOUNDATIONS FOR
POST-WAR ISOLATIONISM
Dr. Seuss
Copyright 1942 Field Publications

53 – December 14, 1942

With a Whole World to Rebuild . . .

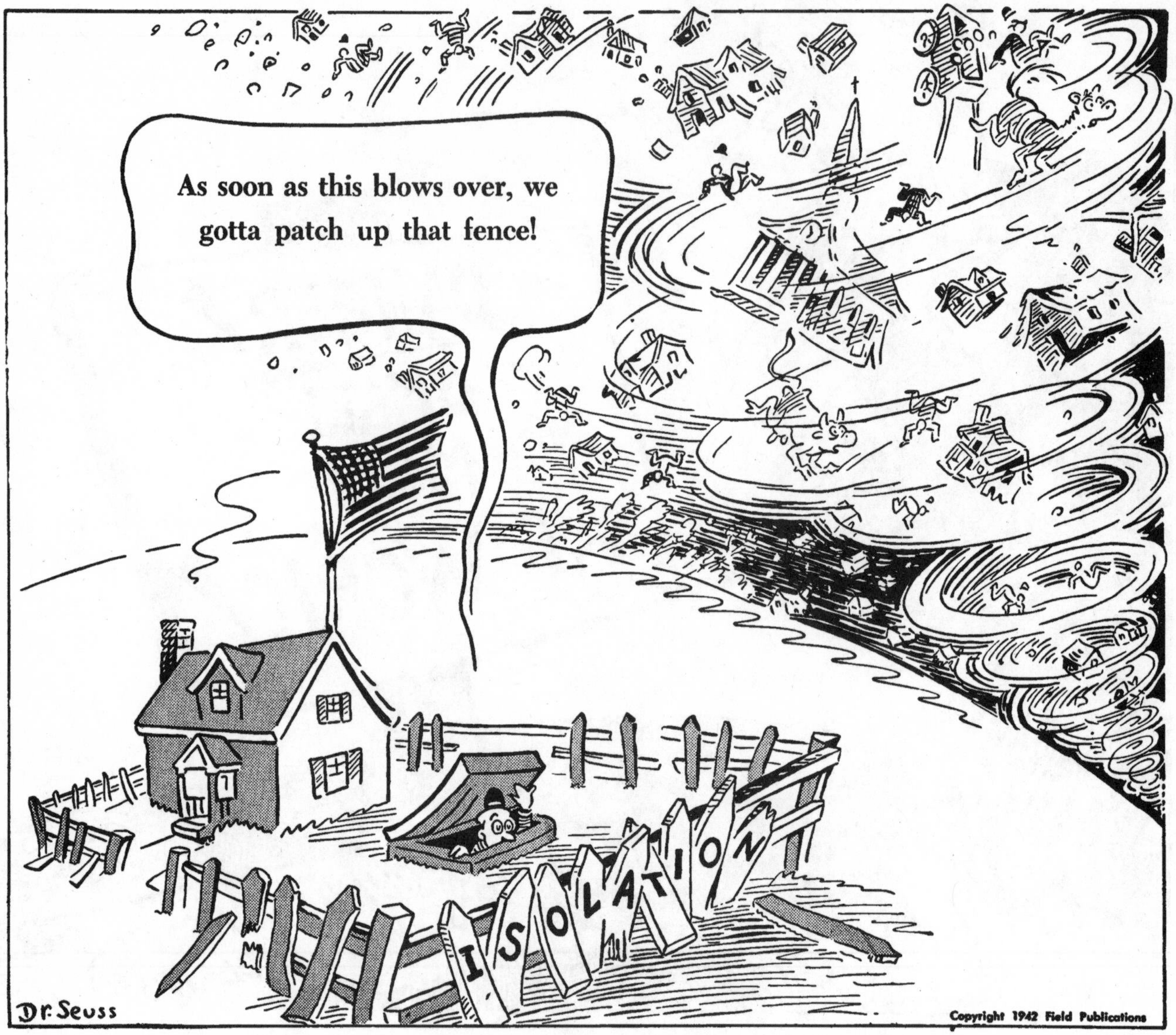
As soon as this blows over, we gotta patch up that fence!
ISOLATION
Dr. Seuss
Copyright 1942 Field Publications

The Kidnaper

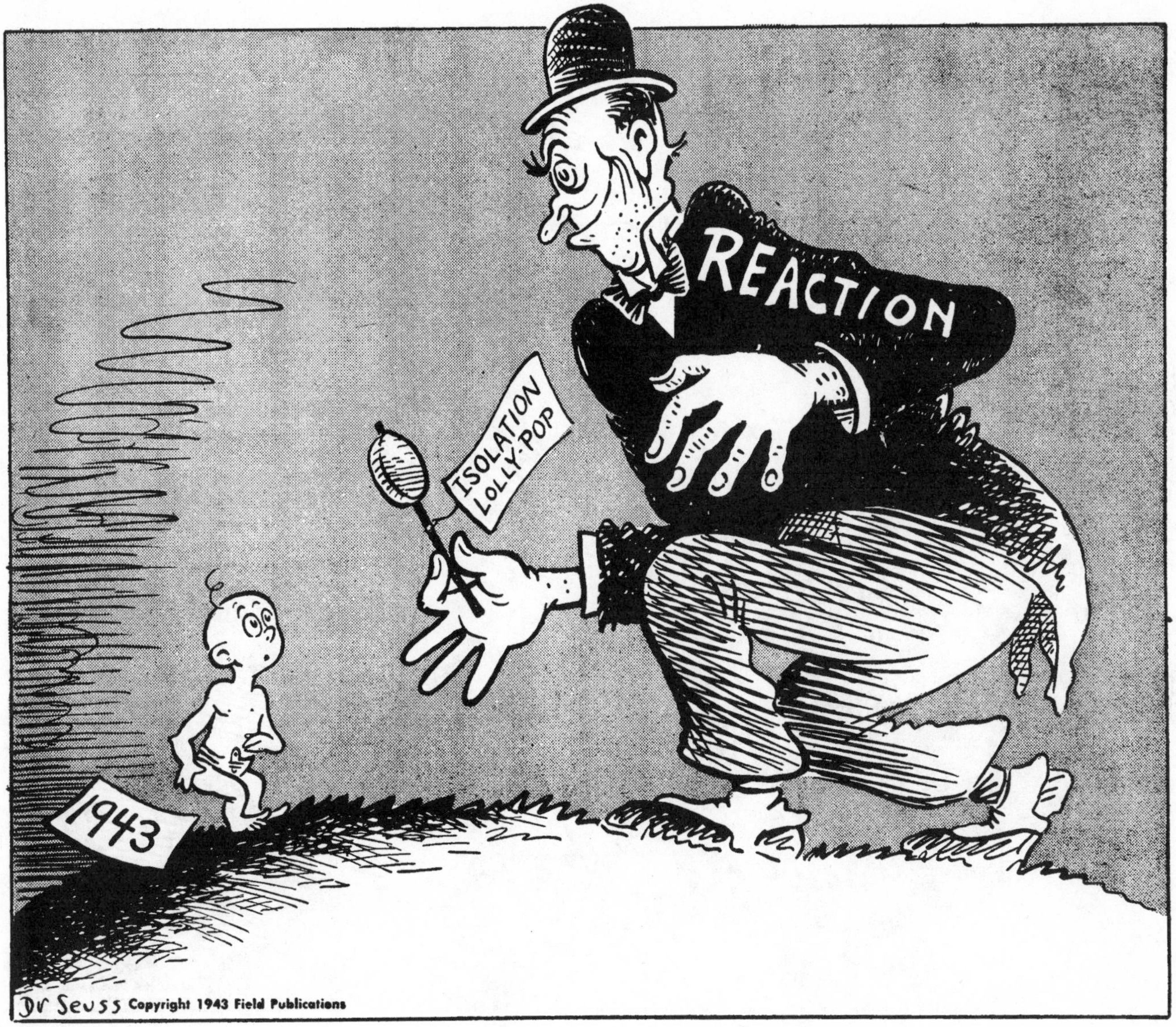
REACTION
ISOLATION LOLLY-POP
1943
Dr Seuss Copyright 1943 Field Publications

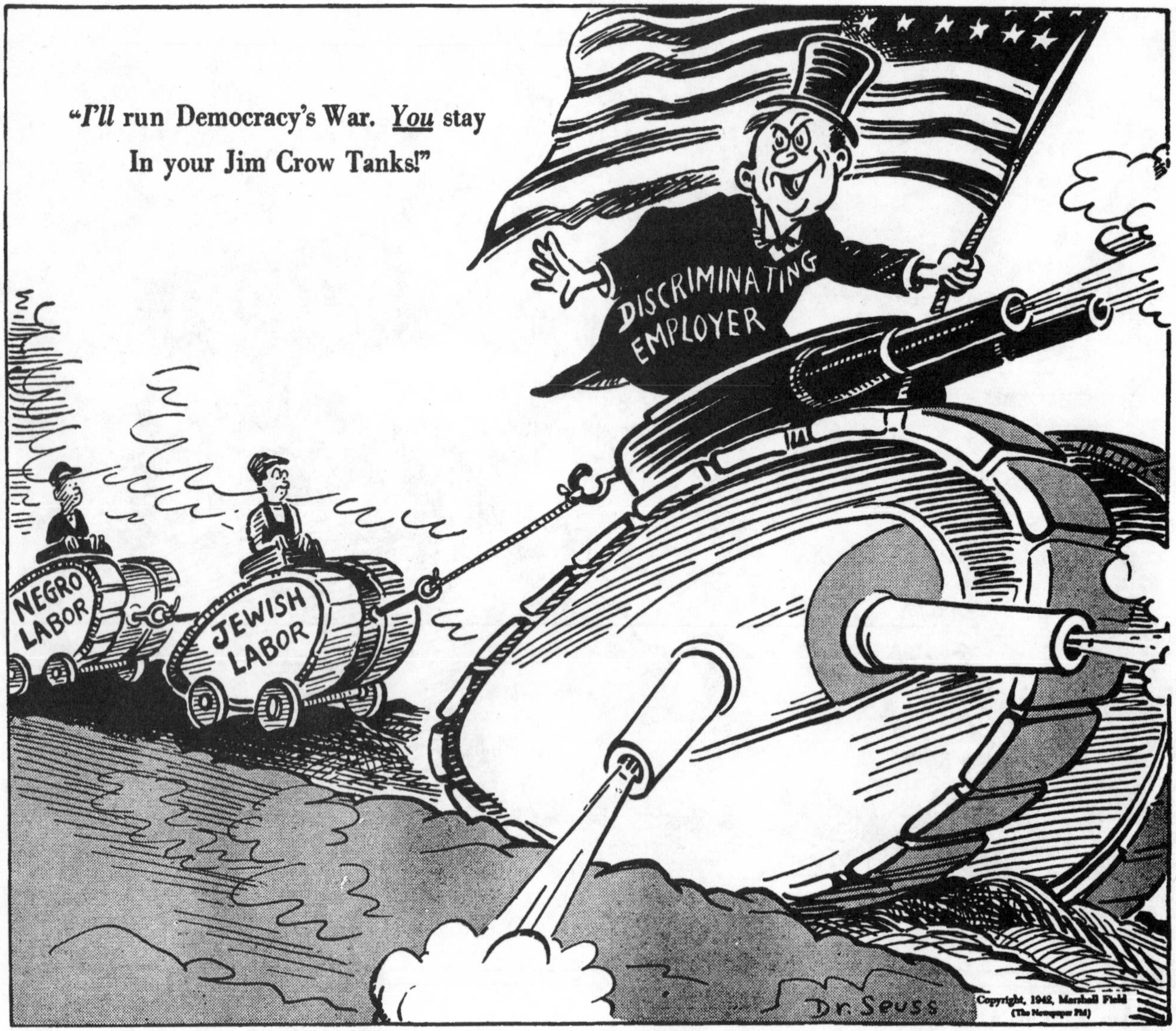
"I'll run Democracy's War. You stay
In your Jim Crow Tanks!"
DISCRIMINATING
EMPLOYER
NEGRO
LABOR
JEWISH
LABOR
Dr. Seuss
Copyright, 1942, Marshall Field

56 – April 14, 1942

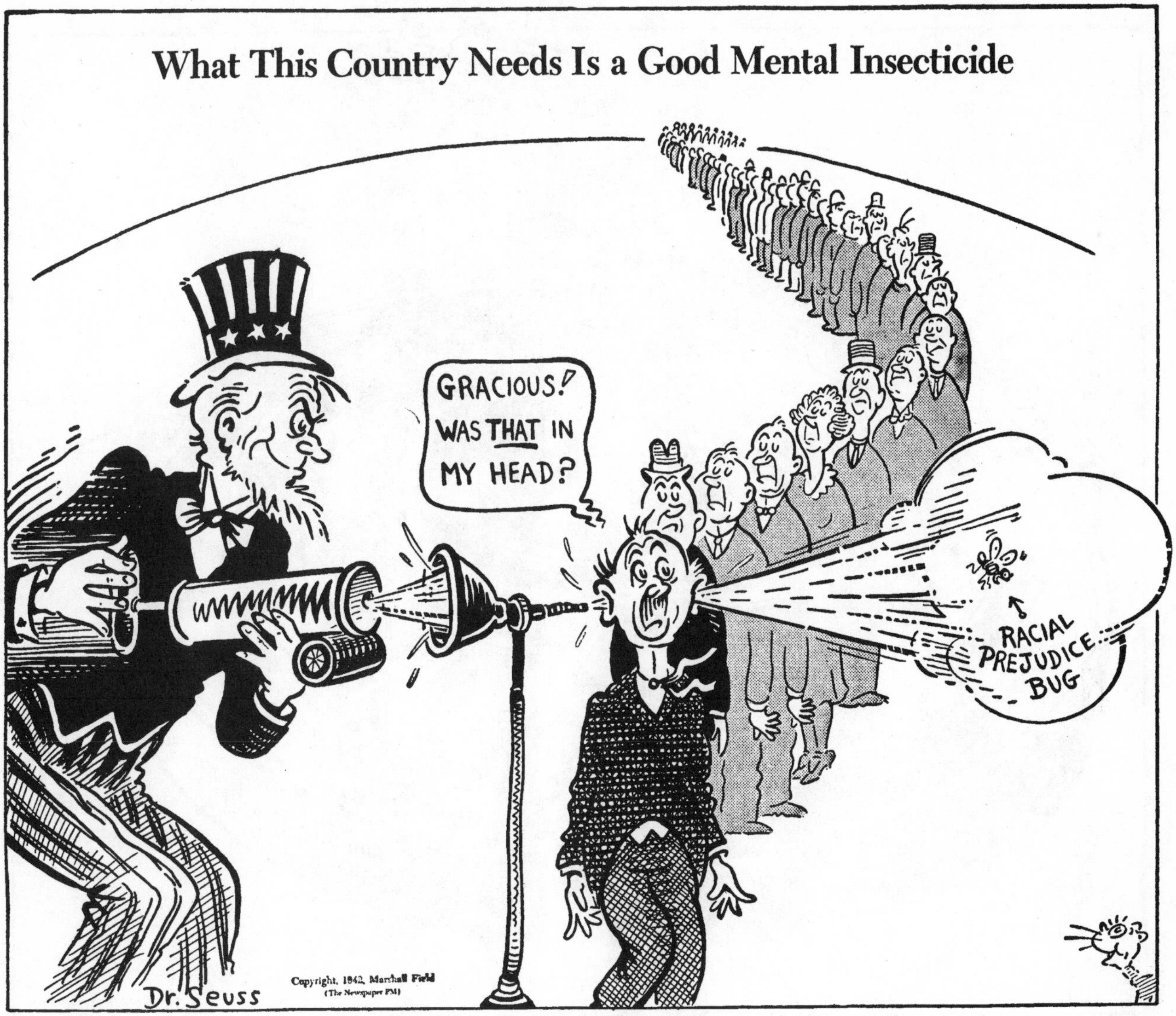
What This Country Needs Is a Good Mental Insecticide
GRACIOUS! WAS THAT IN MY HEAD?
RACIAL PREJUDICE BUG
Dr. Seuss
Copyright, 1942, Marshall Field
(The Newspaper PM)

57 — June 11, 1942

The Old Run-Around

U.S.
WAR
INDUSTRIES
NEGRO
JOB-HUNTERS
ENTER HERE
Copyright 1942, PM Syndicate
Dr. Seuss

58 — June 26, 1942

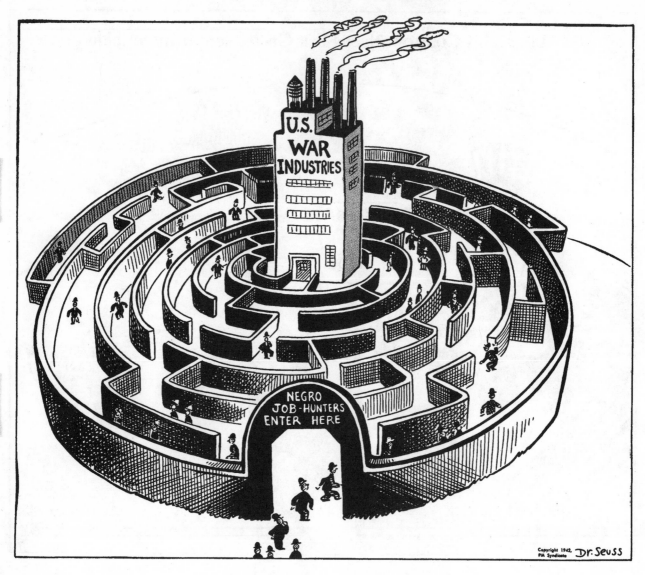

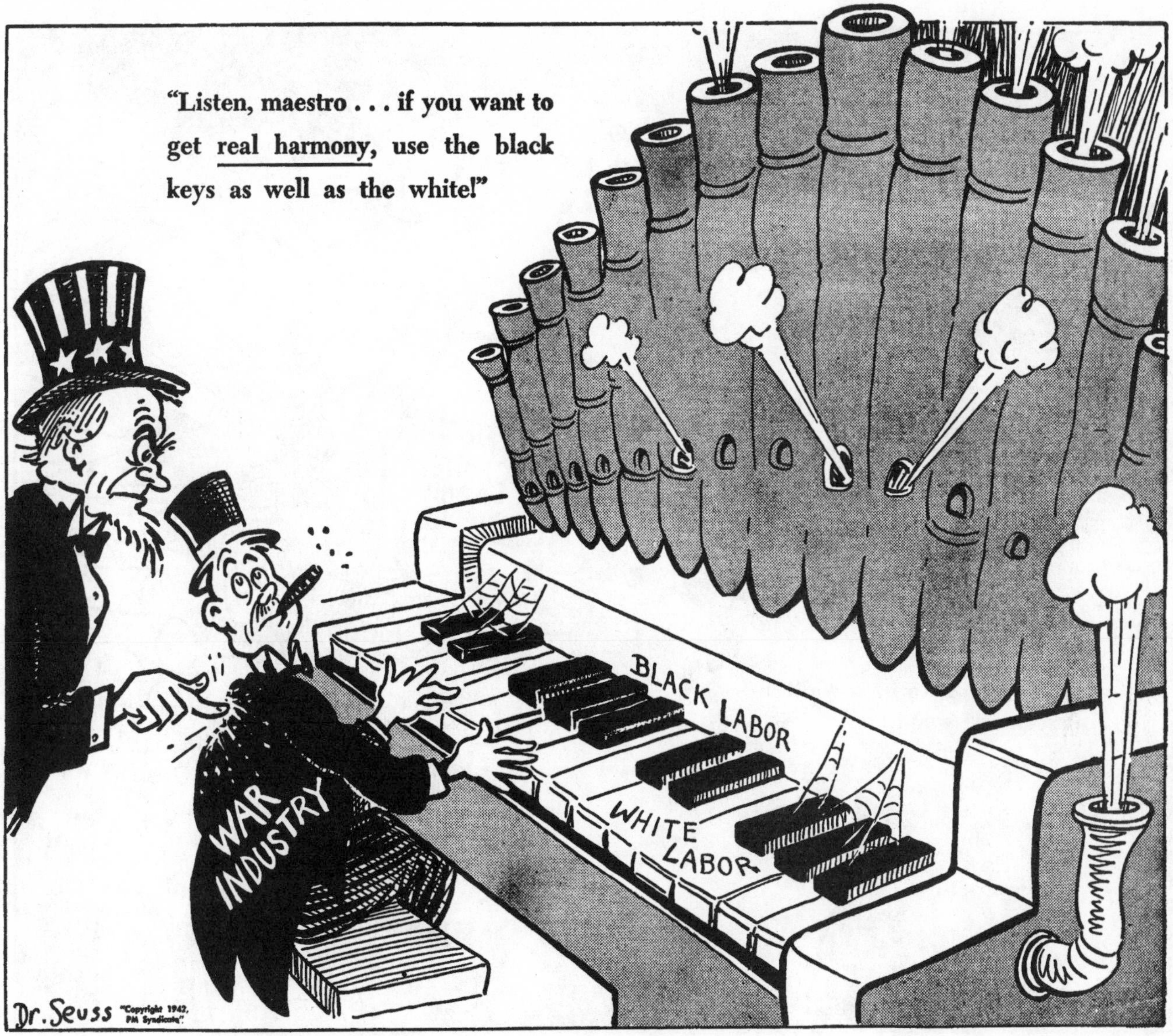
"Listen, maestro . . . if you want to get real harmony, use the black keys as well as the white!"
BLACK LABOR
WHITE LABOR
WAR INDUSTRY
Dr. Seuss
"Copyright 1942, PM Syndicate"

59 — June 29, 1942

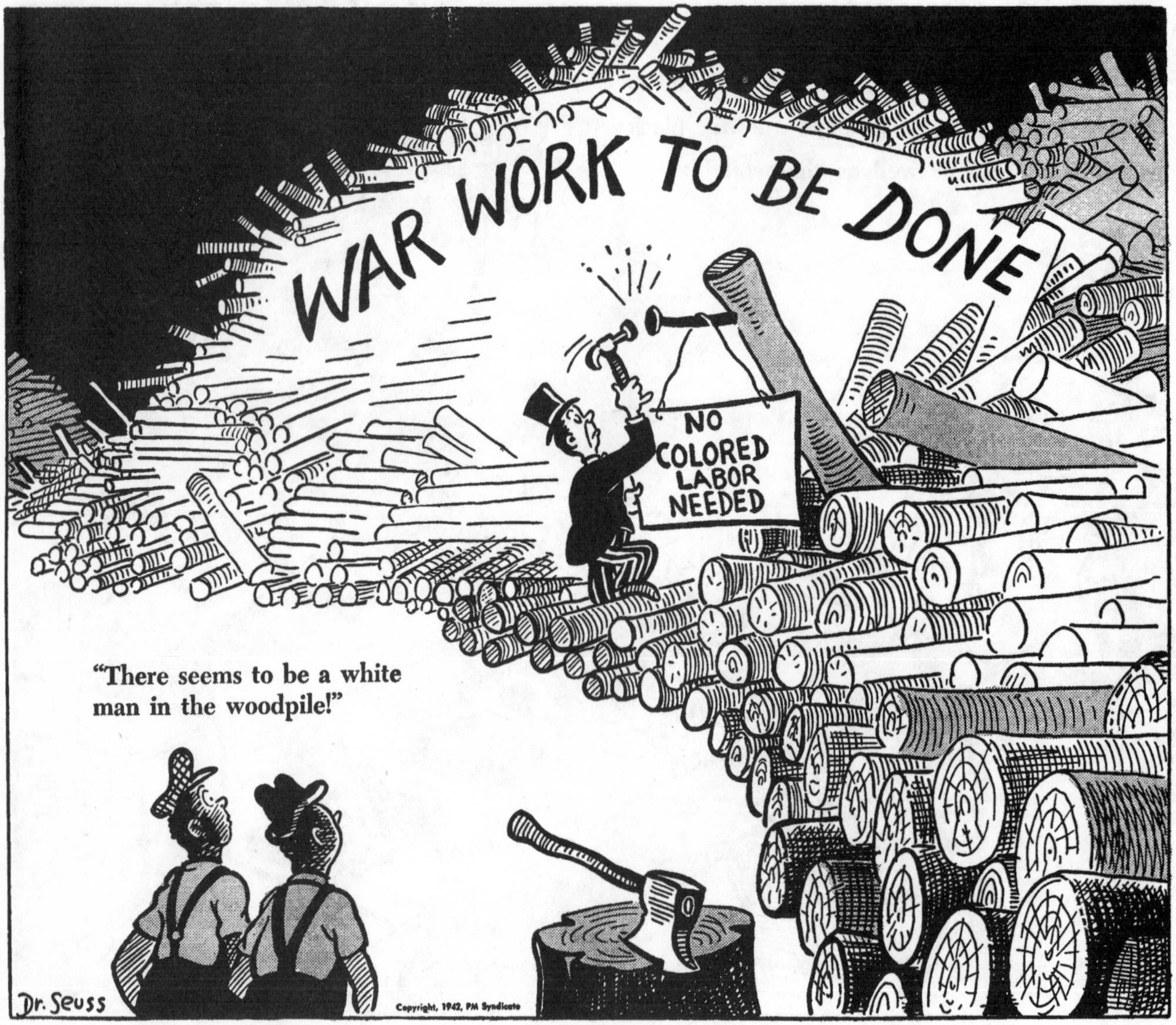
WAR WORK TO BE DONE
NO COLORED LABOR NEEDED
Dr. Seuss
Copyright, 1942, PM Syndicate

"There seems to be a white man in the woodpile!"

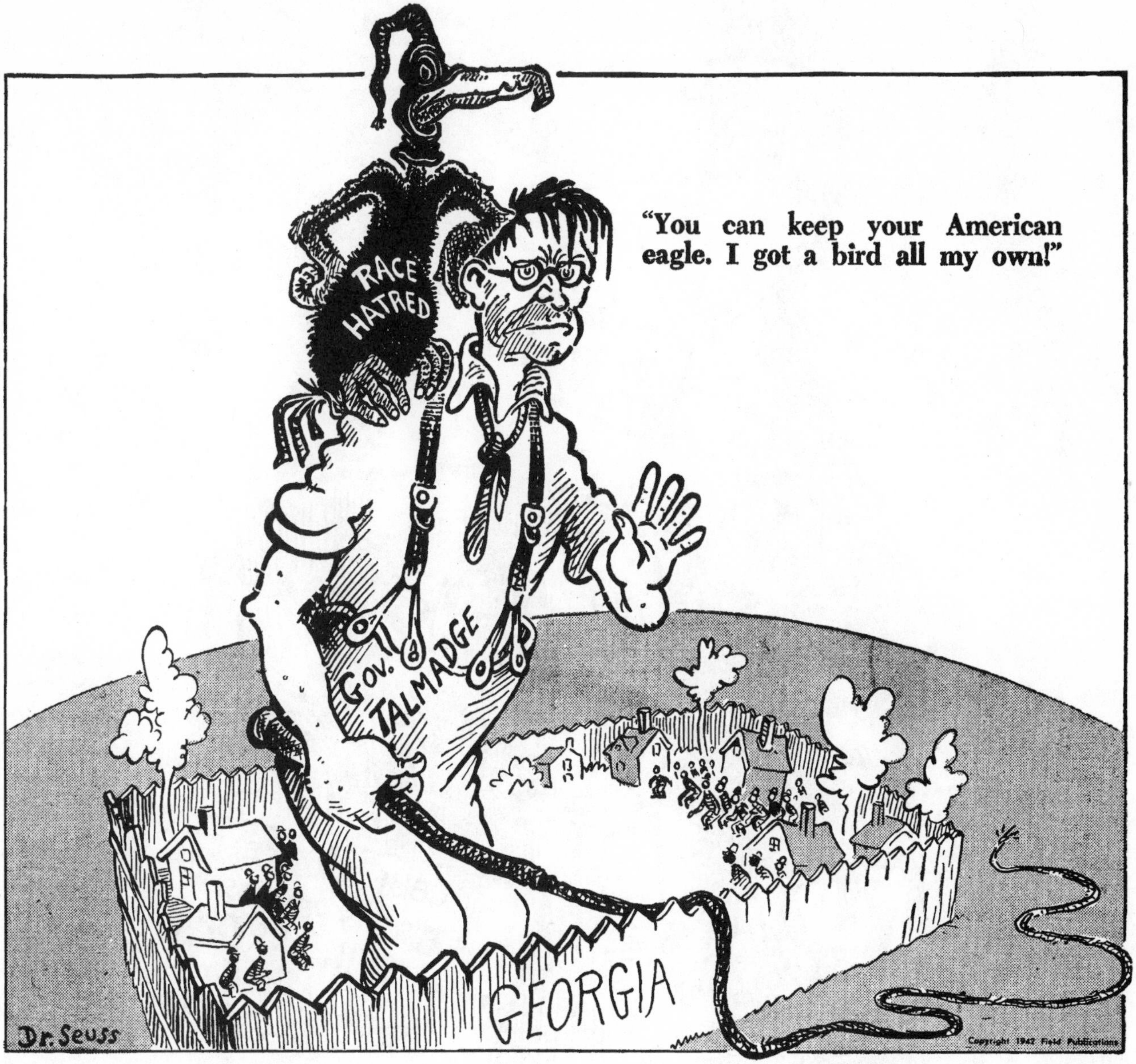
RACE HATRED
GOV. TALMADGE
GEORGIA
Dr. Seuss
Copyright 1942 Field Publications

"You can keep your American eagle. I got a bird all my own!"

61 — August 19, 1942

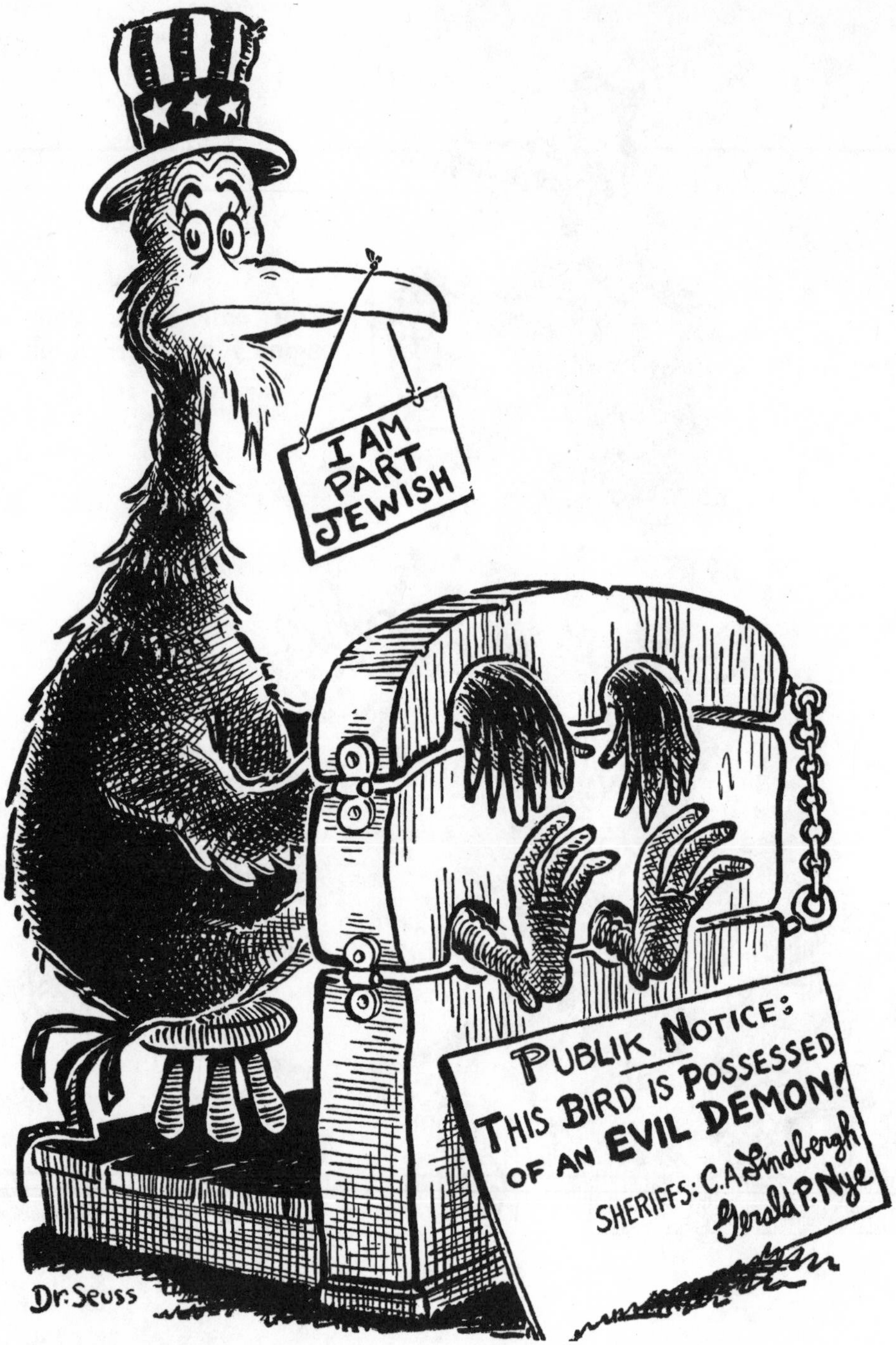
I AM
PART
JEWISH
PUBLIK NOTICE:
THIS BIRD IS POSSESSED
OF AN EVIL DEMON!
SHERIFFS: C.A. Lindbergh
Gerald P. Nye
Dr. Seuss

62 — September 22, 1941

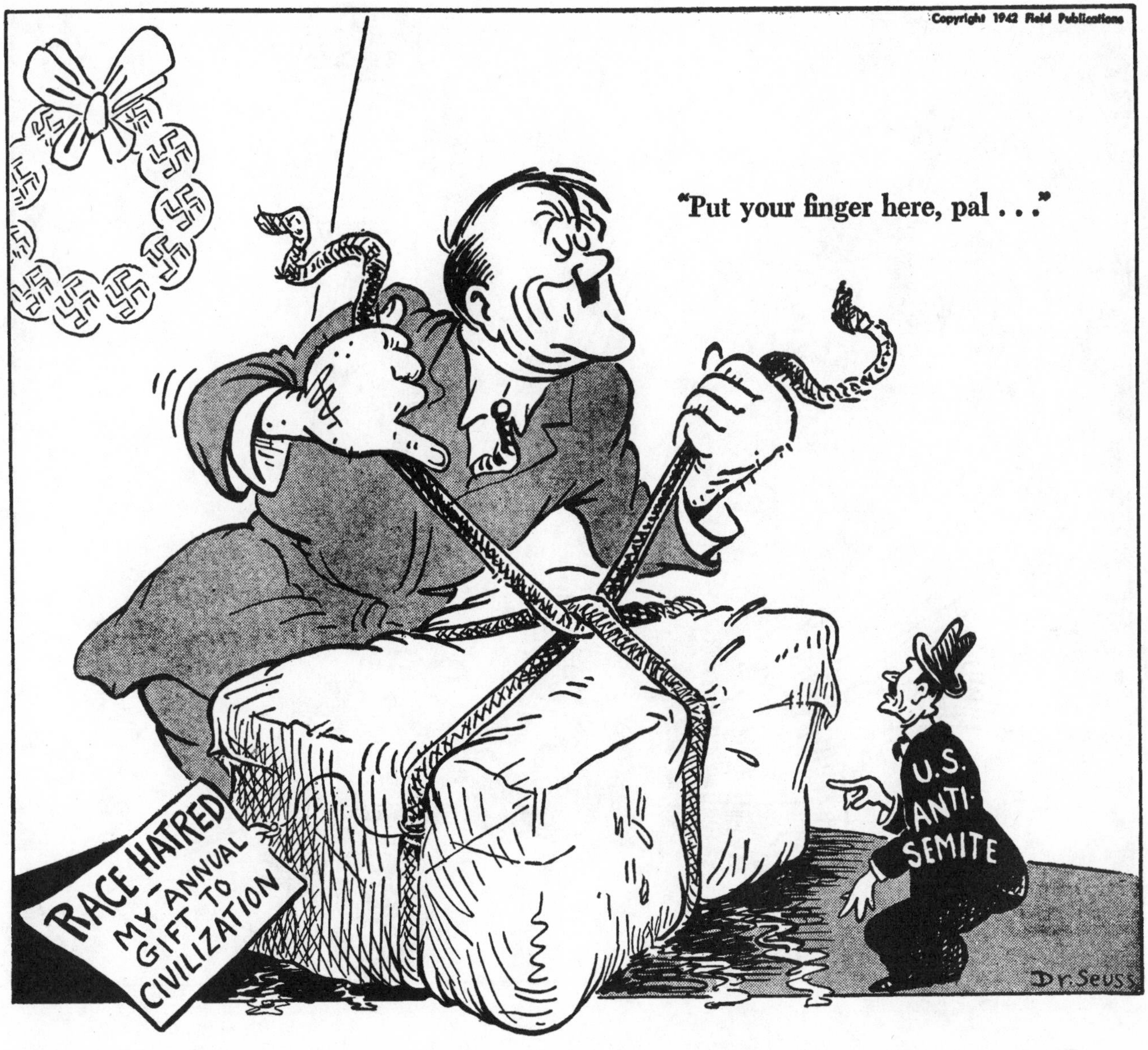
Copyright 1942 Field Publications
"Put your finger here, pal . . ."
RACE HATRED – MY ANNUAL GIFT TO CIVILIZATION
U.S. ANTI-SEMITE
Dr. Seuss

63 – December 16, 1942

We'll Have to Clean a Lot of Stuff Out Before We Put Peace Thoughts In!

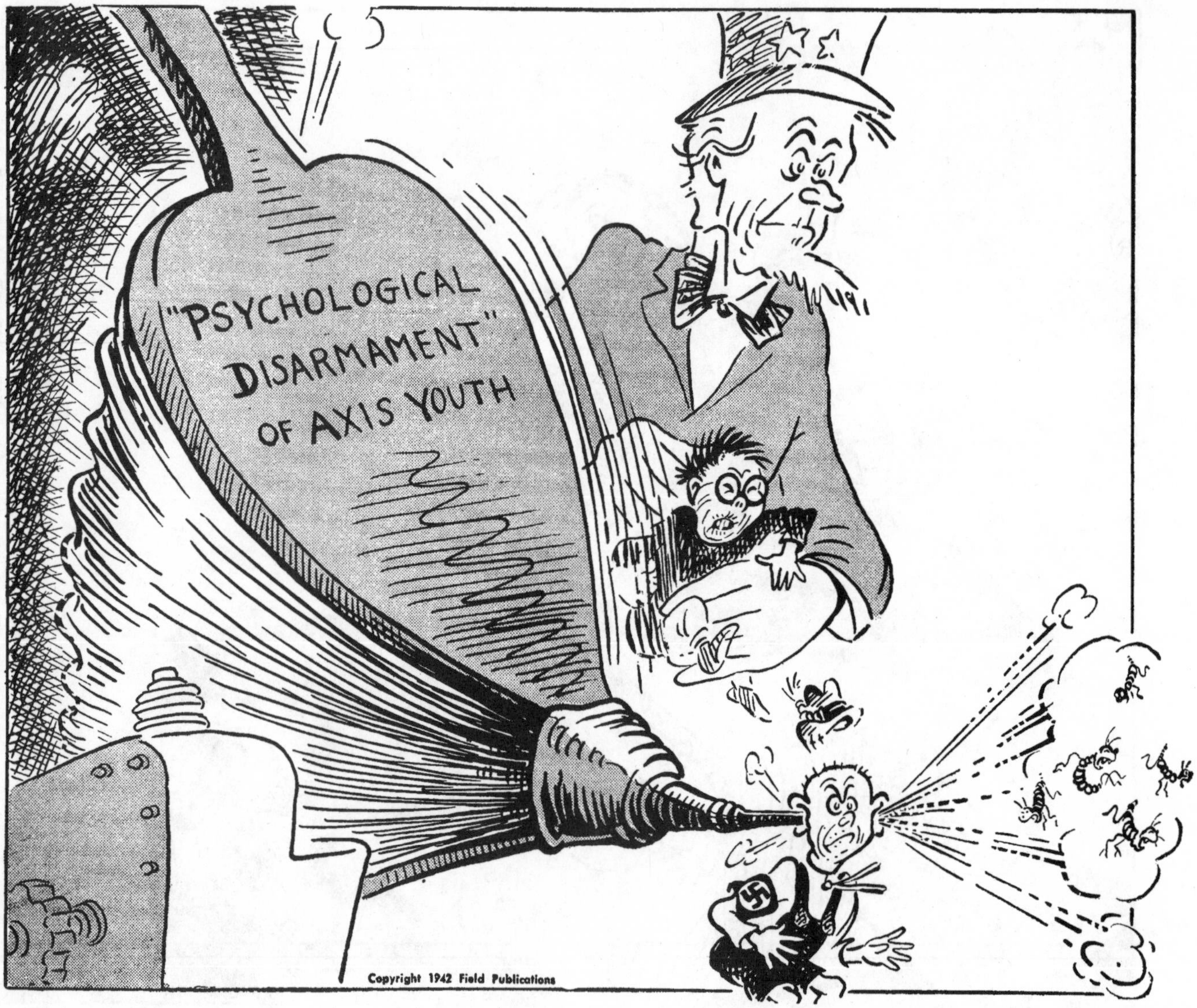
"PSYCHOLOGICAL DISARMAMENT" OF AXIS YOUTH
Copyright 1942 Field Publications

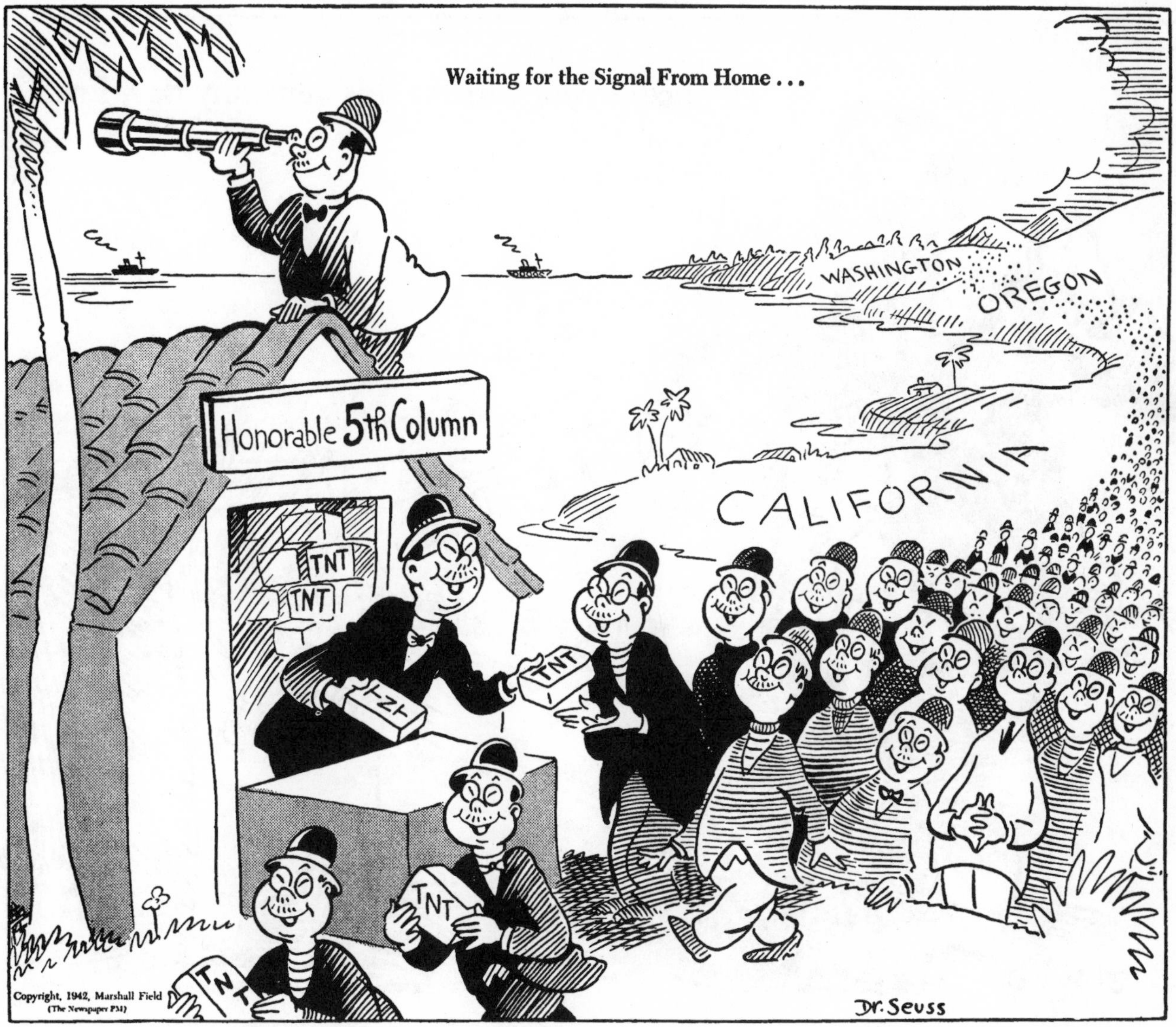
Waiting for the Signal From Home . . .
Honorable 5th Column
TNT
TNT
TNT
TNT
TNT
TNT
WASHINGTON
OREGON
CALIFORNIA
Copyright, 1942, Marshall Field
(The Newspaper PM)
Dr. Seuss

65 — February 13, 1942

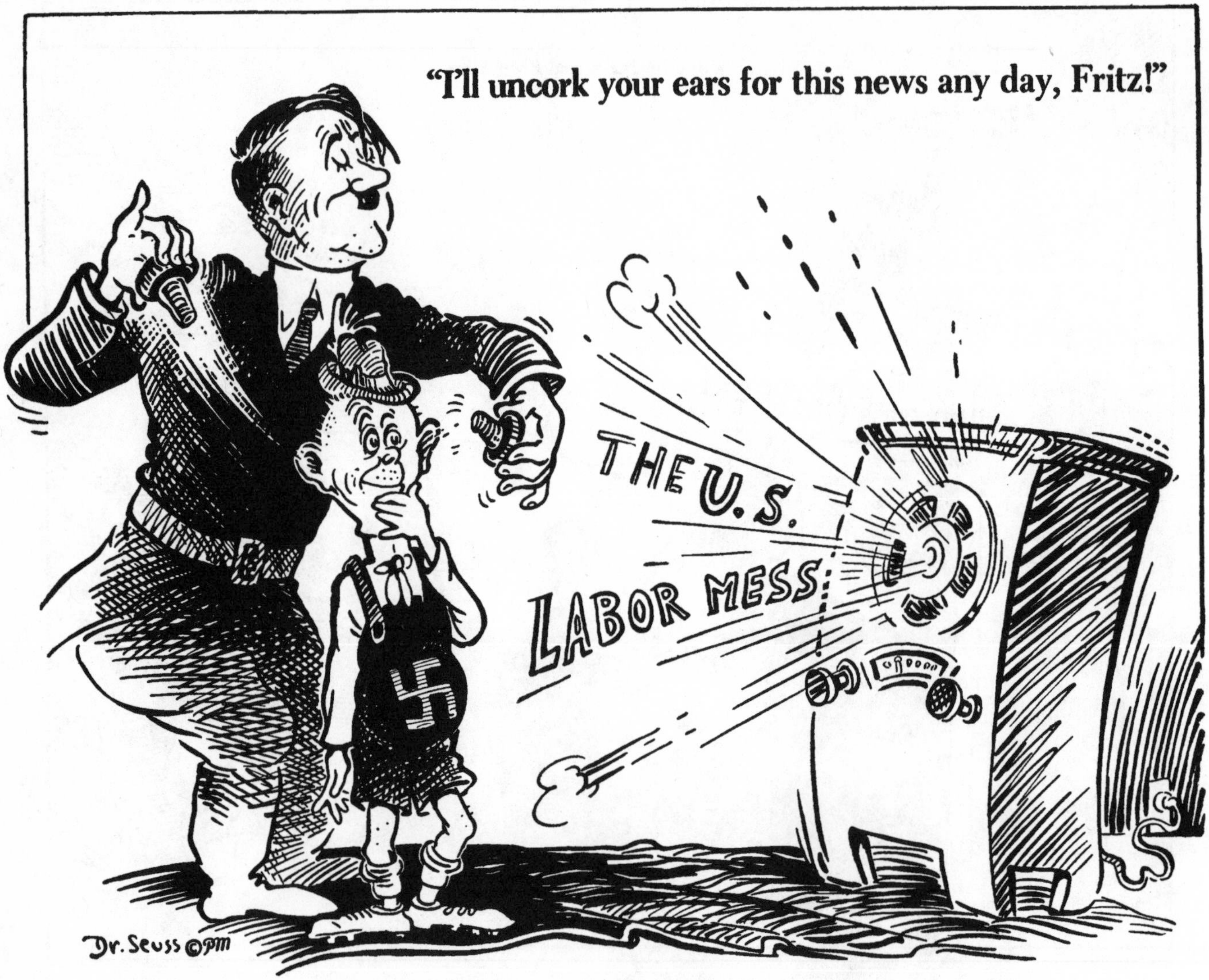
"I'll uncork your ears for this news any day, Fritz!"
THE U.S.
LABOR MESS
Dr. Seuss ©PM

66 — November 19, 1941

Gassing the Troops on Our Own Front Line

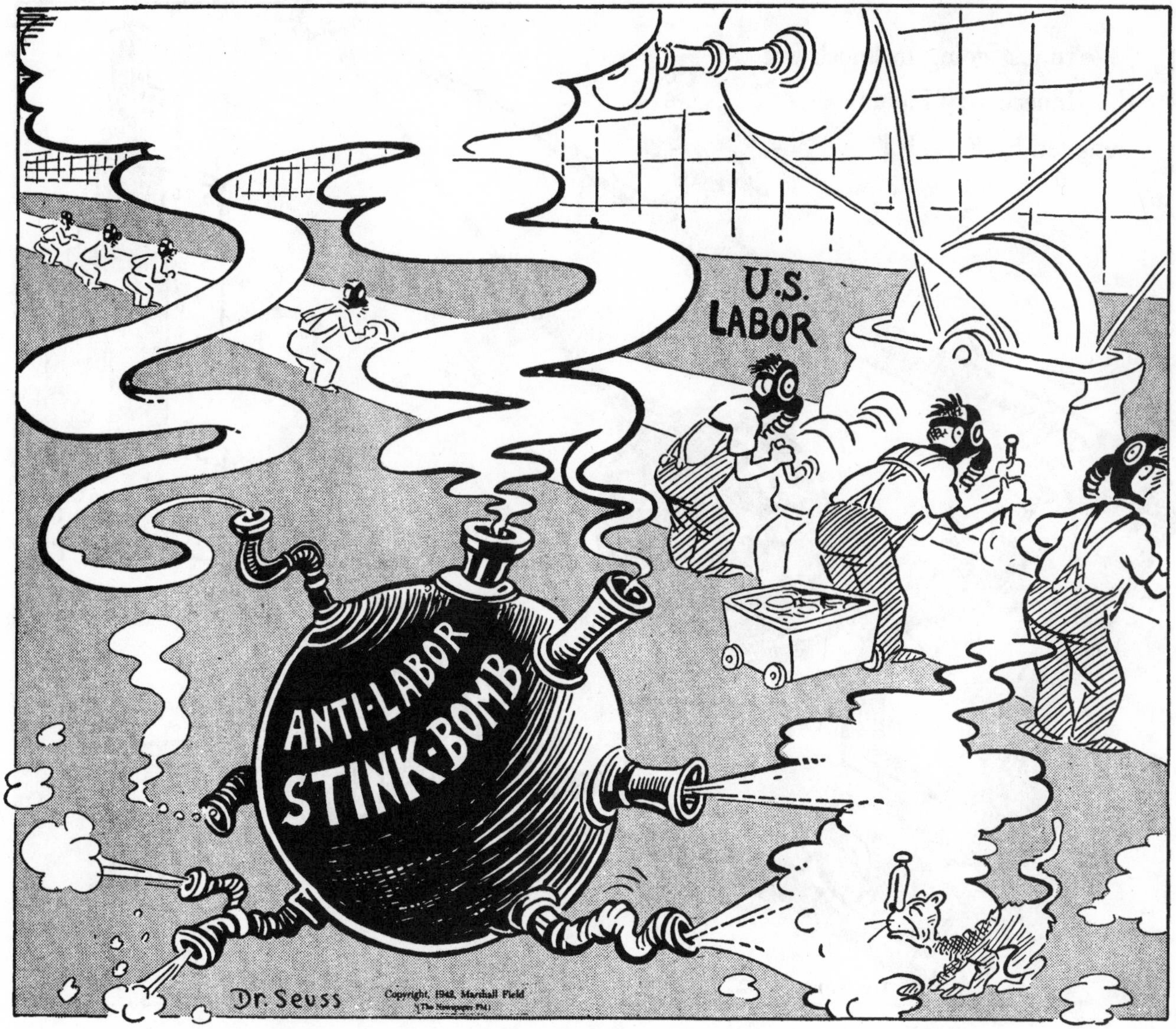
U.S.
LABOR
ANTI-LABOR
STINK-BOMB
Dr. Seuss
Copyright, 1942, Marshall Field
(The Newspaper PM)

67 — March 26, 1942

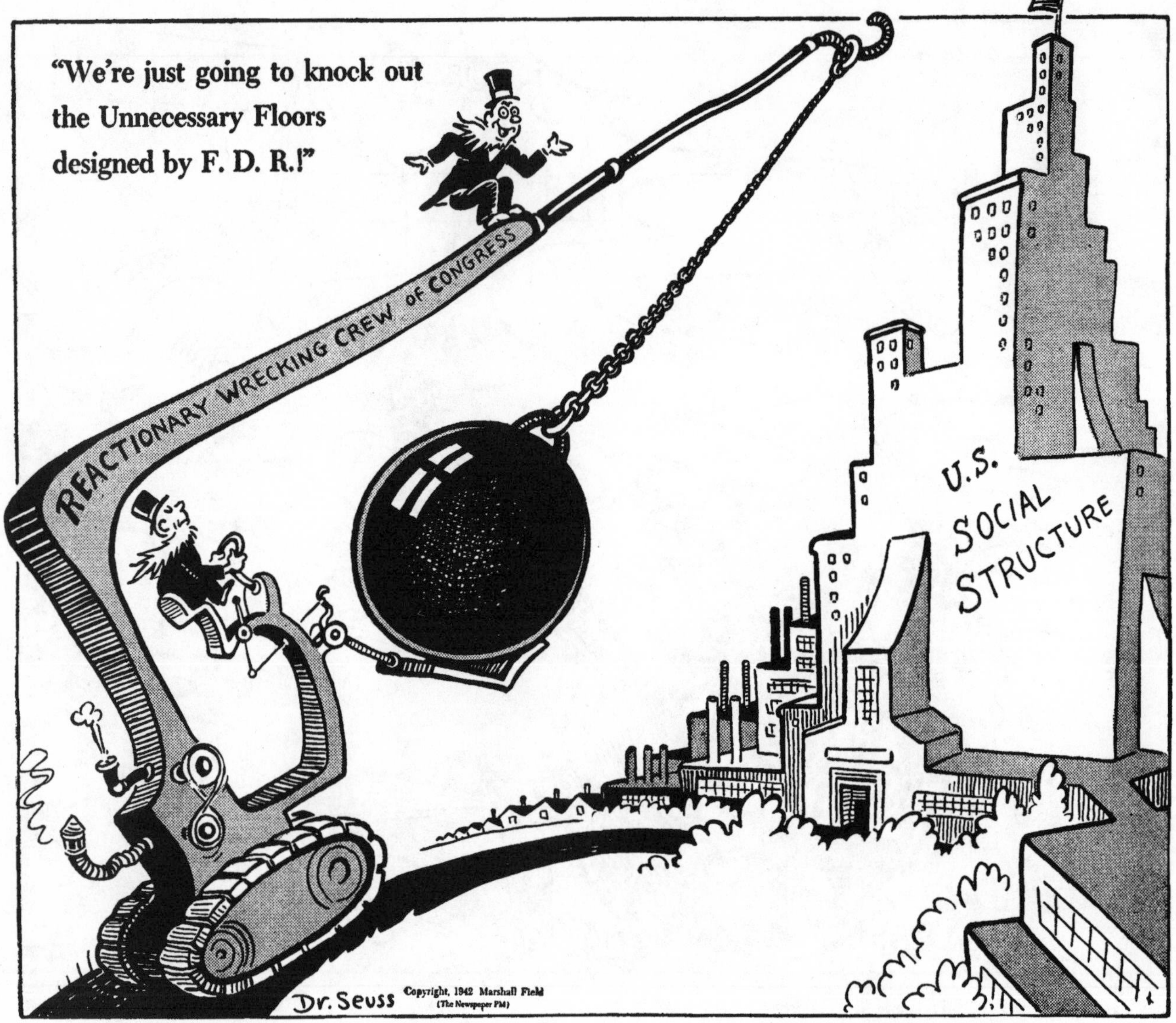
"We're just going to knock out
the Unnecessary Floors
designed by F. D. R.!"
REACTIONARY WRECKING CREW of CONGRESS
U.S.
SOCIAL
STRUCTURE
Dr. Seuss
Copyright, 1942 Marshall Field
(The Newspaper PM)

68 — May 18, 1942

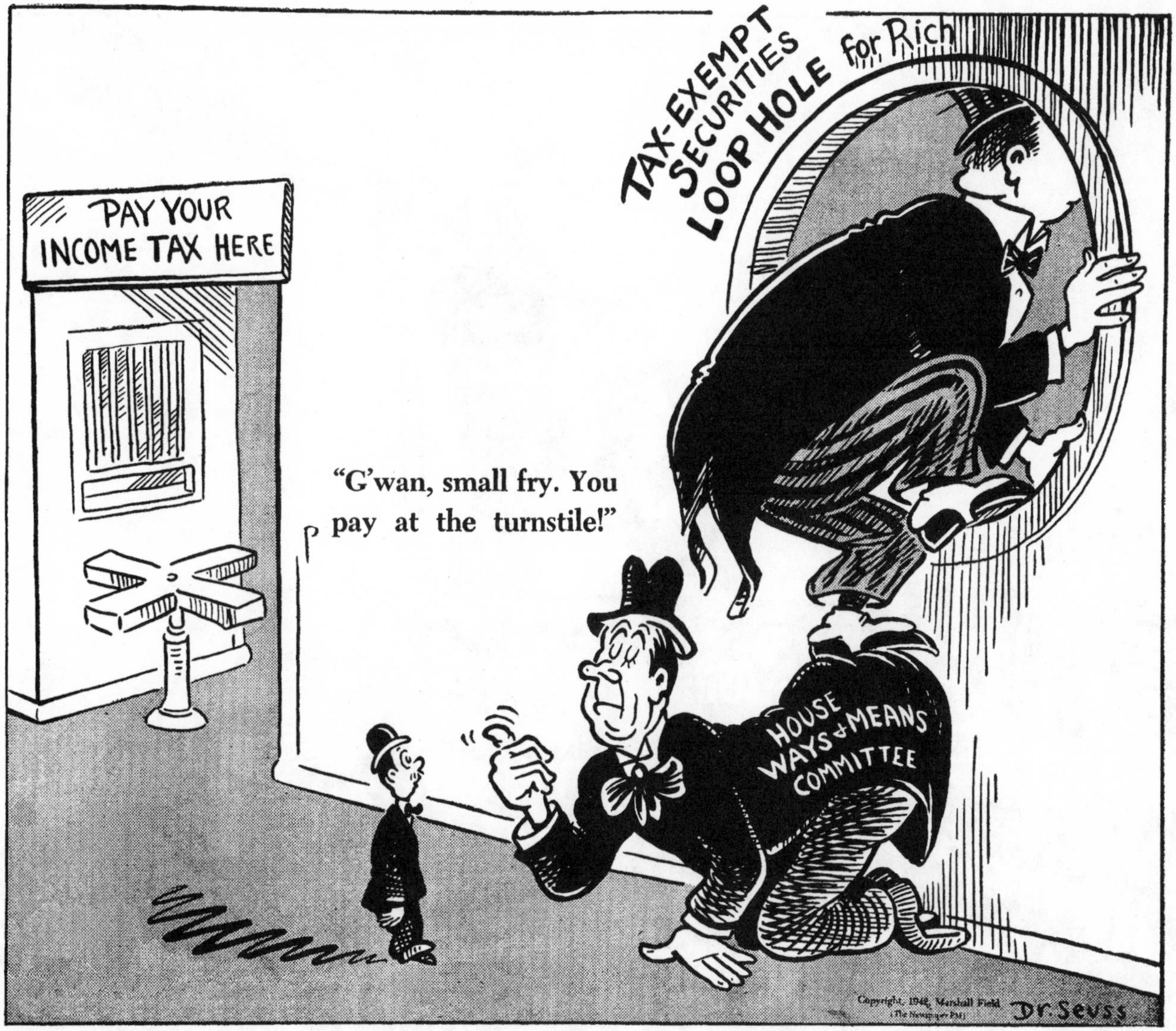
TAX-EXEMPT SECURITIES LOOP HOLE for Rich
PAY YOUR INCOME TAX HERE
HOUSE WAYS & MEANS COMMITTEE
Copyright, 1942, Marshall Field
(The Newspaper PM)
Dr. Seuss

"G'wan, small fry. You pay at the turnstile!"

69 – May 27, 1942

Hey, You Talent Scouts, Give a Look Down!

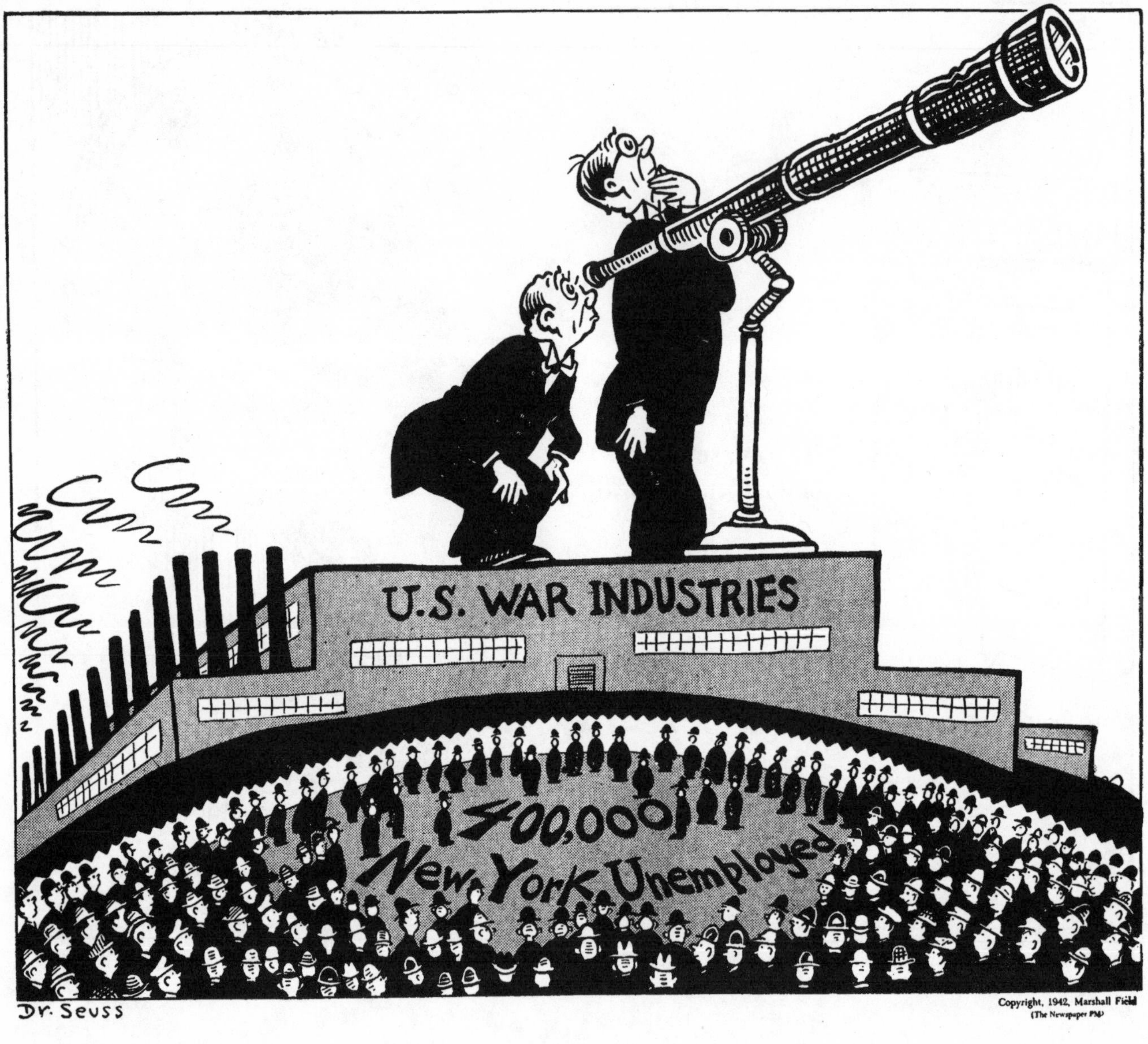
U.S. WAR INDUSTRIES
400,000 New York Unemployed
Dr. Seuss
Copyright, 1942, Marshall Field
(The Newspaper PM)

Democracy's Turnstile

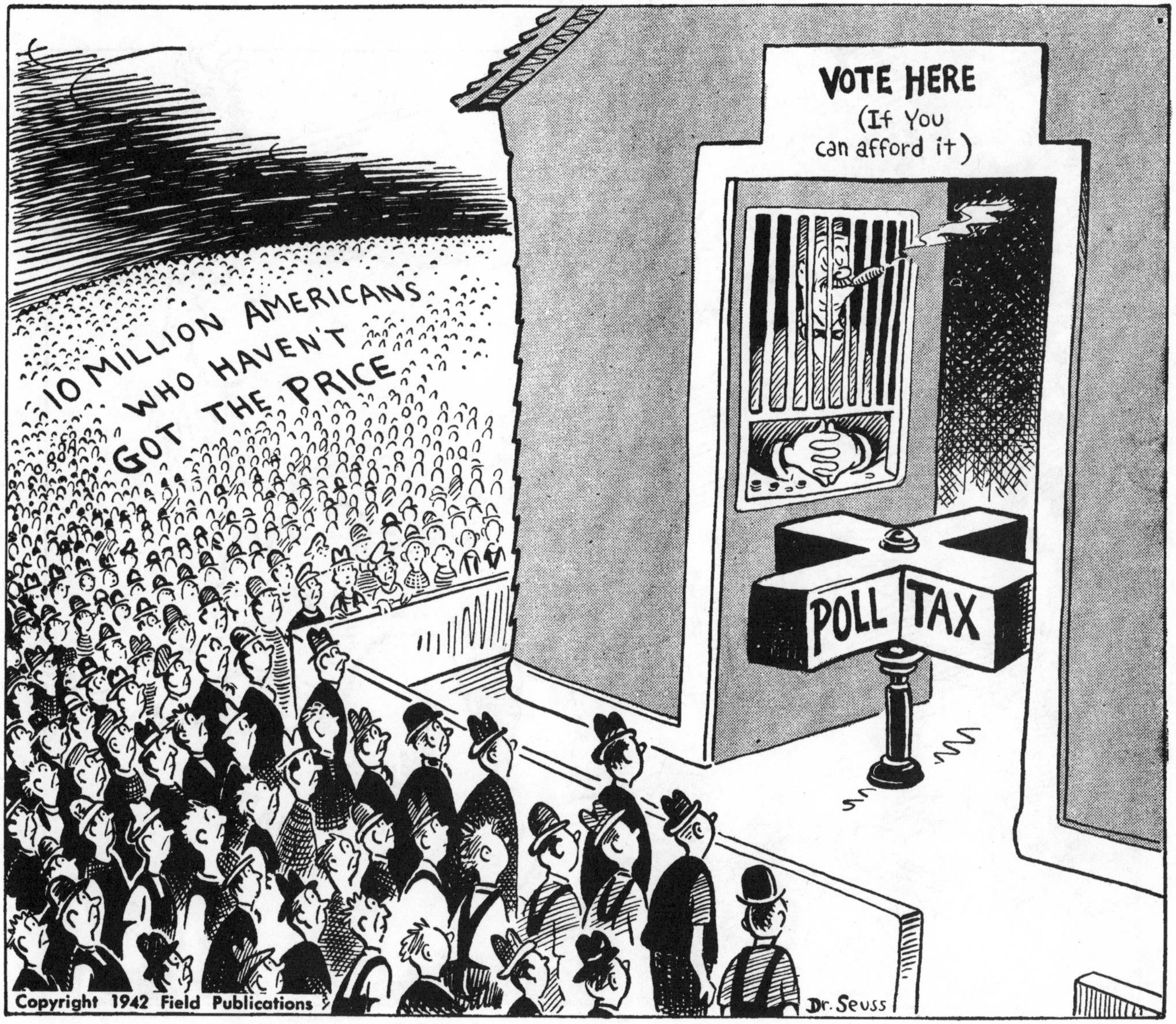

VOTE HERE
(If You
can afford it)
10 MILLION AMERICANS
WHO HAVEN'T
GOT THE PRICE
POLL TAX
Copyright 1942 Field Publications
Dr. Seuss

71 — October 12, 1942

Buck Bilbo Rides Again

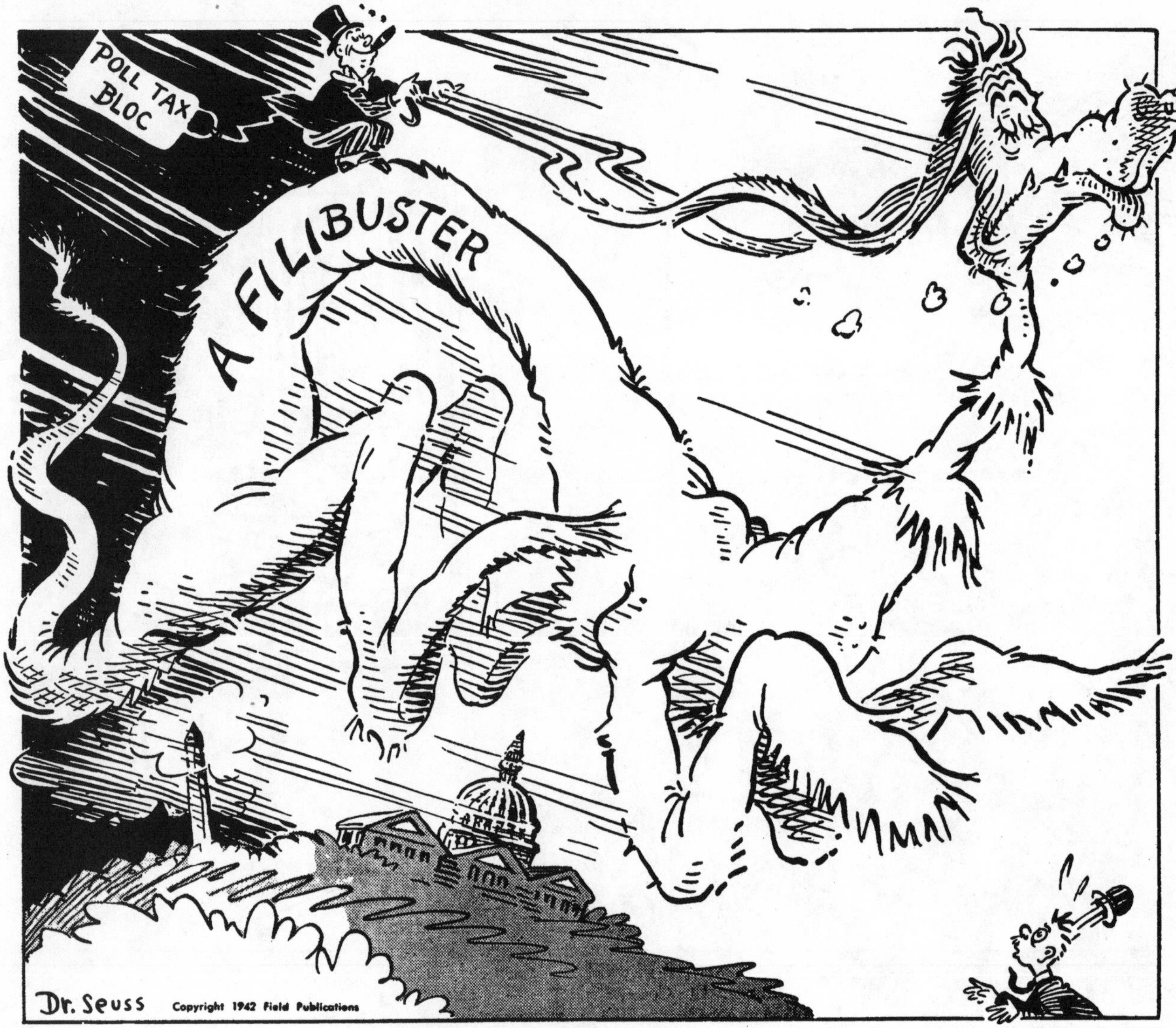
POLL TAX BLOC
A FILIBUSTER
Dr. Seuss
Copyright 1942 Field Publications

72 — November 16, 1942

Hitler and Nazi Germany

Except for the world crisis that began in the 1930s, Dr. Seuss might never have drawn a political cartoon.

German Chancellor Adolf Hitler was at the center of that world crisis. By the spring of 1941 Hitler controlled all of Europe except for England and the neutral nations—Sweden and Switzerland, the Republic of Ireland, Iceland, Greenland, and Spain. Half of France was occupied by Germany, with the other half governed by a collaborationist regime at Vichy. Dr. Seuss's first cartoon featuring Hitler appeared in May 1941. In this first cartoon, "The head eats...the rest gets milked" (May 19), Hitler is the proprietor of "Consolidated World Dairy," and he has "consolidated" eleven conquered nations into one cow. The final (twelfth) hindquarters has a question mark—who's next?

In a July 1941 cartoon captioned "crisis in Berchtesgaden," Hitler is aghast to discover the letter V in his alphabet soup. The British had made the V sign an internationally recognized symbol of victory (and of anti-German activities); Berchtesgaden was Hitler's mountain hideaway. This cartoon refers obliquely to a series of cartoons in the *New Yorker* dealing with highly unexpected situations, but in a note printed directly underneath the cartoon, Dr. Seuss made his apologies to a second *PM* cartoonist, Carl Rose. Dr. Seuss wrote the following note to

Editor Ingersoll: "Here's a sad situation. I finished up this picture yesterday, thinking it one of my best...when, socko! in came your Sunday edition, with an alphabet soup gag in Carl Rose's cartoon. My first impulse was to tear mine up, but I've decided to send it along anyway. If you want to tear it up, go ahead, with my blessing. If, on the other hand, you decide it still warrants running, please do so only after explaining things to Rose, and asking his permission...." In August, Hitler appears as a mighty hunter carrying his outsize moose ("vanquished Europe") home on his shoulders only to have the moose bite him in the rear—"Sabotage." Like the Hitler of the alphabet soup, this Hitler is decidedly unjaunty.

Dr. Seuss depicted Hitler alone; he depicted him among his generals and other Germans; he depicted him with his allies, Benito Mussolini of Italy and Pierre Laval of Vichy France, and, often, a stereotyped "Japan." Of the cartoons depicting Hitler alone, the most striking appeared in late 1941, one before the United States became involved formally in the fighting but long after Hitler had expanded German control throughout Europe, one after America entered the war. The first (November 10) depicts Hitler as one-man band attempting to play a "New World Symphony" of conquered European nations (count them!) and Italy, the nation that had joined his cause. Once again, as in the "Consolidated World Dairy," France gets top billing. Yugoslavia, Rumania, and Greece are now "the Balkans" and Italy—with Japan, Hitler's Axis ally—is a part of the picture, albeit a minor one. (Note Hitler's left boot, cut away to allow Hitler's toes to grasp the hammers to beat the xylophone.)

85   In late November, still before Pearl Harbor, Hitler lines up performing seals—"artists assembled from the twelve great capitals of the world"—to issue an "Anti-Comintern blast." The Comintern was the Communist International, 1919–1943, established by Lenin in an attempt to claim Communist control of the world socialist movement. In 1936, Hitler and the Japanese government had signed an Anti-Comintern Pact, and in late 1941 the two countries were joined by eleven other governments in the pact that is the context for this cartoon. At Thanksgiving 1941 (a cartoon not included here) Hitler is chef, and "Uncle Sam" is the turkey on a platter—crosses in eyes, paper ruffles around ankles: "A Toast to Next Thanksgiving: Here's hoping we're not the bird!"

86   "The Latest Self-Portrait" (December 23), which serves as the cover of this volume, depicts Hitler as simultaneously sculptor, subject, mermaid and *putti* crowning Hitler with knight's helmet. It is the second striking portrait of Hitler alone, and it is a step beyond Hitler as one-man band. This is multiple Hitlers, a jab at Hitler's unlimited ego. Because of the five faces of Hitler, this cartoon gives us a chance to study Dr. Seuss's Hitler. Dr.

Seuss's Hitler is jaunty, almost nonchalant. His chin is raised. His hair is combed straight to the side. A single line sketches his cheek. No mouth is visible beneath the brush mustache. His eyes are shut demurely. Note that even the bird on Hitler's shield—the neck suggests it is a vulture—and the horse echo Hitler's haircut and cheekline. And both bird and horse have Hitler's mustache!

We see Dr. Seuss's Hitler in a variety of situations over a broad stretch of time. A month after Pearl Harbor, on January 2, 1942, Dr. Seuss portrayed Hitler in a dilemma that reflects the unhappy German military situation: simultaneously "frozen" in Russia and "sunburned" in North Africa (a cartoon not included here). In a series of cartoons in early 1942, Dr. Seuss drew Hitler as a baby: "Mein Early Kampf, by Adolf Hitler." In the first and most effective of the series, the baby Hitler ("Adolfikins"—complete with brush mustache and adult forelock) gives the unlucky stork delivering him a hotfoot; at the foot of the panel is Hitler's date of birth. Note the tilt of Hitler's head. In the second cartoon (not included in this volume), Hitler refuses milk from Holstein cows as "non-Aryan." Holsteins are a Dutch breed, not German, but Dr. Seuss may have been playing on the Jewish-sounding name. In the third (also not included), baby Hitler cuts his first tooth on a bust of Otto von Bismarck, the towering figure of German unification in the late nineteenth century and to many the father figure of virulent German nationalism. In a cartoon of March 1942, Dr. Seuss depicted Hitler bringing snakes back to Ireland, eleven snakes aboard his Nazi submarine. The Republic of Ireland maintained neutrality during World War II. British forces did operate

87

88

in Northern Ireland, despite protest from the Republic.

Perhaps because of the slightly comical air of Dr. Seuss's Hitler, his two most foreboding Hitler cartoons do 89 not show Hitler's face. One (March 19, 1942) depicts John Q. Citizen polishing Hitler's boots: "What do YOU expect to be working at after the war?" The shoeshine stand man 90 is roughly the size of one of Hitler's feet. "Second Creation" (April 3, 1942) shows Hitler melting Germans down to recast them in the Nazi mold, heads bowed, right hand raised in the *Sieg Heil* salute. Here again Hitler dwarfs normal people—the people he melts down and the new human beings he casts. Both cartoons are among the truly memorable cartoons of World War II, epitomizing as they do the essential relation between totalitarian dictator and subject and, indeed, the creation of a new race of slaves. But between them, on March 23, came Dr. Seuss's standard Hitler. This is not an editorial cartoon but an illustration for a short and humorous news clip. Hitler's head may be attached to the body of a snake, but he seems a good deal less poisonous than a rattlesnake.

91 In a cartoon of June 1942, Dr. Seuss dressed Hitler in mermaid garb—and five o'clock shadow—to counter false optimism at reverses to German air power in Europe. Hitler as mermaid dwarfs the Allied ships he has impaled on his trident. He also dwarfs the man in the armchair, who in turn dwarfs the buildings among which he sits. Two days later, in "No sign yet of sagging morale,"

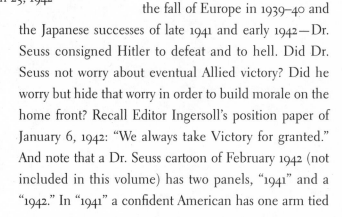

March 23, 1942

Dr. Seuss had Hitler riding a dachshund ("The perilous- 92 ly extended Reich") and supporting the dachshund's belly with a sling at the end of a pole. The Reich may be overextended, but Hitler does not look worried. With rare exceptions, Dr. Seuss's Hitler is impervious to or oblivious of the problems he faces.

Six months after Pearl Harbor, we find a cartoon in 93 which Hitler sends one of his minions to scout out hell: "A lot of us may be going there one of these fine days." The underling carries a trident and wears horns and a tail—camouflage for a spy in hell; but the horns are clearly tied on, and the tail is clearly part of his absurd union suit. These last two cartoons document a fascinating shift in emphasis. Before Pearl Harbor Dr. Seuss consistently painted Hitler as world threat; after Pearl Harbor—indeed, long before the clear positive swing in Allied fortunes away from the disasters of the fall of Europe in 1939–40 and the Japanese successes of late 1941 and early 1942—Dr. Seuss consigned Hitler to defeat and to hell. Did Dr. Seuss not worry about eventual Allied victory? Did he worry but hide that worry in order to build morale on the home front? Recall Editor Ingersoll's position paper of January 6, 1942: "We always take Victory for granted." And note that a Dr. Seuss cartoon of February 1942 (not included in this volume) has two panels, "1941" and a "1942." In "1941" a confident American has one arm tied behind him, and the restraint is labeled "Conceit." In "1942" the same fellow has *both* arms tied behind him, and the second restraint has two labels: "Incompetence" and "Carelessness." Now he is worried: "Hey, I said *one* hand...*not both!*" The cartoon is an attack on all three obstacles to action, but in Dr. Seuss's vision the situation still seems less than desperate.

In July 1942, Dr. Seuss drew two cartoons with the title "With Adolf in Egypt." Hitler himself never set foot in Egypt during the war, but beginning in February 1942 Hitler's Afrika Korps was operating in North Africa. Despite important British bases on its soil, Egypt maintained neutrality into 1945. So the thrust of these cartoons is purely rhetorical: one (July 3, 1942) attributed to Hitler megalomaniac outrage at Muslims praying to Mecca but turning their behinds toward Berlin; the second introduced a Seussian crossbreed—an Aryan camel for Hitler's use, presumably in North Africa—a dachshund with a hump!

Three cartoons in October placed German war fortunes at a low ebb. In one of them Hitler doesn't even appear; in another he is present only as a photograph on the wall. On October 7, a German father clad in lederhosen exclaims to his hungry son, also clad in lederhosen, "Food? We Germans don't eat *food*! We Germans eat countries!" The hardship of the German people is indicated in several ways. The plant on the windowsill is dying, and the stuffed head of an elk mounted on the wall has crosses in its eyes—it is twice dead. In the cartoon of the very next day, a Nazi radio broadcaster introduces "Colonel Schmaltz of the Gestapo" to speak "on his recent experiences in Norway." Colonel Schmaltz is a skeleton. Like Dr. Seuss's Mussolini, Colonel Schmaltz has crossed bandages on the side of his head, but here the bandages rest on his skull. On October 15, Dr. Seuss depicted a nonchalant Hitler "testing das new secret weapon for 1943..."—"Der Skids," with an undersized Hitler hurtling uncontrollably downhill. Mid-October is very early to be predicting the military reverses that beset Hitler in the winter of 1942 and spring of 1943.

One month later, in "Slightly Diverted," Dr. Seuss satirized the two-front war that Hitler was waging against the Soviet Union and in North Africa. As he parachutes into Tunisia, Hitler blithely reads a guidebook to Moscow and states to an incredulous fellow parachutist: "According to my book, boys, der Kremlin from here should be just around der corner!" Also in November Dr. Seuss had Hitler putting "Germany," a figure strikingly different from Hitler in height and face and mustache, through two wringers: the "African wringer" and the "Russian wringer." Indeed, by late 1942 German forces were in serious trouble both in the Soviet Union and in North Africa.

"I would like to take this opportunity to prophesy a white Christmas" (December 4, 1942) has Hitler getting the worst of the Russian winter. But once again Hitler is unaffected. December of 1942 marked the second winter German forces faced in the Soviet Union, and it was a winter fatal to their assault. In January, the Red Army penetrated the siege of Leningrad in the north, and in the south the German army occupying Stalingrad surrendered. Reverses or no, Dr. Seuss's Hitler is rarely angry.

101 Dr. Seuss often drew Hitler with his allies. On July 20, 1942, Dr. Seuss depicted the execution of Jews. Hitler and the French wartime premier Pierre Laval sing from a piece of sheet music. From trees behind them hang the bodies of Jews. The lines of the song are a play on the final line of a then-famous poem by American poet Alfred Joyce Kilmer. His poem "Trees" opens with these lines, "I think that I shall never see/A poem lovely as a tree" and closes, "Poems are made by fools like me/But only God can make a tree." This cartoon is puzzling for several reasons. First, why is Laval on a par with Hitler? Yes, the French regime collaborated with Germany in sending alien Jews and many French Jews to Auschwitz and other concentration camps beginning in March 1942; but is that reason enough to depict the music in Laval's hands?

German persecution of Jews was general knowledge in July 1942, but the death camps—the first of which opened in December 1941—were not. The first credible reports of massive killings of Jews became public in Britain in June (see the *Jewish Chronicle* for June 19 and July 3), but they referred to Poland, not to France. Beginning in early August these reports circulated in the United States, but it was only after a press conference on November 24 in Washington, D. C., convened by Stephen S. Wise, president of the World Jewish Congress, that the Nazi genocide became a subject of general discussion. Why are the cartoon's corpses hanging from trees? There may be no specific incident to which this cartoon refers; Dr. Seuss may simply have conflated Hitler's persecution of the Jews in Europe with the lynchings familiar to Americans. This is Dr. Seuss's only cartoon dealing with Jewish deaths in Europe, but, as we have seen, he targeted anti-Semitism frequently.

102 Two weeks later Hitler dressed down his French ally, Pierre Laval, whom Dr. Seuss depicted as a louse spreading infection. 103 And on December 17, 1942, Dr. Seuss produced one of his grimmest cartoons, about the rounding up of 400,000 French laborers to work in Germany. In this cartoon Hitler sits on a throne in a cave, amidst a pile of skulls, a Valkyrie-like helmet on his head and a sword across his lap, and orders Laval, a lizard-like creature with a very long tail: "Crawl Out and Round Me Up Another 400,000 Frenchmen!" The issue here is not genocide but forced labor; French laborers sent to Germany largely survived.

104 Hitler's Italian ally Mussolini appears in October's "Crisis in the High Command." Hitler consults with his generals about what to do with his Italian ally. Because of defeats abroad and dissension at home, Mussolini was perennially a problem for his German ally, and the late months of 1942 were not a good time for either Hitler or Mussolini. But the truly precipitous decline in Mussolini's fortunes came later, with the Allied invasion of Italy in the summer of 1943. Hitler's general asks, "Should we send him to storage at I. J. Fox...?" (I. J. Fox was a famous furrier on New York's fashionable Fifth Avenue.) Here we see five Germans, including Hitler. The generals all wear their hair in brush-cut fashion; as always, Hitler has his hair long and combed straight to the side. Still, even the generals are not carbon copies of each other. Three wear monocles; two have walrus mustaches, one has a brush mustache, one is clean-shaven. These generals are Pruss-

ian generals, not Nazis; Junkers, not *Wehrmacht* officers. Hence the image—except for Hitler and Mussolini, of course—is of World War I, not World War II. Do cartoonists, like stereotypical military strategists, always fight the last war?

This cartoon includes a visual puzzle (or perhaps a simple mistake?): for the two generals standing *behind* the table, there is only one set of booted legs *under* the table. Several viewers have concluded that the two generals are in fact one person caught in double view: first looking back at "Benito" and asking the first part of the question (note that the dots beneath the question lead directly down to his head) and then looking forward to finish the question to Hitler. But if so, Dr. Seuss is playing games with us, for despite the clear similarities, the two generals are almost a study in differences: the one in front has his monocle in his right eye, not his left, a mustache, no braid on his sleeve, a much larger iron cross, buttons on the inner ends of his epaulettes, a different collar and narrower sash.

138 But most often the ally depicted was a stereotyped "Japan." The first of these appeared on June 13, 1941; we will consider it later in the context of Dr. Seuss's representations of Japan. The Axis Alliance (established by the Tripartite Pact, September 27, 1940) linked Germany, Italy, and Japan. It committed all parties to come to the aid of each other against nations not then at war—a transparent reference to the United States. The actual collaboration between Berlin and Tokyo was far from complete: Berlin didn't notify Tokyo of its plan in summer 1941 to attack the Soviet Union, and Tokyo didn't tell Berlin of its

plan to attack the United States. An October 19, 1941 cartoon finds Hitler and "Japan" bickering over who will 105 push "Uncle Sam" over the other's back. Note the eyes. Hitler's eyes are shut—demurely? "Uncle Sam's" eyes are shut in blithe disregard of imminent danger. "Japan's" eyes are open, huge, and slanted grotesquely.

On December 19, 1941, just twelve days after Pearl 106 Harbor, Dr. Seuss invoked his career as cartoonist for Esso's Flit with a *PM* cover depicting Hitler, "Japan," and Mussolini as insects; an angry Uncle Sam holds a Flit gun labeled "U. S. Defense Bonds and Stamps." Hitler and "Japan" are far larger than Mussolini; note also Hitler's swastika and "Japan's" battle flag with the rays of the rising sun. This wasn't the first time Dr. Seuss depicted the Axis partners as less than human. In May (as we saw in the previous chapter) a lobster, alligator, octopus, and shark—all wearing swastikas—lurked in the "old Family bath tub." In June, Dr. Seuss employed kanga- 33 roos; earlier in December, the Japanese were depicted as 222 cats. He also depicted conquered nations as performing 145 seals or hunting trophies for Hitler. But given the purpose 85, 163 of Flit—extermination—this cartoon marks a change. Its viciousness is tempered, perhaps, by the Flit campaign, which always included an element of whimsy. The first Flit cartoon showed a "medieval tenant" waking up to find a huge beast looming at the foot of his bed: "Darn it all, another Dragon. And just after I'd sprayed the whole castle with Flit!" For most readers of *PM* in 1941, "Quick, Henry, the Flit!" summoned up instantly that ad campaign, and that context may have softened what appears today a very harsh depiction. (*The Tough Coughs as He*

Ploughs the Dough contains many pages of "Quick, Henry, the Flit!" cartoons, including this one.) As we shall see, Dr. Seuss went on to harsher depictions still, particularly of French premier Pierre Laval and "Japan."

107   On December 30, 1941—after Pearl Harbor and after the German declaration of war on the United States—Dr. Seuss drew Hitler and "Japan" as street thugs who mugged "Uncle Sam." In this cartoon, "Uncle Sam" reads "Rules for a Gentleman's Conduct in Combat," but bricks that appear to have just hit him on the head (one is "Pearl Harbor," the other "Manila") indicate that Hitler and "Japan" are anything but gentlemen. Hitler carries a third brick; "Japan" carries both cosh and knife. In these cartoons "Uncle Sam" is the innocent victim of German and Japanese attack.

108   Two days later (January 1, 1942), Hitler, Mussolini, and "Japan" appear as three snake-like beasts, nightmares in the New Year's Day hangover of Uncle Sam. Indeed,
109 on January 1, 1942 the Allied cause did not appear to be thriving. In mid-March 1942, Hitler and "Japan" size up "YOU + ME" for an Axis ball-and-chain. In May ("Giv-
110 ing the Axis a Lift") Hitler and "Japan" ride along with a "U. S. Joy-Rider," that is, a thoughtless consumer of crucial resources. The English is colloquial and flawless—"Step on it, kid; ya got gas and rubber to burn!"—but it is "Japan" whose mouth is open.

We will see further examples of Dr. Seuss's Laval, Mussolini, and "Japan." But let's pause for a moment to consider Dr. Seuss's caricature of Hitler. It is surely less evil-looking than we might expect. It may be that with four grandparents who had been born in Germany (of Protestant, not Jewish, parents), Dr. Seuss was simply unable to depict the German leader as more vicious. It may be that Dr. Seuss's forte is the light touch and that fantasy—after all, Dr. Seuss counts himself the "world's most outstanding writer of fantasy"—is inadequate to the task of portraying evil. Today's overriding concern with the Nazi Holocaust may influence our reaction to all images of Hitler, even those of sixty years ago, before the world knew the full extent of the European Holocaust. Perhaps Dr. Seuss's Hitler shows the influence of Charlie Chaplin's *The Great Dictator*, which came out in 1940. Chaplin bestrode the era (*City Lights* appeared in 1931, and *Modern Times*, in 1936), and Dr. Seuss would surely have known Chaplin's buffoonish Adenoid Hynkel, dictator of Tomania. As we shall see, there are also other Chaplinesque touches in the wartime cartoons, notably in Dr. Seuss's depiction of the stereotypical common man in the derby that Chaplin's tramp wore.

We'll see other Hitler cartoons as we proceed, but we might note here that Dr. Seuss often uses a dachshund to represent Germany. Why not a German shepherd? Perhaps it's too noble a dog, and Dr. Seuss needs an animal he can ridicule. Perhaps it's the German name (the literal translation of *dachshund* is badger dog). We've seen two such dachshunds already, one the "perilously extended Reich" whose belly Hitler supports with a sling 92 suspended from a fishing pole (June 5, 1942), the second cowering under the table as Hitler orders a spy to scout 93 out hell (June 11, 1942). There are many others. In a stunning cartoon of May 1942, Laval is "the man who was SO 111 LOW, he could walk under a Dachshund's belly." In July,

112 Dr. Seuss proclaimed the absurd invention of Hitler's dromedary dachsund. (This is the second of the two-part "With Adolf in Egypt" series.)

113 On November 24, 1942, Dr. Seuss showed Hitler before Stalingrad, deciding to switch into reverse—he sits on skis with a dachshund improbably positioned between Hitler and the skis. In the days before snowmobiles, Dr. Seuss was free to invent his own—powered by an outboard motor. An artillery shell has taken Hitler's hat, and it's not easy to figure out what the hind legs of the dachshund do; for that matter, what do the forelegs do? (The German army's attempt to break Soviet resistance at Stalingrad fell victim to a Soviet counterattack that began November 19 and lasted until the German forces surrendered on January 21, 1943.) At Thanksgiving
114 1942, Dr. Seuss drew Laval atop a coat of arms of dachshunds rampant, asking, apparently of an American audience, "Did you have turkey at your house? I had Dachshund at mine." The drawing is amazing: nineteen dachshunds (in one case, one head sits atop two bodies!), two swastika flags, twelve additional swastikas, five military hats. Laval stands atop a platter with a halo of sausages about his head. None of the dachshunds appears happy with his role; check particularly the four surrounding the large swastika at center bottom. But there are problems. It is Laval, not dachshund, on the platter. If anyone is getting consumed at Thanksgiving 1942, it is Laval and France, not Hitler's Germany. It is a great drawing, but the caption is less than convincing.

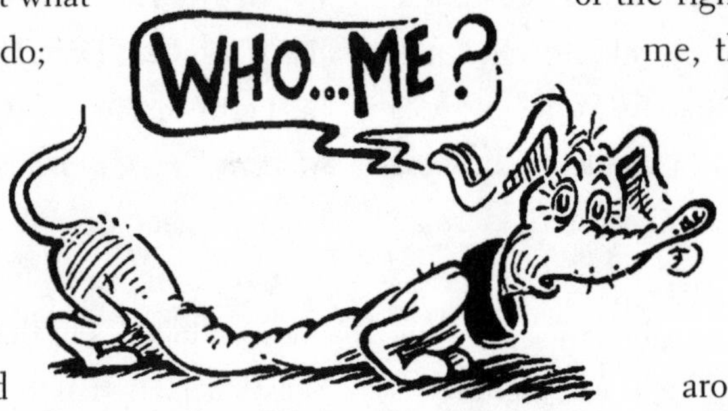
WHO...ME?
December 16, 1942

One *PM* reader who shared his life with a dachshund wrote to the editor to protest Dr. Seuss's slander of the breed: "If this insidious campaign continues, I am afraid people will begin to consider it their patriotic duty to kick my little darling around. And he wouldn't understand; he doesn't read the papers. I call this to your attention because I have always regarded *PM* as a champion of the rights of the underdog. And believe me, than the dachshund there is no dog more under." In response, Dr. Seuss offered only a plea of no-contest: "Note to Mr. Holbrook's dachshund: Sorry, friend. And if anyone kicks you around, sue me. You've got an excellent case.—Dr. Seuss." But he appended a drawing that may have soothed Mr. Holbrook. In his profile of Dr. Seuss in the *New Yorker* (December 17, 1960), E. J. Kahn, Jr., states that after this incident Dr. Seuss "resolved never again to compete, artistically, with photographers and taxidermists." Perhaps not in his war-time cartoons, but of course Dr. Seuss continued to "compete": witness, in the postwar era, Horton of *Horton Hears a Who* or Thidwick of *Thidwick the Big-Hearted Moose*.

Hitler is the prime subject of all of Dr. Seuss's World War II cartoons. Without him, Dr. Seuss might well have remained a successful commercial artist with a sideline in children's literature.

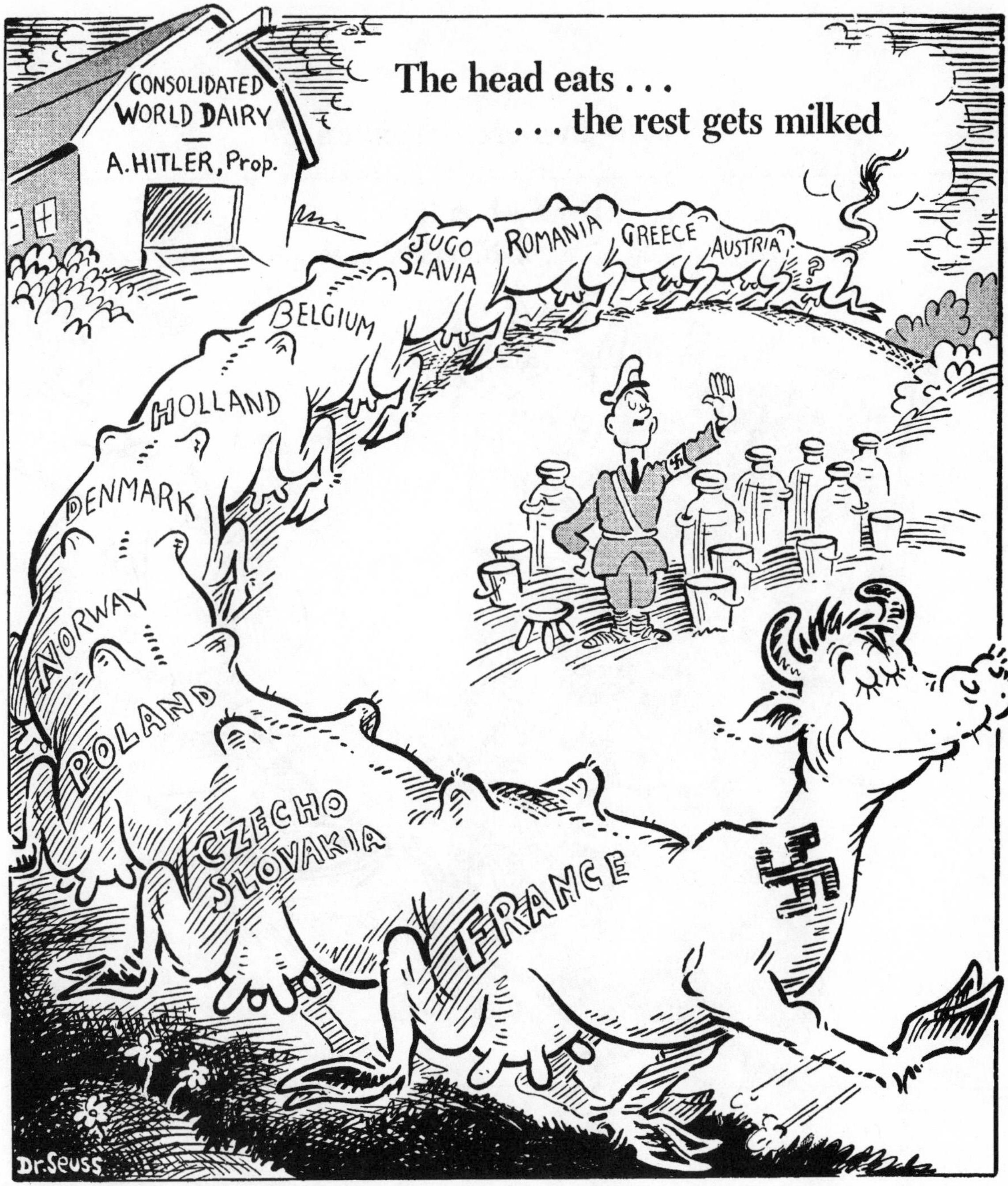
The head eats . . .
. . . the rest gets milked
CONSOLIDATED
WORLD DAIRY
A. HITLER, Prop.
JUGO
SLAVIA
ROMANIA
GREECE
AUSTRIA
?
BELGIUM
HOLLAND
DENMARK
NORWAY
POLAND
CZECHO
SLOVAKIA
FRANCE
Dr. Seuss

81 — May 19, 1941

Crisis in Berchtesgaden

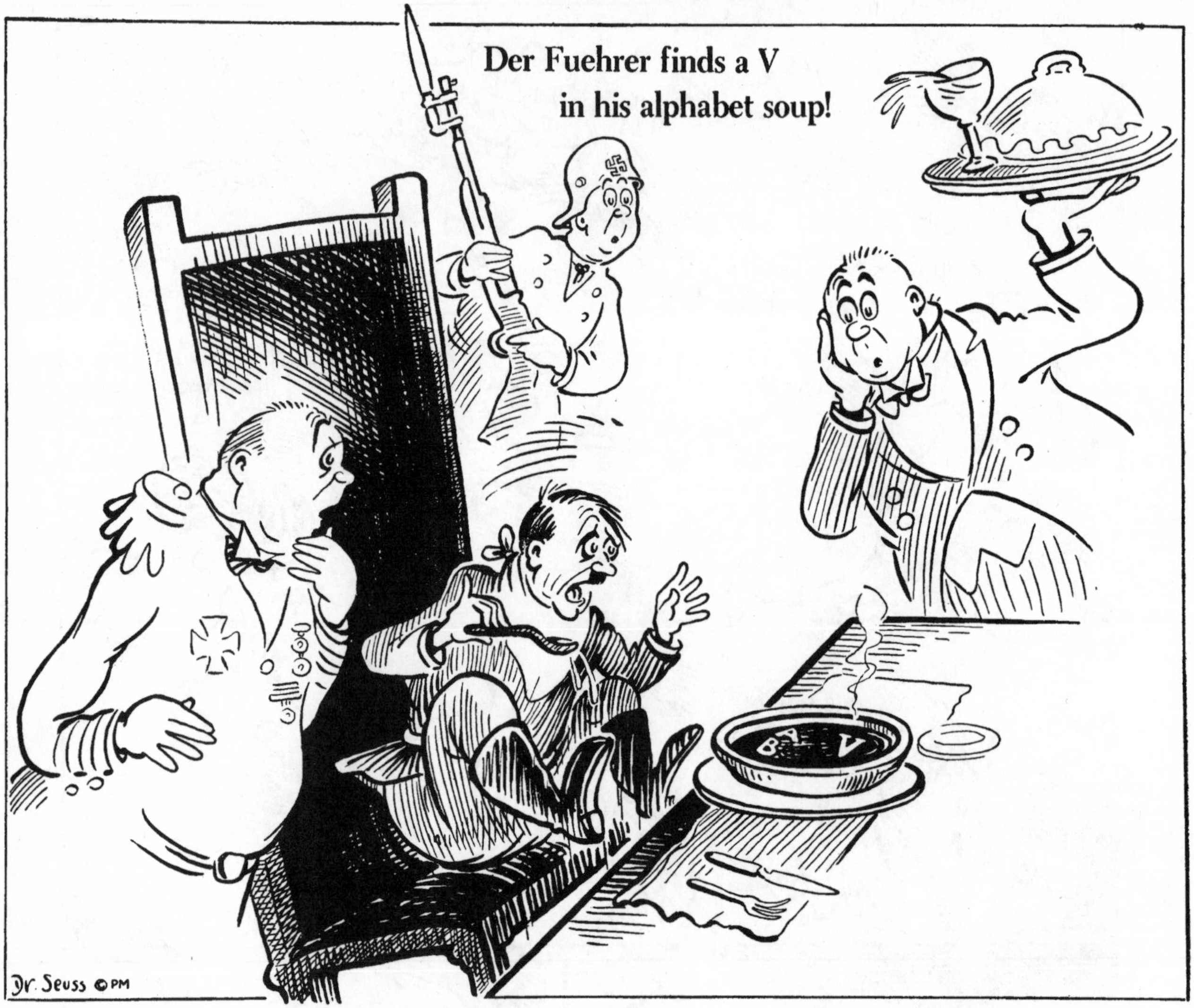
Der Fuehrer finds a V
in his alphabet soup!
Dr. Seuss ©PM

"Quite dead I shoot him . . . unt still, by Himmel, he bites!"

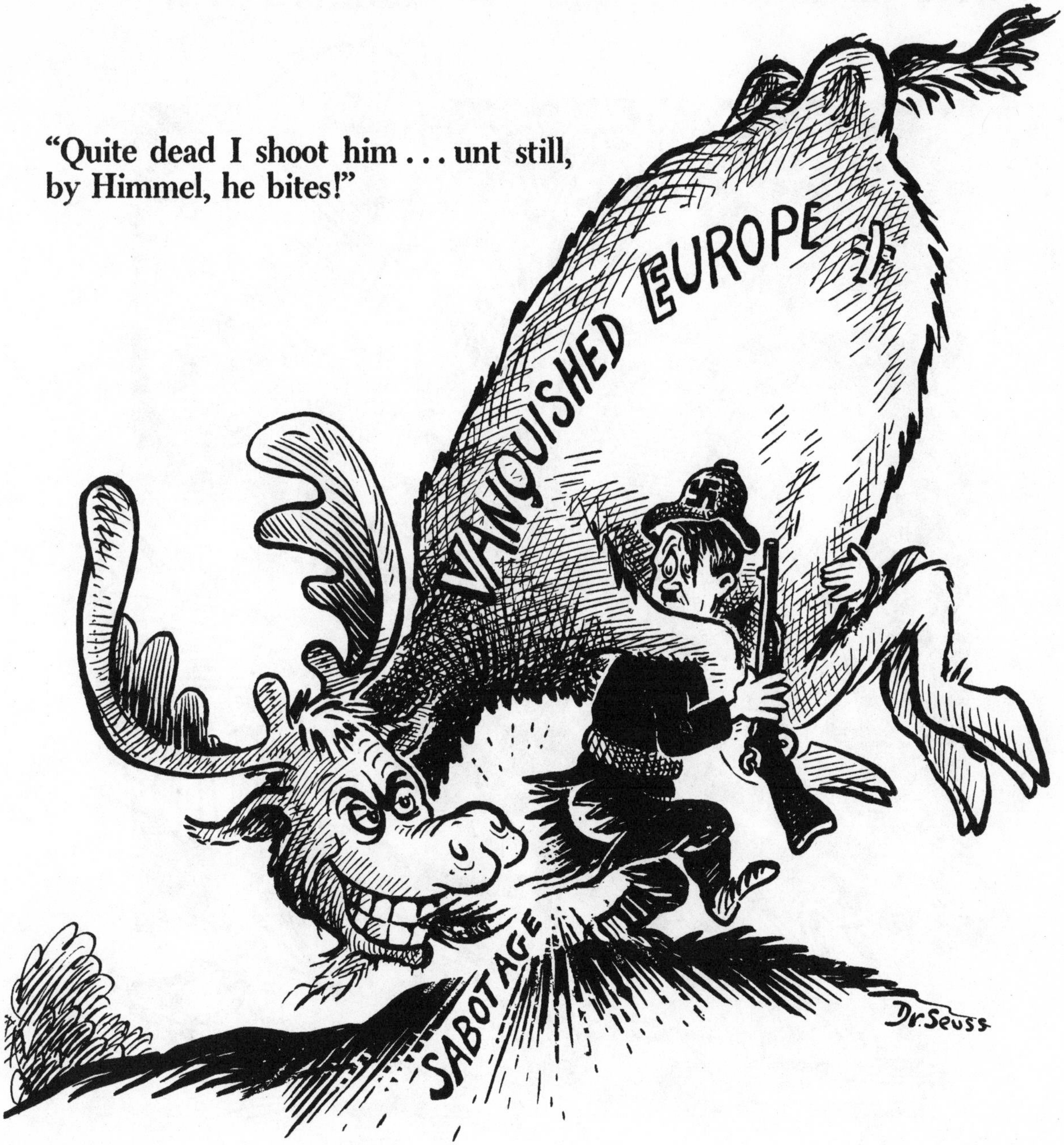
VANQUISHED EUROPE
SABOTAGE
Dr. Seuss

83 — August 18, 1941

It's a Cinch, Adolf . . . Once You Learn to Play It

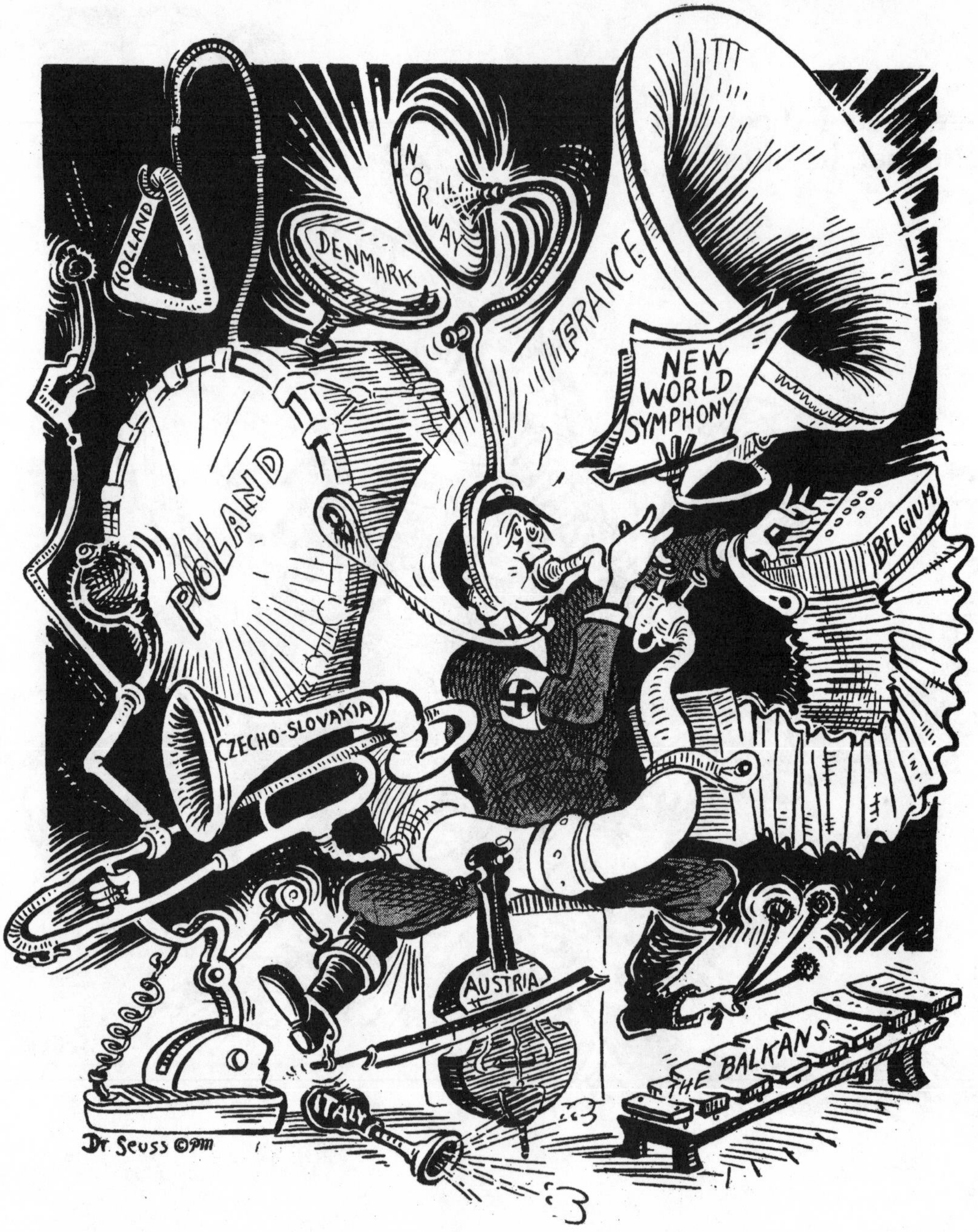
HOLLAND
DENMARK
NORWAY
FRANCE
NEW WORLD SYMPHONY
POLAND
BELGIUM
CZECHO-SLOVAKIA
AUSTRIA
THE BALKANS
ITALY
Dr. Seuss ©PM

84 – November 10, 1941

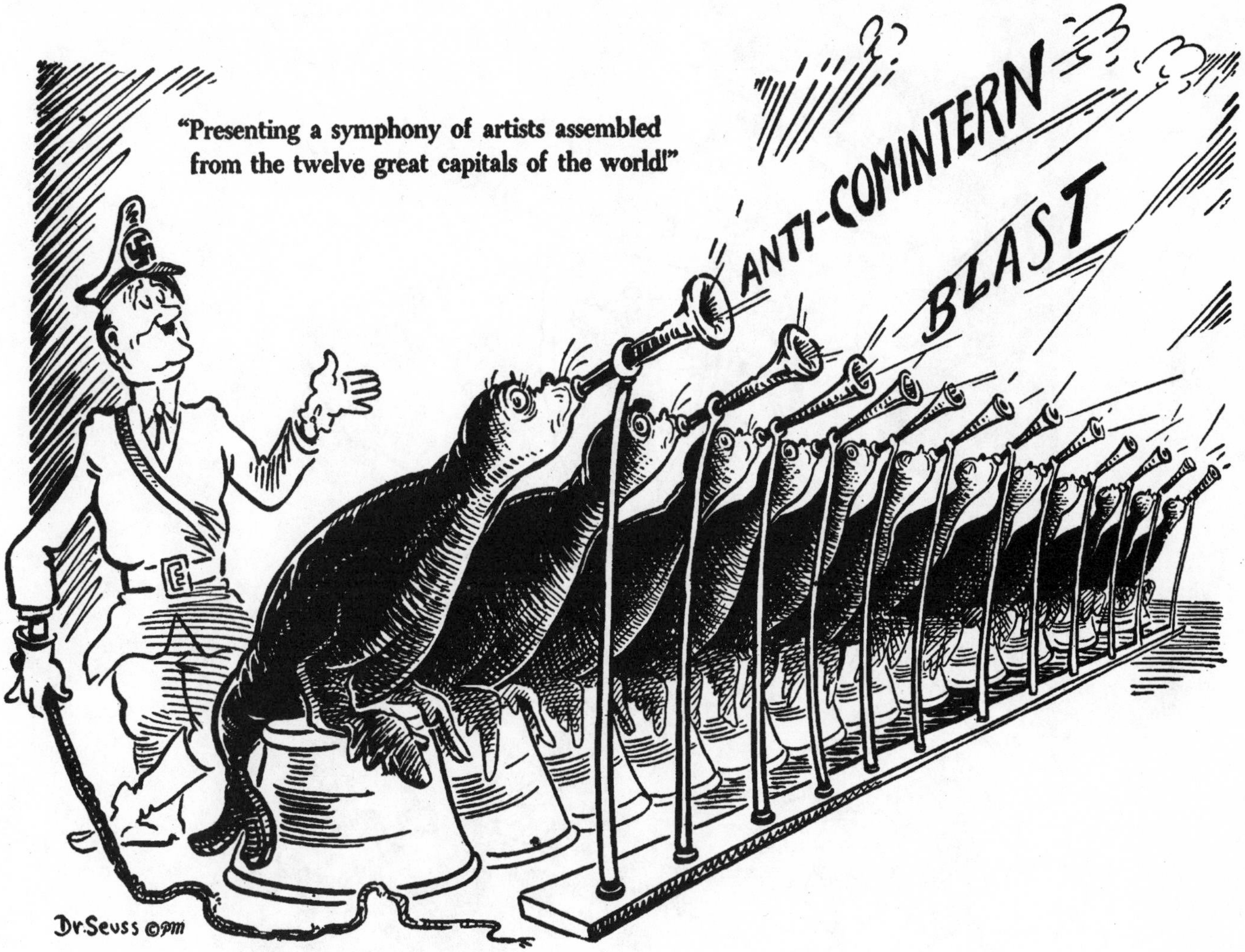
"Presenting a symphony of artists assembled
from the twelve great capitals of the world!"
ANTI-COMINTERN
BLAST
Dr. Seuss ©PM

85 — November 27, 1941

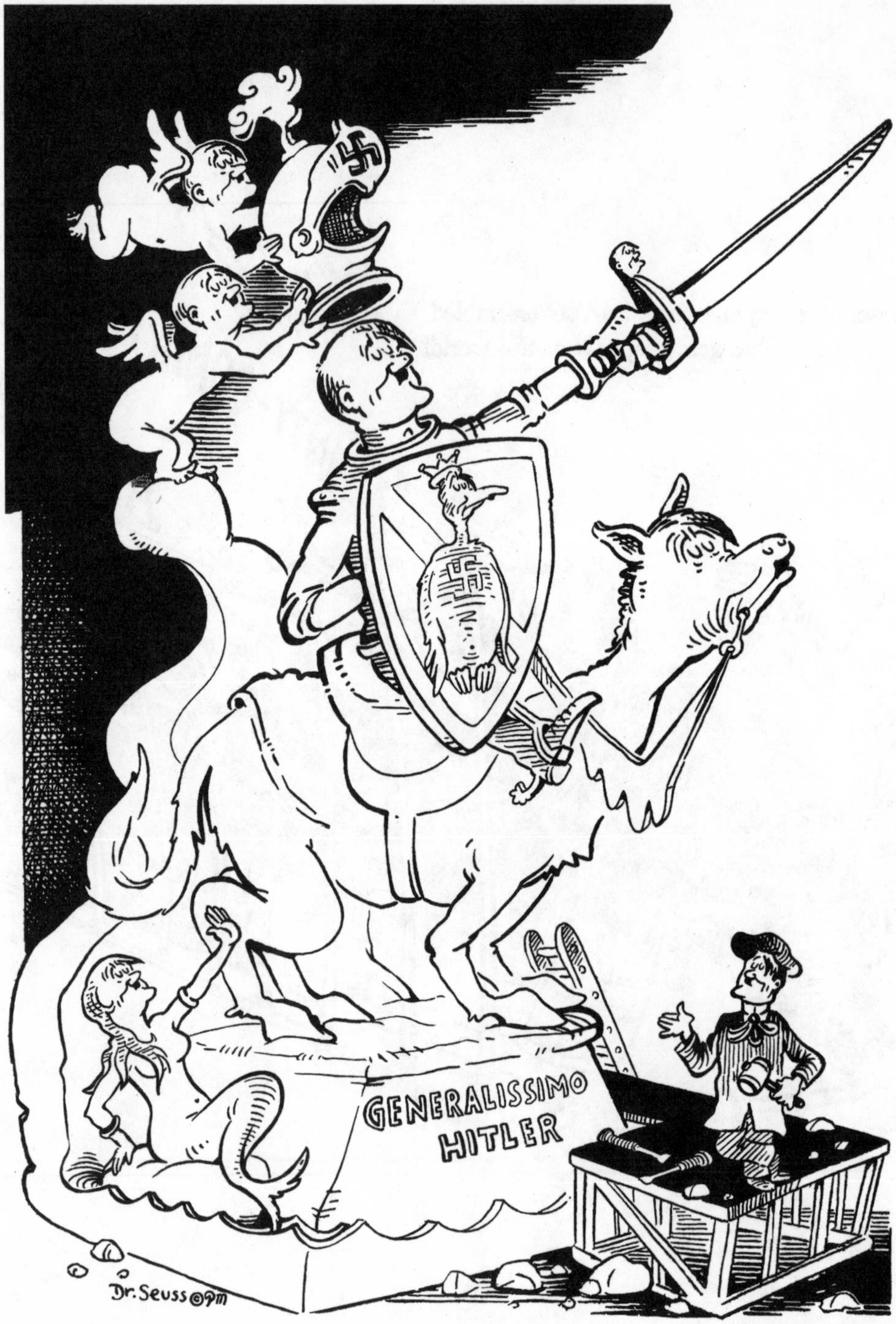
GENERALISSIMO
HITLER
Dr. Seuss © PM

86 – December 23, 1941

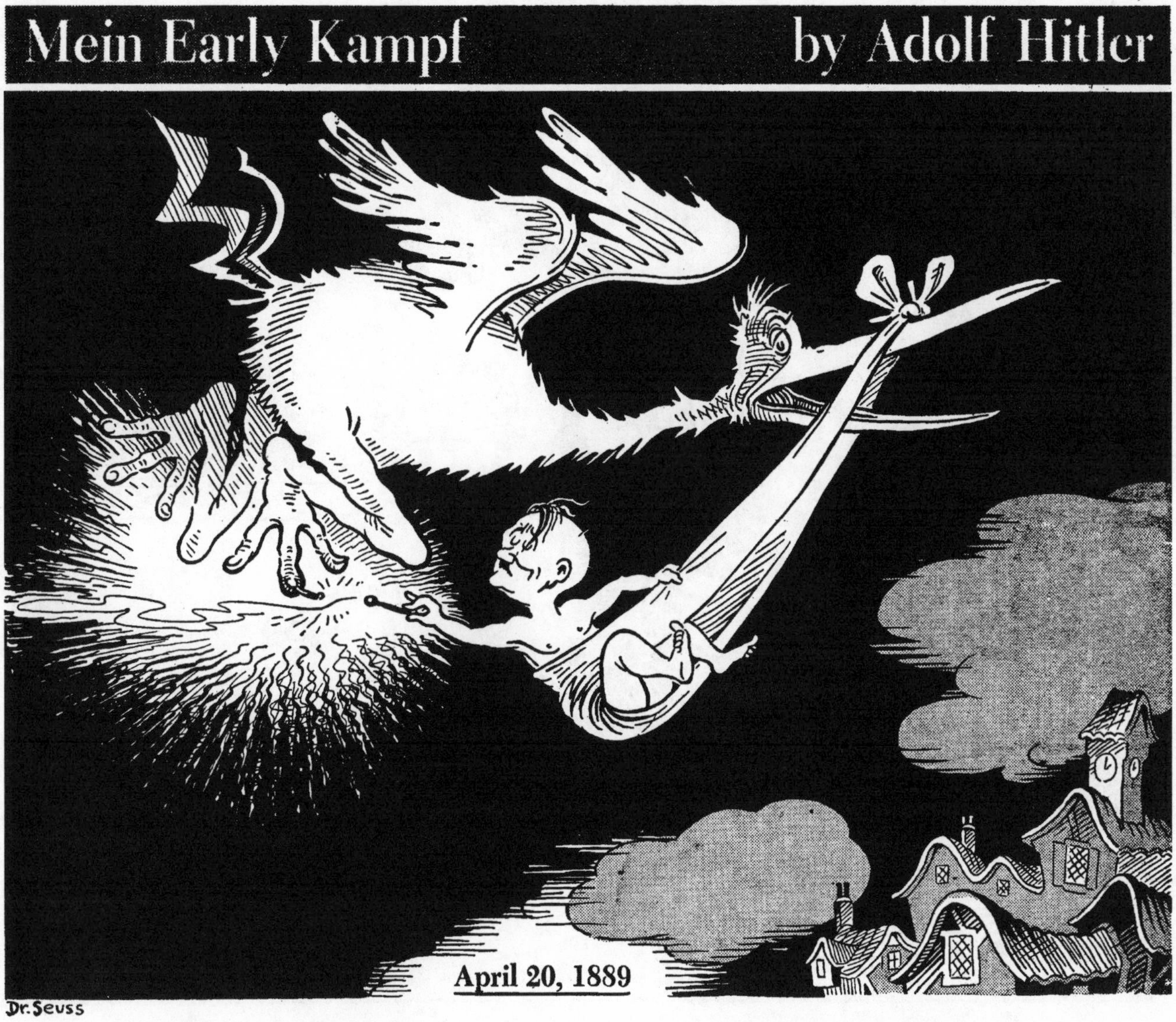
Mein Early Kampf
by Adolf Hitler
April 20, 1889
Dr. Seuss

I give the hotfoot to the stork that brings me.

87 – January 20, 1942

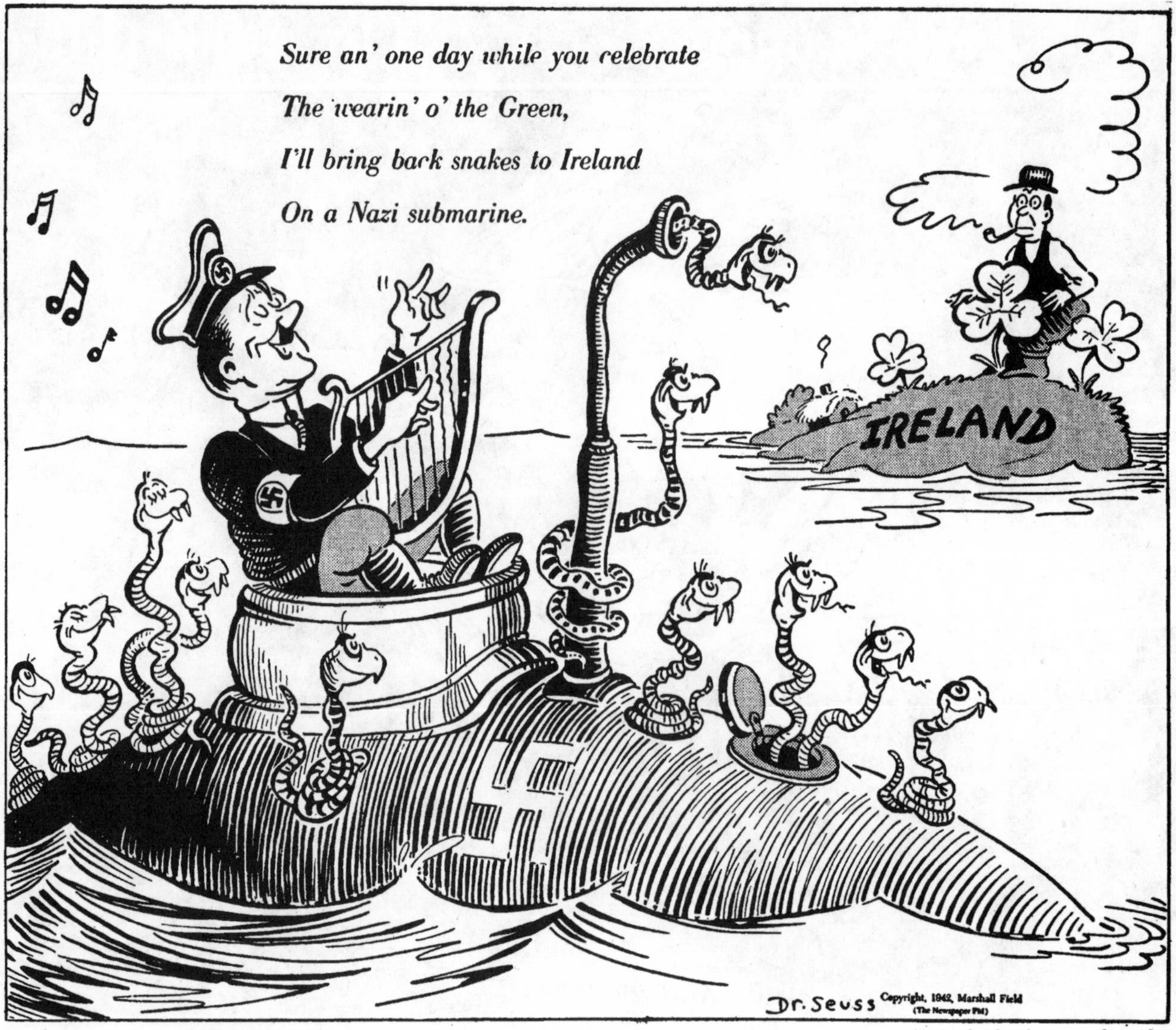
Sure an' one day while you celebrate
The wearin' o' the Green,
I'll bring back snakes to Ireland
On a Nazi submarine.
IRELAND
Dr. Seuss
Copyright, 1942, Marshall Field
(The Newspaper PM)

88 — March 17, 1942

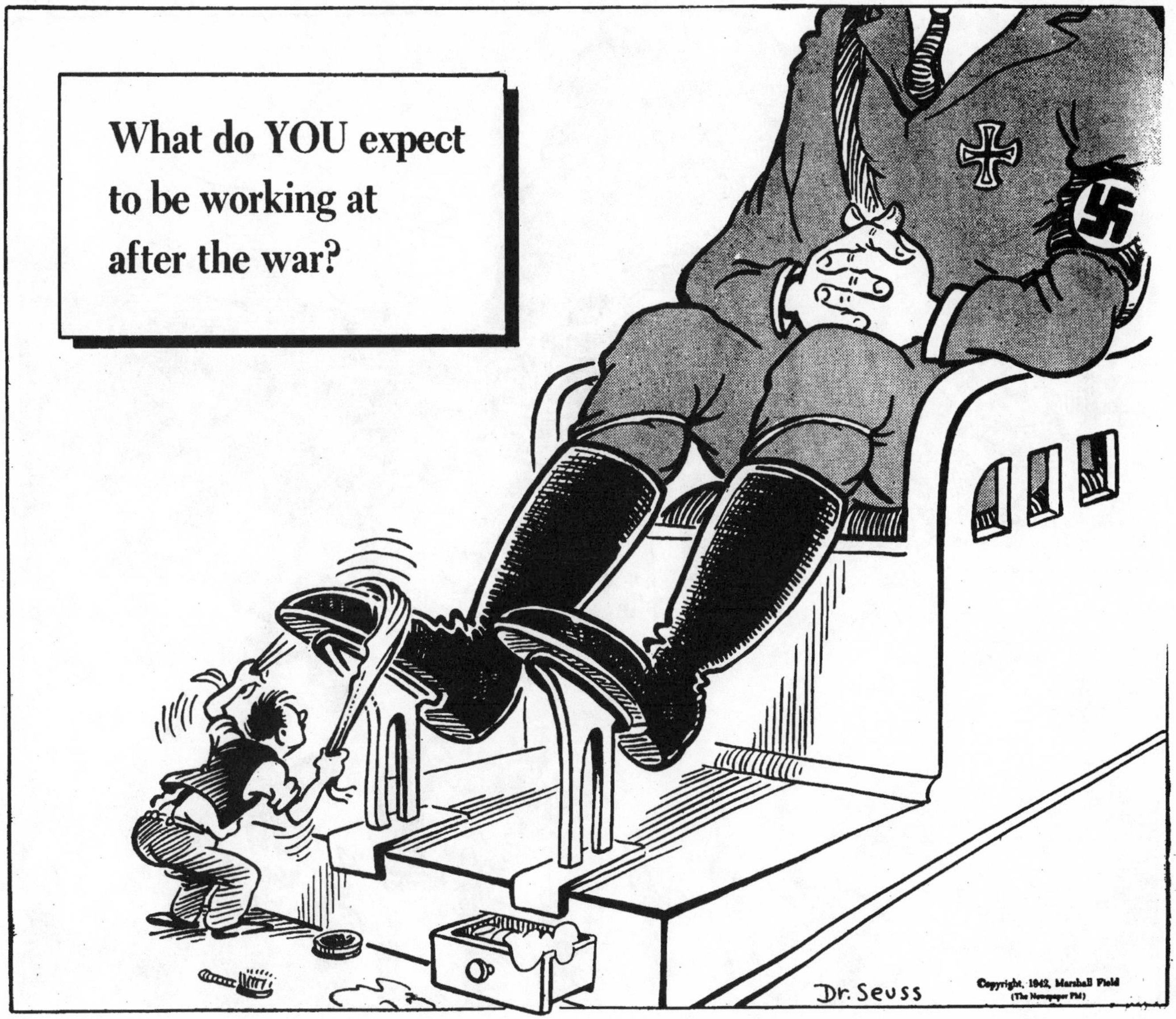
What do YOU expect to be working at after the war?
Dr. Seuss
Copyright, 1942, Marshall Field
(The Newspaper PM)

89 – March 19, 1942

Second Creation

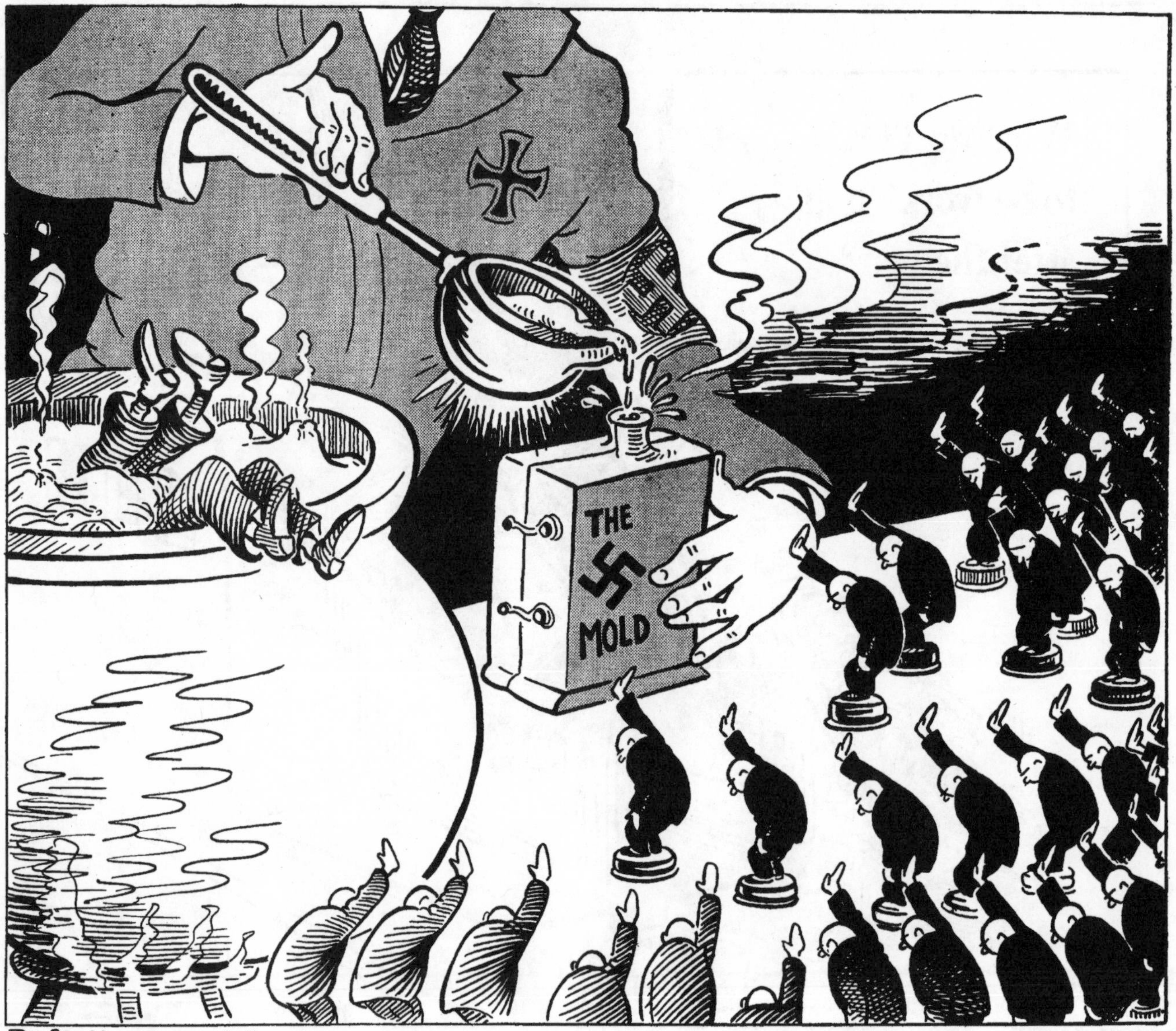
THE
MOLD
Dr Seuss Copyright, 1942, Marshall Field
(The Newspaper PM)

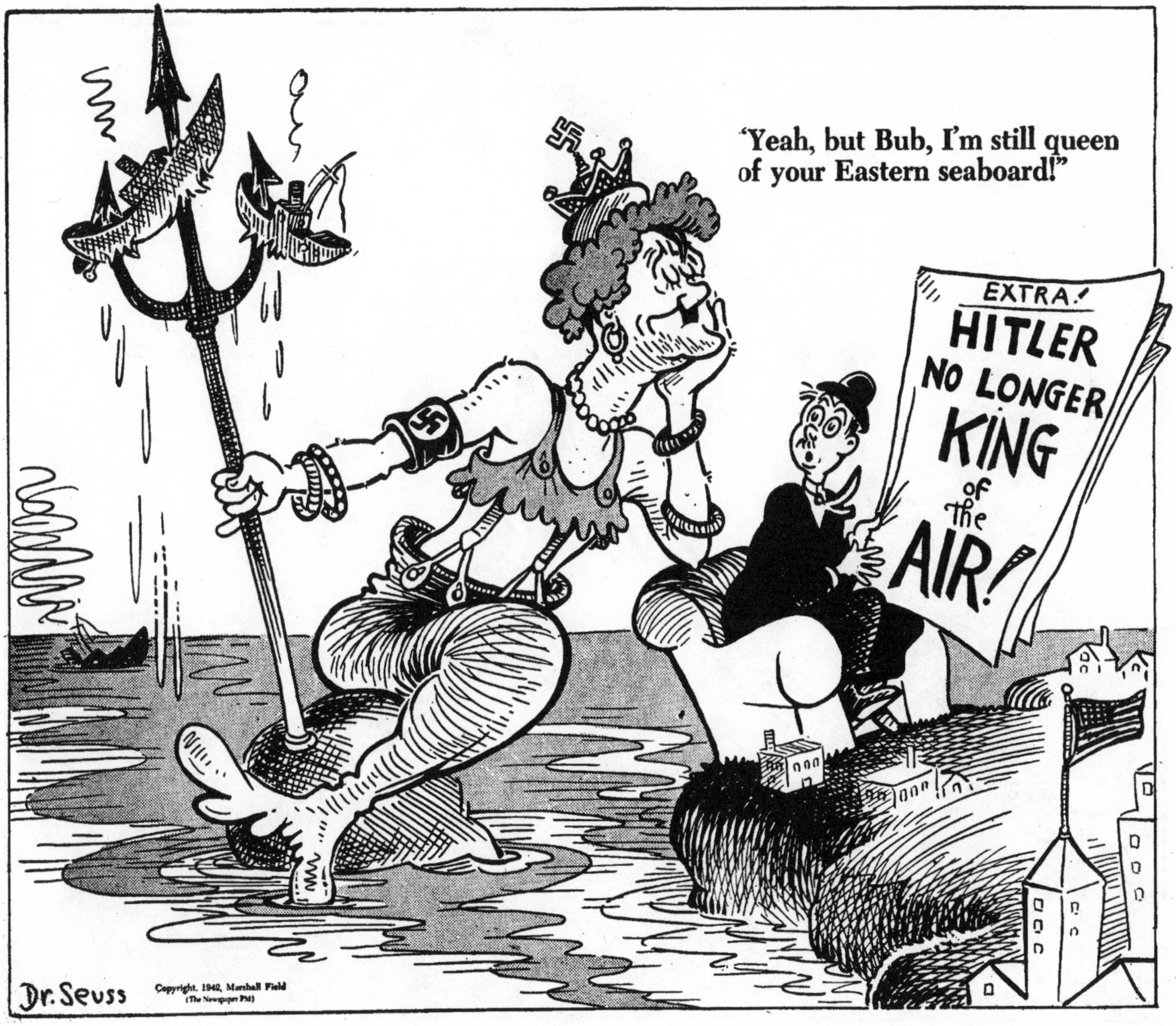
"Yeah, but Bub, I'm still queen of your Eastern seaboard!"
EXTRA!
HITLER NO LONGER KING of the AIR!
Dr. Seuss
Copyright, 1942, Marshall Field (The Newspaper PM)

91 — June 3, 1942

No Sign Yet of Sagging Morale

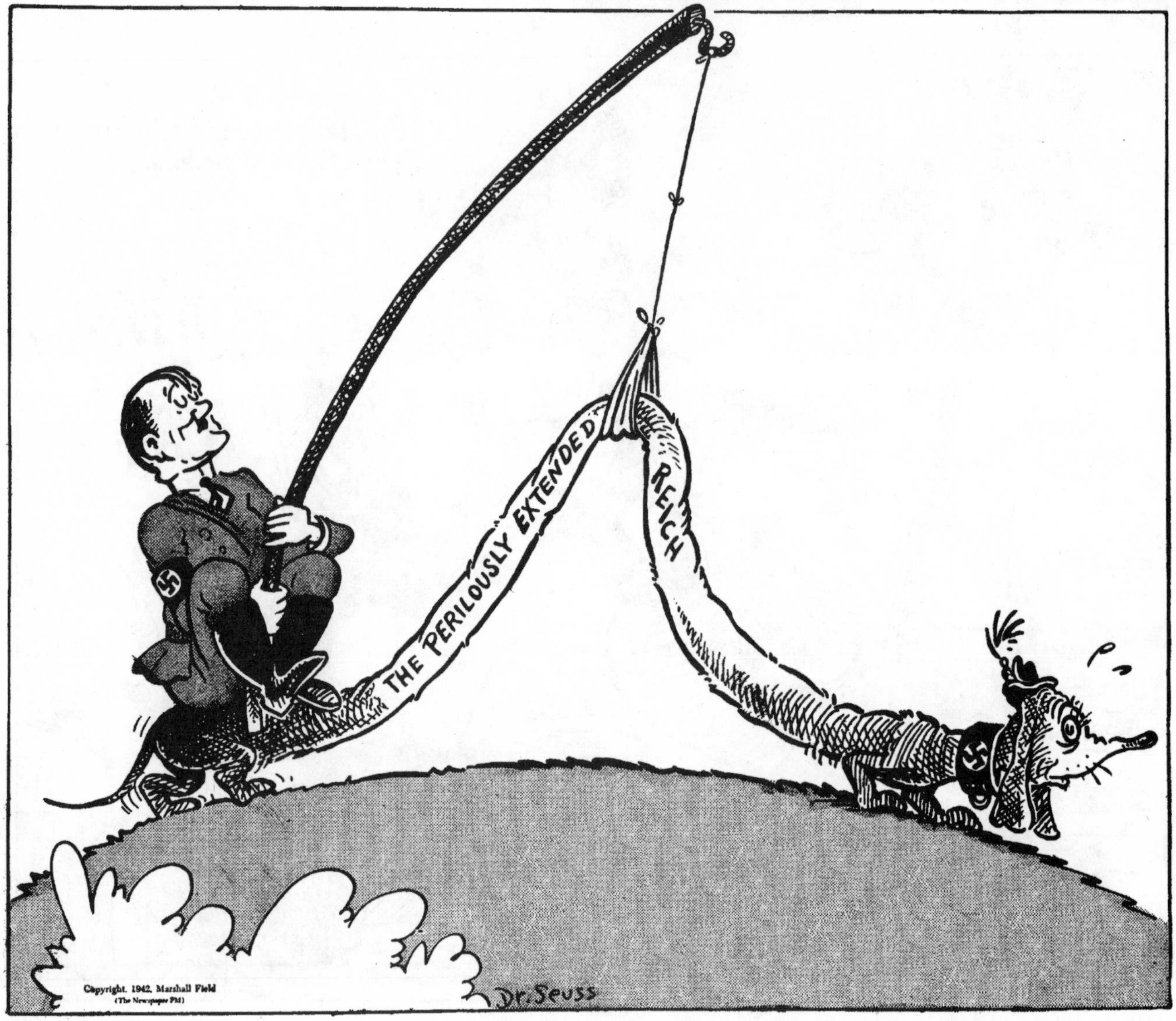
THE PERILOUSLY EXTENDED REICH
Copyright, 1942, Marshall Field
(The Newspaper PM)
Dr. Seuss

92 — June 5, 1942

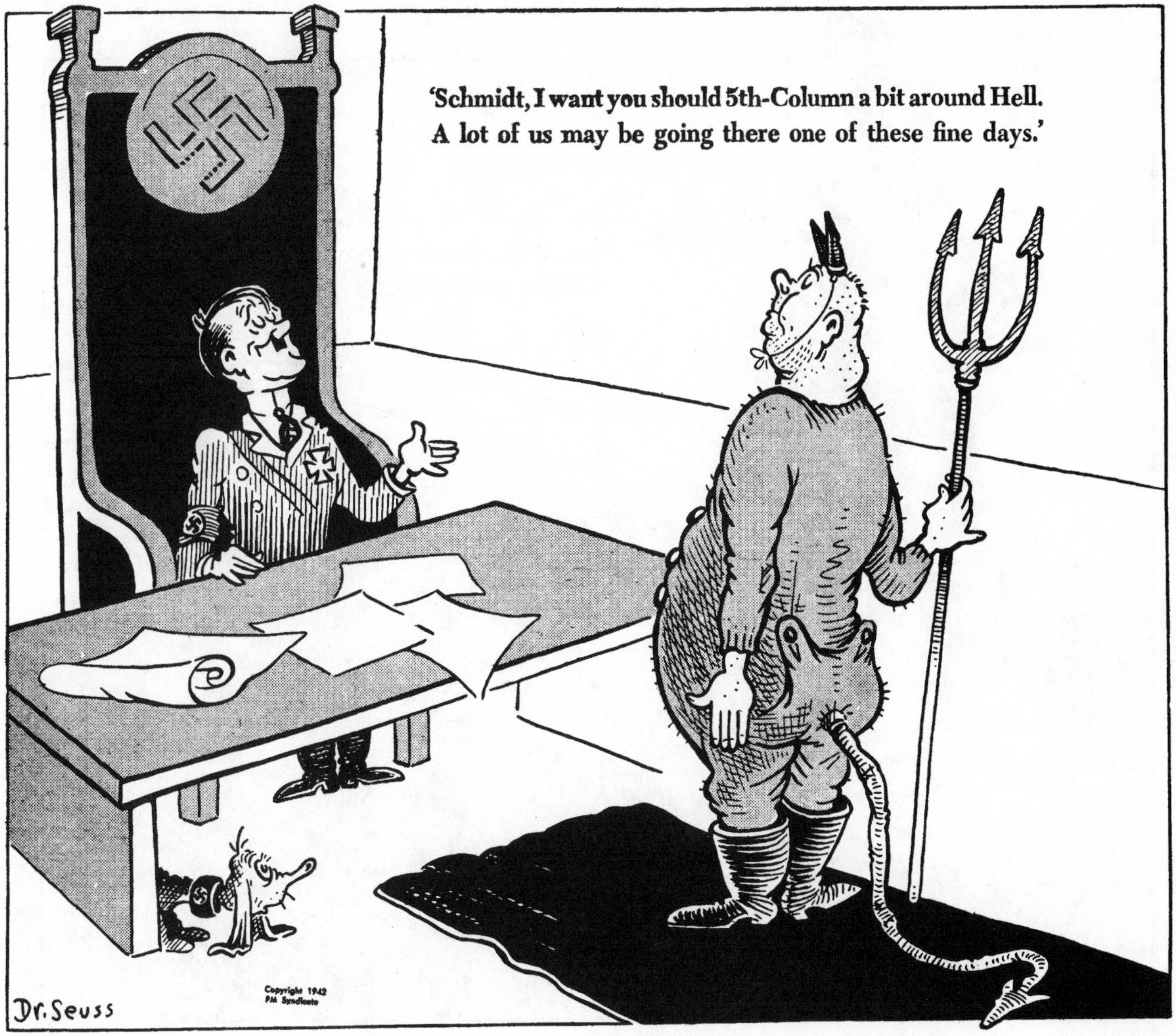
'Schmidt, I want you should 5th-Column a bit around Hell.
A lot of us may be going there one of these fine days.'
Dr. Seuss
Copyright 1942
PM Syndicate

93 — June 11, 1942

With Adolf in Egypt

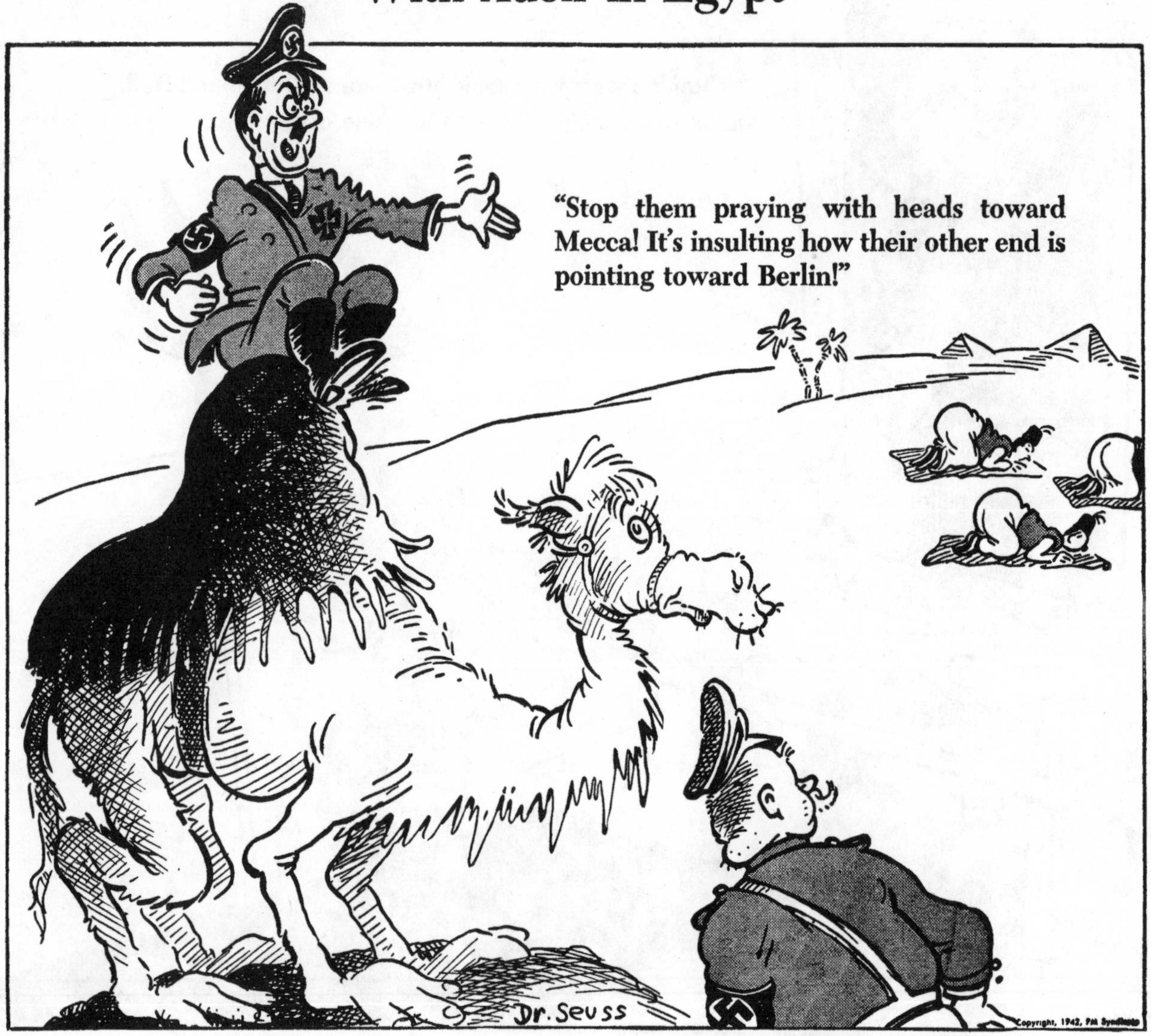
"Stop them praying with heads toward Mecca! It's insulting how their other end is pointing toward Berlin!"
Dr. Seuss
Copyright, 1942, PM

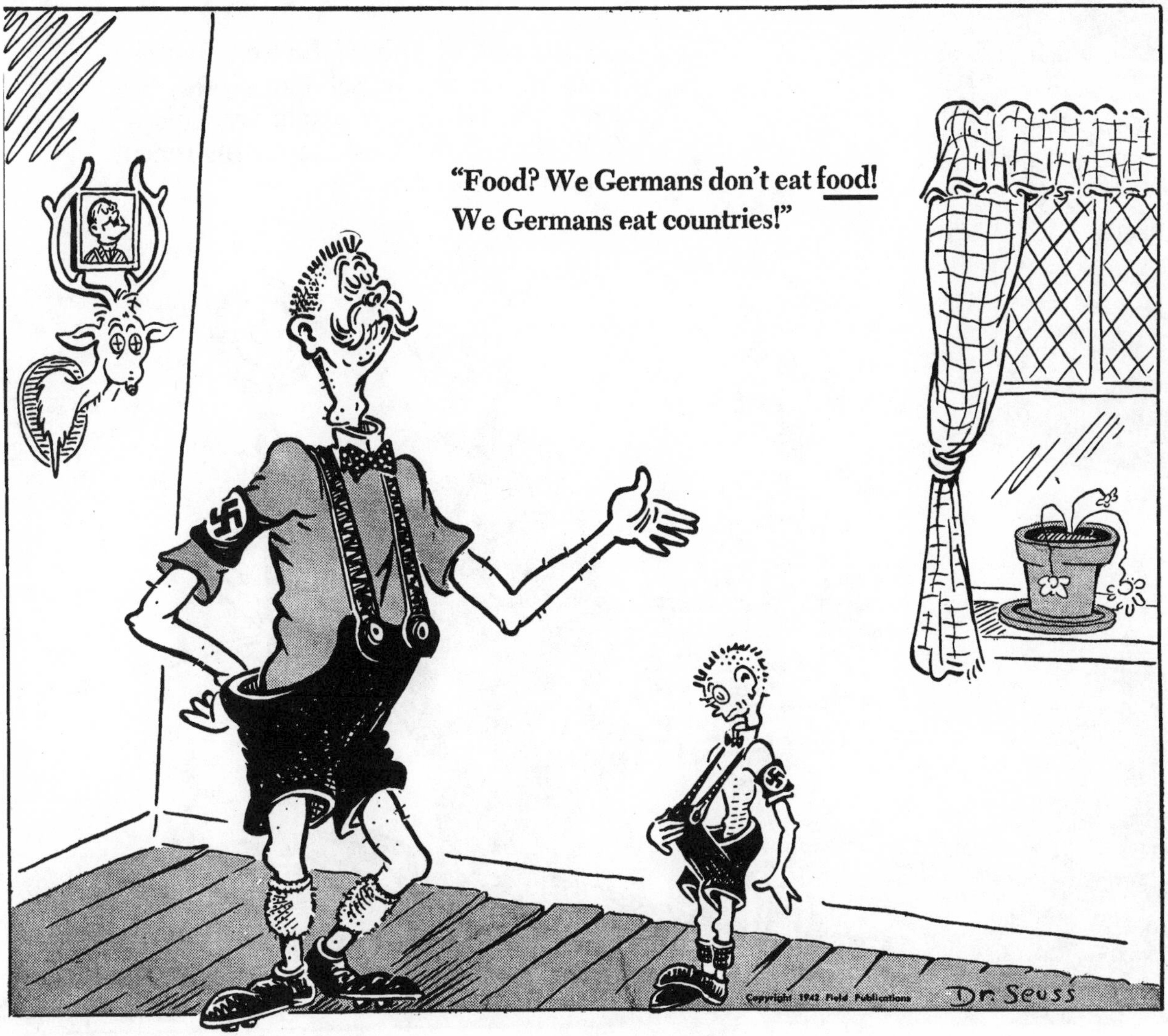
"Food? We Germans don't eat food! We Germans eat countries!"
Copyright 1942 Field Publications
Dr. Seuss

95 — October 7, 1942

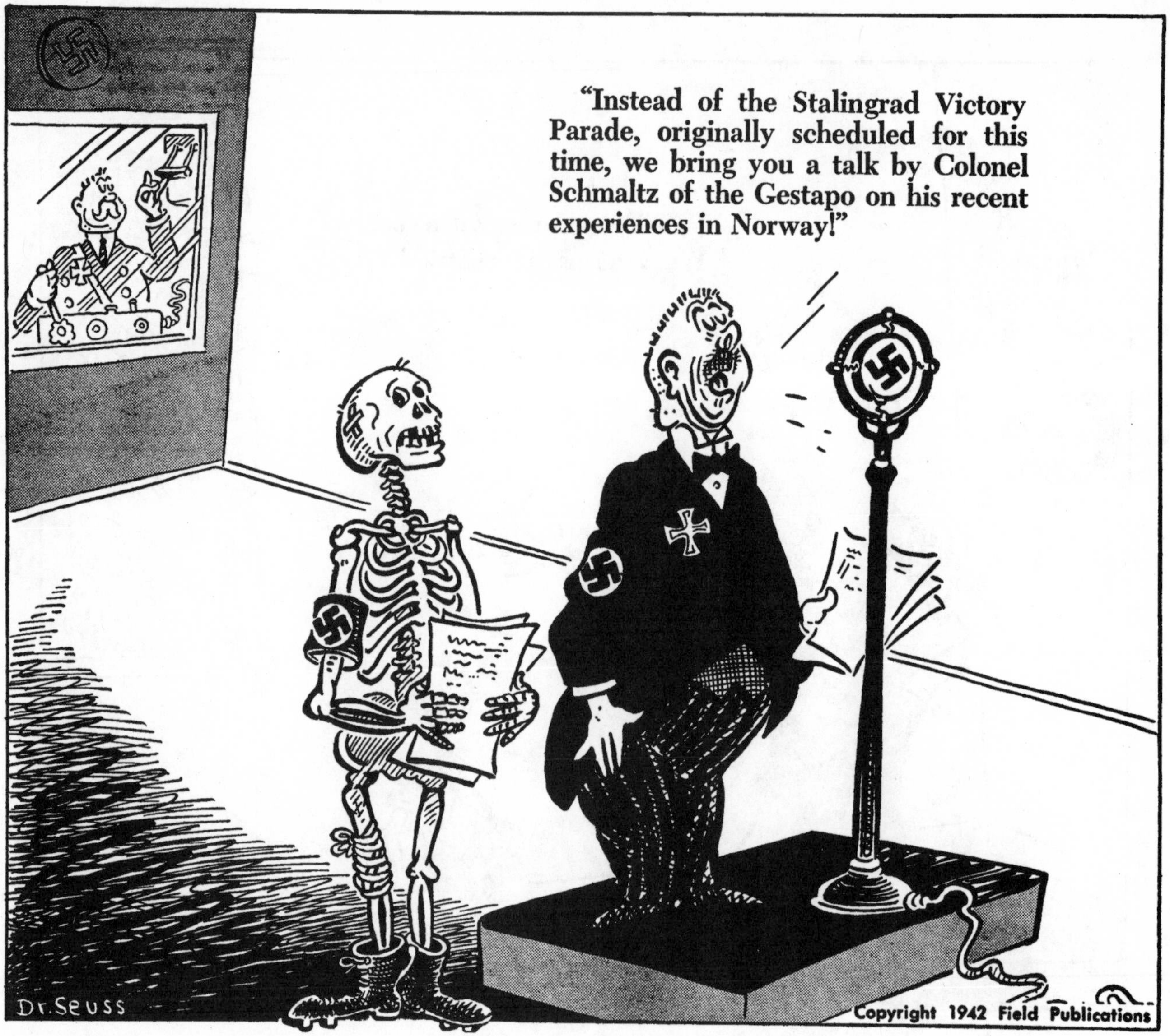
"Instead of the Stalingrad Victory Parade, originally scheduled for this time, we bring you a talk by Colonel Schmaltz of the Gestapo on his recent experiences in Norway!"
Dr. Seuss
Copyright 1942 Field Publications

96 — October 8, 1942

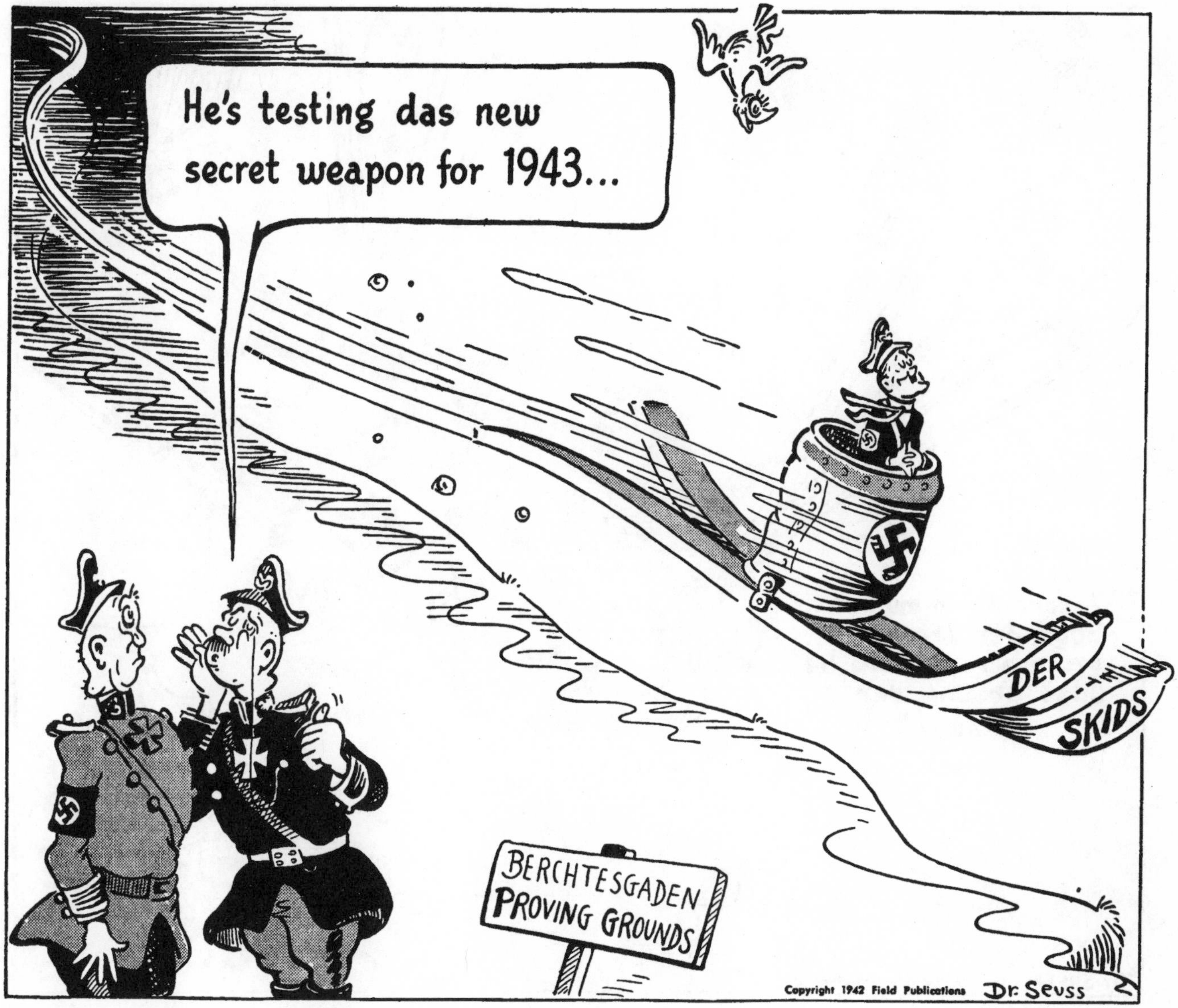
He's testing das new secret weapon for 1943...
DER SKIDS
BERCHTESGADEN PROVING GROUNDS
Copyright 1942 Field Publications
Dr. Seuss

97 — October 15, 1942

Slightly Diverted

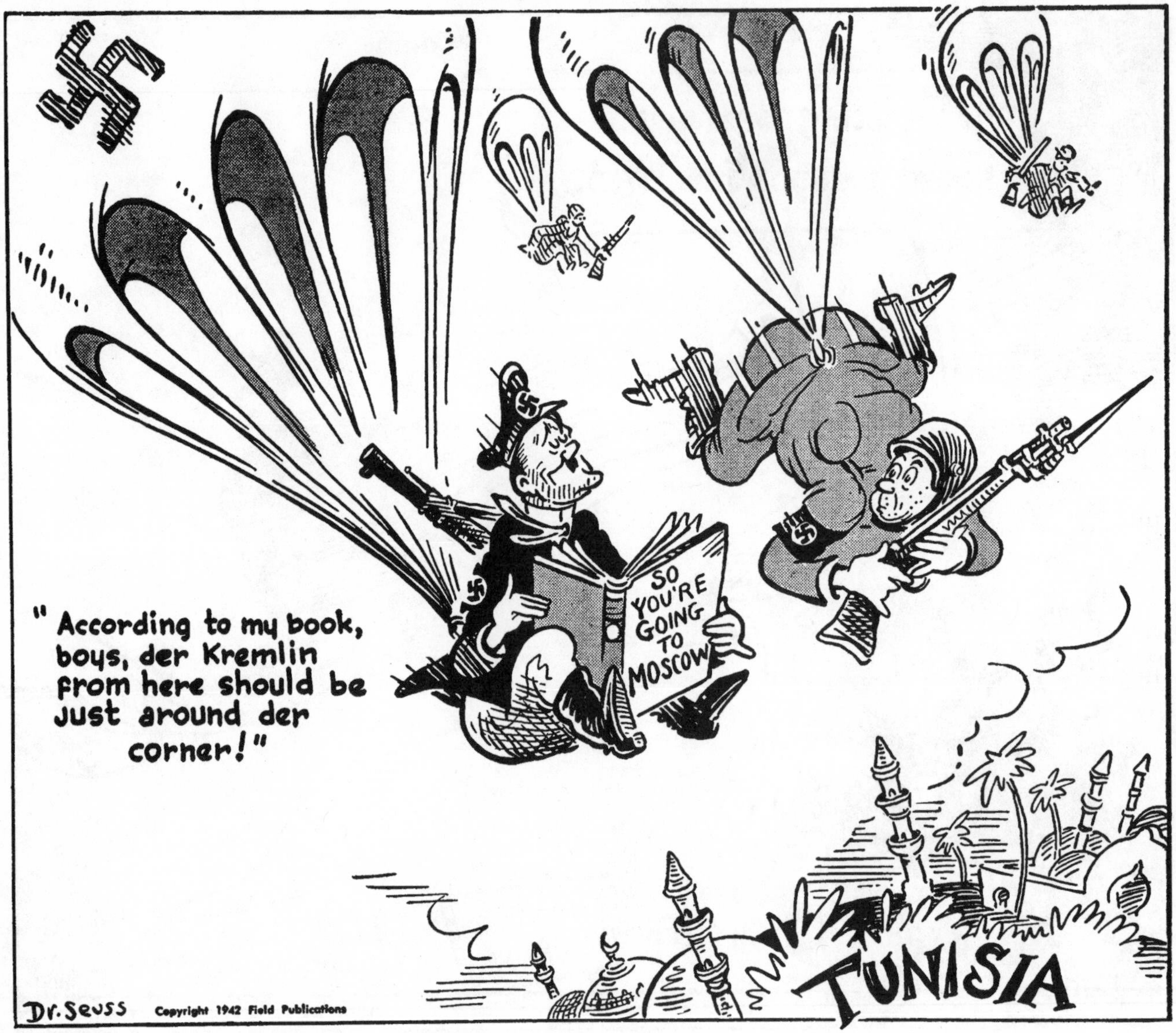
SO YOU'RE GOING TO MOSCOW
" According to my book, boys, der Kremlin from here should be just around der corner!"
TUNISIA
Dr. Seuss
Copyright 1942 Field Publications

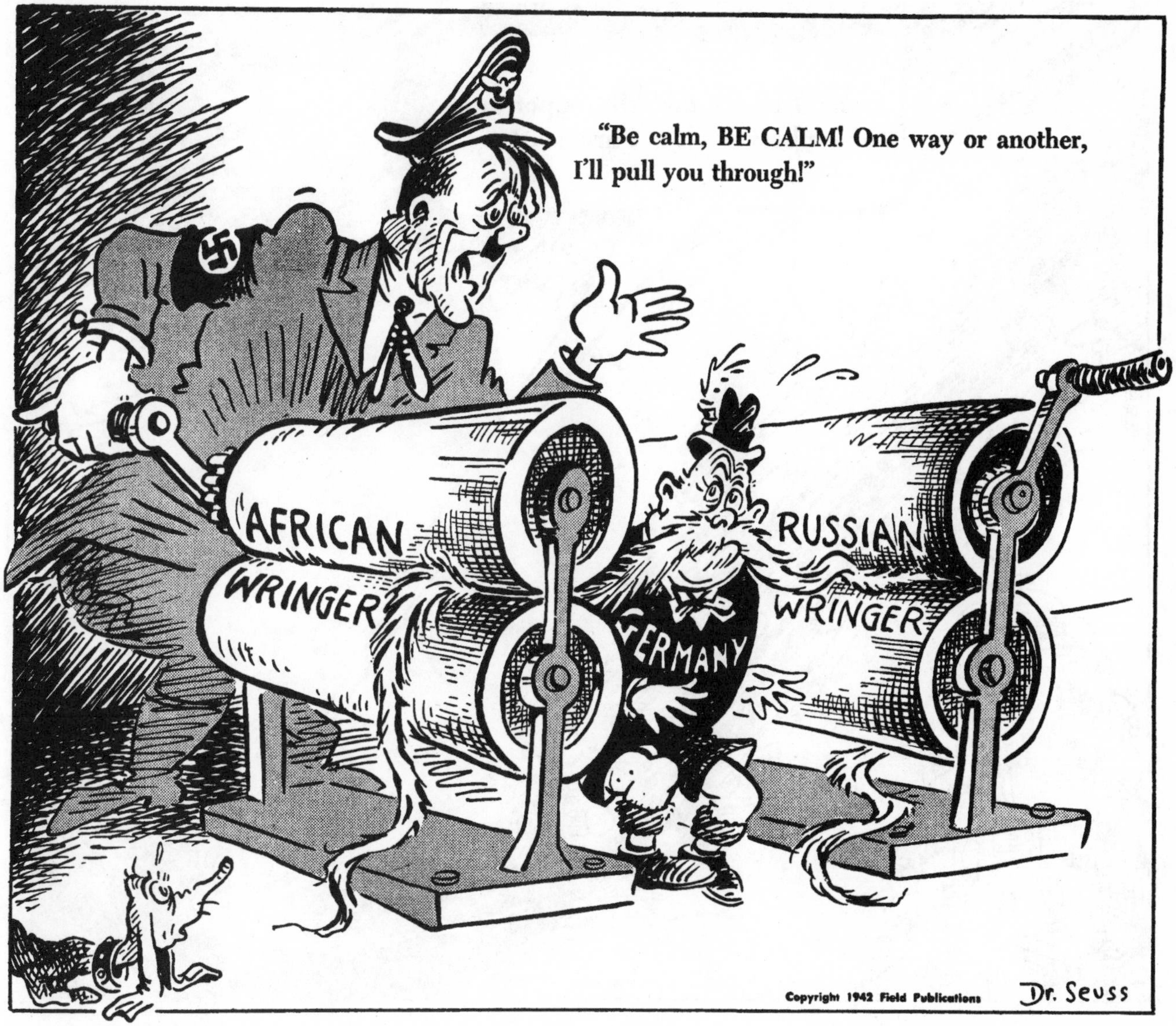
"Be calm, BE CALM! One way or another, I'll pull you through!"
AFRICAN
WRINGER
GERMANY
RUSSIAN
WRINGER
Copyright 1942 Field Publications
Dr. Seuss

99 – November 19, 1942

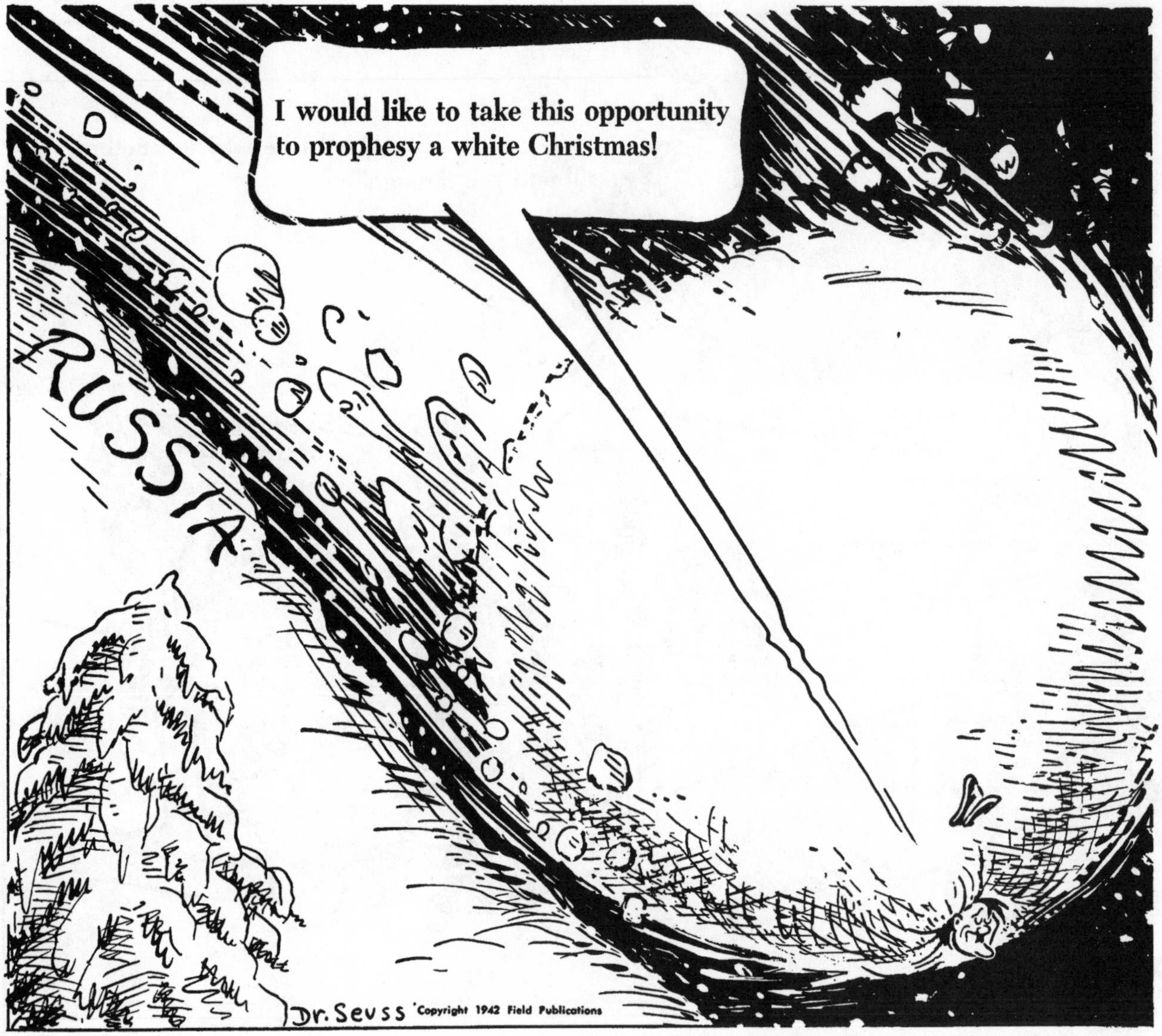
I would like to take this opportunity to prophesy a white Christmas!
RUSSIA
Dr. Seuss
Copyright 1942 Field Publications

100 — December 4, 1942

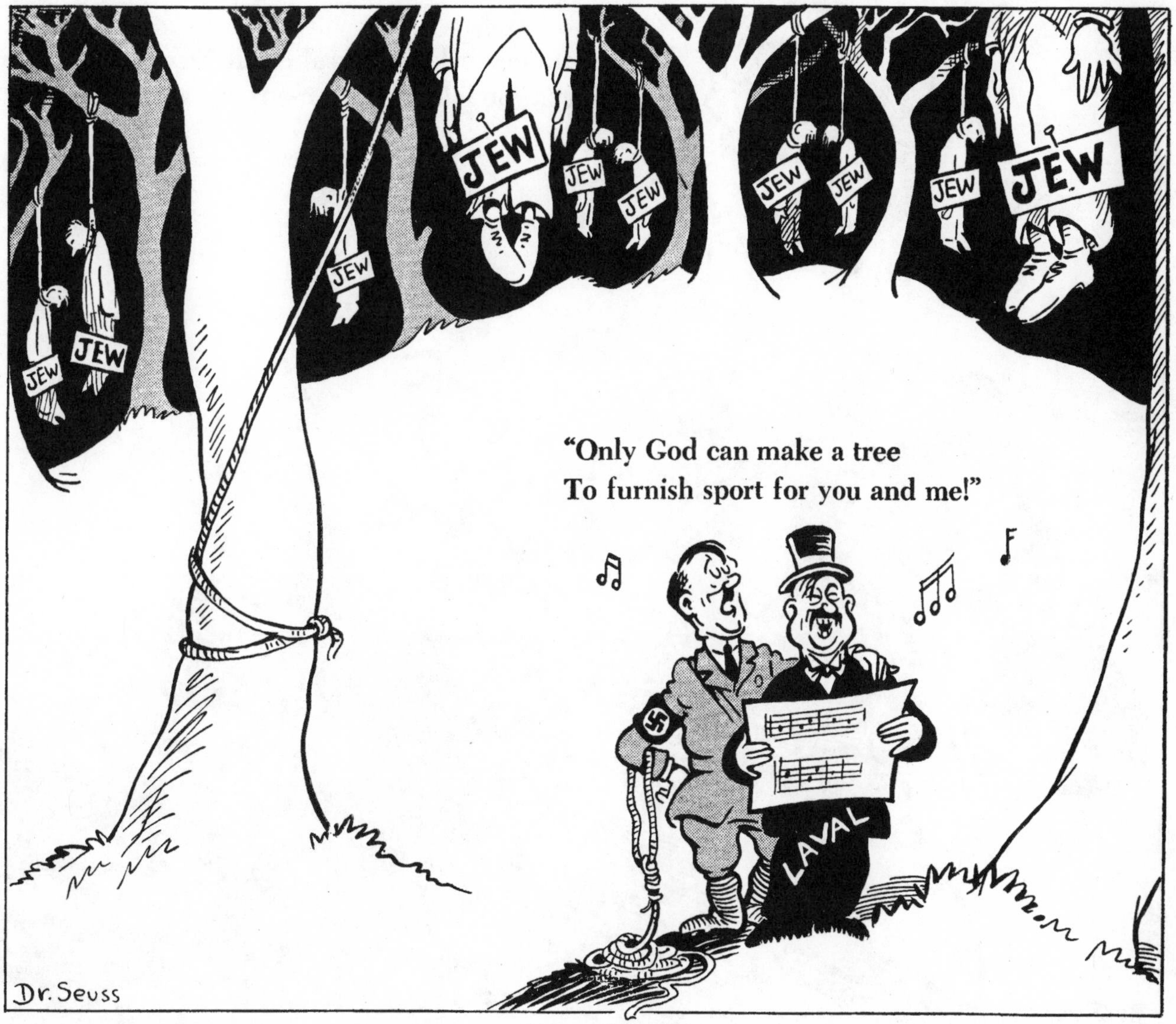
JEW
JEW
JEW
JEW
JEW
JEW
JEW
JEW
JEW
JEW
JEW
"Only God can make a tree
To furnish sport for you and me!"
LAVAL
Dr. Seuss

101 — July 20, 1942

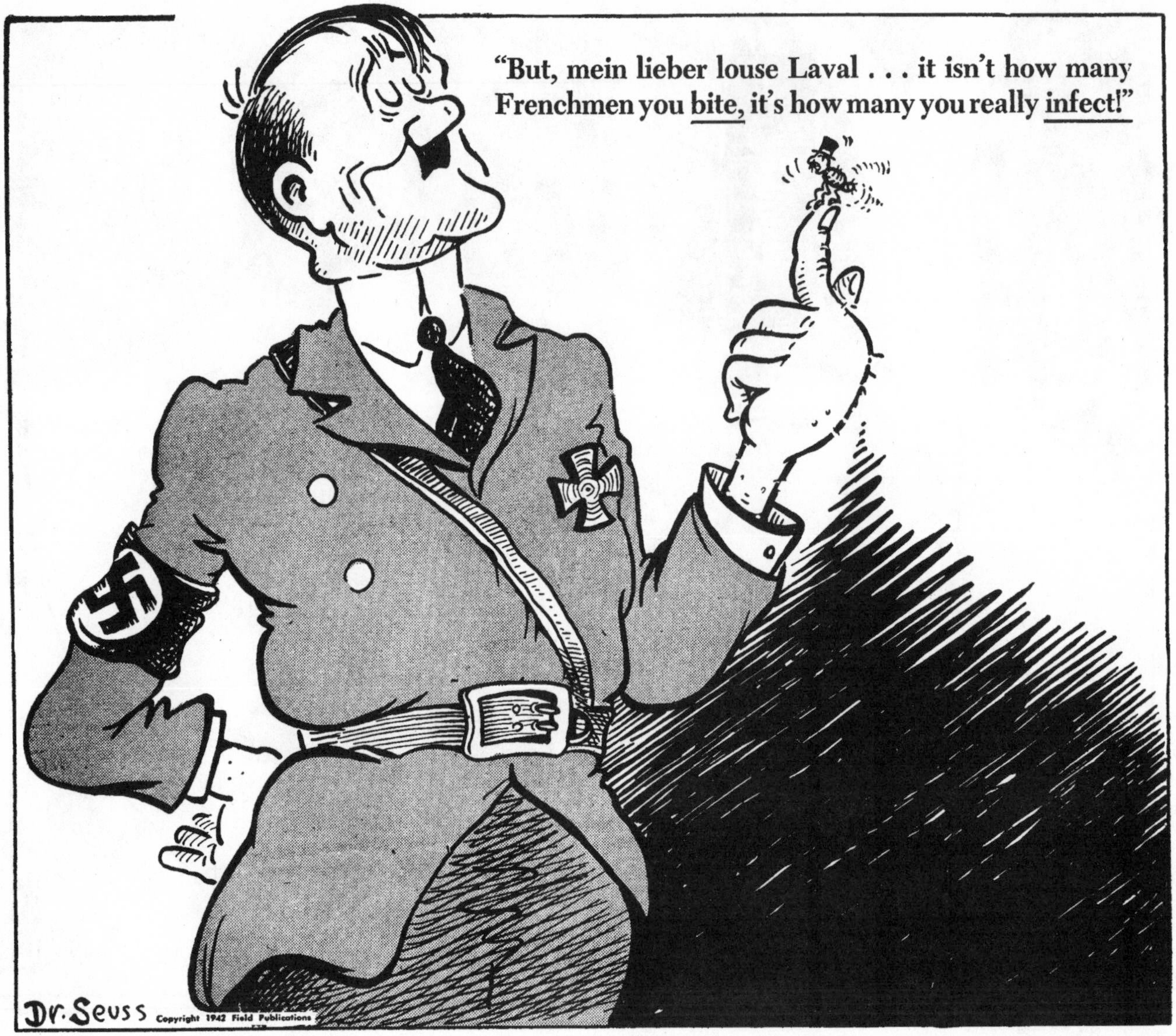
"But, mein lieber louse Laval . . . it isn't how many Frenchmen you bite, it's how many you really infect!"
Dr. Seuss
Copyright 1942 Field Publications

102 — August 7, 1942

"Crawl Out and Round Me Up Another 400,000 Frenchmen!"

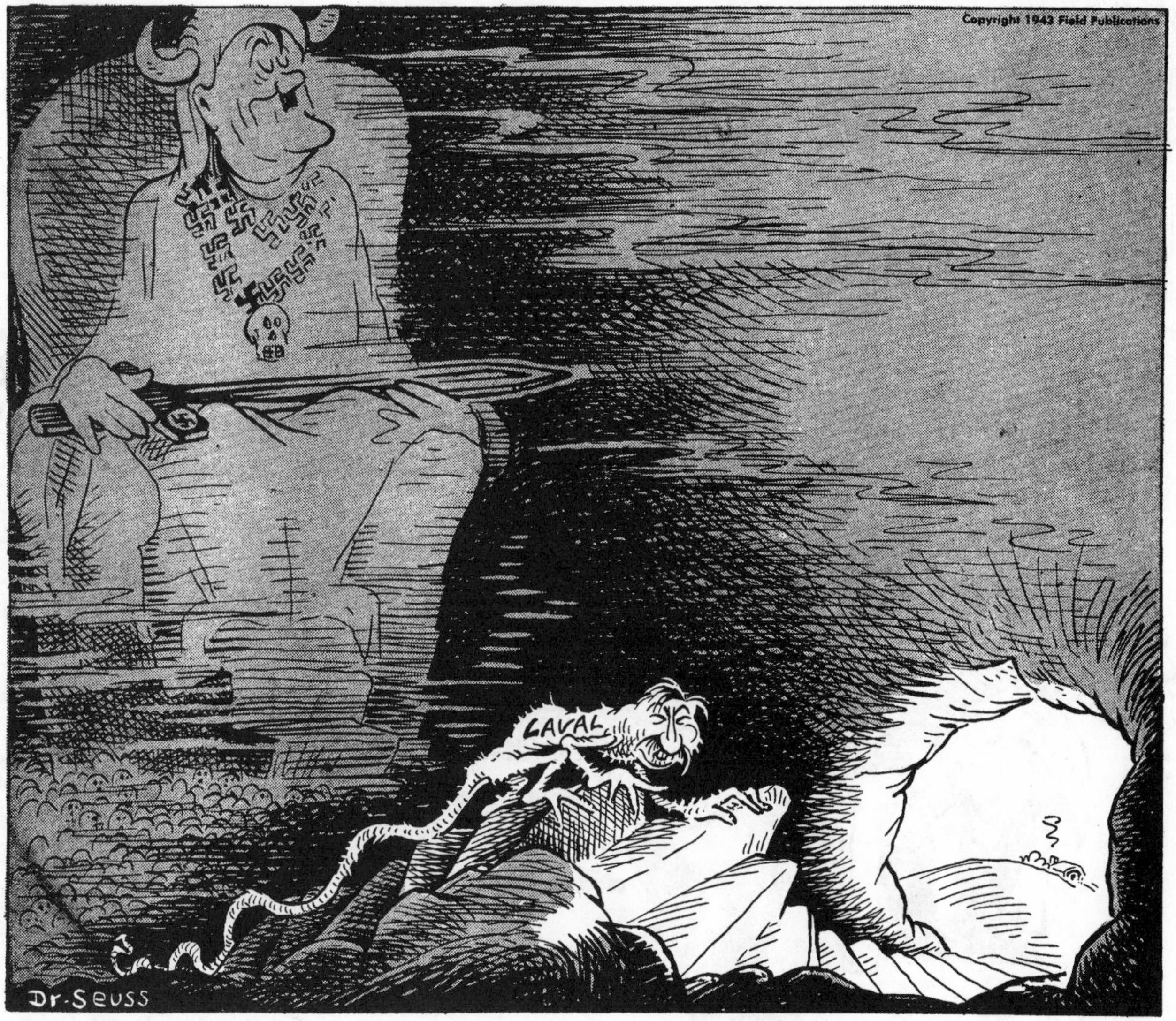
Copyright 1943 Field Publications
LAVAL
DR. SEUSS

103 — December 17, 1942

Crisis in the High Command

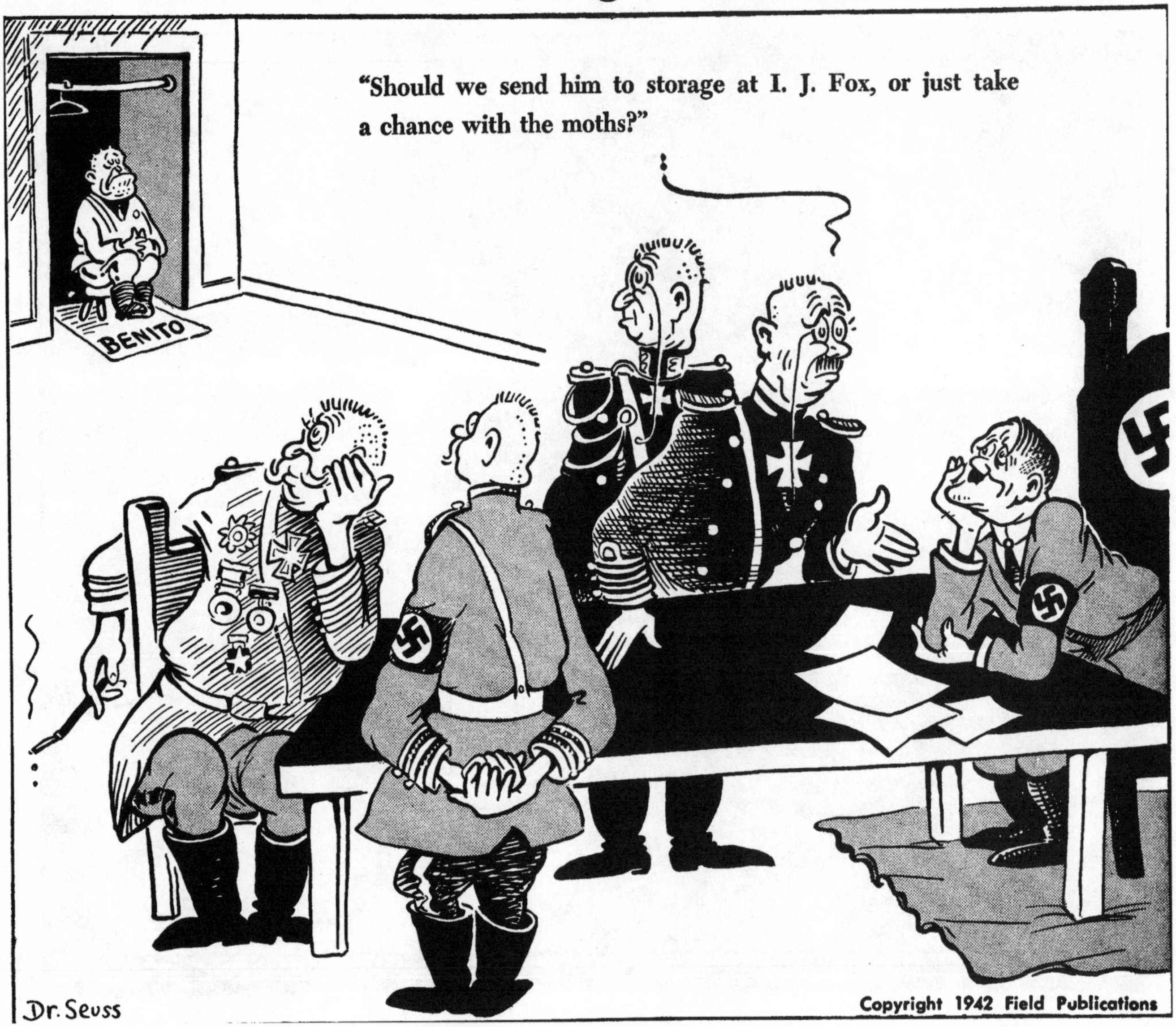
"Should we send him to storage at I. J. Fox, or just take a chance with the moths?"
BENITO
Dr. Seuss
Copyright 1942 Field Publications

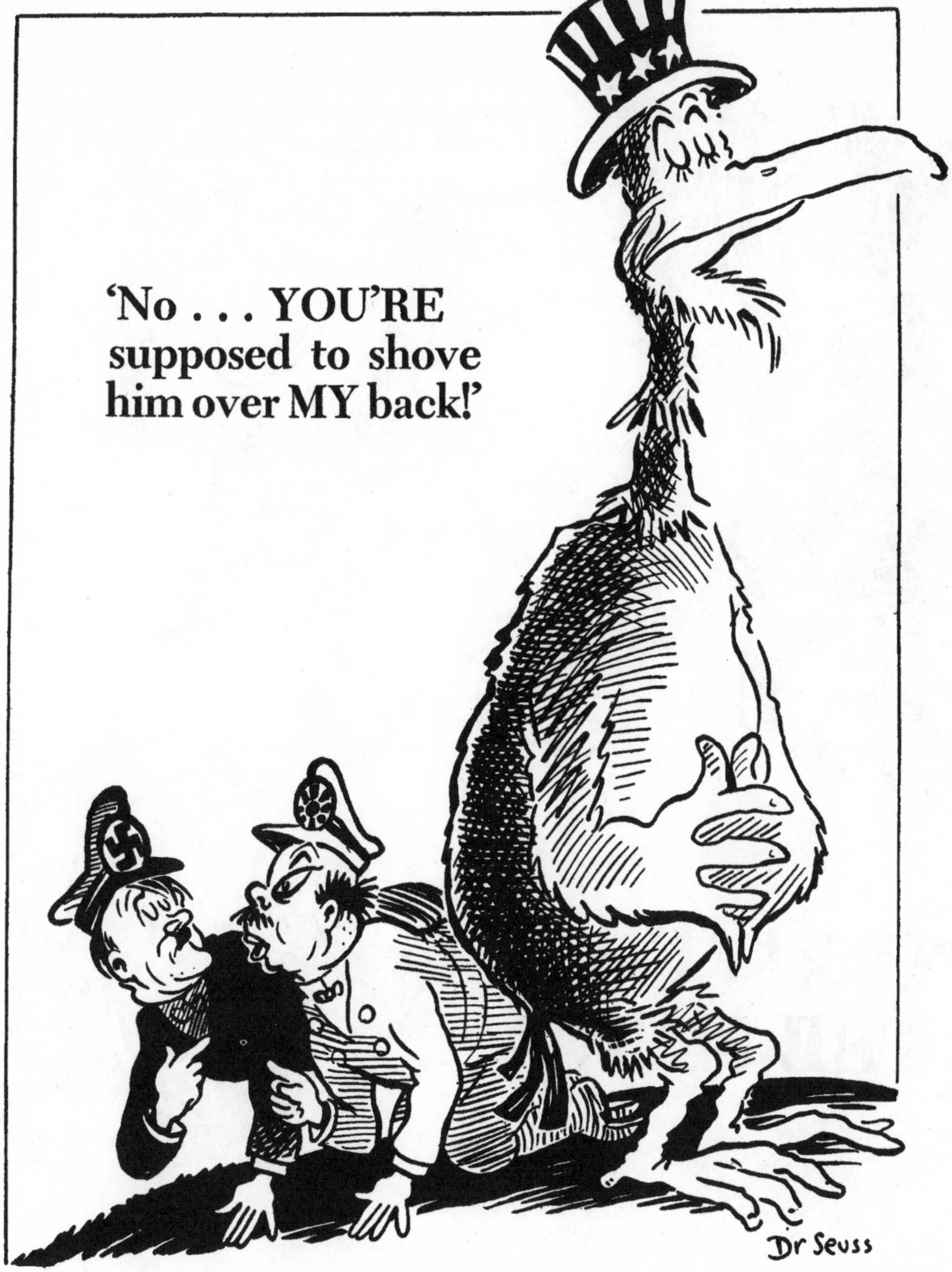
'No . . . YOU'RE supposed to shove him over MY back!'
Dr Seuss

105 — October 19, 1941

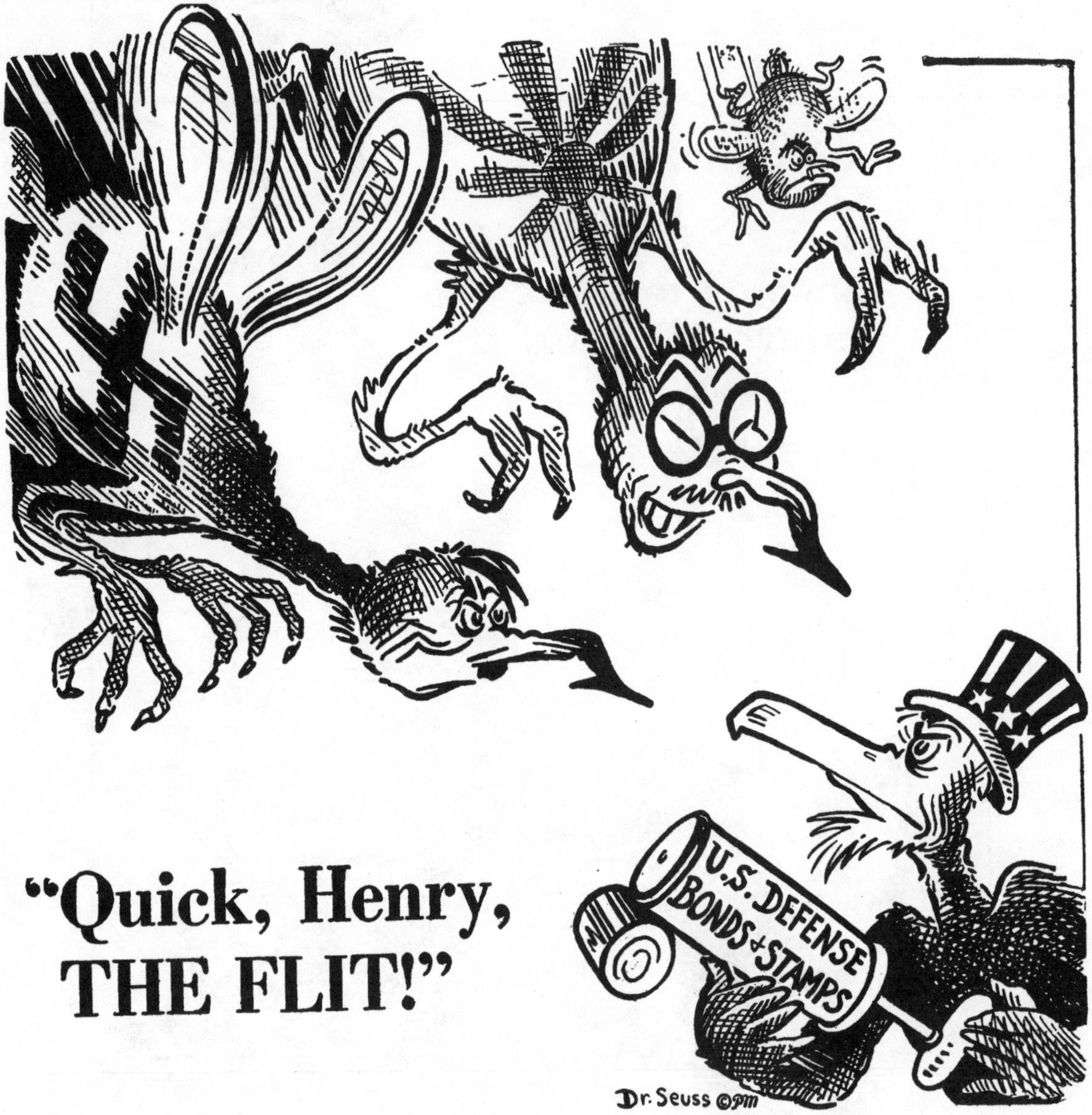
U.S. DEFENSE
BONDS & STAMPS
Dr. Seuss ©PM

"Quick, Henry,
THE FLIT!"

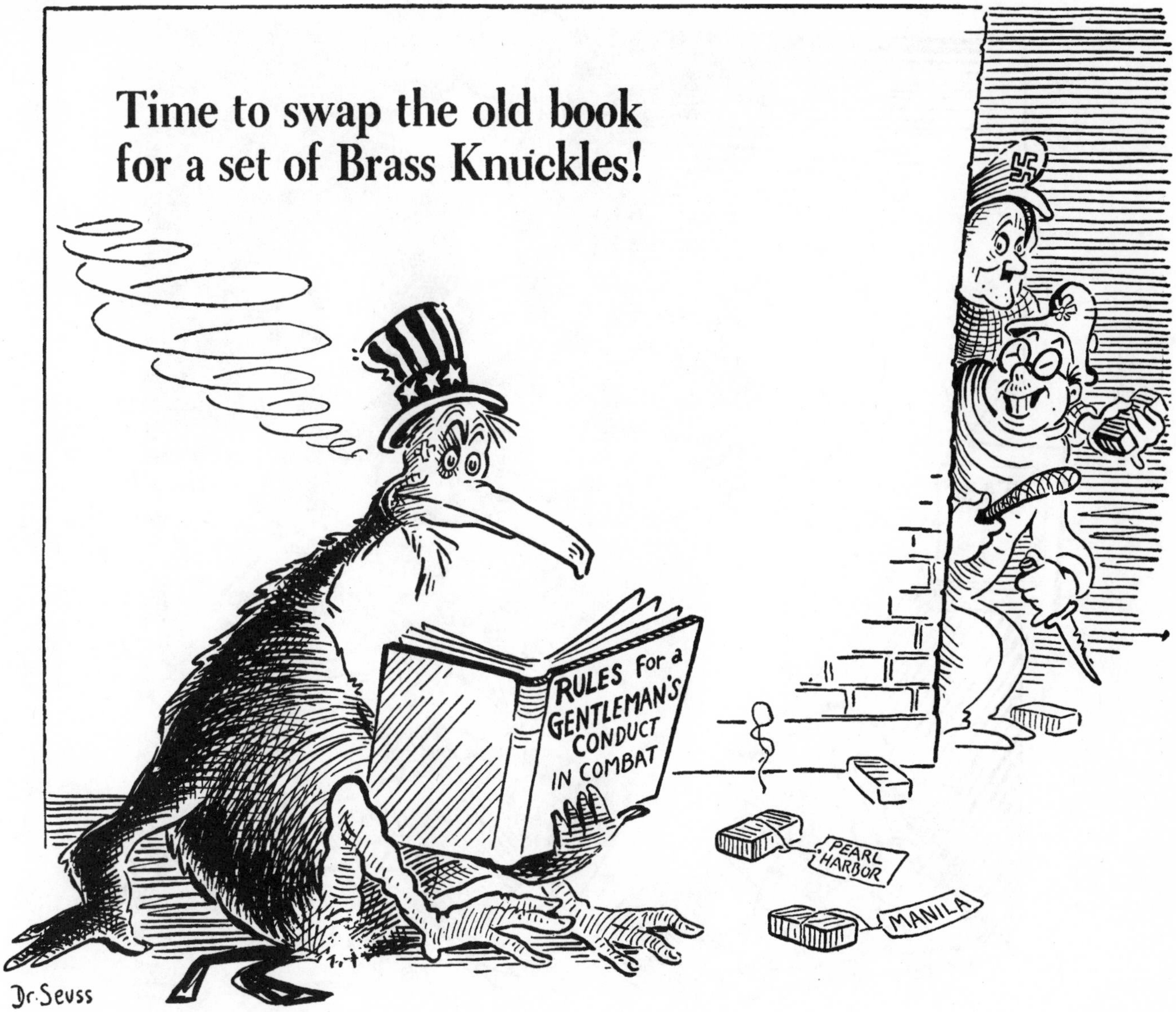
Time to swap the old book
for a set of Brass Knuckles!
RULES For a GENTLEMAN'S CONDUCT IN COMBAT
PEARL HARBOR
MANILA
Dr. Seuss

107 — December 30, 1941

HAPPY NEW YEAR! But, Boy! What a Hangover!

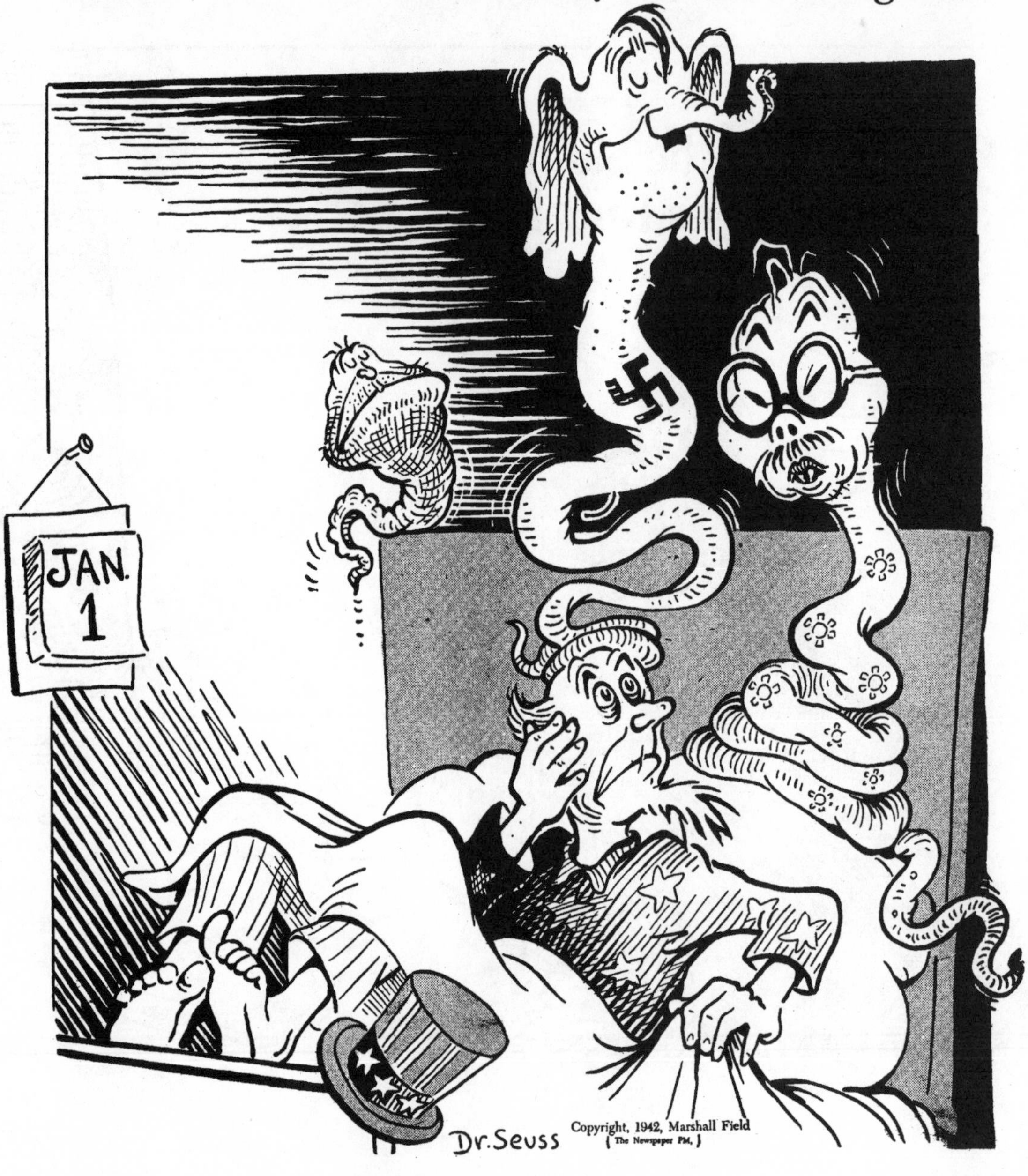
JAN.
1
Dr. Seuss
Copyright, 1942, Marshall Field
(The Newspaper PM,)

Measuring Up a Couple of Prospects

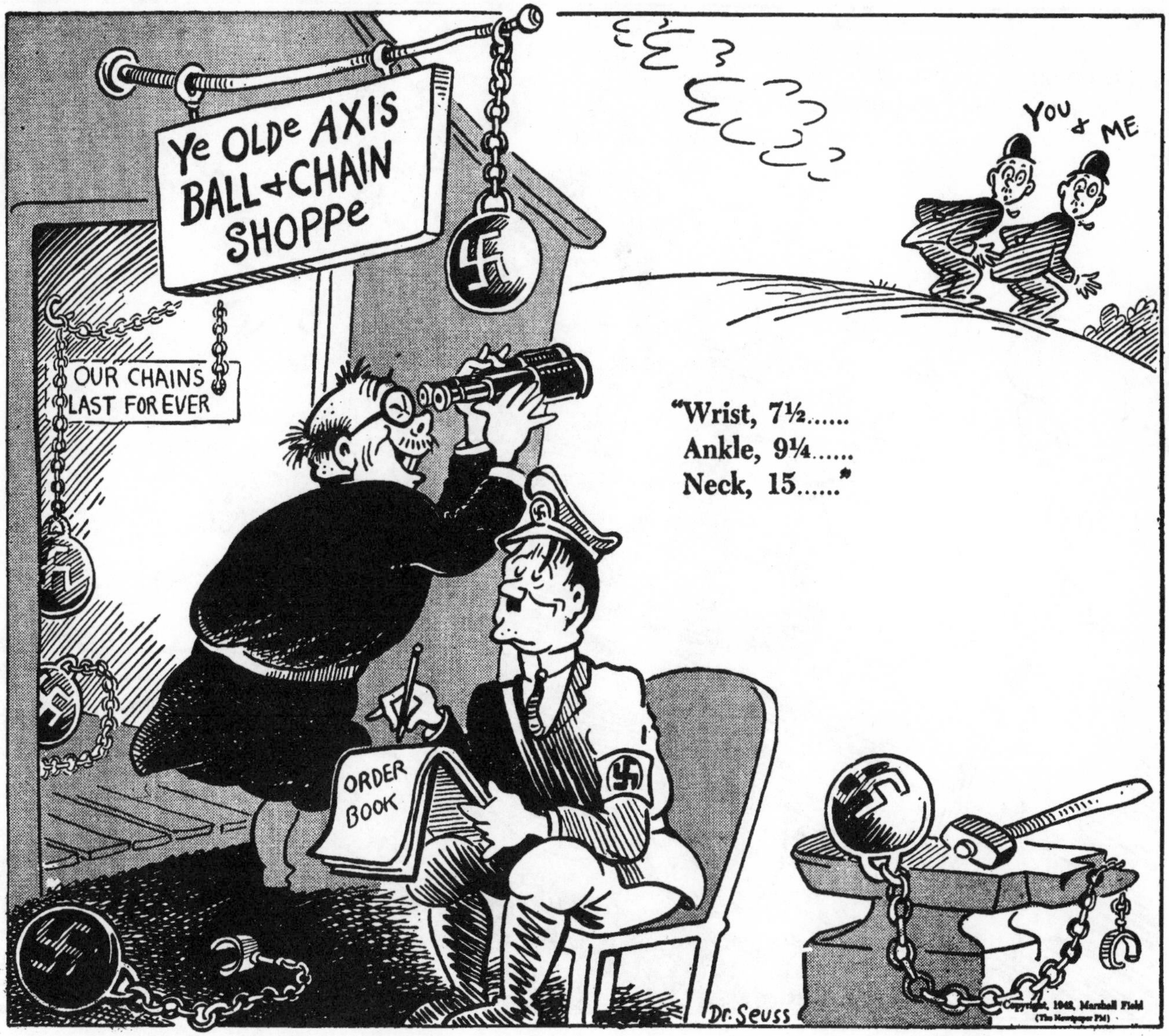
Ye OLDe AXIS
BALL & CHAIN
SHOPPe
OUR CHAINS
LAST FOR EVER
YOU & ME
ORDER
BOOK
Dr. Seuss

"Wrist, 7½......
Ankle, 9¼......
Neck, 15......"

Giving the Axis a Lift

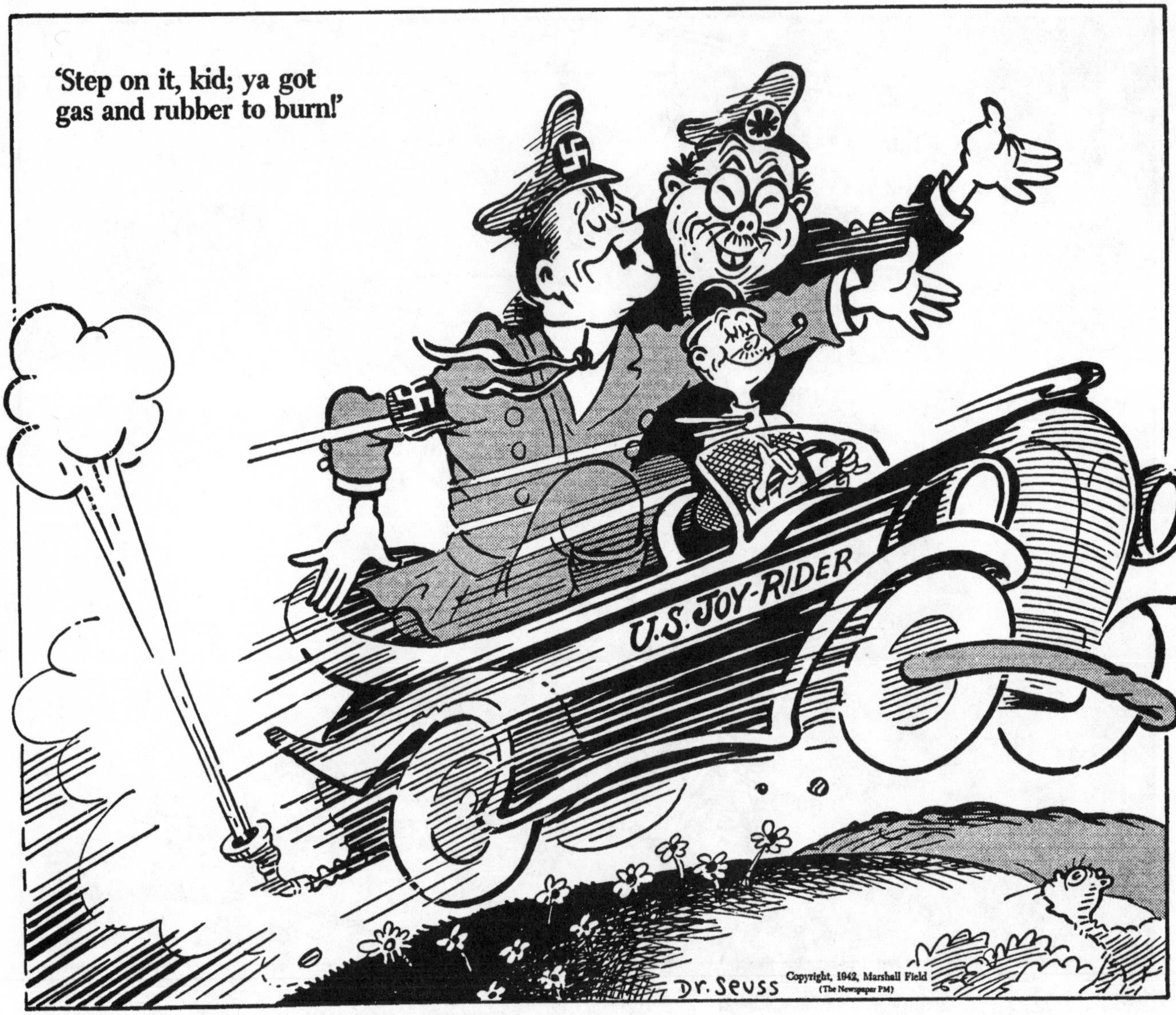
'Step on it, kid; ya got gas and rubber to burn!'
U.S. JOY-RIDER
DR. SEUSS
Copyright, 1942, Marshall Field
(The Newspaper PM)

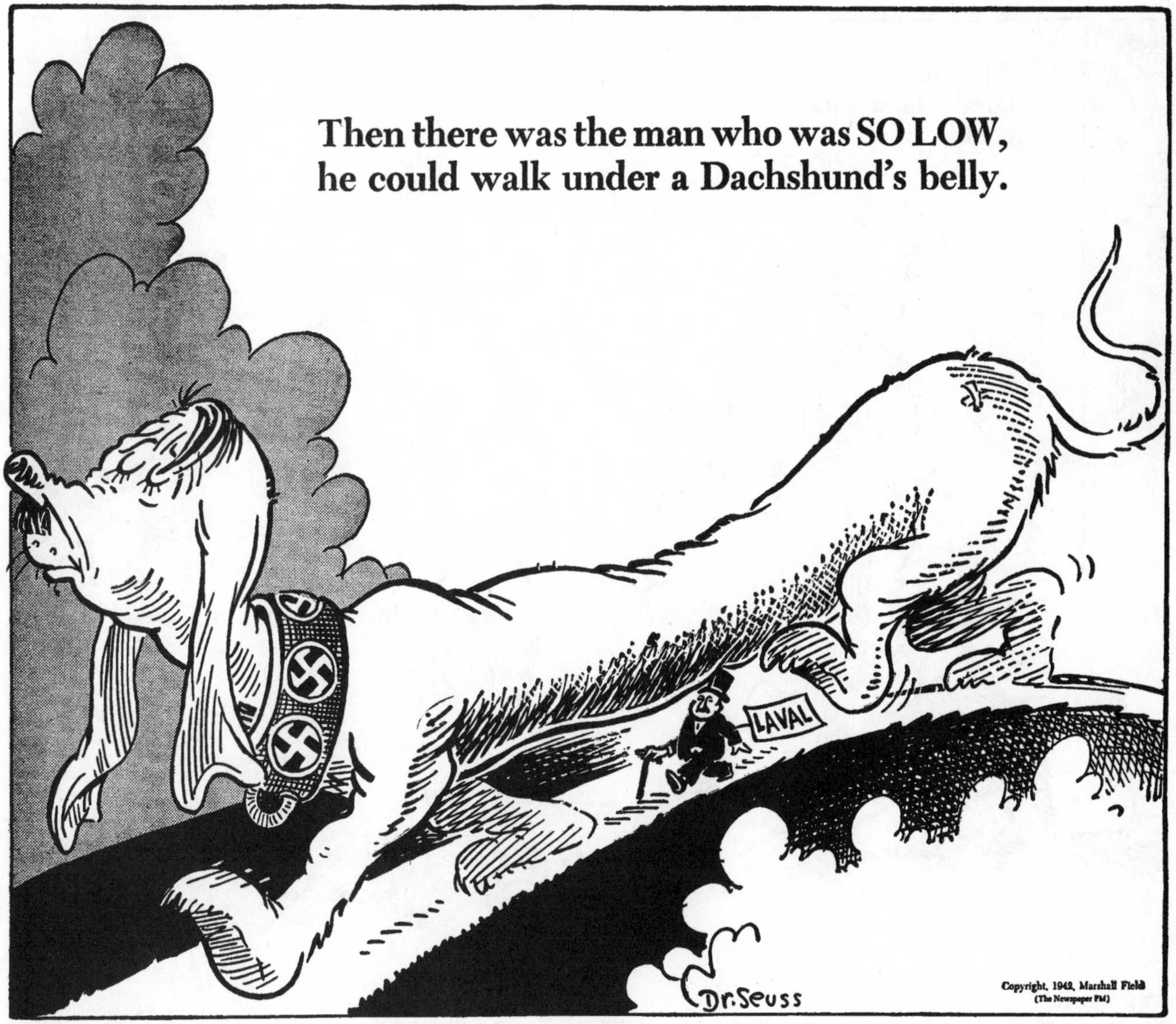
Then there was the man who was SO LOW,
he could walk under a Dachshund's belly.
LAVAL
Dr. Seuss
Copyright, 1942, Marshall Field
(The Newspaper PM)

111 — May 8, 1942

With Adolf in Egypt

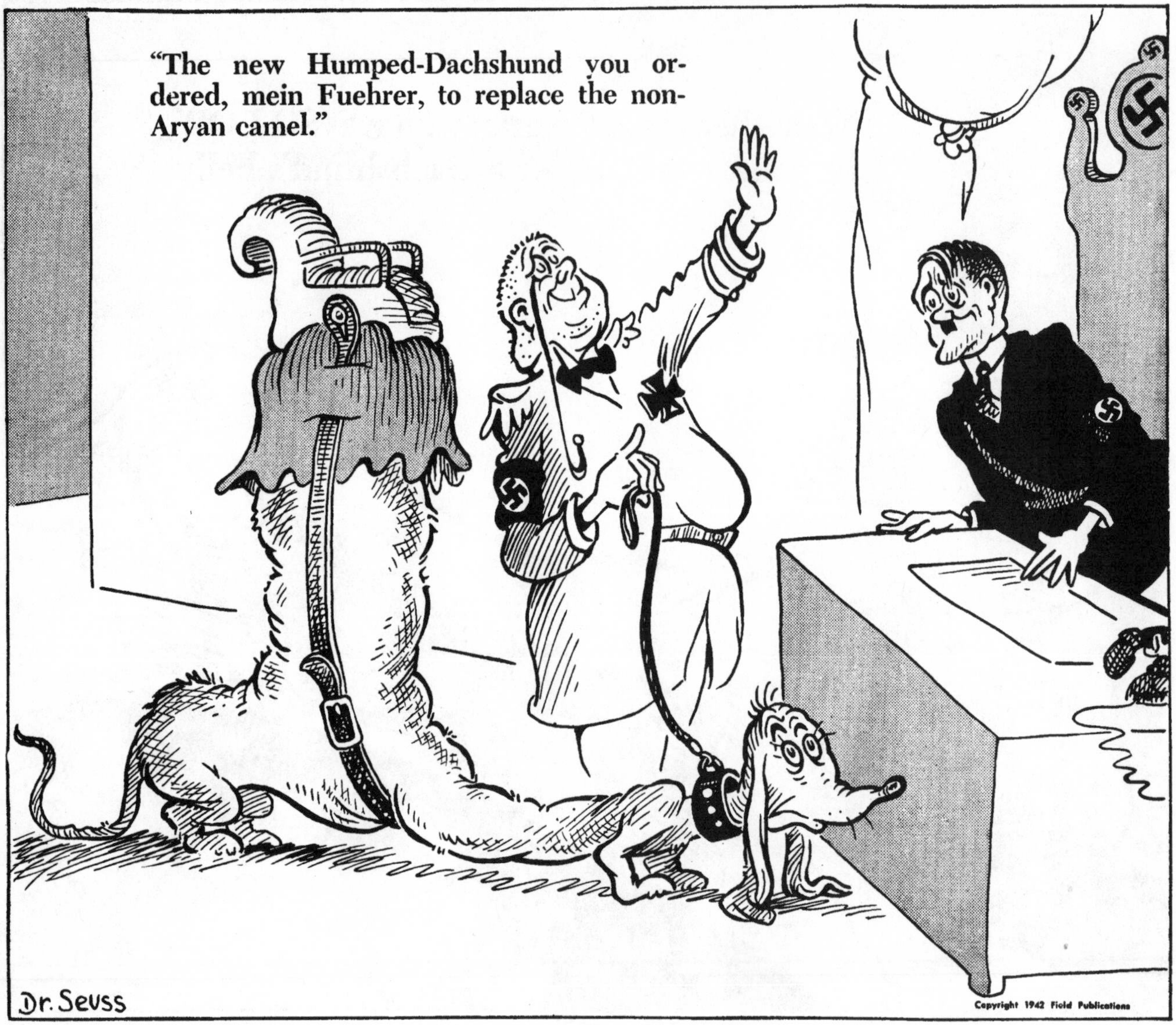

"The new Humped-Dachshund you ordered, mein Fuehrer, to replace the non-Aryan camel."
Dr. Seuss
Copyright 1942 Field Publications

"Hold tight, I'm switching to reverse! . . . Remember the gear we used so much last winter?"

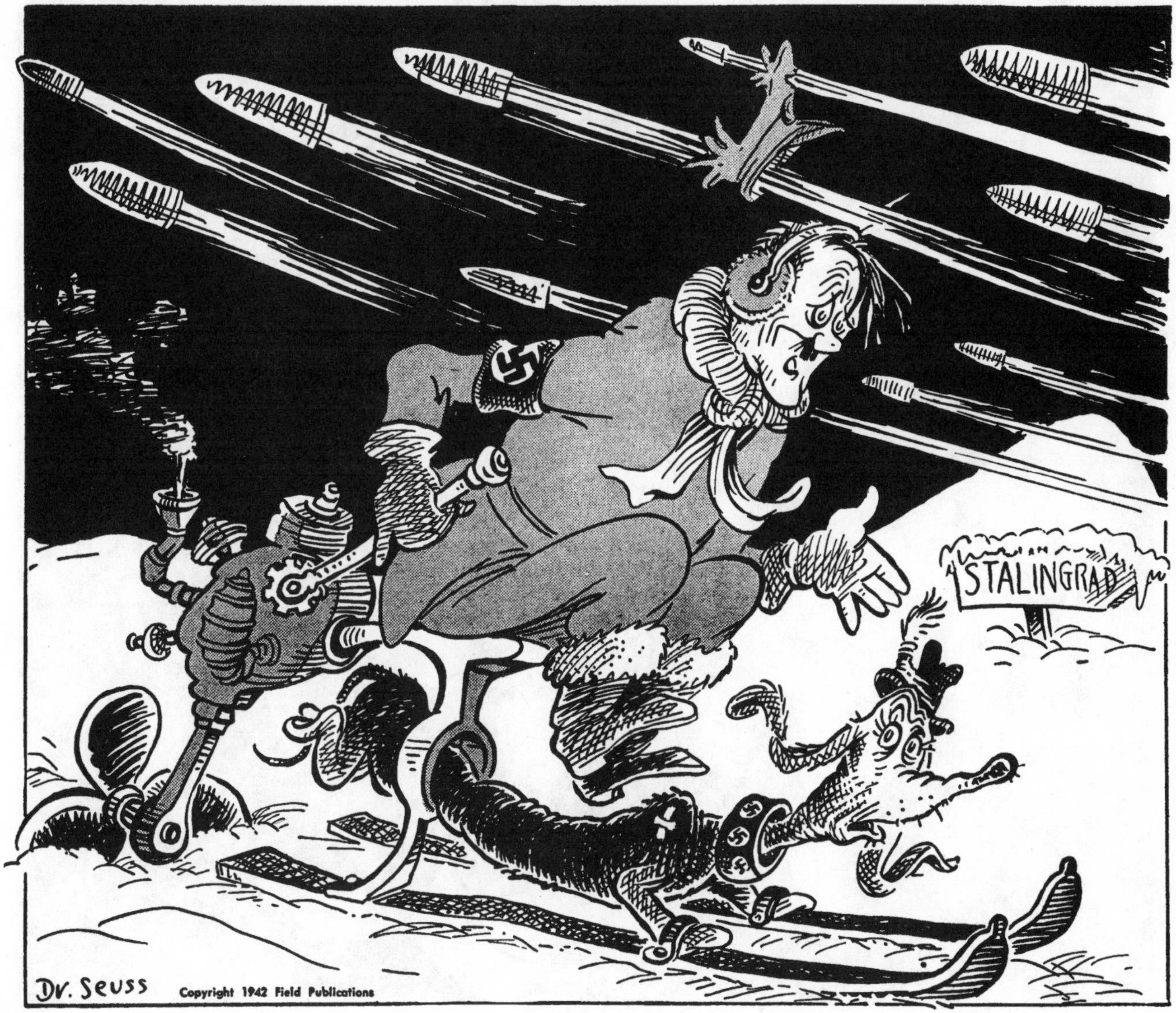
STALINGRAD
Dr. Seuss
Copyright 1942 Field Publications

113 — November 24, 1942

"Did you have turkey at your house? I had Dachshund at mine."

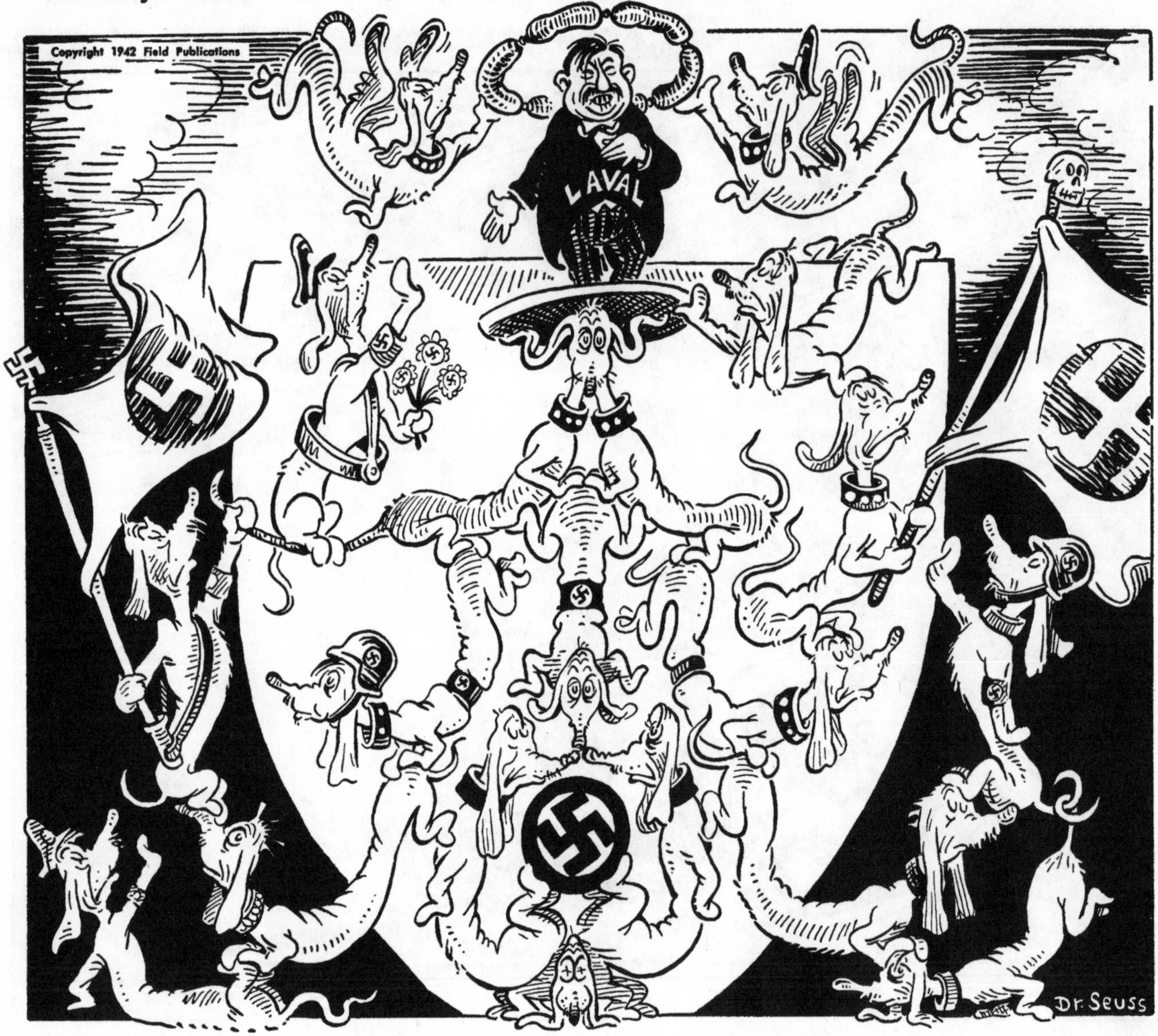
Copyright 1942 Field Publications
LAVAL
Dr. Seuss

114 — November 27, 1942

The Rest of the World

We turn now to the rest of the world. Dr. Seuss depicted much of the world only in passing; he focussed on Hitler's Axis partners—Italy and Japan—and on France, the Soviet Union, and Great Britain. So we shall deal here with those countries in that order.

Italy and its dictator Benito Mussolini were easy targets for Dr. Seuss. In June 1941, Dr. Seuss drew Mussolini making a speech: "Salute to thee, Italia, for thy most victorious year!" Of course, the year had not been victorious, either for Italy or for Mussolini: the Italian invasions of Egypt and Greece had failed, the British had captured Ethiopia on May 16, 1941, and German influence in Italy had risen. Here Mussolini stands atop a wheeled platform, feet strapped down and legs propped up by wooden braces; even his right hand needs an assist from an overhead pulley to salute the assembled multitude. But assembled multitude there is not; in the empty town square below sits only a cat. Dr. Seuss's Mussolini is a two-bit dictator from the start.

Mussolini was Hitler's ally, yet when Hitler invaded the Soviet Union in June 1941 he got less than full Italian assistance. In a ceremony on June 26, Mussolini dispatched the first motorized division of the Italian expeditionary corps. Ultimately, some 200,000 Italian troops took part in the campaign in Russia; perhaps 80,000 did not return. On July 1, Dr. Seuss drew Mussolini claiming a role in the attack on the Soviet Union: "Yoo hoo, Adolf! Lookee! I'm attacking 'em too!" He rides a pedal-driven tank; a toy-sized gun mounted on the handlebars has a cork stopping its barrel. Dr. Seuss's Mussolini is going nowhere: he's still south of the Alps, and his tank is anchored firmly.

As we noted earlier, Dr. Seuss started drawing editorial cartoons because he reacted so strongly against the words of the Fascist publicist Virginio Gayda. On November 14, 1941, less than a month before Pearl Harbor, Dr. Seuss drew Gayda and Mussolini ensconced like hermit crabs in snail shells at the bottom of the ocean; Mussolini's shell has a sign reading "B. Mussolini, Private." Says Mussolini to Gayda: "Write a piece called *Mare Nostrum*, and make it good and strong!" *Mare nostrum* is Latin for "our sea." Mussolini used this Latin phrase to lend classical resonance to his goal of controlling the Mediterranean. In fact, after the British attack on the Italian navy at Taranto (November 11, 1940), the Italian navy played only a minor role in the war, largely in protecting convoys between Italy and North Africa. The Italian navy is a joke, Dr. Seuss seems to be saying, and the talk is hot air. "Good and strong" indeed!

130 After Pearl Harbor, Italy declared war on the United States on December 10, 1941 in tandem with Germany, Japan's other Axis partner. The United States reciprocated on December 11. On December 22, 1941, when Dr. Seuss drew "Bundles for Benito," the basic elements of his Mussolini were already in place: huge underslung jaw, five o-clock shadow, split upper lip, excess poundage. In this cartoon there are crossed bandages on Mussolini's bared hip; in later cartoons the bandages migrate to the

131 side of Mussolini's head. In a January 1942 cartoon, Hitler and "Japan" look to a bouncing Benito as a source of rubber to patch a flat tire; the unidentified booted foot that has sent Benito bouncing may be the British forces in North Africa which in November and December had sent Germany's Afrika Korps under General Rommel retreating westward and, in the process, isolated and captured Italian forces. By speaking of Axis shortages, Dr. Seuss may have hoped to divert attention from shortages on the home front. Dr Seuss continued his mocking assault on Mussolini's classical pretensions in "Caesar and Cleopatra" (not included here). Mussolini is depicted as Caesar, and he has his arm about the waist of Cleopatra, a dressmaker's dummy, headless and legless; a tag labels her "Egyptian booby prize, made in Berlin." In

132 a cartoon of July 21, 1942, Hitler rides the backs of Mus-

solini and Laval, promising them "War Spoils"—the skeleton of a fish. Dr. Seuss added in parentheses "(+ I *do* mean spoiled!)." No matter what Dr. Seuss's attitude toward Hitler, it is clear here that he had only contempt for Mussolini and Laval. In an August image ("Rome-Town Boy Makes Good!") Mussolini vacuums a pyramid. 133 The subtitle, "194? Benito Cleans Up Egypt," mocks Italian ambitions once more. Despite British bases on its territory, Egypt remained neutral until joining the Allies in 1945. Mussolini was fit to be janitor, nothing more.

134 Dr. Seuss's cartoons of October 20, 1942, and November 11, 1942, show Mussolini with crossed bandages on temple, albeit different temples. These cartoons display not only the dictator in all his fecklessness but also other Italians with faces clearly different from Mussolini's. In the former, there are four other Italians. One has glasses, all four have mustaches, and none bears the slightest resemblance to Mussolini. Dr. Seuss underlined the message of hardship on the home front in several ways: the cobweb on the pantry shelf, the lone wisp of smoke rising from the stovepipe, the similarly anemic steam above the pot of water, the hands resting on the stove top, the patch on the coat of the man on the right. On November 11, Dr. Seuss 135 depicted Mussolini pulling wings off butterflies (Ethiopia, Croatia, Albania, Greece—all targets of Italian attack), oblivious of the "Inevitable Invasion of Italy." Note that these (friendly) planes have the same barbed noses as did Hitler and "Japan" in the earlier "Quick, Henry, THE 106 FLIT!" With the Allied invasion of North Africa, the German occupation of the rest of France, and French admiral Darlan's surrender to the Allies in North Africa, the

136 inevitable was several steps closer. On November 17, Dr. Seuss drew "Jitters a la Duce." Comments one Italian general to another as they watch Mussolini in his ornate bathroom: "His hand ain't so steady. These days all he dares shave is his reflection!" Indeed, the cartoon Mussolini is 137 applying lather to the mirror. On December 2, 1942, Dr. Seuss predicted Mussolini's fate: a dodo ("Extinct 249 yrs.") summons him with the words, "Are your bags packed, Sir? They're exhibiting you in the Museum." (Mussolini's actual demise—execution at the hands of Italian partisans—would come more than two years later, in April 1945.) This is not the first time Dr. Seuss relegat- 48 ed a target to museum status: in "Hall of the Extinct," he did similarly with an ostrich labeled "Isolationism."

Among foreign countries Japan is second only to Germany in the number of times it appears in Dr. Seuss's cartoons. From its first appearance in June 1941 to a final appearance on December 7, 1942, Dr. Seuss included figures representing Japan in dozens of cartoons. The first cartoon 138 shows Japan resisting the urging of Hitler, its Axis Alliance partner, to enter the war: "Japan's" feet stick through the hull of his ship to brace against a rock on the ocean floor. In pidgin English, "Japan" says to Hitler: "Please push bit harder. Hon. feet still slightly holding back." In mid-1941 Japan and the United States were engaged in the long negotiations that ended without success in late November, and Dr. Seuss may have had those negotiations in mind here: Japan and the United States were exploring the possibility of moving away from confrontation, but Hitler's interest was clearly in having the Japanese in the war.

This "Japan" is a comic opera figure, owing more to Gilbert and Sullivan than to reality. His uniform has showy epaulets. His tall, cockaded hat has its own gaudy topping, and Japan's imperial battle flag flies above. He wears heavy glasses over his slanted eyes. He has long thin mustaches. The pidgin English would appear in later cartoons, too. The term "Jap" would become almost a staple. The slanted eyes would remain. Indeed, in a cartoon about the Vichy French purchase of some Japanese ships (April 22, 1942; not included here), Dr. Seuss drew the French premier Laval on the operating table directing his doctor, "Doc, give my eyes a slant. I've joined the Japanese Navy." In a late June cartoon not included here, "Japan" has conflicting body tattoos—the "Nazi pact" is the Axis Alliance, and the "Russ pact" is Japan's non-aggression treaty of 1939. Eight days earlier, on June 22, Hitler had invaded the Soviet Union, leaving Japan highly uncomfortable with its nonaggression treaty; and of course, Japan was involved in negotiations with the United States that the United States hoped would make it wish to erase the "Nazi pact" tattoo. In July, "Japan" appeared sick in bed, attended to by Dr. 139 Hitler, who urges him to invade Russia ("a restful little excursion up Vladivostok way"). After Germany invaded the Soviet Union, the Japanese government did face a decision in late June and early July: move north against the Soviet Union (despite its nonaggression treaty with the Soviet Union, Japan's leaders were fiercely anti-Communist) or move south into resource-rich Southeast Asia. Japan chose the latter, and that choice brought with it war against the United States.

Over the months, Dr. Seuss's "Japan" gradually evolved into the caricature we've already encountered in the cartoons of Hitler. A cartoon of Oct. 20, 1941 (not included here) shortened the mustaches (perhaps to ape Hitler?) and turned the nose piggish. These elements became part and parcel of the final "Japan," although there were side trips along the way. Dr. Seuss drew 140 "Japan" as child (November 11, 1941) and as man 141 (November 28, 1941). The child asks for kerosene, Excelsior, and a blow torch—hardly what's needed for a cake. (Excelsior is fine wood shavings once used as a packing material; soaked in kerosene and ignited, the shavings become an arsonist's delight.) The man demands "a brick to bean you with." Strikingly similar in execution, these cartoons both allude to the U.S. freezing of Japanese assets (and hence the end of all trade) in the summer of 1941, against which Japan protested bitterly. Poor in natural resources, Japan got much of its war—and peace—matériel from the United States, and oil was by far the most important single item. The argument *against* such sales to Japan figures in these cartoons: why supply dangerous materiel to a likely enemy? The argument *for* such sales recognized that a desperate Japan would have to take action to secure its own supply of oil; it was a logic that many within the Roosevelt administration understood, and President Roosevelt himself had endorsed it a year earlier, in 1940. In common with much of American opinion at the time, Dr. Seuss showed little awareness of the threat that United States actions posed to Japan. The man of November 28 is far more sinister than the child of November 11. By the latter date, negotiations between the

United States and Japan had broken down completely; Dr. Seuss probably did not know it, but negotiations between the United States and Japan effectively came to an end on November 26.

Dr. Seuss also depicts Japan and the Japanese as cats. On December 1, 1941, Dr. Seuss had Japan as a cat drown- 142 ing because of the heavy weight of China tied to its tail. Japan had been at war with China since 1937; it had proved an unwinnable war. In the cartoon, Japan certainly doesn't *appear* dangerous; indeed, it is drowning and cannot save itself. On December 5, 1941, two days before Pearl Harbor, 143 Dr. Seuss drew Japan as a monkey to Hitler's organ-grinder, perhaps effective propaganda but a misreading of the actual relation. Depicting the Japanese as monkeys or apes was a common practice of American and British political cartoons of the war era; the choice of cats, I think, is unique to Dr. Seuss. These last cartoons of late 1941 raise an issue for which there is no answer: Did Dr. Seuss really take Japan so lightly? or was he whistling in the dark? Was he truly confident of U. S. power vis-à-vis Japan? or did he simply not believe that Japan would attack? Recent scholarship— see, for example, Paul Kennedy's *The Rise and Fall of the Great Powers* (1987)—suggests strongly that Japanese victory was impossible, that given U. S. economic strength and Japan's economic weakness, the eventual outcome of the war was never in doubt. But the view from today and the view from 1941 are not the same. Had Dr. Seuss thought the issue through? Probably not.

By Pearl Harbor Dr. Seuss's "Japan" is complete, and we see it most clearly in his cartoon of December 9, 1941. 144 This is his second cartoon after Pearl Harbor and the first to treat Japan. As in "The Latest Portrait" of Hitler, so here: "Japan" appears *five* times. The Hitler portrait was a gibe at the German dictator's ego. Here we realize that for Dr. Seuss there is only one Japanese. Hitler and Mussolini stand among other Germans and other Italians, who are usually visually distinct. But there are no other Japanese. Is this why Dr. Seuss's cartoons of Japan have more bite than his cartoons of Hitler?

This "Japan" is not a portrait of a specific Japanese leader. It is not the emperor; it is not General Tojo Hideki, the wartime prime minister; it is not Foreign Minister Togo Shigenori (despite the caption on the cartoon of June 20, 1941 that shows Hitler, Stalin, and Togo). All three of those faces appeared regularly in the American media, as did—particularly in the final weeks before Pearl Harbor—the faces of Japan's negotiators in Washington, Kurusu Saburo and Nomura Kichisaburo. Yet, rather than a specific person, Dr. Seuss draws "Japan"—piggish nose, coke-bottle eyeglasses, slanted eyes, brush mustache, lips parted (usually in a smile). On its face it is not a particularly sinister depiction, so when one version, used to sell war bonds, received the caption, "Wipe that sneer off his face!" there was a disconnect of sorts between drawing and caption. Surely it is more smile than sneer.

But notice the activities of the "Japan" figures. They employ slingshot, hotfoot, hammer-on-head, drill-in-back, trapdoor. These are hardly life-threatening assaults and seem more in the nature of Laurel and Hardy slapstick. Of course, it is true that the censors blocked full reporting of U. S. losses at Pearl Harbor, but this cartoon seems if anything *less* sinister than Dr. Seuss's depictions

of Japan before Pearl Harbor. Finally, the cartoon as Dr. Seuss draws it (the original is in the San Diego collection) bears a subtitle: "Good God! I've been raped!" Given the relative tolerance of the time toward rape, the assault is clearly meant to seem something less than life-threatening.

Two of the most powerful of all the editorial cartoons are monumental juxtapositions of this "Japan" and Hitler. The first appeared almost immediately after Pearl Harbor (December 12, 1942), when Dr. Seuss drew Hitler and "Japan" as enormous faces on a new Mt. Rushmore. Note the swastika flag flying above the U. S. flag and the four figures (none of them labeled "You") that stand and regard the statues.

The stunning Japanese gains of late 1941 and early 1942—Hong Kong surrendered on December 24, Singapore surrendered on February 15, and fighting continued in the Philippines, Borneo, and other parts of the Pacific—must be behind a cartoon of February 17: "*Keep count of those fox-holes!*" The losses to Japan were hardly fox-holes, nor did they come at the hands of tanks (note the swastika on the barrel of the gun); but Hitler made no startling gains in the European fighting in January-February, so the cartoon must refer to Japan. The day before Dr. Seuss had drawn a cartoon—not included here—showing Hitler and "Japan" as cattle rustlers who comment, "Funny...Some people never learn to keep their barn doors locked." The barns in the background carry labels: "Singapore," "Pearl Harbor," "Maginot Line." But of course the end run around the Maginot Line was already nearly two years in the past.

In March 1942, in the second of the monumental juxtapositions, Dr. Seuss depicted Hitler and "Japan" as faces on a billboard and asked,"What have YOU done to help save your country from them?" (March 5, 1942). Note that the John Q. Public figure now has "YOU" inscribed on his back. "Japan" is missing his glasses in a cartoon of April 20, 1942, in which Dr. Seuss celebrated the quixotic bombing of Japan by General James Doolittle's "Doolittle's Raiders." The glasses are missing for a very specific reason: to enable an American pilot to spit in "Japan's" eye. Still, one line from "Japan's" forehead curls around his right eye, forming almost a vestigial eyeglass.

In tracing Dr. Seuss's "Japan" from December 9 until April 1942 we have skipped over an important cartoon of December 10, 1941. It shows Uncle Sam under siege by literally hundreds of cats in "JAP ALLEY": "Maybe only alley cats, but Jeepers! a hell of a lot of 'em!" All of the cats have slanted eyes, and one of the cats takes a prodigious leap from the middle of the crowd up and over the corner of the fence to descend on Uncle Sam from behind his back. We might conclude that this cat represents the attack at Pearl Harbor, but Uncle Sam already has one cat in his grasp, so the flying cat is not the first.

It remains for us to examine several later "Japans." Three months later Japan had made even more gains: the Dutch surrendered in the Dutch East Indies on March 5, in the Philippines Bataan surrendered on April 9, the Japanese landed in Northern New Guinea in April. But the Battle of the Coral Sea (May 4–8) represented Japan's first strategic defeat, and it may be behind the optimism of a cartoon on May 12. Dr. Seuss acknowledged Japan's

successful springboarding around Asia and the Pacific—China, Java, Sumatra, Burma, the Philippines, New Guinea—but still forecasted Japan's ultimate defeat. The final springboard reads, "To Complete and Utter Destruction," and the "Japan" waiting to jump on it says, "ME…? Oh, I'm the Climax of the Act!" On Aug. 13, 1942, Hitler, "Japan," and "YOU" appeared "Playing Musical Chairs…For Keeps, and With Experts." Here it is the "YOU" figure (note the suspender buttons) that is small compared with the figures of "Japan," Hitler, and Mars, the god of war playing a song titled "War." Three contestants, two seats: "YOU" know he's in deep trouble.

The Japanese captured eight of the fliers of Doolittle's Raiders and in October 1942, claiming that they had strafed a schoolyard, announced dire threats: "If enemy fliers, in disregard of humanitarian principles, persist in their cruel, inhuman 'what the hell' attitude in the future they will face death or some other severe punishment." Although the news was not made known until April 1943, on October 15 the Japanese did execute three of the American fliers. In reaction—to the threat, not to the fact of the deaths—comes the nadir in Dr. Seuss's renderings of "Japan." The face we've come to know. But this time his teeth are jagged, a skull hangs from his top hat, his arms end in lobster claws, and his legs, in bear paws. His left claw squeezes a human figure, and three other figures are on the ground, presumably dead.

In November 1942, Dr. Seuss reverted almost to the Gilbert and Sullivan "Japan" with which he began, and in a cartoon from November 18, the gaudy epaulets and hat are back on the figure reporting naval disaster to the emperor. The throne on which the Son of Heaven sits sports matching guardian beasts (with eyeglasses, no less), a paper lantern dangling overhead, and a rising sun emblem on the headrest. This is the sole Japan cartoon where there are distinct differences *among* Japanese. The emperor has no mustache—all the more startling because of course Emperor Hirohito *did* wear a mustache. The 40,000 dead are apparently the Japanese dead in the fighting in the Solomon Islands in the Southwest Pacific, for that is the only naval battle at the time. On December 7, in his final cartoon featuring Japan, Dr. Seuss regresses still further. December 7 is the anniversary of Pearl Harbor (not the anniversary of the alliance between Japan and Germany), and Dr. Seuss portrays husband Hitler, ugly wife "Japan" (no glasses, no mustache, piggish nose, outsized breasts), and in a cradle beside them, "Hashimura Frankenstein." The baby is a misshapen buck-toothed monster with mustache, flaps for ears, and legs that end in claws; his adult right hand wields an axe.

Perhaps it is no surprise that American cartoonists during the Pacific War painted Japan in overtly racist ways. However, it is a surprise that a person who denounces anti-black racism and anti-Semitism so eloquently can be oblivious of his own racist treatment of Japanese and Japanese Americans. And to find such cartoons—largely unreproached—in the pages of the leading left newspaper of New York City and to realize that the cartoonist is the same Dr. Seuss we celebrate today for his imagination and tolerance and breadth of vision: this is a sobering experience.

France posed cartooning challenges somewhat different from those presented by Hitler's Axis partners. In 1941, the northern half France was occupied by the Germans; the southern half was in theory independent under a government located at Vichy. It had not one leader but two: Marshall Henri Philippe Pétain, the aged hero of World War I who became the first chief of state of the Vichy regime, and Pierre Laval, who in 1942 assumed dictatorial power in Vichy. Dr. Seuss also drew cartoons (not included here) featuring Admiral Jean-Louis-Xavier-François Darlan, minister of the navy in the Vichy regime and—briefly in late 1942—collaborator with the Allies, and Jacques Doriot, leading collaborator. An early cartoon shows Hitler picking the pocket of a totally befuddled Pétain. The French leader wears his marshall's cap from World War I and dress uniform of striped trousers, jacket, and cape. Pétain looks skyward toward Hitler's *Sieg Heil* salute, but the saluting arm is a prop, and Hitler's real right hand reaches out to relieve Pétain of his watch. In June 1941, Dr. Seuss drew France as a battered prizefighter ("François") whom Hitler and Mussolini summon to new battle against Britain.

Pierre Laval served as vice-premier and foreign minister in the Vichy government of Marshall Pétain from its inception in July 1940 until December, when Pétain, doubting his loyalty, dismissed him. Based in Occupied France, Laval advocated collaboration with the Nazis and Hitler. In April 1942, apparently under Nazi pressure, Pétain reinstated him in the Vichy government, and in November Laval assumed dictatorial powers. Laval approved the shipping of French workers to Germany, the creation of French fascist militia, and the establishment of a highly repressive regime. (In 1944, he followed the retreating German army into Germany, and in 1945, back in France, he was executed by firing squad.) In April 1942, Dr. Seuss commemorated his return to Vichy in

157 "Marianne...look what the cat brought back!" The cat, complete with three swastikas cut into his fur, is Hitler, and the cat's foul-smelling burden is Laval, hand raised in salute. Leaning on his cane, Marshall Pétain speaks to Marianne, the symbol of France's Third Republic (1870–1940), which ended with the fall of France.

Laval becomes the subject of some of Dr. Seuss's most vitriolic depictions. A cartoon in June 1942 shows

158 Hitler playing Laval like a violin. (The original drawing in the Dr. Seuss Collection of the University of California at San Diego has an alternate caption: "Amazing what tone I can get out of such a cheap instrument!") Note here the swastikas on Hitler's cufflinks and on the

159 very notes! In October, Laval sells a caged France "Down the River." (That expression comes from the practice of American slave owners in the upper South of selling difficult slaves down the Mississippi to a worse fate in

160 Louisiana.) Also in October Hitler and Laval combine to put "France" through the wringer of war. And Laval figures in two of the most brutal of all Dr. Seuss's cartoons

101 of Hitler: singing with Hitler as Jewish bodies hang from trees in the background, and slouching out of a cave to

103 round up 400,000 Frenchmen to labor in Germany. Indeed, if one were to judge only from the cartoons of Dr. Seuss, one might conclude that Pierre Laval—not Adolf Hitler—is the most evil figure of World War II in Europe.

Compared with his craven Laval, Dr. Seuss's Mussolini is a buffoon pure and simple.

The Soviet Union posed complex issues for any cartoonist, let alone one drawing cartoons for *PM*. American policy had been resolutely anti-Soviet, but on the Left there was great sympathy for the Soviet Union. The Soviet Union had signed a non-aggression treaty with Hitler, and then, in 1939, assisted Hitler in the destruction of Poland. Until the very end of the war, the Soviet Union had a nonaggression treaty with America's enemy Japan. When Germany attacked Russia in June 1941, the Soviet Union gained more favor with the American public, and Soviet casualties in the war far outstripped those of any European or American ally—indeed, all European and American Allied casualties combined. One's attitude toward the Soviet Union often had immediate consequences for one's attitude toward the American Communists, and vice versa. Though Communists were a major element in Denning's Popular Front of the 1930s and early 1940s, Dr. Seuss seems to have been skeptical of both.

Dr. Seuss portrayed the Soviet Union in four images. One is as a dinosaur to Hitler's caveman (August 16, 1941): 161 clad in animal skin, Hitler whacks away at the dinosaur's tail, oblivious to the danger of riling the monster. Here Dr. Seuss had the big picture right: that the Soviet Union, albeit at enormous cost, would prove to be Hitler's downfall. But in August 1941, only eight weeks into the German assault, that was far from certain. In a second image, the Soviet Union is winter personified. In his cartoon of February 6, 1942, "Russian Winter," an ice- 162 bound giant sitting atop Hitler holds a stopwatch registering (improbably) "February." In the background "YOU + ME" wonder, "Yeah...but who takes over when the big guy's time is up?" Indeed, it would be the *second* Russian winter, 1942–43, that saw the crumbling of the German forces. (Think back to the cartoon on page 104, showing a giant Russian snowball taking a tiny Hitler down the mountainside; that cartoon appeared ten months after this cartoon, during that second Russian winter.) Dr. Seuss also depicted Russia as a bear. In a cartoon of June 25, 1941, 163 the Soviet bear resists the intentions of "A. Hitler, Taxidermist." Among the trophy heads already adorning his wall is Italy. Why Italy? It is hard to say. Hitler did intervene in Italy to prop up Mussolini, but those events came in 1943, not 1941. Note that unlike the other stuffed heads, all with antlers, Italy is a pelt, unmounted, stretched on tacks; its genus—skunk? polecat? squirrel?—is hard to judge, but it is certainly several steps down the scale from the animals on the rest of the wall. In "The Unexpected Target" (July 164 4, 1941), Dr. Seuss suggests opportunity for Uncle Sam, not in alliance with the bear—that would come later, but incidental to the German attack. A cartoon one week later comments on Soviet casualties, but in a backhanded fashion. 165 ion. Hitler is cheerleader ("Sis! Boom! Bah! Rah!") to his Minister of Propaganda Joseph Goebbels, who uses an adding machine to tally Soviet deaths. The figures start at 9,128,275 and climb higher, sometimes by fractions and decimals, soon reaching 87,429,387,256. The figures are clearly spurious, a product of the Nazi propaganda mill. But Soviet casualties were real casualties, not mere statistics, and even without Nazi inflation they soon reached

staggering proportions. Indeed, postwar estimates of Soviet civilian and military deaths in World War II often exceed 20,000,000, nearly *one hundred times higher* than U. S. civilian and military deaths. Of that sobering fact there is little inkling here.

But for Dr. Seuss the Soviet Union is preeminently its dictator Joseph Stalin, whom we have encountered already. Just before the German attack on the Soviet Union, Dr. Seuss had Stalin hopelessly entangled in pacts with Hitler and "Japan." In this cartoon, Stalin 166 wears a Cossack-style costume with billowy pants and blousy top. Says Hitler (with his mouth closed!): "In other words, gentlemen, Togo won't hit Joe and Joe won't hit Togo...unless they take a poke at each other when I start socking Joe." Hands, toes, teeth: all come in handy in holding five sheets of paper labeled "Pact." In fact, there were only three pacts, and three of the sheets in the cartoon perform the same task of linking Stalin and "Japan," but visual impact trumps exactitude. Dr. Seuss's Stalin appears happy in this Axis company.

Two days after this cartoon appeared Germany attacked the Soviet Union, just as Dr. Seuss predicted, and Dr. Seuss overcame his initial anti-Communist concerns to draw a benevolent Stalin. On August 11, in one of his limerick cartoons, Dr. Seuss showed Stalin knitting a huge 167 sock: "In Russia a chap, so we're told,/Knits an object strange to behold./Asked what is his gag,/He says 'This is the bag/That the great Adolf will hold!'" Russia will defeat all invaders. Here Stalin wears the military shirt he often wore, not the Cossack outfit we noted earlier. Again, on December 24, 1941, Dr. Seuss depicted Stalin as a

168 chef/headwaiter, hammer and sickle in hand, serving "Roast Adolf"—a pig. Two months later, Dr. Seuss's sympathy is clearly with Stalin, as a dowager on Uncle Sam's

169 arm expresses disdain for Stalin the redcap, who carries an impossible load. In addition to a huge trunk labeled "Our War Load," Stalin carries eighteen pieces of luggage—and two umbrellas! The dowager is "Our Cliveden set," a reference to a pejorative coinage of the Communist journalist Claud Cockburn in 1937 to refer to pro-appeasement British nobility supposed to meet at Cliveden, the country home of Viscount Astor and his American-born wife Nancy. Lord Astor owned the *Observer*; his brother controlled the *Times*. Note the striking difference in tone between these three cartoons and the earlier ones. Like Dr. Seuss's Hitler, his mature Stalin has no visible mouth. His hook nose bends down over an immense mustache. His eyebrows stand out below a low hairline; his chin is full—indeed, double. The only other Russian Dr. Seuss mentioned by name is Vyacheslav Molotov, and he does not appear in a cartoon; instead, he is a recipient of membership in the Society of Red Tape Cutters.

170 On August 6, 1942, Hitler walks a "Velvet carpet" of human bodies to reach the oil wells of the Caucasus, Soviet territory. The bodies are all male and wear boots and swastika armbands, so the reference seems to be to German soldiers killed in the campaign. The German offensive in the Caucasus began July 25 and bogged down in the mountains during the winter of 1942–43. By April 1943, the Red Army had almost restored the military status quo ante. Hitler's forces never did reach their target—the oil fields of Baku. Note that Dr. Seuss focused exclusively

on German casualties, perhaps to emphasize Hitler's indifference to the cost. But where are the Soviet casualties? As with "Sis! Boom! Bah! Rah!" so here: Soviet casualties are not foremost in Dr. Seuss's thinking.

In August Dr. Seuss predicted trouble for Germany in 171 its campaign in the Soviet Union. Stalin does not appear in this cartoon, nor does Hitler, but two German underlings, one a military officer and the other a civilian, read a letter from Hitler asking that they send him his winter underwear: "Tck, Tck! Now he writes it looks like he'll need dot Historical Underwear back!" The underwear in question, now on display in Room XXIV of "Adolf's Museum," was "worn by Der Fuehrer before Moscow in 1941." It is displayed with right arm raised in *Sieg Heil* stance.

At first Dr. Seuss's Russia was the enemy of his enemy. Over time it metamorphosed into a more positive image, but even late in 1942 there was ambivalence in Dr. Seuss's depictions of the Soviet Union.

Dr. Seuss rarely drew Britain. In the Munich Pact of September 30, 1938, Great Britain and France acceded to Hitler's demands on Czechoslovakia as the price for avoiding general war. But thereafter Great Britain took a strong stand against Hitler and bore the brunt of his air attacks in 1940-41. Given the role of Great Britain in the war and particularly in the American run-up to the war, this relative absence is itself noteworthy. Nor did Dr. Seuss ever draw British leader Winston Churchill, the focus of so many wartime cartoons that emphasized his cigar, his paunch, and his "V for Victory" sign. Since Dr. Seuss drew cartoons only between January 1941 and January 1943, there was no call for him to castigate Neville Chamberlain for Munich (although we have seen his cartoon lampooning the "Cliveden Set") or mourn the British-French evacuation of Dunkirk or celebrate the Battle of Britain and the Royal Air Force. Yet Churchill and Britain are front and center in the events of 1941 and 1942. Why so little Britain in the cartoons? It is hard to say.

In the early cartoons of 1941, Britain is the largely-unseen recipient (more often than not, nonrecipient) of U. S. aid. President Roosevelt had promised "All-out aid to Britain," and Dr. Seuss quoted him in a *PM* cover of May 4, 1941. Two weeks later Herbert Hoover stands atop a vast pile of war materiel—planes, tanks, artillery, shells, crates—and hollers: "It's all yours, dear lads! (If you can dope out a way to get it.)" England is an island in flames in the far distance, and on the ocean between Hoover and England four freighters are sinking. In the foreground, a lazy stevedore blows smoke rings. Herbert Hoover, the former president, was hostile to President Roosevelt and opposed intervention. But he favored relief aid (food) to all of Europe and aid to Britain so long as that aid did not involve convoy duty for American ships. A cover of a September *PM* depicts U. S. aid under the Lend-Lease Act. Lend-Lease, which President Roosevelt signed into law on March 11, 1941, was one of the "steps short of war" by which the Roosevelt administration sought to keep the British afloat. In the cartoon, a sinuous highway on stilts gets the goods "Two Thirds of the way to England." (How do the trucks turn around?)

On October 10 the "U. S. S. Neutrality Act" steams in a tight circle. The Neutrality Act of 1935 banned ship-

ments of war materiel to belligerents. Revisions in 1936 prohibited loans to belligerents and in 1937 covered civil war situations (read: Spain). In 1939 the Roosevelt administration succeeded in convincing Congress to amend the law to allow "cash and carry" trade, which favored naval superpower Britain over Germany. Lend-Lease marked a further revision, so that by the time of Pearl Harbor the United States had moved far from true neutrality. But to Dr. Seuss, aid short of war was not enough.

Britain is a lion on a *PM* cover of November 1941. Here a very boyish "Japan" with a slingshot emerges between two towering giants, each with a cigar and a confident smile: Uncle Sam on the left, the British lion on the right. Note that the boy's eyes do *not* slant—the only instance in all Dr. Seuss's cartoon depictions of Japan. This cartoon must have caused the perfectionist Dr. Seuss true anguish, for the typesetter misread Dr. Seuss's handwritten caption, "Looks Like the Mighty Hunter Has Us Cornered," rendering the final word, nonsensically, "convinced."

After Pearl Harbor "Gnawing at Our Lifeline" (March 11) shows Russia, the United States, and Britain as rock climbers roped together, Russia leading the United States and Britain up a cliff, but Britain is almost out of the picture. A mountain goat labeled "Propaganda attempts to cut us apart" nibbles at the rope between Russia and the United States.

To support Britain was to support in some degree the British empire. On February 23, 1942, amid the stunning early Japanese victories in the Pacific, Dr. Seuss drew "Hurry Up With That Ark!" This cartoon shows the U. S.

172

173

174

175

176

177

178 in the role of Noah, with Africa (a giraffe), the Near East (a camel), Australia (a kangaroo), India (an elephant up a tree, shades of Horton), and the East Indies (already submerged in the flood). That many of these areas were under British colonial control does not figure in the cartoon. (For most of the parts of the world in this cartoon, notably Africa, the Near East, and Australia, this cartoon is about the extent of Dr. Seuss's treatment.) That Dr. Seuss was torn on how to depict Britain is clear from cartoons two days apart in the spring of 1942. The first, "A

179 Chance to Fight For His OWN Freedom" (March 31) shows Caucasians arming an angry elephant ("India") to fight a Japanese tank; Sir Richard Stafford Cripps, the left-wing British politician Winston Churchill had sent to India with a plan for self-government that did not reach fruition, saws away at the elephant's leg irons. Two

180 days later (April 2) Dr. Seuss set the Cripps mission in a very different light. "Awkward Place to Be Arguing About Contracts" has the Indian elephant sitting on the back of a bent-over figure labeled "Britain," and Britain is teetering on a tightrope. He followed these two cartoons with a third (April 17) showing a snake charmer (is it

181 Cripps?) charming a small snake ("India's Home Prob-lem") while a huge boa constrictor ("Japan") approaches from behind, drooling at the prospect of devouring the snake charmer. Says snake to charmer: "Don't look now, pal, but you'll be needing a much larger Flute!" In a fourth (May 4), Dr. Seuss depicted the development in 182 India that he saw as opening "The Gateway to India" for Japanese troops. India's politicians had to choose between their colonial overlord, Great Britain, and Japan. Days before, anticipating a Japanese invasion, India's Congress Party had adopted a policy toward Japan of "non-violent non-cooperation." In fact, Japanese troops got beyond Burma only barely and briefly, and that happened in 1944.

This about-face leads us to ask a more general question: What were the connections between White House and *PM* during Dr. Seuss's tenure on the newspaper? As Paul Milkman reports, President Roosevelt played an important role in finding Ralph Ingersoll the financial backing for *PM*; but did the contact continue thereafter? Did *PM* take editorial or cartoon cues from the White House? Whatever the situation, Dr. Seuss's cartoons about Britain are remarkably few in number and ambivalent in content.

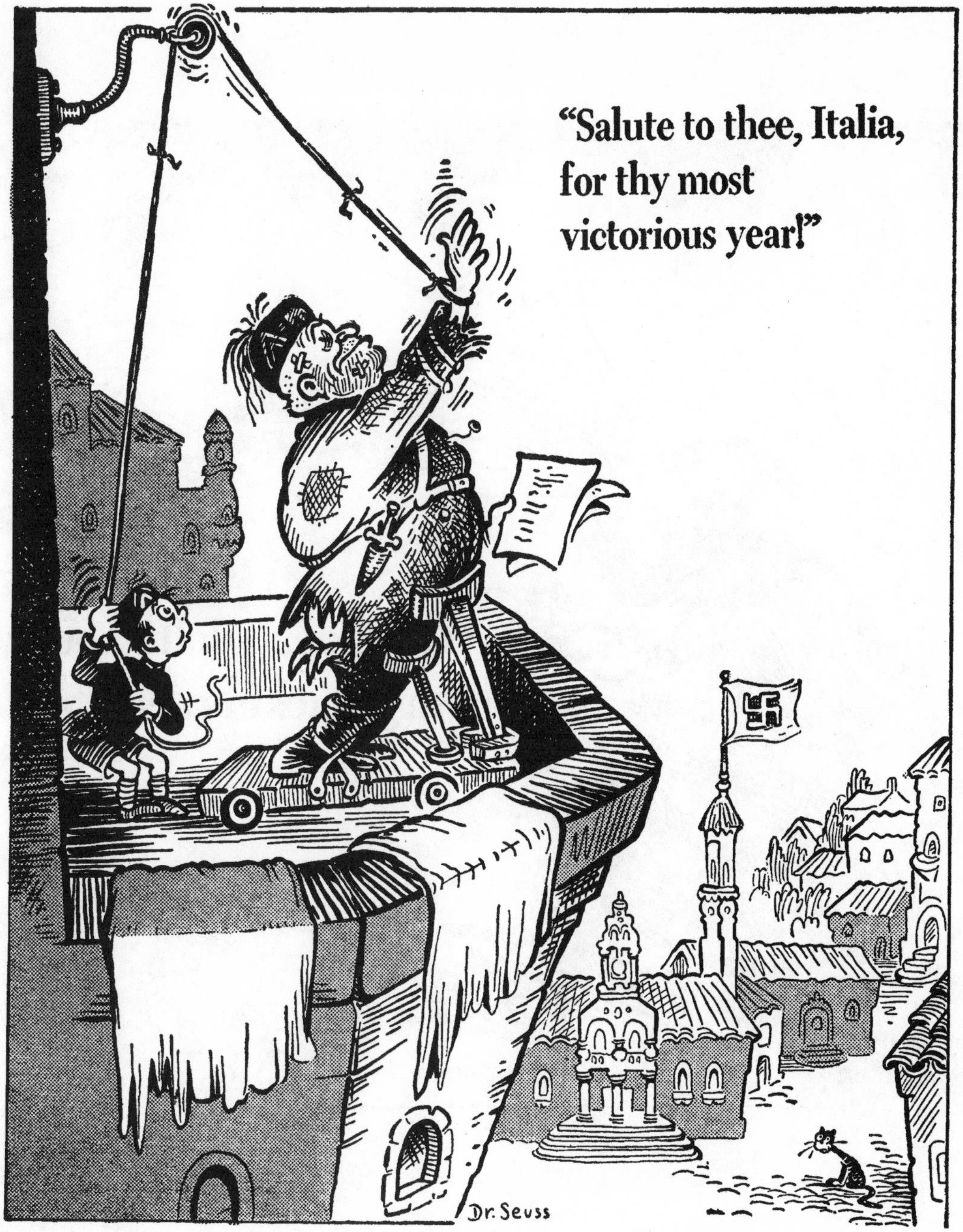
"Salute to thee, Italia, for thy most victorious year!"
Dr. Seuss

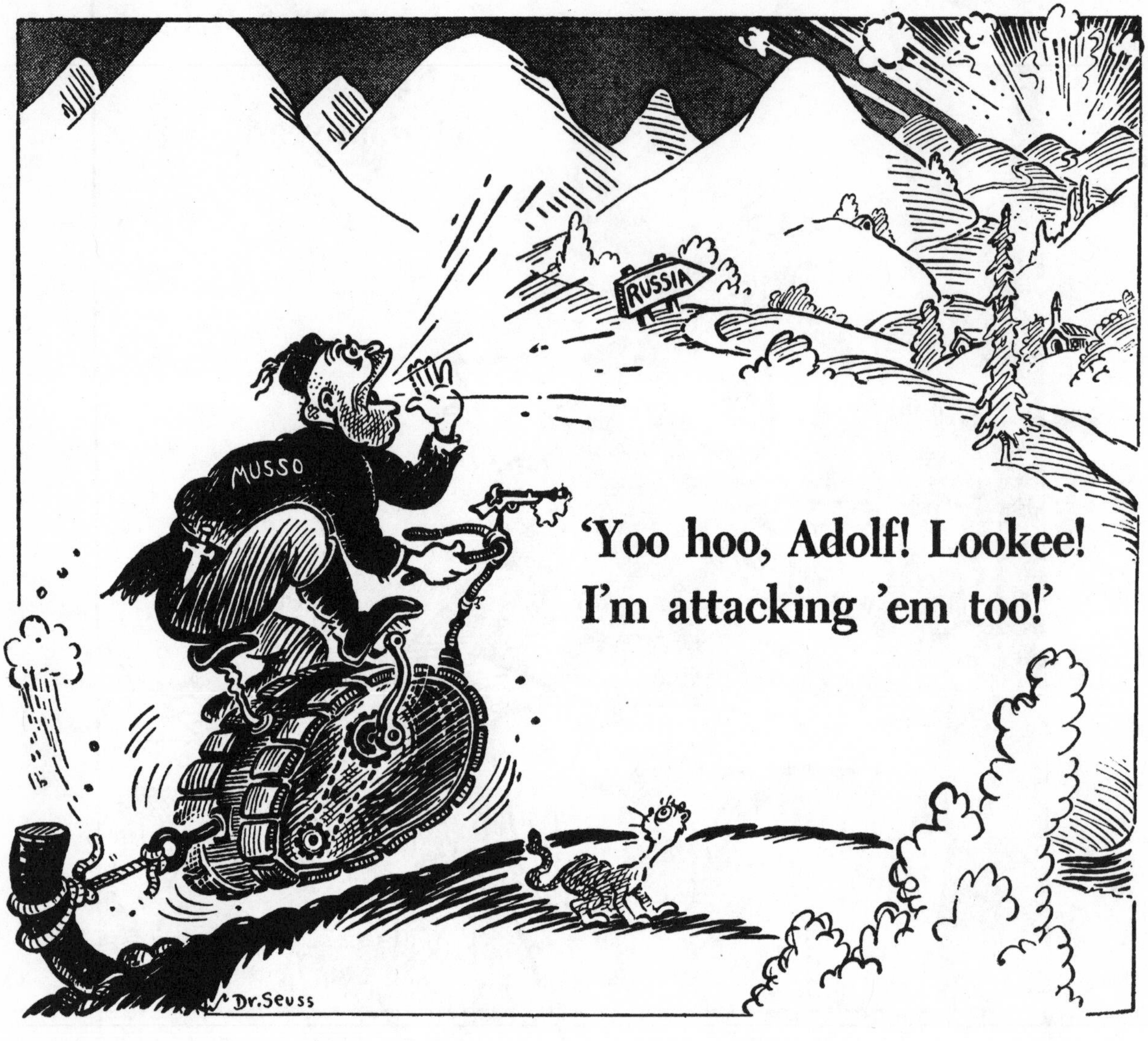
RUSSIA
MUSSO
'Yoo hoo, Adolf! Lookee!
I'm attacking 'em too!'
Dr. Seuss

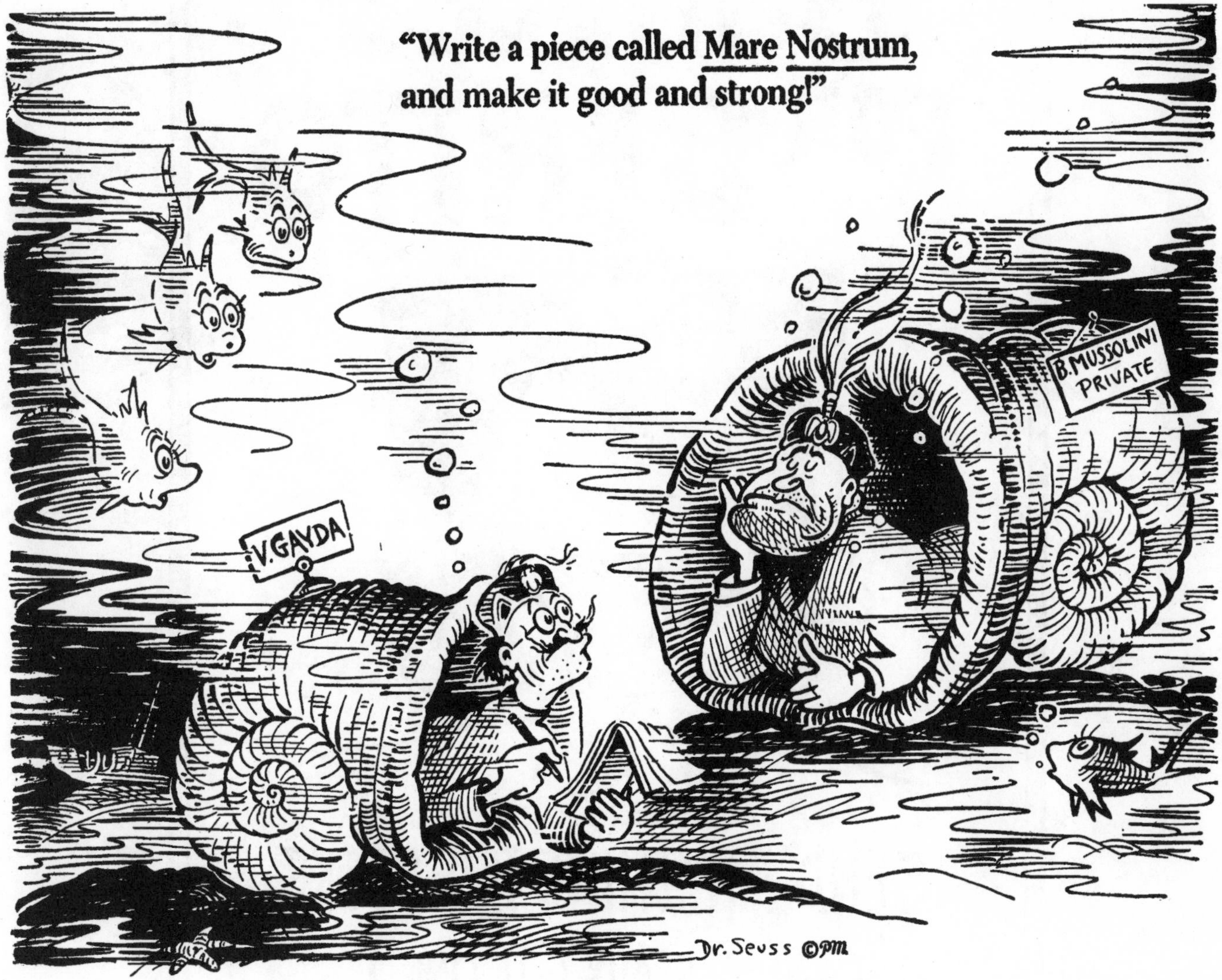
"Write a piece called Mare Nostrum, and make it good and strong!"
V. GAYDA
B. MUSSOLINI PRIVATE
Dr. Seuss ©PM

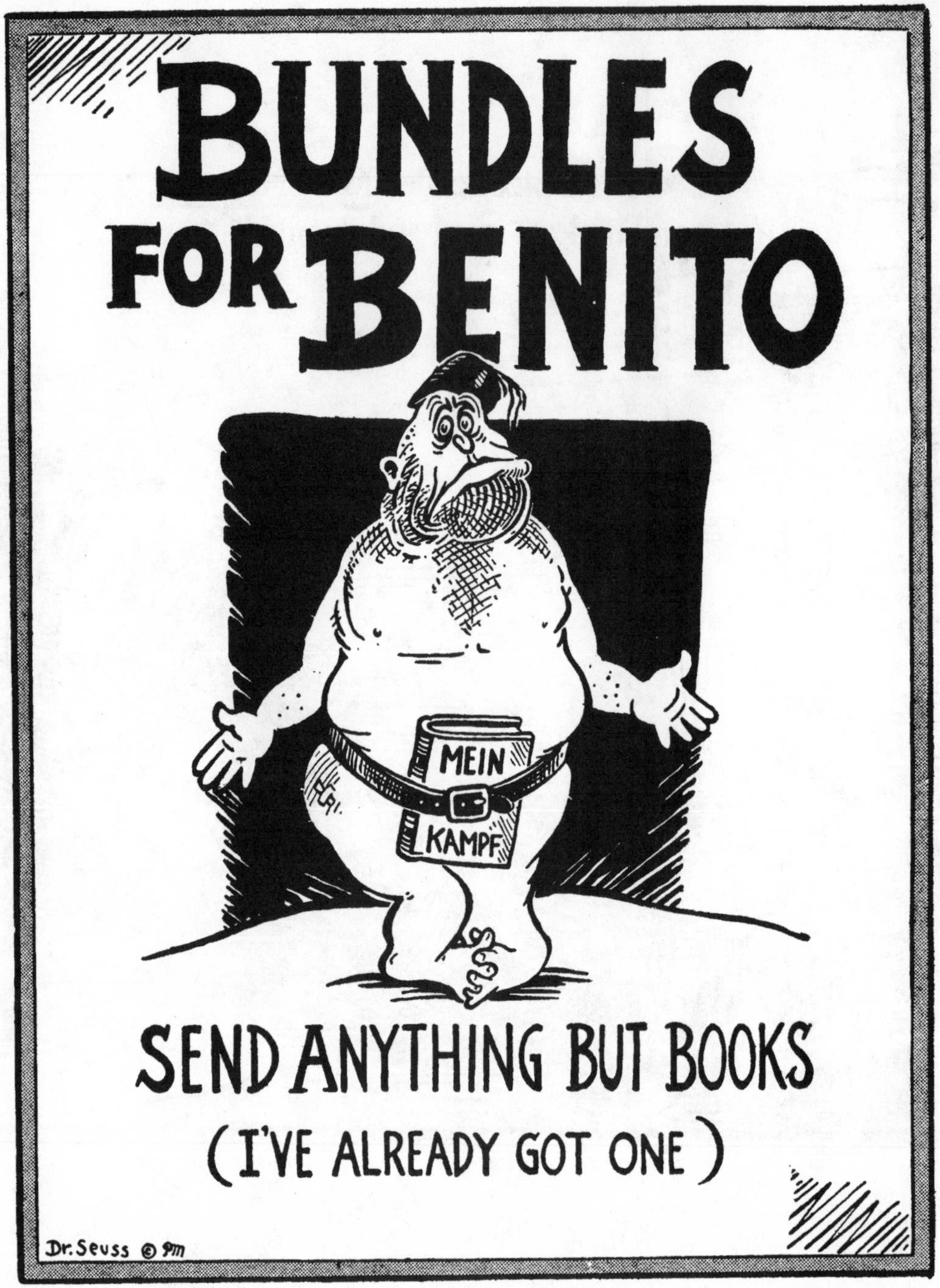
BUNDLES FOR BENITO
MEIN KAMPF
SEND ANYTHING BUT BOOKS
(I'VE ALREADY GOT ONE)
Dr. Seuss © PM

130 — December 22, 1941

Tire Shortage Solved

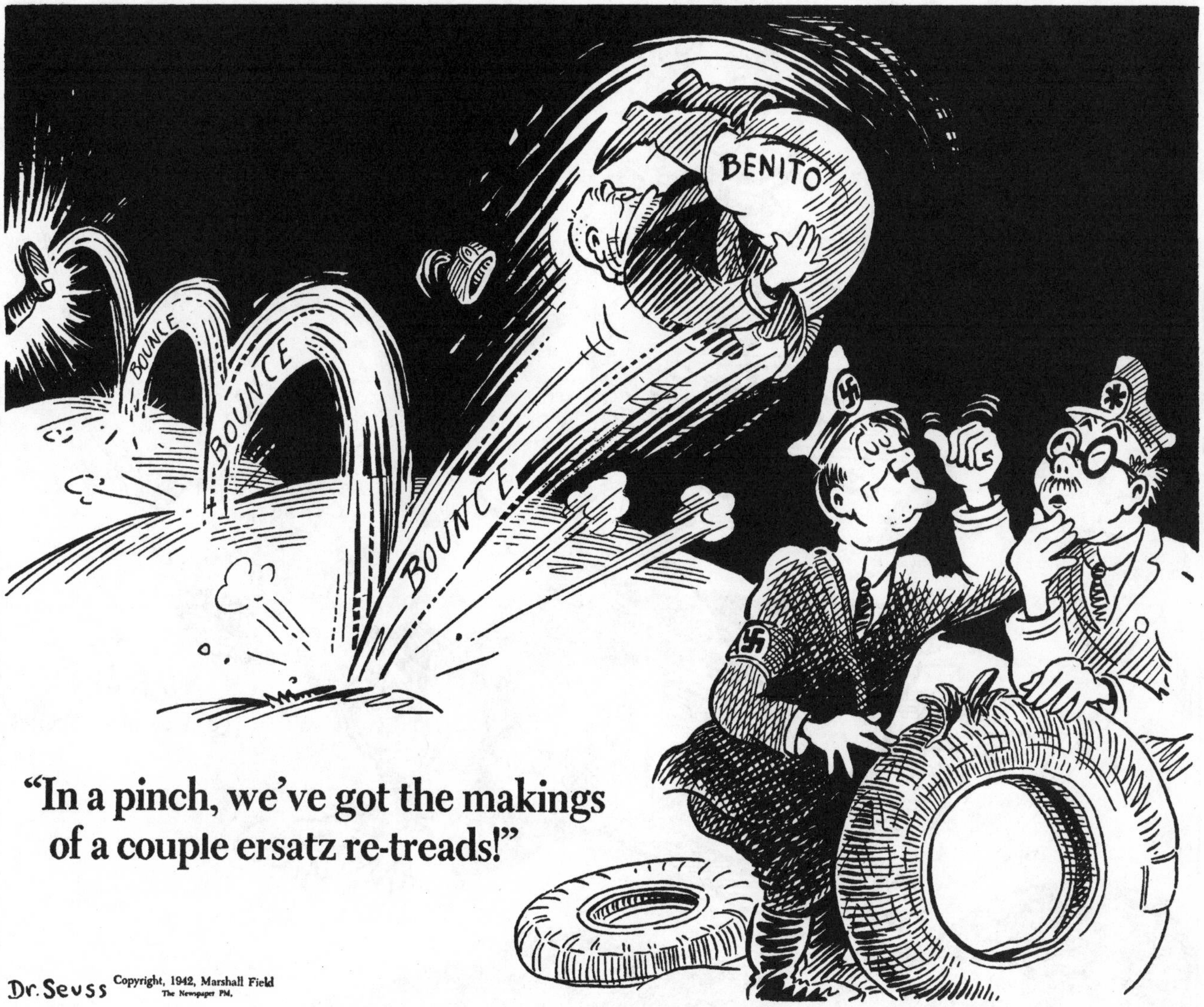
BENITO
BOUNCE
BOUNCE
BOUNCE
BOUNCE
Dr. Seuss
Copyright, 1942, Marshall Field
The Newspaper PM.

"In a pinch, we've got the makings
of a couple ersatz re-treads!"

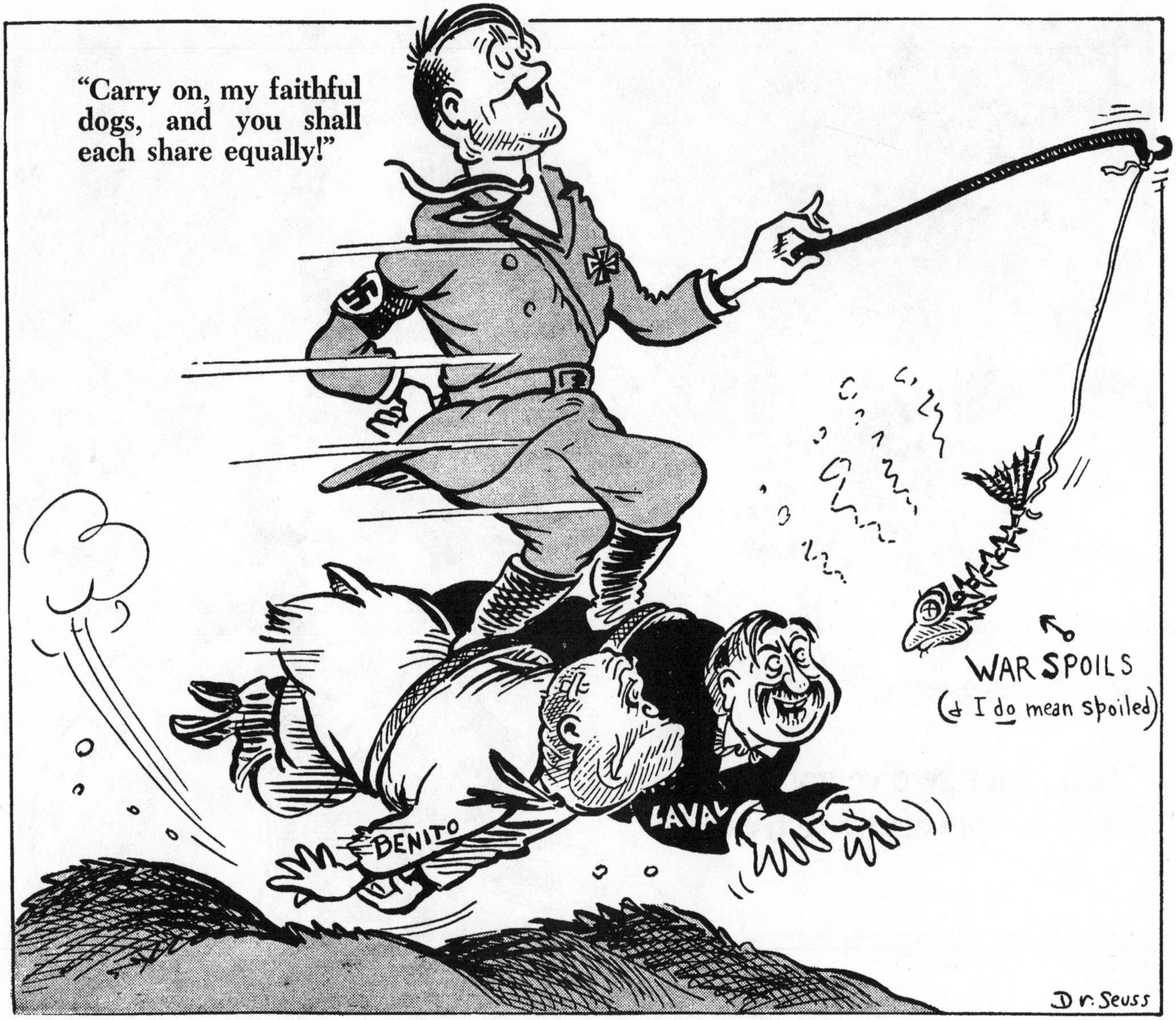
"Carry on, my faithful dogs, and you shall each share equally!"
WAR SPOILS
(& I do mean spoiled)
BENITO
LAVAL
Dr. Seuss

ROME TOWN BOY MAKES GOOD!
194? Benito Cleans Up Egypt

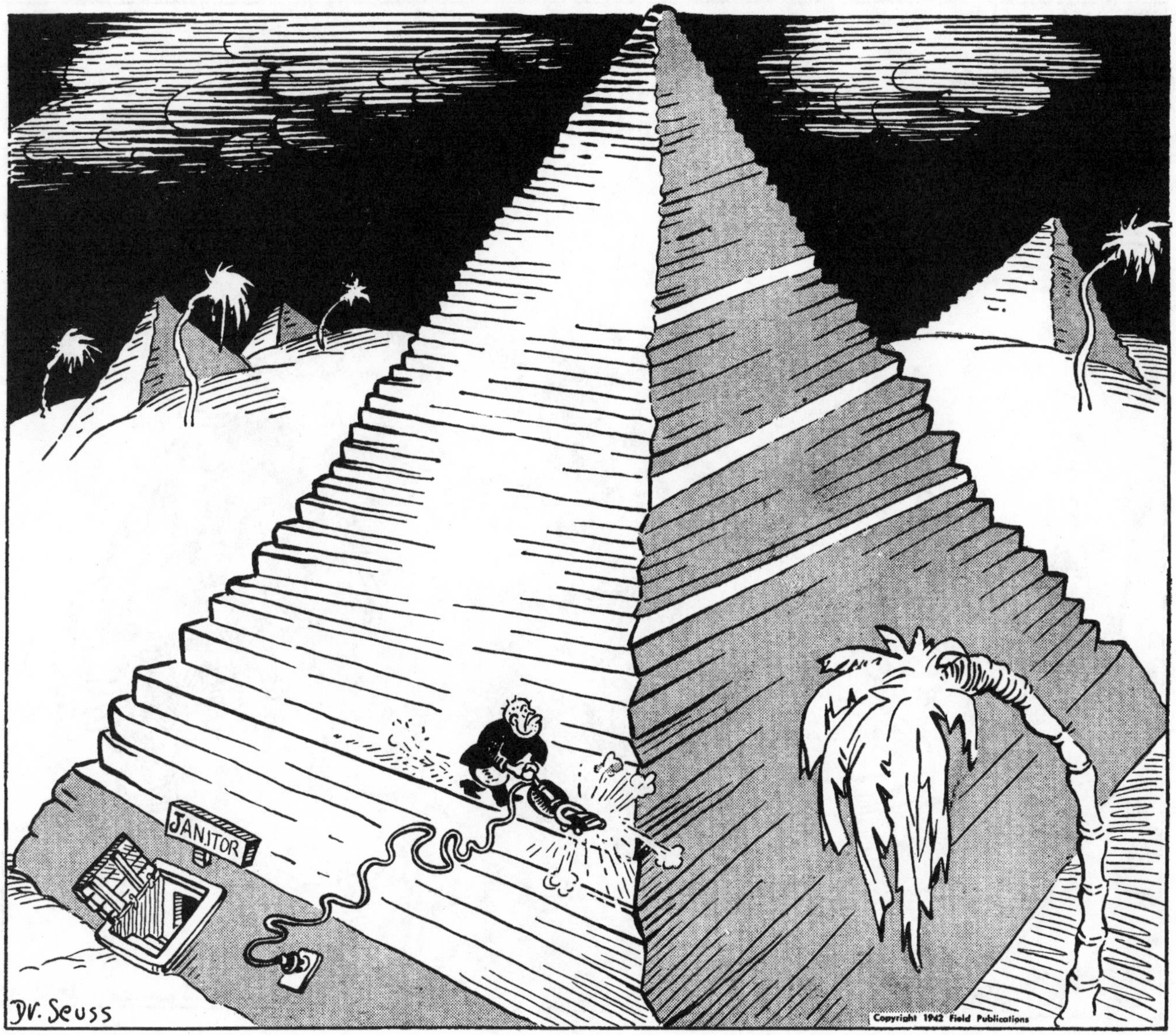
JANITOR
Dr. Seuss
Copyright 1942 Field Publications

133 — August 4, 1942

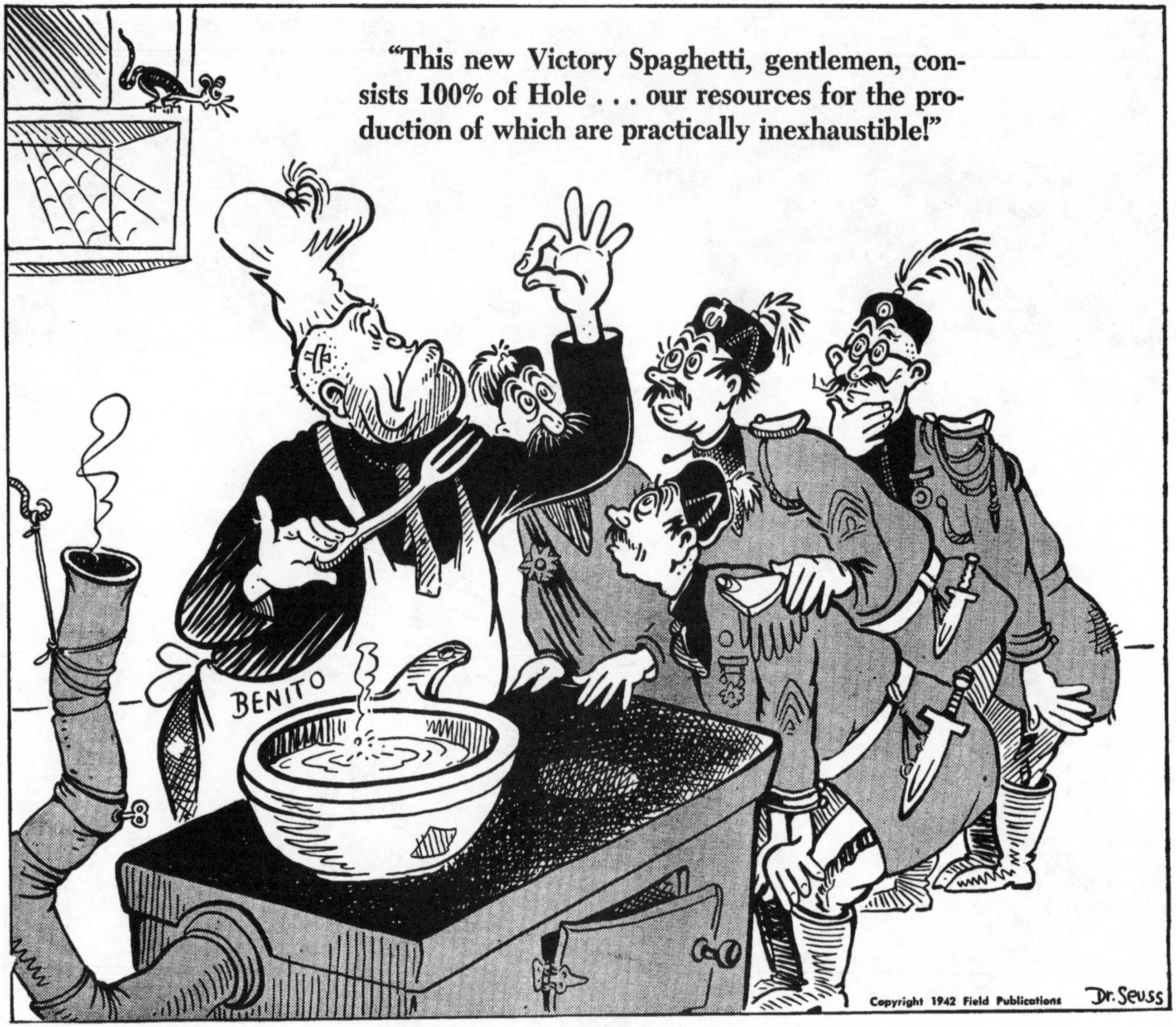
"This new Victory Spaghetti, gentlemen, consists 100% of Hole . . . our resources for the production of which are practically inexhaustible!"
BENITO
Copyright 1942 Field Publications
Dr. Seuss

134 — October 20, 1942

Try and Pull the Wings Off These Butterflies, Benito!

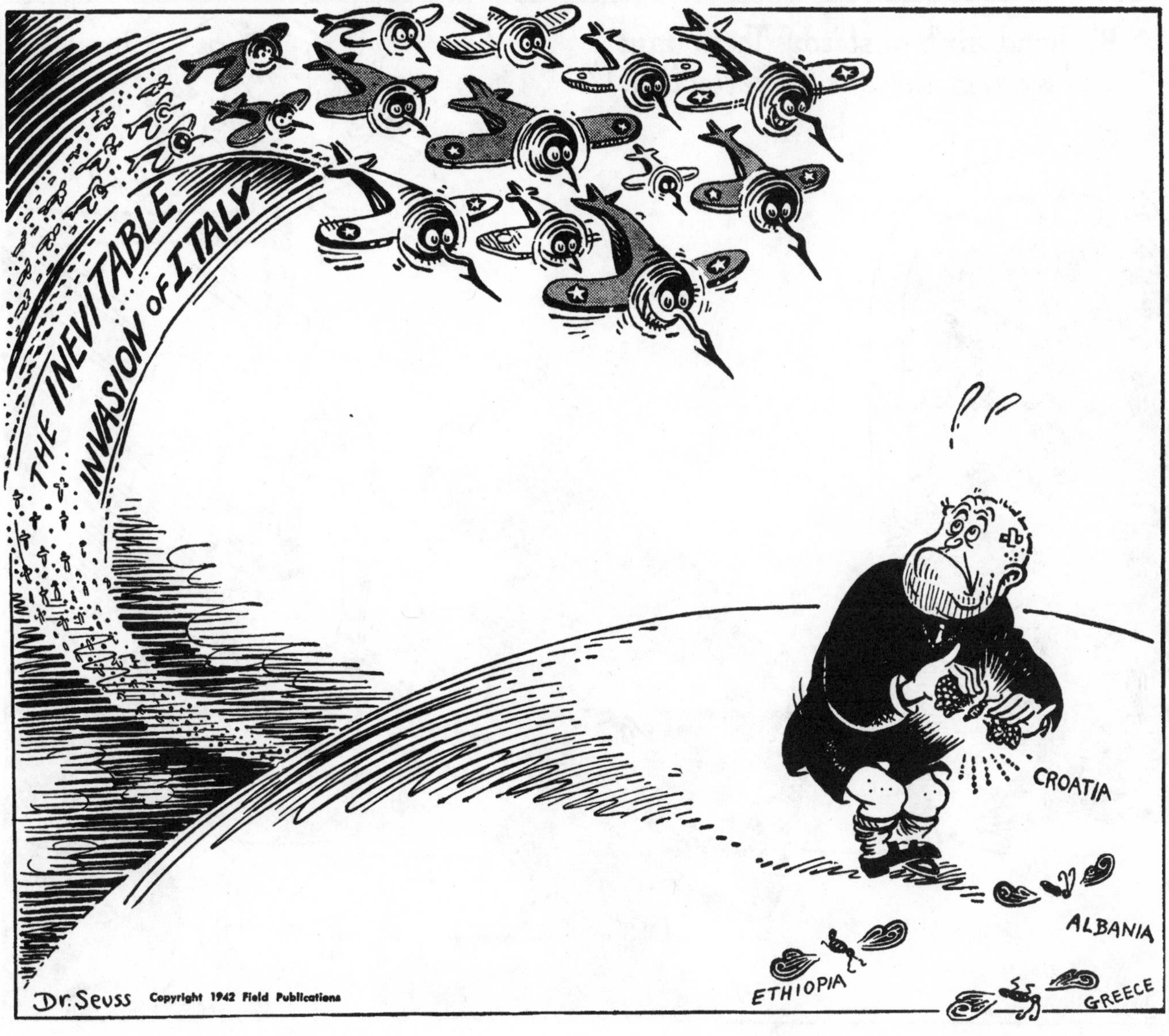
THE INEVITABLE INVASION OF ITALY
CROATIA
ALBANIA
ETHIOPIA
GREECE
Dr. Seuss
Copyright 1942 Field Publications

135 — November 11, 1942

Jitters a la Duce

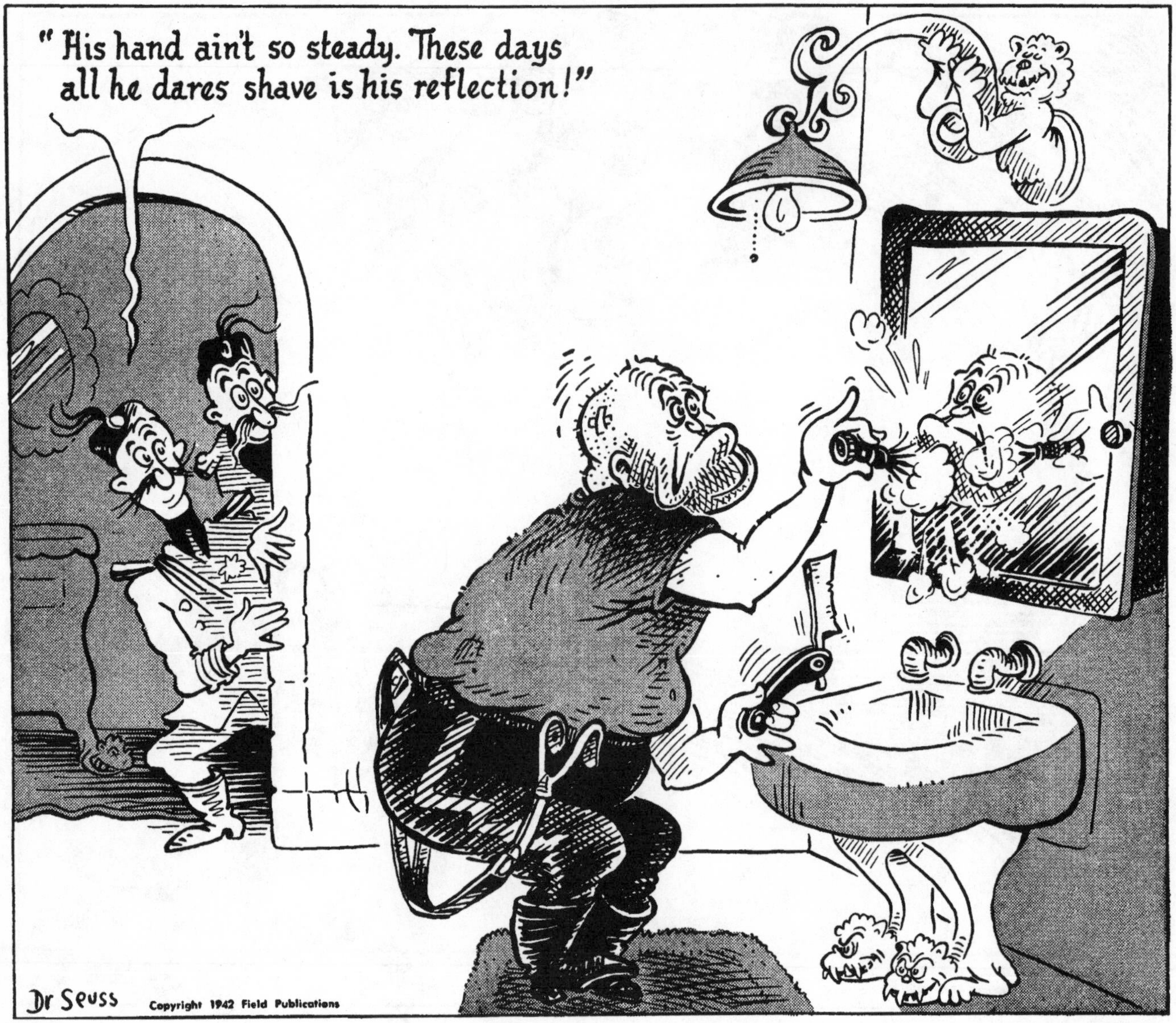
"His hand ain't so steady. These days all he dares shave is his reflection!"
Dr Seuss
Copyright 1942 Field Publications

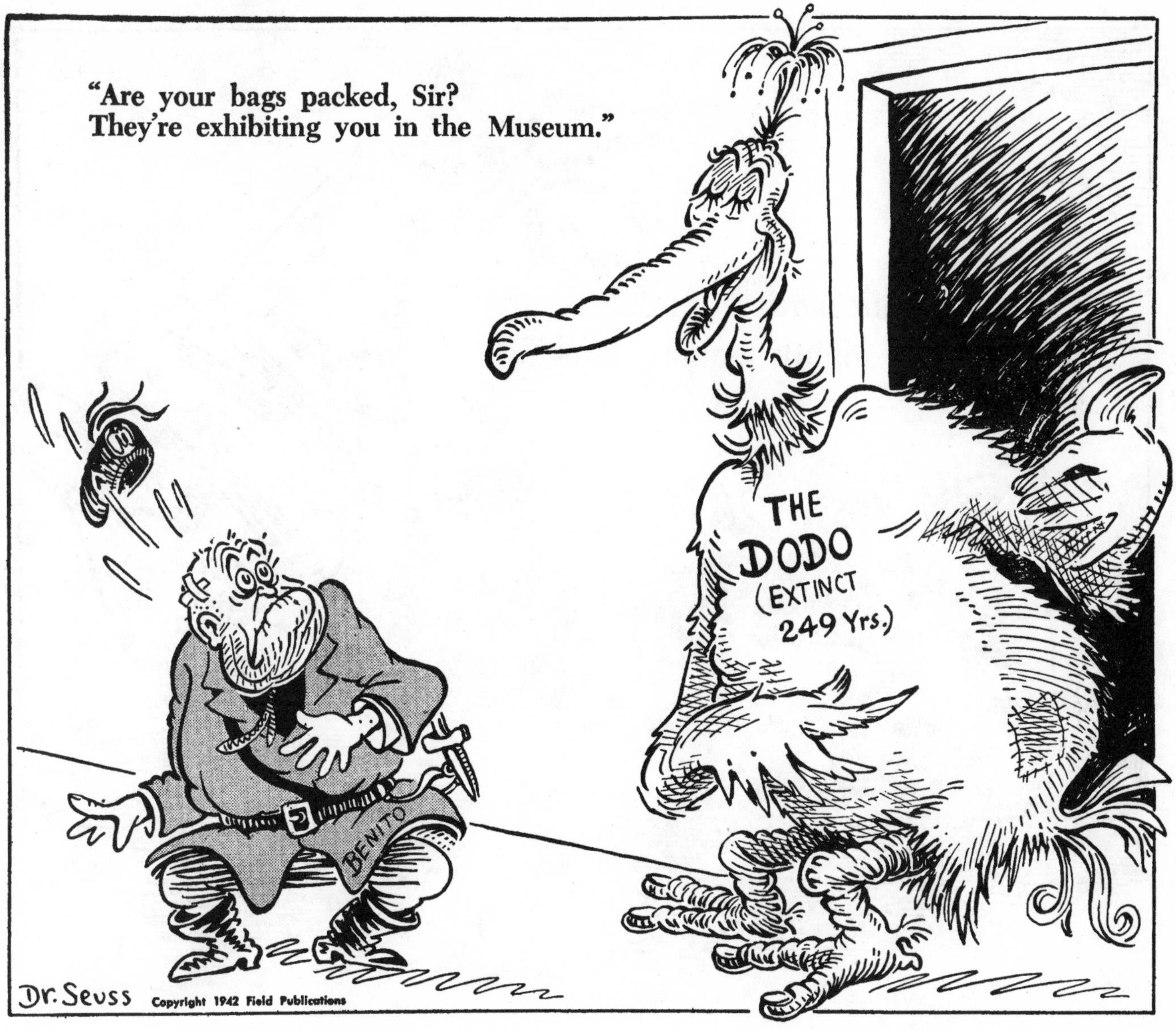
"Are your bags packed, Sir?
They're exhibiting you in the Museum."
THE
DODO
(EXTINCT
249 Yrs.)
BENITO
Dr. Seuss
Copyright 1942 Field Publications

137 — December 2, 1942

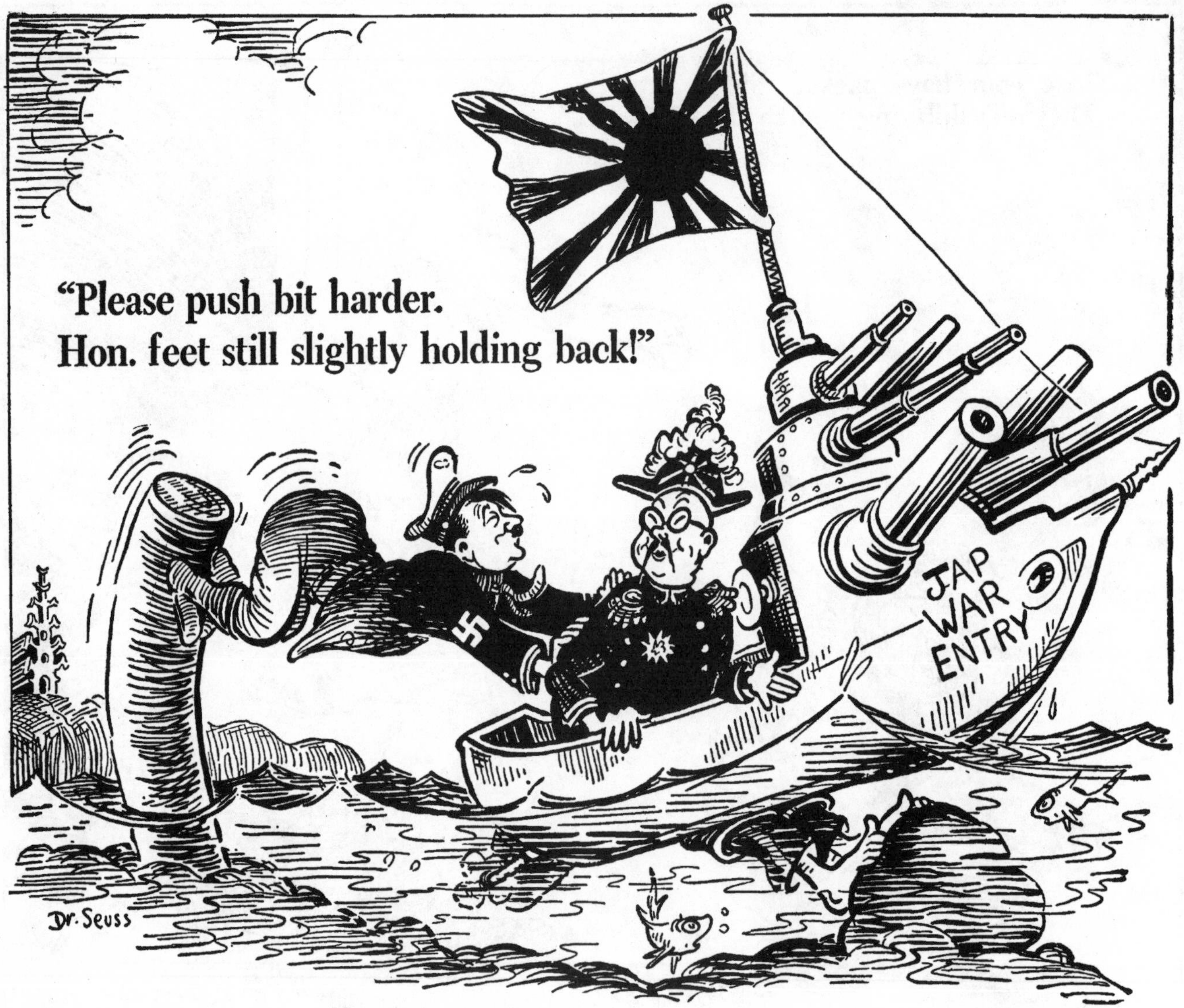
JAP WAR ENTRY
Dr. Seuss

"Please push bit harder.
Hon. feet still slightly holding back!"

By Dr. Seuss

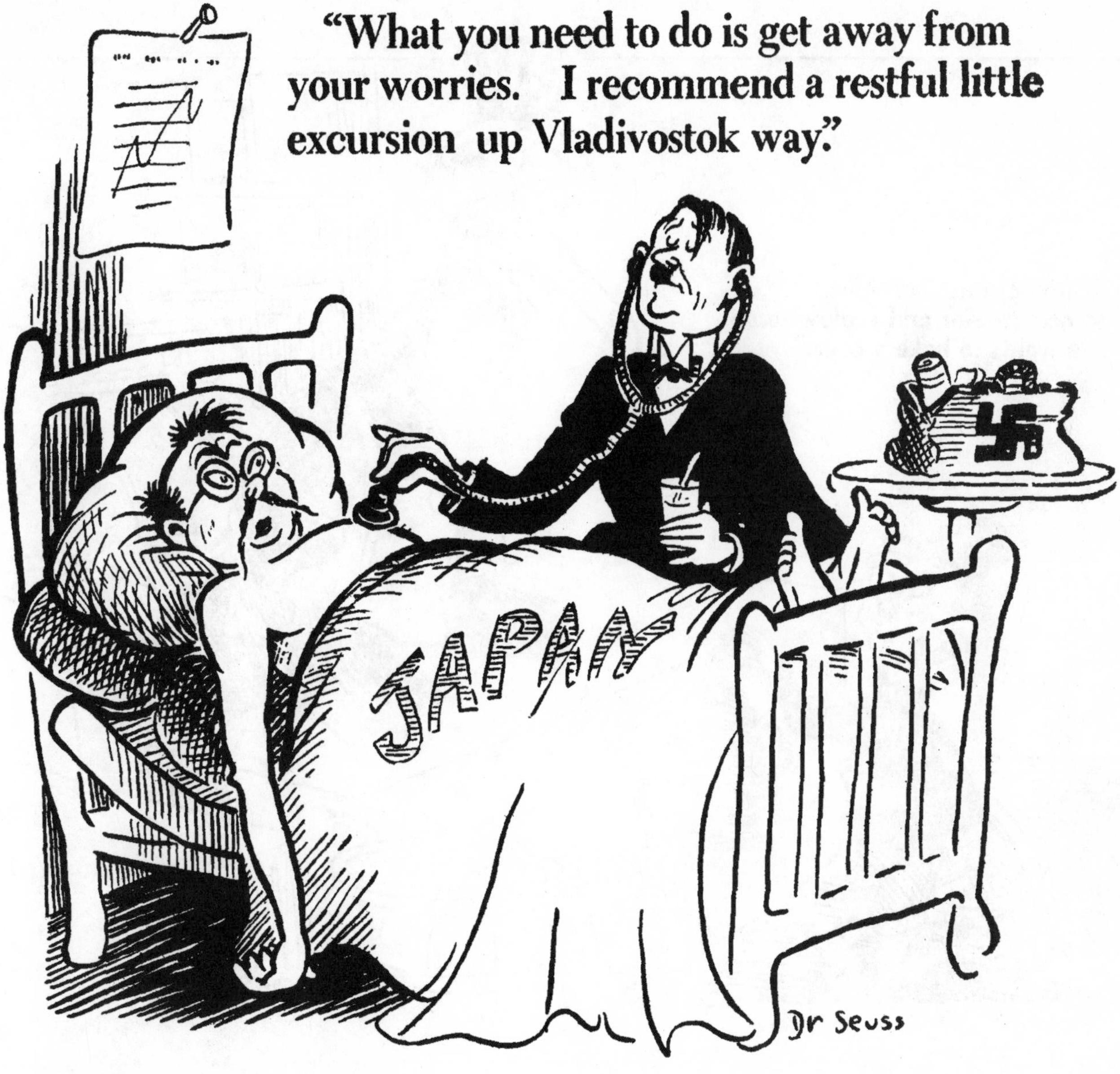
JAPAN
Dr Seuss

"What you need to do is get away from your worries. I recommend a restful little excursion up Vladivostok way."

139 — July 23, 1941

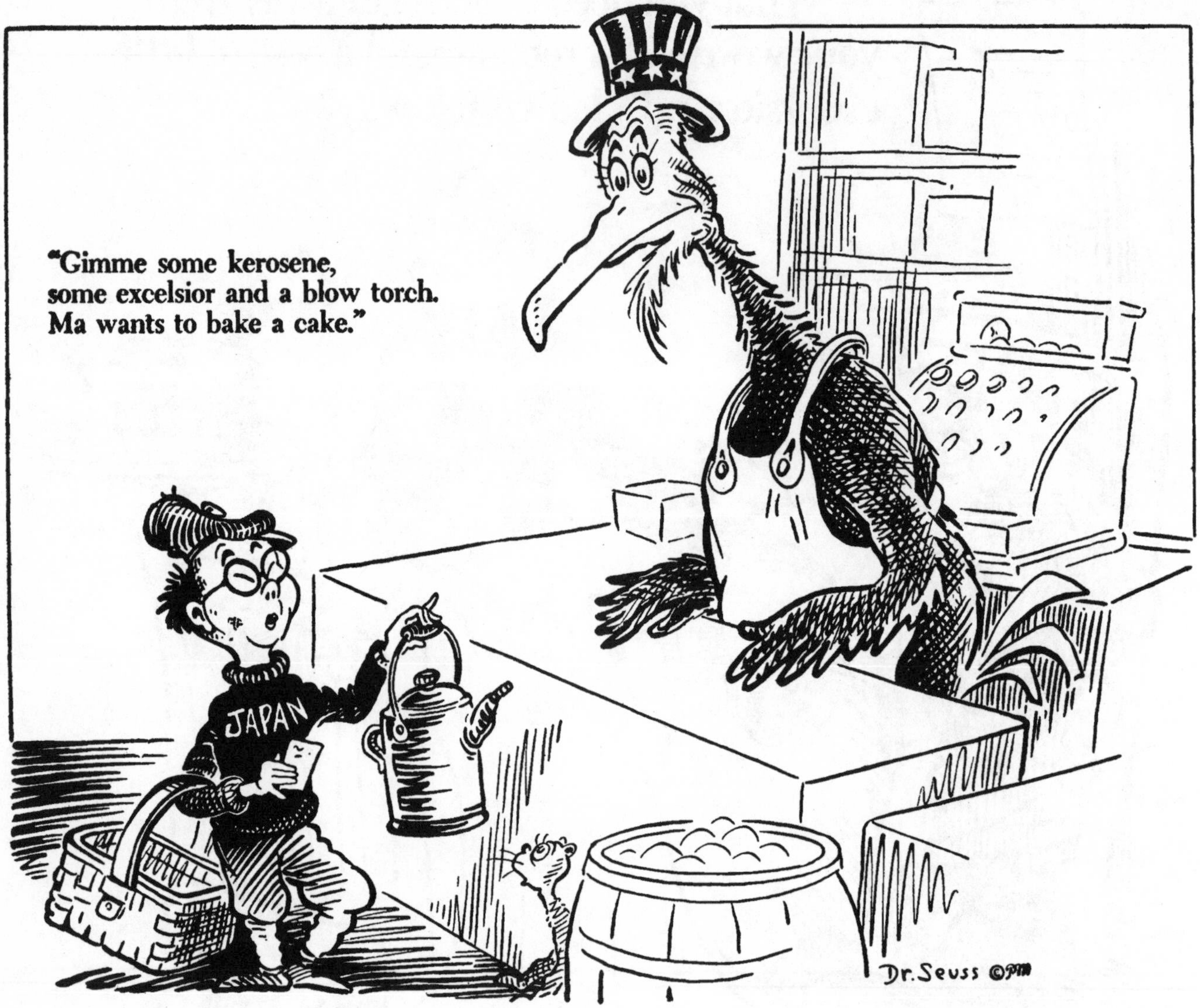
"Gimme some kerosene,
some excelsior and a blow torch.
Ma wants to bake a cake."
JAPAN
Dr. Seuss ©PM

140 — November 11, 1941

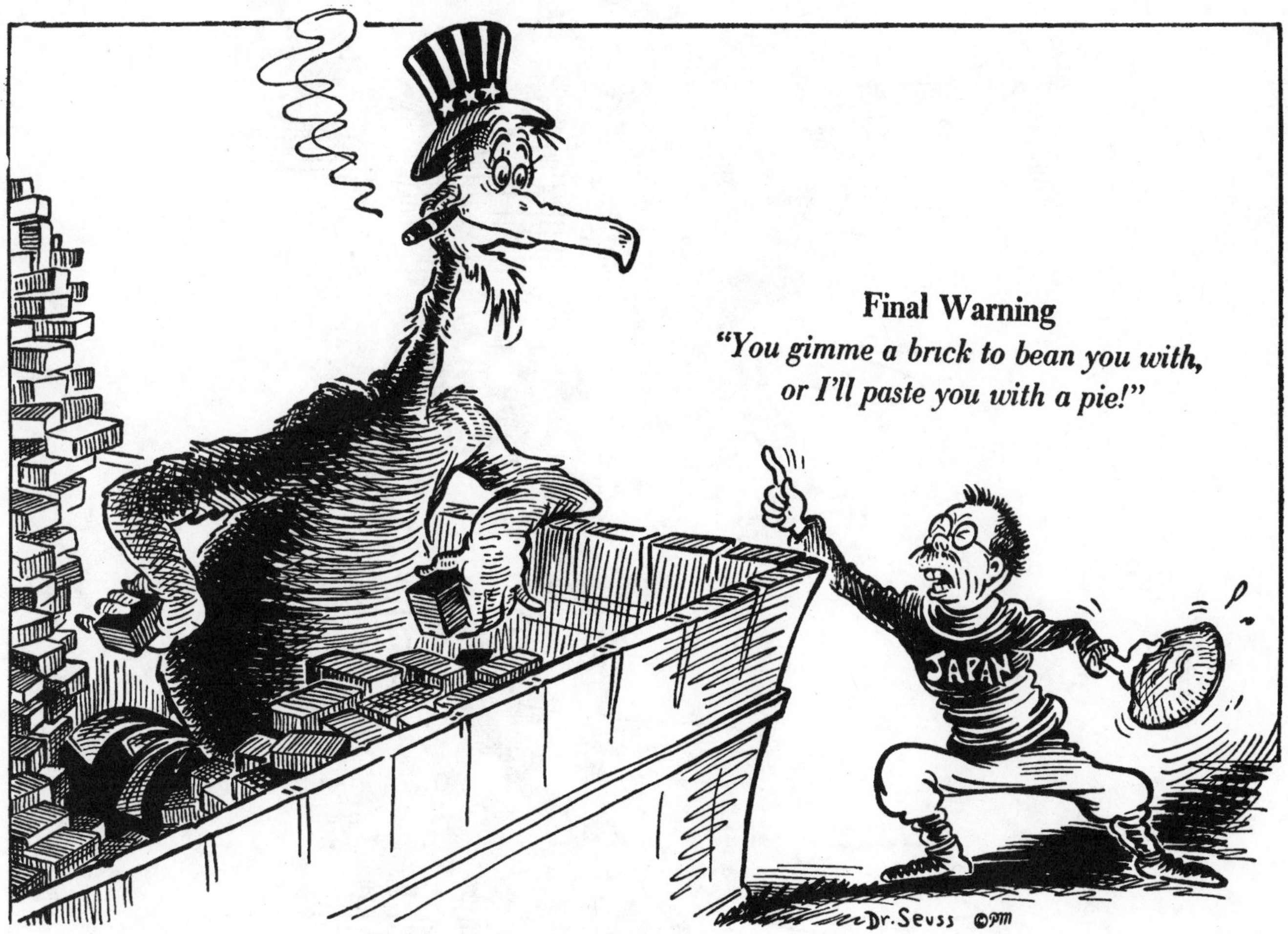
JAPAN
Dr. Seuss ©PM

Final Warning
"You gimme a brick to bean you with, or I'll paste you with a pie!"

141 — November 28, 1941

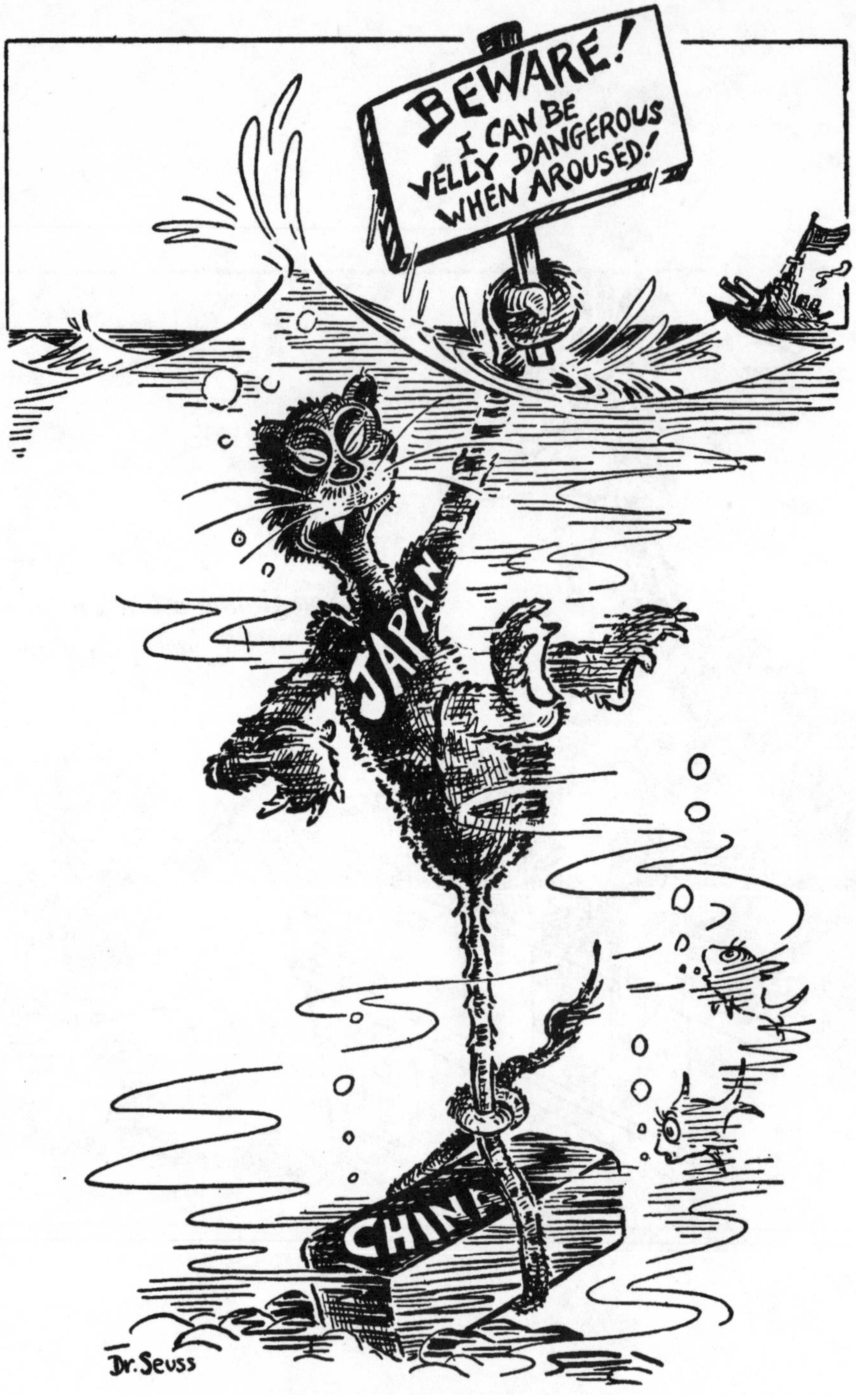
BEWARE!
I CAN BE
VELLY DANGEROUS
WHEN AROUSED!
JAPAN
CHINA
Dr. Seuss

142 — December 1, 1941

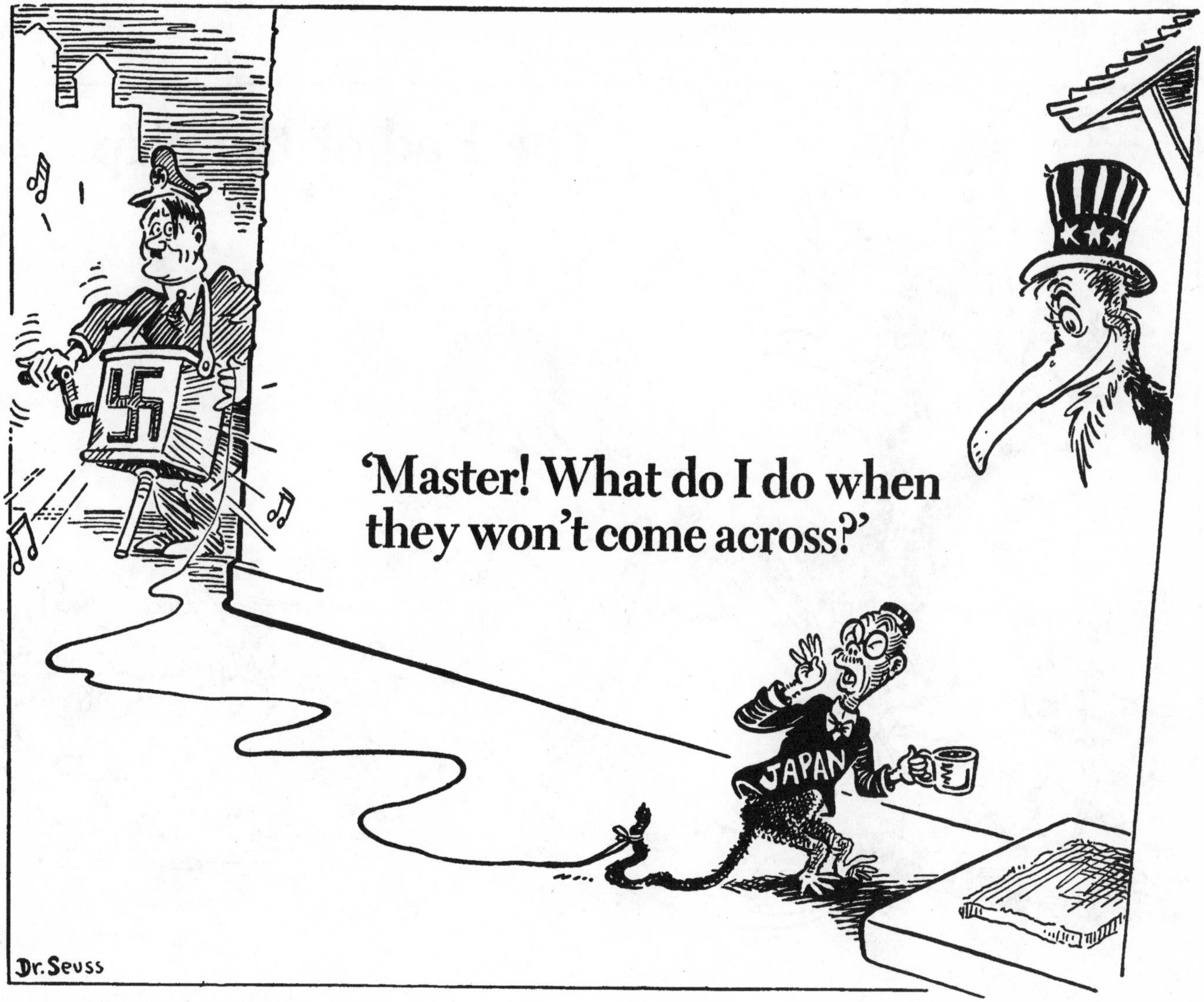
'Master! What do I do when they won't come across?'
JAPAN
Dr. Seuss

143 — December 5, 1941

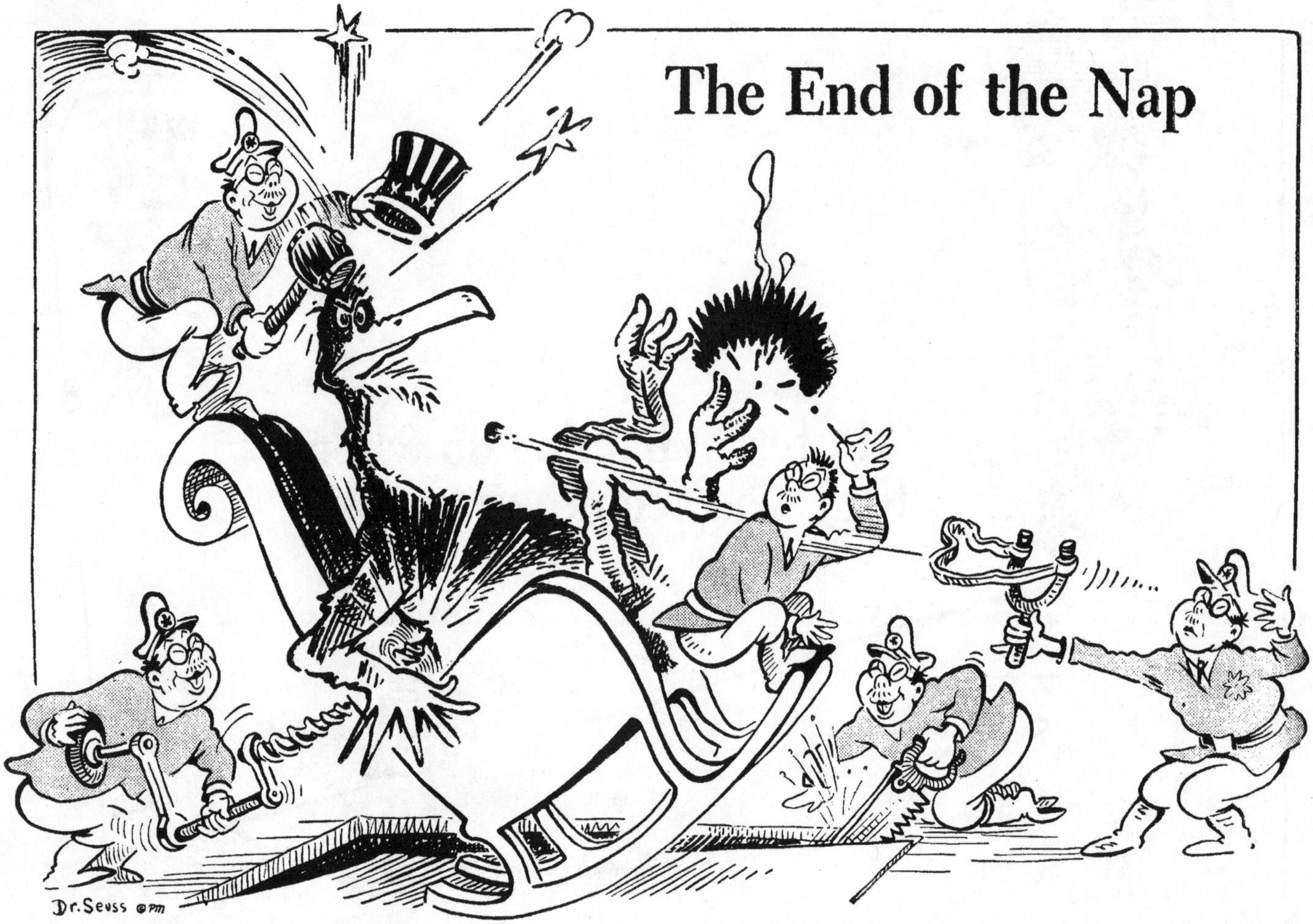
The End of the Nap
Dr. Seuss ©PM

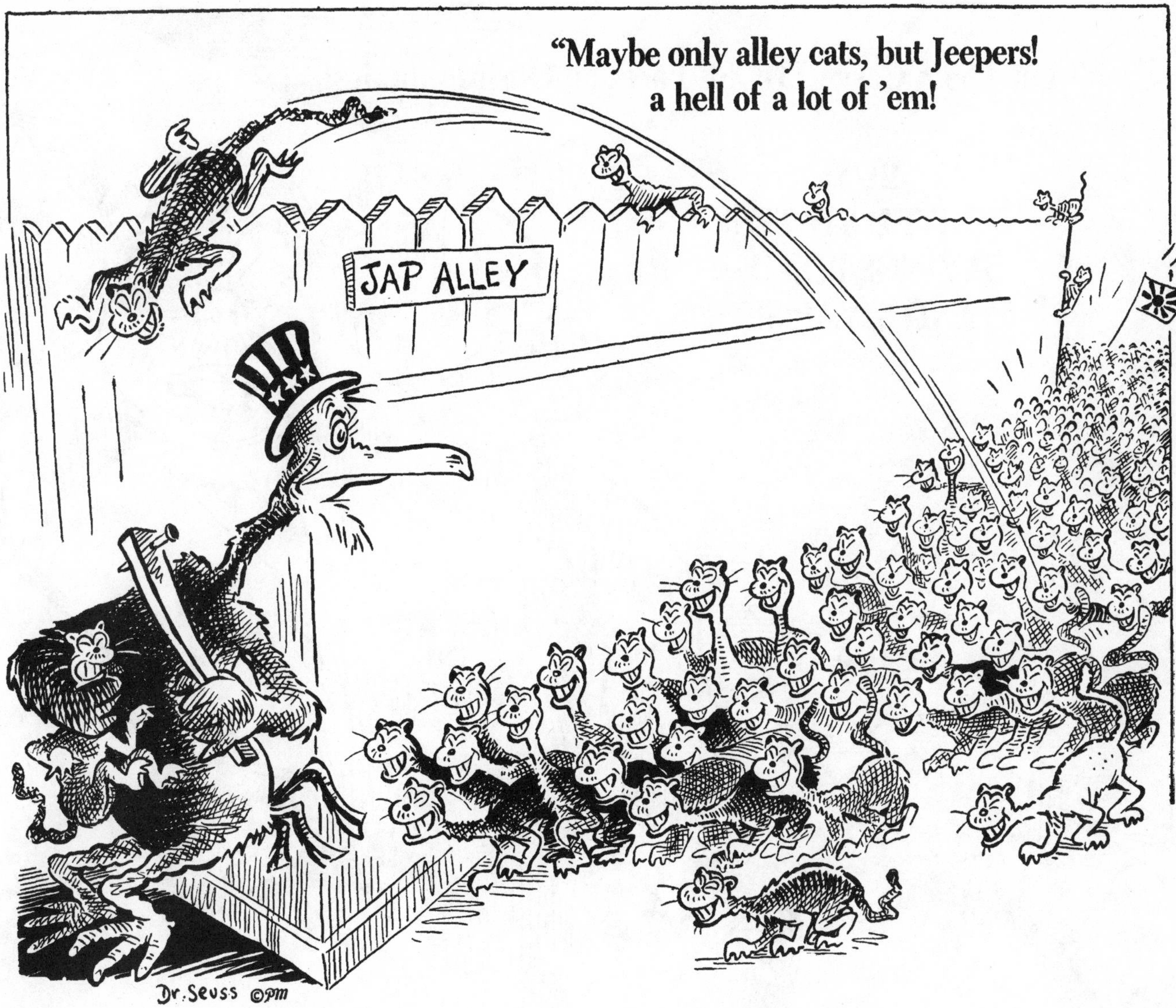
"Maybe only alley cats, but Jeepers!
a hell of a lot of 'em!
JAP ALLEY
Dr. Seuss ©PM

145 — December 10, 1941

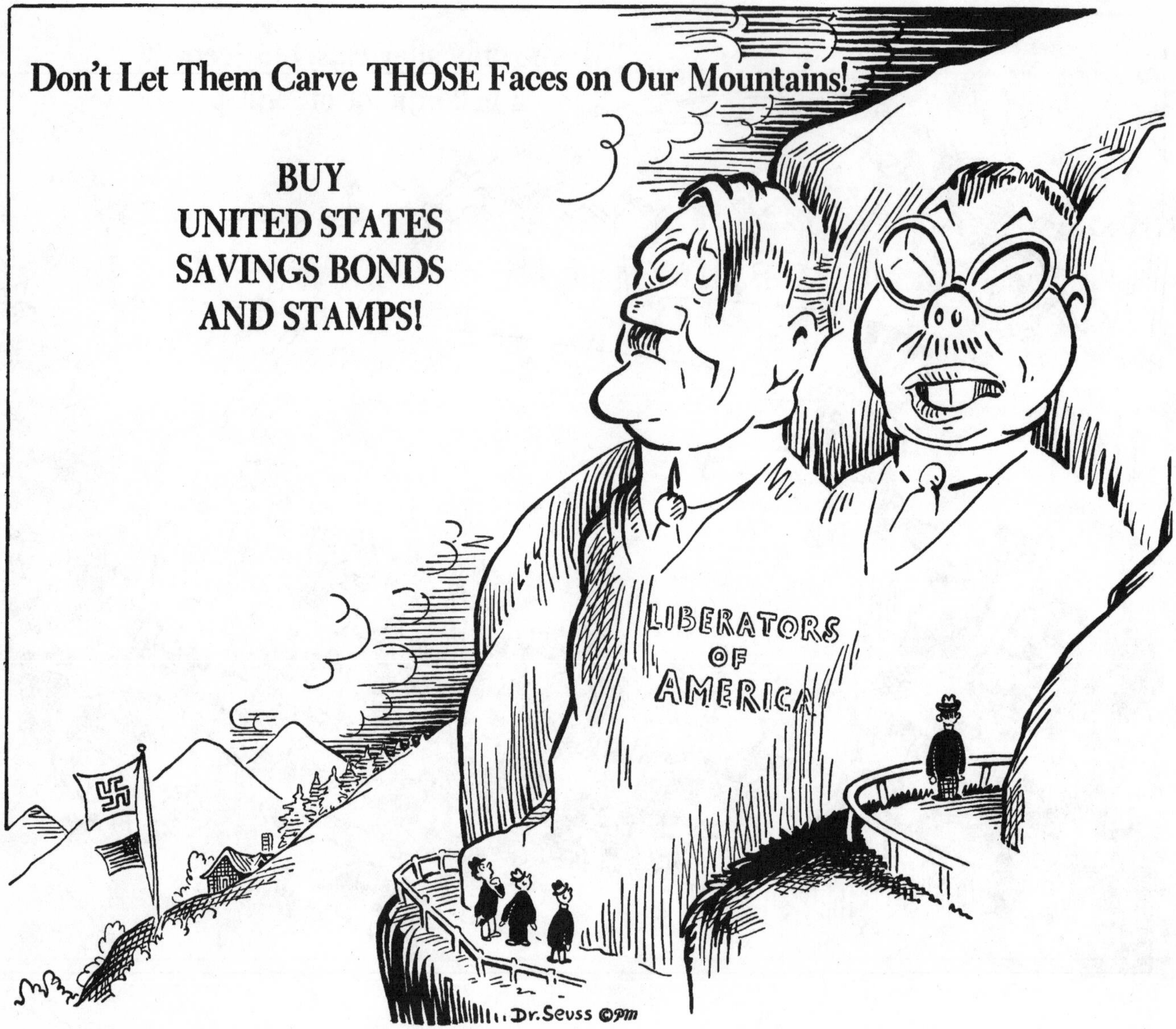
Don't Let Them Carve THOSE Faces on Our Mountains!
BUY
UNITED STATES
SAVINGS BONDS
AND STAMPS!
LIBERATORS
OF
AMERICA
Dr. Seuss

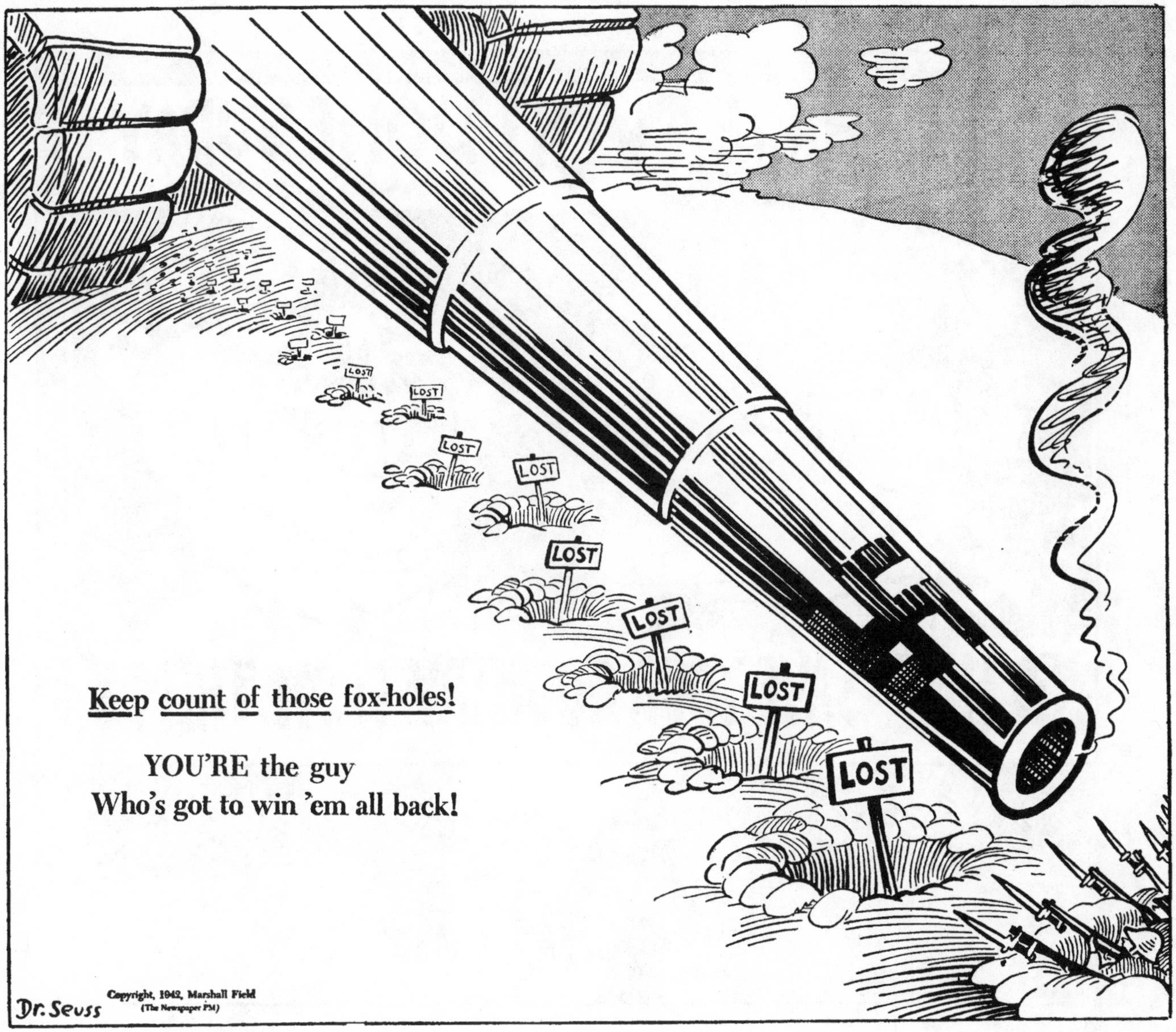
LOST
LOST
LOST
LOST
LOST
LOST
LOST
LOST
Keep count of those fox-holes!
YOU'RE the guy
Who's got to win 'em all back!
Dr. Seuss
Copyright, 1942, Marshall Field
(The Newspaper PM)

147 — February 17, 1942

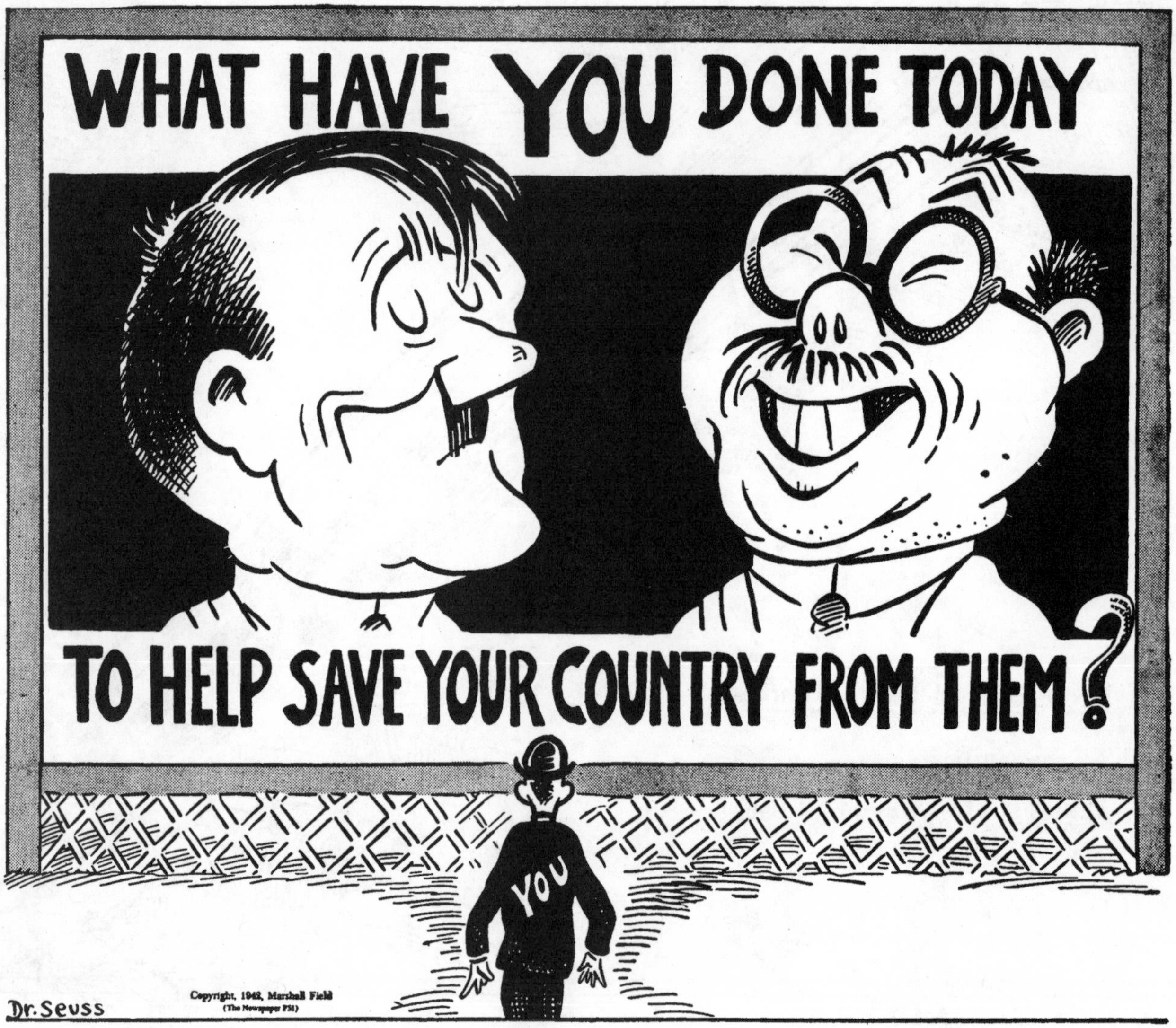
WHAT HAVE YOU DONE TODAY
TO HELP SAVE YOUR COUNTRY FROM THEM?
YOU
Dr. Seuss
Copyright, 1942, Marshall Field
(The Newspaper PM)

The Old Tobacco Juice Where It Counts!

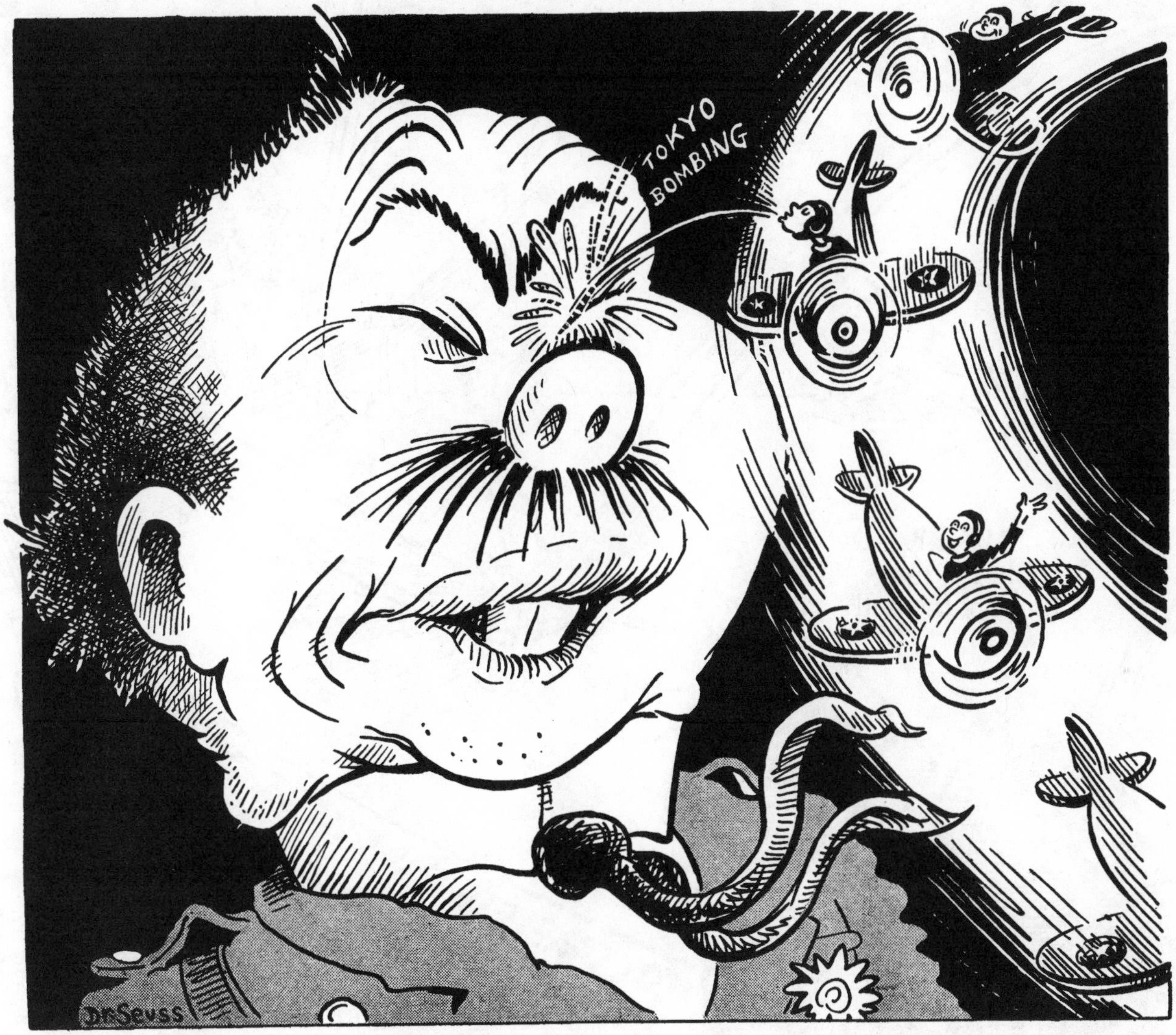
TOKYO BOMBING
DR. SEUSS

149 — April 20, 1942

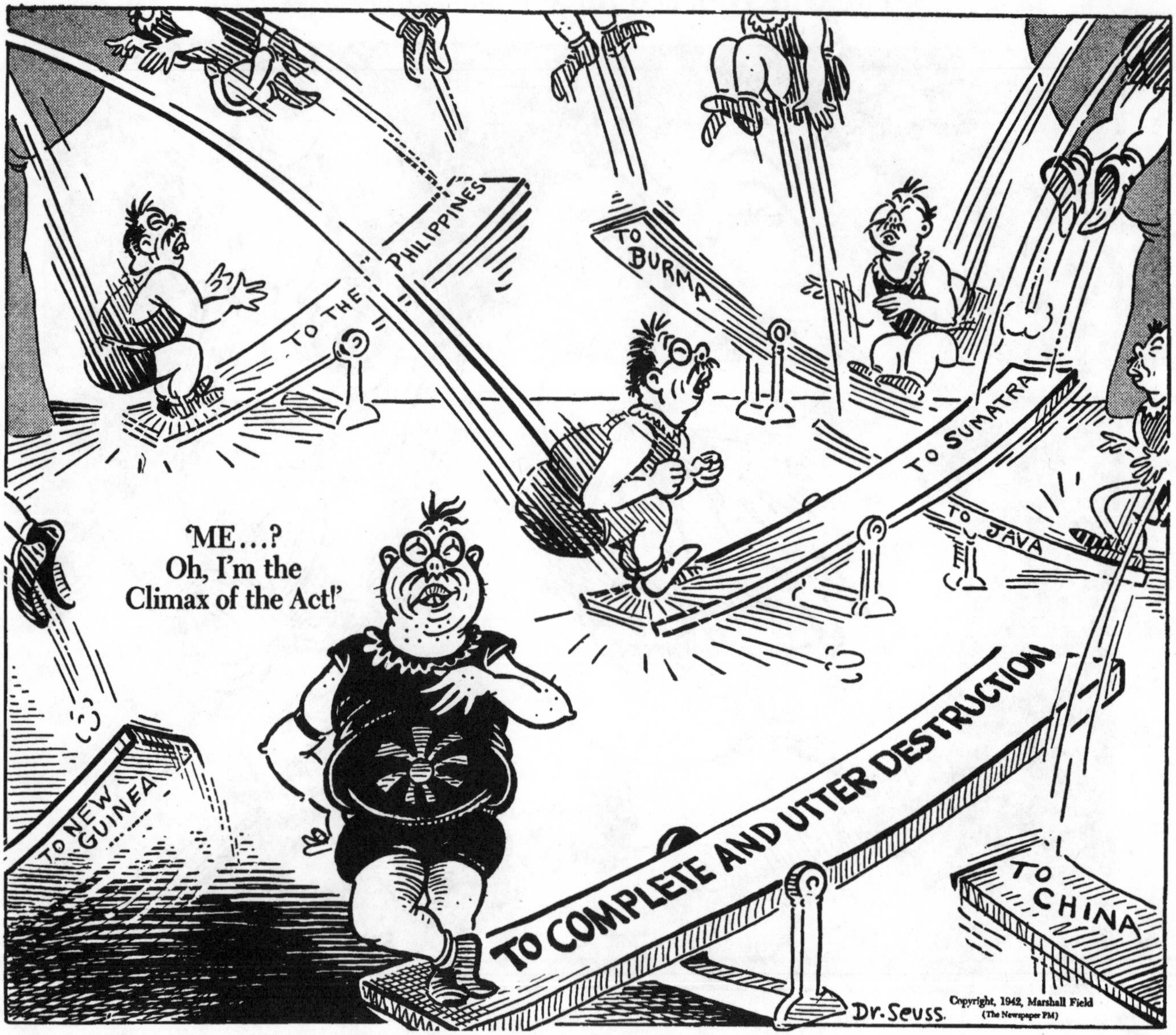
TO THE PHILIPPINES
TO BURMA
TO SUMATRA
TO JAVA
'ME...? Oh, I'm the Climax of the Act!'
TO NEW GUINEA
TO COMPLETE AND UTTER DESTRUCTION
TO CHINA
Dr. Seuss.
Copyright, 1942, Marshall Field (The Newspaper PM)

Playing Musical Chairs . . . For Keeps, and With Experts

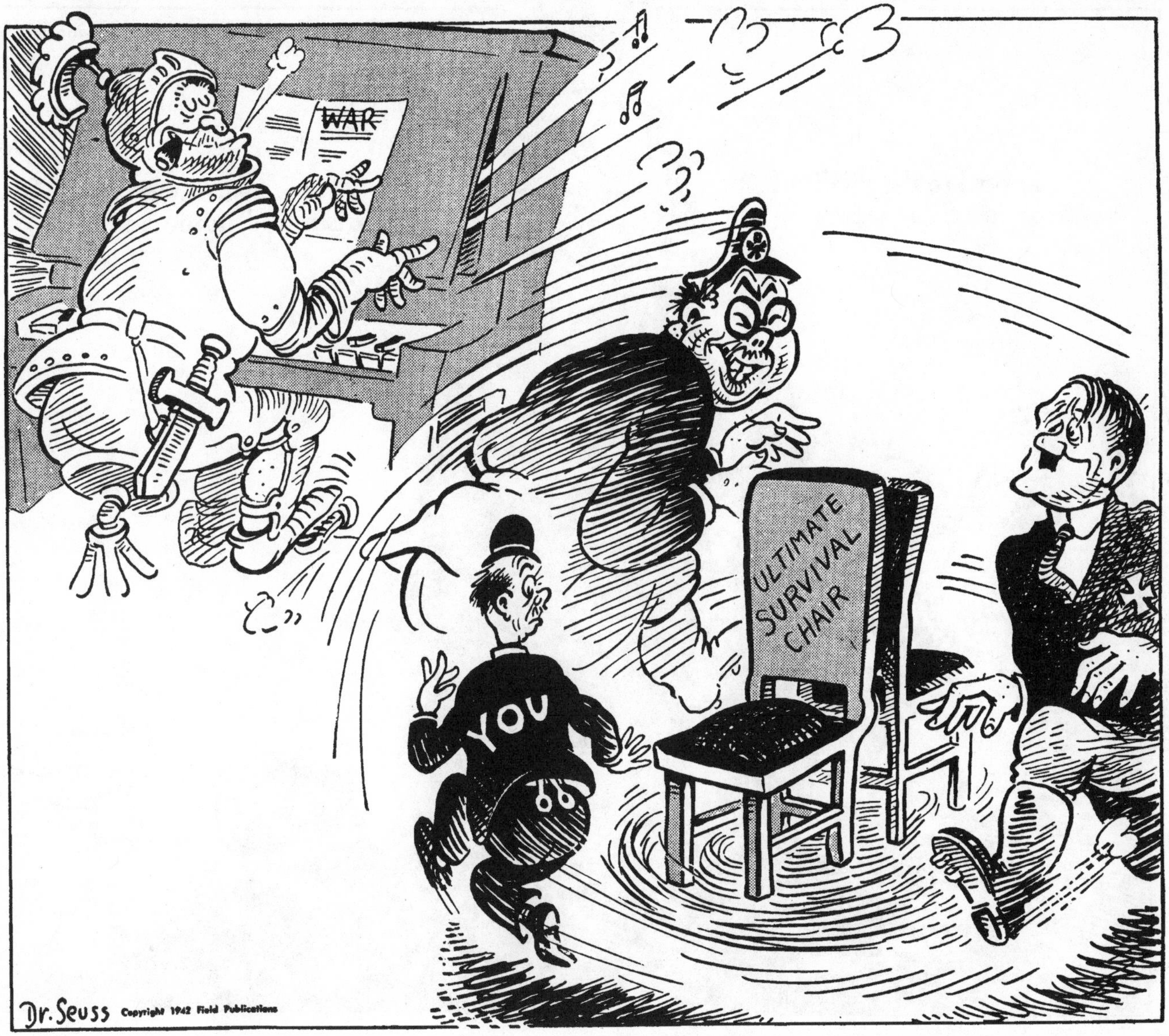
WAR
ULTIMATE SURVIVAL CHAIR
YOU
Dr. Seuss
Copyright 1942 Field Publications

151 — August 13, 1942

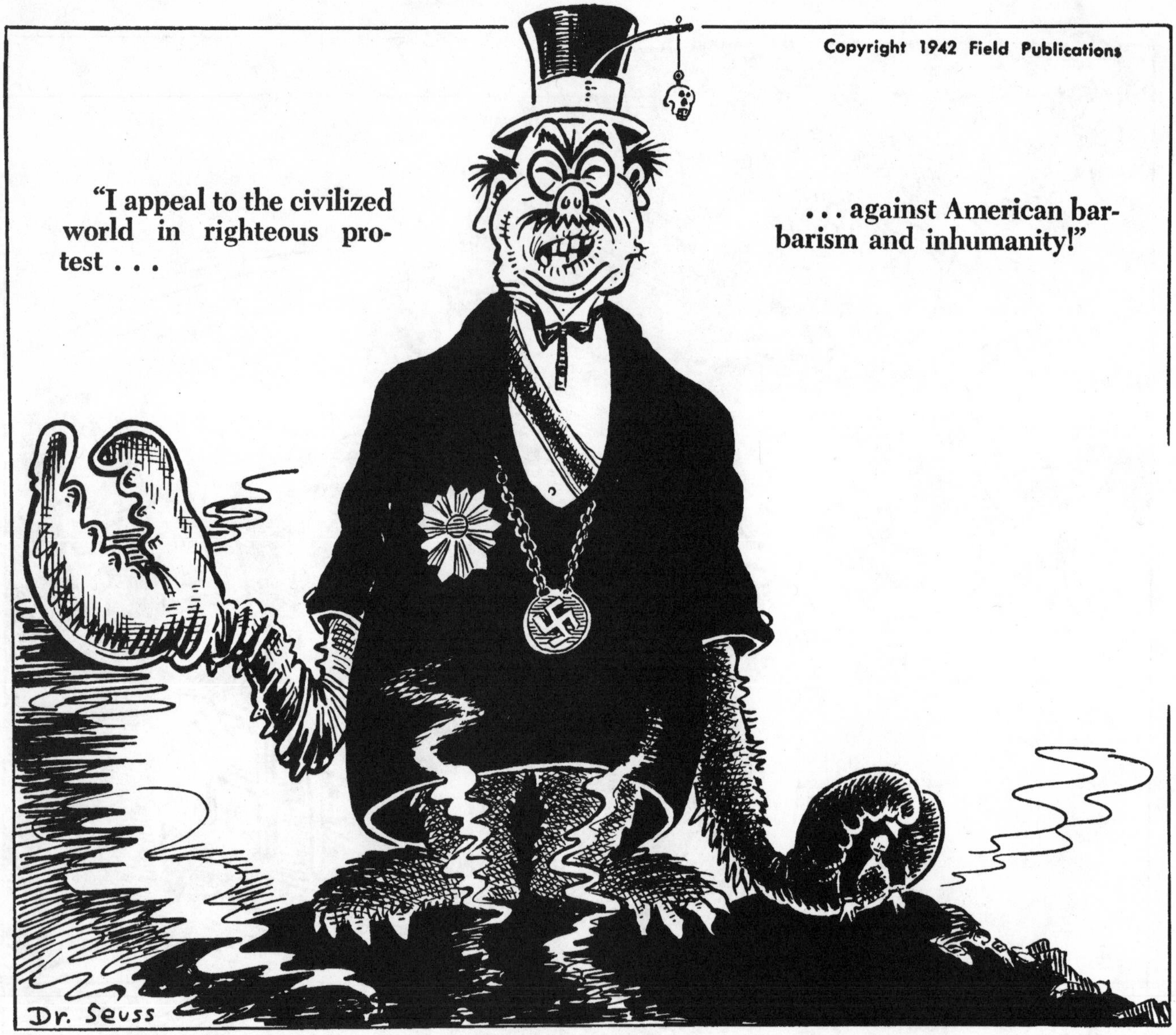
Copyright 1942 Field Publications
"I appeal to the civilized world in righteous pro-test . . .
. . . against American bar-barism and inhumanity!"
Dr. Seuss

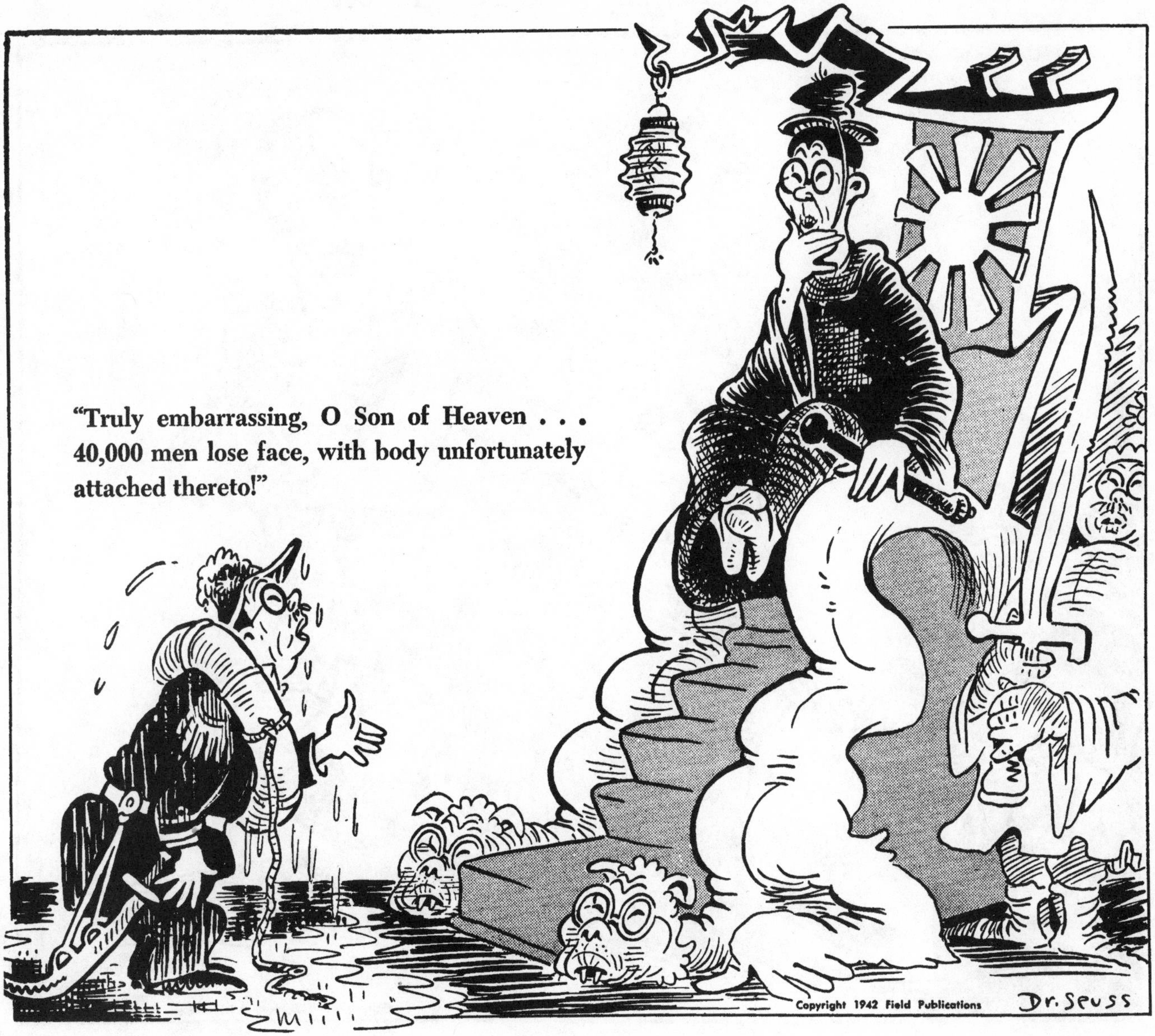
"Truly embarrassing, O Son of Heaven . . .
40,000 men lose face, with body unfortunately
attached thereto!"
Copyright 1942 Field Publications
Dr. Seuss

153 — November 18, 1942

Married Exactly One Year Todav

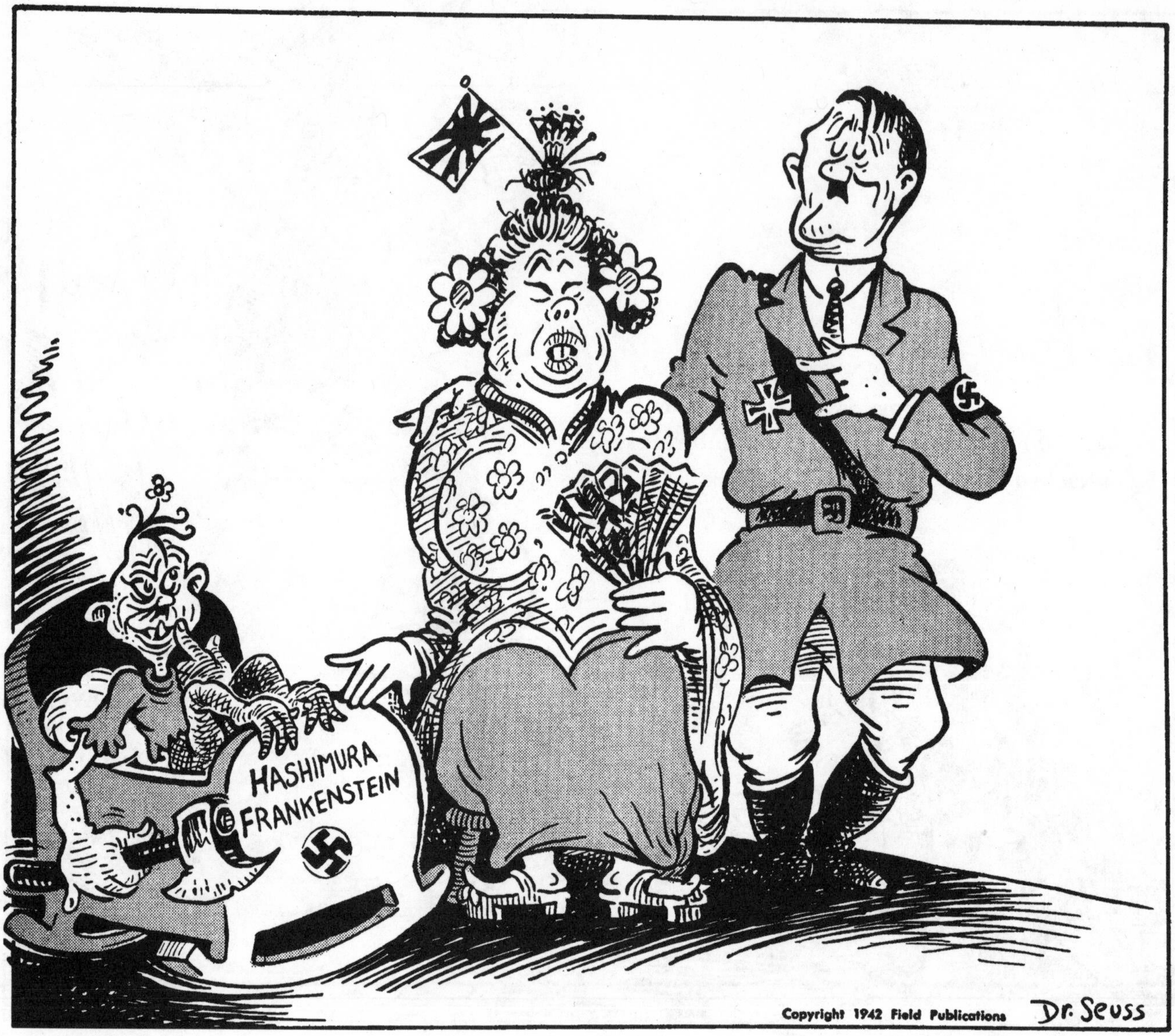
HASHIMURA
FRANKENSTEIN
Copyright 1942 Field Publications
Dr. Seuss

154 — December 7, 1942

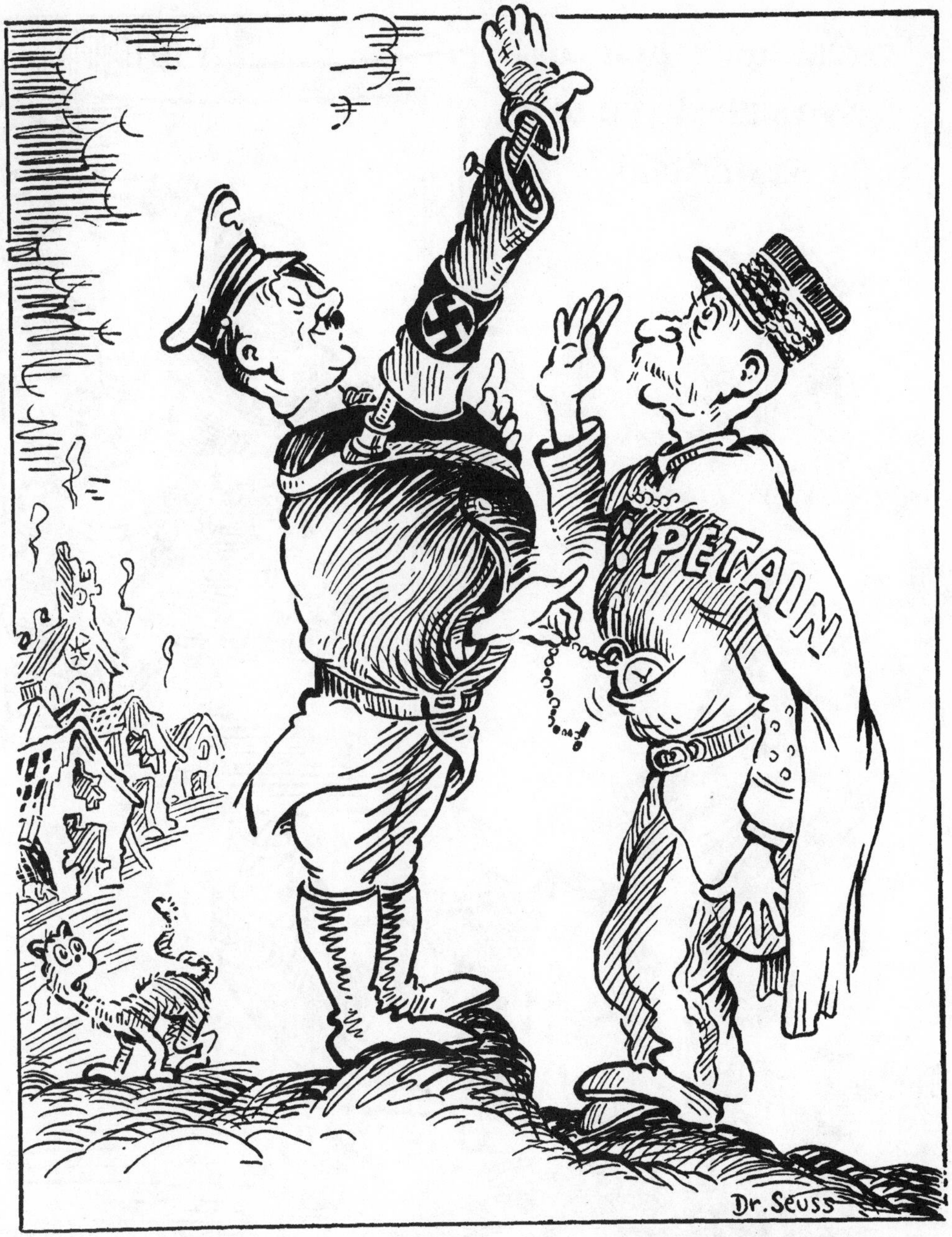
PETAIN
DR. SEUSS

"Put your arm up like this, and your troubles are over . . ."
By Dr. Seuss

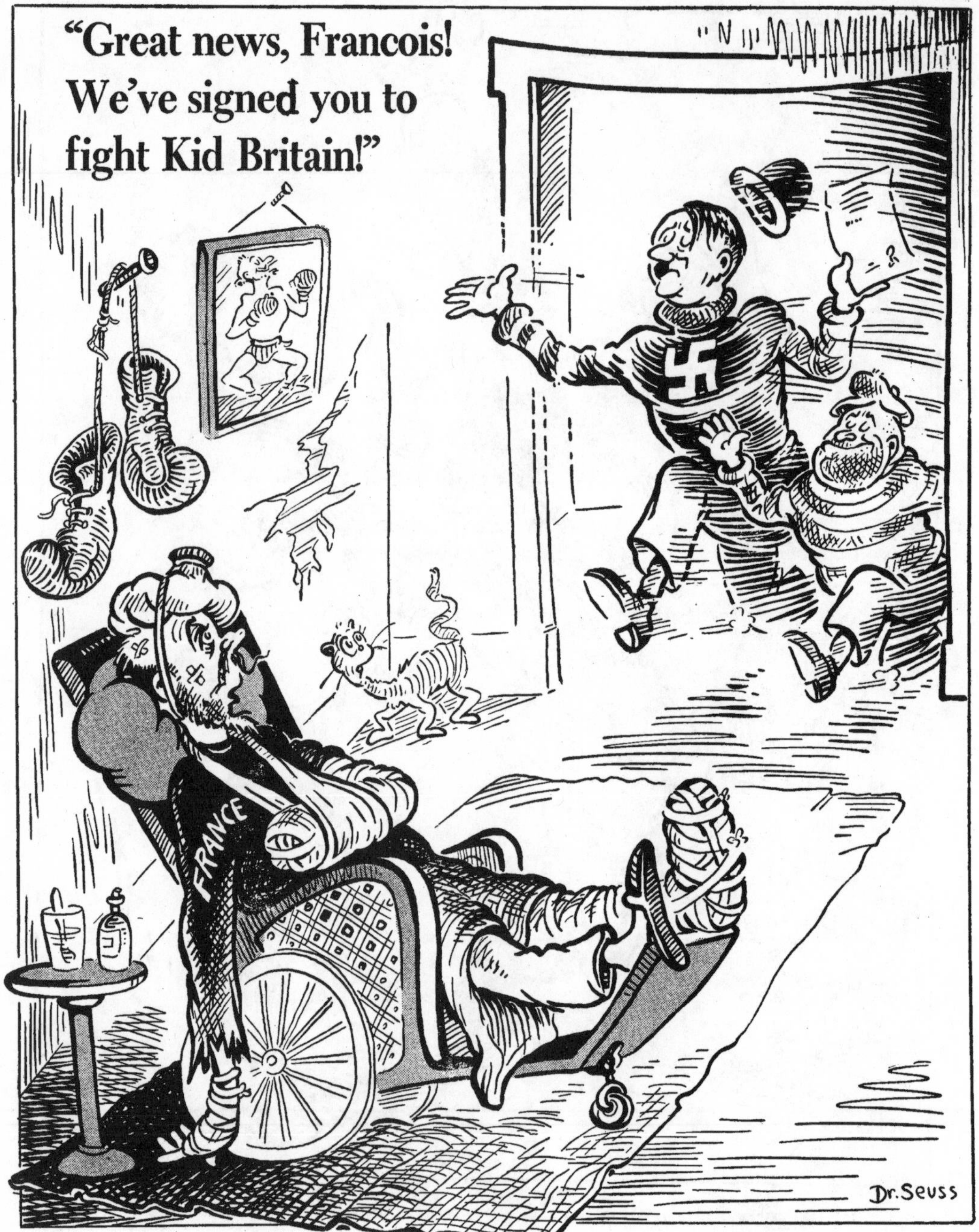
"Great news, Francois! We've signed you to fight Kid Britain!"
FRANCE
Dr. Seuss

156 — June 6, 1941

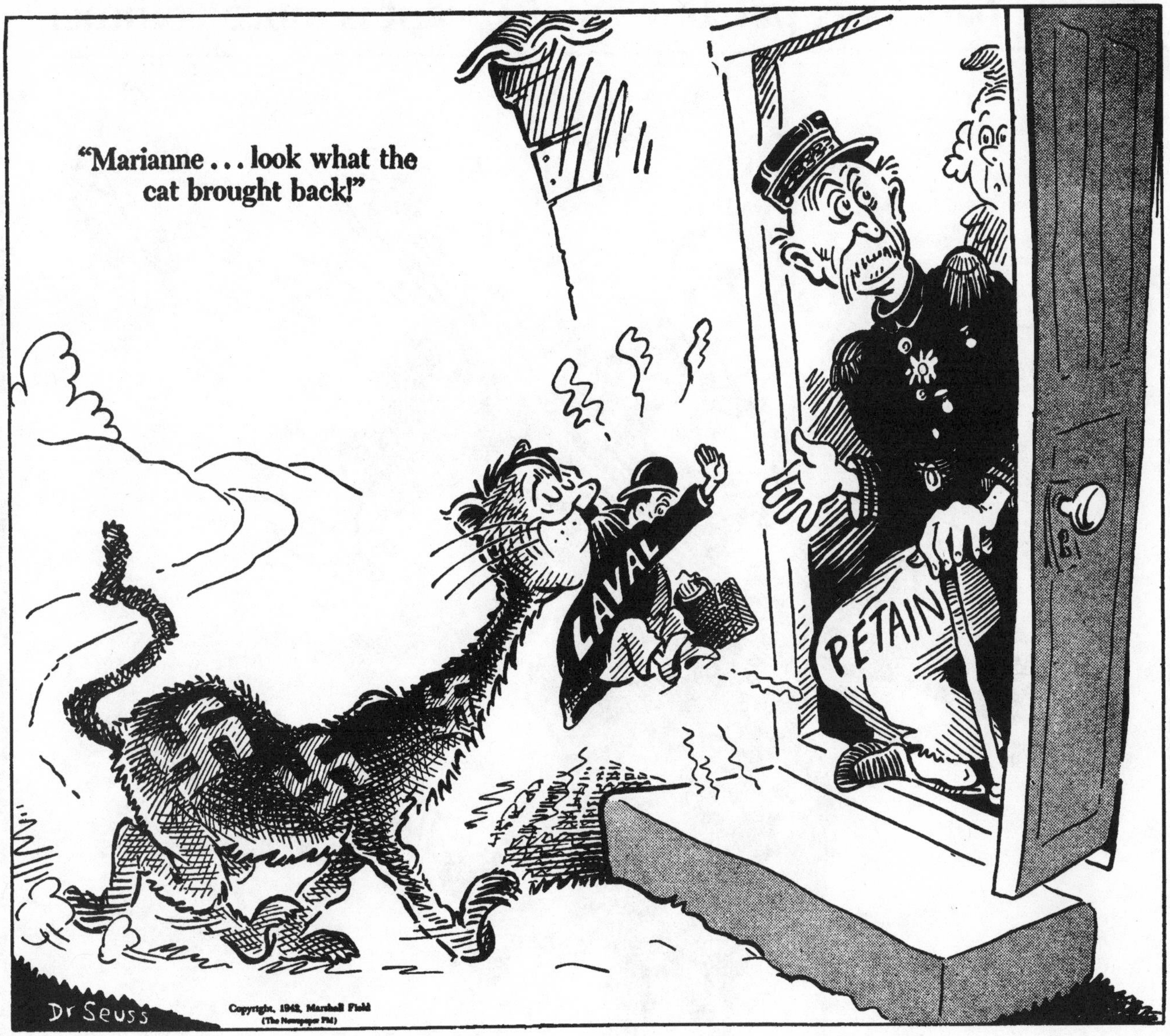
"Marianne . . . look what the cat brought back!"
LAVAL
PETAIN
Dr Seuss
Copyright, 1942, Marshall Field
(The Newspaper PM)

157 — April 15, 1942

'Not a bad tone, pal, but what I want is more volume!'

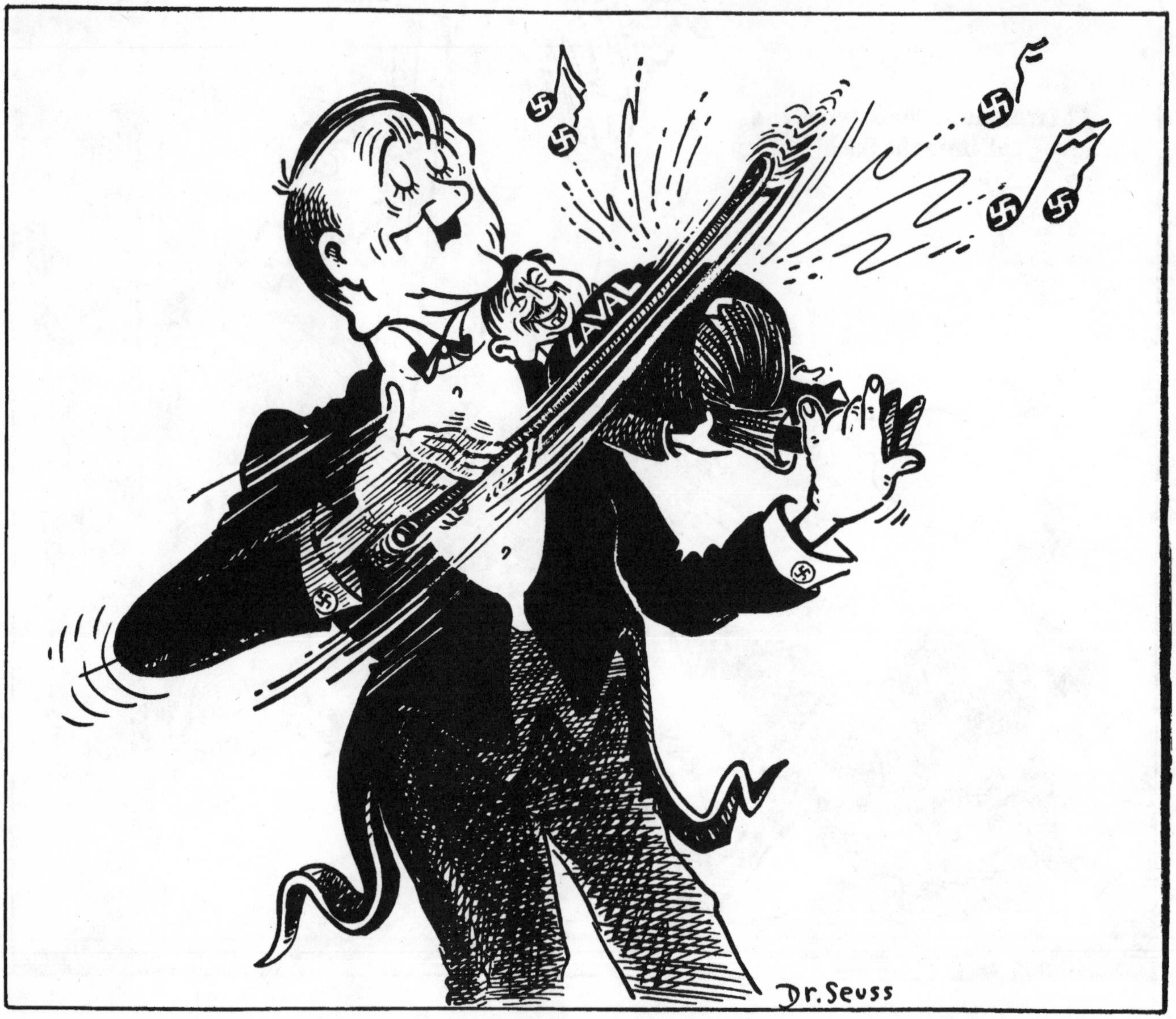
LAVAL
Dr. Seuss

158 — June 19, 1942

Down the River

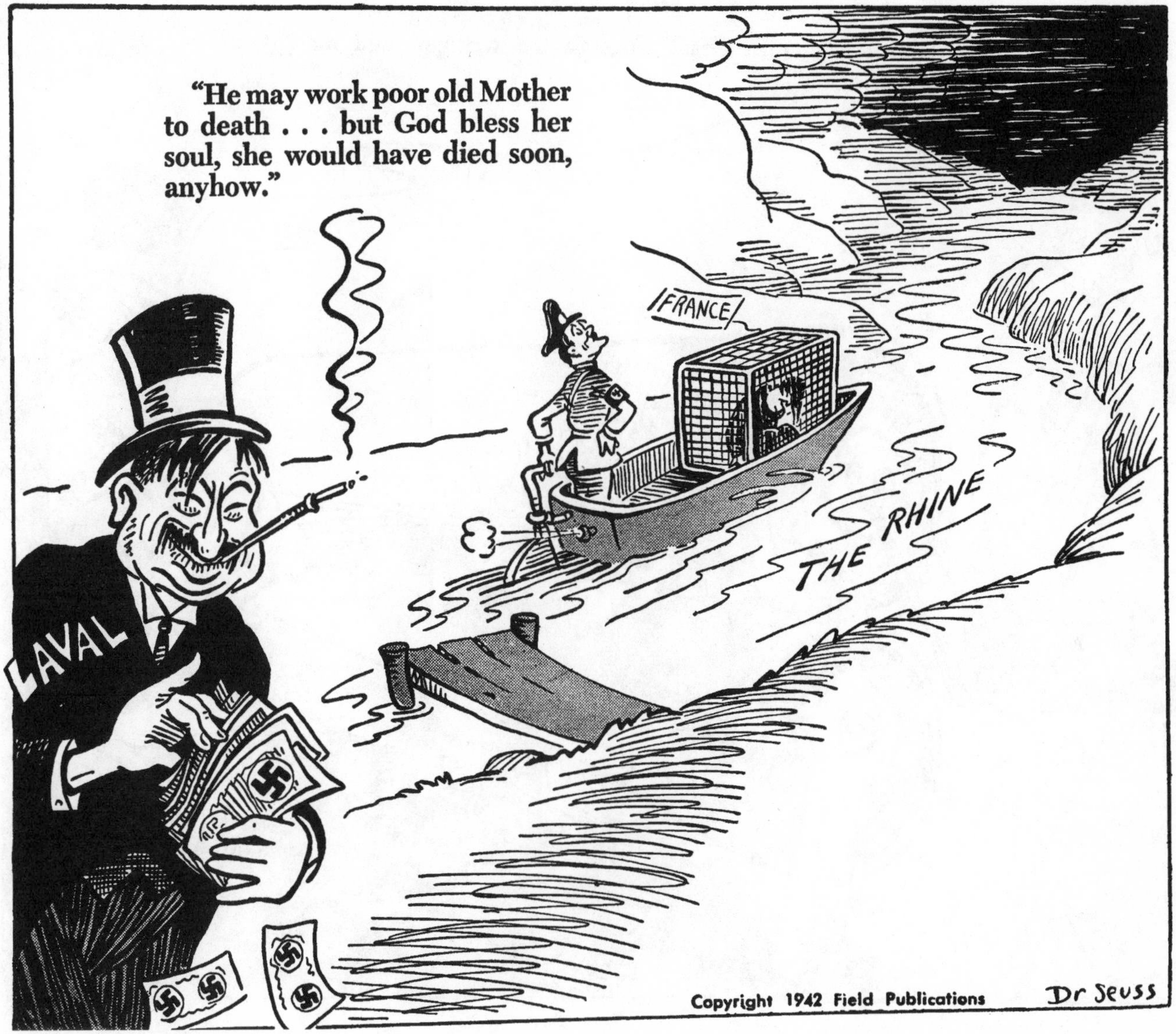
"He may work poor old Mother to death . . . but God bless her soul, she would have died soon, anyhow."
FRANCE
THE RHINE
LAVAL
Copyright 1942 Field Publications
Dr Seuss

159 – October 9, 1942

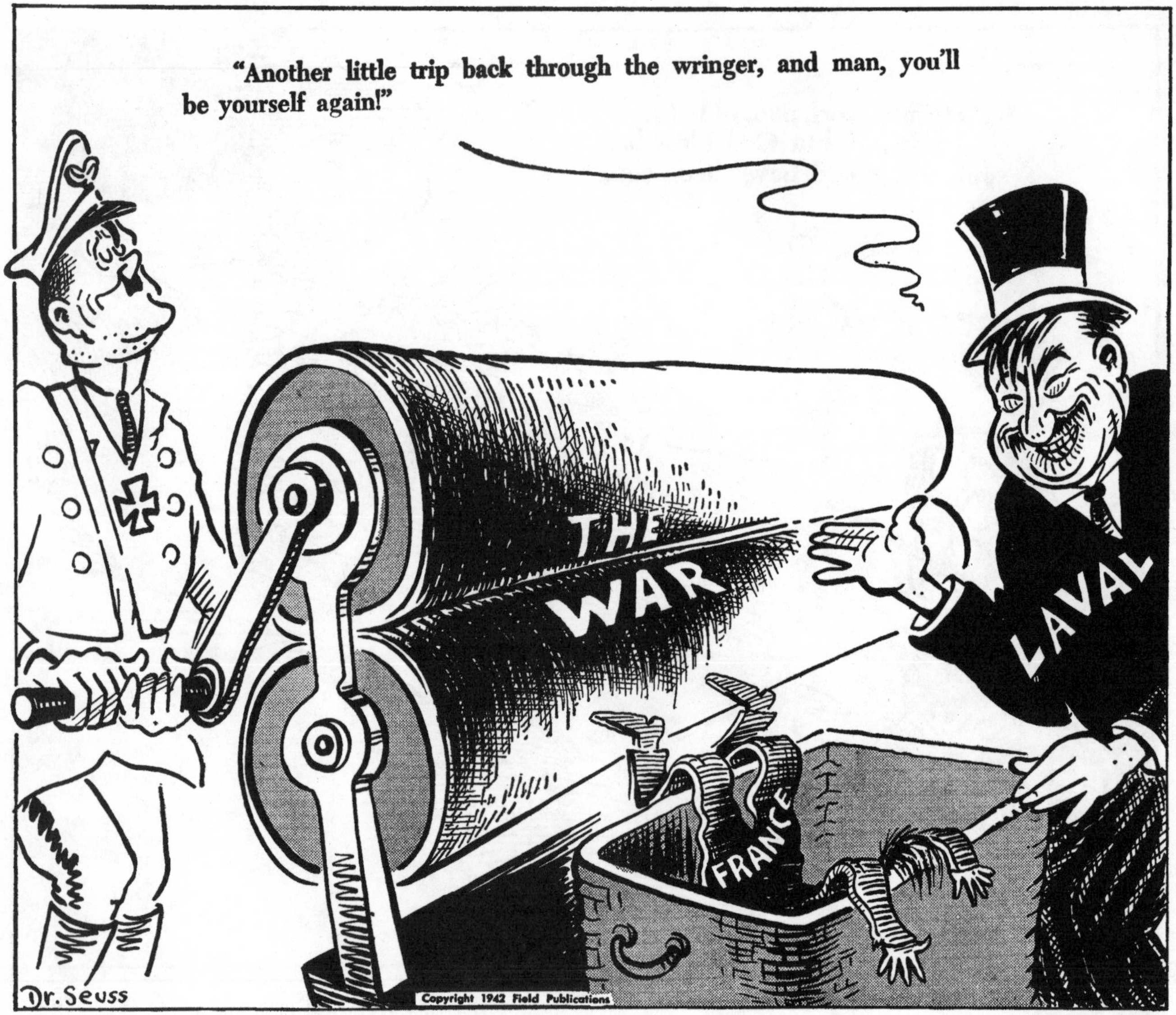
THE WAR
LAVAL
FRANCE
Dr. Seuss
Copyright 1942 Field Publications

"Another little trip back through the wringer, and man, you'll be yourself again!"

160 — October 19, 1942

Communique: "The annihilation is proceeding according to schedule."

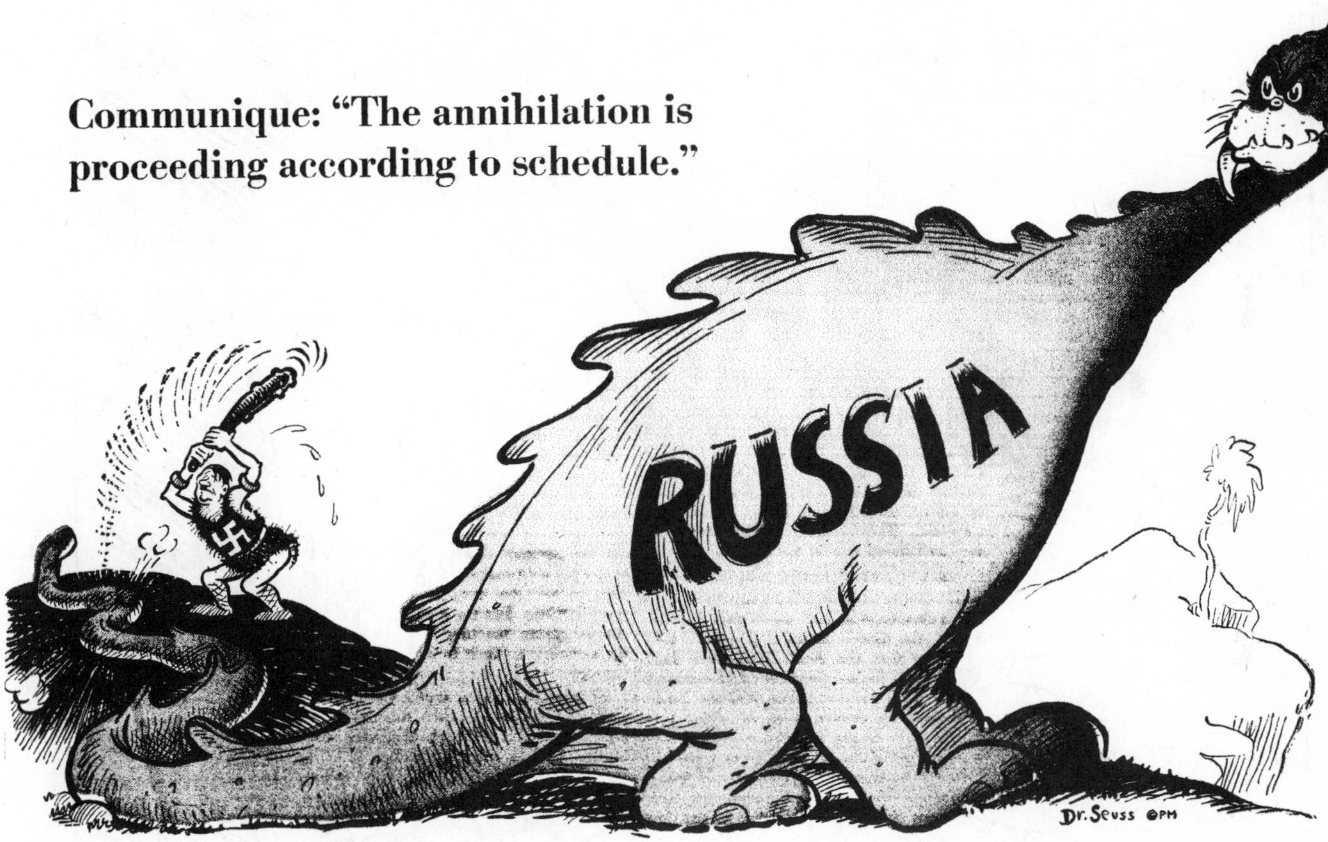
RUSSIA
Dr. Seuss ©PM

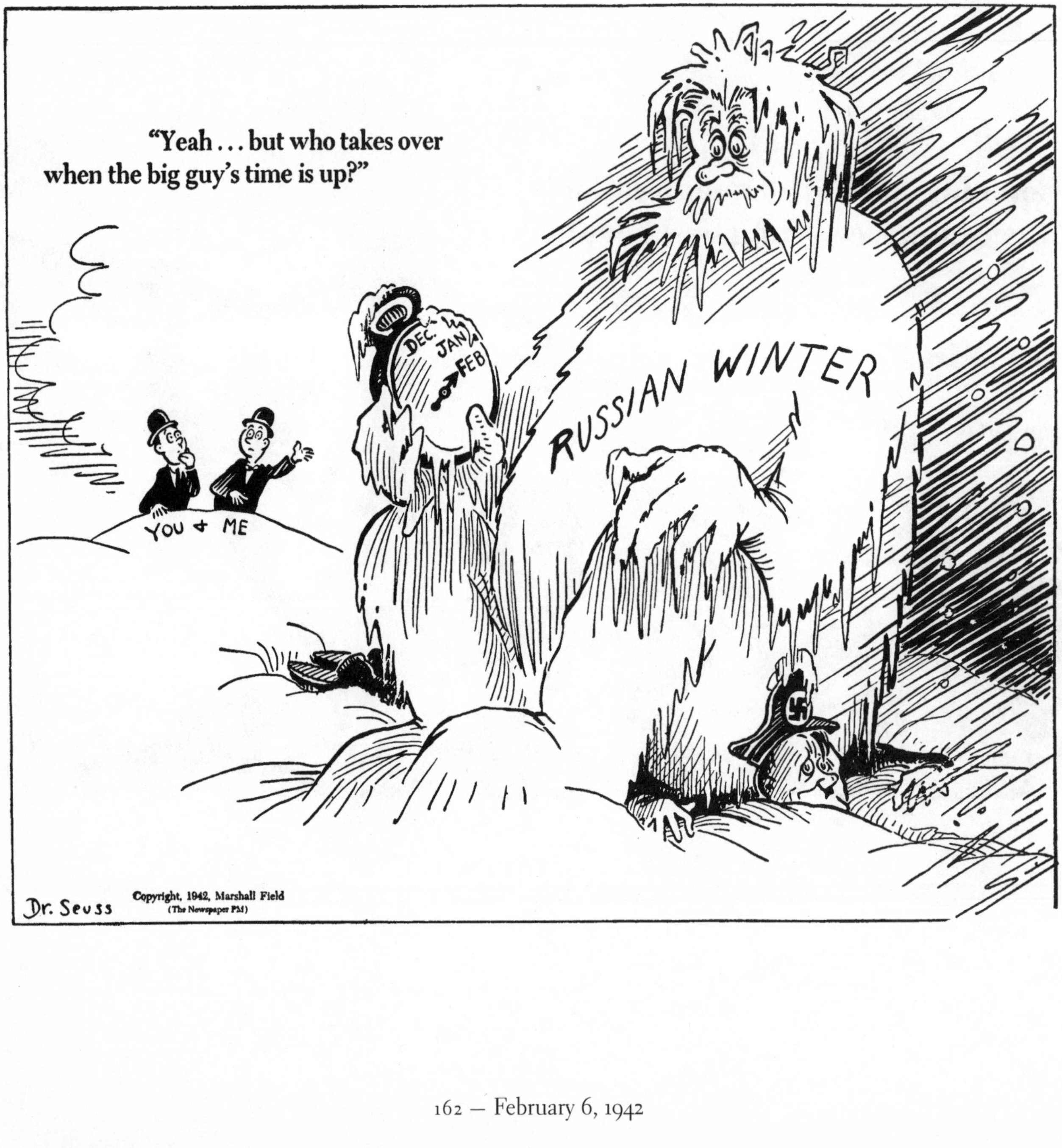
DEC.
JAN
FEB
RUSSIAN WINTER
YOU + ME
Dr. Seuss
Copyright, 1942, Marshall Field
(The Newspaper PM)

"Yeah . . . but who takes over when the big guy's time is up?"

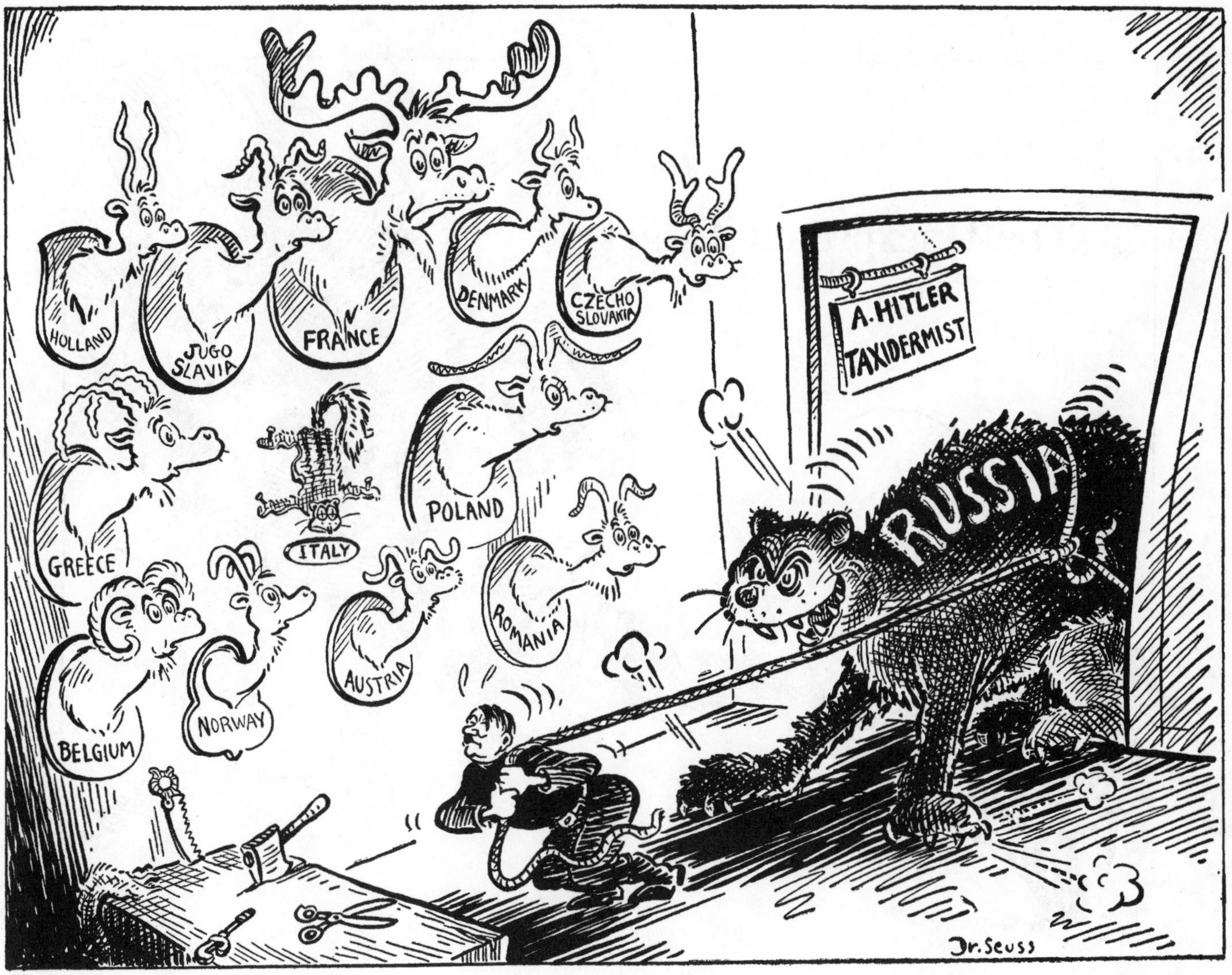
HOLLAND
JUGO SLAVIA
FRANCE
DENMARK
CZECHO SLOVAKIA
A. HITLER TAXIDERMIST
GREECE
ITALY
POLAND
RUSSIA
BELGIUM
NORWAY
AUSTRIA
ROMANIA
Dr. Seuss

163 – June 25, 1941

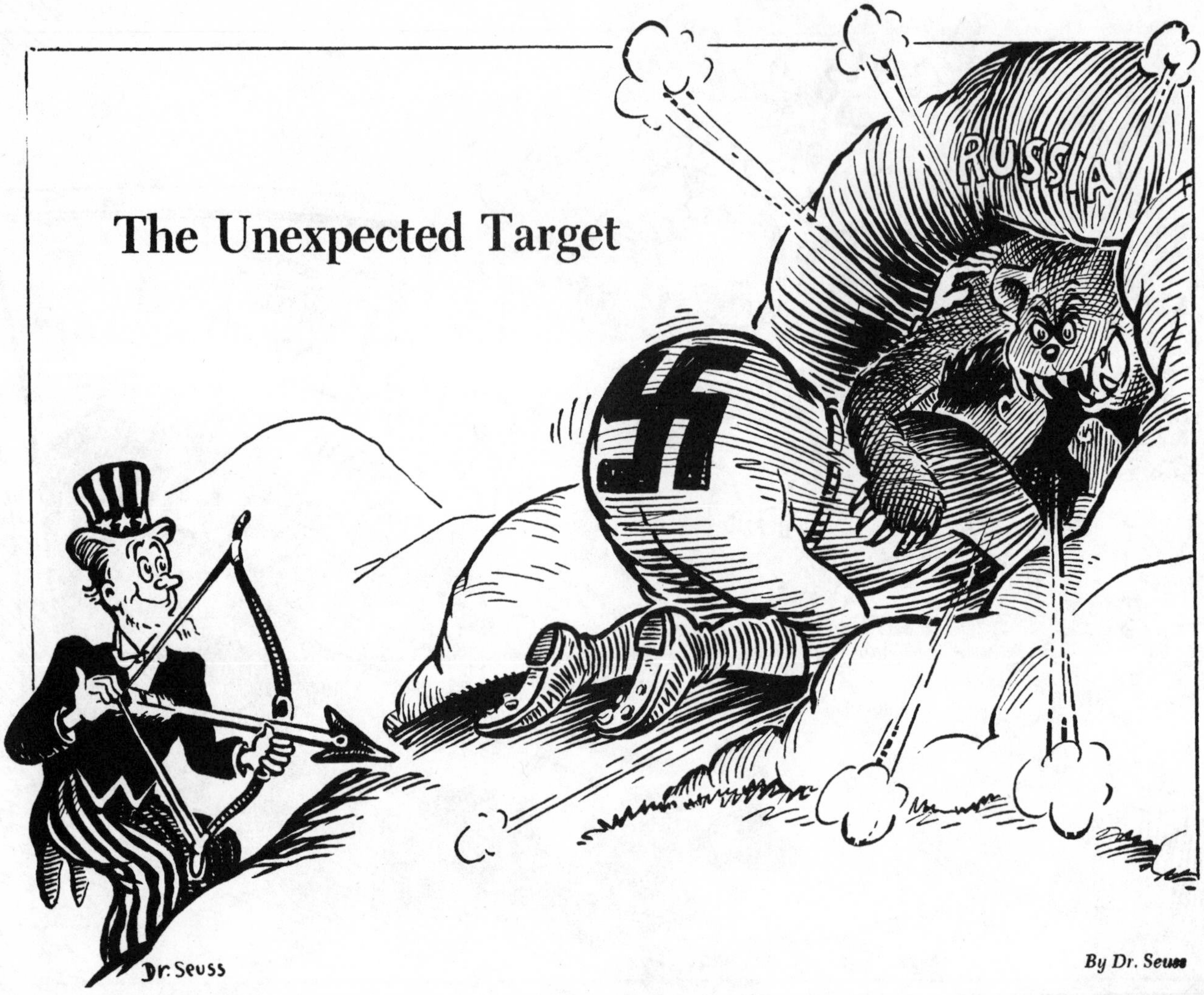
The Unexpected Target
RUSSIA
Dr. Seuss
By Dr. Seuss

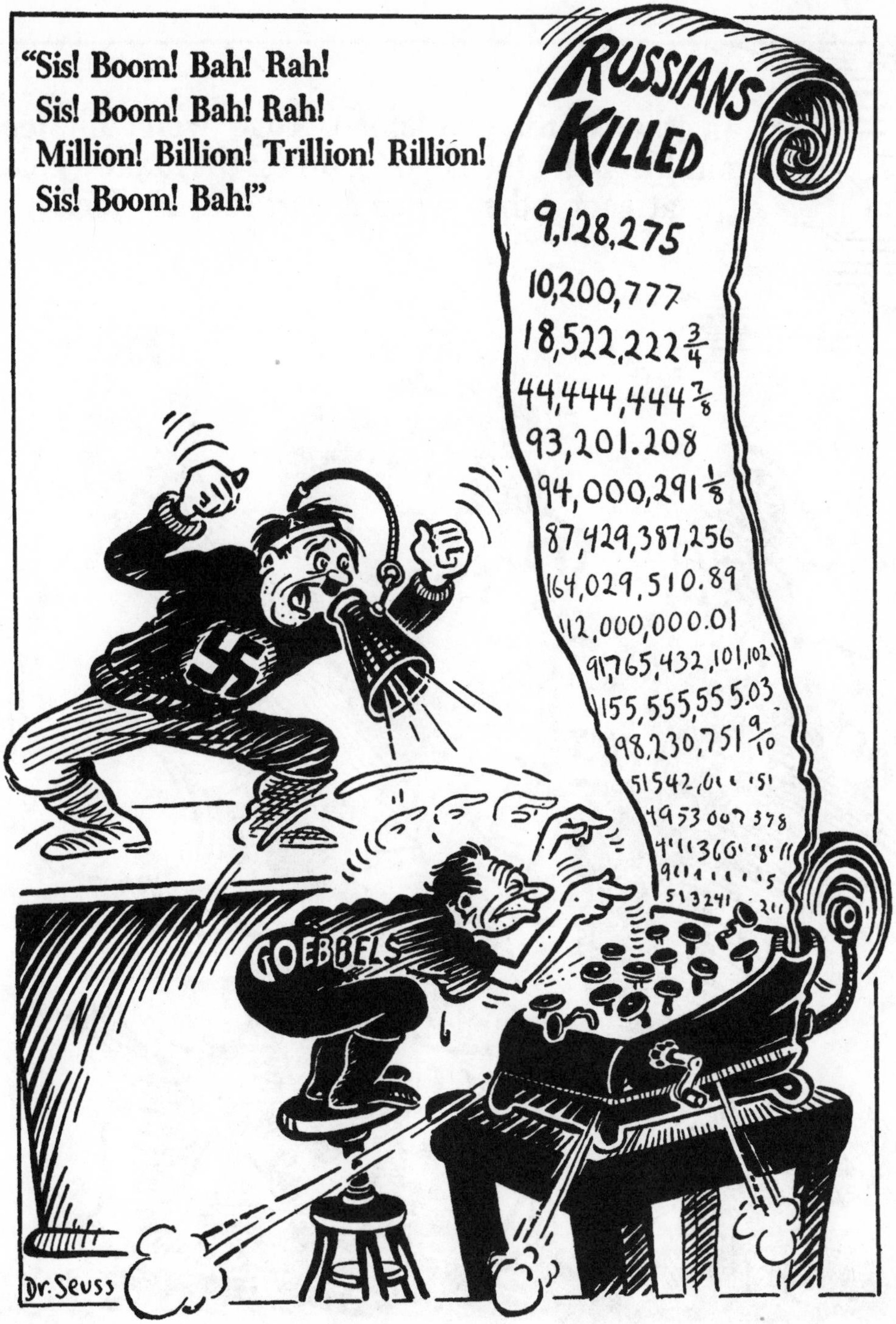
"Sis! Boom! Bah! Rah!
Sis! Boom! Bah! Rah!
Million! Billion! Trillion! Rillion!
Sis! Boom! Bah!"
RUSSIANS KILLED
9,128,275
10,200,777
18,522,222 3/4
44,444,444 7/8
93,201.208
94,000,291 1/8
87,429,387,256
164,029,510.89
112,000,000.01
91,765,432,101,102
155,555,555.03
98,230,751 9/10
GOEBBELS
Dr. Seuss

165 — July 10, 1941

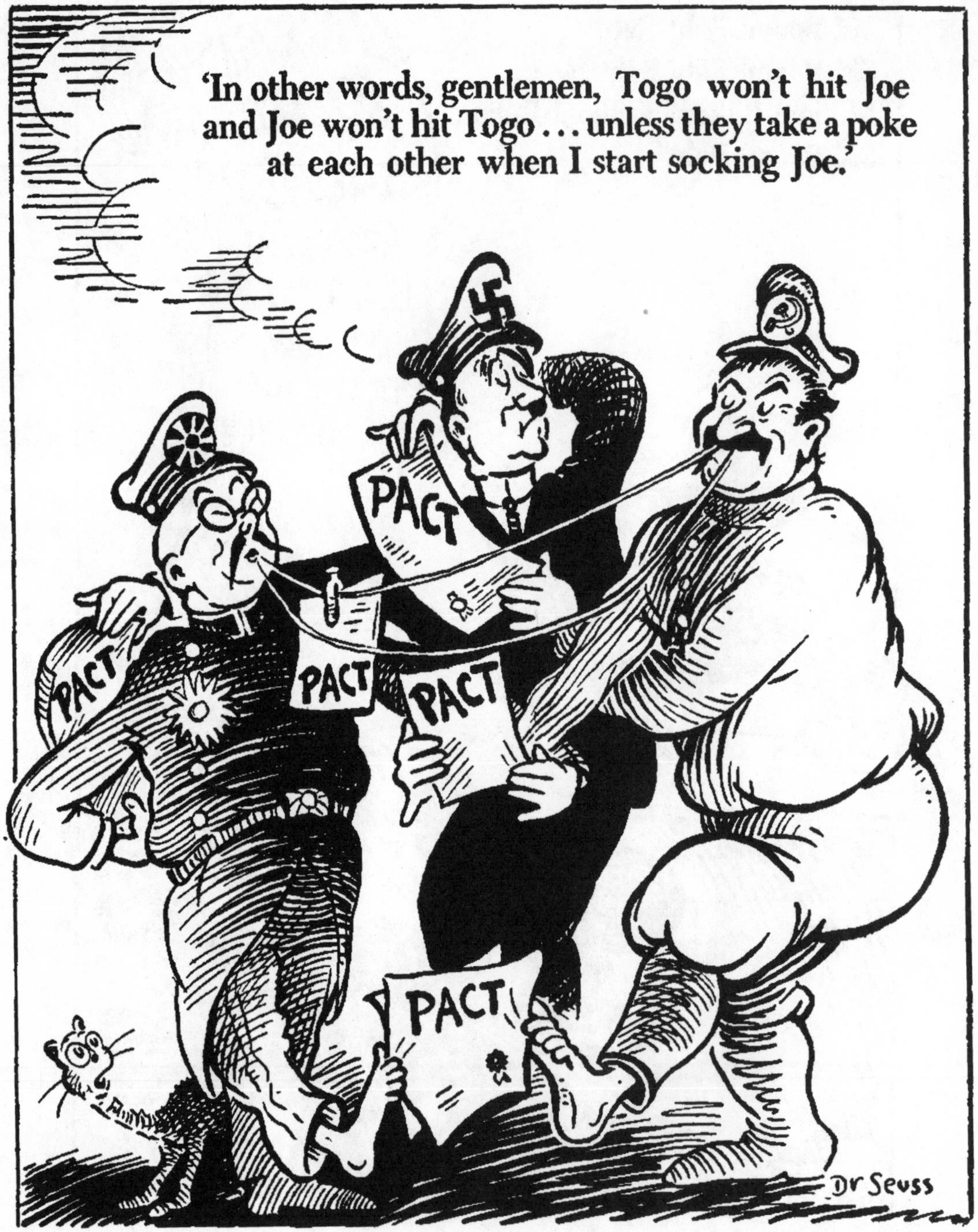
'In other words, gentlemen, Togo won't hit Joe and Joe won't hit Togo . . . unless they take a poke at each other when I start socking Joe.'
PACT
PACT
PACT
PACT
PACT
Dr Seuss

166 — June 20, 1941

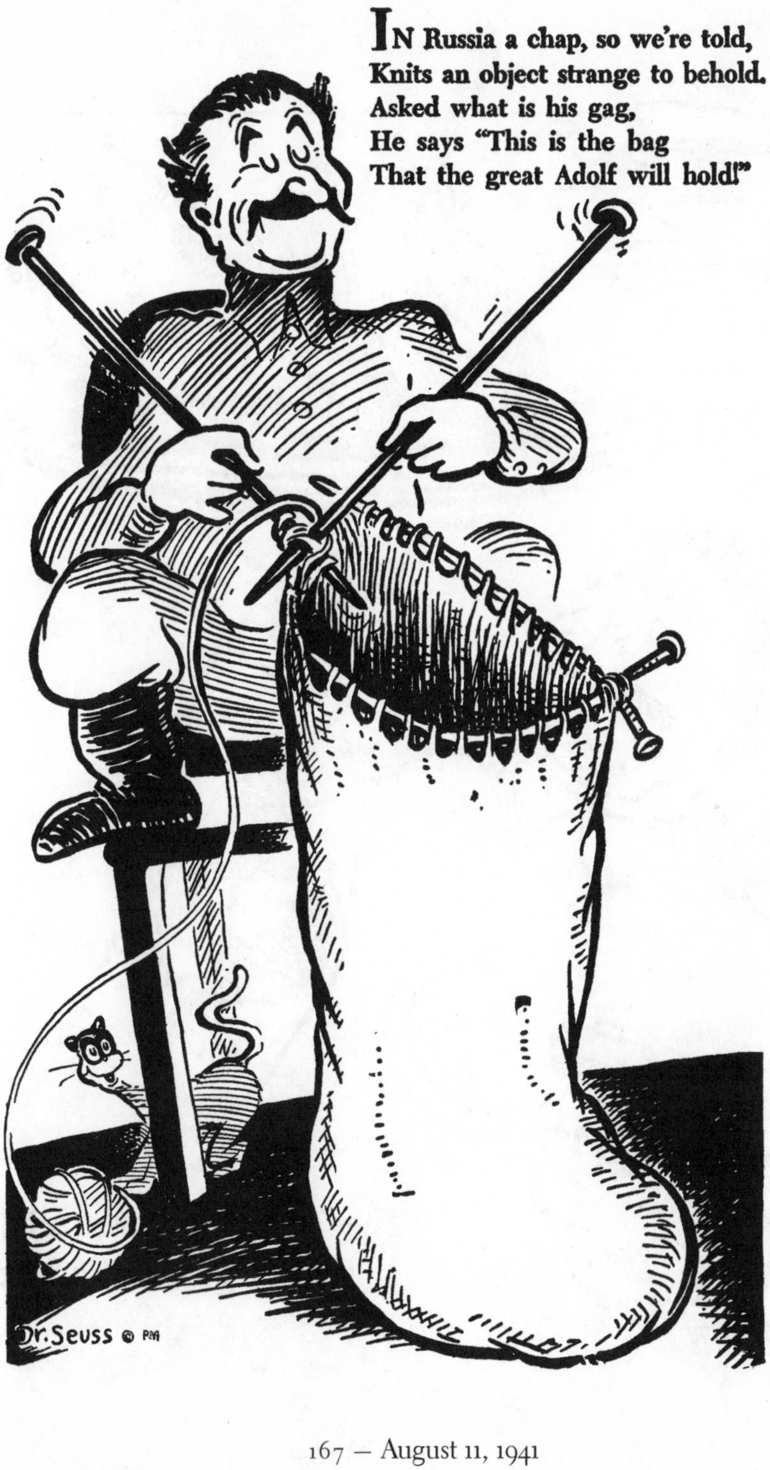
IN Russia a chap, so we're told,
Knits an object strange to behold.
Asked what is his gag,
He says "This is the bag
That the great Adolf will hold!"
Dr. Seuss © PM

167 — August 11, 1941

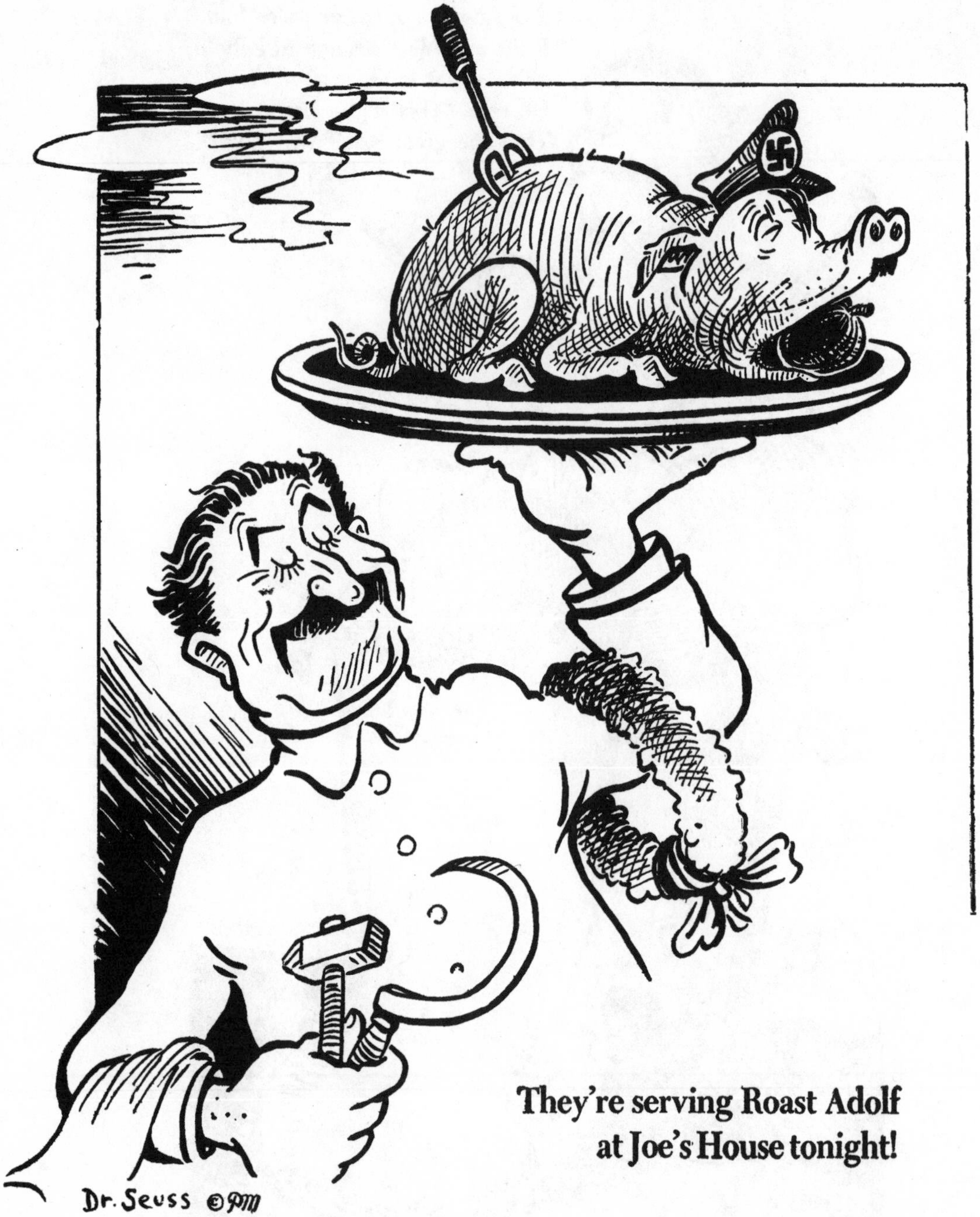
Dr. Seuss ©PM

They're serving Roast Adolf
at Joe's House tonight!

168 – December 24, 1941

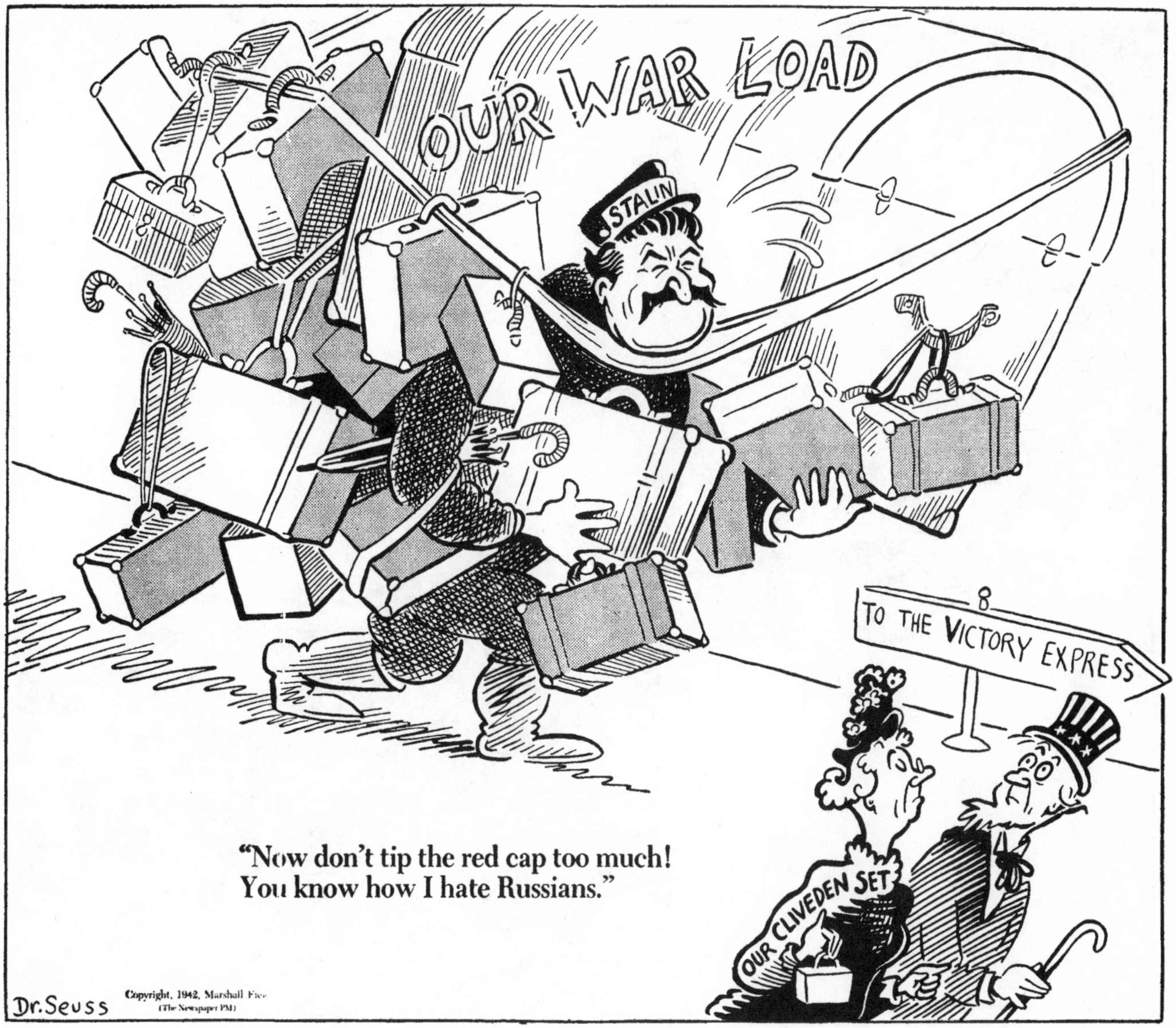
OUR WAR LOAD
STALIN
TO THE VICTORY EXPRESS
OUR CLIVEDEN SET
Dr. Seuss
Copyright, 1942, Marshall Fie
(The Newspaper PM)

"Now don't tip the red cap too much!
You know how I hate Russians."

169 — February 19, 1942

Velvet Carpet to the Oil Well

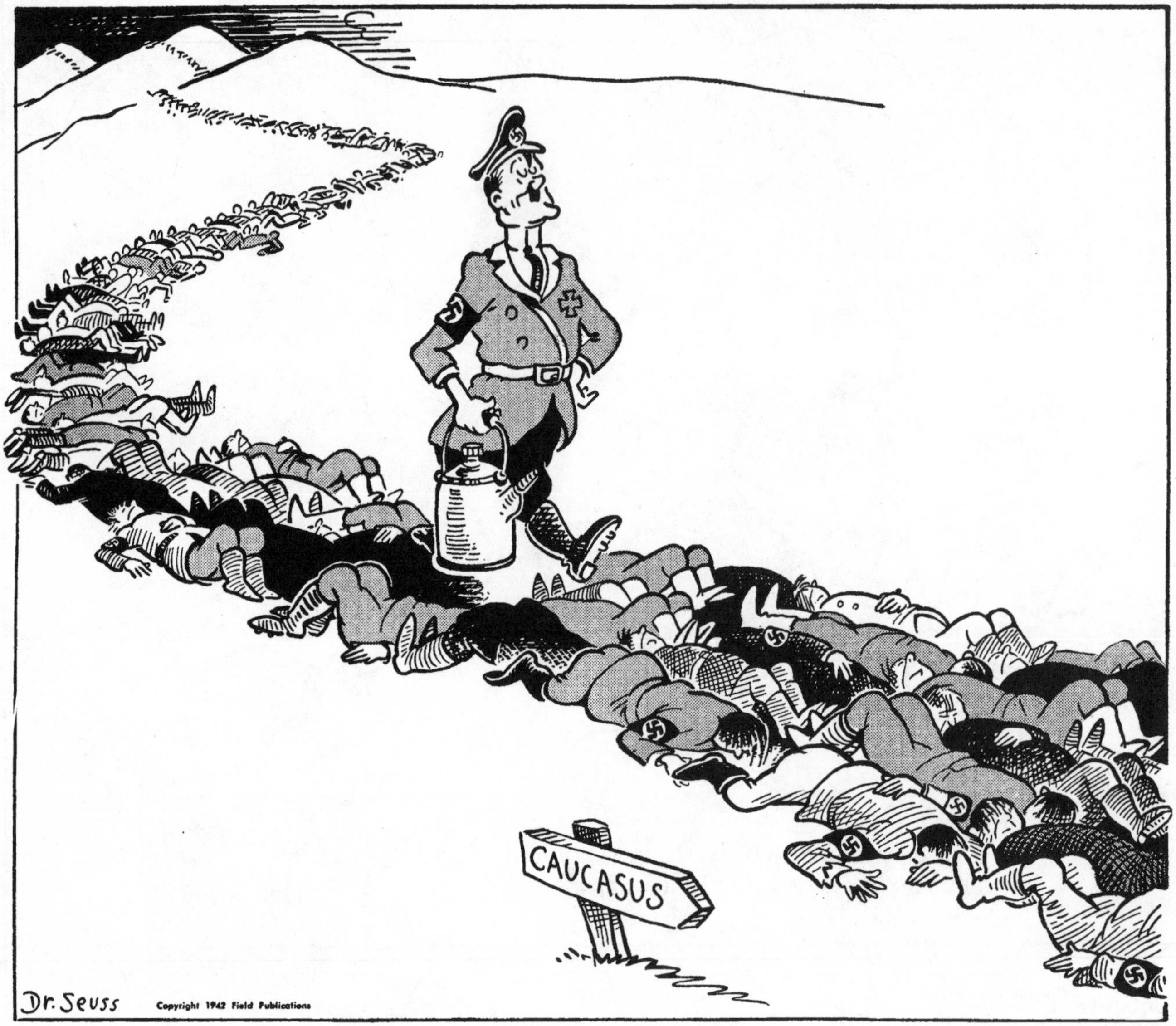
CAUCASUS
Dr. Seuss
Copyright 1942 Field Publications

170 — August 6, 1942

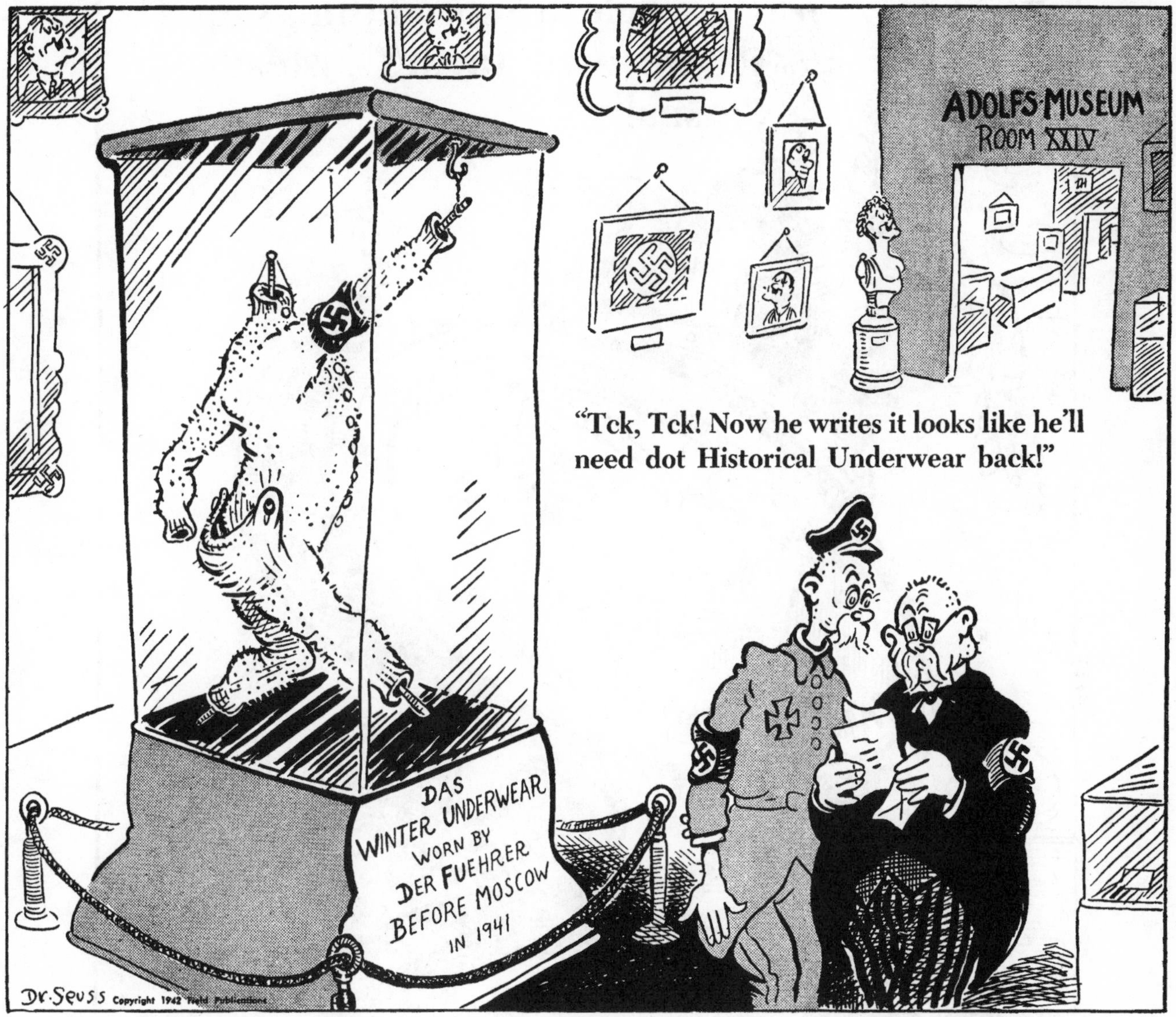
ADOLFS·MUSEUM
ROOM XXIV
DAS
WINTER UNDERWEAR
WORN BY
DER FUEHRER
BEFORE MOSCOW
IN 1941
Dr. Seuss Copyright 1942 Field Publications
"Tck, Tck! Now he writes it looks like he'll need dot Historical Underwear back!"

171 — August 27, 1942

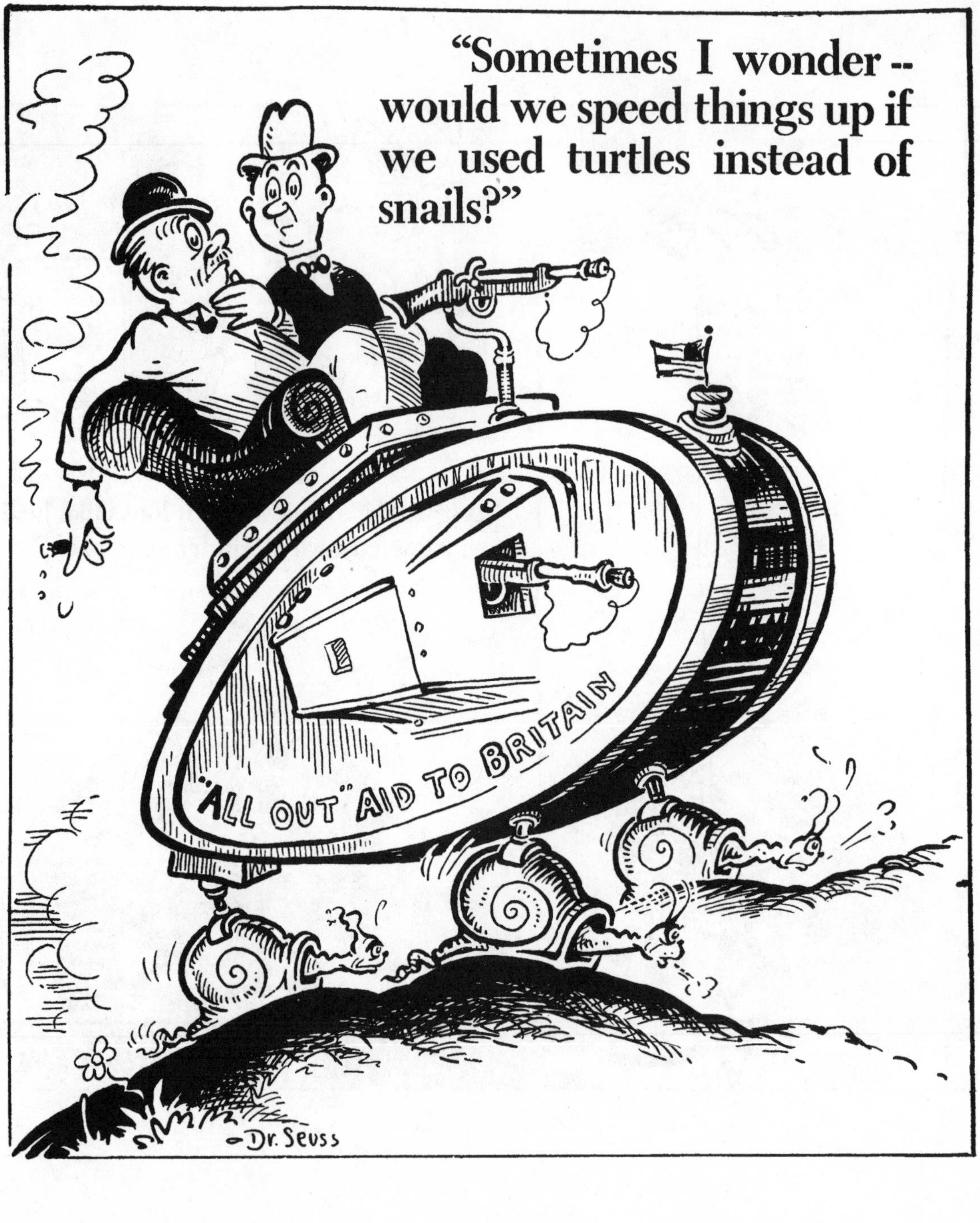
"Sometimes I wonder -- would we speed things up if we used turtles instead of snails?"
"ALL OUT" AID TO BRITAIN
Dr. Seuss

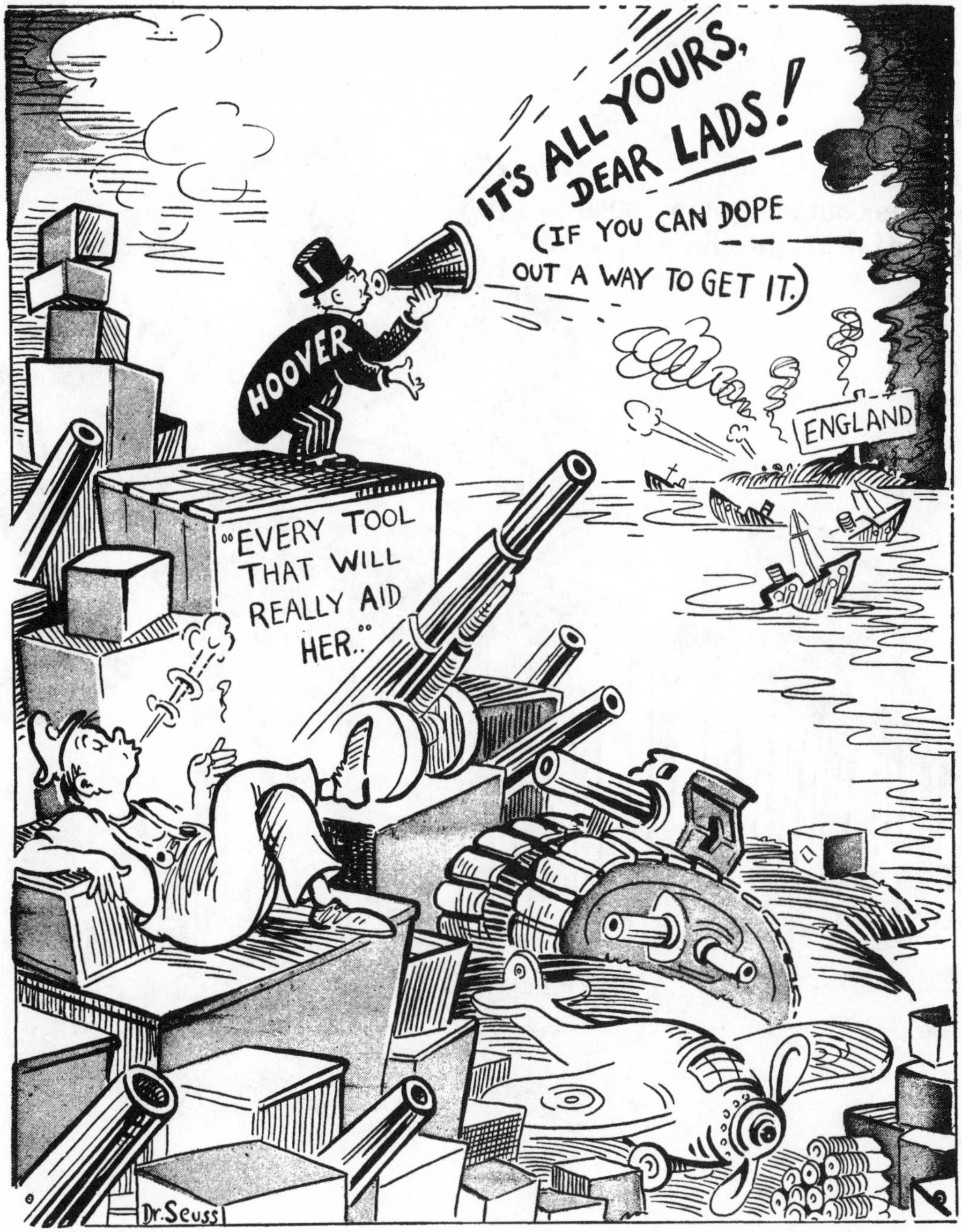
IT'S ALL YOURS, DEAR LADS!
(IF YOU CAN DOPE OUT A WAY TO GET IT.)
HOOVER
ENGLAND
"EVERY TOOL THAT WILL REALLY AID HER."
Dr. Seuss

173 — May 13, 1941

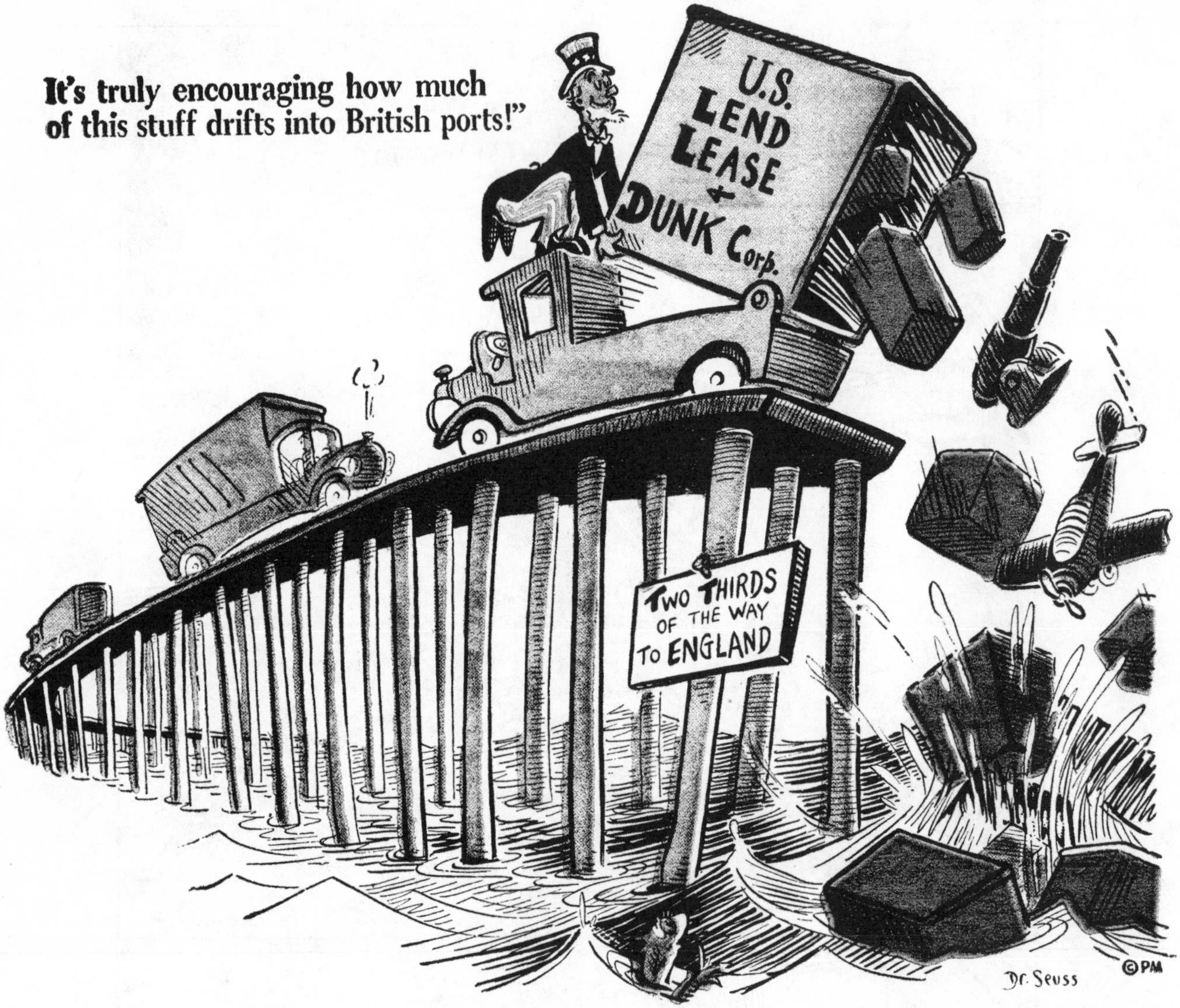
It's truly encouraging how much of this stuff drifts into British ports!"
U.S. LEND LEASE + DUNK Corp.
TWO THIRDS OF THE WAY TO ENGLAND
Dr. Seuss
©PM

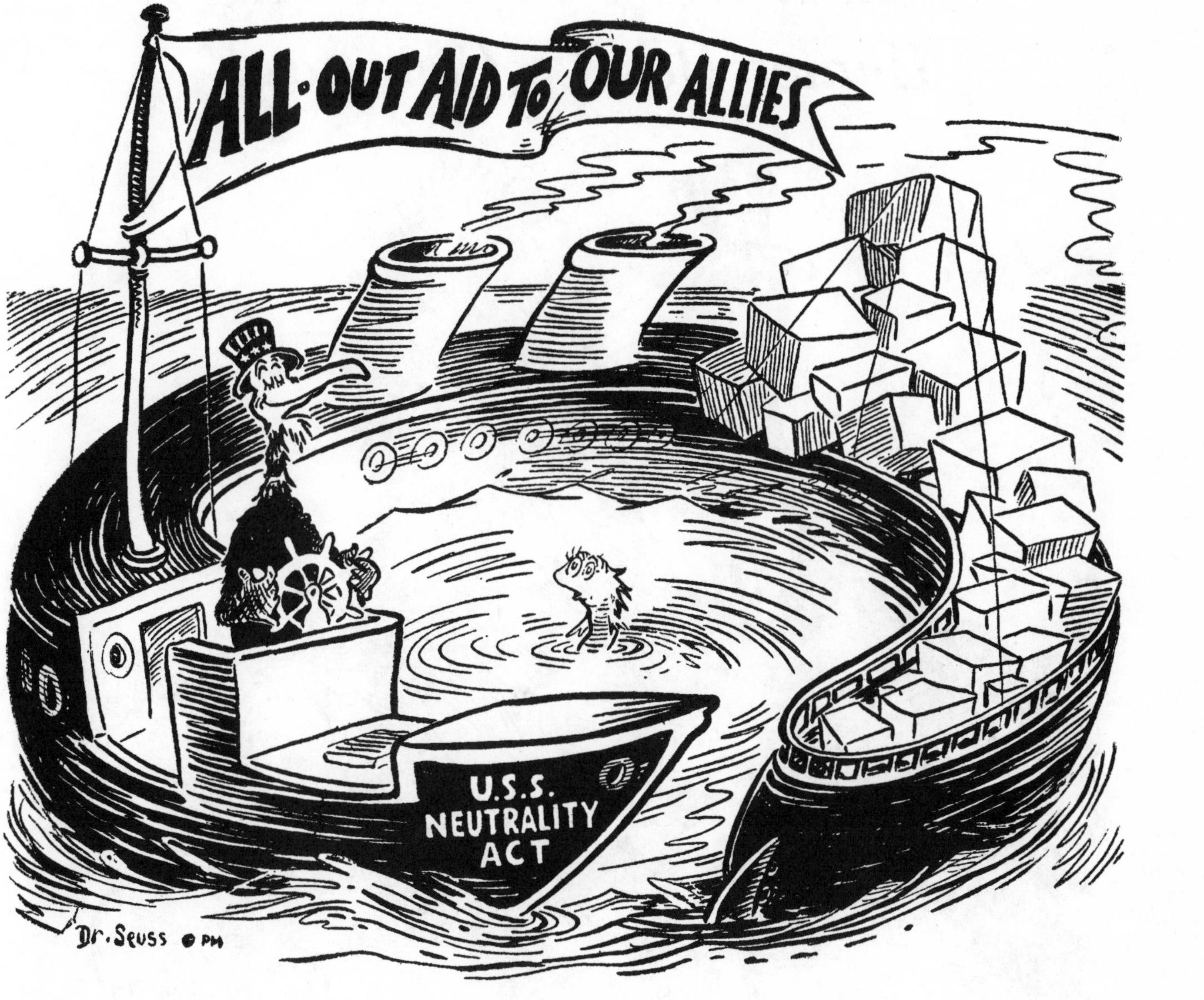
ALL-OUT AID TO OUR ALLIES
U.S.S.
NEUTRALITY
ACT
Dr. Seuss © PM

175 — October 10, 1941

'Well, It Looks Like the Mighty Hunter Has Us Convinced'

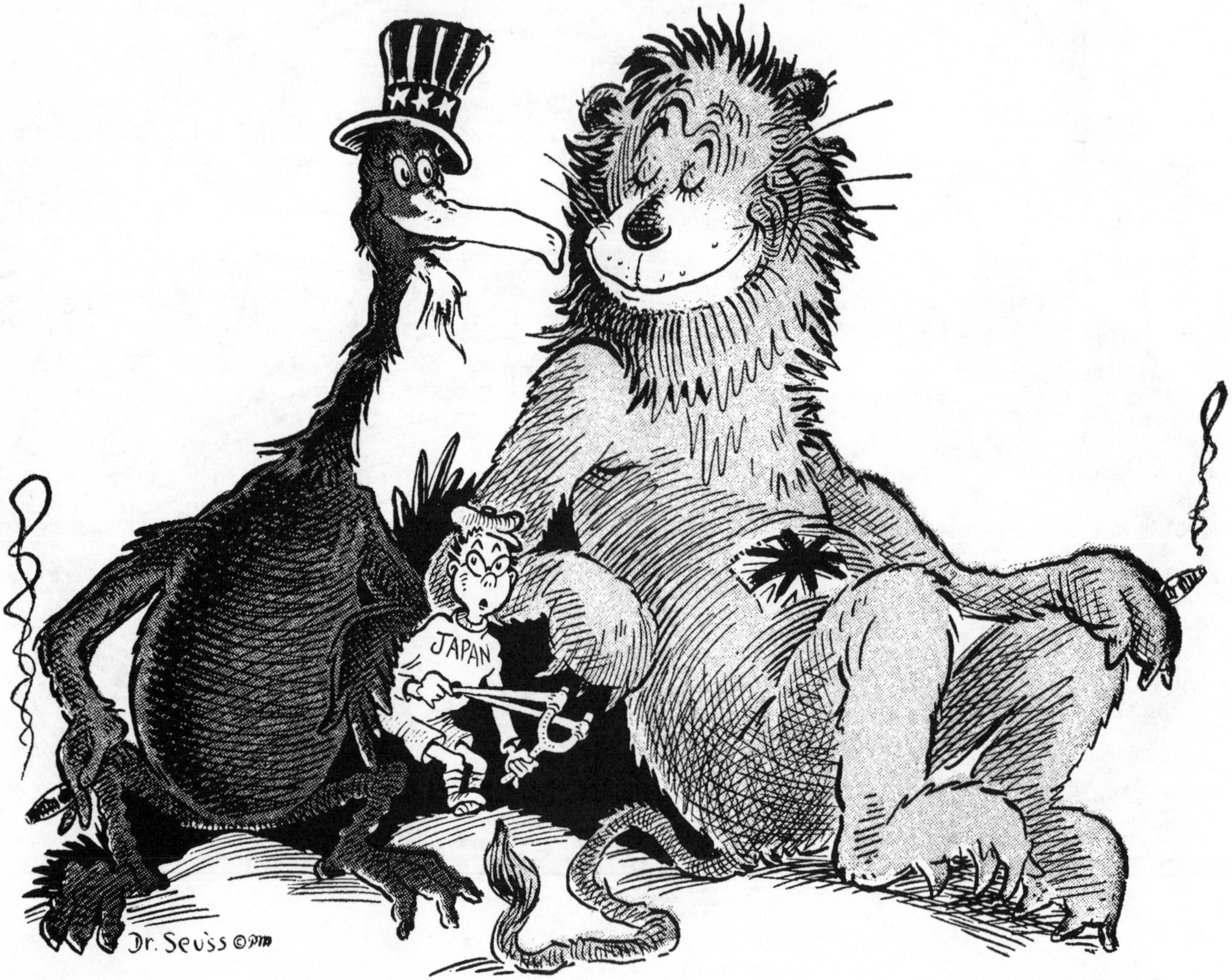
JAPAN
Dr. Seuss ©PM

Gnawing at Our Life Line

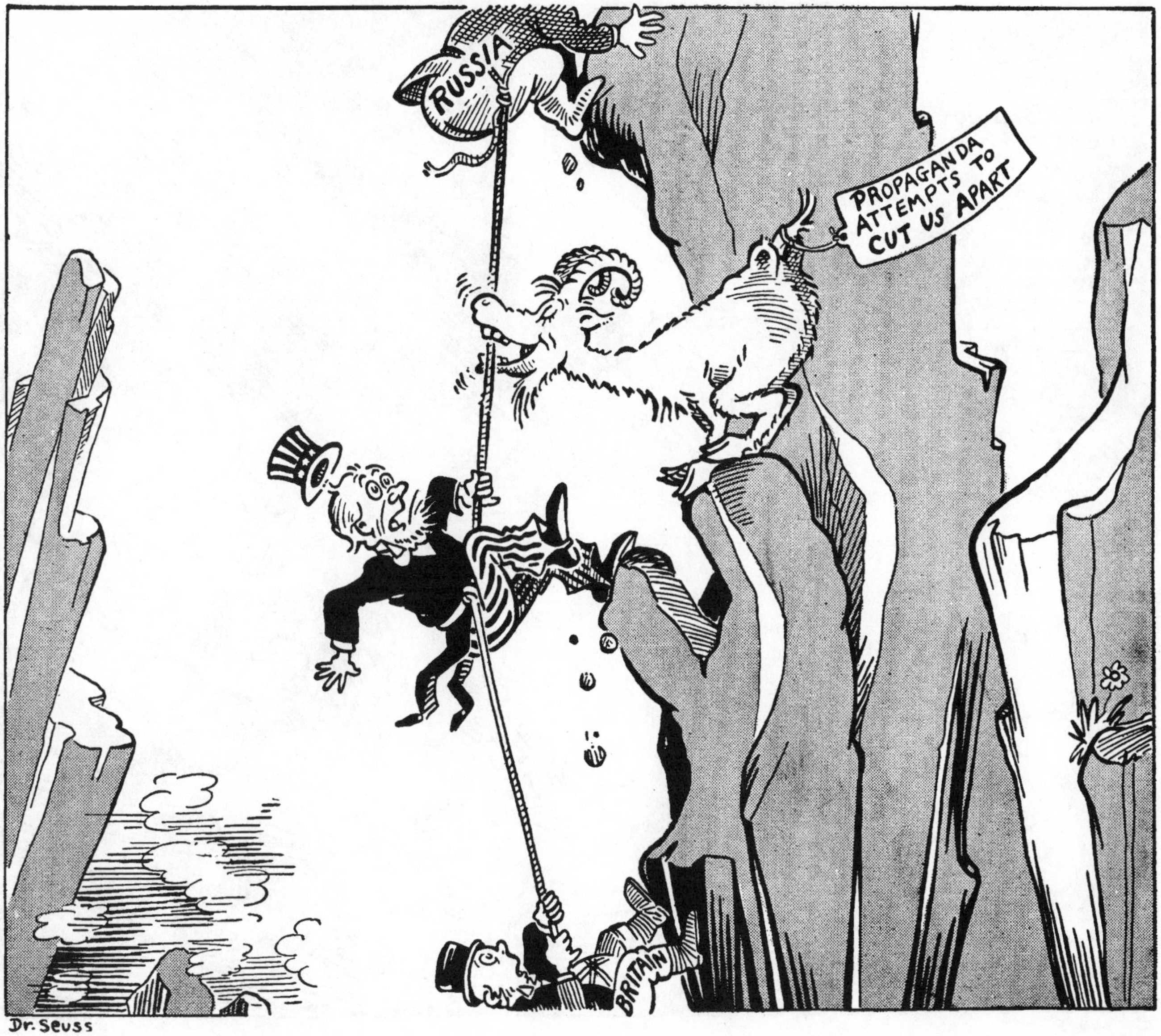
RUSSIA
PROPAGANDA ATTEMPTS TO CUT US APART
BRITAIN
Dr. Seuss

177 – March 11, 1942

"Hurry Up With That Ark!"

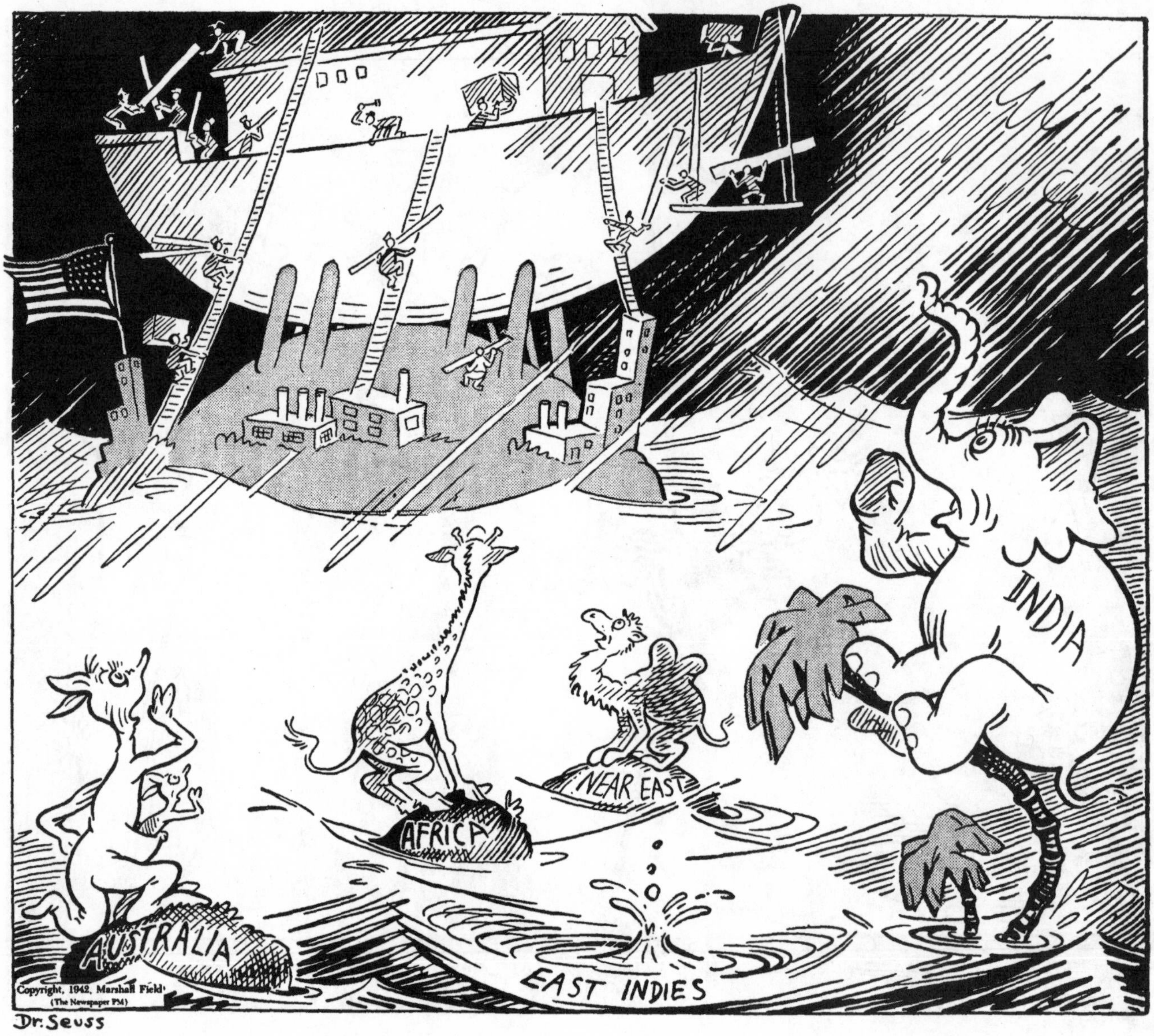
INDIA
NEAR EAST
AFRICA
AUSTRALIA
EAST INDIES
Copyright, 1942, Marshall Field
(The Newspaper PM)
Dr. Seuss

A Chance to Fight for His OWN Freedom

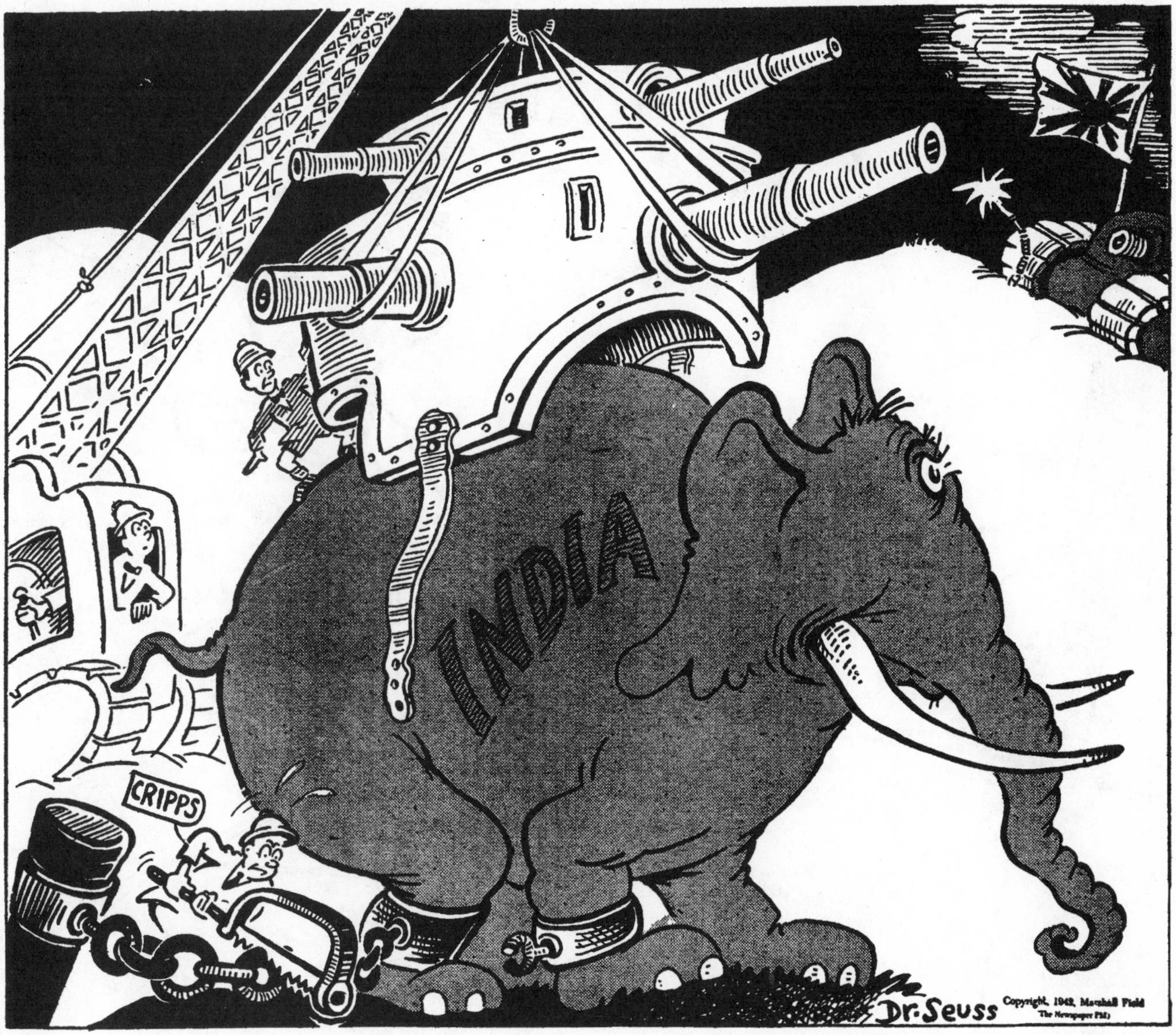
INDIA
CRIPPS
Dr. Seuss
Copyright, 1942, Marshall Field
The Newspaper PM)

Awkward Place to Be Arguing About Contracts

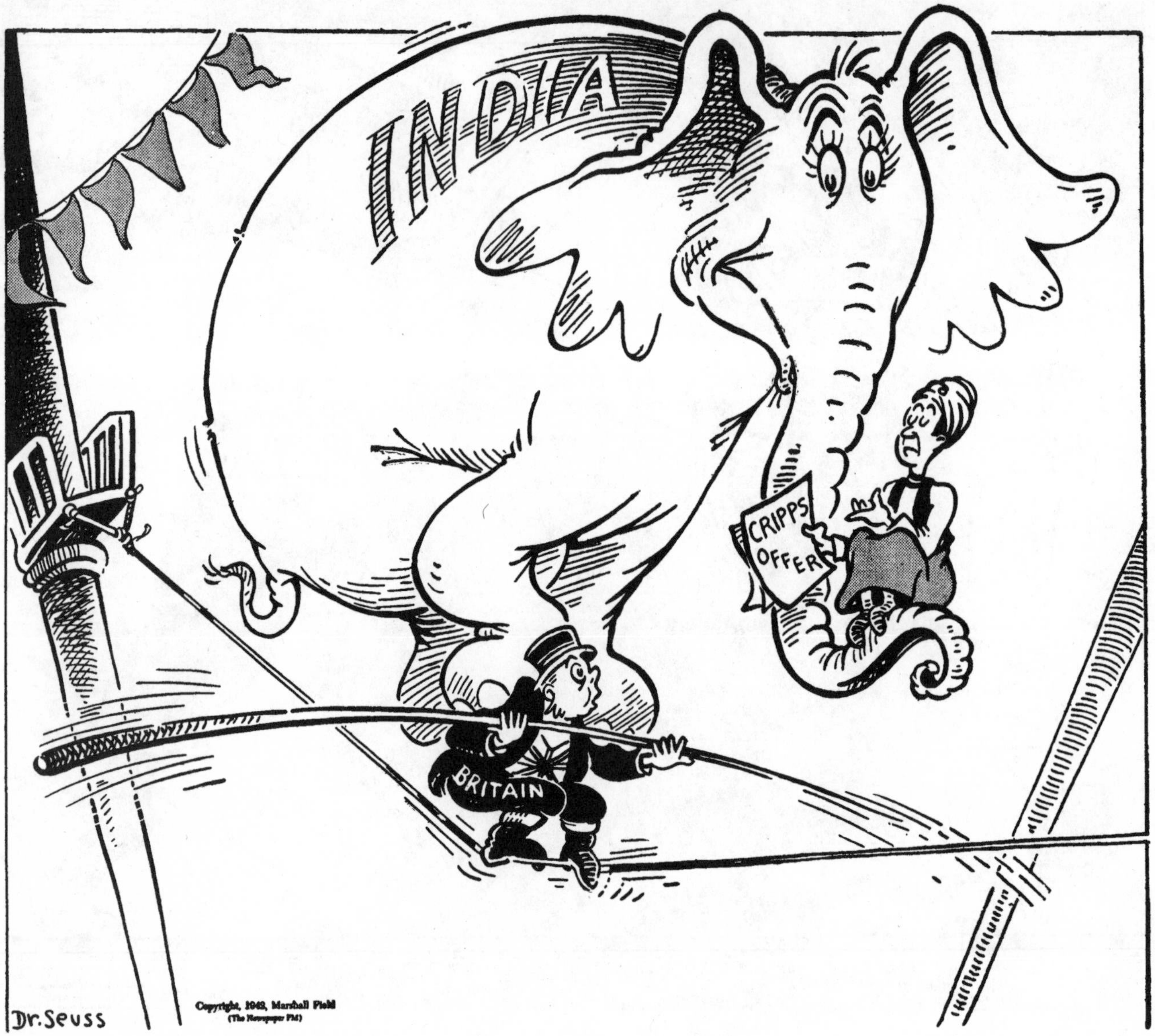
INDIA
CRIPPS OFFER
BRITAIN
Dr. Seuss
Copyright, 1942, Marshall Field
(The Newspaper PM)

180 – April 2, 1942

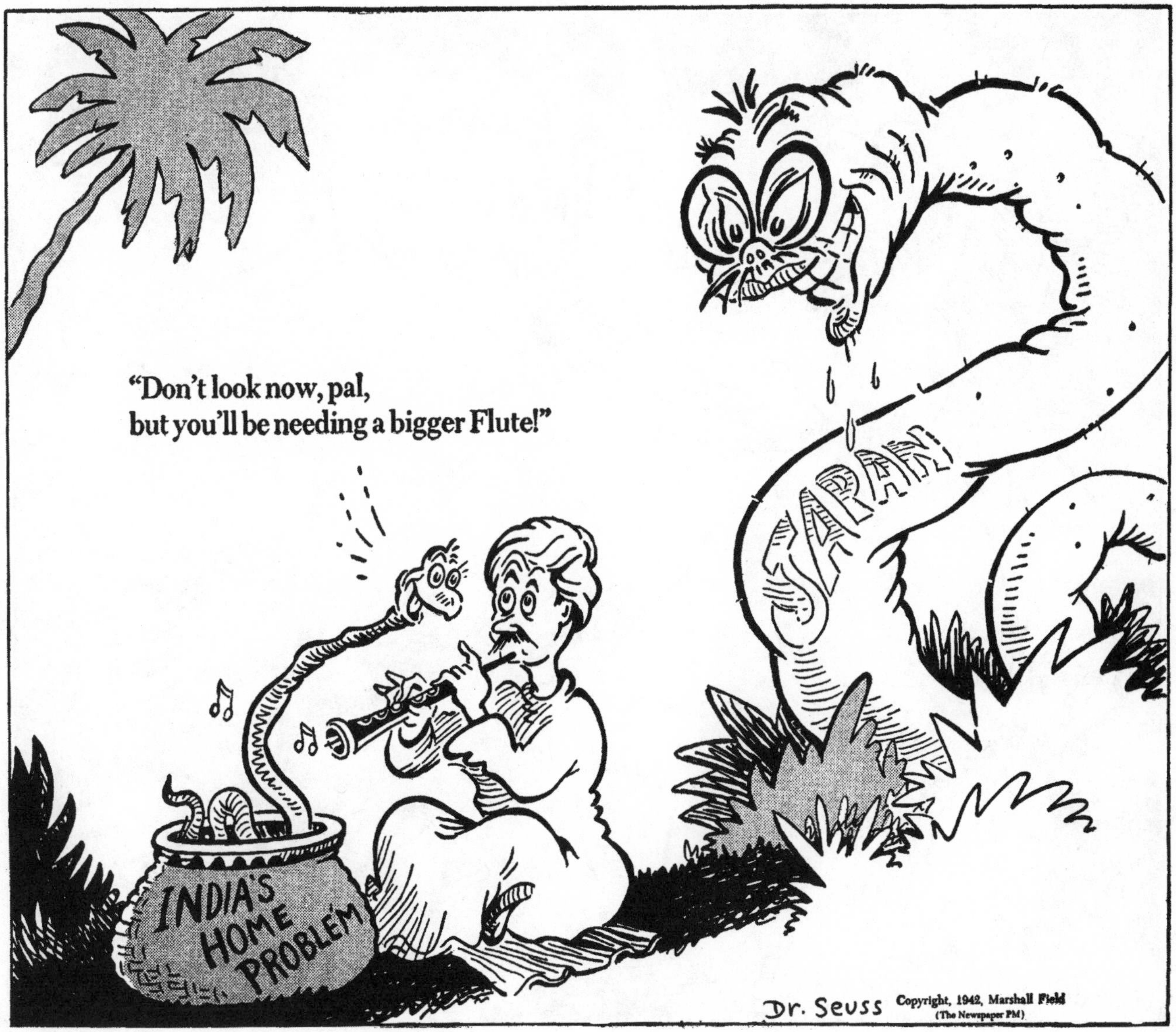
"Don't look now, pal,
but you'll be needing a bigger Flute!"
INDIA'S HOME PROBLEM
JAPAN
Dr. Seuss
Copyright, 1942, Marshall Field
(The Newspaper PM)

181 – April 17, 1942

The Gateway to India

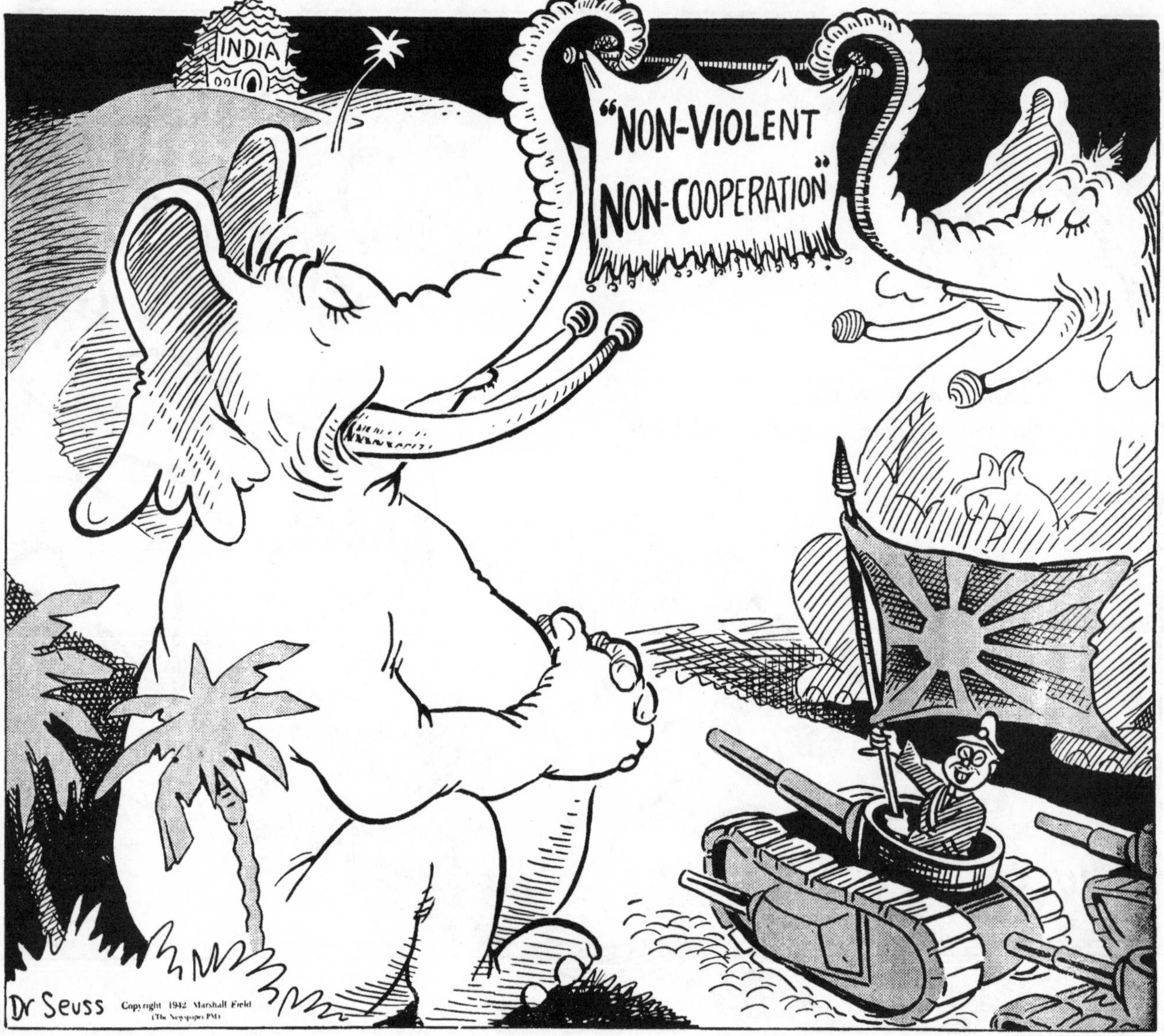

INDIA
"NON-VIOLENT NON-COOPERATION"
Dr Seuss
Copyright 1942 Marshall Field
(The Newspaper PM)

Winning The War

In 1942, the government's Office of Civilian Defense distributed a pamphlet entitled "What Can I Do?"

It promised "V-Home Certificates" to "those families which have made themselves into a fighting unit on the home front." The V-Home certificate reads:

> We in this home are fighting...we solemnly pledge all our energies and all our resources to fight for freedom and against fascism. We serve notice to all that we are personally carrying the fight to the enemy, in these ways:
>
> I. *This home follows the instructions of its air-raid warden....*
>
> II. This home *conserves* food, clothing, transportation, and health, in order to hasten an unceasing flow of war materials to our men at the front.
>
> III. This home *salvages* essential material, in order that they may be converted to immediate war uses.
>
> IV. This home *refuses to spread rumors* designed to divide our Nation.
>
> V. This home *buys* War Savings Stamps and Bonds *regularly*.
>
> We are doing these things because we know we must *Win This War*.

On December 8, 1941, the day after Pearl Harbor and long before "What Can I Do?" appeared, *PM* editor Ralph Ingersoll exhorted his staff: "Today we begin a new task...WINNING THE WAR." Dr. Seuss performed yeoman service in that cause. Most of Dr. Seuss's cartoons after Pearl Harbor had as their purpose building morale to win the war.

During his two years at *PM*, Dr. Seuss drew four cartoon series: the lampooning of Virginio Gayda that we examined in the first chapter and the Society of Red Tape Cutters, both repetitions of the same drawing, albeit with different quotations or honorees; the "Mein Early Kampf" series depicting Hitler as a baby; and the "War Monuments" series in January 1942. There are also several cases in which Dr. Seuss used the same title for two separate cartoons. "War Monuments" is both the most ambitious series and the most successful. Here Dr. Seuss spelled out the themes of much of his campaign on the home front. The series is drenched in satire. The first "monument" (January 5) is to "John F. Hindsight, master strategist of yesterday's battles, famed for his great words, 'We coulda.. + We shoulda..'" The statue has Hindsight leaning back in a rocking chair, legs crossed, squinting through a telescope that takes a U-turn to aim directly behind him. Two bemused onlookers underline the sarcasm. The second

11

188

87

195-199

195

196 "monument" (January 6) is to "Walter Weeper: generously over-subscribing his quota of tears, he enabled others to furnish the blood and the sweat." On his shoulder, a stone bird adds his tears. Once again, two onlookers seem to

197 speak for the artist. Two days later (January 8) came "Dame Rumor, Minister of Public Information." Two housewives gossip over a clothesline, in the process divulging alarmist misinformation. In the background, a group on a tour bus looks on as the guide holds forth. (Note with what economy Dr. Seuss establishes the setting—New York, likely Central Park.)

198   The fourth "monument" appeared on January 13: "To JOHN HAYNES HOLMES who spoke the beautiful words: 'The Unhappy People of Japan are Our Brothers!' " The statue is of an orator (head not visible) standing with left arm in the breast of his jacket and right arm around the shoulder of "Japan." "Japan" has a jury-rigged halo over his head, and in his right hand he holds a dagger and a severed head. Unlike the cartoon depicting Japanese Americans lining up to receive bricks of TNT, this cartoon drew angry response from many readers ("Letters to and from the Editor," January 21 and 28, 1942). Some of them spoke up for John Haynes Holmes, a prominent Protestant pacifist minister. Some protested on more basic grounds. Wrote one: "I protest the Dr. Seuss cartoon on John Haynes Holmes.... Beyond the sheer bad taste is something even deeper. That is, the implied rejection of the basic Christian principle of the universal brotherhood of man." Wrote another: "I am not a pacifist, but I do not need to be one to find myself in complete sympathy with Dr. Holmes's belief in the essential brotherhood of man. For what else are you fighting,

PM?" A third spoke of "PM's grotesque incitement to hatred. It's OK to remember Pearl Harbor; why not remember our war aims, too?" A fourth: "In my abysmal ignorance the thought that the Japanese people (and all people for that matter) were no worse than and no better than any other people on the globe was deeply etched in my mind. The absurd notion that the common people of these war-driven countries, the working masses, were the first real sufferers of a terroristic Fascist-capitalist regime has been replaced by the scientific actuality that those people are inherently militaristic and savage as suggested by your Dr. Seuss." A fifth: "Your Dr. Seuss has long been a thorn in PM's pages.... If the Japanese people are not 'our brothers,' what are they to us? Our 'mortal enemies'?"

To the letters Dr. Seuss responded Jan. 21, 1942 (ellipses in original):

In response to the letters defending John Haynes Holmes... sure, I believe in love, brotherhood and a cooing white pigeon on every man's roof. I even think it's nice to have pacifists and strawberry festivals...in between wars.

But right now, when the Japs are planting their hatchets in our skulls, it seems like a hell of a time for us to smile and warble: "Brothers!" It is a rather flabby battlecry.

If we want to win, we've got to kill Japs, whether it depresses John Haynes Holmes or not. We can get palsy-walsy afterward with those that are left.

—Dr. Seuss

Letters continued to come in, con and pro. On the con side: "Dr. Holmes is against those who push other people around—and therefore is for the people of Japan as you should be. Disagreement becomes possible only as to the best methods of relieving them of their Fascist oppressors—or helping them to help themselves." And pro: "More power to Seuss's cartoons. They're well done, original and carry a real meaning. Why don't those pacifists stop trying to 'keep their Holmes fires burning.'" In their biography, the Morgans report that Dr. Seuss "was stunned by the virulence of the backlash from isolationists. He had spurred Americans into war, they argued, because, at thirty-eight, he was too old for the draft; his battles were only on paper." This may be Dr. Seuss's recollection (the Morgans don't give a footnote for this passage; it is not absolutely clear that this recollection applies specifically to the issue of John Haynes Holmes), but these critical letters in PM are hardly from isolationists.

199   The fifth and final "monument" is to "Wishful Listeners: They Spent the War Listening for the Sudden Cracking of German Morale." Four men, hands to ears, listen in the direction of Germany (a helpful sign points "To Germany"); one carries a banner, "It won't be long now!" A Seussian cat (also part of the statue) holds an ear trumpet in the same direction, while a Seussian dog leads its nonplussed master past the base of the statue.

Let's look more closely at Dr. Seuss's effort to win the war. It occupied Dr. Seuss both before and after the "War Monuments" series. There are three general categories: effort, unity, and the economy.

Effort is obviously a crucial factor on the home front. Defeatism is a grave danger. So is over-optimism. Doing nothing, letting others do the heavy lifting, going about business as usual: all work against the common good. Dr. Seuss set out to illustrate these dangers. Doing nothing included, of course, taking no action against Hitler; that was a major part of Dr. Seuss's attack on the "isolationists." On a PM cover of May 8, 1941, Dr. Seuss drew "Uncle   200 Sam" talking at full steam—talking and not doing. Note how long the eagle's neck is, how conveniently his wings become hands with thumbs he can twiddle, and how happy he appears. In late August, Dr. Seuss drew the third   201 of three cartoons (two, not included here, appeared in July) dealing with aspects of the American army. It attributes low morale in the military to low pay. Doctors examining a draftee with the aid of an x-ray machine see ribs, spine, arm bones—and empty purse: "He has Pursis Emptosis, or Empty Purse...a disease that's very very bad for Morale!" Neither "empty" nor "purse" has Latin roots, so "Pursis Emptosis" is Dr. Seuss-speak, pure and simple. At the end of August, President Roosevelt signed the first supplemental defense appropriation bill. The eagle's neck is back to normal size on September 25—more than two   202 months before Pearl Harbor—in "Stop Wringing The Hands that Should Wring Hitler's Neck!" Says a despairing "Uncle Sam," "The democracies are finished! Ah Woe!" Once again, wings end in hands that boast fingers, even fingernails. In November, "Windbags of America"   203 hold forth as the world burns. It is a classic portrait of civic leaders; each holds pages of speech. Wearing a fireman's hat, "Uncle Sam" heads for the conflagration, but he has to drag the "Windbags" along, too.

Dr. Seuss was a genius at ridiculing pomposity and pretensions. In these cartoons he did so time and again.

204 On December 16, 1941, less than ten days after Pearl Harbor, he depicted a chubby man leaning back in his armchair, bow tie on and martini in hand, saying: "Now let ME tell you what's wrong!" The title: "You Can't Kill Japs Just by Shooting Off Your Mouth!" Two weeks later, in "The Battle of the Easy Chair," a man of leisure tells his

205 manservant, "Wake me, Judkins, when the Victory Parade comes by!" He holds one flag in his hand; another is under his arm. He wears buttons that read "V", "Hooray for Our Side," "Hitler Can't Take It!" and "We Can't Lose," but it is perfectly clear that he himself is not about to take any action at all. In January and February, the papers are full of discussion of military training,

206 expansion, appropriations. In February, Dr. Seuss helped recruit men of action as pilots for the U. S. Army Air Corps (the Air Force was not yet an independent service). The exhortation reads, *Out-blitz the Blitzer! Fly for Uncle Sam!* A monstrous four-engine plane with thirteen cannons large and small bears down on a worried Hitler in his Piper Cub.

207 Several cartoons on the theme of business-as-usual deserve careful study. In "Red Tape" (February 3, 1942) Dr. Seuss traced water on its way from a hydrant to a fire, which he labels "The War." A first man (coat, tie, and hat) labors with a hand pump to bring water up into a wooden tank. A second man (top hat, bow tie, jacket, vest) scoops the water into a sieved container over a second tank, which empties in turn into buckets. Three men (top hats, suits) examine the buckets with jeweler's loupe and magnifying glass. Then comes a bearded old man to push one bucket at a time in a baby carriage to a man (bow tie, cut-

away) who empties the buckets into a vat that decants into a beaker over a flame. The resultant steam condenses a drop at a time into a teacup on a turtle's back. The turtle carries the cup to a fireman on a ladder who—pinkie extended—throws the water on the fire. The cartoon is a tour de force: eight humans, three turtles, a pump, and twelve containers—a profusion of elements yet a unity of conception and purpose.

208 Eight days later Dr. Seuss drew giant eyeglasses (he labeled them, helpfully, "rose colored") for a cartoon with the title "Complacency." One man asks the other: "What

209 if we lose a bit today? We'll snatch it back tomorrow!" The next day complacency is one barrel of "Our Big Bertha," a cannon with six barrels. Four of the barrels are useless: "Carelessness," "Red Tape," "Complacency," and "Blunders." One—"Political Squabbles"—is counterproductive, blowing smoke back into Uncle Sam's face. A side vent emits "Just Plain Gas." Only one of the six barrels is "For Hitler + the Japs," and it emits only a lame "Pip!"

210 On February 24, Dr. Seuss drew two figures buried under a huge down comforter ("Our Warm, Warm Cot") against the icy drafts of "The Grim Cold Facts." (The corner of the blanket reaches down to envelop the cat on

211 the floor.) In April, Dr. Seuss asked: "Do YOU Belong to One of These Groups?" The three groups in question are: "The Creepers," "The Weepers," and "The Sleepers." Among the Creepers is a man smoking a cigarette— unusual for Dr. Seuss (himself a chain-smoker); the sleepers are eight men and a cat, who have posted a sign on their bed: "Do Not Disturb Until After the War." In a

212 May 1942 cartoon, a happy newspaper reader reads the

headline "Hitler on Skids" while leaning, blissfully unaware, against the huge snake form of "Japan," in the act of swallowing "China." The message: Things may be going all right in Europe, (though that was hardly the case); but the Pacific is another matter entirely. This cartoon is noteworthy as Dr. Seuss's only depiction of a Chinese person. The headline "Hitler on Skids" prefigures the cartoon of October 15, 1942, which has Hitler testing the new secret weapon: skids. But it is not clear whether Dr. Seuss had actual headlines in mind, for Hitler suffered no major defeats in May. Also in May, six straw-hatted men (and a dog) at "The Optimist's Picnic" celebrate finding a clover leaf ("A Little Good News") even as, offshore, ten ships sink in the background.

97

213

Having drawn the devastating cartoon of "Red Tape" in February, Dr. Seuss joins Ingersoll in dreaming up in May a "Society of Red Tape Cutters" (see following page). The entire cartoon is devoted to a statement about red tape and the society—two-thirds certificate, one-third text. The text reads, in part: "The Society of Red Tape Cutters, an organization which would love to be nation-wide, today elected as its first Honorary Member the President of the U. S. A., Franklin Delano Roosevelt. Roosevelt...was nominated and elected for cutting the red tape which impeded our war effort. By persistent work with the red tape shears, he has boosted production, streamlined our fighting forces, and brought closer our day of victory. Membership...is open to all public workers and officials...." The text ends: "There is no limit on the number of members; indeed, we would be delighted to elect thousands of them. So cut, boys, cut."

(In the ensuing months the Society would "elect" to membership Senator Harry S. Truman, Admiral Chester Nimitz, Russian Foreign Minister Vyacheslav Molotov, Secretary of State Cordell Hull, and six lesser lights.)

The certificate itself is a work of art. In the center: the name of the honoree and the citation and the name of the society and "Awarded by the Readers of the Newspaper *PM*," with a circular seal to one side and the signature of Ralph Ingersoll below. On the left, from the top: the legs of two men, presumably hanged by red tape; a deskworker with tape around neck and body; a pilot in an airplane, with red tape around both wings and the propeller; two men in a tank, with red tape around both necks and one gun barrel; an infantryman, with red tape around body and rifle. At the bottom: a war factory, red tape around its smokestacks. On the right: a cheerful bird greeting the sun as it comes out from behind a cloud, and giant hands holding giant scissors reaching down from behind that cloud to cut red tape and send a ship and its happy skipper off on their business. The cartoon appeared a dozen times, only the honoree changing, but it never lost its freshness.

July brought an otherworldly "Dream of a Short War," surely one of the most magical of all Dr. Seuss's war-time cartoons. Winged horse, canopied chariot, and ethereal driver come straight out of some Utopia, perhaps the *Arabian Nights*, but the dream is over: "End of the line, sir. From here on you walk." One week later Dr. Seuss drew "The Alibi Boys—That Favorite Song-and-Dance Team of the Democratic Nations." As two patrons look on skeptically, "We could of," "We would of," and

214

215

Society of Red Tape Cutters Elects Roosevelt

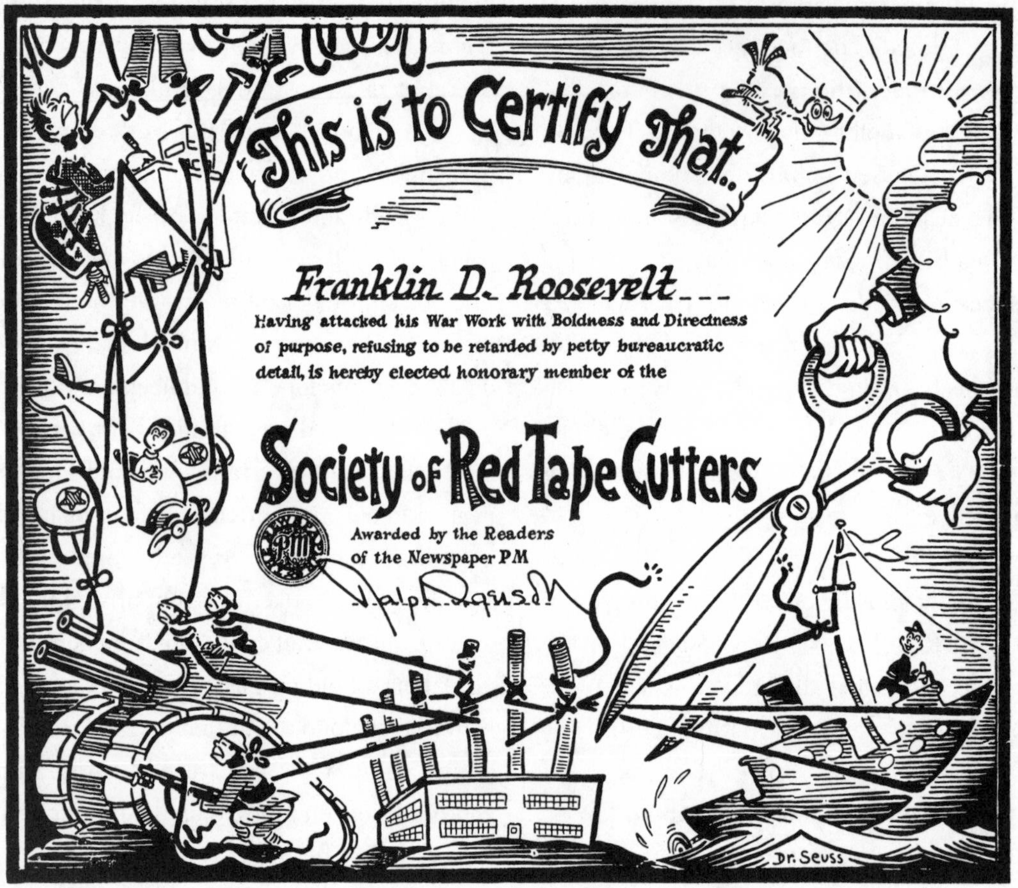
This is to Certify That..
Franklin D. Roosevelt
Having attacked his War Work with Boldness and Directness of purpose, refusing to be retarded by petty bureaucratic detail, is hereby elected honorary member of the
Society of Red Tape Cutters
Awarded by the Readers of the Newspaper PM
PM
Dr. Seuss

May 26, 1942

"We should of" do a song-and-dance turn. Despite the placard reading "democratic nations," this cartoon seems to focus on *this* democratic nation.

In the summer of 1942, Congress faced a major
216 issue—taxes. In late July, Dr. Seuss produced a third cartoon that calls for a road map: "The Knotty Problem of Capitol Hill: Finding a Way to Raise Taxes Without Losing a Single Vote." Here a bemused Uncle Sam, normal-sized, looks in through a window as top-hatted Congressmen—dwarves and a cat—attempt the impossible. One studies a model of an atom; one, standing in a trash basket, goes through the waste paper. Four work atop a table with surveyor's instruments. One examines blueprints; one eyes an assayer's scales. Five crowd around a sheet of

paper with a lone zero in its middle. Two enter formulas in a record book decorated as well with games of tic-tac-toe. One lies supine—presumably asleep—under the table; we see only his feet.

217 A fourth cartoon in the same vein is "Speaking of Giant Transports..." (August 5, 1942). An overburdened Uncle Sam pilots the single-engine, open-cockpit plane. "Red Tape" is one of a dozen gliders he has in tow. The other drags on progress are "Talk Against Our Allies" (a phonograph going full-blast); "Peanut Politics;" "Our Ham Fishes," that is, political critics of the administration—Hamilton Fish was a longtime Republican Congressman from New York; "The Great Rubber Puzzle" (likely a reference to the shortage of rubber once Japan severed the trade routes between Southeast Asia and the United States); "Racial Prejudice;" "6th Column Press" (a subject to which we return in a minute); and "Inflation" (again, stay tuned). In the midst of things is a man in a hammock: "Sleeper: Do not disturb until after the war." And Dr. Seuss crammed all these elements into a cartoon measuring perhaps 6" x 7"! Note that Dr. Seuss represented "6th Column Press" with an outhouse, complete with a carved moon in the door.

218 In August, Dr. Seuss showed the dangers that lurk when a "defeatist" falls for Hitler's "peace poseys." "We'll Need Changes in the Old Victory Band Before We 219 Parade in Berlin" (August 21, 1942) shows a man with cigarette holder in his smiling mouth and tinkling away on a triangle ("Most of us doing too little") and a much smaller man trying his best with the assistance of two hard-pressed cats to carry and blow a tuba ("Few of us

going full blast"). In September the subject was "Our Placid Conceit"—a gentleman (vest, cutaway, and cigar) 220 can't accept that "We can't win this war without sacrifice." Note that it is Uncle Sam—we see only his gigantic hands—who "Can't Pound it Into His Head!"

Unity during wartime is an obvious goal and dissent a problem. We have seen already that *PM* waged a campaign to silence Father Coughlin's *Social Justice*, a magazine that sympathized openly with fascism abroad. But the United States was a free country, and one of its arguments with Hitler and the fascists was their suppression of dissent. In May 1942, Dr. Seuss drew a crowd of men 221 thumbing their noses at Hitler. One man carries a huge banner: "So long as men can do THIS they're FREE!" Even the bird atop the pole thumbs its nose at Hitler! Freedom includes the freedom to dissent. The original drawing carries the title "The Fifth Freedom." In his State of the Union speech on January 6, 1941 President Roosevelt had spoken of "Four Freedoms": freedom of speech, freedom of religion, freedom from want, and freedom from fear; they became a major focus of American domestic propaganda. With this cartoon Dr. Seuss added one more freedom: the freedom to thumb one's nose. At least in the cartoon, this freedom is strikingly white, male, middle-class, and violent—a dozen or so men carry cudgels.

How to foster unity? This was Dr. Seuss's goal. Before Pearl Harbor Dr. Seuss rarely dealt with the issue, except—a truly major exception—in his attacks on Lindbergh and the "isolationists." America First was the major organization dedicated to nonintervention. In one cartoon of June 1941, Dr. Seuss linked America First not only with Nazis and fascists (as we have seen him do before) but also with Communists. In "Relatives? Naw...Just three fellers going along for the ride!" Dr. Seuss shows a kangaroo "America First" carrying in its pouch a second kangaroo ("Nazis"), carrying in *its* pouch a third kangaroo ("Fascists"), carrying in *its* pouch a fourth kangaroo ("Communists"). It is startling for a *PM* cartoonist to connect Communists with the other three, since *PM* itself was so much a part of the Popular Front, which included Communists. But in his later manuscript about *PM* (archived at Boston University), Ralph Ingersoll blames unnamed Communists for the labor woes that hobbled *PM* virtually from the start, and we shall see that Dr. Seuss seems never to have gotten over his own suspicions of communists.

At the end of August 1941 came a cartoon showing German submariners deciding *not* to fire on the good ship "U. S. S. Disunity." The ship carries four men, two of whom row in opposing directions and two of whom puff into the sails, again in opposing direction. Says one German to the other: "Don't waste a torpedo, Fritz, we can take this gang with a butterfly net!"

After Pearl Harbor Dr. Seuss presses for unity. In February 1942 it was "That Cheap Gunning for Eleanor Roosevelt," which leaves Hitler and "Japan" delighted. Eleanor Roosevelt was perhaps the most influential presidential spouse of the twentieth century. In a radio broadcast of a week or so earlier, she had suggested that American housewives make do with less sugar; she was aston-

ished to find herself the target of sharp criticism, including the charge that she had encouraged hoarding. Later that month Dr. Seuss stigmatized those who didn't pull together. The "Sniper" (February 25, 1942) depicts "Our Lifeboat" in high seas. It has an American flag but no captain, and an onboard sniper uses his slingshot to bean one of the men setting the pace. The assailant's only complaint is "the color of that guy's tie."

As in his campaign against *Social Justice*, Dr. Seuss inveighed frequently against Nazi propaganda, notably in cartoons of March 1942. "Why Do We Sit and Take It?" (March 9) shows "You" and "Me" in a car at a filling station. The station is "Adolf's Service—Free Air"; Hitler pumps "Anti-Roosevelt, Anti-Russian, Anti-British Propaganda" into an already-bulging tire. The next day Dr. Seuss showed the Dies Committee trapping a rabbit but missing "the Big Ones" in the "subversive activities jungle"—a huge fanged snake with a "Japanese" face, a swastika-branded beast of uncertain genus, and a rhinoceros. The padlock on the cage is as big as the rabbit, but that fact does not affect the pride of the committee. The "Special House Committee for the Investigation of Un-American Activities" (1938–1944) was known as the Dies Committee, after its chair, Martin Dies (D., Texas). In late February it released a report on Japanese activities. Dr. Seuss poked fun at the Dies Committee, but was the "jungle" the external world? And was Dr. Seuss opposed to witch-hunts at home? The cartoon is not clear. (In June Dr. Seuss drew a somewhat clearer cartoon [not included here]: "After him, Sam! It's a Robin RED-Breast!" pillories the Dies Committee's fixation on all things red. Riding a cat, swinging a lasso, and firing a toy gun, a figure labeled Dies races through the bowlegs of a bemused Uncle Sam in hot pursuit of a robin.) In March 228 "Our Internal Wrangles" meant stripping massive gears, and again Hitler and "Japan" exult.

217 We've seen already (in the cartoon "Speaking of Giant Transports..." August 5, 1942) that Dr. Seuss dubs part of the press a "sixth column." (The phrase "sixth column," perhaps original with Dr. Seuss, is a play on "fifth column," a phrase that got its start during the Spanish Civil War meaning sympathizers behind enemy lines.) 229 On April 21, 1942, Dr. Seuss drew the *New York Daily News*, the *Chicago Tribune*, and the *Washington Times-Herald* lying in ambush for President Roosevelt. The three newspapers were an interlocking family conglomerate: Eleanor Medill Patterson of the *Washington Times-Herald* and Joseph Patterson, owner of the *New York Daily News*, were sister and brother; Colonel Robert McCormick, who owned the *Chicago Tribune*, was their cousin. Their newspapers had the largest circulations of all American dailies, and they had been anti-Roosevelt for years. Paul Milkman refers to the *News* and the Hearst press as "jingoistic, xenophobic, and hysterical." New York's 42nd Street was home to the *New York Daily News* 230 (April 30, 1942), instrument of Joseph Patterson; Milkman quotes a rival newspaper's description of the editorial policy of the *Daily News* as "folksy fascism."

We have noted Dr. Seuss's ambivalence toward the Soviet Union. Still, once the United States joined the shooting war and became allied with the Soviet Union, Dr. Seuss softened his criticism of Communists. A cartoon of June 4, 1942 (not included here) is one result of that change. A tiny gun ("U. S. aid to Russia") goes to Stalin, while a huge weapon ("Justice Department anti-red blunderbuss") is to "pepper the seat of [Stalin's] breeches." How contradictory to be aiding the Soviet Union and at the same time persecuting domestic Communists! But is the problem the very fact of hunts for domestic Reds? Or, is it that the hunts for domestic Reds—the difference in the size of the weapons highlights the issue—receive more support than the Soviet ally abroad? In a cartoon of June 1942, Dr. Seuss returns 231 to the theme of the "Sixth Column" press, depicting Hitler and an American newspaperman wearing two-man shoes. Says the newsman: "Me? Why I'm just going my own independent American way!"

In June and July Dr. Seuss pilloried the "Congressional Sling-shot Club"—first (a cartoon of June 30, not included here) for killing a bird labeled "National Harmony," second, for pelting Uncle Sam in a battlefield trench, from behind (July 15). Says Uncle Sam, directly to 232 the reader: "If you expect me to win this war, Mr. Voter, keep your Katzenjammer Kids at home!" (The original Katzenjammer Kids were the pesky stars of a cartoon strip of that name.) In "Easy, There, EASY! NO ACROBAT IS 233 FALL-PROOF!" Uncle Sam teeters on a high wire over a vast abyss. An arrow hanging from the wire reads: "Victory Plenty Far Ahead." On one end of Uncle Sam's pole two cats engage in "Cheap Political Cat-Squabbles." These cartoons make clear the tactical usefulness of *not* portraying President Roosevelt. Portray Roosevelt, and the attacks of the "Sling-shot Club" are directed at a politician; portray only Uncle Sam, and the attacks become assaults on the war effort and national unity.

Early in August, Representative Holland (D-Pennsylvania) declared on the floor of the House: "The Pattersons and their ilk must go. We want no Quislings in America." Joseph Patterson responded two days later with a headline: "You're a liar, Congressman Holland." A few days later came the charge that the *Chicago Tribune* had printed a news dispatch that included confidential military information. (By the end of the month, an investigation cleared the *Chicago Tribune*.) Needless to say, these charges were music to Dr. Seuss's ears, and he responded with "Cissy, Bertie, and Joe" ("Still Spraying Our Side With Disunity Gas," Aug. 10). Cissy is Eleanor Patterson of the *Washington Times-Herald*; Bertie is Colonel Robert McCormick of the *Chicago Tribune*; Joe is Joseph Patterson of the *New York Daily News*. In August 1942, Dr. Seuss draws a louse labeled "The Anti-Roosevelt Bug" boasting about giving McCormick "the greatest all-time itch on record!" Note the superiority—in body size and complexity—of the "anti-Roosevelt bug" over the "just *plain* bugs." And remember that in the forties, "bugs" was colloquial for "crazy." In August, Dr. Seuss found the "endless cat fights on our own home front" distracting: "Gee, It's All Very Exciting...*But it Doesn't Kill Nazi Rats*."

234

235

236

Unity, dissent, and propaganda—Dr. Seuss supported the Roosevelt administration, opposed the "Sixth Column" press, and sought to unite Americans in pursuit of these goals. If he sometimes contradicted himself, so also did the Roosevelt administration.

The wartime economy affected everyone, whether in the form of shortages, inflation, or inequity. The war brought economic prosperity to the United States, but in the long run, not in the two years Dr. Seuss was drawing his cartoons. He focused instead on ways the war effort affected folks in the short run: war taxes, shortages of goods, problems of production, inflation, malingering. Perhaps better than other, more objective indicators, his cartoons tell us how the war affected many lives at home.

In August 1941, before Pearl Harbor and before the U. S. involvement in the war, Dr. Seuss drew two wealthy club men lamenting new taxes: "And with new WAR Taxes, mind you, we'll soon be going THREES on our dollar cigars." A cartoon of November 18, 1941, "Blitz Buggy De Luxe," shows "Uncle Sam" driving a tank. He has cigar in one hand, martini in the other; behind him stands a butler before a table set with linen and candelabra, and a bottle of champagne chills in a bucket on the floor. The subtitle: "Destroy Hitler (IN PERFECT COMFORT)." And this is before Pearl Harbor!

237

238

Soon after Pearl Harbor, on December 26, 1941, Dr. Seuss urged his readers to buy war bonds. A man at home reads somber headlines: "Japs Sink U. S. Ships." A moose head mounted on the wall leans down and speaks: "Boss, maybe you'd better hock me and buy more U. S. Defense Bonds and Stamps!" Even before Pearl Harbor the Treasury financed the defense buildup in part with "Defense Bonds." Once the United States entered the war, "Defense Bonds" became "War Bonds," to be bought at one's place of work by authorizing deductions from paychecks. In January 1942, Dr. Seuss pushed this payroll sav-

239

240

ings plan: "If you're not in it, ask your boss!" That same month Dr. Seuss made light of tightened belts in a hilarious cartoon (January 12, 1942). It shows a hefty matron clad in fur coat confronting the rubber shortage. She wishes to buy a girdle, and the only one available is far too small. The solution awaits her in the fitting room: two store clerks ready with outsize tongs and crane-like apparatus with huge hook. "The Old Easy Life" (January 19, 1942; not included here) had to go: Uncle Sam as boxer with one boxing glove already on has to choose for his second hand between manicure ("The Old Easy Life") and a second boxing glove. Dr. Seuss wanted "PRO-DUCTION PRODUCTION PRODUCTION PRO-DUCTION" (March 4, 1942), and he transformed the smokestacks of factories into blowtorches scorching the posteriors of Hitler and "Japan."

Dr. Seuss attacked slackers (March 6, 1942): "Too blamed many of us" have not speeded up, and victory is still "Miles + Miles + Miles ahead." In a cartoon of March 20, 1942, "You Can't Build a Substantial V Out of Turtles!", it is "Dawdling Producers" who are turtles. Almost all the turtles look happy or at least complacent, but Dr. Seuss clearly was not. This V of turtles prefigures the much higher tower of turtles that after the war leads to the downfall of Yertle, king of the turtles, in *Yertle the Turtle and Other Stories* (1958). On April 8, 1942, Dr. Seuss drew a happy umbrella salesman ringing up his profits as he sells umbrellas to people stranded in a flood. A swastika in the storm identifies the cause of the flood. The caption: "Beware the Man Who Makes a Fortune in a Flood!" Later that month (April 29, 1942), Dr. Seuss

drew a cartoon with a similar theme. A lifeboat ("U. S. life-boat") is already crowded. It holds eighteen people, including six sailors doing the rowing, six men passengers, one woman, and five children. Their dilemma: whether to rescue a businessman in a life jacket, complete with cigar and huge cash register labeled "High net incomes + profits." Says one sailor to the group already in the boat: "He thinks we oughta save his cash register, too!"

In May, Dr. Seuss criticized New Yorkers—and by extension all Americans—for not maintaining blackout and hence aiding Nazi submarines. The Nazi submarine has already released a torpedo toward a freighter it has spotted against the lights of "N. Y. City." In June, he attacked slackers in the workforce: "YOU + ME" is the label on the hat of the complacent fellow in a hospital bed, phoning in to take sick leave. On the wall above his head a "Home Front Health Chart" traces a downward trajectory. In late June, Dr. Seuss drew "Phony Optimism." A man and woman with fatuous smiles on their faces stroll along holding eleven balloons, while in the lower left corner one cat remarks to another: "A balloon barrage...but not against bombs. It's designed to protect the mind against facts!" (Barrage balloons were tethered by cable around likely targets as a defense against low-flying enemy aircraft.) In July, Dr. Seuss attacked inflation: a worried Uncle Sam reads a child-care book ("How to Bubble the Baby") as he seeks to restrain a baby whose huge belly—'Inflation'—makes him float to the ceiling. Even the cat pitches in.

In August, Dr. Seuss connected the shortage of goods and the shortage of effort. Wearing a chef's hat and standing over a stove, Uncle Sam laments, "If we had some

241

242

243

244

245

246

247

248

249

250

251

ham, we could have a Real Production Omelette right now...if we had some eggs..." and his sidekick cat, pointing to "effort shortage" in the firebox, adds, "...if we had 252 a bigger fire." Two days later, Dr. Seuss ridiculed those who talked but didn't act, in this case, to collect the scrap metal the war effort needed. Says the puzzled cat on the backyard scrap heap: "But nobody wants to attack the scrap right in his own back yard!" In September (a cartoon not included here) a "war materials bootlegger" wears a decoration around his neck. On the decoration is a dollar sign. The bootlegger speaks or sings: "Oh, the lowly private swims/Through pools of blood and loses limbs/Just to get a D.S.O. hung round his collar./But, hell, why die for tin/When it's easier to win/The Exalted Order of the Stinking Dollar!" (D.S.O. stands for Dis- 253 tinguished Service Order.) Three days later Dr. Seuss responded to Congressional talk of price and wage ceilings with one of his most startling cartoons: floor has become ceiling and ceiling, floor. (The door hasn't 254 changed!) In October, Dr. Seuss illustrated the scrap drives that became a feature of wartime life: a truckload of scrap metal—radiator, bedstead, boiler, gear, bathtub, bike, rake, clock, trumpet, and assorted pots and pans—

with a matronly lady riding on top. The zipper of her dress extends down the front of her dress from neck to hem, and she offers it as scrap—but only if the government can get it unzipped!

Just before Christmas, three enchanting reindeer addressed the reader: "Maybe it's none of our busi- 255 ness...but How much are YOU giving This Christmas in U. S. War Bonds and Stamps?" The next day, December 23, Dr. Seuss urged his readers not to travel at Christmas. 256 The crowd charging "Track 25" is one of Dr. Seuss's great crowd scenes: a swirling scrimmage of men (and a few women) who carry gift boxes large and super-large and even a Christmas tree with all its decorations. Hats, gift-wrapped parcels, and three men fly; men stand on each other's backs and step on each other's heads. Three men in the lower right have given up the fight. Shortly after Christmas (December 28, 1942), Dr. Seuss drew a most 257 repulsive hoarder–alone in his well-stocked warehouse, with huge cigar and enormous stomach. Dr. Seuss's penultimate cartoon, in January 1943, is dated 1973, thir- 258 ty years after "the Battle of 1943." A bearded veteran with cane boasts to his grandson of having "groused about the annoying shortage of fuel oil!" A skeptical cat looks on.

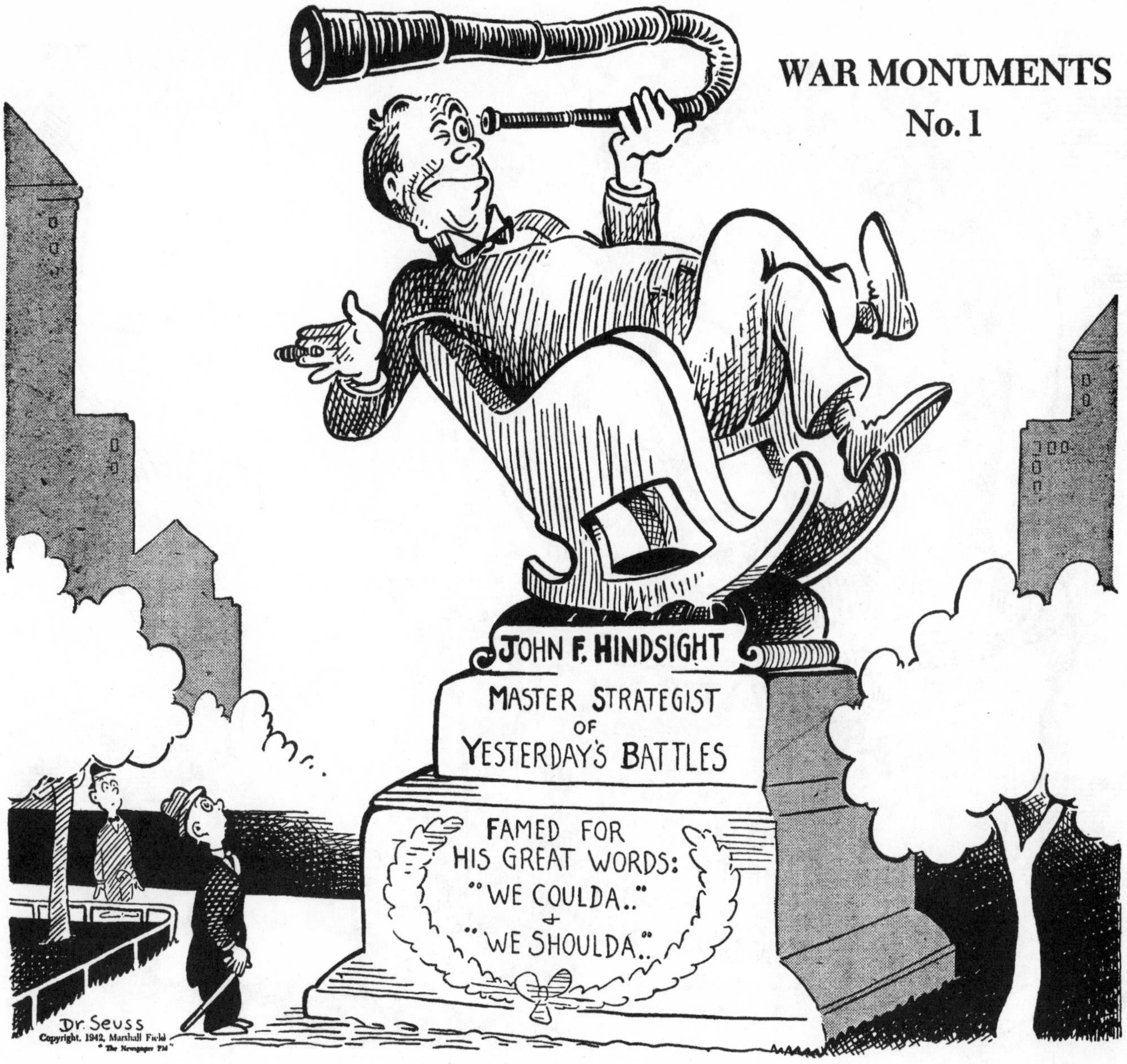
WAR MONUMENTS
No. 1
JOHN F. HINDSIGHT
MASTER STRATEGIST OF YESTERDAY'S BATTLES
FAMED FOR HIS GREAT WORDS:
"WE COULDA.."
+
"WE SHOULDA."
Dr. Seuss
Copyright, 1942, Marshall Field

195 — January 5, 1942

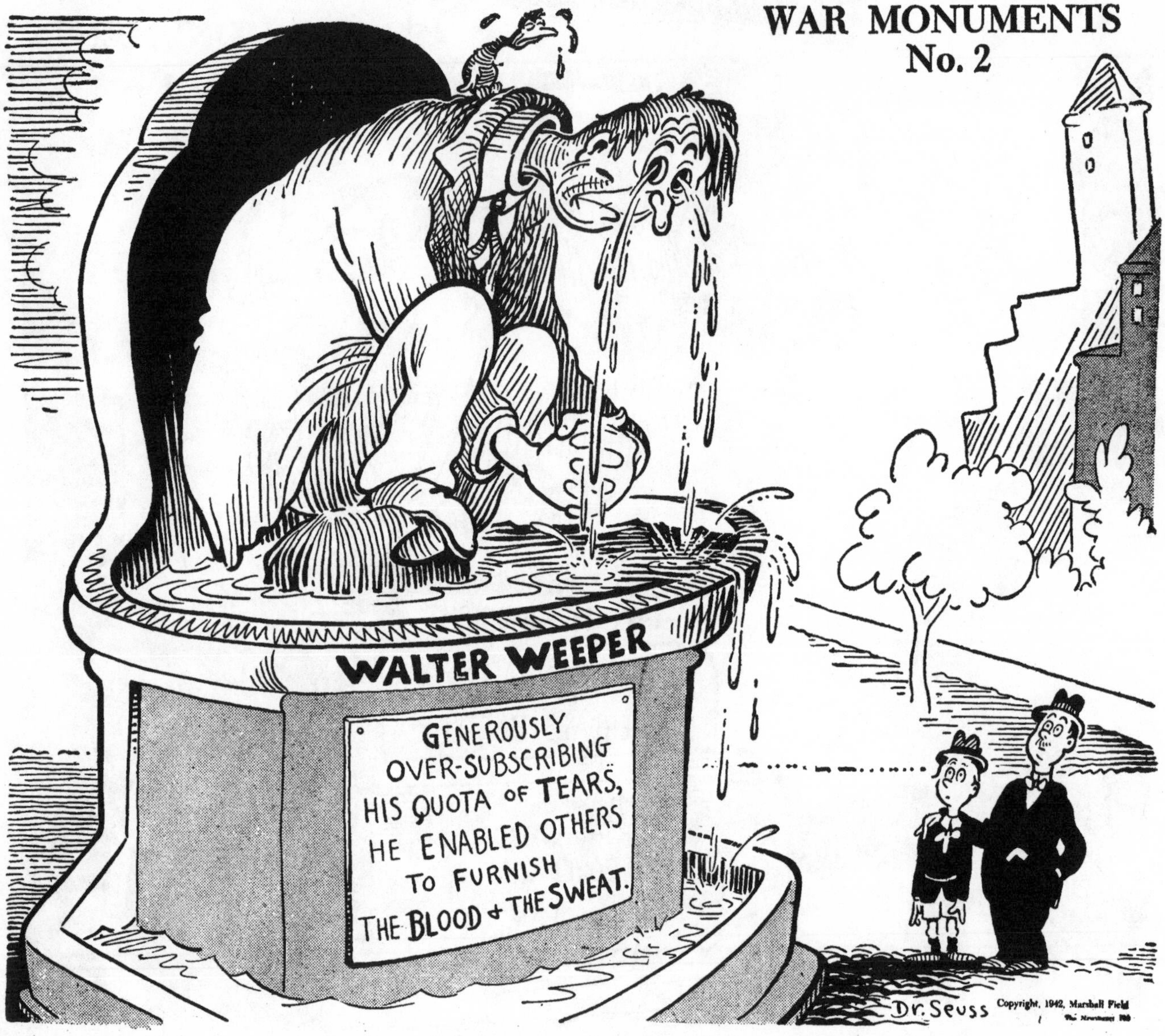
WAR MONUMENTS
No. 2
WALTER WEEPER
GENEROUSLY
OVER-SUBSCRIBING
HIS QUOTA OF TEARS,
HE ENABLED OTHERS
TO FURNISH
THE BLOOD & THE SWEAT.
Dr. Seuss
Copyright, 1942, Marshall Field

196 — January 6, 1942

WAR MONUMENTS No. 3

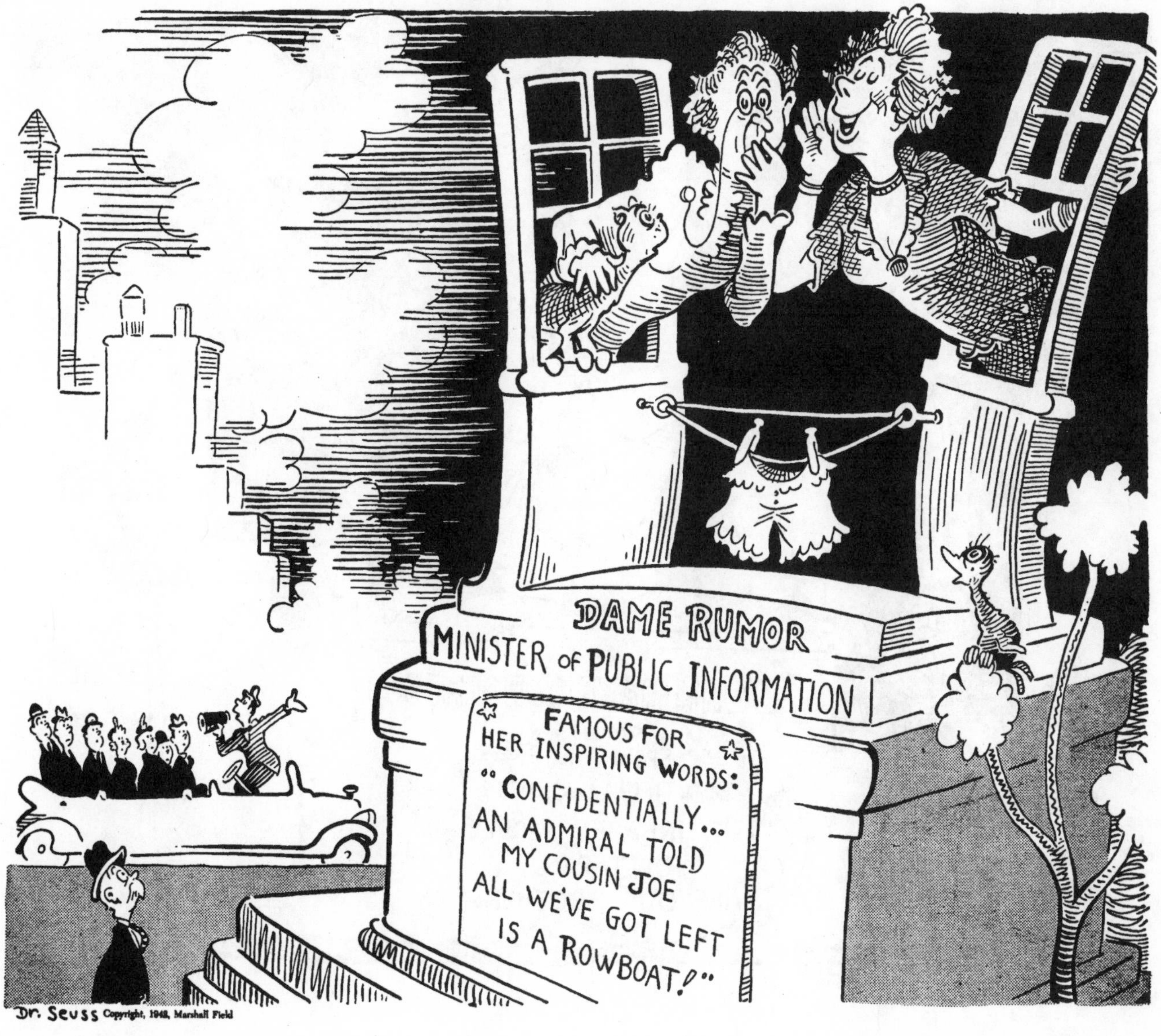

DAME RUMOR
MINISTER of PUBLIC INFORMATION
FAMOUS FOR HER INSPIRING WORDS: "CONFIDENTIALLY... AN ADMIRAL TOLD MY COUSIN JOE ALL WE'VE GOT LEFT IS A ROWBOAT!"
Dr. Seuss Copyright, 1942, Marshall Field

197 – January 8, 1942

WAR MONUMENTS No. 4

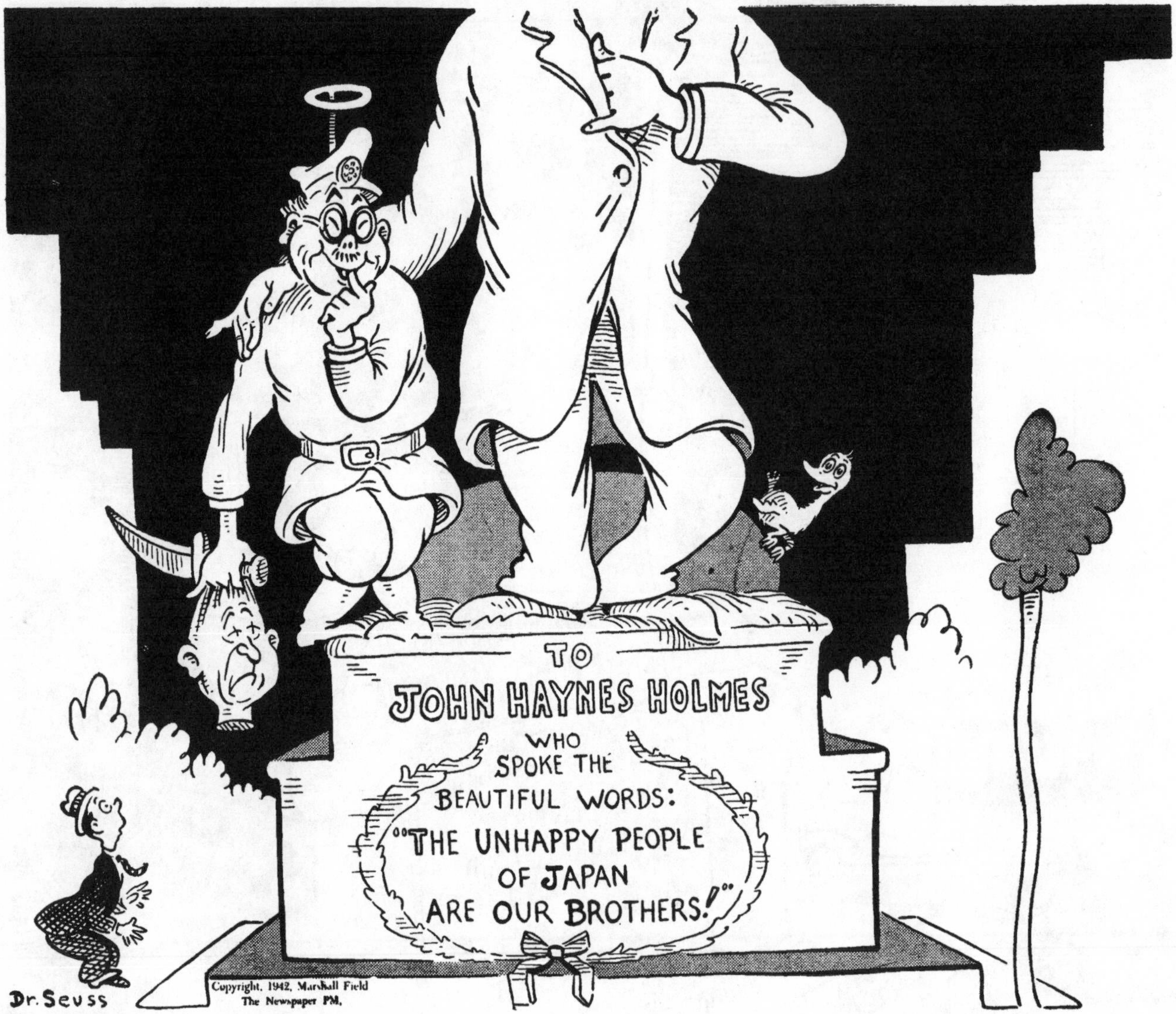
TO
JOHN HAYNES HOLMES
WHO
SPOKE THE
BEAUTIFUL WORDS:
"THE UNHAPPY PEOPLE
OF JAPAN
ARE OUR BROTHERS!"
Dr. Seuss
Copyright, 1942, Marshall Field
The Newspaper PM.

198 — January 13, 1942

WAR MONUMENTS No. 5

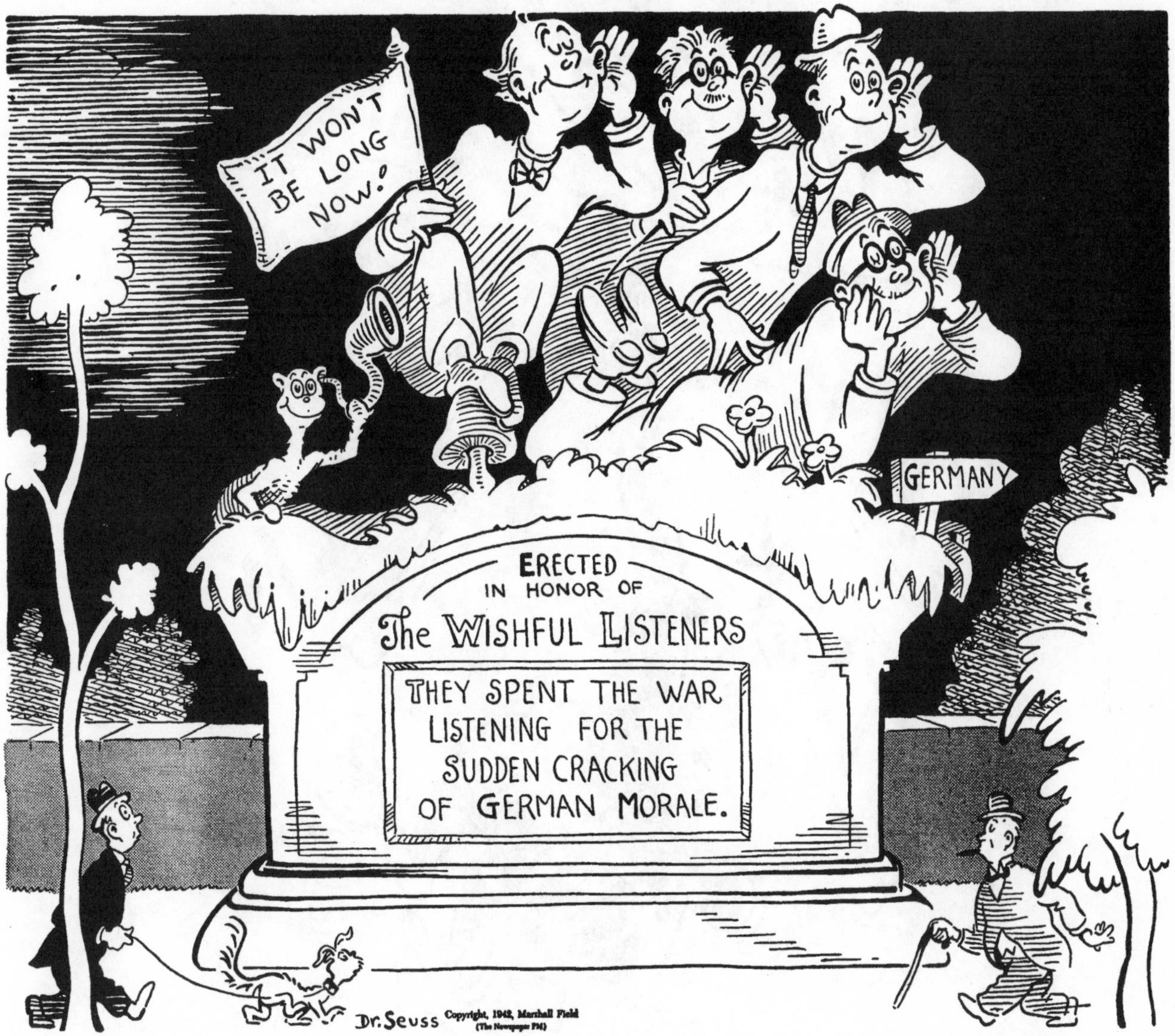
IT WON'T BE LONG NOW!
GERMANY
ERECTED IN HONOR OF
The WISHFUL LISTENERS
THEY SPENT THE WAR LISTENING FOR THE SUDDEN CRACKING OF GERMAN MORALE.
Dr. Seuss
Copyright, 1942, Marshall Field (The Newspaper PM)

199 – January, 18, 1942

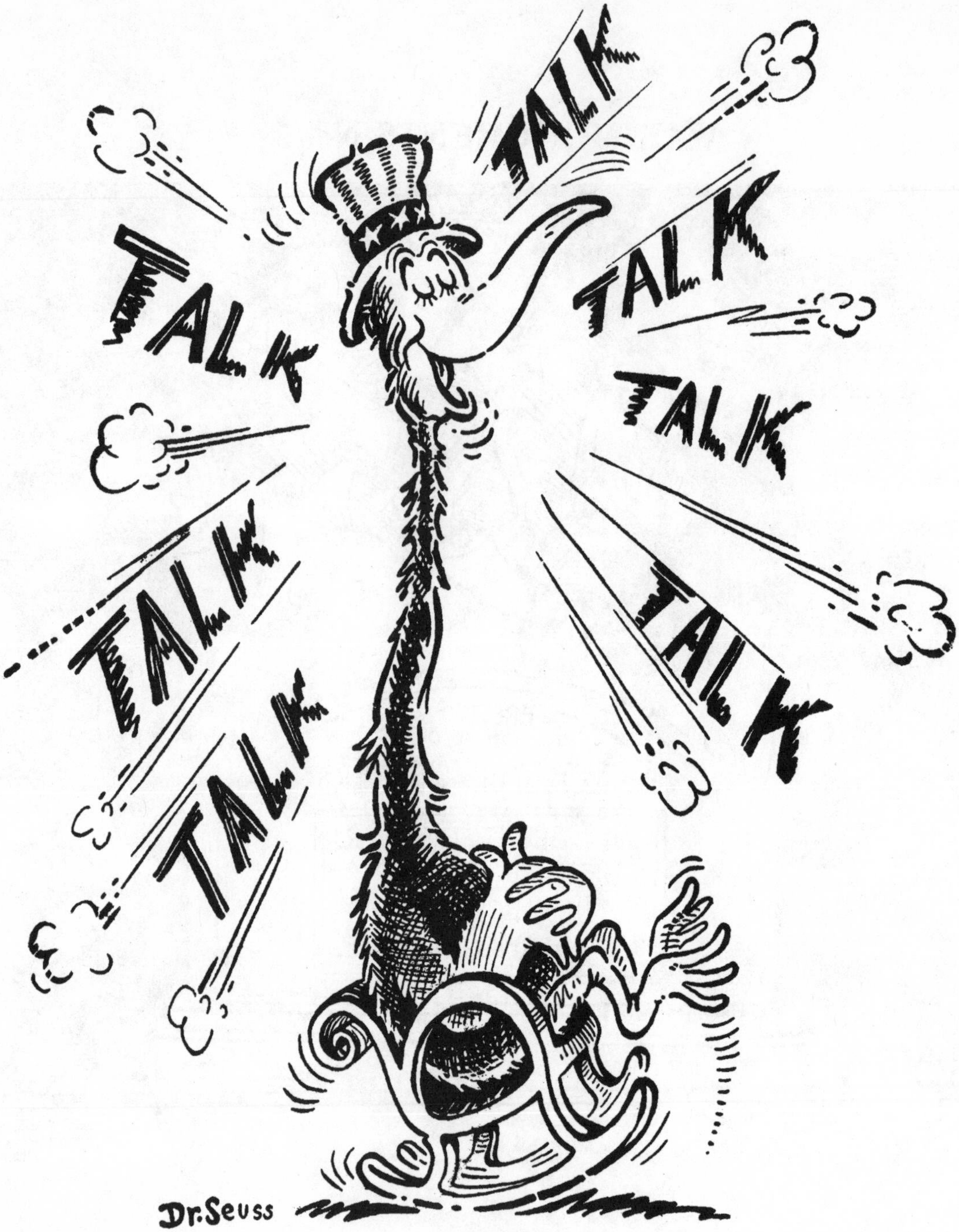
TALK
TALK
TALK
TALK
TALK
TALK
TALK
Dr. Seuss

"He has *Pursis Emptosis,* or Empty Purse . . .
a disease that's very very bad for Morale!"

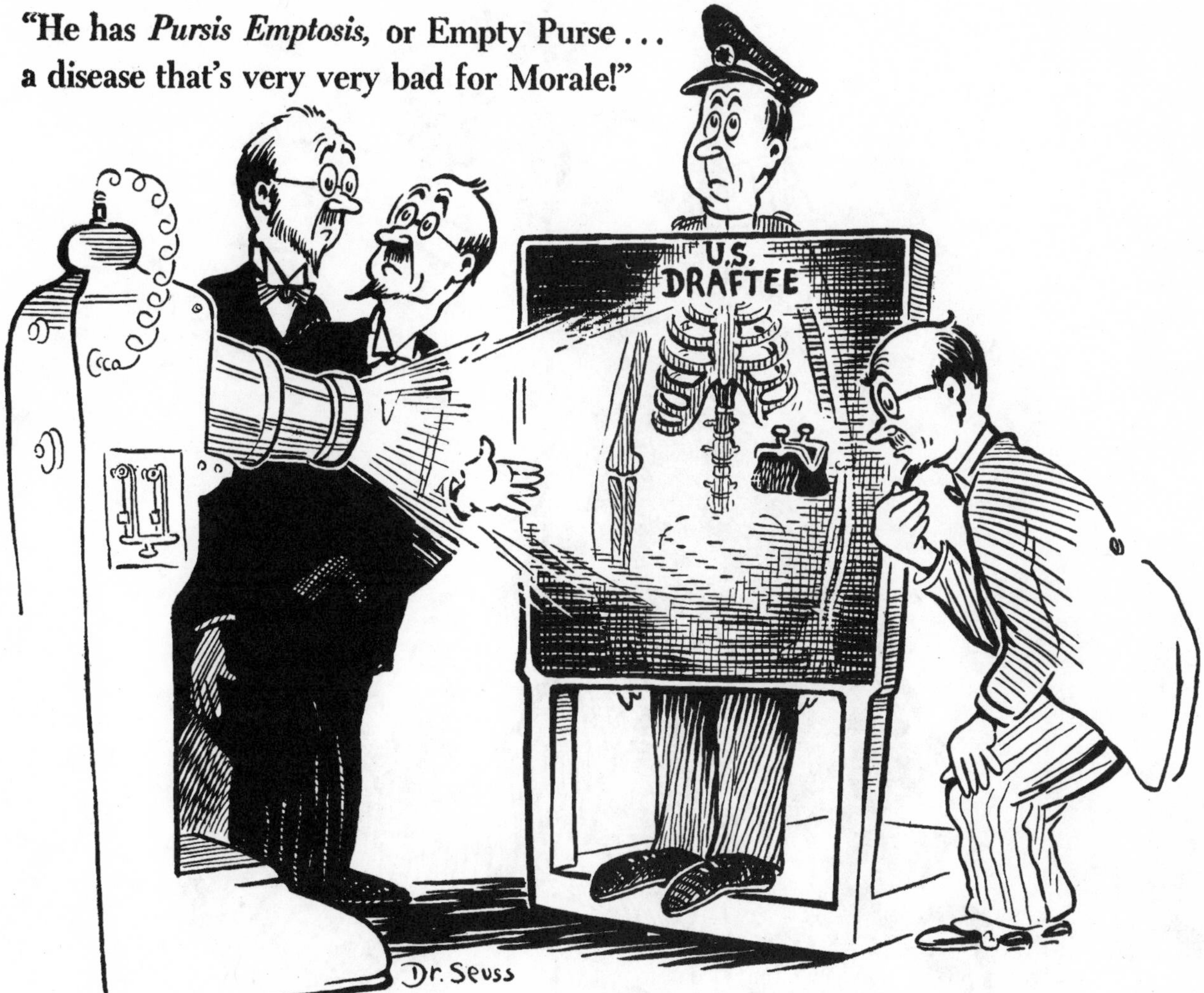
U.S.
DRAFTEE
Dr. Seuss

Stop Wringing the Hands That Should Wring Hitler's Neck!

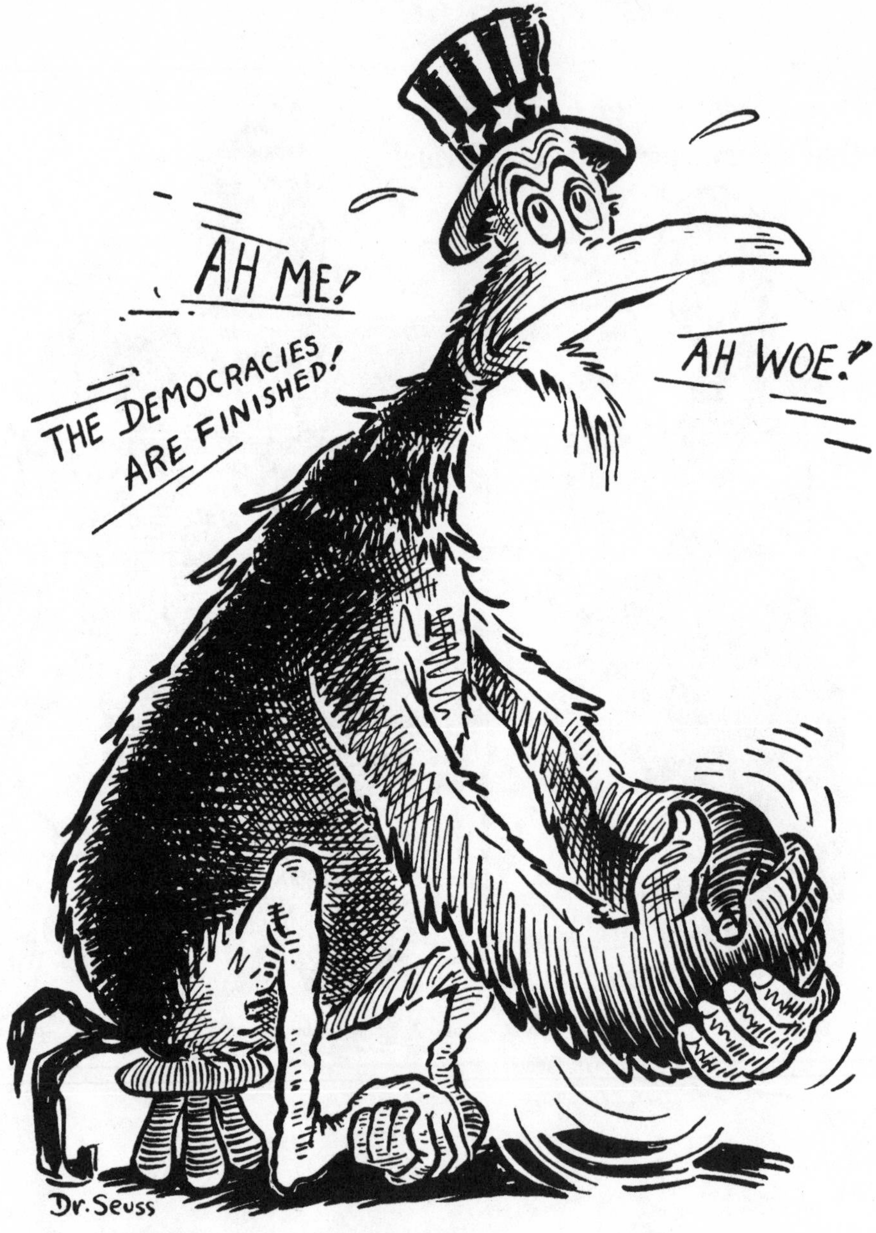
AH ME!
AH WOE!
THE DEMOCRACIES ARE FINISHED!
Dr. Seuss

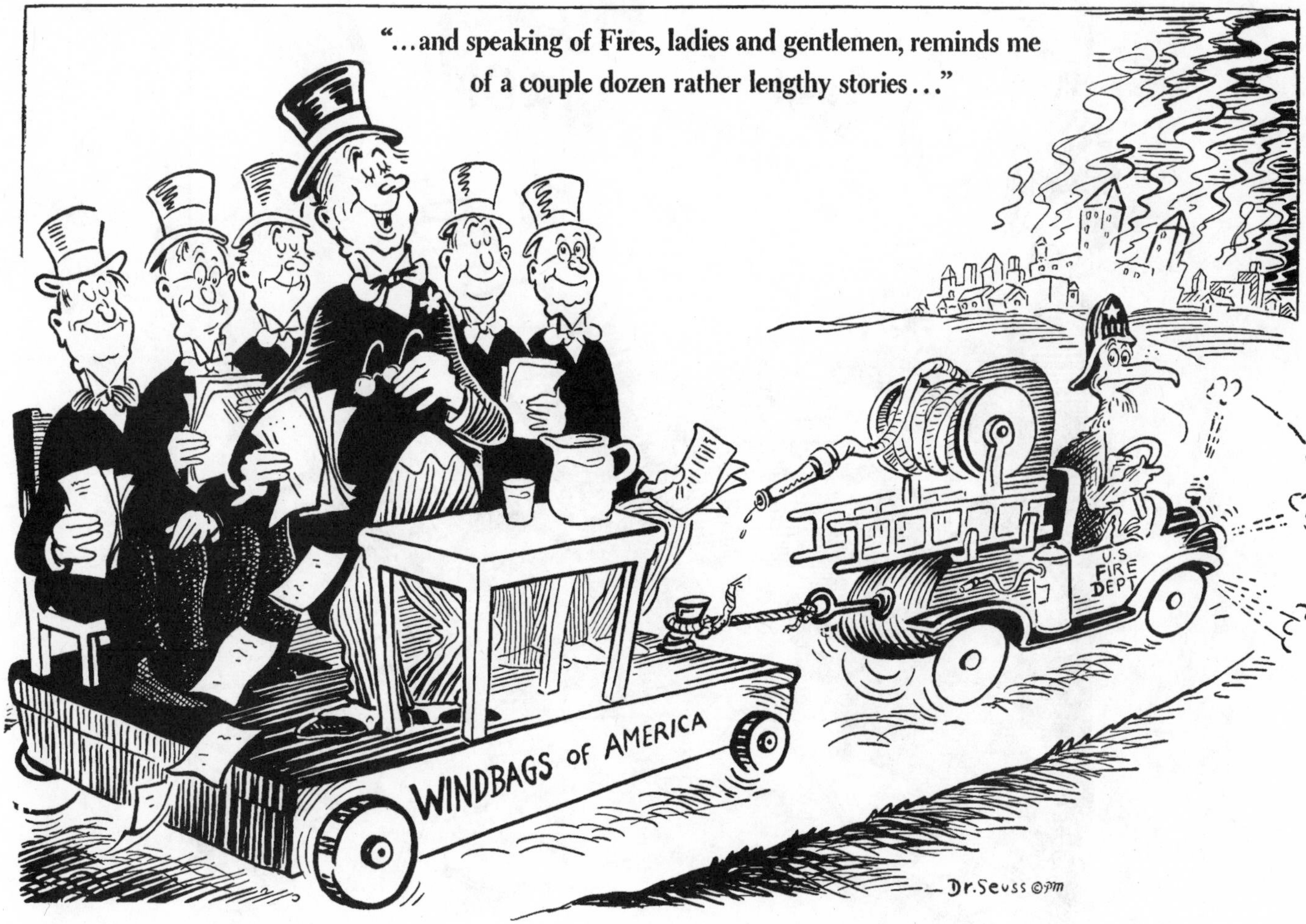
"...and speaking of Fires, ladies and gentlemen, reminds me of a couple dozen rather lengthy stories..."
WINDBAGS OF AMERICA
U.S. FIRE DEPT
Dr. Seuss ©pm

You Can't Kill Japs Just by Shooting Off Your Mouth!

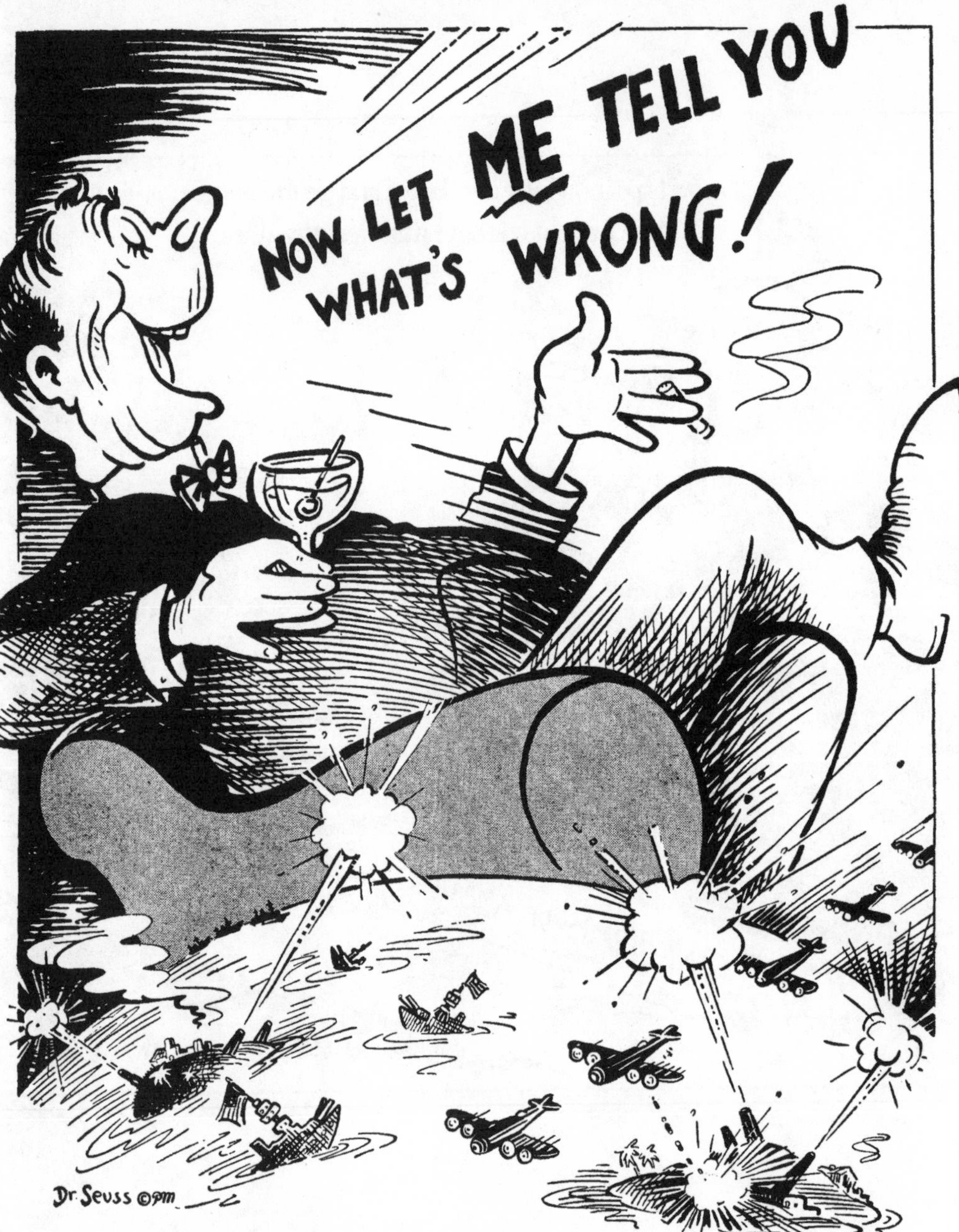
NOW LET ME TELL YOU WHAT'S WRONG!
DR. SEUSS ©PM

The Battle of the Easy Chair

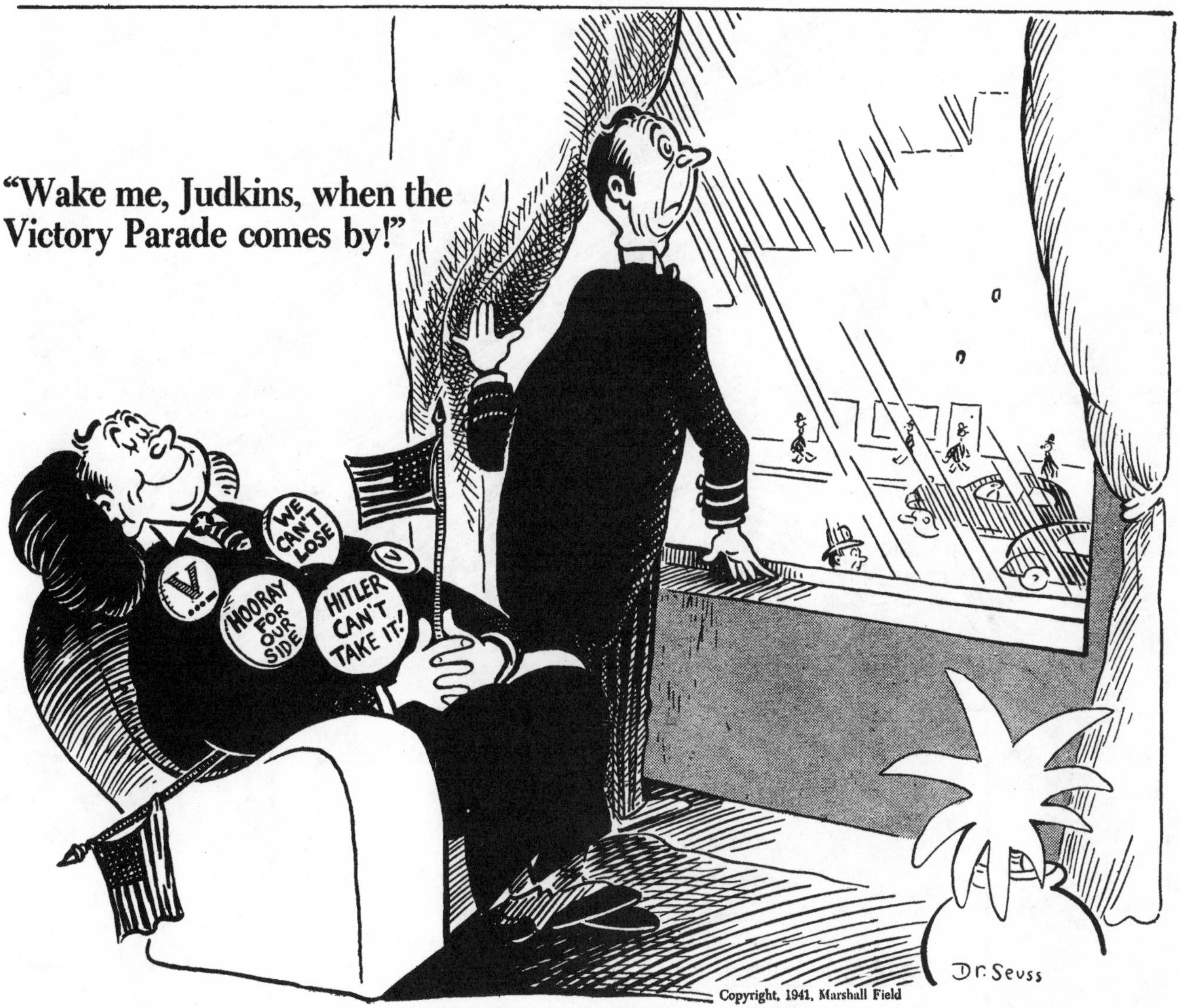
WE CAN'T LOSE
V
HOORAY FOR OUR SIDE
HITLER CAN'T TAKE IT!
V
Dr. Seuss
Copyright, 1941, Marshall Field

"Wake me, Judkins, when the Victory Parade comes by!"

205 – December 31, 1941

Fly Him Out of the Sky!

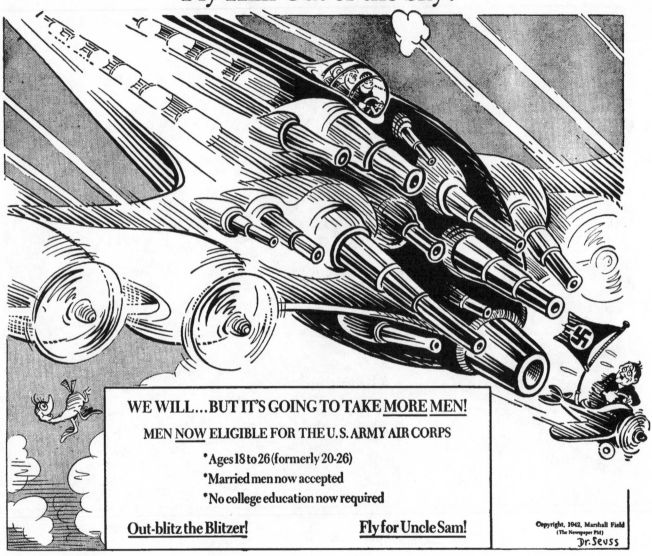

WE WILL...BUT IT'S GOING TO TAKE <u>MORE</u> MEN!

MEN <u>NOW</u> ELIGIBLE FOR THE U.S. ARMY AIR CORPS

* Ages 18 to 26 (formerly 20-26)
* Married men now accepted
* No college education now required

<u>Out-blitz the Blitzer!</u>   <u>Fly for Uncle Sam!</u>

Copyright, 1942, Marshall Field
(The Newspaper PM)
Dr. Seuss

Red Tape

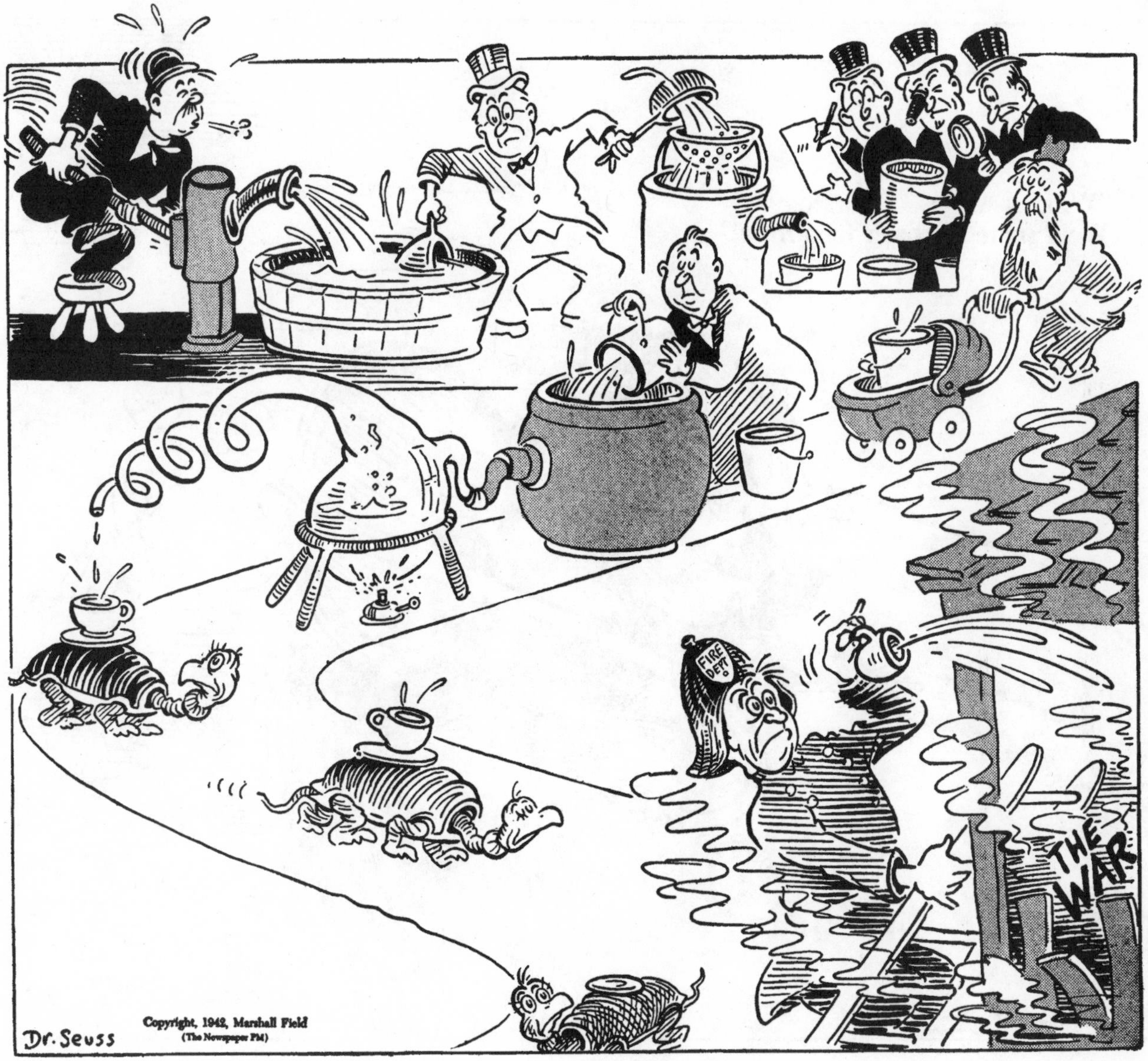
FIRE DEPT
THE WAR
Dr. Seuss
Copyright, 1942, Marshall Field (The Newspaper PM)

Complacency

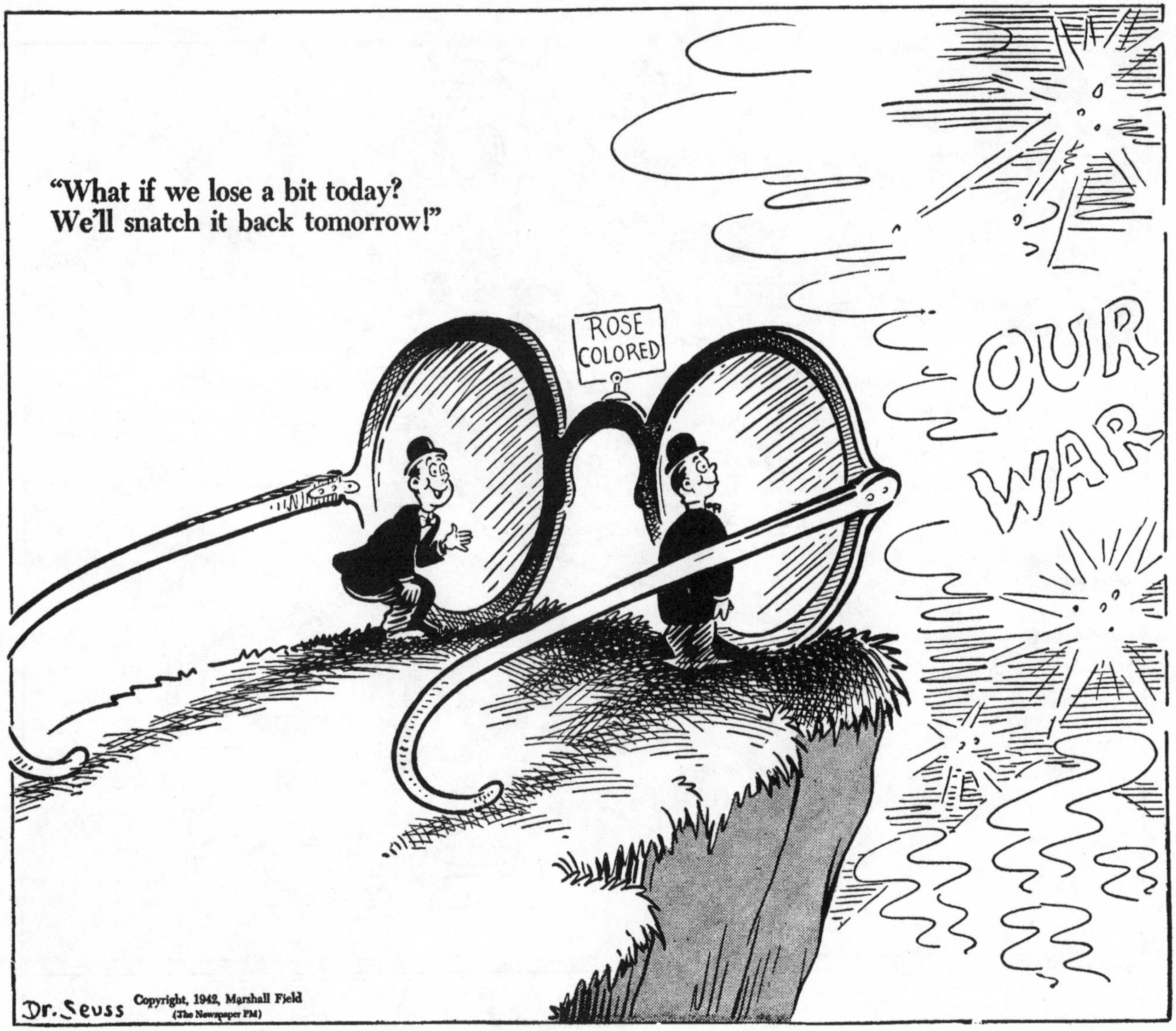
"What if we lose a bit today?
We'll snatch it back tomorrow!"
ROSE
COLORED
OUR
WAR
Dr. Seuss
Copyright, 1942, Marshall Field
(The Newspaper PM)

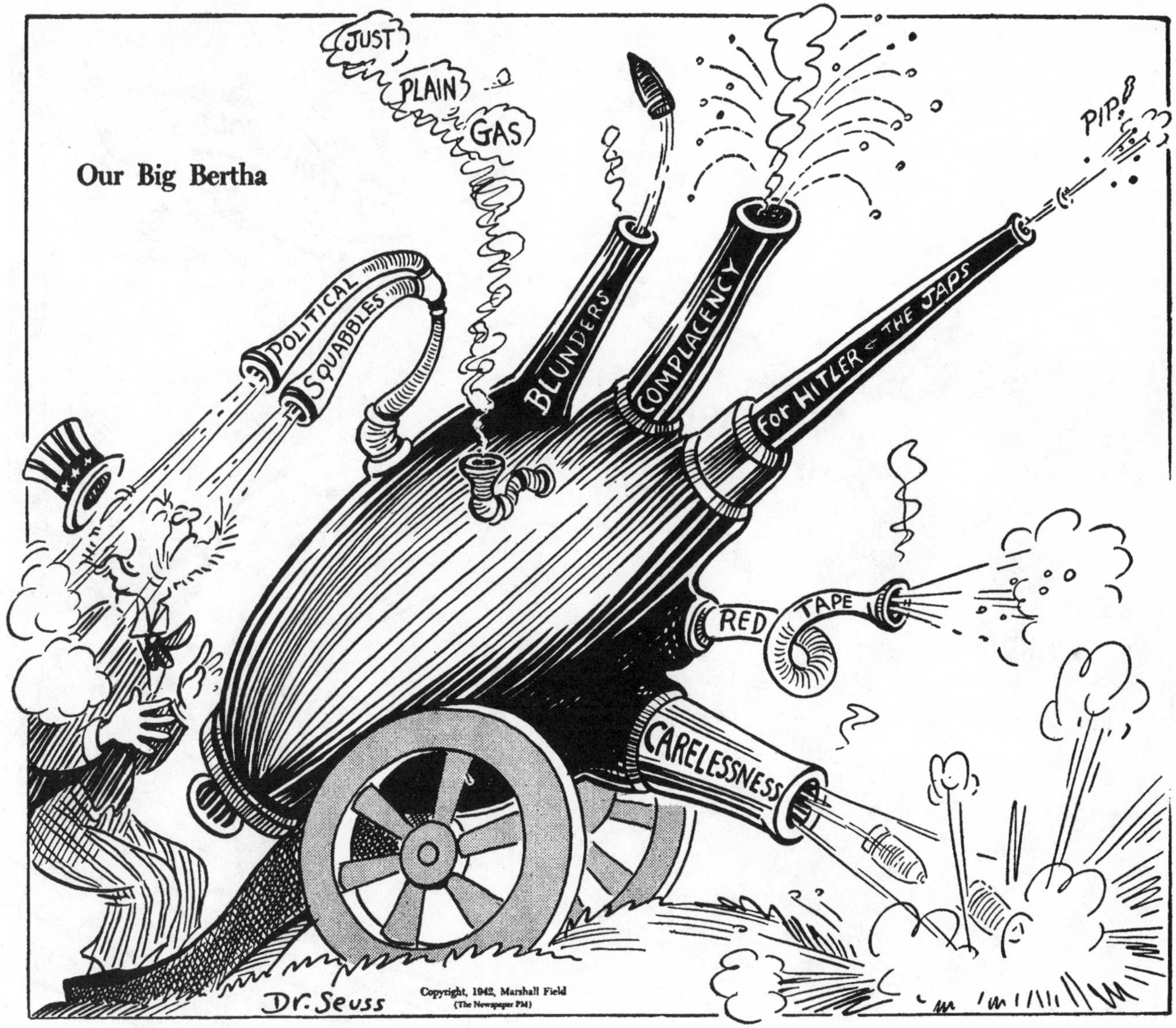
Our Big Bertha
JUST
PLAIN
GAS
PIP!
POLITICAL
SQUABBLES
BLUNDERS
COMPLACENCY
for HITLER & THE JAPS
RED
TAPE
CARELESSNESS
?
Dr. Seuss
Copyright, 1942, Marshall Field
(The Newspaper PM)

209 — February 18, 1942

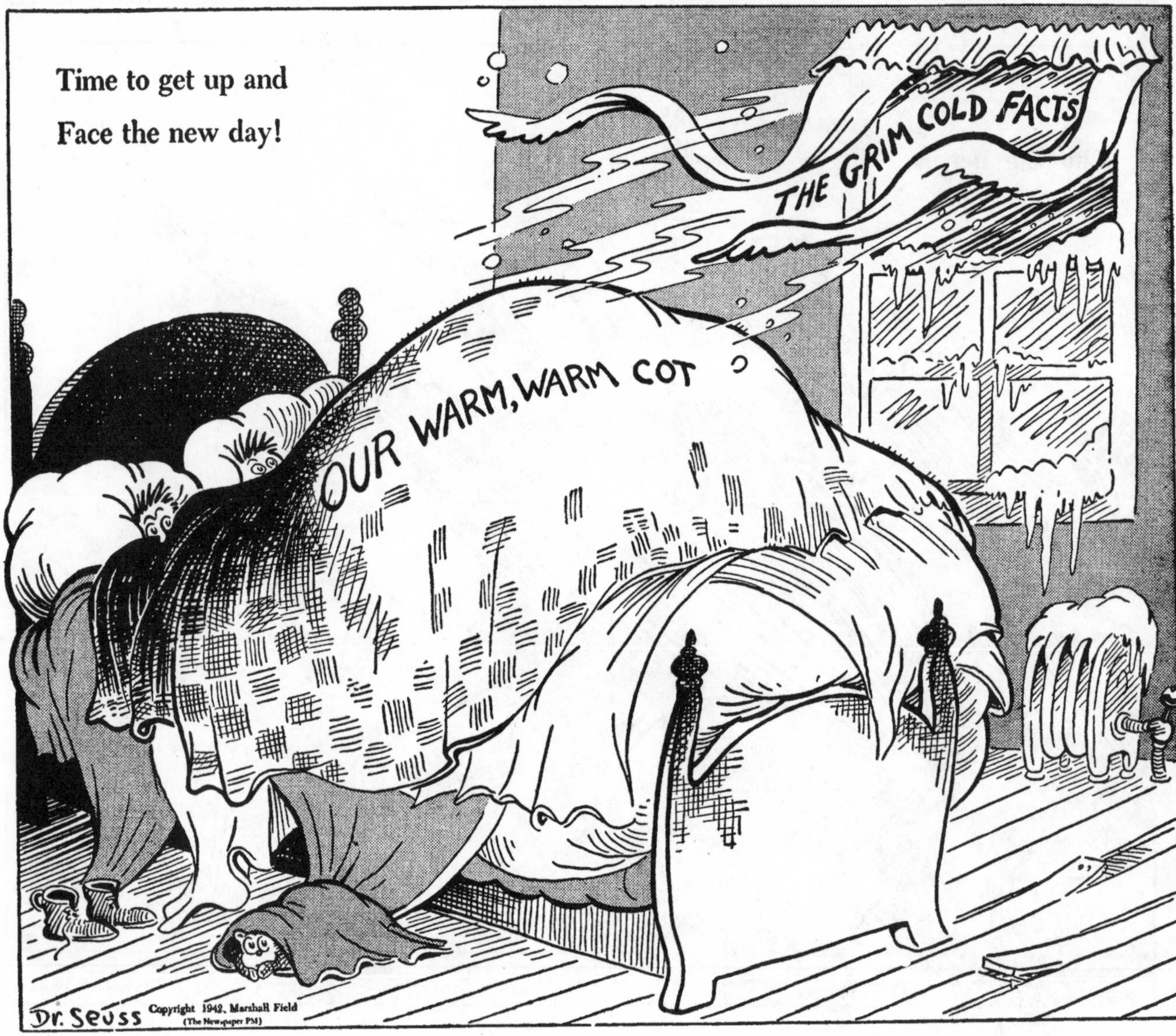
Time to get up and
Face the new day!
THE GRIM COLD FACTS
OUR WARM, WARM COT
Dr. Seuss
Copyright 1942, Marshall Field
(The Newspaper PM)

Do YOU Belong to One of These Groups?

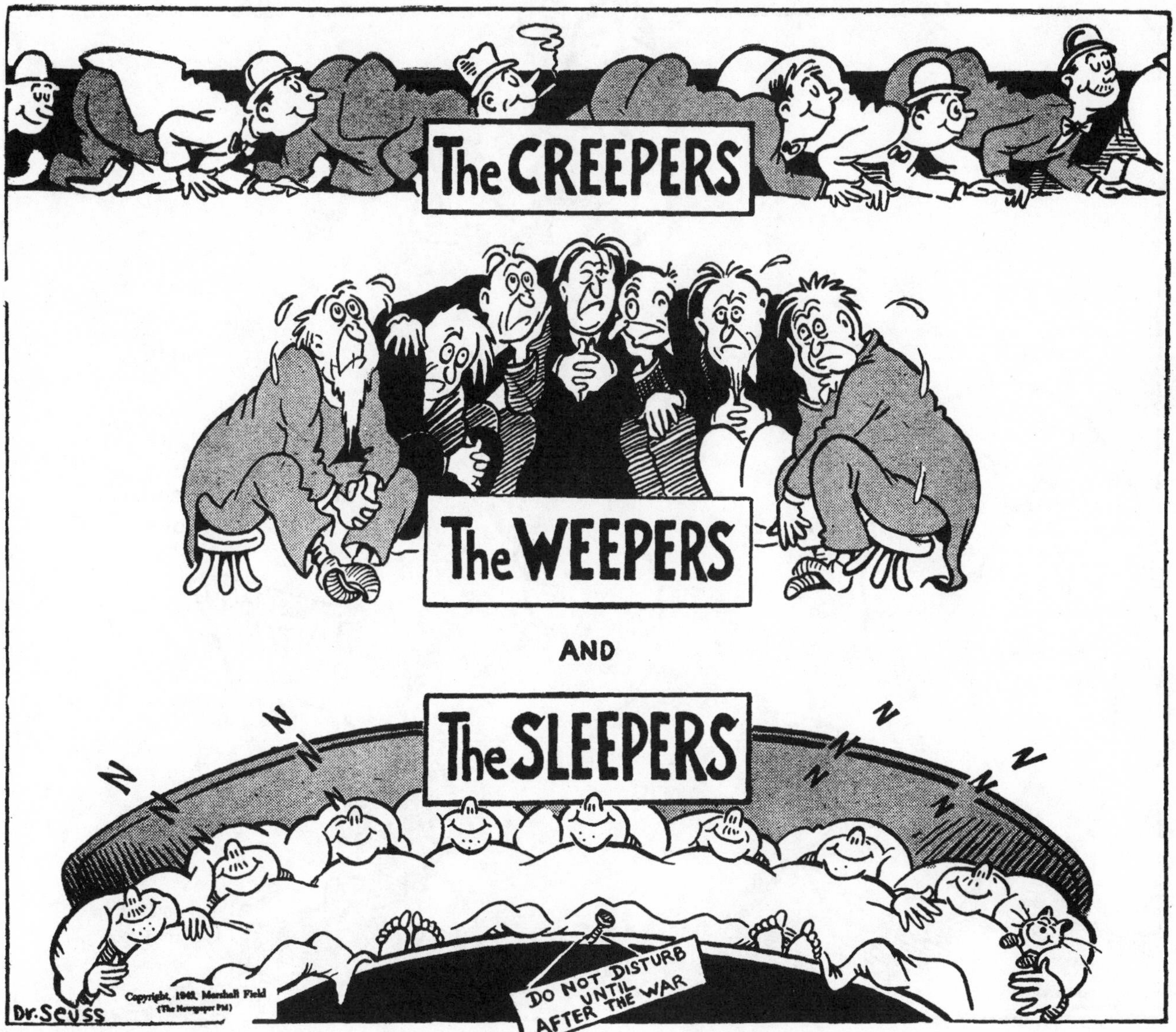
The CREEPERS
The WEEPERS
AND
The SLEEPERS
DO NOT DISTURB UNTIL AFTER THE WAR
Dr. Seuss
Copyright, 1942, Marshall Field
(The Newspaper PM)

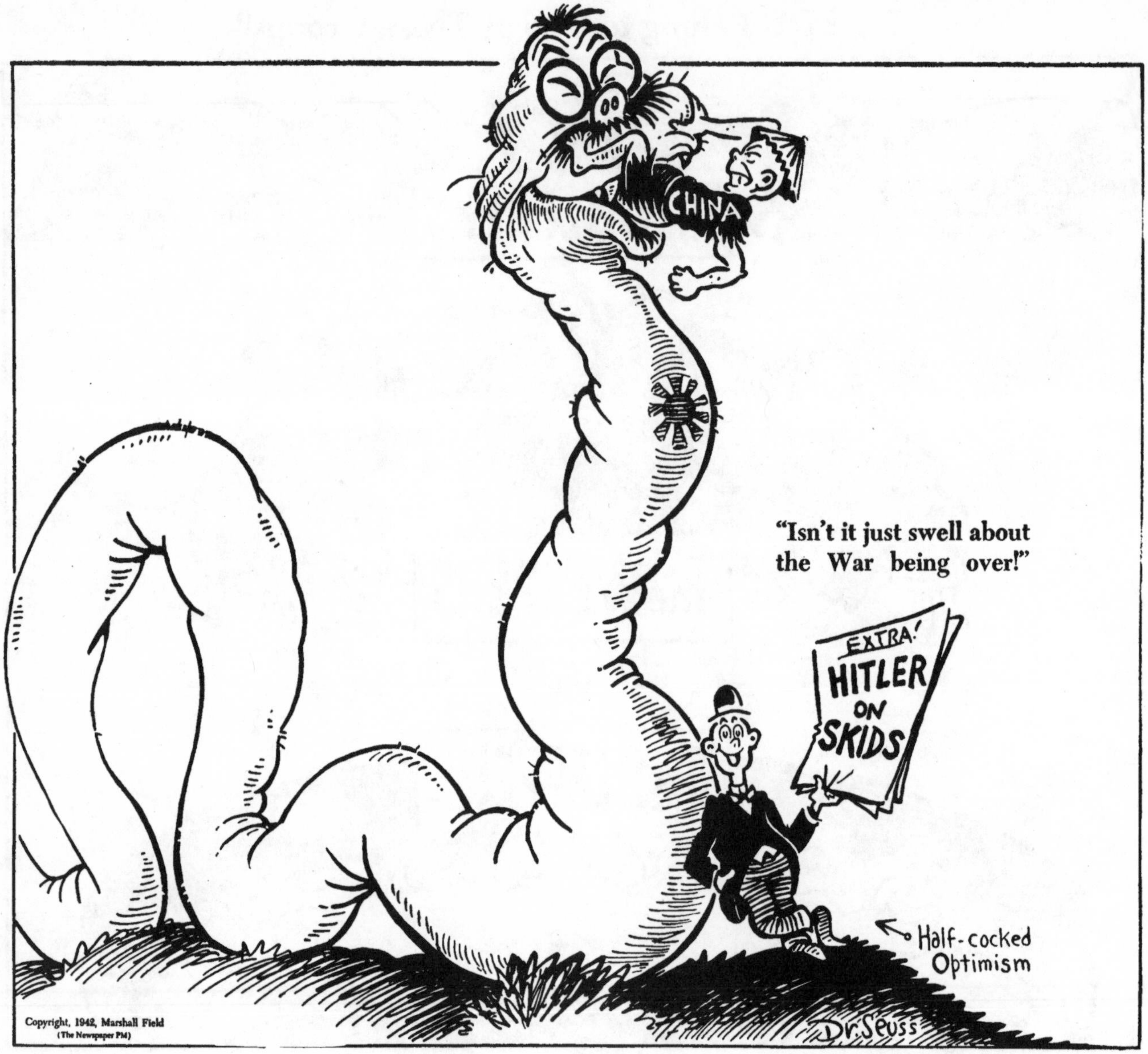
CHINA
EXTRA!
HITLER ON SKIDS
"Isn't it just swell about the War being over!"
Half-cocked Optimism
Dr. Seuss
Copyright, 1942, Marshall Field
(The Newspaper PM)

The Optimist's Picnic

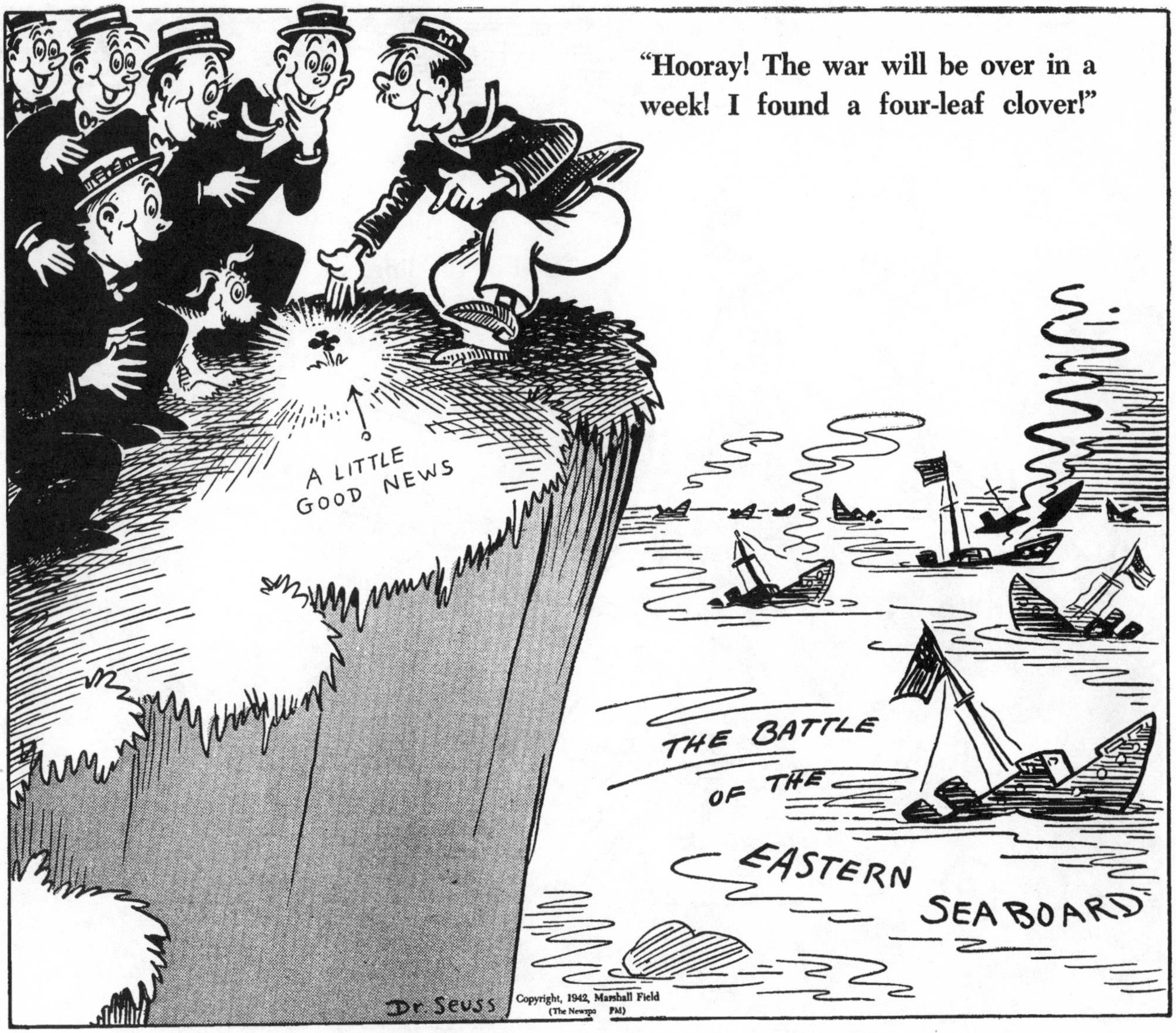
"Hooray! The war will be over in a week! I found a four-leaf clover!"
A LITTLE GOOD NEWS
THE BATTLE OF THE EASTERN SEABOARD
Dr. Seuss
Copyright, 1942, Marshall Field
(The Newspa PM)

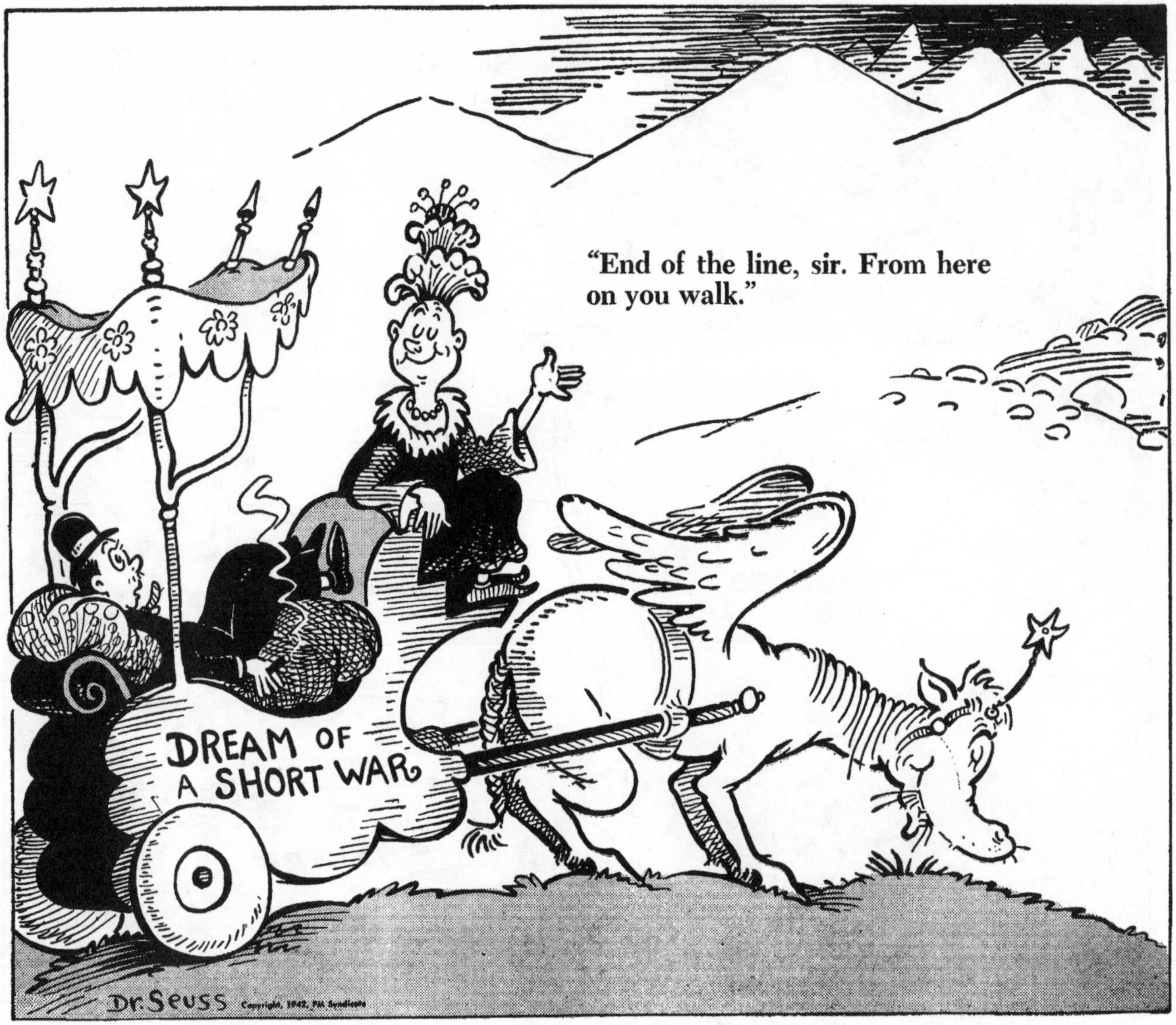
"End of the line, sir. From here on you walk."
DREAM OF A SHORT WAR
Dr. Seuss

214 — July 7, 1942

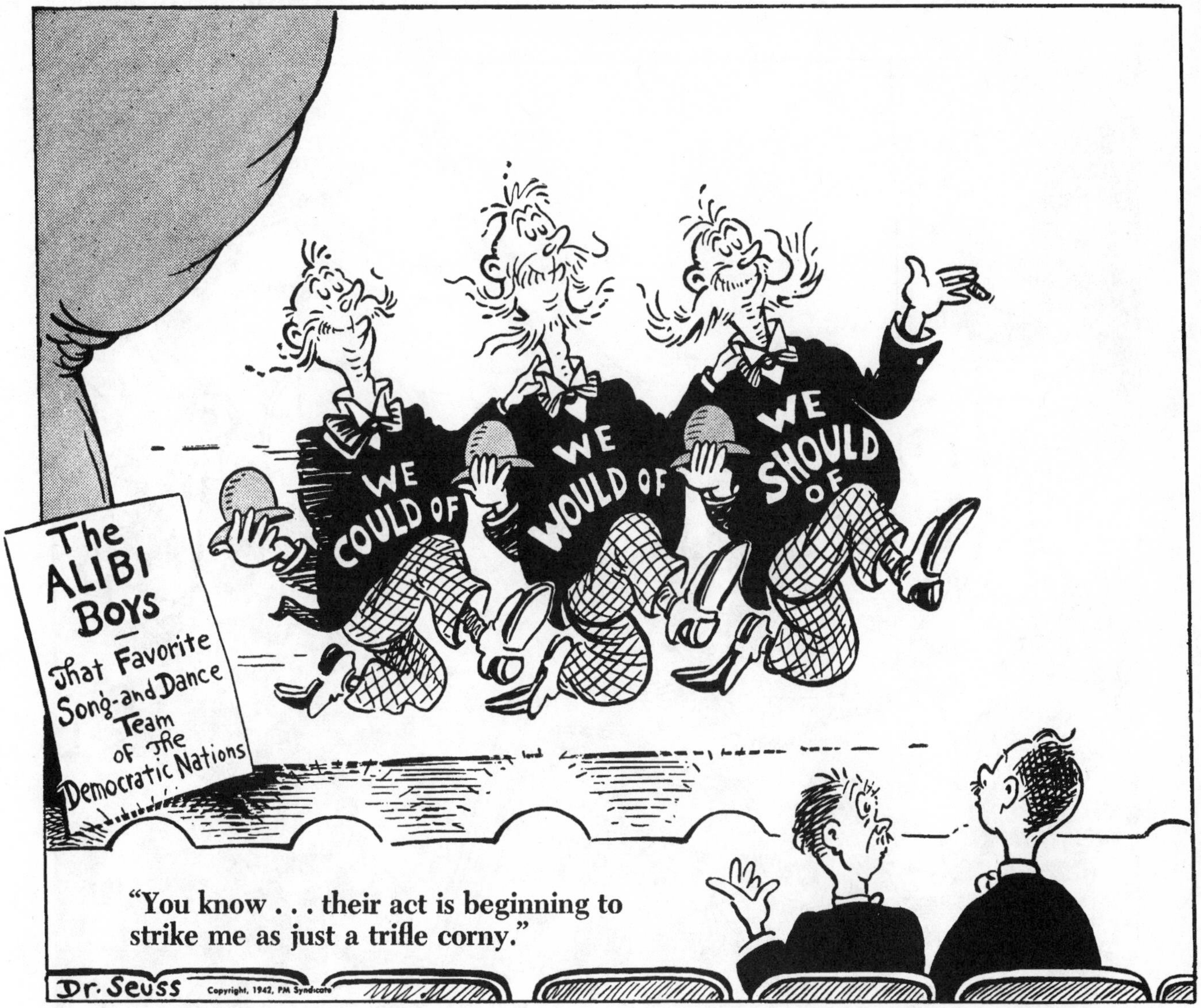
The ALIBI BOYS
That Favorite Song-and Dance Team of The Democratic Nations
WE COULD OF
WE WOULD OF
WE SHOULD OF
Dr. Seuss
Copyright, 1942, PM Syndicate
"You know . . . their act is beginning to strike me as just a trifle corny."

215 — July 14, 1942

THE KNOTTY PROBLEM OF CAPITOL HILL
Finding a Way to Raise Taxes Without Losing a Single Vote

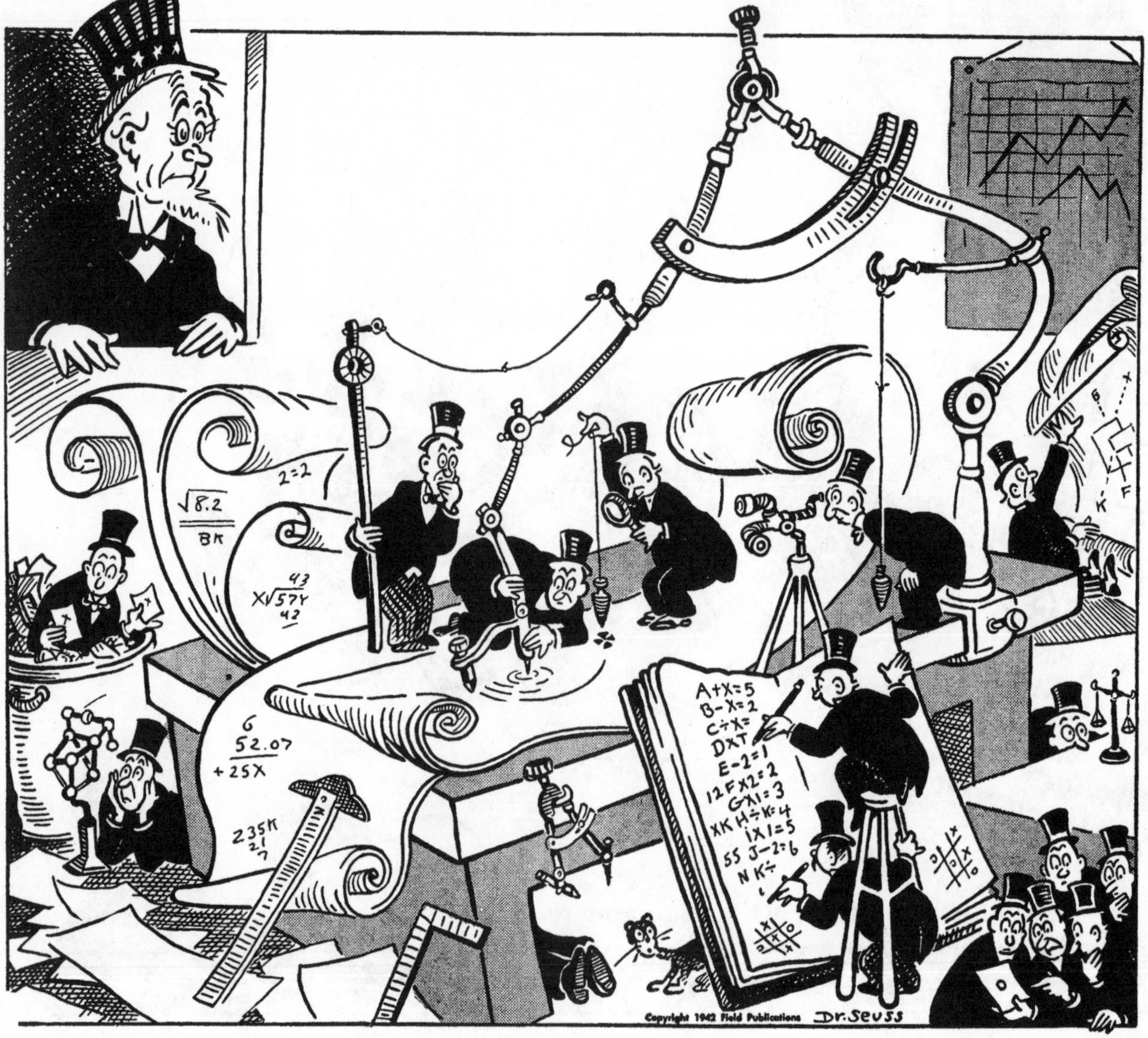
2=2
√8.2
BK
43
X√57Y
42
6
52.07
+25X
235K
A+X=5
B−X=2
C÷X=
DXT
E−2=1
12 F X2=2
GXI=3
XK H÷K=4
IXI=5
55 J−2=6
N K÷
Copyright 1942 Field Publications
Dr. Seuss

Speaking of Giant Transports . . .

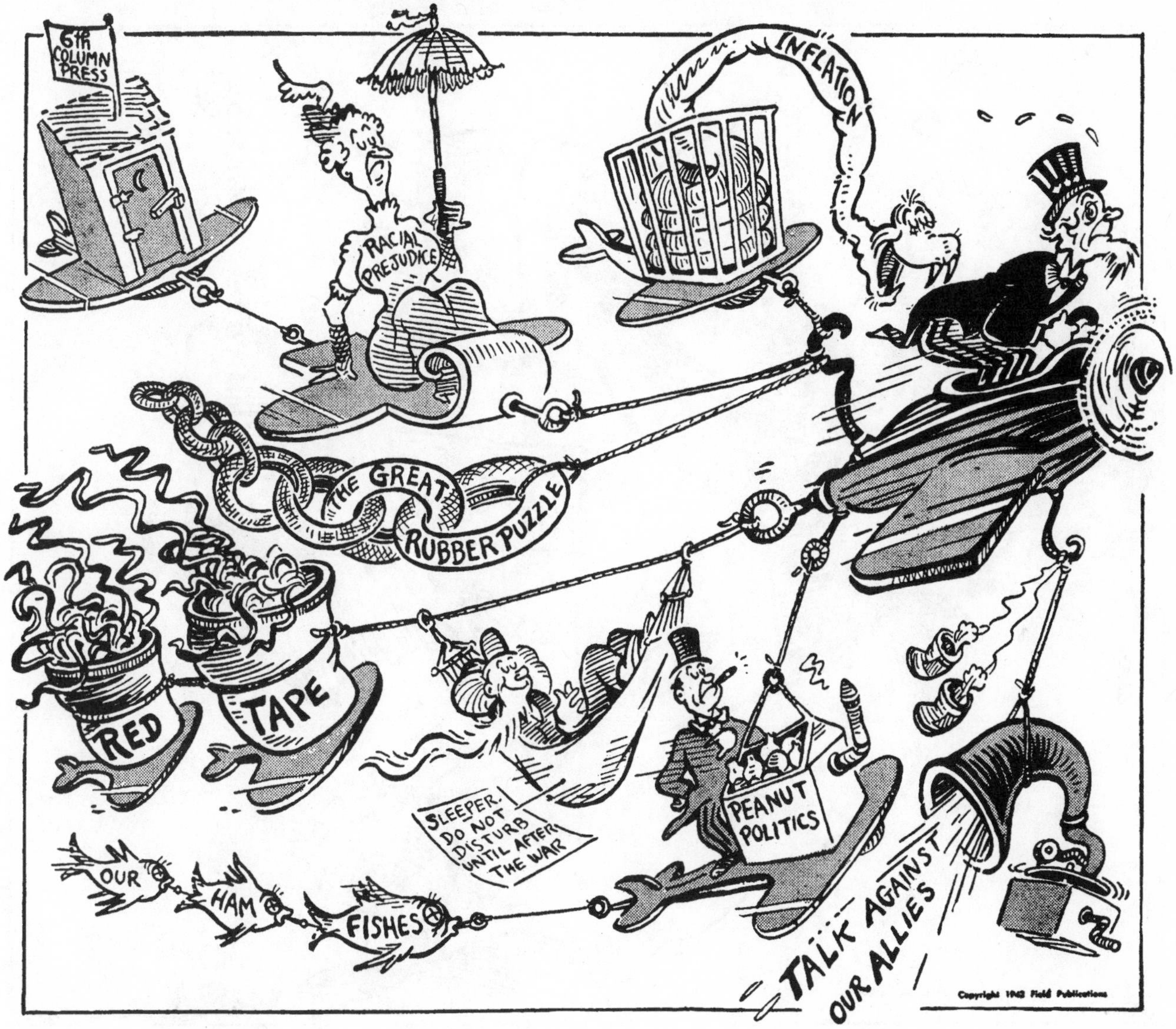
6th COLUMN PRESS
RACIAL PREJUDICE
INFLATION
THE GREAT RUBBER PUZZLE
RED
TAPE
SLEEPER. DO NOT DISTURB UNTIL AFTER THE WAR
PEANUT POLITICS
OUR
HAM
FISHES
TALK AGAINST OUR ALLIES
Copyright 1942 Field Publications

It Won't Be Long Now Before He Trots THIS Out Again!

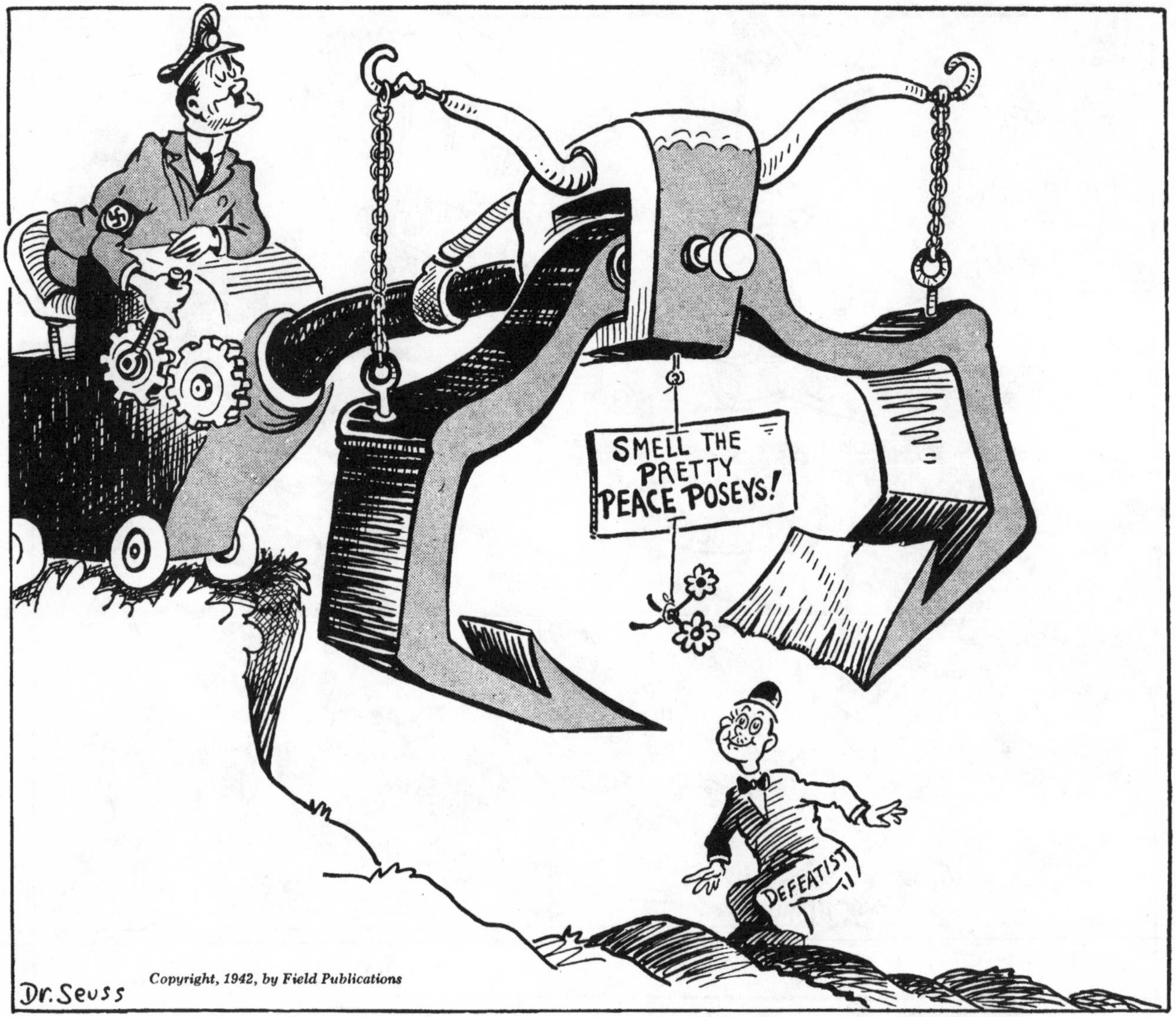
SMELL THE PRETTY PEACE POSEYS!
DEFEATIST
Dr. Seuss
Copyright, 1942, by Field Publications

We'll Need Changes in the Old Victory Band Before We Parade in Berlin

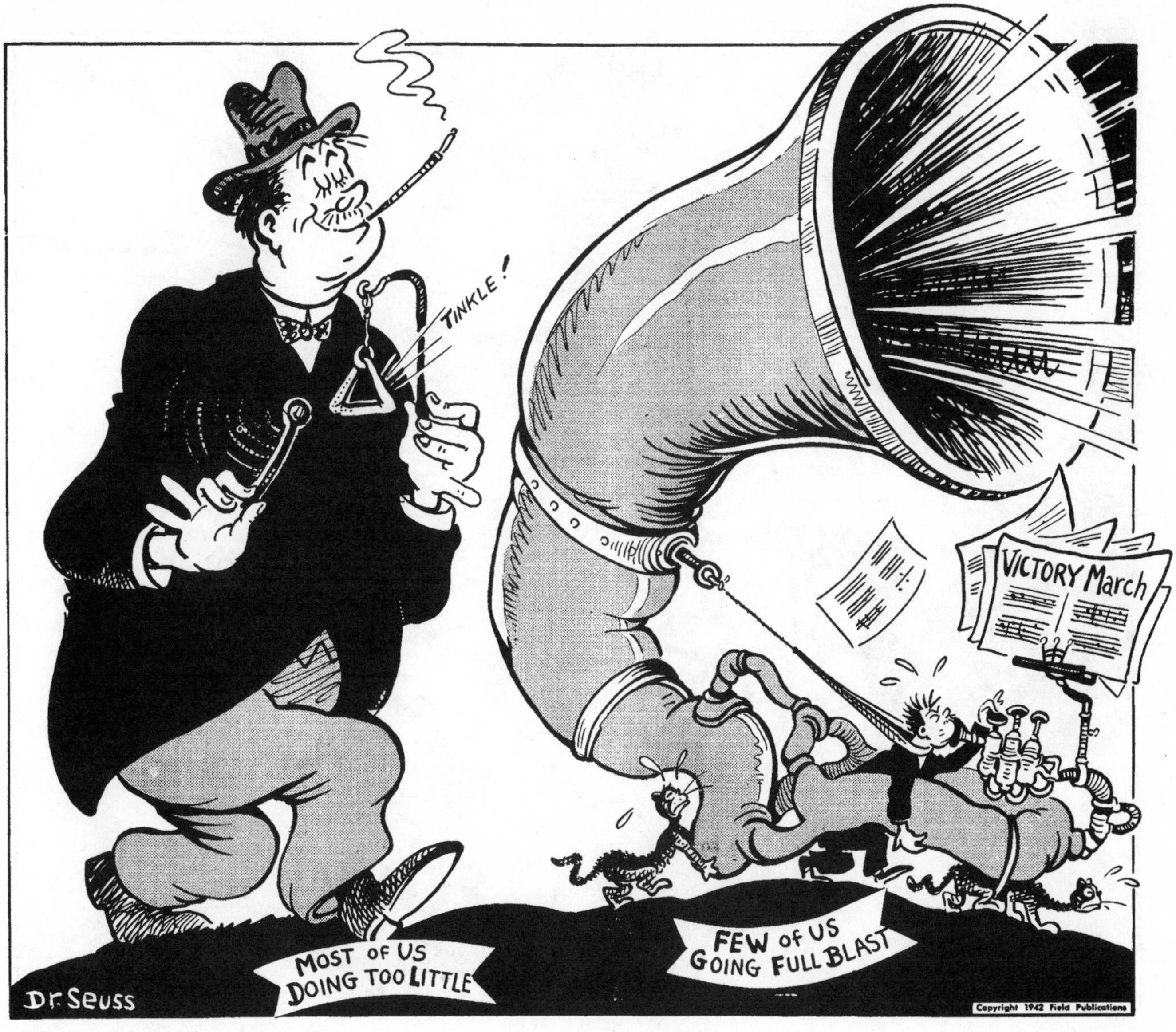
TINKLE!
VICTORY March
MOST OF US DOING TOO LITTLE
FEW OF US GOING FULL BLAST
Dr. Seuss
Copyright 1942 Field Publications

219 — August 21, 1942

Can't Pound It Into His Head!

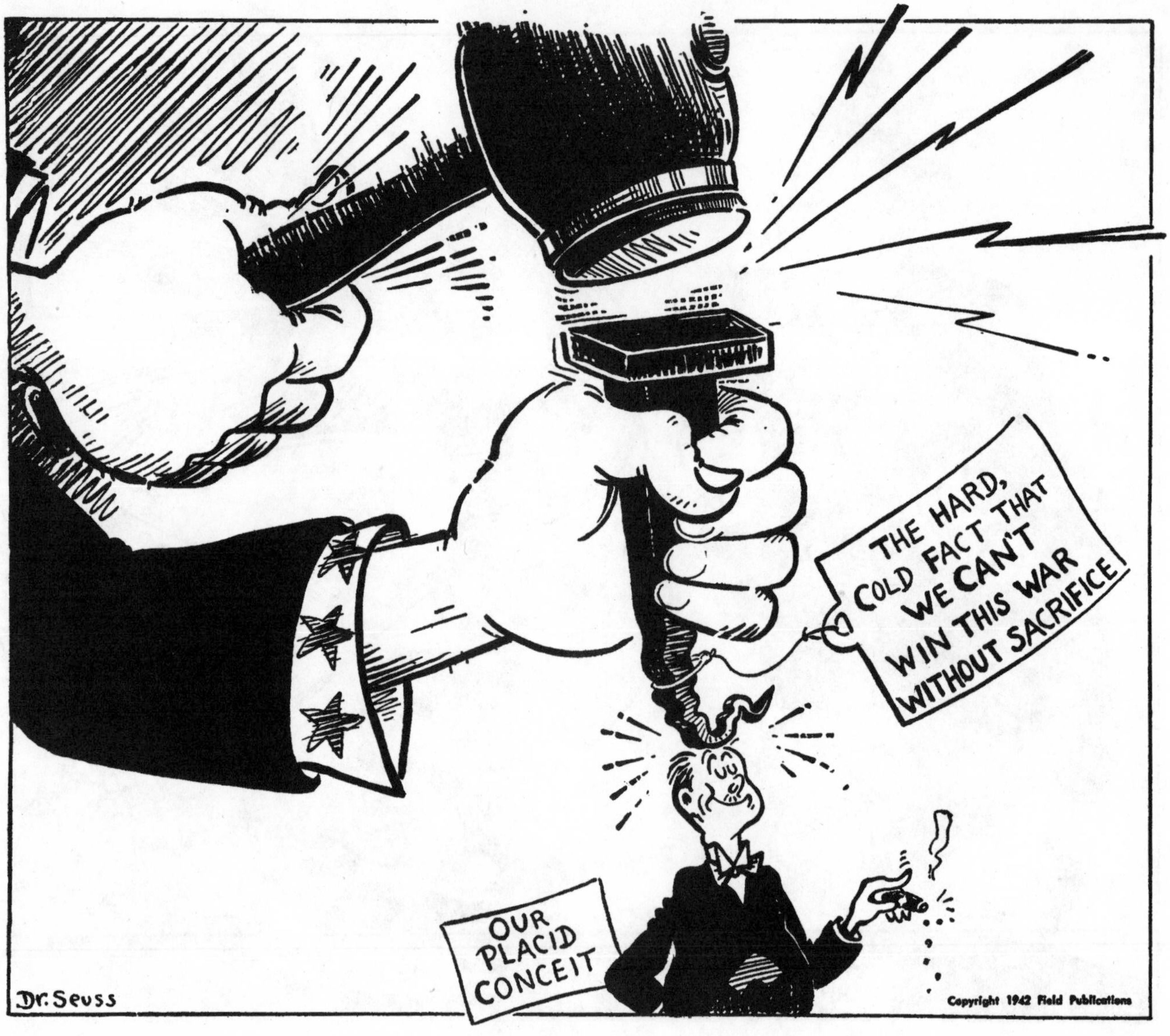
THE HARD, COLD FACT THAT WE CAN'T WIN THIS WAR WITHOUT SACRIFICE
OUR PLACID CONCEIT
Dr. Seuss
Copyright 1942 Field Publications

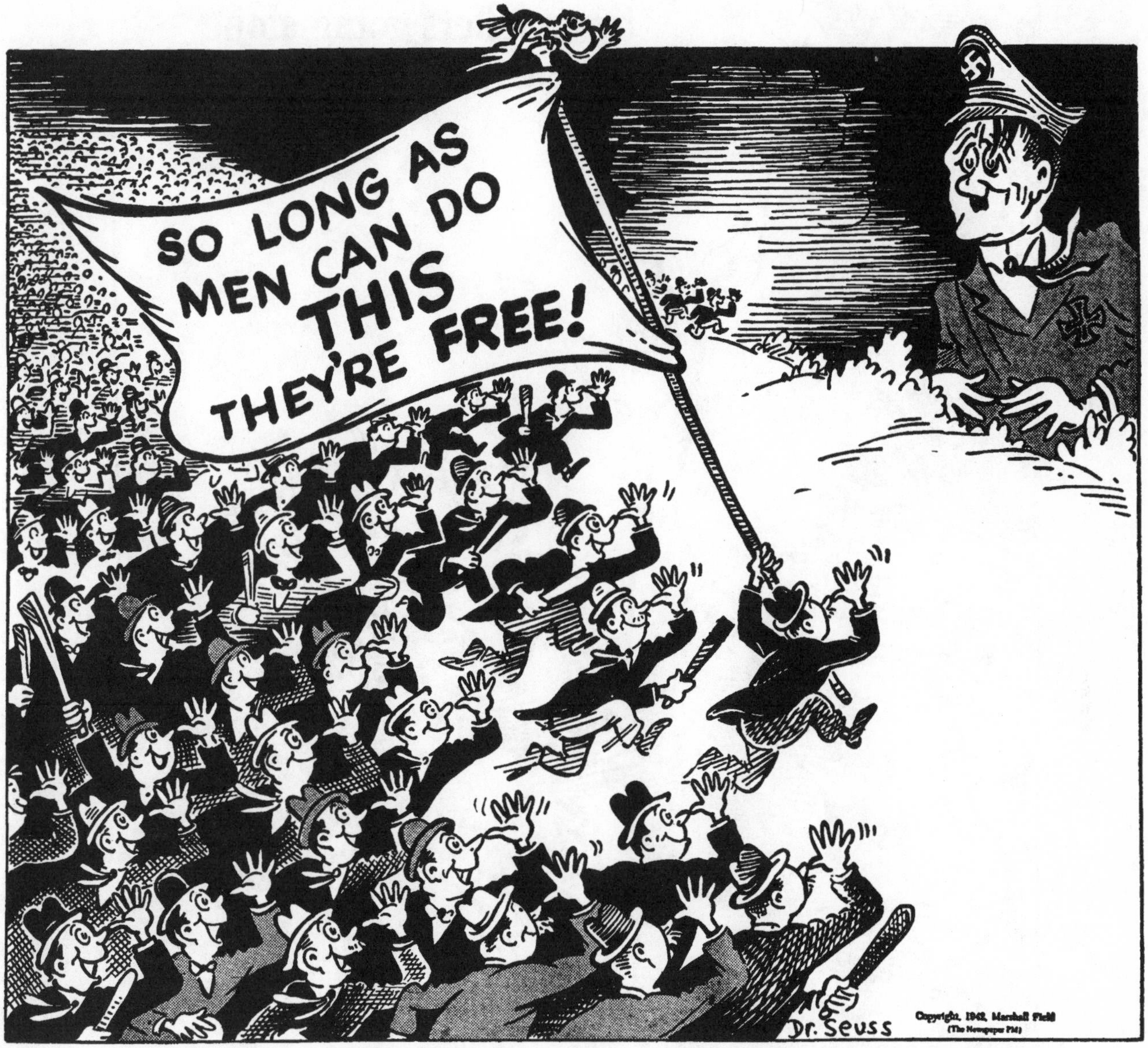
SO LONG AS
MEN CAN DO
THIS
THEY'RE FREE!
Dr. Seuss
Copyright, 1942, Marshall Field
(The Newspaper PM)

221 — May 14, 1942

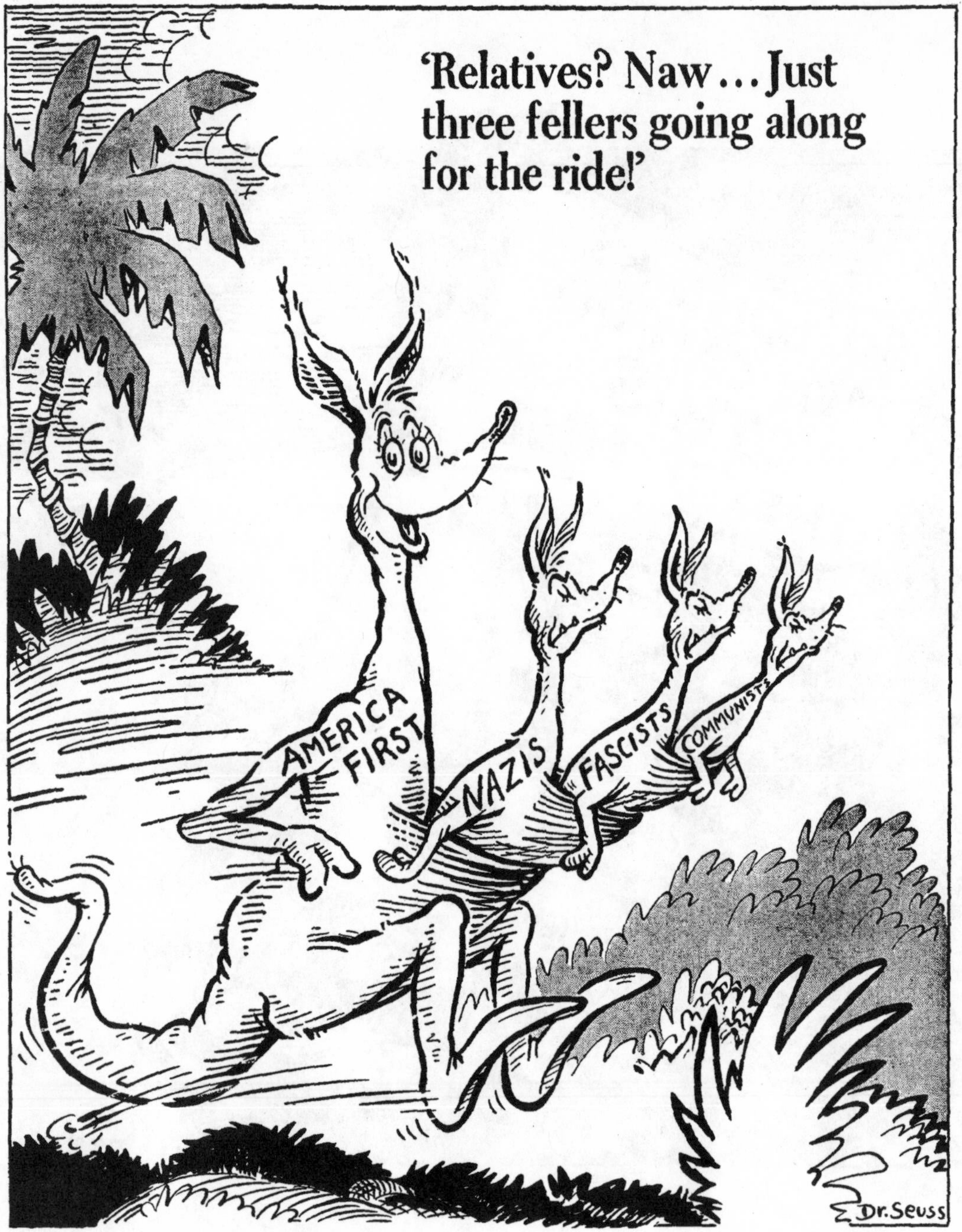
'Relatives? Naw... Just three fellers going along for the ride!'
AMERICA FIRST
NAZIS
FASCISTS
COMMUNISTS
Dr. Seuss

222 — June 18, 1941

"Don't waste a torpedo, Fritz, we can take this gang with a butterfly net!"

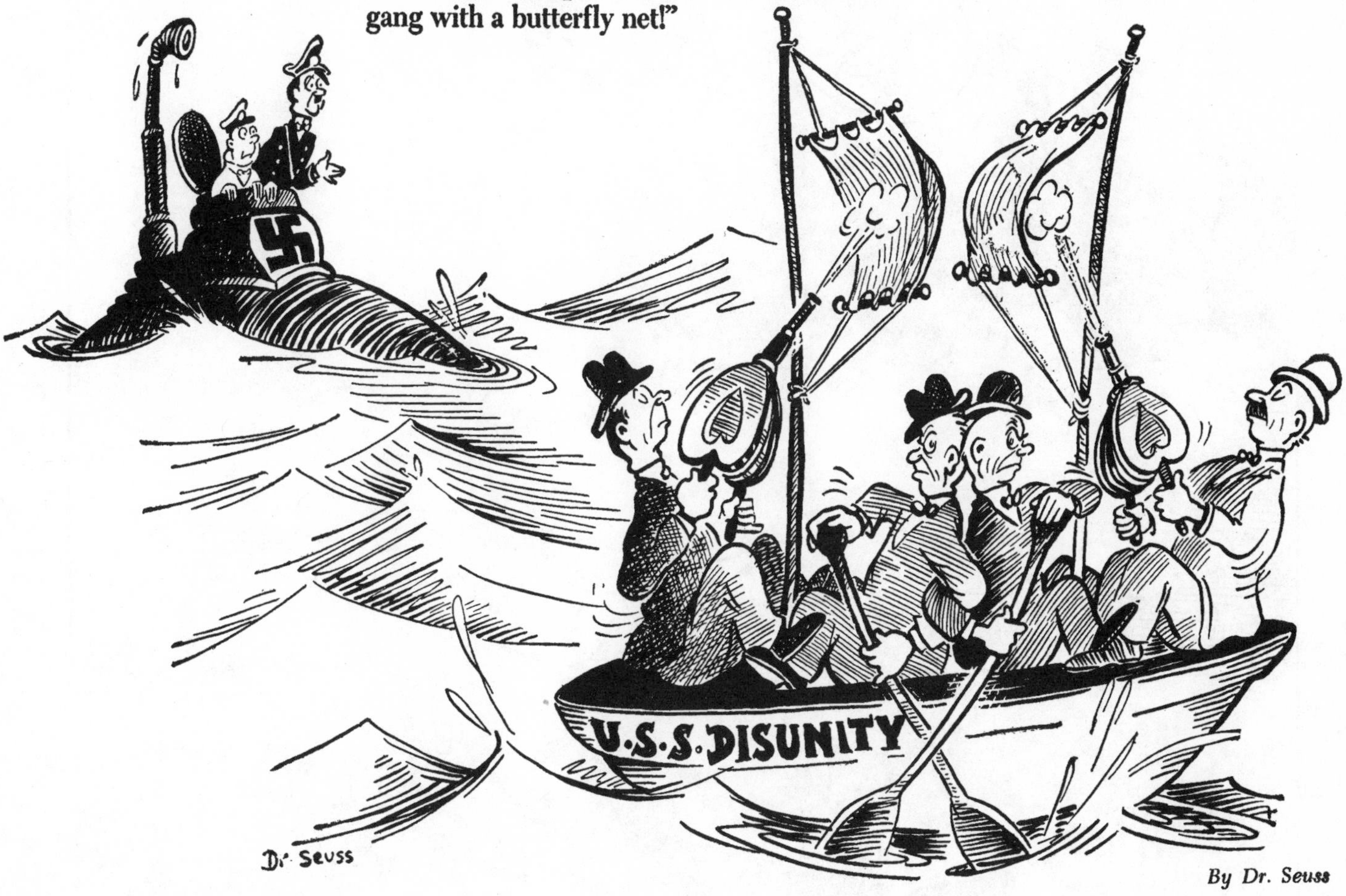
U.S.S. DISUNITY
Dr. Seuss
By Dr. Seuss

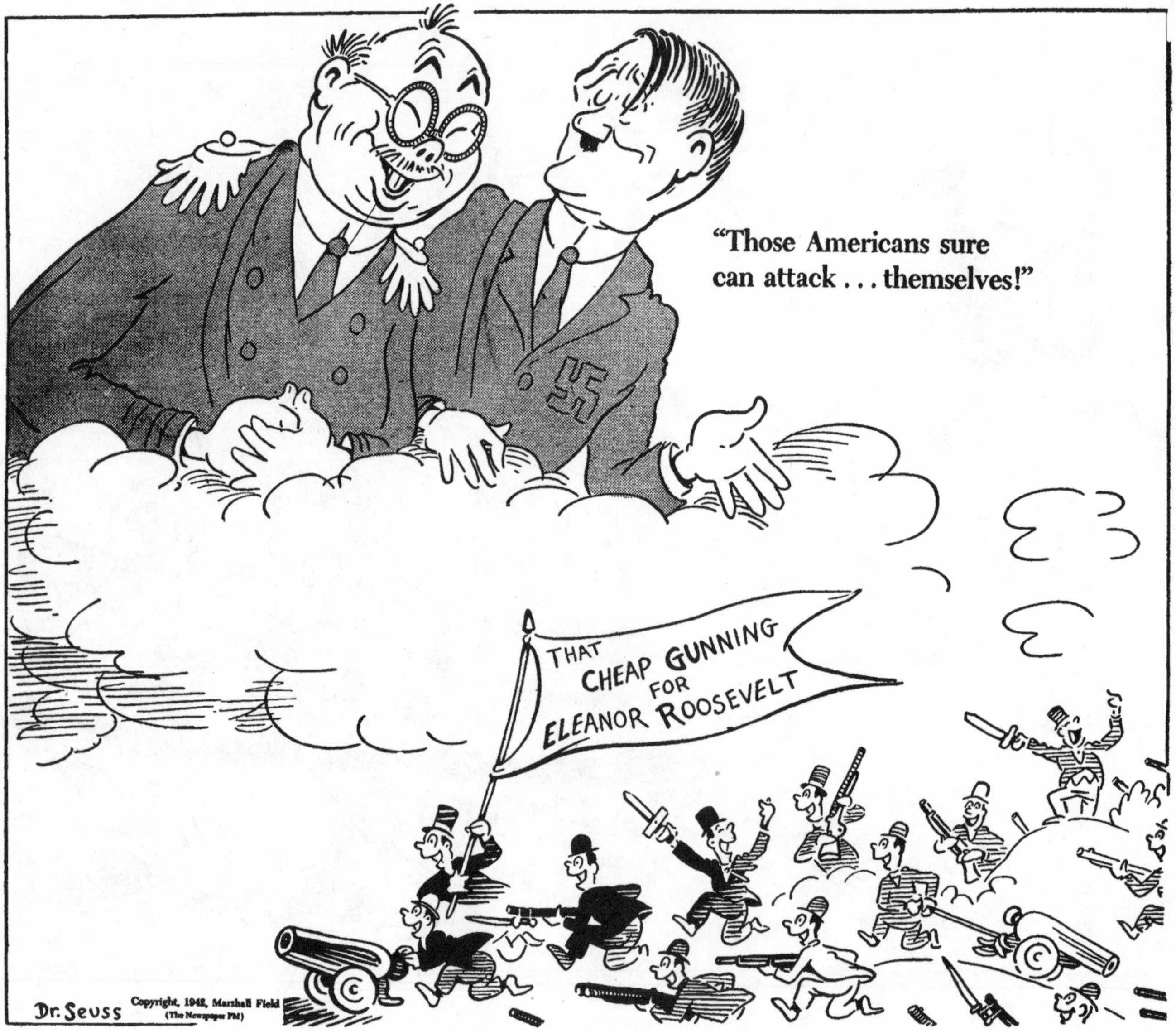
"Those Americans sure can attack . . . themselves!"
THAT CHEAP GUNNING FOR ELEANOR ROOSEVELT
Dr. Seuss
Copyright, 1942, Marshall Field (The Newspaper PM)

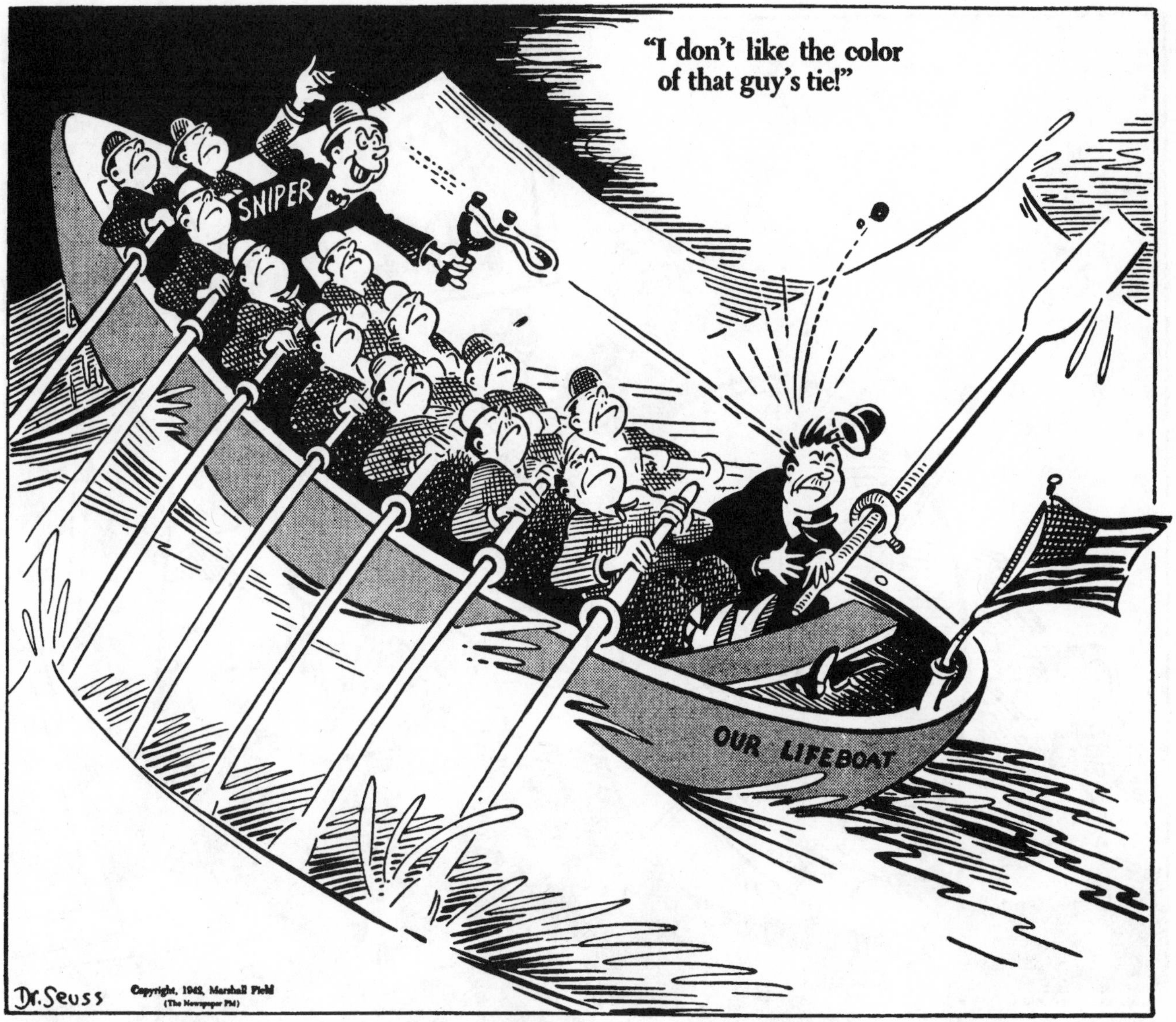
"I don't like the color
of that guy's tie!"
SNIPER
OUR LIFEBOAT
Dr. Seuss
Copyright, 1942, Marshall Field
(The Newspaper PM)

225 — February 25, 1942

Why Do We Sit and Take It?

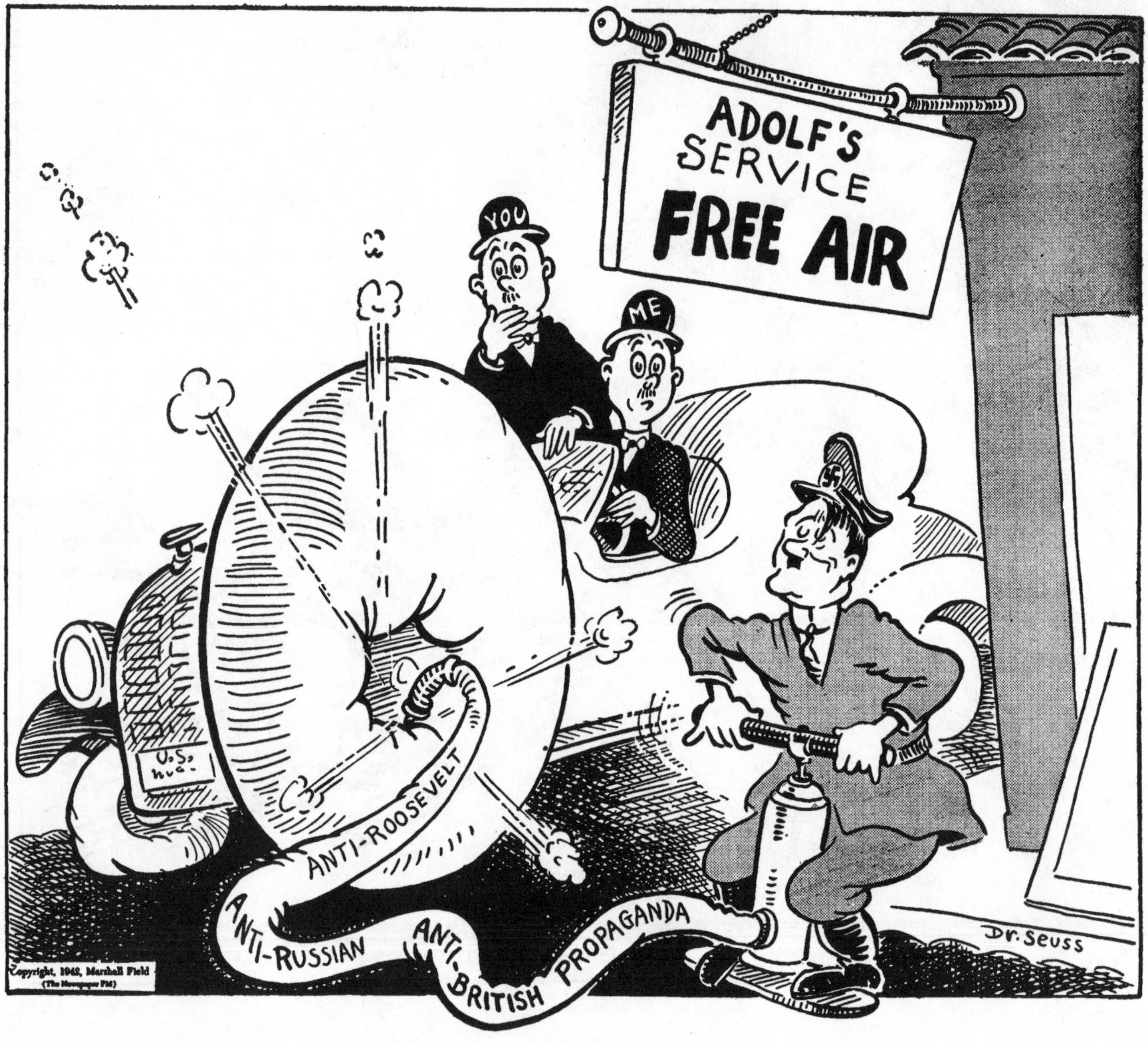
ADOLF'S
SERVICE
FREE AIR
YOU
ME
U.S.
ANTI-ROOSEVELT
ANTI-RUSSIAN
ANTI-BRITISH
PROPAGANDA
Dr. Seuss
Copyright, 1942, Marshall Field

Mighty Trapper . . . But He Misses the Big Ones

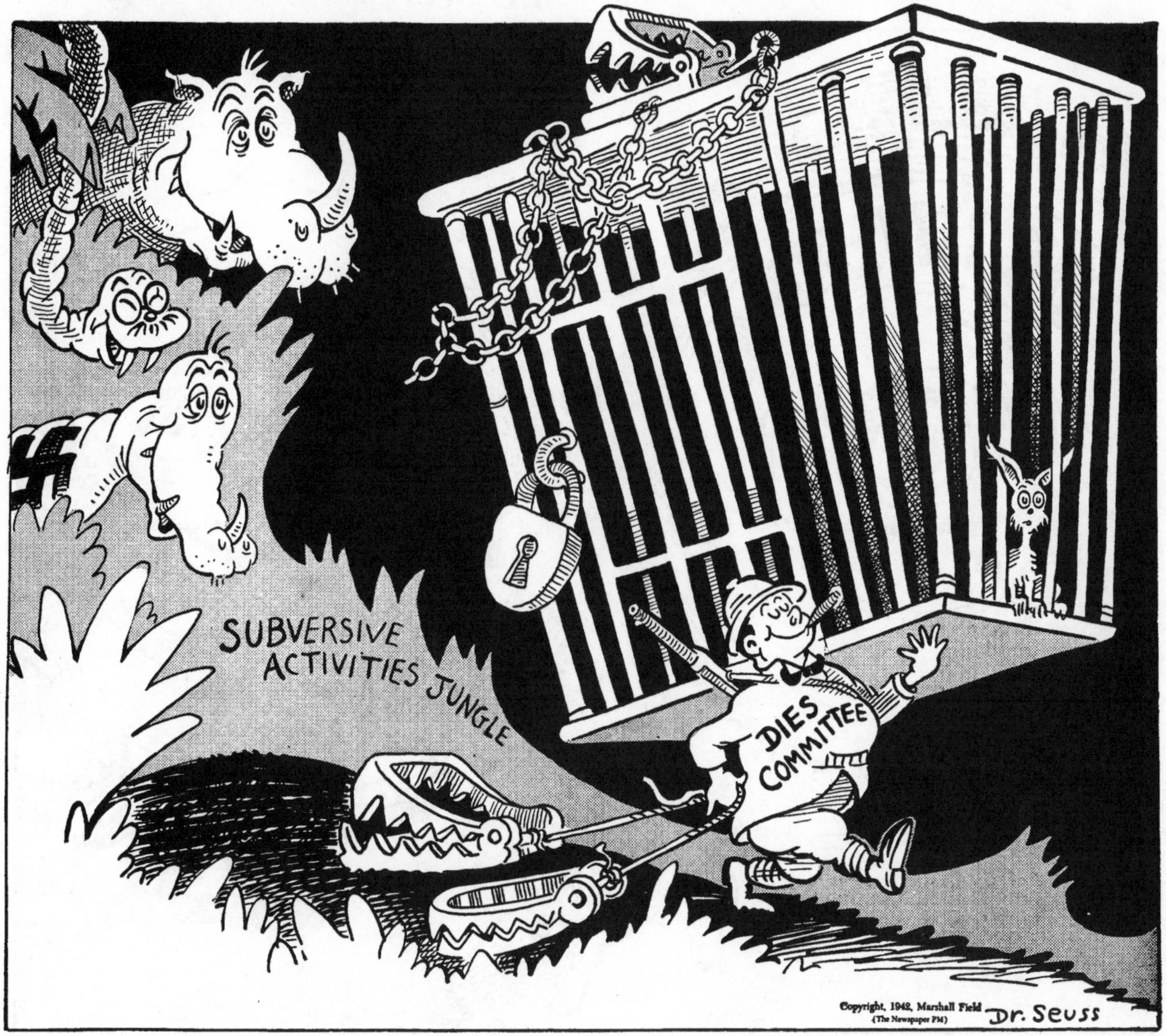
SUBVERSIVE ACTIVITIES JUNGLE
DIES COMMITTEE
Copyright, 1942, Marshall Field (The Newspaper PM)
Dr. Seuss

227 – March 10, 1942

'I Hear the Americans Are Stripping Their Gears Again!'

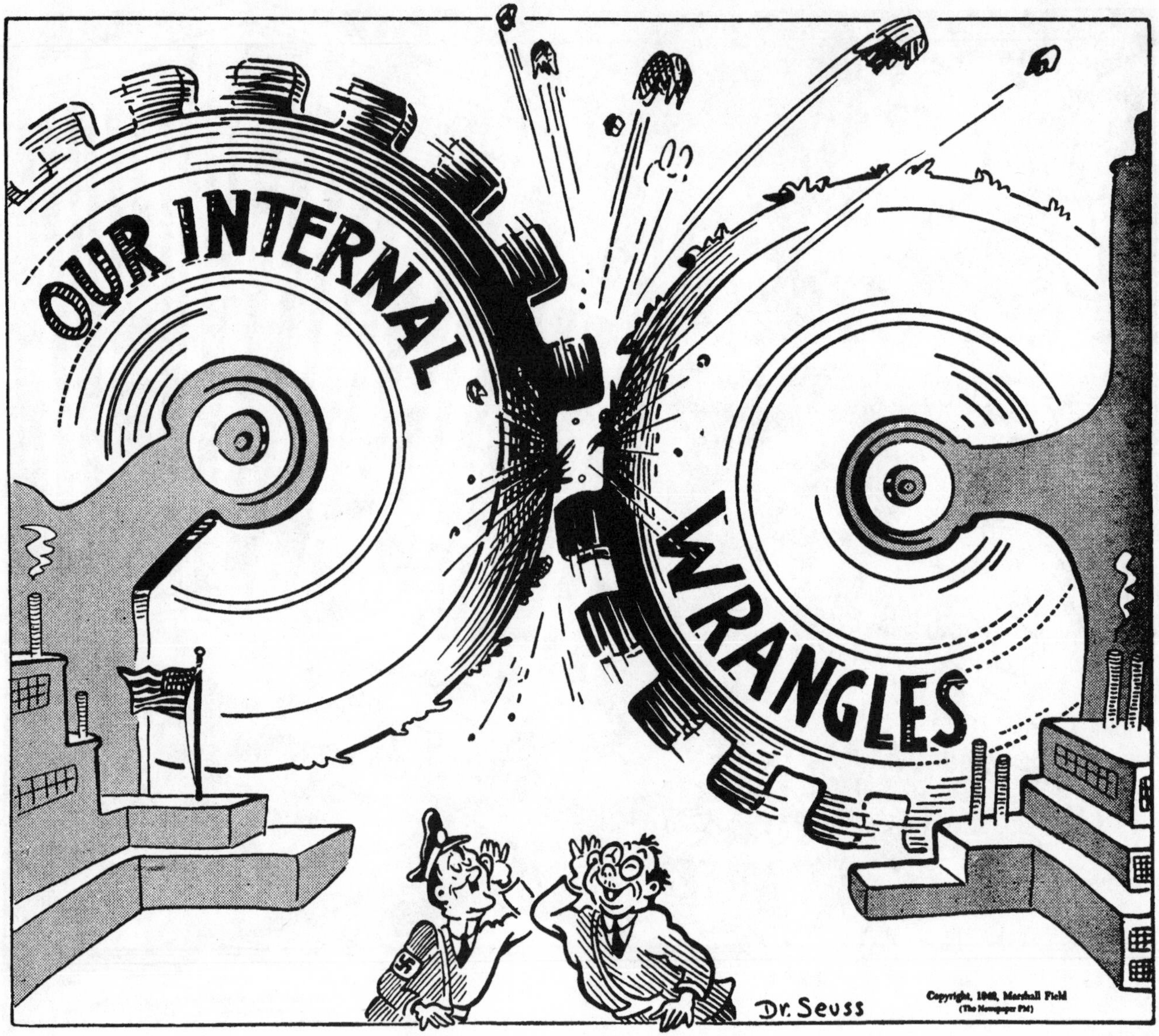
OUR INTERNAL
WRANGLES
Dr. Seuss
Copyright, 1942, Marshall Field
(The Newspaper PM)

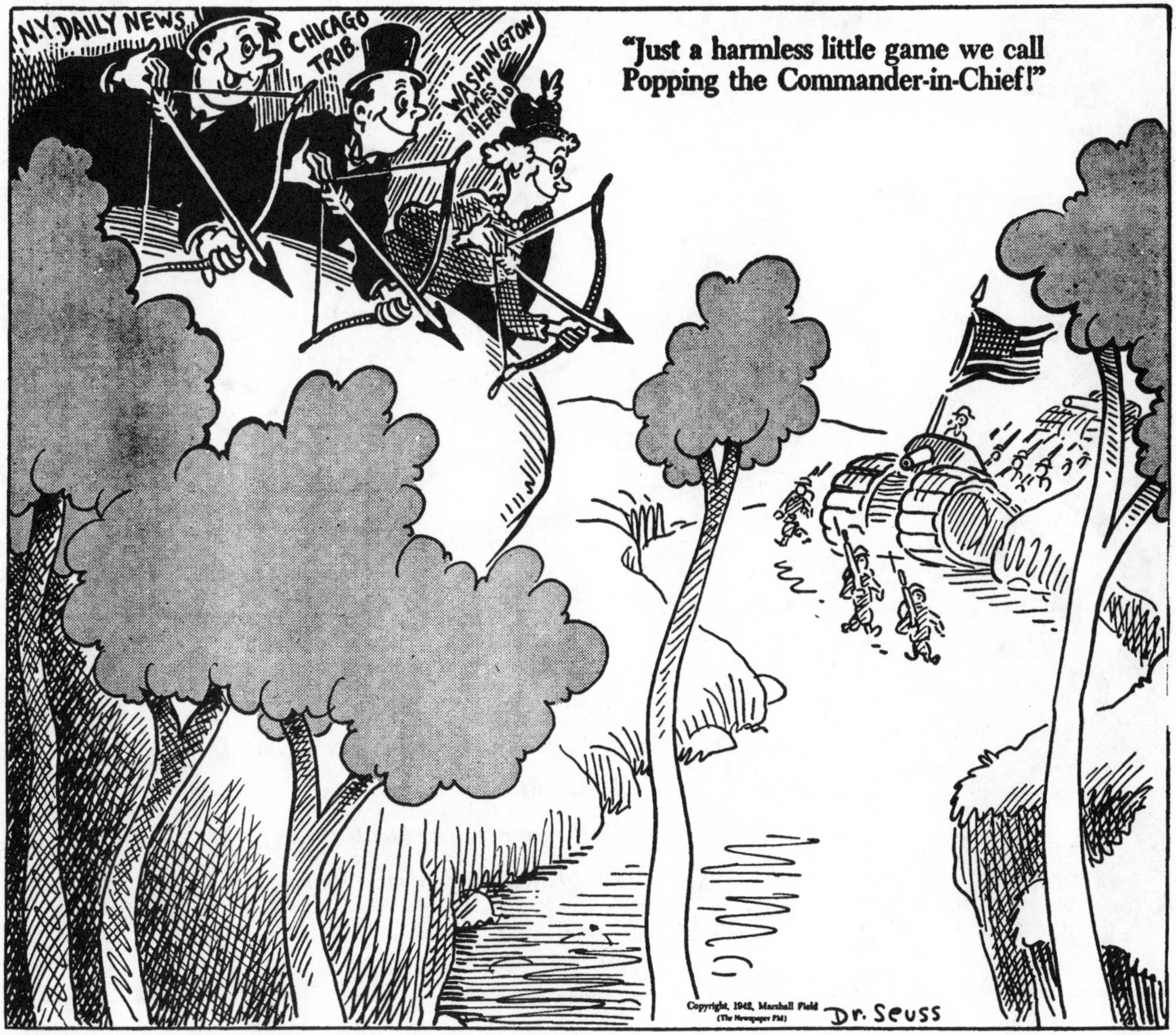
N.Y. DAILY NEWS
CHICAGO TRIB.
WASHINGTON TIMES HERALD
"Just a harmless little game we call Popping the Commander-in-Chief!"
Copyright, 1942, Marshall Field (The Newspaper PM)
Dr. Seuss

229 — April 21, 1942

The OLD GRUDGE of 42d Street

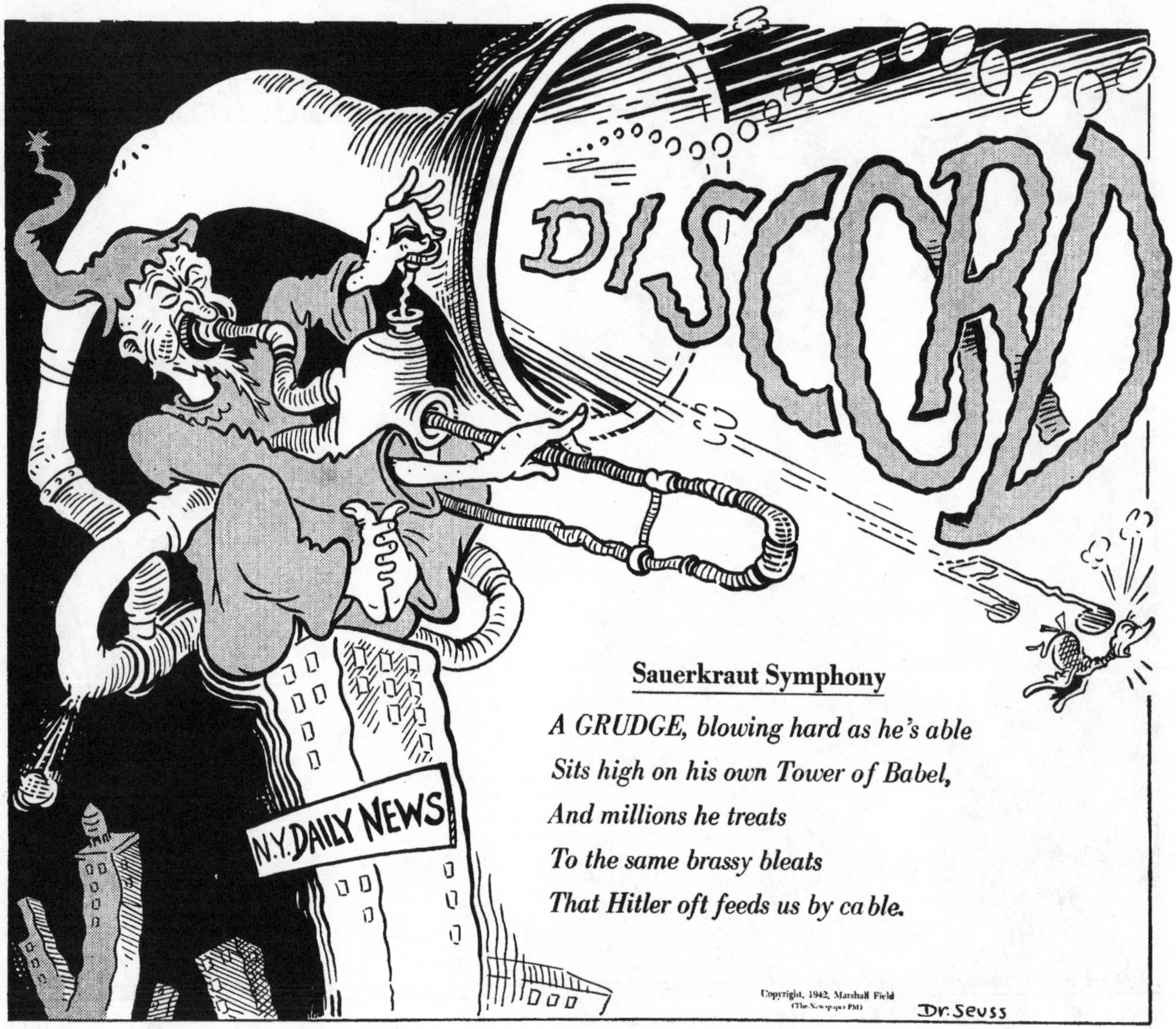
DISCORD
N.Y. DAILY NEWS
Sauerkraut Symphony
A GRUDGE, blowing hard as he's able
Sits high on his own Tower of Babel,
And millions he treats
To the same brassy bleats
That Hitler oft feeds us by ca ble.
Copyright, 1942, Marshall Field
(The Newspaper PM)
Dr. Seuss

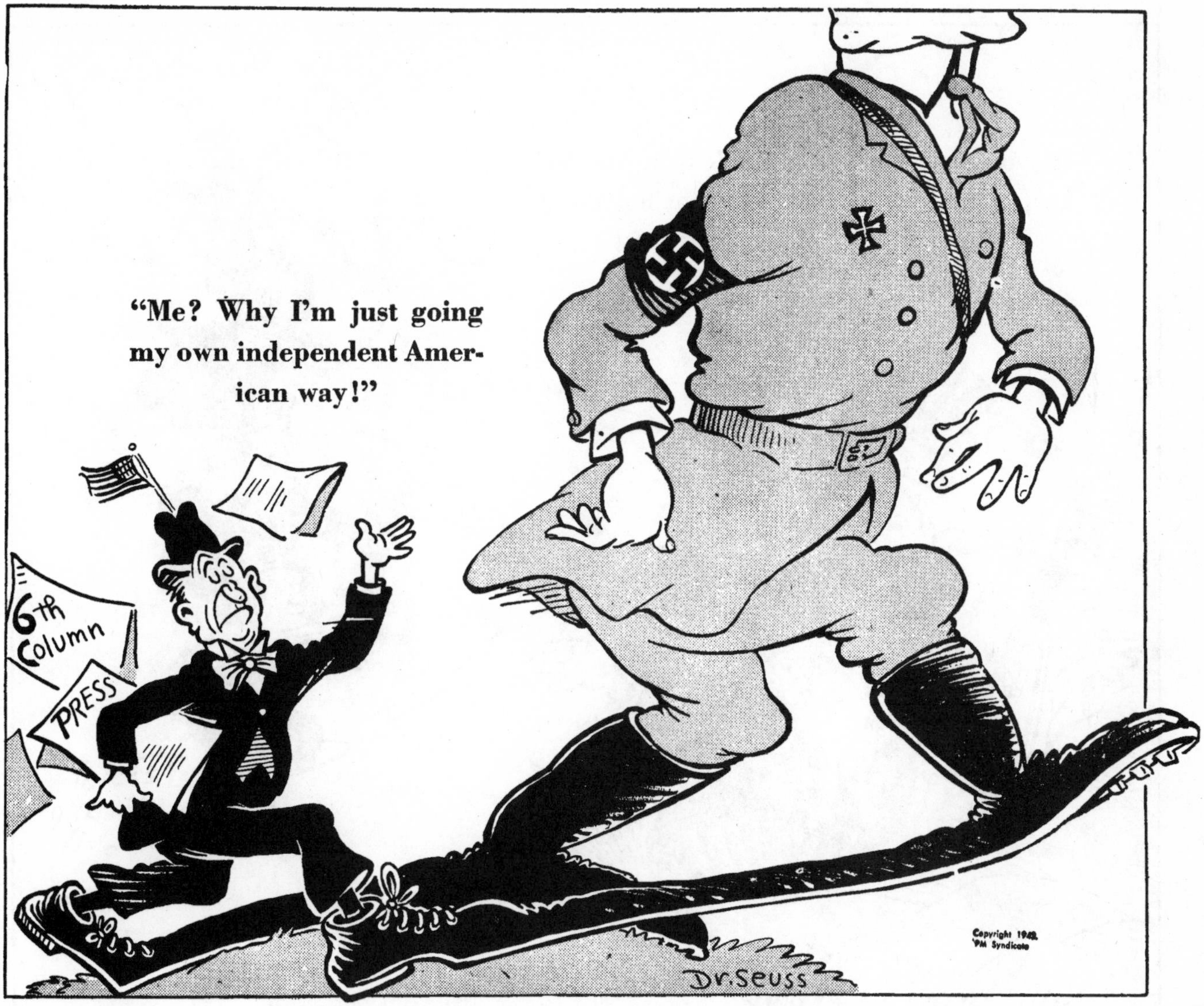
"Me? Why I'm just going my own independent American way!"
6th Column
PRESS
Copyright 1942 PM Syndicate
Dr. Seuss

231 — June 15, 1942

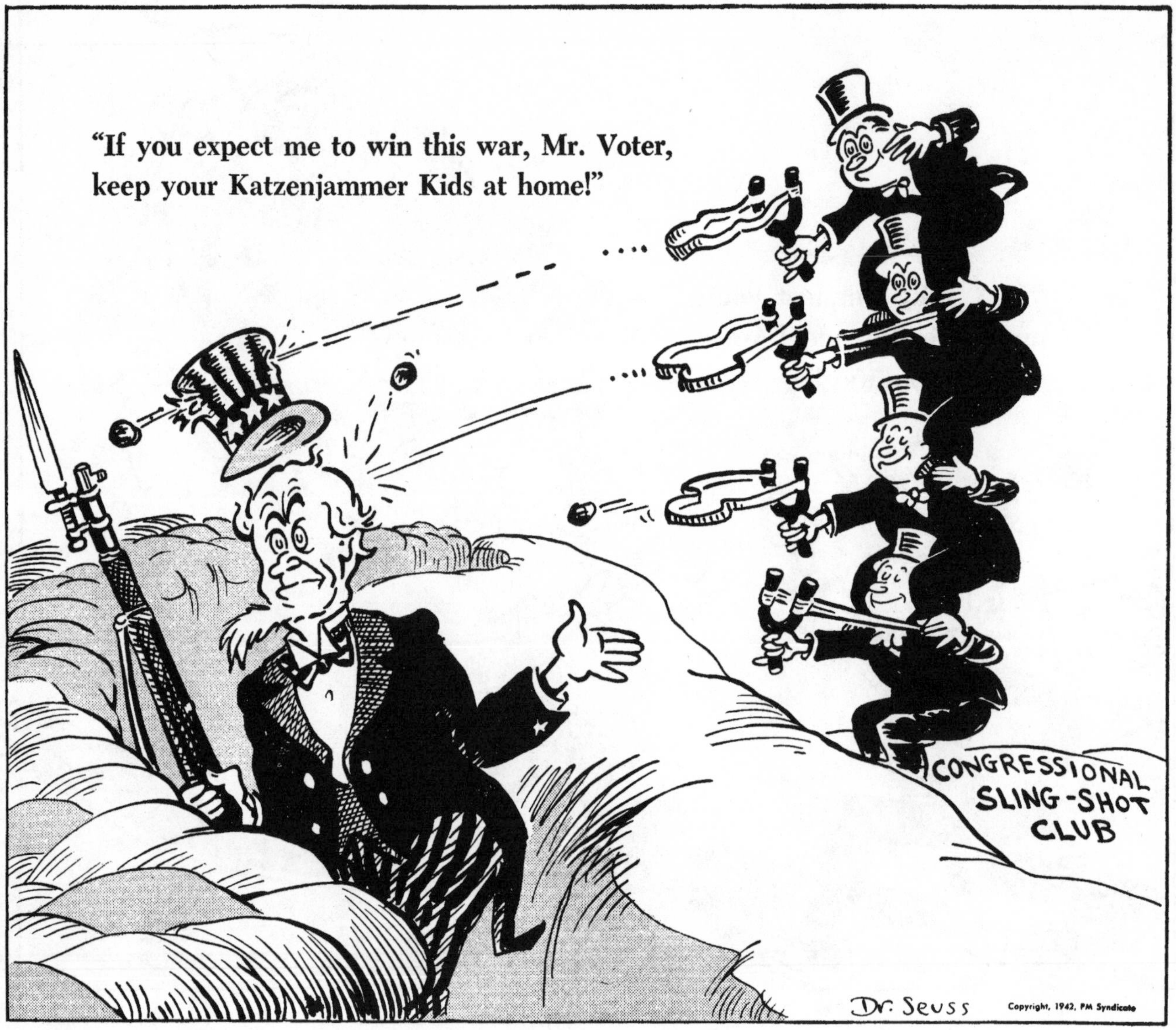
"If you expect me to win this war, Mr. Voter,
keep your Katzenjammer Kids at home!"
CONGRESSIONAL
SLING-SHOT
CLUB
Dr. Seuss
Copyright, 1942, PM Syndicate

'Easy, There, EASY! No Acrobat Is Fall-Proof!'

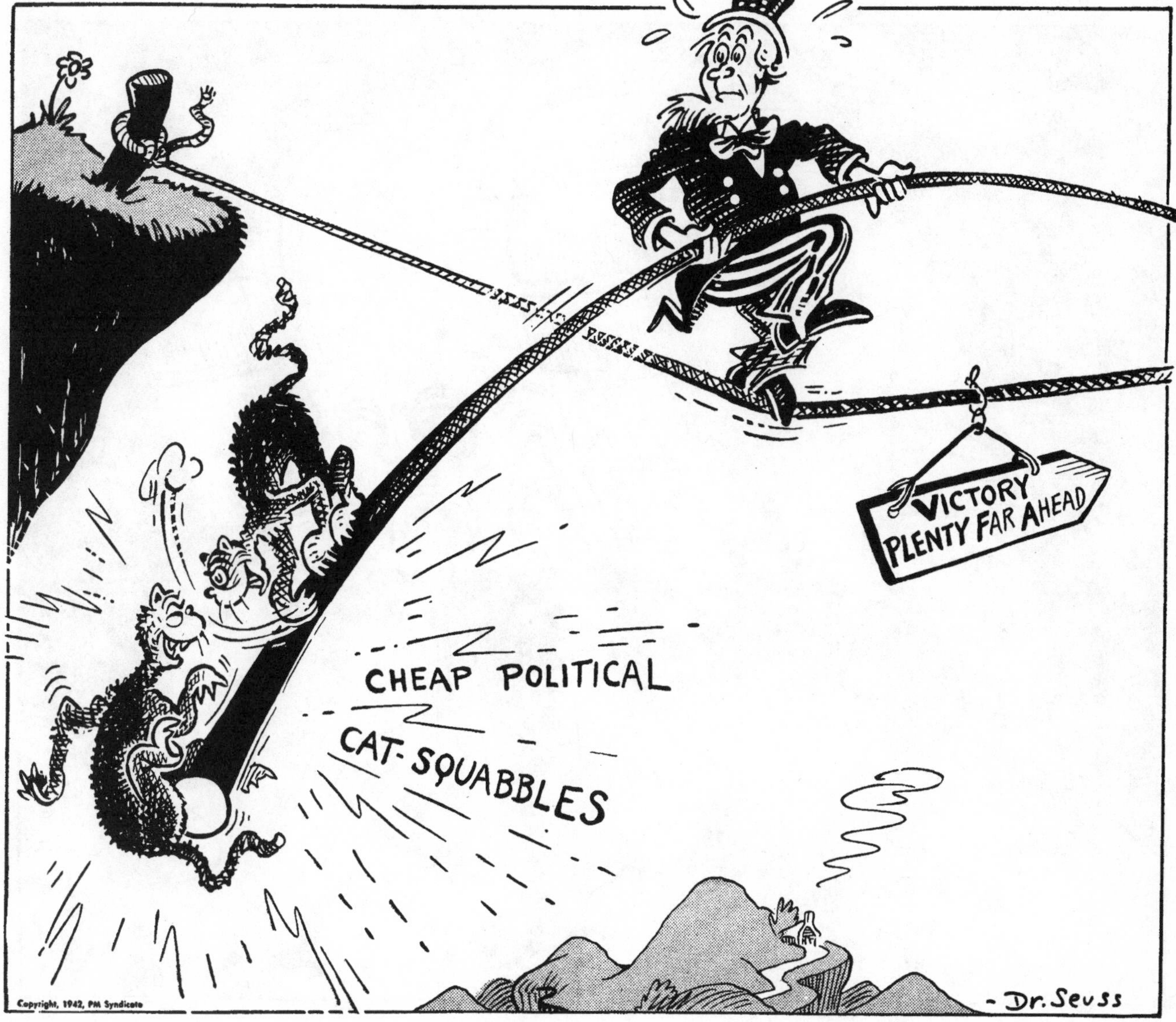

VICTORY PLENTY FAR AHEAD
CHEAP POLITICAL
CAT-SQUABBLES
Copyright, 1942, PM Syndicate
- Dr. Seuss

Still Spraying Our Side With Disunity Gas!

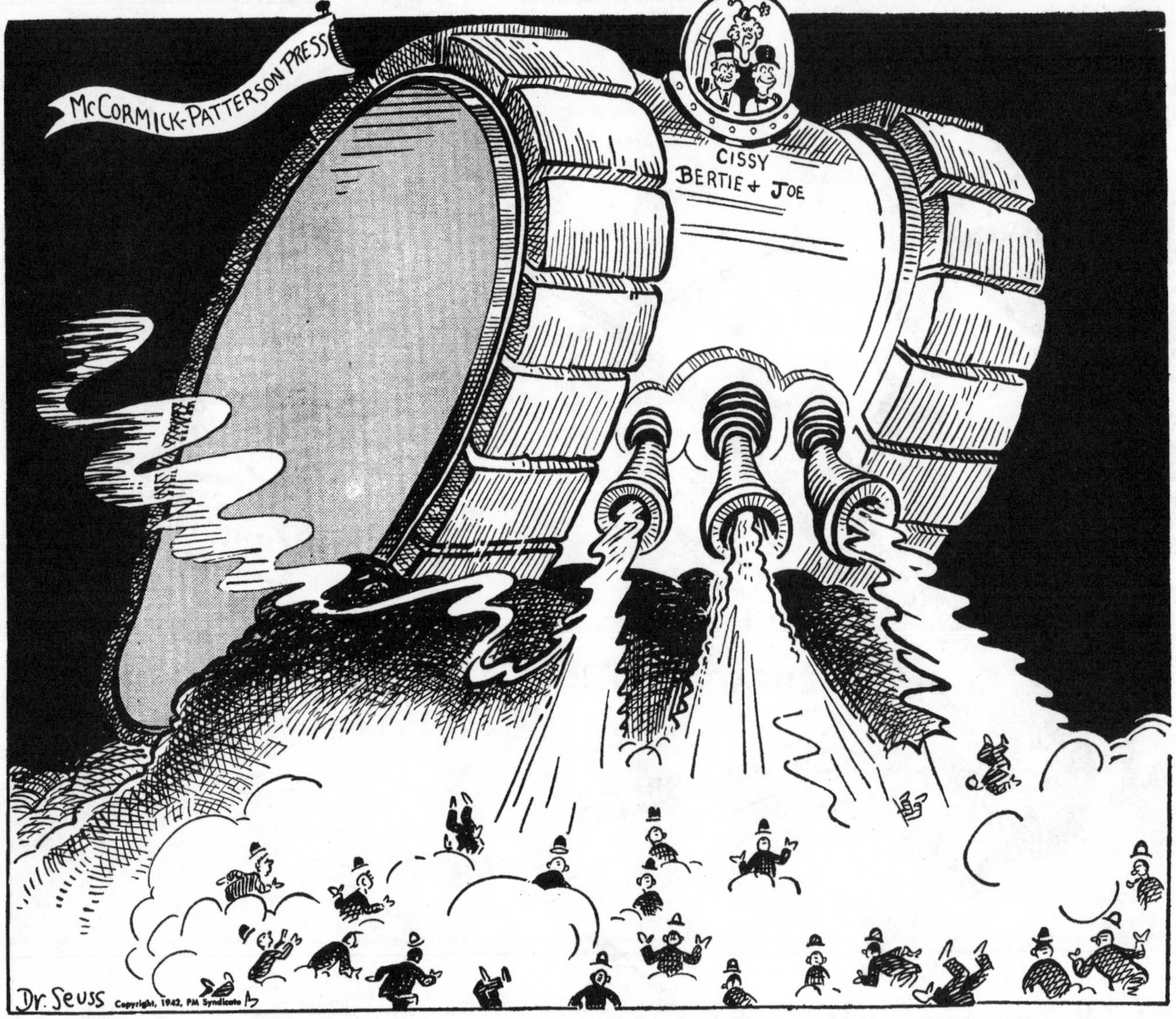
McCORMICK-PATTERSON PRESS
CISSY
BERTIE + JOE
Dr. Seuss
Copyright, 1942, PM Syndicate

234 — August 10, 1942

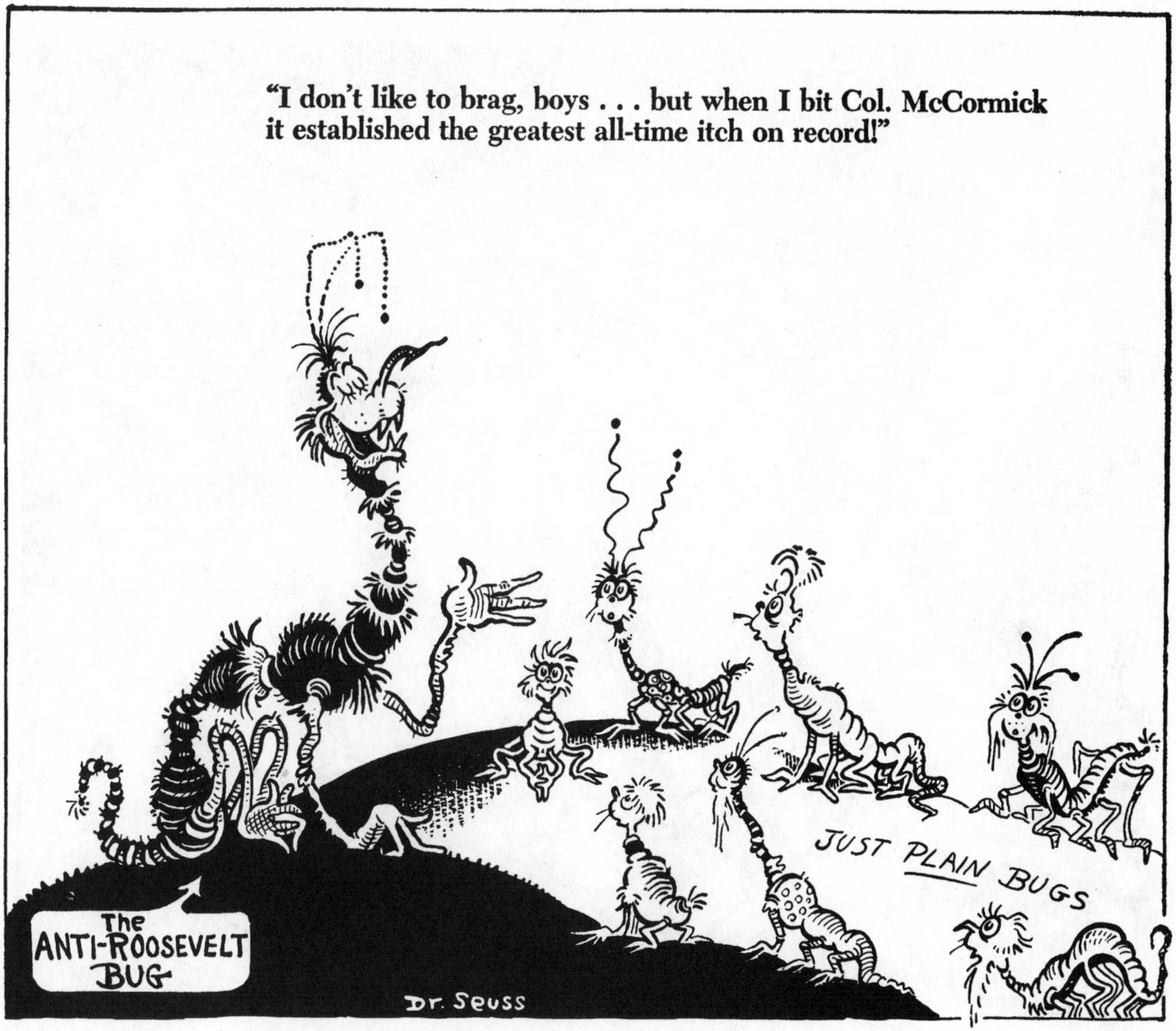
The ANTI-ROOSEVELT BUG
JUST PLAIN BUGS
Dr. Seuss

"I don't like to brag, boys . . . but when I bit Col. McCormick it established the greatest all-time itch on record!"

235 — August 17, 1942

"Gee, It's All Very Exciting . . . But It Doesn't Kill Nazi Rats."

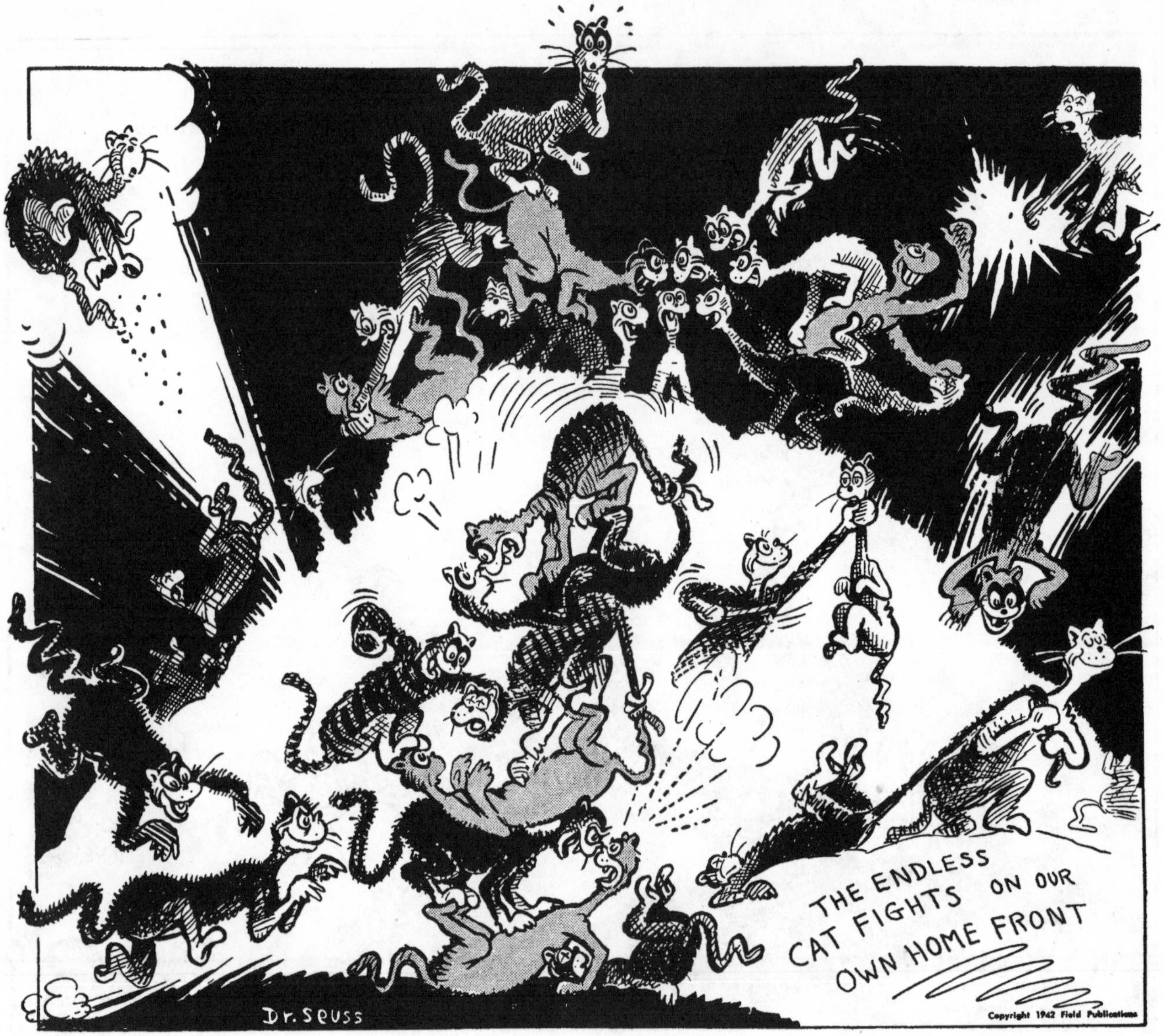
THE ENDLESS CAT FIGHTS ON OUR OWN HOME FRONT
DR. SEUSS
Copyright 1942 Field Publications

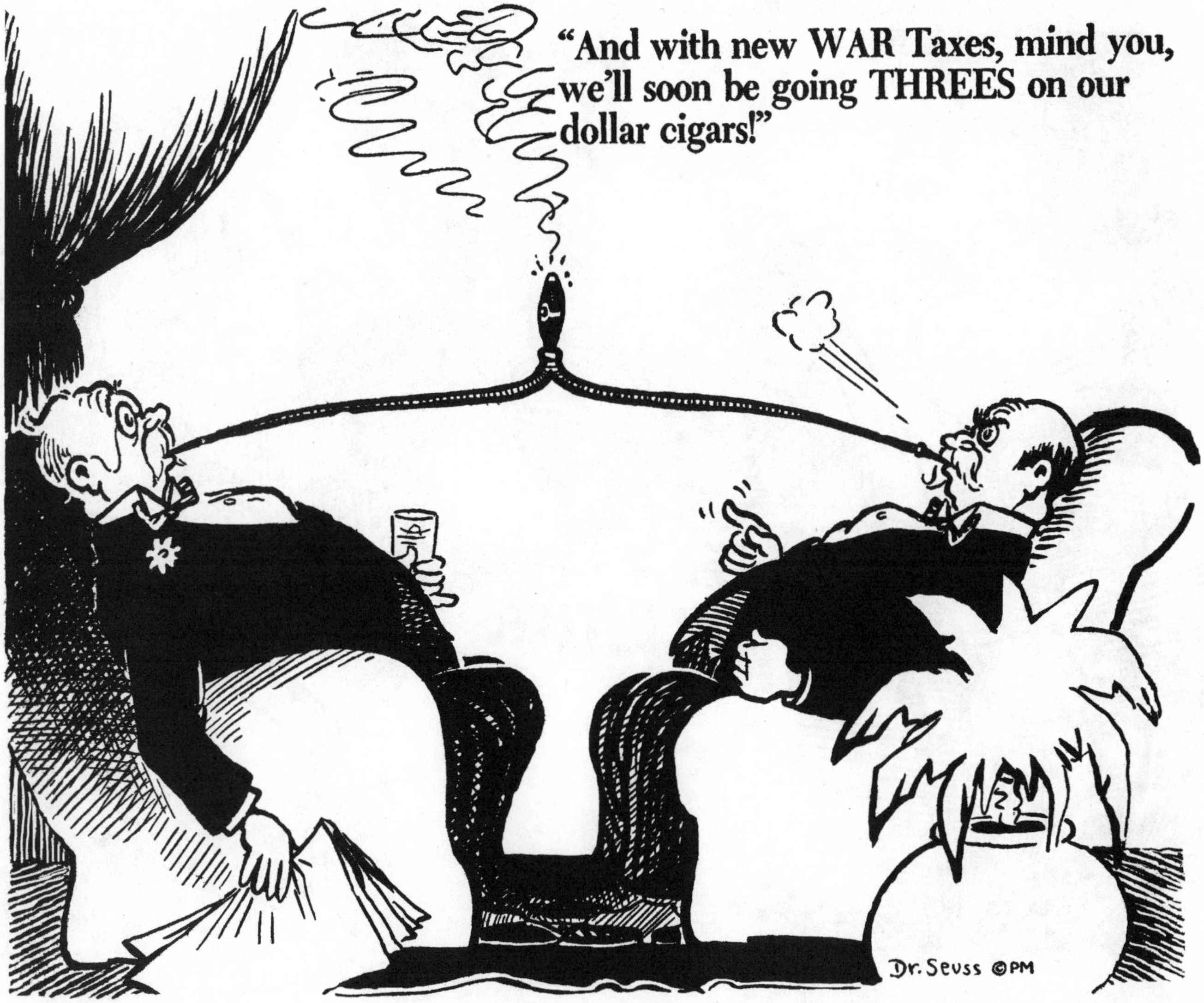
"And with new WAR Taxes, mind you, we'll soon be going THREES on our dollar cigars!"
Dr. Seuss ©PM

237 – August 5, 1941

BLITZ BUGGY DE LUXE

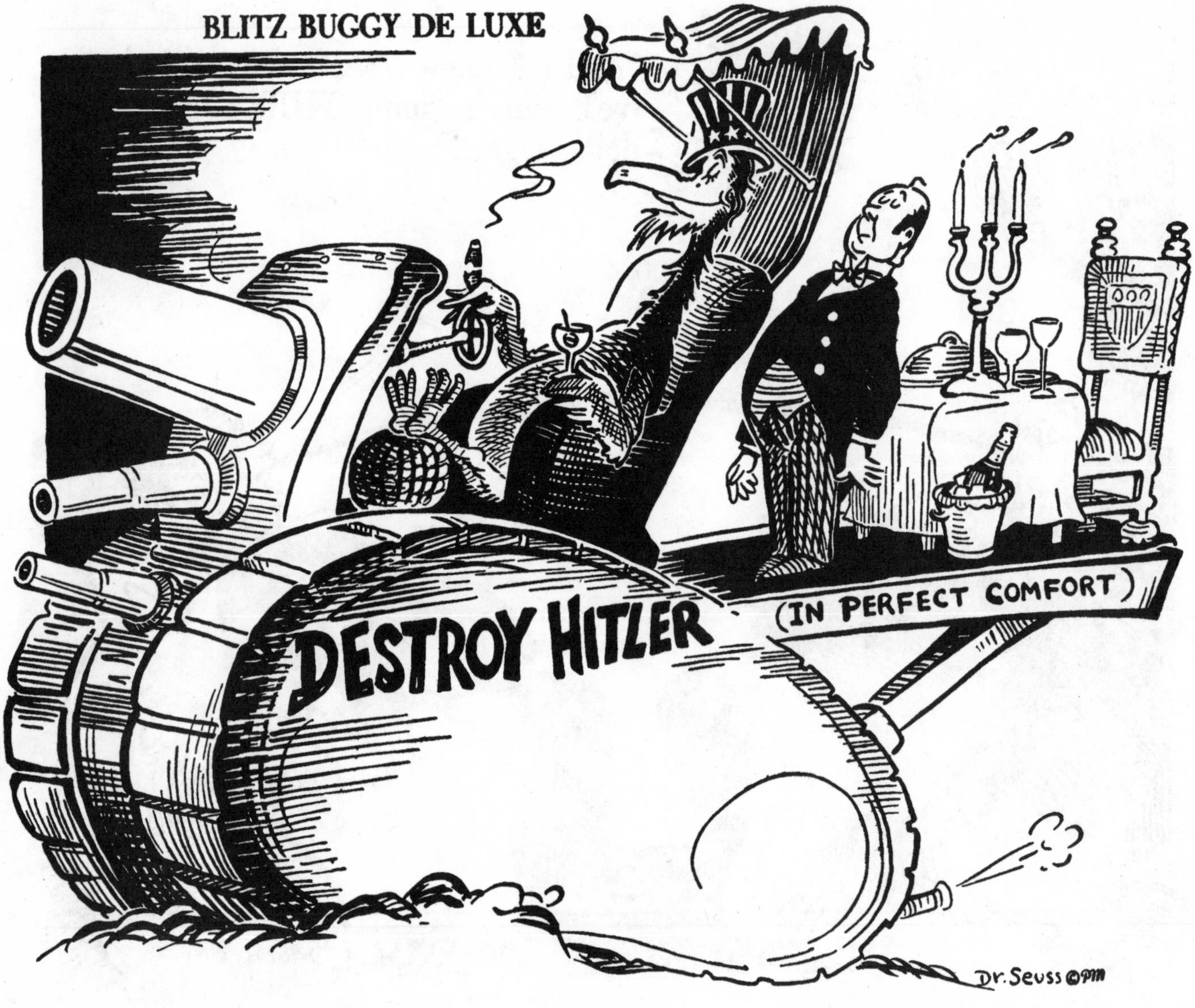
DESTROY HITLER
(IN PERFECT COMFORT)
Dr. Seuss ©PM

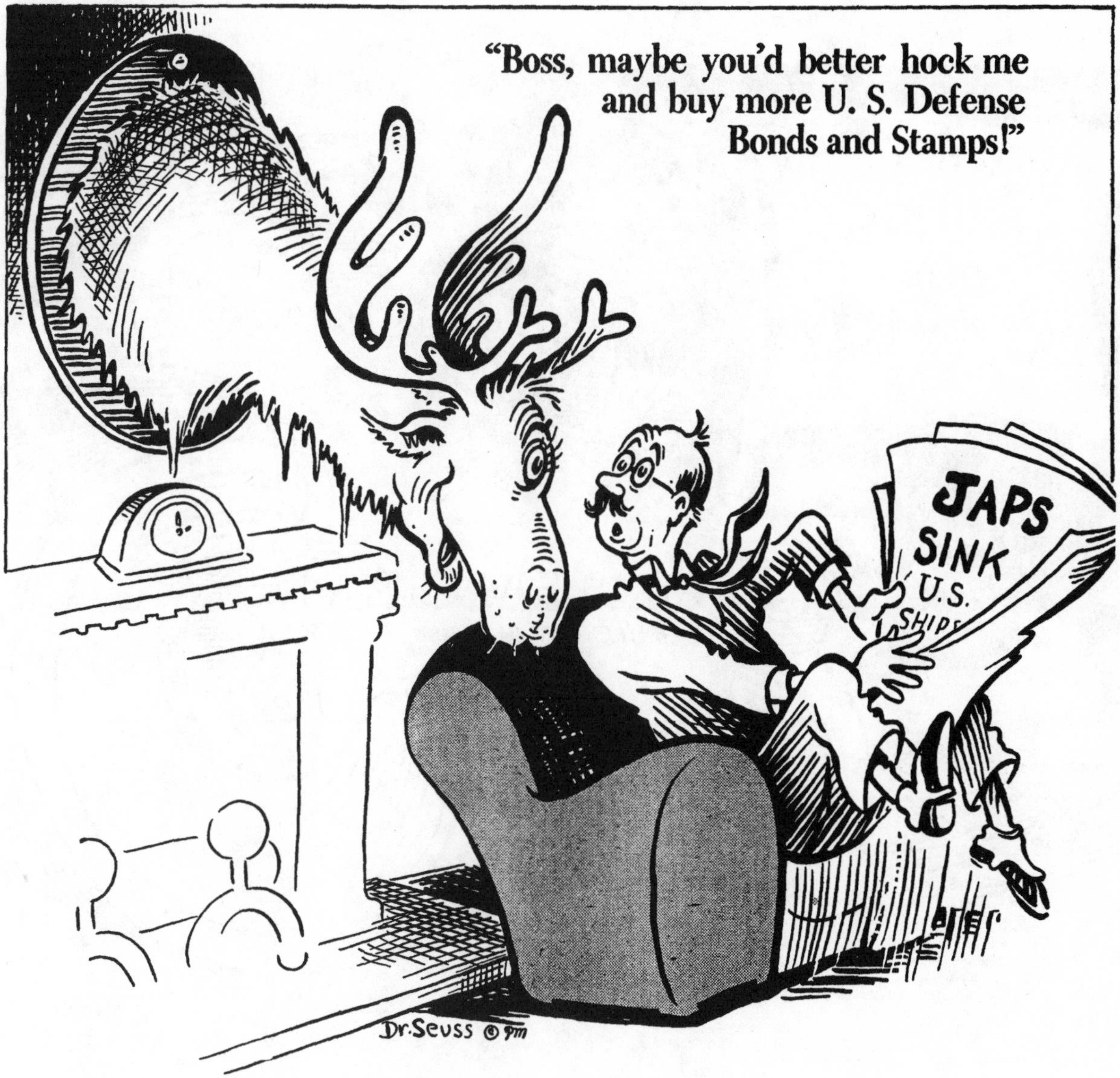
"Boss, maybe you'd better hock me and buy more U. S. Defense Bonds and Stamps!"
JAPS SINK U.S. SHIPS
Dr. Seuss

239 — December 26, 1941

ROLL HIM FLAT WITH THE OLD PAY-ROLLER
PAYROLL SAVINGS PLAN
(IF YOU'RE NOT IN IT, ASK YOUR BOSS!)
ADOLF
Dr. Seuss
Copyright, 1942, Marshall Field
1941, The Newspaper PM, Inc.

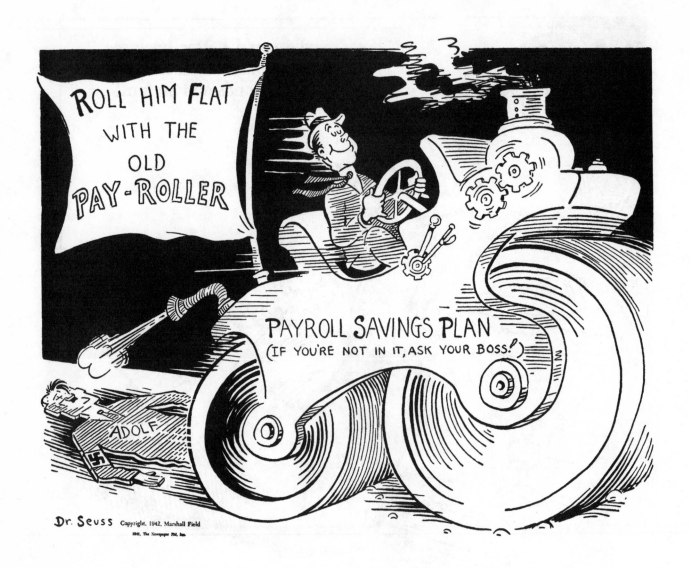

Girdle Shortage

'If madam will step into the fitting room . . .'

Dr. Seuss Copyright, 1942, Marshall Field Newspaper PM

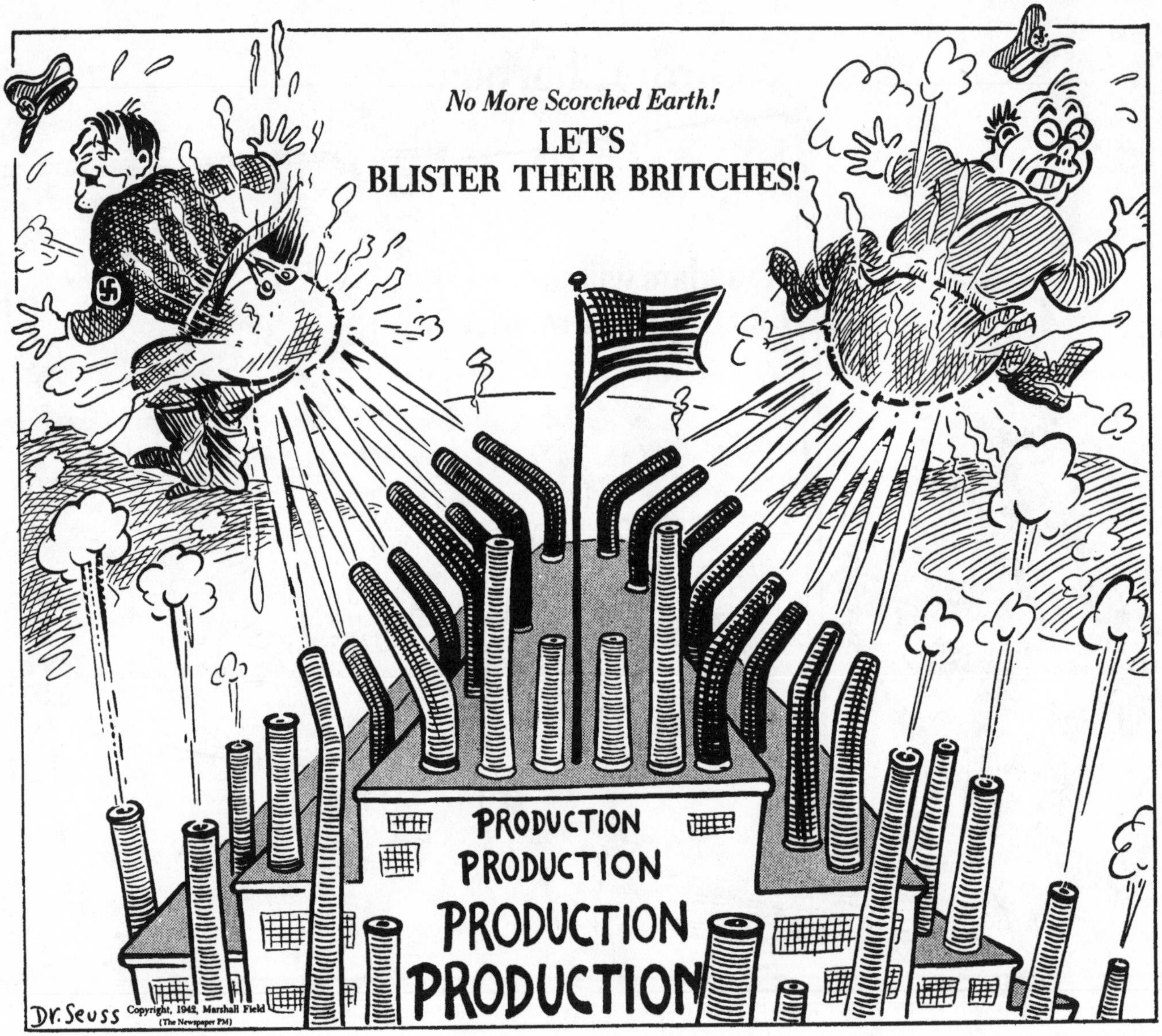
No More Scorched Earth!
LET'S
BLISTER THEIR BRITCHES!
PRODUCTION
PRODUCTION
PRODUCTION
PRODUCTION
Dr. Seuss
Copyright, 1942, Marshall Field
(The Newspaper PM)

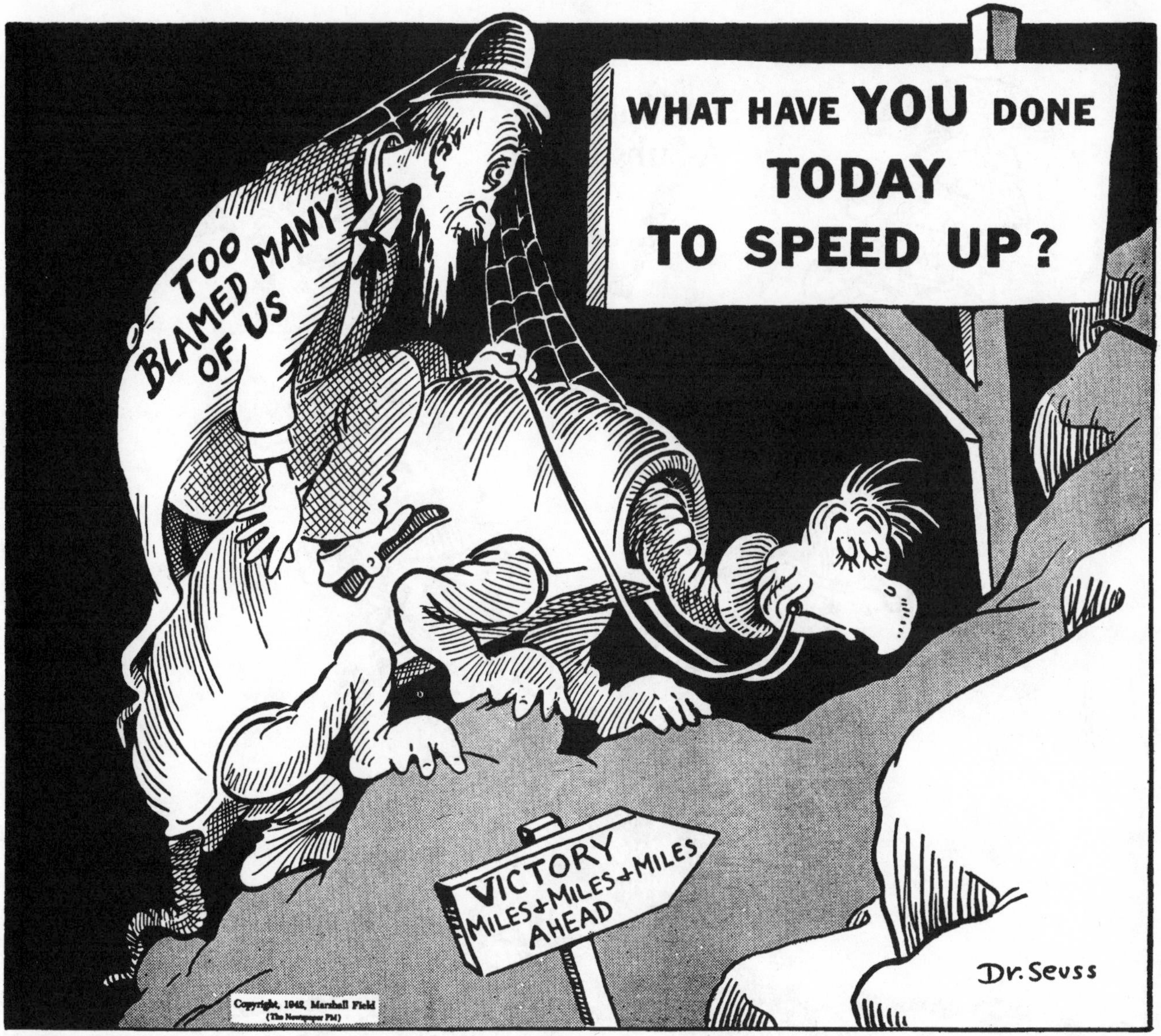
WHAT HAVE YOU DONE TODAY TO SPEED UP?
TOO BLAMED MANY OF US
VICTORY MILES & MILES & MILES AHEAD
Dr. Seuss
Copyright, 1942, Marshall Field (The Newspaper PM)

243 – March 6, 1942

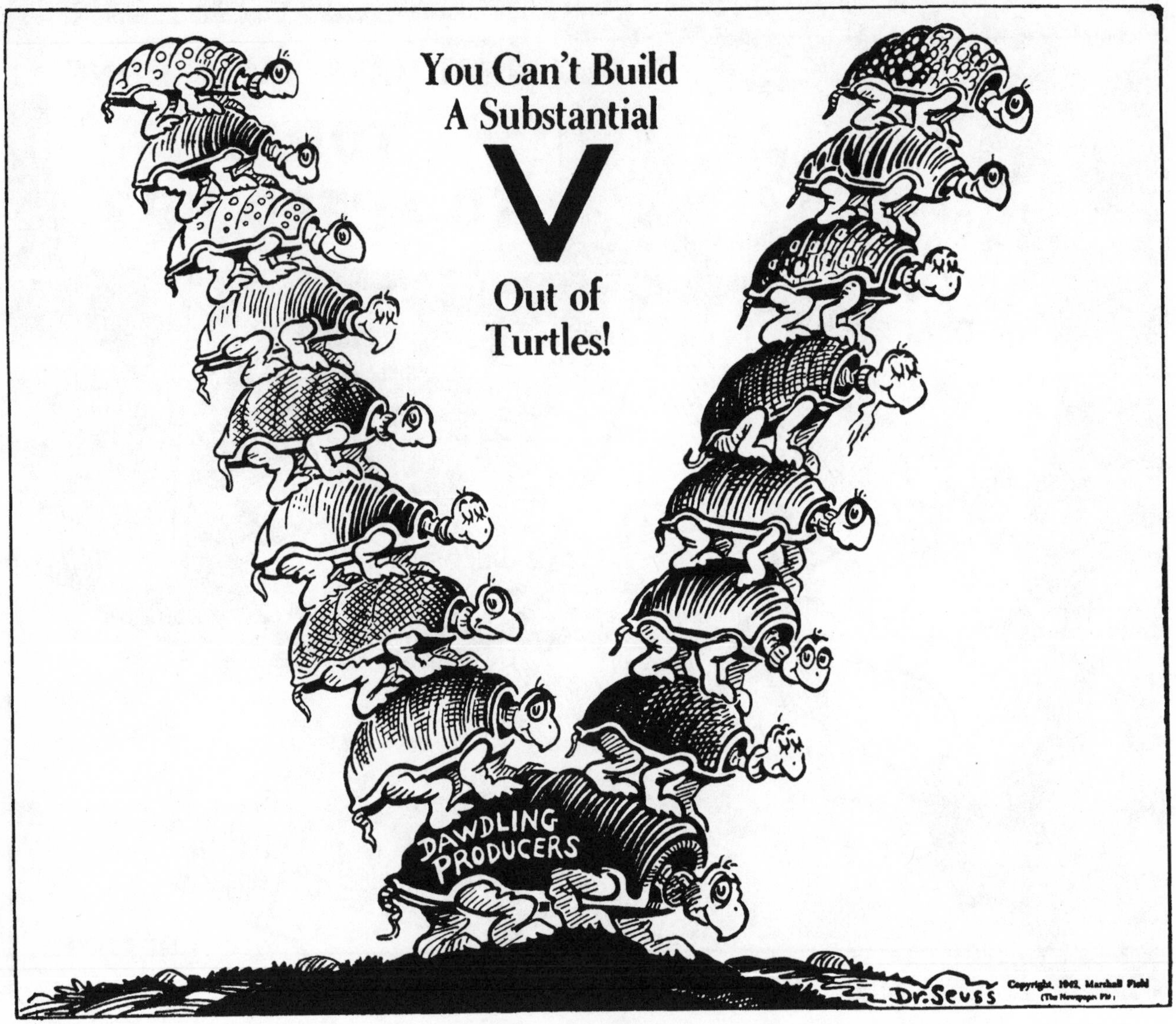
You Can't Build
A Substantial
V
Out of
Turtles!
DAWDLING PRODUCERS
Dr. Seuss
Copyright, 1942, Marshall Field

244 — March 20, 1942

Beware the Man Who Makes a Fortune in a Flood!

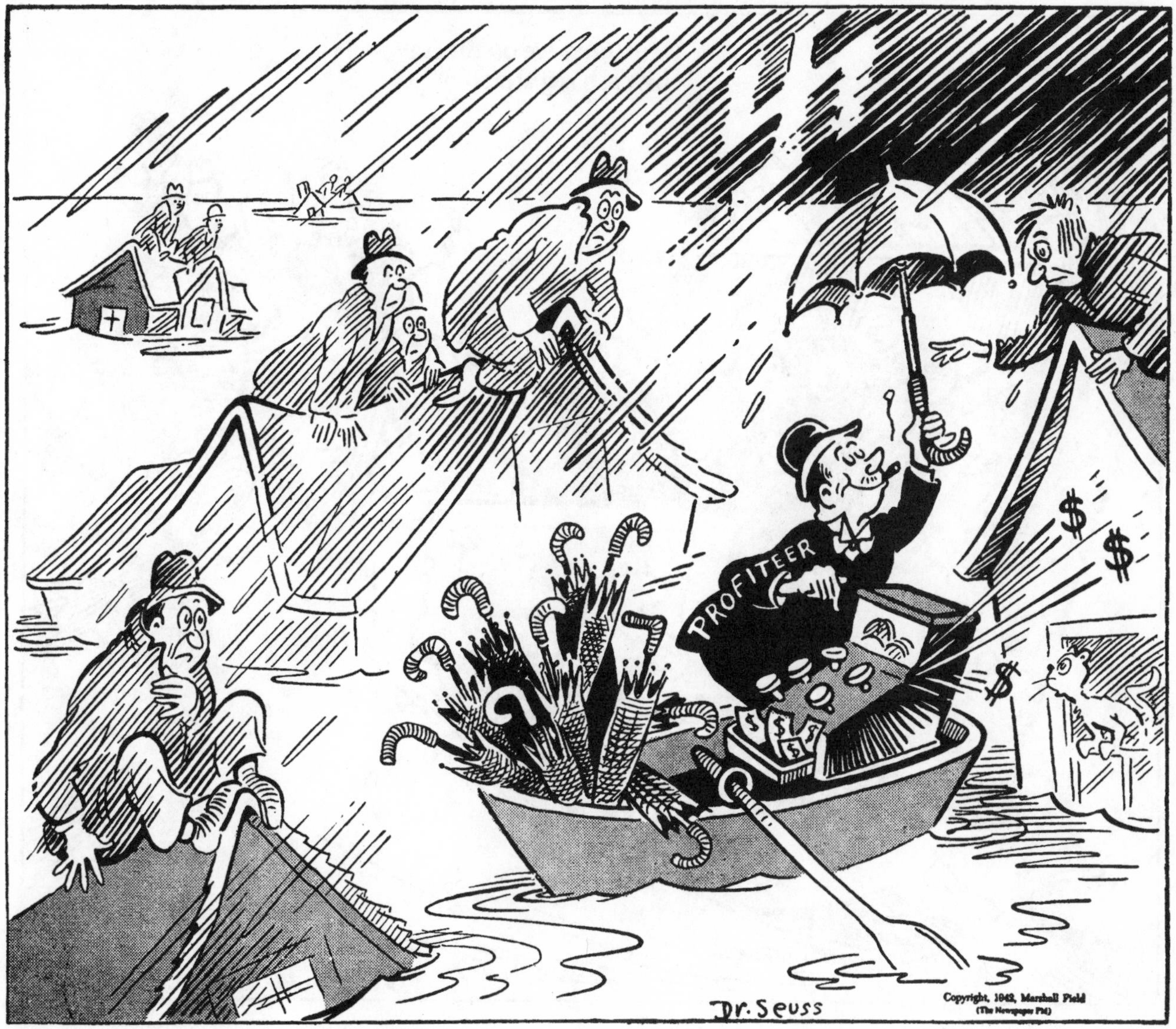
PROFITEER
$
$
$
Dr. Seuss
Copyright, 1942, Marshall Field
(The Newspaper PM)

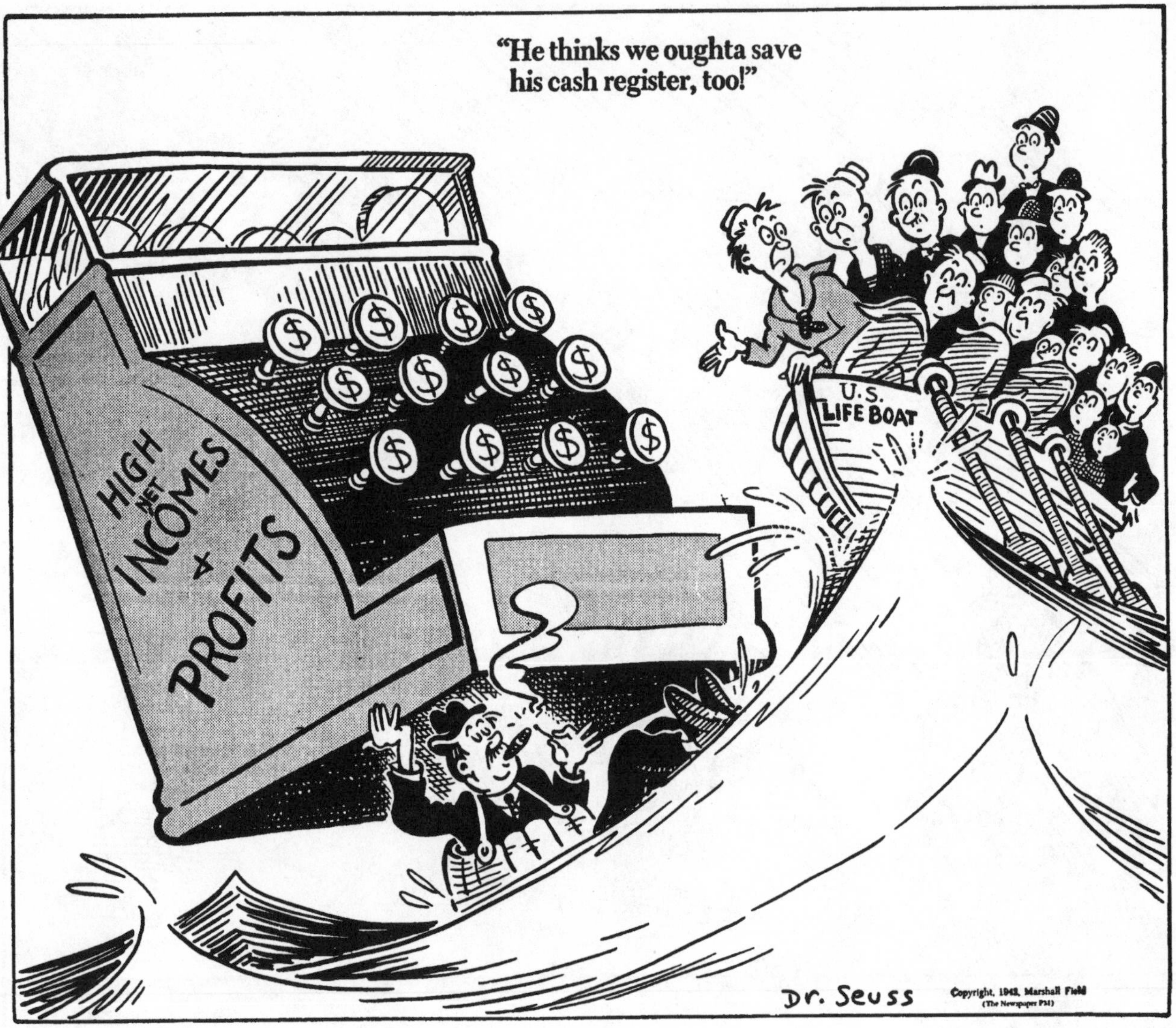
HIGH NET INCOMES + PROFITS
U.S. LIFE BOAT
Dr. Seuss
Copyright, 1942, Marshall Field
(The Newspaper PM)
"He thinks we oughta save his cash register, too!"

Illumination for the Shooting Gallery

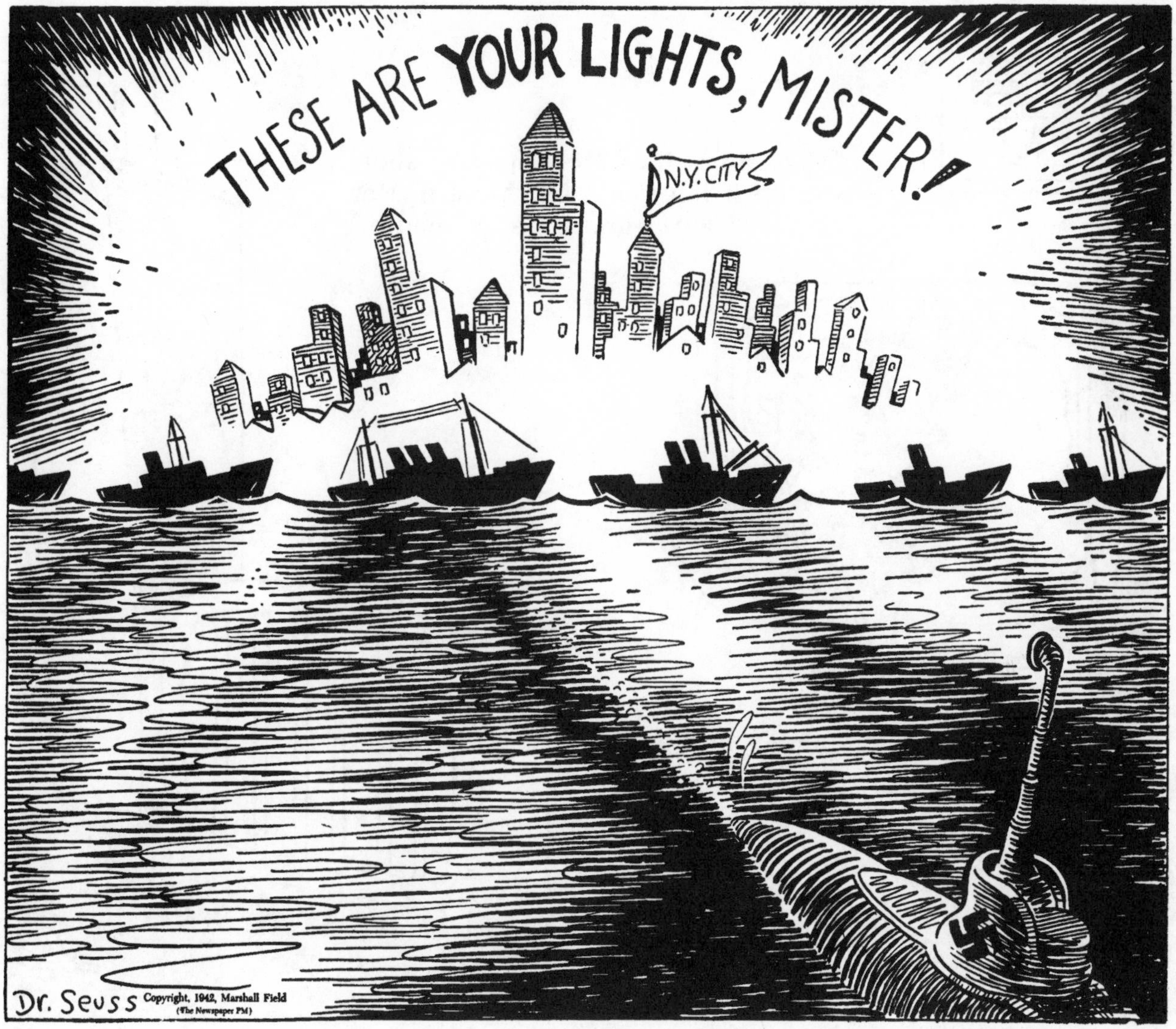
THESE ARE YOUR LIGHTS, MISTER!
N.Y. CITY
Dr. Seuss
Copyright, 1942, Marshall Field
(The Newspaper PM)

247 – May 20, 1942

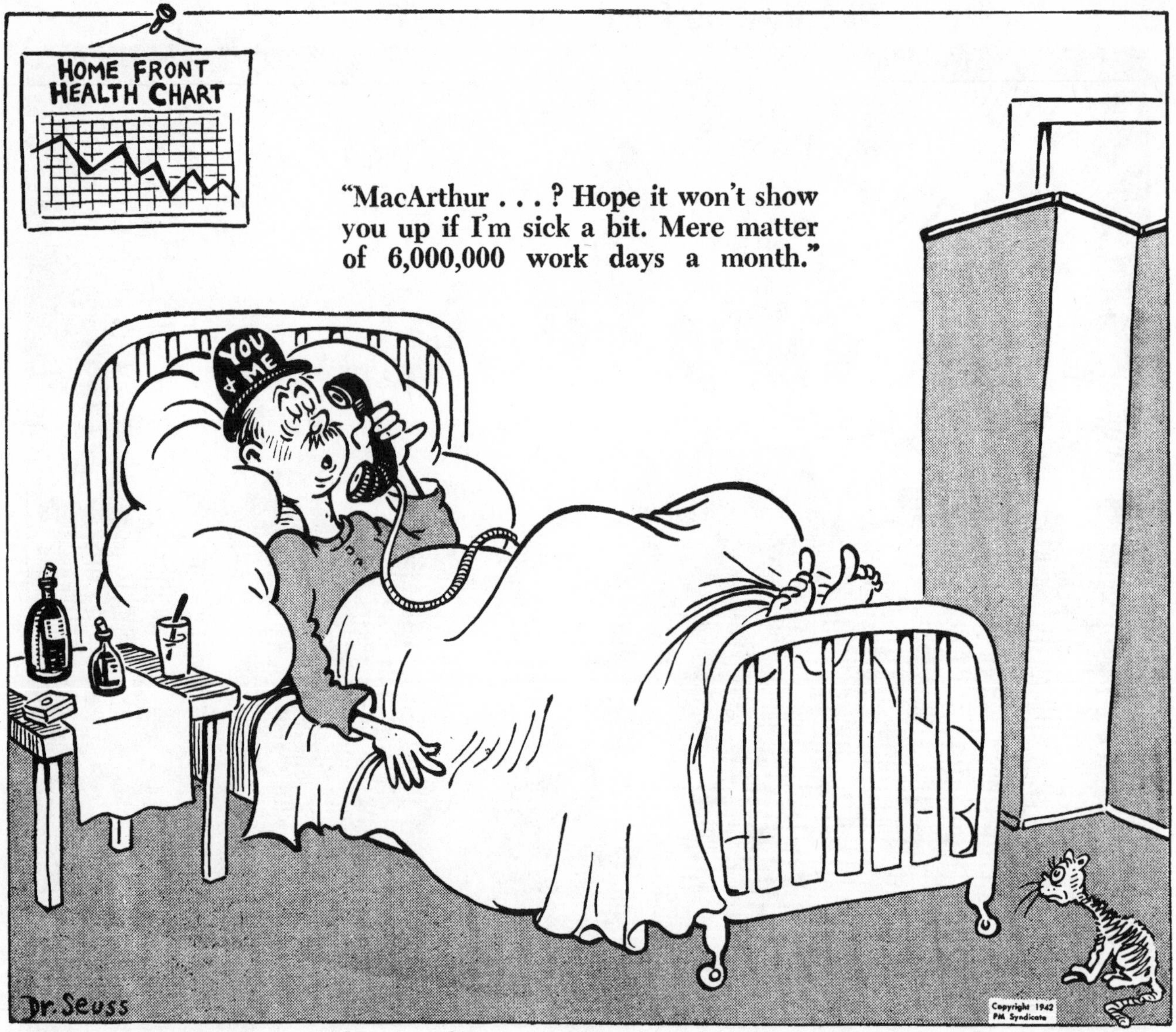
HOME FRONT HEALTH CHART
"MacArthur . . . ? Hope it won't show you up if I'm sick a bit. Mere matter of 6,000,000 work days a month."
YOU & ME
Dr. Seuss
Copyright 1942 PM Syndicate

NEWS NOTE: War production drives report sick and injured war workers lose 6,000,000 work days every month.

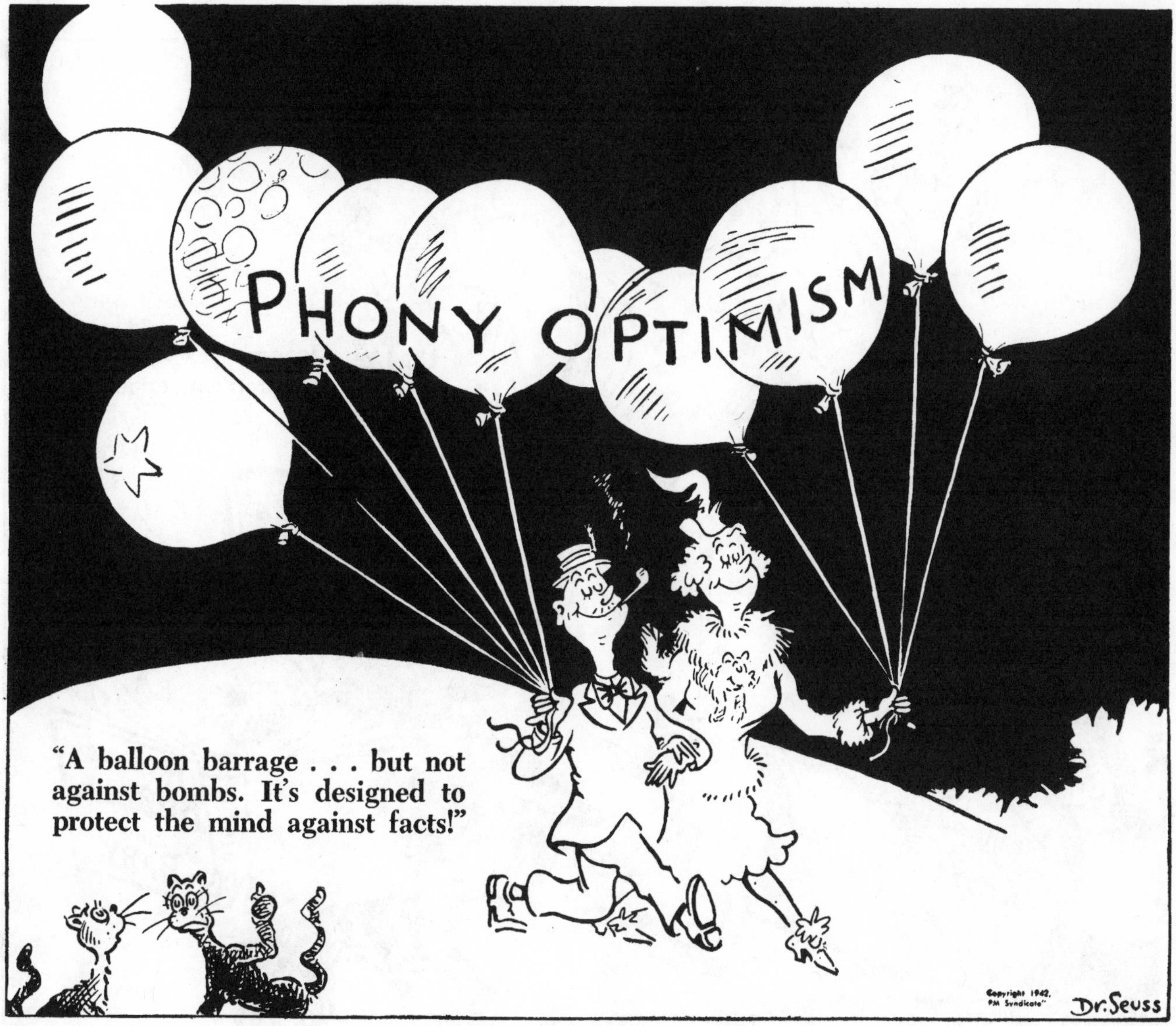
PHONY OPTIMISM
Copyright 1942, PM Syndicate
Dr. Seuss

"A balloon barrage . . . but not against bombs. It's designed to protect the mind against facts!"

249 — June 25, 1942

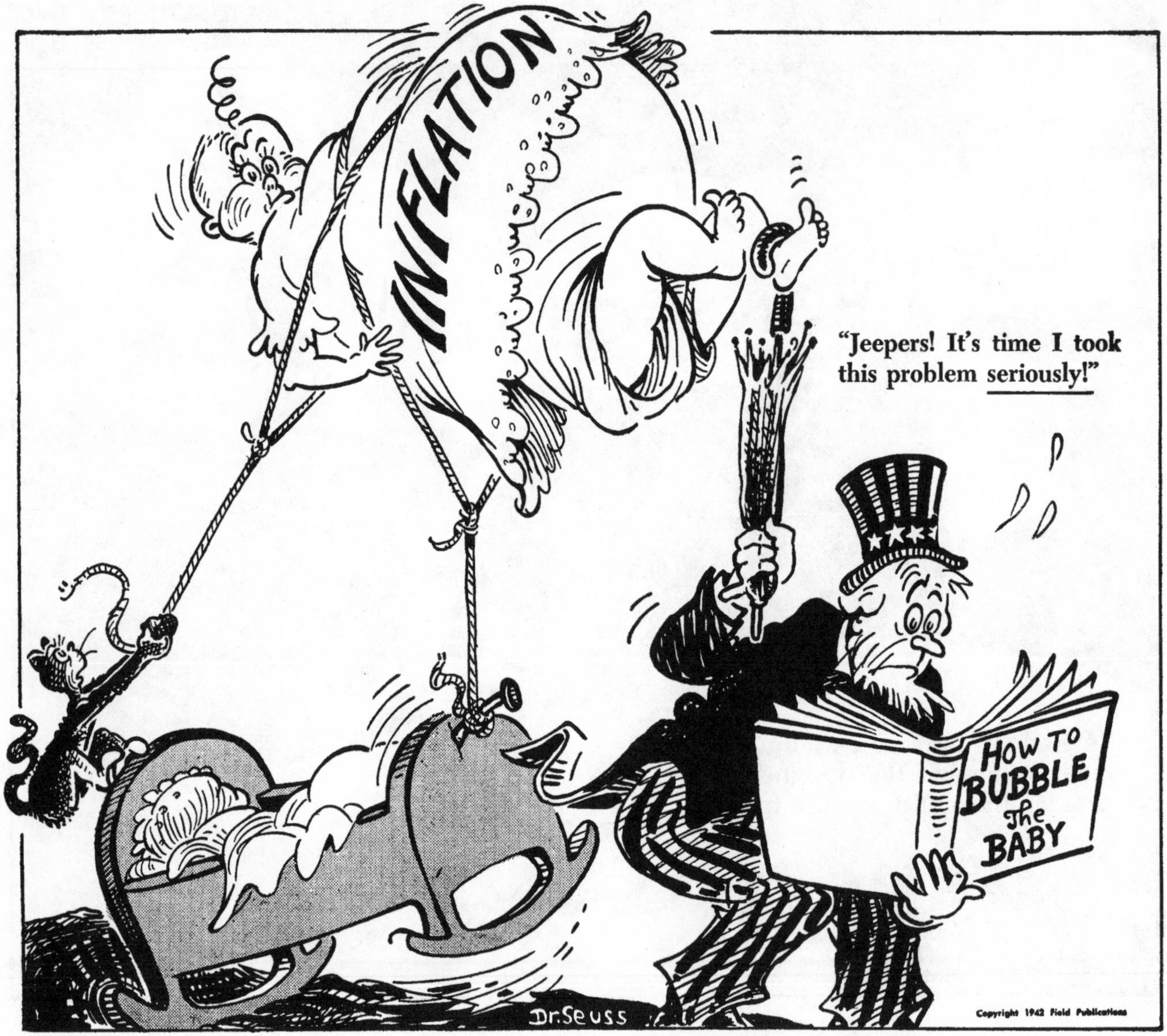
INFLATION
"Jeepers! It's time I took this problem seriously!"
HOW TO BUBBLE The BABY
Dr. Seuss
Copyright 1942 Field Publications

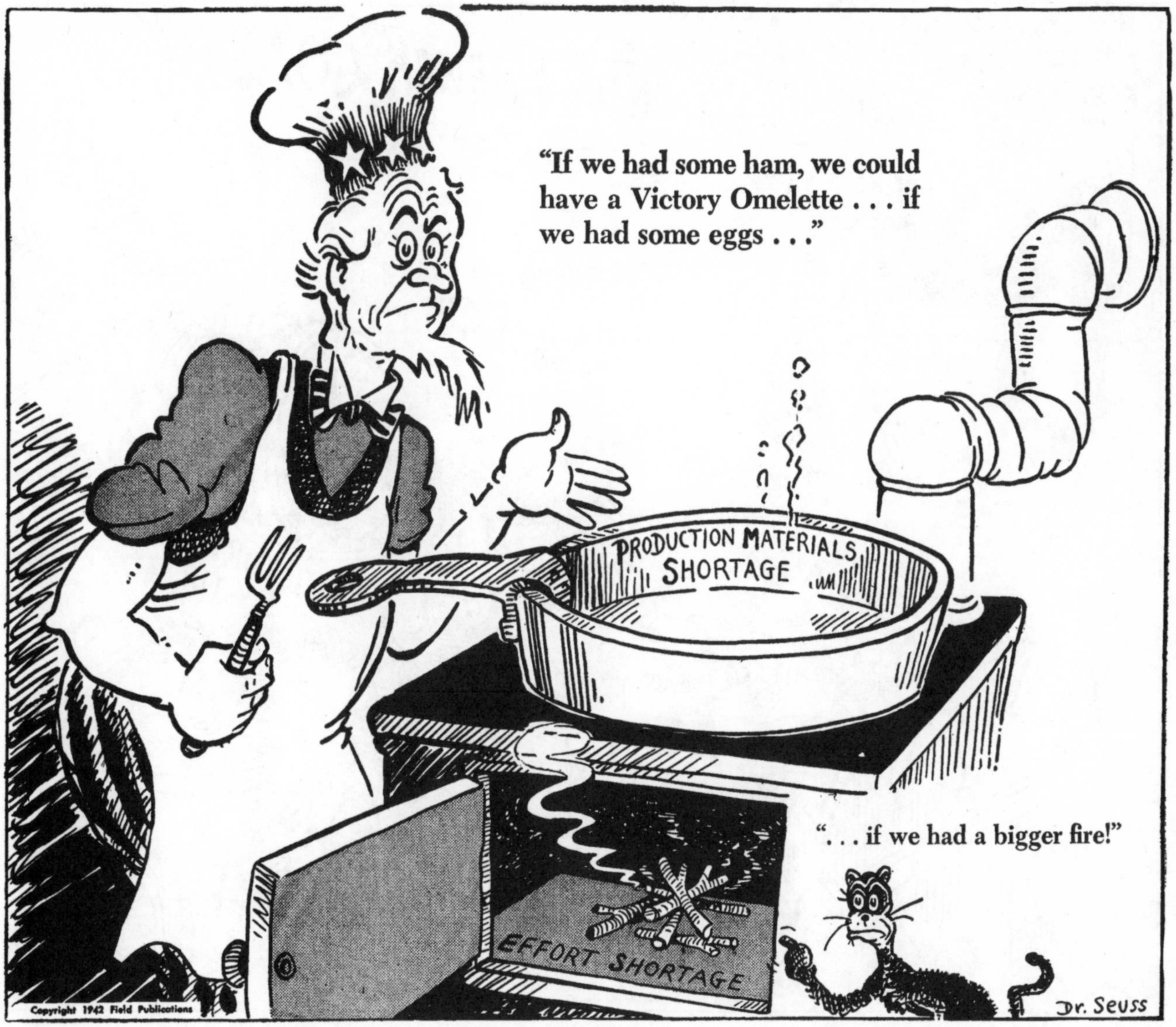
"If we had some ham, we could have a Victory Omelette . . . if we had some eggs . . ."
PRODUCTION MATERIALS SHORTAGE
EFFORT SHORTAGE
". . . if we had a bigger fire!"
Copyright 1942 Field Publications
Dr. Seuss

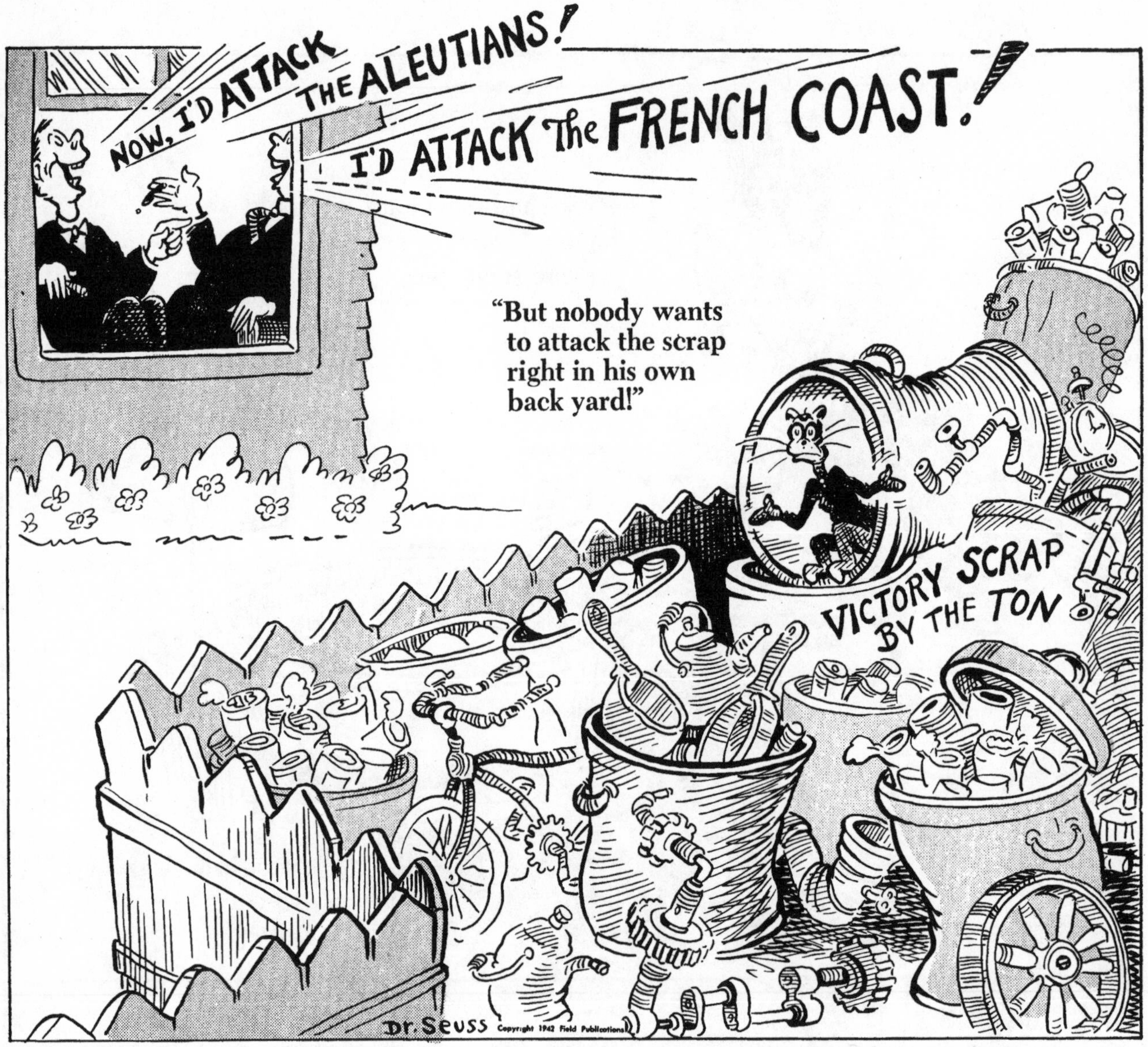
NOW, I'D ATTACK THE ALEUTIANS!
I'D ATTACK the FRENCH COAST!
VICTORY SCRAP BY THE TON
DR. SEUSS
Copyright 1942 Field Publications

"But nobody wants to attack the scrap right in his own back yard!"

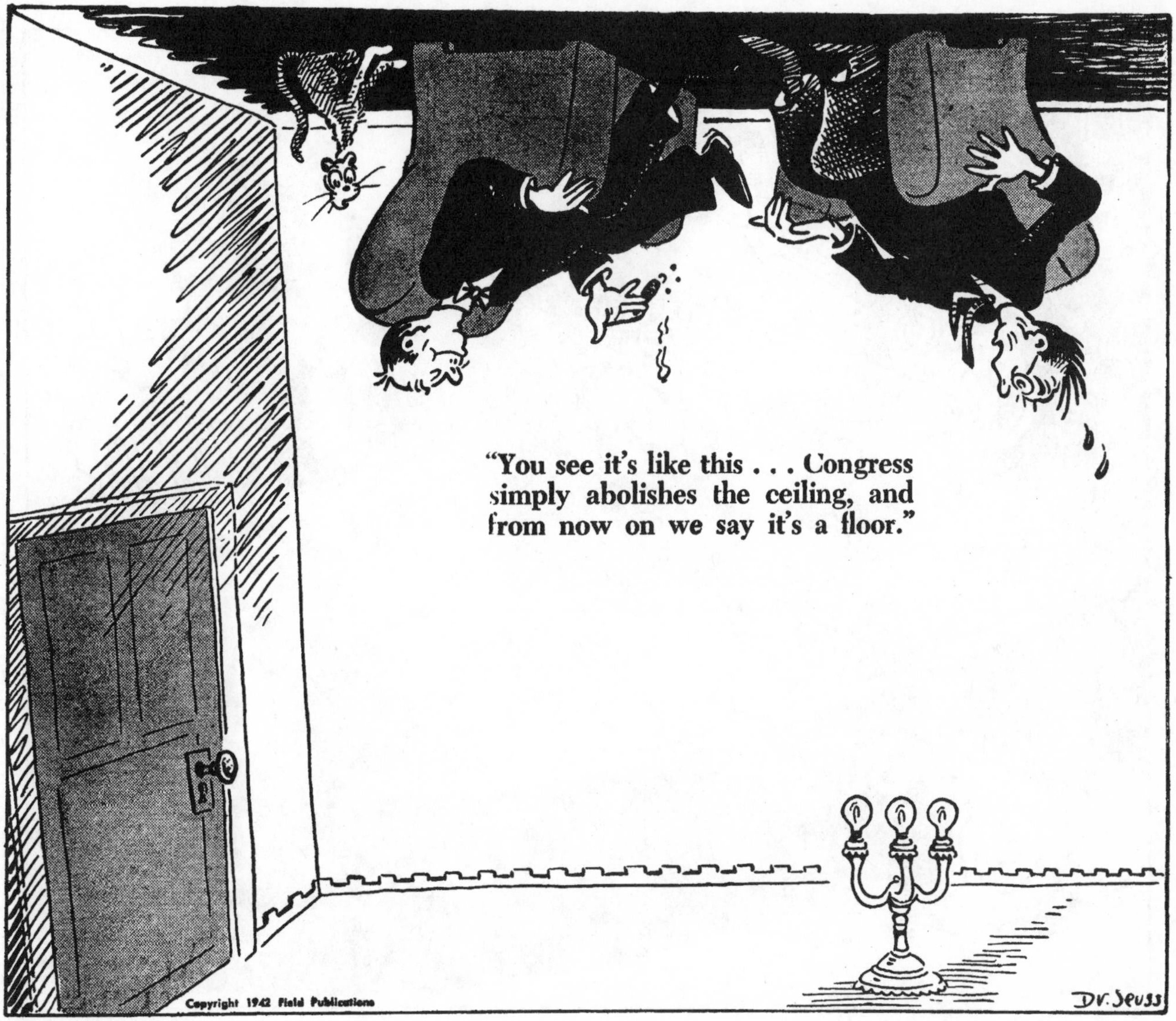
Copyright 1942 Field Publications
Dr. Seuss

"You see it's like this . . . Congress simply abolishes the ceiling, and from now on we say it's a floor."

253 — September 25, 1942

"She Says the Government Can Have Her Zipper, If the Government Can Get It Un-jammed!"

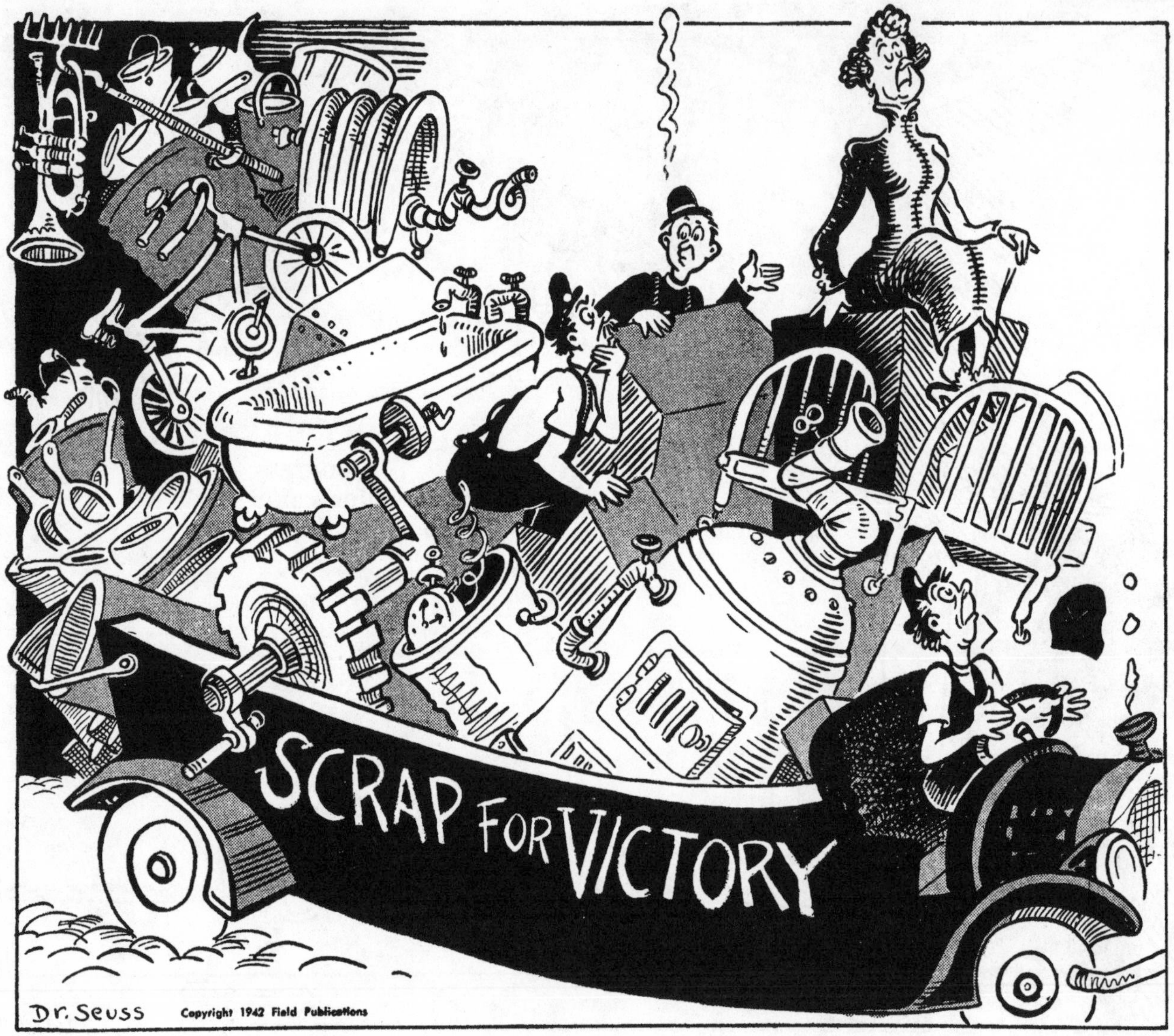
SCRAP FOR VICTORY
Dr. Seuss
Copyright 1942 Field Publications

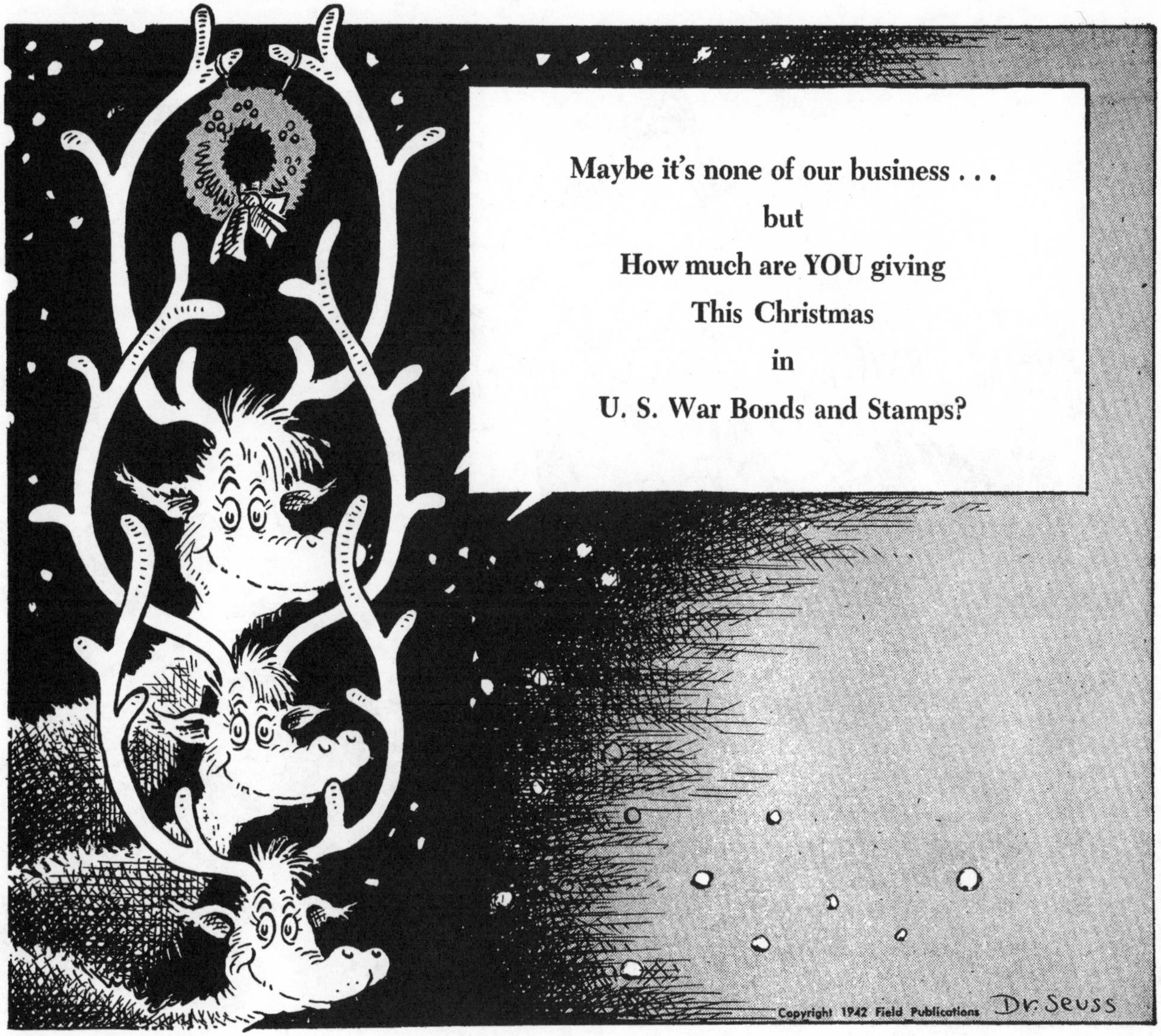
Maybe it's none of our business . . .
but
How much are YOU giving
This Christmas
in
U. S. War Bonds and Stamps?
Copyright 1942 Field Publications
Dr. Seuss

255 — December 22, 1942

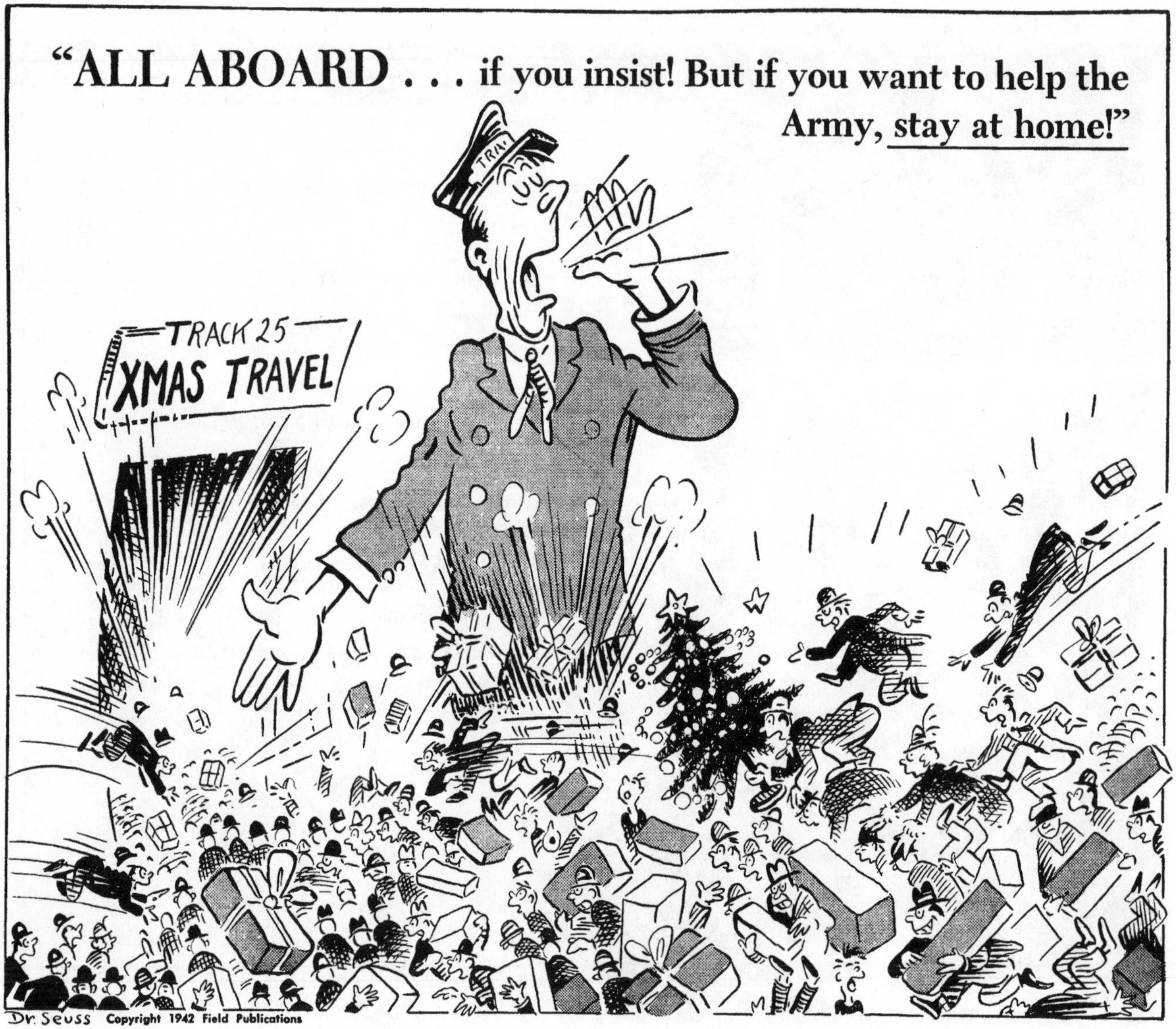
TRACK 25
XMAS TRAVEL
Dr. Seuss Copyright 1942 Field Publications

"ALL ABOARD . . . if you insist! But if you want to help the Army, stay at home!"

The Man Who Wears His Flag Upon His Belly

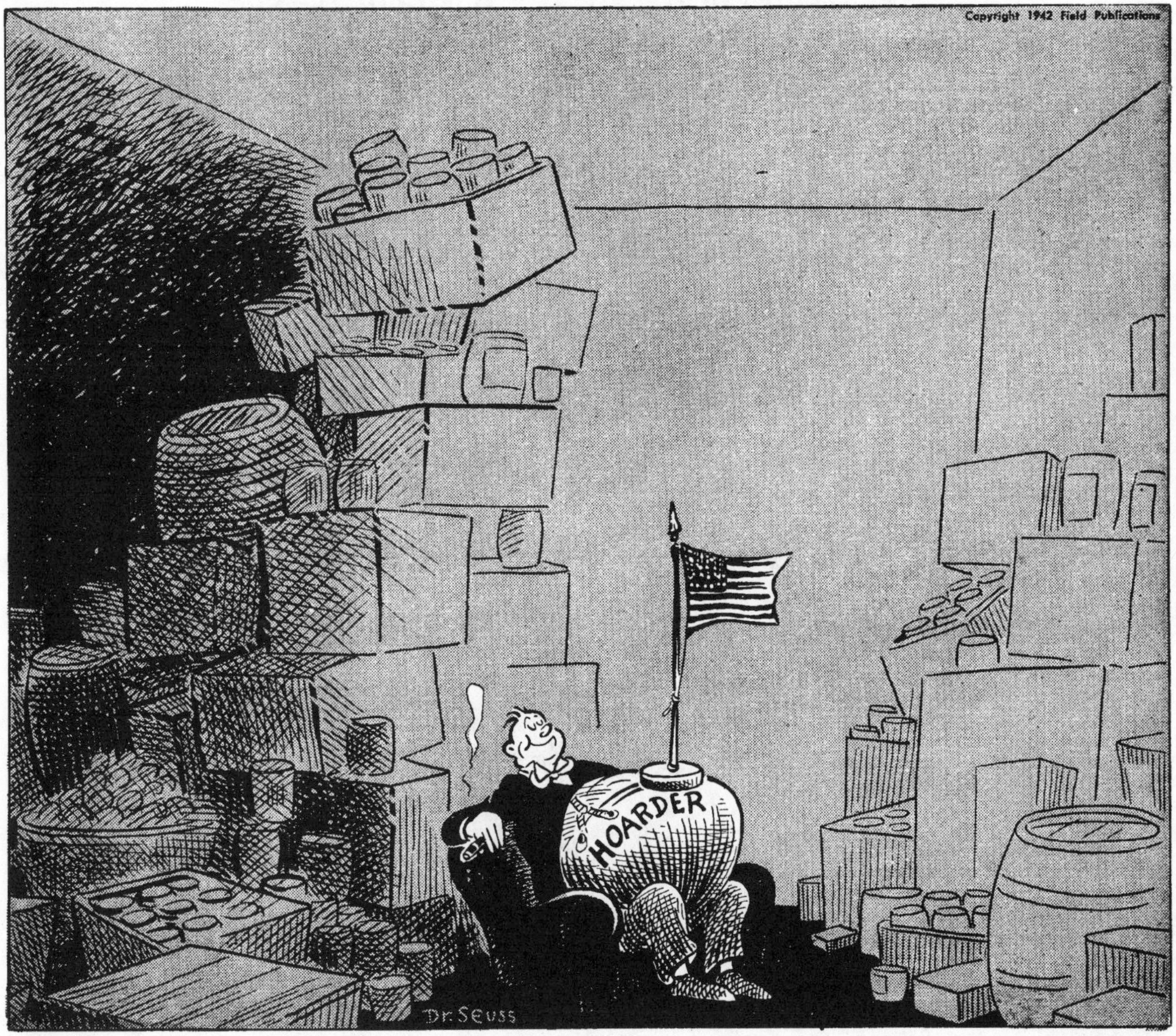
Copyright 1942 Field Publications
HOARDER
Dr. SEUSS

257 – December 28, 1942

The Veteran Recalls the Battle of 1943

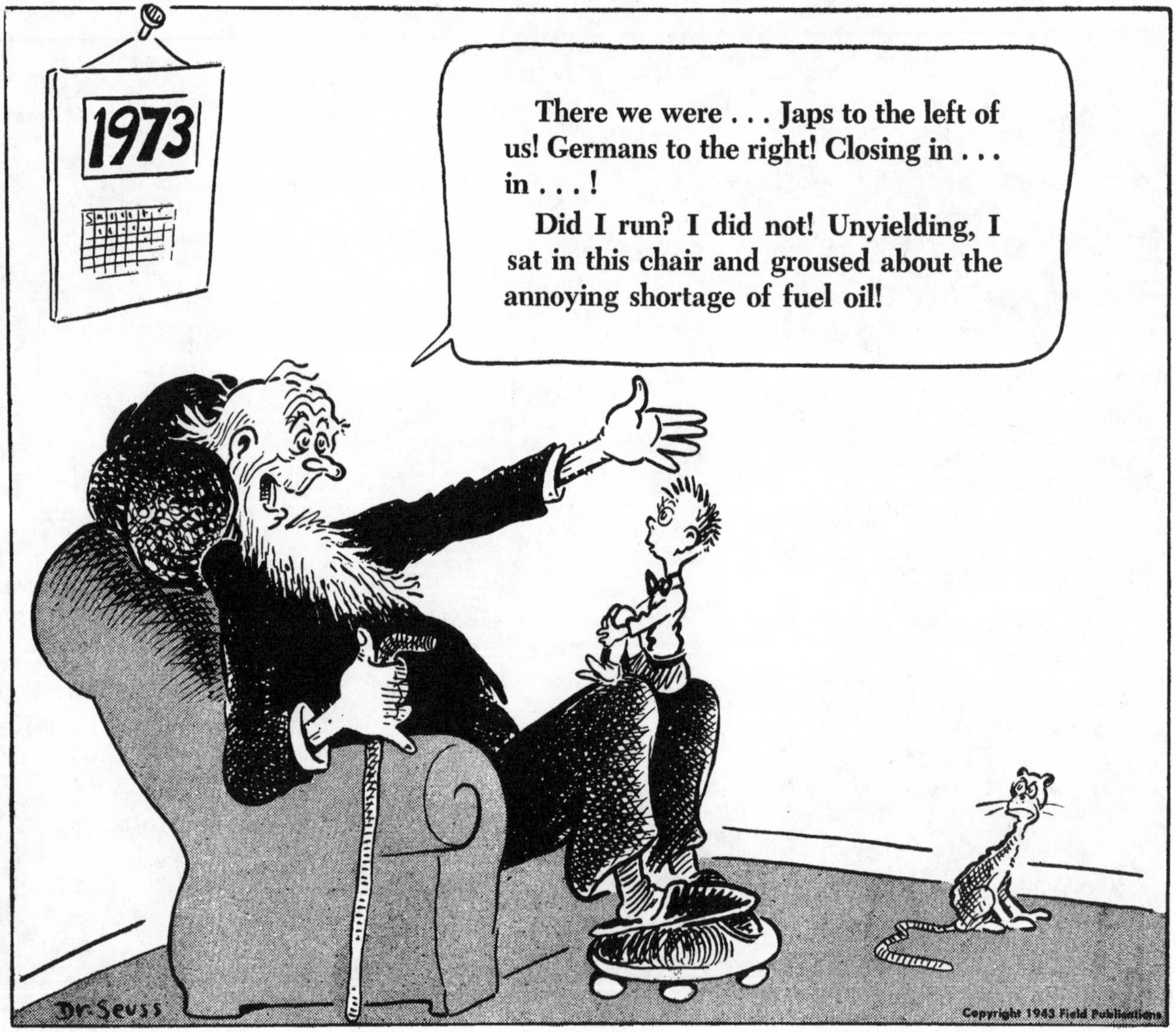
1973
There we were . . . Japs to the left of us! Germans to the right! Closing in . . . in . . . !
Did I run? I did not! Unyielding, I sat in this chair and groused about the annoying shortage of fuel oil!
Dr. Seuss
Copyright 1943 Field Publications

Concluding Thoughts

In January 1943, Dr. Seuss accepted a commission in the U. S. Army.

He had preferred Navy intelligence, but the background investigation took weeks. One account has a navy investigator asking a Standard Oil executive about Dr. Seuss's work with *PM*, to which the executive replied: "Oh, Geisel isn't a Communist; he just does it for the money!" Working at *PM* was an issue: that fact tells something about *PM* and something about the tenor of the day. By the time he passed Navy muster, as he did, he had a commission in the Army to work with Frank Capra's Signal Corps unit. In fact, the Morgans report that Dr. Seuss apparently began working for the government in summer 1942, doing drawings and posters for the Treasury Department and the War Production Board. In any case, Dr. Seuss left *PM* and never returned. He had drawn his last editorial cartoon.

Frank Capra was one of Hollywood's most successful directors. During the war he became the army's premiere propagandist and produced "Why We Fight," the series of films that sets out to explain to the American people—military and civilians—what the war was about. Then almost thirty-nine, Dr. Seuss spent the next years making films, including two we shall consider shortly. He returned to civilian life in January 1946, five months after the fighting ended. His subsequent career took place in California, his residence from the war years until his death in 1991. There

were books: *Bartholomew and the Oobleck* (1949), *If I Ran the Zoo* (1950), *Scrambled Eggs Super* (1953), *How the Grinch Stole Christmas* (1957), and many others. There were movies and three Oscars, for *Hitler Lives?* (1946), *Design for Death* (1947), and *Gerald McBoing-Boing* (1951). There was his campaign for literacy: *The Cat in the Hat* (1958), *Green Eggs and Ham* (1962), *Fox in Socks* (1965), and the rest, with elevation to a cultural prominence perhaps unique in twentieth-century America. In his postwar drawings, lovers of Dr. Seuss will find all sorts of echoes of his wartime cartoons. We focus here on only two postwar echoes: *Yertle the Turtle*, which reprises his cartoons about Hitler, and two films and a book, which track Dr. Seuss's continuing encounter with Japan.

Dr. Seuss published *Yertle the Turtle and Other Stories* in 1958. It has delighted readers ever since. It is the story of a turtle king, Yertle, who wants to see and rule beyond his pond. He orders his subject turtles to stand on each other's backs, with Yertle, of course, on top. The taller the tower, the more overweening the ambitions of Yertle and the heavier the weight pressing down on the unfortunate turtles low down in the tower. At the bottom is a turtle named Mack. At the climax of the tale Mack burps, and tower and Yertle come tumbling down. The story concludes: "And the turtles, of course...all the turtles are free/As turtles and, maybe, all creatures should be." We noted the cartoon of March 20, 1942: "You Can't Build a Substantial V Out of Turtles." That shaky tower of turtles prefigures the tower of turtles that fifteen years later leads to the fall of Yertle. How many of those delighted readers—children or their parents and grandparents—see in Yertle...Hitler? Yet that's who he is.

244

In an interview of 1987, Dr. Seuss commented: "Yertle was Hitler or Mussolini. Originally, Yertle had a moustache, but I took it off. I thought it was gilding the lily a little bit." Yertle is dictator plain and simple, expansionist in his desire to see farther and farther until he is toppled because—in Dr. Seuss's words of 1987—"Mack, the turtle holding up the throne from the bottom, burps. Just to show you how things have changed, my publisher, Random House, had a directors meeting to decide if I should be allowed to use the word 'burp.' The top man, good old sophisticated Bennett Cerf, felt it might be offensive to readers. *Burp?* Can you imagine?"

However, the parallel with Hitler is far from exact. Although he, too, overextended himself, Hitler was toppled not from below but by outside force. And nowhere in *Yertle the Turtle* is there any reference to that other aspect of Hitler's legacy, the Nazi Holocaust. To be sure, the current concern with the European Holocaust developed largely *after* 1958. Still, the question we've asked before arises once again: Is Dr. Seuss's Hitler adequate to the task of representing the real Hitler? Many years later, in a 1980 interview, Dr. Seuss had this to say about his general approach: "I always want the good guys to win....

I don't deal in tragedies.... I tell the kids to forget it and go on to the next tragedy." He went on to speak of fantasy and whimsy: "Fantasy is a necessary ingredient to living. It's a way of looking at life through a distorted telescope, and that's what makes you laugh at the terrible realities. Whimsy, which is a deliberate contradiction of reality, is pure escapism. And without whimsy, none of us can live." Fantasy and whimsy are not merely necessary for life; they are Dr. Seuss's stock-in-trade. But there are limits to their reach. (We have noted resonances between Dr. Seuss's wartime cartoons of Hitler and Charlie Chaplin's *The Great Dictator* of 1940, in which the character Adenoid Hynkel, Dictator of Tomania, is an obvious caricature of Hitler. Writing in 1974 in *My Life in Pictures*, Chaplin states: "Had I known of the actual horrors of the Nazi concentration camps, I could not have made *The Great Dictator*. I wanted to ridicule their mystic bilge about a pure-blooded race.")

Dr. Seuss's encounter with Japan after his *PM* cartoons involves films and *Horton Hears a Who*. When Dr. Seuss entered the Army and went to work for Frank Capra, he was involved with two films about Japan: *Know Your Enemy: Japan* (1945; there was also a *Know Your Enemy: Germany*) and *Our Job in Japan* (1945-46). The latter film was made at the end of the war for indoctrinating (or reindoctrinating) U. S. servicemen headed for service in occupied Japan. It is not possible to identify precisely Dr. Seuss's role in either film, but *Our Job in Japan* focuses on the reeducation of the Japanese. One leitmotif echoes almost precisely Dr. Seuss's cartoon showing Uncle Sam using a bellows to purge the brains of Axis youth, and as we have seen, that cartoon echoed an earlier cartoon about purging *American* brains of their racism.

The narrator of *Our Job in Japan* speaks with a tough-guy city accent and before the film ends will identify himself as an American soldier. The film opens with the surrender ceremony in Tokyo Bay on the battleship *Missouri*, September 2, 1945. Once General Douglas MacArthur has spoken, the narrator says: "The end of the war, the beginning of another peace—peace *if* we can solve the problem of seventy million Japanese people. Here's where we clinch our victory, or we muff it. Here's our job in Japan." He continues:

> What *does* a conquering army do with seventy million people? What *does* a conquering army do with the family of the Japanese soldier—fathers, brothers, mothers, cousins of the soldier? What *do* we do with the soldiers themselves, back now in civilian clothes as part of the Japanese family? What to do with these people?—people trained to play follow the leader, people trained to follow blindly wherever their leaders led them, people who were led into waging a war so disgusting, so revolting, so obscene that it turned the stomach of the entire civilized world. What do we do with the Japanese people when the military leaders they followed are gone? They can still make trouble...or...they can make sense. We have decided to make sure they make sense, and that job starts here.

As these words come over the soundtrack, the images are of Japanese brutality interspersed with scenes of Japan's home front. But with the last sentence, the camera focuses on a middle-aged balding Japanese man working at a desk. As we watch, his skull dissolves to reveal the brain

beneath, and then that brain detaches itself from the man's body and moves toward the front of the screen. The fuzzy background clarifies into a mass of similar brains, which start to move about. In the final shot in this sequence, the one brain in the foreground has become indistinguishable from the many brains in the background, and the screen is one large scene of brain tissue. While this eerie spectacle unfolds, the narrator carries on: "Our problem's in the brain inside of the Japanese head. There are seventy million of these in Japan, physically no different than any other brains in the world, actually all made of exactly the same stuff as ours. These brains, like our brains, can do good things, or bad things, all depending on the kind of ideas that are put inside."

The film eventually urges American soldiers to help prove that "our idea is better than the Japanese idea" and to do so by "being ourselves." The narrator speaks of "what we like to call the American way, or democracy, or just plain old Golden Rule common sense," which includes the idea that "most Americans don't believe in pushing people around, even when we happen to be on top." *PM* had opposed "people who push other people around." The narrator speaks of "a fair break for everybody, regardless of race or creed or color." On the screen, we see two black soldiers and a Hispanic soldier in a chow line—this in an American army that still practiced segregation!

Our Job in Japan is a film to train American troops for their mission in Japan. It is not fair to expect other than very broad strokes—and that is what it offers. It drips with ethnocentrism. But that is not our point here. Our point is that Dr. Seuss worked on it, and the sequence that we have examined fits in neatly with his wartime cartoons showing Uncle Sam sanitizing the brains first of Americans and then of Axis youth.

This sequence lends itself to two readings. The first is of the United States (at least, Dr. Seuss's ideal "America") as the standard of good and bad and as psychologist to the world. In this reading, the United States has a civilizing mission in the world, and the backward Japanese are lucky to have the advanced United States as conqueror. (We can find varieties of this message not only in the popular literature of the late 1940s but also in the writings of many academic experts on Japan. Recall Henry Wallace's speech of December 1942 calling for "psychological disarmament" of the Axis.) The second reading emphasizes the other side of the same coin: the human bond despite the bitter enmities of the war just ended. All human brains are the same. Not only is that an important message for American servicemen in 1945; it also opens a path away from ethnocentric treatment of the Japanese. But it is likely that in 1945 and 1946 the former message drowned out the latter.

In 1947, at the invitation of RKO, Dr. Seuss and his wife Helen produced a third film on Japan: *Design for Death*. That film won Dr. Seuss the second of his three Oscars, but critical response was less enthusiastic. Wrote Bosley Crowther in the *New York Times* (June 11, 1948): "This film...received the Academy Award for the best feature-length documentary of 1947. Apparently competition in that category was nil." In 1998, prints of *Design for Death* are very hard to find (fortunately, the Library of Congress holds a copy).

The general theme of *Design for Death* is that throughout history the little people of Japan have been the victims of the big people. The film is narrated by Kent Smith; the character actor Hans Conried reads the parts calling for a "Japanese" accent. Here is part of the opening narration: "The setting of this story was the islands of Japan. The characters in this story were dressed in Japanese costume. The plot had to do with the Japanese war, but not just the Japanese war. It was a blueprint of aggression, of the racket behind all wars. No matter what country they happen to start in. The racket that thrives in any country when too much power gets into the hands of too few. The same old swindle that's been going on, making murderers out of peaceful men since the beginning of time. A simple racket, but people somehow never seem to get wise to it." The narration concludes: "We learned that this racket is everybody's business, no matter what country it starts in. The racket that lies behind all wars of aggression—Japanese wars...Italian wars...German wars...Spanish wars...wars on every continent...present wars and past wars. The old racket of too much power in the hands of the few. The same racket that is threatening us today with World War III. And it will go on giving us more and more graves until the day when we, the people, who do the bleeding, have the will and the courage to say, 'This thing must stop!' It will only stop when we take more responsibility, responsibility for the things that go on everywhere." The narrator lists the problems: "building true representative government," "developing and electing honest leaders," "learning to recognize the truth when we hear it," and so on. *PM*'s wartime commitments live on in Dr. Seuss in the postwar world.

In the words of a second writer in the *New York Times*, the theme of *Design for Death* is "that power and privilege in the hands of a few bred the last war and will breed another war unless checked. The producers foresaw political pitfalls, worked carefully to avoid them, and finally finished their job before the recent Congressional investigation of Communism in Hollywood." Bosley Crowther commented astutely that with this message the film "obviously avoids a careful analysis." Crowther doesn't elaborate, but any analysis of the war that focuses only on *Japan's* actions and insists on reading Japan's history as the story of "the old racket of too much power in the hands of too few" is not particularly helpful.

As with the disembodied brain of *Our Job in Japan*, so with *Design for Death*: there are at least two messages audiences can take away. The first is the simple and ethnocentric message that the "American way" is right and the "Japanese way" is wrong. After all, who will *choose* as a way of life a "Design for Death"? But the second builds in a different direction. The script lists Japan and Italy and Germany and Spain and "wars on every continent" and "present wars and past wars." Is it so great a stretch to read "the old racket of too much power in the hands of the few" as including the United States? Is it so great a stretch to apply the film's "lessons" to this country as well as to the rest of the world? Perhaps not. And perhaps—given the threatened Congressional investigation of Communism in Hollywood—this is an important facet of the film.

After 1946, Dr. Seuss resumed his travels. In 1953, the year after the American Occupation of Japan came to a formal end, Dr. Seuss visited Japan. In 1954 he published *Horton Hears a Who*. This is the story of a friendly elephant (the Horton of *Horton Hatches the Egg*) who hears a tiny voice and realizes, as no one else does, that the voice comes from a speck of dust and that the speck of dust houses a whole civilization of tiny beings. Only by enlisting every last person of Who-ville in a communal shout—"Yopp!"—does that civilization demonstrate to the outside world (apart from Horton) that it exists: "And the elephant smiled, 'Do you see what I mean? ...They've proved they ARE persons, no matter how small.'" In an interview published in 1987, Dr. Seuss acknowledged that "I conceived the idea of *Horton Hears a Who* from my experiences there [Japan]. ... Well, Japan was just emerging, the people were voting for the first time [since the war, perhaps—Japan had had elections since the nineteenth century and universal male suffrage since 1926], running their own lives—and the theme was obvious: 'A person's a person no matter how small,'" though I don't know how I ended up using elephants. And of course when the little boy stands up and yells 'Yopp!' and saves the whole place, that's my statement about voting—*everyone* counts."

Dr. Seuss ties this emphasis to his wartime civics films for the Army, in which he stressed to American troops the importance of voting; but a less sympathetic reading is possible, of the Japanese as small people needing instruction in democracy—which, of course, was the operative premise of the American Occupation. And there is another aspect of *Horton Hears a Who* that is disturbing. If Who-ville is Japan, Horton must stand for the United States. During 1944 and 1945, the United States pursued a campaign of bombing of cities in Japan unprecedented in its thoroughness and in the devastation it caused. Even before the atomic bombings of Hiroshima and Nagasaki, the United States had destroyed an average of more than half of Japan's sixty largest cities. The major means was firebombing—dropping napalm to set the cities ablaze. More than 500,000 civilians died. Yet the mayor of Who-ville says to Who-ville's guardian Horton:

> "My friend," came the voice, "you're a *very* fine friend.
> You've saved all us folks on this dust speck no end.
> You've saved all our houses, our ceilings and floors.
> You've saved all our churches and grocery stores."

For an American in 1954 to write these lines—even in an allegory—calls for willful amnesia.

Other reactions to *Horton Hears a Who* are possible. In her careful analysis of the writings of Dr. Seuss, Ruth K. MacDonald says Horton "represents postwar United States in the international community of nations. The Whos of Who-ville are Dr. Seuss's characterization of the Japanese after Hiroshima, a people whom he found optimistic, hardworking, and particularly eager to vote in their elections." MacDonald notes that the evil figure in the tale is a "black-bottomed" eagle, named Vlad Vlad-i-koff (at the height of the Cold War, a suspiciously Slavic name), and contrasts Dr. Seuss's opinion of 1954 with U. S. public opinion: "Knowledge of the historical parallels is not necessary to see the point of the story, and some readers may be shocked to see the Japanese, propagandized during the war as evil, inscrutable devils, portrayed so favorably. Though the Japanese did not have to prove their existence, they did have to justify it before the world, given the atrocities committed by their government in

World War II; Seuss, who saw through the wartime propaganda, successfully helps their cause here by using American commonplaces to describe former enemies." Of course, MacDonald has not studied Dr. Seuss's wartime cartoons, so she can argue that Dr. Seuss "saw through the wartime propaganda." The need to redress the American image of Japan by "using American commonplaces to describe" Japan is in part the result of wartime images such as the cartoons Dr. Seuss himself drew.

It would be unfair to expect Dr. Seuss between 1941 and 1955 to be qualitatively different from his contemporaries. As John W. Dower has shown in *War Without Mercy*, racism was an ingredient in much if not all of American wartime thinking about Japan, including that of the few supposed experts on Japan. In visceral fashion, Dr. Seuss's cartoons, films, and books from that era take us back into a mind-set that reminds us painfully but usefully of the pitfalls of racism, of the distance we have traveled since the war in our images of Japan, and—in the case of more recent enemies, mainly in the Middle East—of the distance we still have to travel.

Dr. Seuss's cartoons appeared in *PM*, and *PM* was, in Denning's phrase, "the Popular Front tabloid." However, as we have seen, Dr. Seuss seems a good deal less staunchly left-wing than the Popular Front. His cartoons are ambivalent in their portrayal of Communists and the Soviet Union and ambivalent in their portrayal of labor. His cartoons depict mainly middle-class or wealthy figures, mainly whites, mainly men. Perhaps, then, the Popular Front is less useful as context for Dr. Seuss's wartime cartoons than the broader movement that Michael Kazin calls, in a book of this title, "The Populist Persuasion." Kazin defines populism as "a language whose speakers conceive of ordinary people as a noble assemblage not bounded narrowly by class, view their elite opponents as self-serving and undemocratic, and seek to mobilize the former against the latter." Populism is "a grand form of rhetorical optimism: once mobilized, there is nothing ordinary Americans cannot accomplish." Populists "protest social and economic inequities without calling the entire system into question."

Kazin's populism sheds important light on aspects of Dr. Seuss's wartime cartoons. Dr. Seuss's ordinary person wears a Chaplinesque derby, rather than the top hat or homburg of Dr. Seuss's fat cats; he wears a suit, not tuxedo or spats; his suspenders often show. We understand anew the thrust of the "YOU" and "YOU + ME" figures, who place the reader explicitly within the frame, with the effect that the cartoons' messages become more pointed still. Sometimes Dr. Seuss achieves the same effect without labeling the figure "YOU:" witness the lone individual standing before the new Mt. Rushmore. How many cartoonists before or since address "YOU" in words, as Dr. Seuss does? The practice seems particularly suitable for *PM*, the newspaper that stated repeatedly its axiom: "We are against people who push other people around." In Dr. Seuss's cartoons, the little man—always male, though on occasion he has wife and child alongside—is front and center. He is the democrat whom Dr. Seuss seeks to mobilize against the elite. Dr. Seuss is part scold, part cheerleader, but even in the dark days of the war, he possesses a rock-solid confidence in Uncle Sam and in democracy. He is an optimist.

Margin notes: 69, 208 / 226 / 146 / 211, 232

Many years later Dr. Seuss recalled the folks at *PM* as "a bunch of honest but slightly cockeyed crusaders." To a Dartmouth interviewer, he said: "They were understaffed and didn't have the time and energy to monkey with everybody's stuff.... It was a short-order business." And although he thought the cartoons "rather shoddy" as art, he did say: "The one thing I do like about them...is their honesty and frantic fervor." In unpublished papers the Morgans quote, Dr. Seuss commented: "I was intemperate, un-humorous in my attacks...and I'd do it again."

Before leaving the cartoons, we need to pause and review some of their distinguishing characteristics. First and foremost is their sheer quality. With over 400 cartoons in a two-year period, Dr. Seuss was certain to fail on occasion and to repeat himself from time to time, but how many cartoonists can boast of having drawn so many truly great cartoons? Among cartoonists active during World War II, Bill Mauldin, Herblock, and the British cartoonist David Low come to mind, but are there others? And is there any question that Dr. Seuss belongs in the company of these very greatest political cartoonists of that era? Not in my mind. These men are famous in part because we know their work: their cartoons have been collected, reprinted, anthologized. Not so the editorial cartoons of Dr. Seuss. Nearly sixty years after they first appeared, this book is the first general survey.

A second characteristic is their simplicity-in-complexity. As we have noted Dr. Seuss's drawings are often highly complex, and sometimes he adds lengthy titles and spoken words. But Dr. Seuss does not muddy the message or confuse the reader. Third is Dr. Seuss's humor and whimsy. As we have noted in discussing Dr. Seuss's depictions of Hitler, humor and whimsy both have their limits when confronting truly evil acts. But Dr. Seuss undoubtedly brightened the days of thousands of 29 *PM* readers with his Lindbergh quarter and its ostrich, 38 head in the sand, his "America First" joined by "Siamese beard" to a man with a swastika, his cow with thirteen 81 pairs of legs and twelve udders, his "new Humped dachs-112 hund" for Hitler to replace the "non-Aryan camel."

Like many of his cartoonist contemporaries and like cartoonists down to the present day, Dr. Seuss reduces many of his enemies to subhuman status: lice and other insects, cats, snakes. That is a practice that can open the door to virulent racism. But Dr. Seuss's cartoons seem less egregious than many cartoons of the World War II era. For one thing, he depicts non-enemies too as non-human—witness his Uncle Sam eagle and his dachs-hund for the German people. For another, taken as a whole and with the exceptions we've seen, Dr. Seuss's cartoon characters are remarkably gentle.

Next, consider the tiny animals Dr. Seuss uses to 45 underline his editorial slant. The cat that peeks around the couch as "America First" reads *Adolf the Wolf* to her fright-ened children, the fish astonished by Senator Wheeler's 47 underwater impersonation of Admiral Dewey, the dachs-93 hund under the table as Hitler sends one of his minions off to "Fifth Column a bit around hell," the mouse astonished at Mussolini's kitchen act, the bird gawking at the statue of 134
197 "Dame Rumor"—they add a contrapuntal dimension not found regularly in other cartoons. (Among today's car-toonists, only Oliphant comes immediately to mind.)

Finally, consider a few more technical matters of car-toon art. Among these I would note the boldness of the line: for example, in "Speaking of Railroads...*Here's* One 50 to Take Over!", "Velvet Carpet to the Oil Well", or "You 170 Can't Kill Japs Just by Shooting Off Your Mouth!" Also 204 note the frequent use of patches of black and solid black backgrounds—not only for grim subjects such as "Crawl Out and Round Me Up Another 400,000 Frenchmen!", 103 but also for less grim subjects such as "Gee, It's All Very Exciting...But It Doesn't Kill Nazi Rats." Consider also 236 his truncation of figures, as in the headless Hitlers of his greatest Hitler cartoons: "What do YOU expect to be 89 working at after the war?" and "Second Creation." What 90 cartoonist of his time was so daring? Think, too, of his readiness to break the frame. Some of his cartoons are conventional, entirely within four clearly-marked sides, but in many Dr. Seuss draws no sides. In how many car-toons with frames does the image break out of the frame? In a number, he seems to draw sides only to breach them: "HAPPY NEW YEAR! But, Boy! What a Hangover!" and 108 "The End of the Nap" breach the frame on three sides; 144 "Sis! Boom! Bah! Rah!" and "Speaking of Giant Trans-165 ports..." breach the frame on all four sides. In short, Dr. 217 Seuss is an innovator, always pushing the envelope.

As we have seen, these cartoons tell us a great deal about Dr. Seuss and about American public opinion in 1941 and 1942. But strip away the artist's name, forget about his accomplishments before and after, and these cartoons stand the test of time. Dr. Seuss's wartime car-toons are important in their own right, as *cartoons*.

ACKNOWLEDGMENTS AND SOURCES

My hearty thanks to a very large number of people for all kinds of assistance. They include: colleagues at the History Department of the University of Massachusetts for criticism, encouragement, and other help: Kevin Boyle, Milton Cantor, Bob Jones, Kathy Peiss, Charles Rearick, Roland Sarti, Ron Story, Mary Wilson; librarians at the W. E. B. DuBois Library: the good people at the Reference and Interlibrary Loan desks and, for special support, Stás Radosh; librarians and archivists elsewhere: at the Film Division of the Library of Congress; at Special Collections, Boston University; at the Nieman Foundation at Harvard; and, most notably, at the Mandeville Special Collections Library of the University of California, San Diego, Lynda Claassen and Richard H. F. Lindemann. Richard drew up the invaluable list of all Dr. Seuss's *PM* cartoons, scanned the cartoons for this volume digitally, and retouched them with great care. He is responsible for the high quality of these reproductions; others for criticism, advice, and technical assistance: Aaron Berman, John Dower, Tom Engelhardt, Anita Fahrni, Paul Milkman, my parents Gladys and Paul Minear, Larry Minear, Susan Rabiner, Ned Rosenthal, Edgar Sabogal; the professionals at The New Press: André Schiffrin, who reacted immediately and enthusiastically, Jessica Blatt, Hall Smyth, who designed the book and allowed me a voice in the final decisions, Janey Tannenbaum, Grace Farrell. Mistakes, misinterpretations, and other shortcomings are not theirs but mine.

Unless I have indicated otherwise (usually by citing the date of an interview or article), information on Dr. Seuss comes from the fine book by Judith and Neil Morgan, *Dr. Seuss and Mr. Geisel* (New York: Random House, 1995); it is the starting point for all discussion of Dr. Seuss's life and work. Other sources include: Ruth K. MacDonald, *Dr. Seuss* (Boston: Twayne, 1988); Edward Connery Latham, ed., *Theodor Seuss Geisel: Reminiscences and Tributes* (Hanover, N. H.: Dartmouth College, 1996); Richard Marschall, ed., *The Tough Coughs As He Ploughs the Dough: Early Writings and Cartoons by Dr. Seuss* (New York: William Morrow/REMCO Worldservice Books, 1987); *Dr. Seuss From Then To Now: A Catalogue of the Retrospective Exhibition* (San Diego: San Diego Museum of Art, 1986); Paul Milkman, PM: *A New Deal in Journalism 1940-1948* (New Brunswick: Rutgers University Press, 1997). *PM* is available on microfilm. Important articles include "Malice in Wonderland," *Newsweek*, Feb. 9, 1942; E. J. Kahn, Jr., "Children's Friend," *The New Yorker*, Dec. 17, 1960; Marian Christy, "Muse on the Loose," *Boston Globe*, July 20, 1980; David Sheff, "Seuss on Wry..." *Parenting* (Feb. 1987). The "official" Dr. Seuss website (there are also many others) is www.randomhouse.com/seussville. The University of California, San Diego will post eventually all the *PM* cartoons, not simply those in this volume, and the original drawings in its collection on www.ucsd.edu (click to Mandeville Special Collections, and then Online Exhibits).

RICHARD H. MINEAR, *Amherst, Massachusetts, July 1999*

CHRONOLOGICAL LIST OF EDITORIAL CARTOONS IN THIS VOLUME

1942